PEARSON   ALWAYS LEARNING

CSC 1301
Principles of Computer Science I

Second Custom Edition for Georgia State University

Taken from:
Computer Science: An Overview, Twelfth Edition
by J. Glenn Brookshear and Dennis Brylow

Building Java Programs: A Back to Basics Approach, Third Edition
by Stuart Reges and Marty Stepp

Building Java Programs: A Back to Basics Approach, Fourth Edition
by Stuart Reges and Marty Stepp

Cover Art: (left) Courtesy of Dimitar Todorov/Alamy; (right) Courtesy of Mykota/Mazuryk/Fotolia.

Taken from:

Computer Science: An Overview, Twelfth Edition
by J. Glenn Brookshear and Dennis Brylow
Copyright © 2015, 2012, 2009 by Pearson Education, Inc.
New York, New York 10013

Building Java Programs: A Back to Basics Approach, Third Edition
by Stuart Reges and Marty Stepp
Copyright © 2014, 2011, 2008 by Pearson Education, Inc.
Publishing as Addison-Wesley
Upper Saddle River, New Jersey 07458

Building Java Programs: A Back to Basics Approach, Fourth Edition
by Stuart Reges and Marty Stepp
Copyright © 2017, 2014, 2011 by Pearson Education, Inc.
New York, New York 10013

This special edition published in cooperation with Pearson Education, Inc.

All trademarks, service marks, registered trademarks, and registered service marks are the property of their respective owners and are used herein for identification purposes only.

Pearson Education, Inc., 330 Hudson Street, New York, New York 10013
A Pearson Education Company
www.pearsoned.com

Printed in the United States of America

1   16

000200010272038823

CM

ISBN 10: 1-323-42479-2
ISBN 13: 978-1-323-42479-7

Preface

This book presents an introductory survey of computer science. It explores the breadth of the subject while including enough depth to convey an honest appreciation for the topics involved.

Audience

We wrote this text for students of computer science as well as students from other disciplines. As for computer science students, most begin their studies with the illusion that computer science is programming, Web browsing, and Internet file sharing because that is essentially all they have seen. Yet computer science is much more than this. Beginning computer science students need exposure to the breadth of the subject in which they are planning to major. Providing this exposure is the theme of this book. It gives students an overview of computer science—a foundation from which they can appreciate the relevance and interrelationships of future courses in the field. This survey approach is, in fact, the model used for introductory courses in the natural sciences.

This broad background is also what students from other disciplines need if they are to relate to the technical society in which they live. A computer science course for this audience should provide a practical, realistic understanding of the entire field rather than merely an introduction to using the Internet or training in the use of some popular software packages. There is, of course, a proper place for that training, but this text is about educating.

While writing previous editions of this text, maintaining accessibility for nontechnical students was a major goal. The result was that the book has been used successfully in courses for students over a wide range of disciplines and educational levels, ranging from high school to graduate courses. This 12th edition is designed to continue that tradition.

New in the 12th Edition

The underlying theme during the development of this 12th edition has been incorporating an introduction to the Python programming language into key chapters. In the earliest chapters, these supplementary sections are labeled optional.

Taken from: *Java Foundations: Introduction to Program Desighn & Data structures,* Third Edition
by John Lewis, Peter DePasquale, and Joseph Chase

By Chapter 5, we replace the previous editions' Pascal-like notation with Python and Python-flavored pseudocode.

This represents a significant change for a book that has historically striven to sidestep allegiance to any specific language. We make this change for several reasons. First, the text already contains quite a bit of code in various languages, including detailed pseudocode in several chapters. To the extent that readers are already absorbing a fair amount of syntax, it seems appropriate to retarget that syntax toward a language they may actually see in a subsequent course. More importantly, a growing number of instructors who use this text have made the determination that even in a breadth-first introduction to computing, it is difficult for students to master many of the topics in the absence of programming tools for exploration and experimentation.

But why Python? Choosing a language is always a contentious matter, with any choice bound to upset at least as many as it pleases. Python is an excellent middle ground, with:

- a clean, easily learned syntax,
- simple I/O primitives,
- data types and control structures that correspond closely to the pseudocode primitives used in earlier editions, and
- support for multiple programming paradigms.

It is a mature language with a vibrant development community and copious online resources for further study. Python remains one of the top 10 most commonly used languages in industry by some measures, and has seen a sharp increase in its usage for introductory computer science courses. It is particularly popular for introductory courses for non-majors, and has wide acceptance in other STEM fields such as physics and biology as the language of choice for computational science applications.

Nevertheless, the focus of the text remains on broad computer science concepts; the Python supplements are intended to give readers a deeper taste of programming than previous editions, but not to serve as a full-fledged introduction to programming. The Python topics covered are driven by the existing structure of the text. Thus, Chapter 1 touches on Python syntax for representing data—integers, floats, ASCII and Unicode strings, etc. Chapter 2 touches on Python operations that closely mirror the machine primitives discussed throughout the rest of the chapter. Conditionals, loops, and functions are introduced in Chapter 5, at the time that those constructs are needed to devise a sufficiently complete pseudocode for describing algorithms. In short, Python constructs are used to reinforce computer science concepts rather than to hijack the conversation.

In addition to the Python content, virtually every chapter has seen revisions, updates, and corrections from the previous editions.

Organization

This text follows a bottom-up arrangement of subjects that progresses from the concrete to the abstract—an order that results in a sound pedagogical presentation in which each topic leads to the next. It begins with the fundamentals of information encoding, data storage, and computer architecture (Chapters 1 and 2); progresses to the study of operating systems (Chapter 3) and computer networks

(Chapter 4); investigates the topics of algorithms, programming languages, and software development (Chapters 5 through 7); explores techniques for enhancing the accessibility of information (Chapters 8 and 9); considers some major applications of computer technology via graphics (Chapter 10) and artificial intelligence (Chapter 11); and closes with an introduction to the abstract theory of computation (Chapter 12).

Although the text follows this natural progression, the individual chapters and sections are surprisingly independent and can usually be read as isolated units or rearranged to form alternative sequences of study. Indeed, the book is often used as a text for courses that cover the material in a variety of orders. One of these alternatives begins with material from Chapters 5 and 6 (Algorithms and Programming Languages) and returns to the earlier chapters as desired. I also know of one course that starts with the material on computability from Chapter 12. In still other cases, the text has been used in "senior capstone" courses where it serves as merely a backbone from which to branch into projects in different areas. Courses for less technically-oriented audiences may want to concentrate on Chapters 4 (Networking and the Internet), 9 (Database Systems), 10 (Computer Graphics), and 11 (Artificial Intelligence).

On the opening page of each chapter, we have used asterisks to mark some sections as optional. These are sections that cover topics of more specific interest or perhaps explore traditional topics in more depth. Our intention is merely to provide suggestions for alternative paths through the text. There are, of course, other shortcuts. In particular, if you are looking for a quick read, we suggest the following sequence:

Section	Topic
1.1–1.4	Basics of data encoding and storage
2.1–2.3	Machine architecture and machine language
3.1–3.3	Operating systems
4.1–4.3	Networking and the Internet
5.1–5.4	Algorithms and algorithm design
6.1–6.4	Programming languages
7.1–7.2	Software engineering
8.1–8.3	Data abstractions
9.1–9.2	Database systems
10.1–10.2	Computer graphics
11.1–11.3	Artificial intelligence
12.1–12.2	Theory of computation

There are several themes woven throughout the text. One is that computer science is dynamic. The text repeatedly presents topics in a historical perspective, discusses the current state of affairs, and indicates directions of research. Another theme is the role of abstraction and the way in which abstract tools are used to control complexity. This theme is introduced in Chapter 0 and then echoed in the context of operating system architecture, networking, algorithm development, programming language design, software engineering, data organi and computer graphics.

To Instructors

There is more material in this text than students can normally cover in a single semester so do not hesitate to skip topics that do not fit your course objectives or to rearrange the order as you see fit. You will find that, although the text follows a plot, the topics are covered in a largely independent manner that allows you to pick and choose as you desire. The book is designed to be used as a course resource—not as a course definition. We suggest encouraging students to read the material not explicitly included in your course. We underrate students if we assume that we have to explain everything in class. We should be helping them learn to learn on their own.

We feel obliged to say a few words about the bottom-up, concrete-to-abstract organization of the text. As academics, we too often assume that students will appreciate our perspective of a subject—often one that we have developed over many years of working in a field. As teachers, we think we do better by presenting material from the student's perspective. This is why the text starts with data representation/storage, machine architecture, operating systems, and networking. These are topics to which students readily relate—they have most likely heard terms such as JPEG and MP3; they have probably recorded data on CDs and DVDs; they have purchased computer components; they have interacted with an operating system; and they have used the Internet. By starting the course with these topics, students discover answers to many of the "why" questions they have been carrying for years and learn to view the course as practical rather than theoretical. From this beginning it is natural to move on to the more abstract issues of algorithms, algorithmic structures, programming languages, software development methodologies, computability, and complexity that those of us in the field view as the main topics in the science. As already stated, the topics are presented in a manner that does not force you to follow this bottom-up sequence, but we encourage you to give it a try.

We are all aware that students learn a lot more than we teach them directly, and the lessons they learn implicitly are often better absorbed than those that are studied explicitly. This is significant when it comes to "teaching" problem solving. Students do not become problem solvers by studying problem-solving methodologies. They become problem solvers by solving problems—and not just carefully posed "textbook problems." So this text contains numerous problems, a few of which are intentionally vague—meaning that there is not necessarily a single correct approach or a single correct answer. We encourage you to use these and to expand on them.

Other topics in the "implicit learning" category are those of professionalism, ethics, and social responsibility. We do not believe that this material should be presented as an isolated subject that is merely tacked on to the course. Instead, it should be an integral part of the coverage that surfaces when it is relevant. This is the approach followed in this text. You will find that Sections 3.5, 4.5, 7.9, 9.7, and 11.7 present such topics as security, privacy, liability, and social awareness in the context of operating systems, networking, software engineering, database systems, and artificial intelligence. You will also find that each chapter includes a collection of questions called *Social Issues* that challenge students to think about the relationship between the material in the text and the society in which they live.

Thank you for considering our text for your course. Whether you do or do not decide that it is right for your situation, I hope that you find it to be a contribution to the computer science education literature.

Pedagogical Features

This text is the product of many years of teaching. As a result, it is rich in pedagogical aids. Paramount is the abundance of problems to enhance the student's participation—over 1,000 in this 12th edition. These are classified as Questions & Exercises, Chapter Review Problems, and Social Issues. The Questions & Exercises appear at the end of each section (except for the introductory chapter). They review the material just discussed, extend the previous discussion, or hint at related topics to be covered later. These questions are answered in Appendix F.

The Chapter Review Problems appear at the end of each chapter (except for the introductory chapter). They are designed to serve as "homework" problems in that they cover the material from the entire chapter and are not answered in the text.

Also at the end of each chapter are the questions in the Social Issues category. They are designed for thought and discussion. Many of them can be used to launch research assignments culminating in short written or oral reports.

Each chapter also ends with a list called Additional Reading that contains references to other material relating to the subject of the chapter. The websites identified in this preface, in the text, and in the sidebars of the text are also good places to look for related material.

Supplemental Resources

A variety of supplemental materials for this text are available at the book's companion website: www.pearsonhighered.com/brookshear. The following are accessible to all readers:

- Chapter-by-chapter activities that extend topics in the text and provide opportunities to explore related topics
- Chapter-by-chapter "self-tests" that help readers to rethink the material covered in the text
- Manuals that teach the basics of Java and C+ in a pedagogical sequence compatible with the text

In addition, the following supplements are available to qualified instructors at Pearson Education's Instructor Resource Center. Please visit www.pearsonhighered.com or contact your Pearson sales representative for information on how to access them:

- Instructor's Guide with answers to the Chapter Review Problems
- PowerPoint lecture slides
- Test bank

Errata for this book (should there be any!) will be available at www.mscs.mu.edu/~brylow/errata/.

To Students

Glenn Brookshear is a bit of a nonconformist (some of his friends would say *more* than a bit) so when he set out to write this text he didn't always follow the advice he received. In particular, many argued that certain material was too advanced for beginning students. But, we believe that if a topic is relevant, then it is relevant even if the academic community considers it to be an "advanced topic." You deserve a text that presents a complete picture of computer science—not a watered-down version containing artificially simplified presentations of only those topics that have been deemed appropriate for introductory students. Thus, we have not avoided topics. Instead, we've sought better explanations. We've tried to provide enough depth to give you an honest picture of what computer science is all about. As in the case of spices in a recipe, you may choose to skip some of the topics in the following pages, but they are there for you to taste if you wish—and we encourage you to do so.

We should also point out that in any course dealing with technology, the details you learn today may not be the details you will need to know tomorrow. The field is dynamic—that's part of the excitement. This book will give you a current picture of the subject as well as a historical perspective. With this background you will be prepared to grow along with technology. We encourage you to start the growing process now by exploring beyond this text. Learn to learn.

Thank you for the trust you have placed in us by choosing to read our book. As authors we have an obligation to produce a manuscript that is worth your time. We hope you find that we have lived up to this obligation.

Acknowledgments

First and foremost, I thank Glenn Brookshear, who has shepherded this book, "his baby," through eleven previous editions, spanning more than a quarter century of rapid growth and tumultuous change in the field of computer science. While this is the first edition in which he has allowed a co-author to oversee all of the revisions, the pages of this 12th edition remain overwhelmingly in Glenn's voice and, I hope, guided by his vision. Any new blemishes are mine; the elegant underlying framework is all his.

I join Glenn in thanking those of you who have supported this book by reading and using it in previous editions. We are honored.

David T. Smith (Indiana University of Pennsylvania) played a significant role in co-authoring revisions to the 11th edition with me, many of which are still visible in this 12th edition. David's close reading of this edition and careful attention to the supplemental materials have been essential. Andrew Kuemmel (Madison West), George Corliss (Marquette), and Chris Mayfield (James Madison) all provided valuable feedback, insight, and/or encouragement on drafts for this edition, while James E. Ames (Virginia Commonwealth), Stephanie E. August (Loyola), Yoonsuck Choe (Texas A&M), Melanie Feinberg (UT-Austin), Eric D. Hanley (Drake), Sudharsan R. Iyengar (Winona State), Ravi Mukkamala (Old Dominion), and Edward Pryor (Wake Forest) all offered valuable reviews of the Python-specific revisions.

Others who have contributed in this or previous editions include J. M. Adams, C. M. Allen, D. C. S. Allison, E. Angel, R. Ashmore, B. Auernheimer, P. Bankston, M. Barnard, P. Bender, K. Bowyer, P. W. Brashear, C. M. Brown, H. M Brown, B. Calloni, J. Carpinelli, M. Clancy, R. T. Close, D. H. Cooley, L. D. Cornell, M. J. Crowley, F. Deek, M. Dickerson, M. J. Duncan, S. Ezekiel, C. Fox, S. Fox, N. E. Gibbs, J. D. Harris, D. Hascom, L. Heath, P. B. Henderson, L. Hunt, M. Hutchenreuther, L. A. Jehn, K. K. Kolberg, K. Korb, G. Krenz, J. Kurose, J. Liu, T. J. Long, C. May, J. J. McConnell, W. McCown, S. J. Merrill, K. Messersmith, J. C. Moyer, M. Murphy, J. P. Myers, Jr., D. S. Noonan, G. Nutt, W. W. Oblitey, S. Olariu, G. Riccardi, G. Rice, N. Rickert, C. Riedesel, J. B. Rogers, G. Saito, W. Savitch, R. Schlafly, J. C. Schlimmer, S. Sells, Z. Shen, G. Sheppard, J. C. Simms, M. C. Slattery, J. Slimick, J. A. Slomka, J. Solderitsch, R. Steigerwald, L. Steinberg, C. A. Struble, C. L. Struble, W. J. Taffe, J. Talburt, P. Tonellato, P. Tromovitch, P. H. Winston, E. D. Winter, E. Wright, M. Ziegler, and one anonymous. To these individuals we give our sincere thanks.

As already mentioned, you will find Java and C++ manuals at the text's Companion Website that teach the basics of these languages in a format compatible with the text. These were written by Diane Christie. Thank you, Diane. Another thank you goes to Roger Eastman who was the creative force behind the chapter-by-chapter activities that you will also find at the companion website.

I also thank the good people at Pearson who have supported this project. Tracy Johnson, Camille Trentacoste, and Carole Snyder in particular have been a pleasure to work with, and brought their wisdom and many improvements to the table throughout the process.

Finally, my thanks to my wife, Petra—"the Rock"—to whom this edition is dedicated. Her patience and fortitude all too frequently exceeded my own, and this book is better for her steadying influence.

D.W.B.

Contents

Taken from *Computer Science: An Overview*, Twelfth Edition
by J. Glenn Brookshear and Dennis Brylow

Asterisks indicate suggestions for optional sections.

Taken from *Building Java Programs: A Back to Basics Approach*, Fourth Edition
by Stuart Reges and Marty Stepp

Chapter 1 Introduction to Java Programming 1

Taken from *Computer Science: An Overview*, Twelfth Edition
by J. Glenn Brookshear and Dennis Brylow

Taken from *Building Java Programs: A Back to Basics Approach*, Fourth Edition
by Stuart Reges and Marty Stepp

Taken from:
Computer Science: An Overview, Twelfth Edition
by J. Glenn Brookshear and Dennis Brylow

Introduction

In this preliminary chapter we consider the scope of computer
science, develop a historical perspective, and establish a
foundation from which to launch our study.

Computer science is the discipline that seeks to build a scientific foundation for such topics as computer design, computer programming, information processing, algorithmic solutions of problems, and the algorithmic process itself. It provides the underpinnings for today's computer applications as well as the foundations for tomorrow's computing infrastructure.

This book provides a comprehensive introduction to this science. We will investigate a wide range of topics including most of those that constitute a typical university computer science curriculum. We want to appreciate the full scope and dynamics of the field. Thus, in addition to the topics themselves, we will be interested in their historical development, the current state of research, and prospects for the future. Our goal is to establish a functional understanding of computer science—one that will support those who wish to pursue more specialized studies in the science as well as one that will enable those in other fields to flourish in an increasingly technical society.

0.1   The Role of Algorithms

We begin with the most fundamental concept of computer science—that of an **algorithm.** Informally, an algorithm is a set of steps that defines how a task is performed. (We will be more precise later in Chapter 5.) For example, there are algorithms for cooking (called recipes), for finding your way through a strange city (more commonly called directions), for operating washing machines (usually displayed on the inside of the washer's lid or perhaps on the wall of a laundromat), for playing music (expressed in the form of sheet music), and for performing magic tricks (Figure 0.1).

Before a machine such as a computer can perform a task, an algorithm for performing that task must be discovered and represented in a form that is compatible with the machine. A representation of an algorithm is called a **program.** For the convenience of humans, computer programs are usually printed on paper or displayed on computer screens. For the convenience of machines, programs are encoded in a manner compatible with the technology of the machine. The process of developing a program, encoding it in machine-compatible form, and inserting it into a machine is called **programming.** Programs, and the algorithms they represent, are collectively referred to as **software,** in contrast to the machinery itself, which is known as **hardware.**

The study of algorithms began as a subject in mathematics. Indeed, the search for algorithms was a significant activity of mathematicians long before the development of today's computers. The goal was to find a single set of directions that described how all problems of a particular type could be solved. One of the best known examples of this early research is the long division algorithm for finding the quotient of two multiple-digit numbers. Another example is the Euclidean algorithm, discovered by the ancient Greek mathematician Euclid, for finding the greatest common divisor of two positive integers (Figure 0.2).

Once an algorithm for performing a task has been found, the performance of that task no longer requires an understanding of the principles on which the algorithm is based. Instead, the performance of the task is reduced to the process of merely following directions. (We can follow the long division algorithm to find a quotient or the Euclidean algorithm to find a greatest common divisor without

Figure 0.1   An algorithm for a magic trick

Effect: The performer places some cards from a normal deck of playing cards face down on a table and mixes them thoroughly while spreading them out on the table. Then, as the audience requests either red or black cards, the performer turns over cards of the requested color.

Secret and Patter:

Step 1.   From a normal deck of cards, select ten red cards and ten black cards. Deal these cards face up in two piles on the table according to color.

Step 2.   Announce that you have selected some red cards and some black cards.

Step 3.   Pick up the red cards. Under the pretense of aligning them into a small deck, hold them face down in your left hand and, with the thumb and first finger of your right hand, pull back on each end of the deck so that each card is given a slightly *backward* curve. Then place the deck of red cards face down on the table as you say, "Here are the red cards in this stack."

Step 4.   Pick up the black cards. In a manner similar to that in step 3, give these cards a slight *forward* curve. Then return these cards to the table in a face-down deck as you say, "And here are the black cards in this stack."

Step 5.   Immediately after returning the black cards to the table, use both hands to mix the red and black cards (still face down) as you spread them out on the tabletop. Explain that you are thoroughly mixing the cards.

Step 6.   As long as there are face-down cards on the table, repeatedly execute the following steps:

    6.1. Ask the audience to request either a red or a black card.

    6.2. If the color requested is red and there is a face-down card with a concave appearance, turn over such a card while saying, "Here is a red card."

    6.3. If the color requested is black and there is a face-down card with a convex appearance, turn over such a card while saying, "Here is a black card."

    6.4. Otherwise, state that there are no more cards of the requested color and turn over the remaining cards to prove your claim.

Figure 0.2   The Euclidean algorithm for finding the greatest common divisor of two positive integers

Description: This algorithm assumes that its input consists of two positive integers and proceeds to compute the greatest common divisor of these two values.

Procedure:

Step 1. Assign M and N the value of the larger and smaller of the two input values, respectively.

Step 2. Divide M by N, and call the remainder R.

Step 3. If R is not 0, then assign M the value of N, assign N the value of R, and return to step 2; otherwise, the greatest common divisor is the value currently assigned to N.

understanding why the algorithm works.) In a sense, the intelligence required to solve the problem at hand is encoded in the algorithm.

Capturing and conveying intelligence (or at least intelligent behavior) by means of algorithms allows us to build machines that perform useful tasks. Consequently, the level of intelligence displayed by machines is limited by the intelligence that can be conveyed through algorithms. We can construct a machine to perform a task only if an algorithm exists for performing that task. In turn, if no algorithm exists for solving a problem, then the solution of that problem lies beyond the capabilities of machines.

Identifying the limitations of algorithmic capabilities solidified as a subject in mathematics in the 1930s with the publication of Kurt Gödel's incompleteness theorem. This theorem essentially states that in any mathematical theory encompassing our traditional arithmetic system, there are statements whose truth or falseness cannot be established by algorithmic means. In short, any complete study of our arithmetic system lies beyond the capabilities of algorithmic activities. This realization shook the foundations of mathematics, and the study of algorithmic capabilities that ensued was the beginning of the field known today as computer science. Indeed, it is the study of algorithms that forms the core of computer science.

0.2 The History of Computing

Today's computers have an extensive genealogy. One of the earlier computing devices was the abacus. History tells us that it probably had its roots in ancient China and was used in the early Greek and Roman civilizations. The machine is quite simple, consisting of beads strung on rods that are in turn mounted in a rectangular frame (Figure 0.3). As the beads are moved back and forth on the rods, their positions represent stored values. It is in the positions of the beads that this "computer" represents and stores data. For control of an algorithm's execution, the machine relies on the human operator. Thus the abacus alone is merely a data storage system; it must be combined with a human to create a complete computational machine.

In the time period after the Middle Ages and before the Modern Era, the quest for more sophisticated computing machines was seeded. A few inventors began to experiment with the technology of gears. Among these were Blaise Pascal (1623–1662) of France, Gottfried Wilhelm Leibniz (1646–1716) of Germany, and Charles Babbage (1792–1871) of England. These machines represented data through gear positioning, with data being entered mechanically by establishing initial gear positions. Output from Pascal's and Leibniz's machines was achieved by observing the final gear positions. Babbage, on the other hand, envisioned machines that would print results of computations on paper so that the possibility of transcription errors would be eliminated.

As for the ability to follow an algorithm, we can see a progression of flexibility in these machines. Pascal's machine was built to perform only addition. Consequently, the appropriate sequence of steps was embedded into the structure of the machine itself. In a similar manner, Leibniz's machine had its algorithms firmly embedded in its architecture, although the operator could select from a variety of arithmetic operations it offered. Babbage's Difference Engine

Figure 0.3   Chinese wooden abacus (Pink Badger/Fotolia)

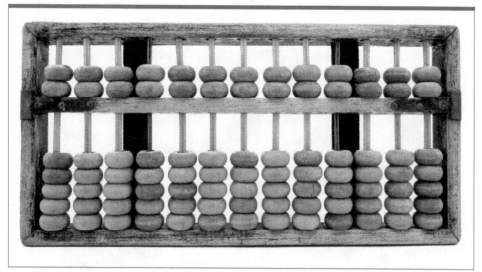

(of which only a demonstration model was constructed) could be modified to perform a variety of calculations, but his Analytical Engine (never funded for construction) was designed to read instructions in the form of holes in paper cards. Thus Babbage's Analytical Engine was programmable. In fact, Augusta Ada Byron (Ada Lovelace), who published a paper in which she demonstrated how Babbage's Analytical Engine could be programmed to perform various computations, is often identified today as the world's first programmer.

The idea of communicating an algorithm via holes in paper was not originated by Babbage. He got the idea from Joseph Jacquard (1752–1834), who, in 1801, had developed a weaving loom in which the steps to be performed during the weaving process were determined by patterns of holes in large thick cards made of wood (or cardboard). In this manner, the algorithm followed by the loom could be changed easily to produce different woven designs. Another beneficiary of Jacquard's idea was Herman Hollerith (1860–1929), who applied the concept of representing information as holes in paper cards to speed up the tabulation process in the 1890 U.S. census. (It was this work by Hollerith that led to the creation of IBM.) Such cards ultimately came to be known as punched cards and survived as a popular means of communicating with computers well into the 1970s.

Nineteenth-century technology was unable to produce the complex gear-driven machines of Pascal, Leibniz, and Babbage cost-effectively. But with the advances in electronics in the early 1900s, this barrier was overcome. Examples of this progress include the electromechanical machine of George Stibitz, completed in 1940 at Bell Laboratories, and the Mark I, completed in 1944 at Harvard University by Howard Aiken and a group of IBM engineers. These machines made heavy use of electronically controlled mechanical relays. In this sense they were obsolete almost as soon as they were built, because other researchers were applying the technology of vacuum tubes to construct totally

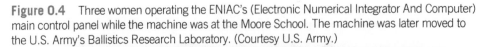

Figure 0.4   Three women operating the ENIAC's (Electronic Numerical Integrator And Computer) main control panel while the machine was at the Moore School. The machine was later moved to the U.S. Army's Ballistics Research Laboratory. (Courtesy U.S. Army.)

electronic computers. The first of these vacuum tube machines was apparently the Atanasoff-Berry machine, constructed during the period from 1937 to 1941 at Iowa State College (now Iowa State University) by John Atanasoff and his assistant, Clifford Berry. Another was a machine called Colossus, built under the direction of Tommy Flowers in England to decode German messages during the latter part of World War II. (Actually, as many as ten of these machines were apparently built, but military secrecy and issues of national security kept their existence from becoming part of the "computer family tree.") Other, more flexible machines, such as the ENIAC (electronic numerical integrator and calculator) developed by John Mauchly and J. Presper Eckert at the Moore School of Electrical Engineering, University of Pennsylvania, soon followed (Figure 0.4).

From that point on, the history of computing machines has been closely linked to advancing technology, including the invention of transistors (for which physicists William Shockley, John Bardeen, and Walter Brattain were awarded a Nobel Prize) and the subsequent development of complete circuits constructed as single units, called integrated circuits (for which Jack Kilby also won a Nobel Prize in physics). With these developments, the room-sized machines of the 1940s were reduced over the decades to the size of single cabinets. At the same time, the processing power of computing machines began to double every two years (a trend that has continued to this day). As work on integrated circuitry progressed, many of the components within a computer became readily available on the open market as integrated circuits encased in toy-sized blocks of plastic called chips.

A major step toward popularizing computing was the development of desktop computers. The origins of these machines can be traced to the computer hobbyists who built homemade computers from combinations of chips. It was within this "underground" of hobby activity that Steve Jobs and Stephen Wozniak

Babbage's Difference Engine

The machines designed by Charles Babbage were truly the forerunners of modern computer design. If technology had been able to produce his machines in an economically feasible manner and if the data processing demands of commerce and government had been on the scale of today's requirements, Babbage's ideas could have led to a computer revolution in the 1800s. As it was, only a demonstration model of his Difference Engine was constructed in his lifetime. This machine determined numerical values by computing "successive differences." We can gain an insight to this technique by considering the problem of computing the squares of the integers. We begin with the knowledge that the square of 0 is 0, the square of 1 is 1, the square of 2 is 4, and the square of 3 is 9. With this, we can determine the square of 4 in the following manner (see the following diagram). We first compute the differences of the squares we already know: $1^2 - 0^2 = 1$, $2^2 - 1^2 = 3$, and $3^2 - 2^2 = 5$. Then we compute the differences of these results: $3 - 1 = 2$, and $5 - 3 = 2$. Note that these differences are both 2. Assuming that this consistency continues (mathematics can show that it does), we conclude that the difference between the value $(4^2 - 3^2)$ and the value $(3^2 - 2^2)$ must also be 2. Hence $(4^2 - 3^2)$ must be 2 greater than $(3^2 - 2^2)$, so $4^2 - 3^2 = 7$ and thus $4^2 = 3^2 + 7 = 16$. Now that we know the square of 4, we could continue our procedure to compute the square of 5 based on the values of 1^2, 2^2, 3^2, and 4^2. (Although a more in-depth discussion of successive differences is beyond the scope of our current study, students of calculus may wish to observe that the preceding example is based on the fact that the derivative of $y = x^2$ is a straight line with a slope of 2.)

x	x^2	First difference	Second difference
0	0		
1	1	1	
2	4	3	2
3	9	5	2
4	16	7	2
5			2

built a commercially viable home computer and, in 1976, established Apple Computer, Inc. (now Apple Inc.) to manufacture and market their products. Other companies that marketed similar products were Commodore, Heathkit, and Radio Shack. Although these products were popular among computer hobbyists, they were not widely accepted by the business community, which continued to look to the well-established IBM and its large mainframe computers for the majority of its computing needs.

In 1981, IBM introduced its first desktop computer, called the personal computer, or PC, whose underlying software was developed by a newly formed company known as Microsoft. The PC was an instant success and legitimized

Augusta Ada Byron

Augusta Ada Byron, Countess of Lovelace, has been the subject of much commentary in the computing community. She lived a somewhat tragic life of less than 37 years (1815–1852) that was complicated by poor health and the fact that she was a nonconformist in a society that limited the professional role of women. Although she was interested in a wide range of science, she concentrated her studies in mathematics. Her interest in "compute science" began when she became fascinated by the machines of Charles Babbage at a demonstration of a prototype of his Difference Engine in 1833. Her contribution to computer science stems from her translation from French into English of a paper discussing Babbage's designs for the Analytical Engine. To this translation, Babbage encouraged her to attach an addendum describing applications of the engine and containing examples of how the engine could be programmed to perform various tasks. Babbage's enthusiasm for Ada Byron's work was apparently motivated by his hope that its publication would lead to financial backing for the construction of his Analytical Engine. (As the daughter of Lord Byron, Ada Byron held celebrity status with potentially significant financial connections.) This backing never materialized, but Ada Byron's addendum has survived and is considered to contain the first examples of computer programs. The degree to which Babbage influenced Ada Byron's work is debated by historians. Some argue that Babbage made major contributions, whereas others contend that he was more of an obstacle than an aid. Nonetheless, Augusta Ada Byron is recognized today as the world's first programmer, a status that was certified by the U.S. Department of Defense when it named a prominent programming language (Ada) in her honor.

the desktop computer as an established commodity in the minds of the business community. Today, the term PC is widely used to refer to all those machines (from various manufacturers) whose design has evolved from IBM's initial desktop computer, most of which continue to be marketed with software from Microsoft. At times, however, the term PC is used interchangeably with the generic terms *desktop* or *laptop*.

As the twentieth century drew to a close, the ability to connect individual computers in a world-wide system called the **Internet** was revolutionizing communication. In this context, Tim Berners-Lee (a British scientist) proposed a system by which documents stored on computers throughout the Internet could be linked together producing a maze of linked information called the **World Wide Web** (often shortened to "Web"). To make the information on the Web accessible, software systems, called **search engines,** were developed to "sift through" the Web, "categorize" their findings, and then use the results to assist users researching particular topics. Major players in this field are Google, Yahoo, and Microsoft. These companies continue to expand their Web-related activities, often in directions that challenge our traditional way of thinking.

At the same time that desktop and laptop computers were being accepted and used in homes, the miniaturization of computing machines continued. Today, tiny computers are embedded within a wide variety of electronic appliances and devices. Automobiles may now contain dozens of small computers running Global Positioning Systems (GPS), monitoring the function of the engine, and providing

Google

Founded in 1998, Google Inc. has become one of the world's most recognized technology companies. Its core service, the Google search engine, is used by millions of people to find documents on the World Wide Web. In addition, Google provides electronic mail service (called Gmail), an Internet-based video-sharing service (called YouTube), and a host of other Internet services (including Google Maps, Google Calendar, Google Earth, Google Books, and Google Translate).

However, in addition to being a prime example of the entrepreneurial spirit, Google also provides examples of how expanding technology is challenging society. For example, Google's search engine has led to questions regarding the extent to which an international company should comply with the wishes of individual governments; YouTube has raised questions regarding the extent to which a company should be liable for information that others distribute through its services as well as the degree to which the company can claim ownership of that information; Google Books has generated concerns regarding the scope and limitations of intellectual property rights; and Google Maps has been accused of violating privacy rights.

voice command services for controlling the car's audio and phone communication systems.

Perhaps the most revolutionary application of computer miniaturization is found in the expanding capabilities of **smartphones,** hand-held general-purpose computers on which telephony is only one of many applications. More powerful than the supercomputers of prior decades, these pocket-sized devices are equipped with a rich array of sensors and interfaces including cameras, microphones, compasses, touch screens, accelerometers (to detect the phone's orientation and motion), and a number of wireless technologies to communicate with other smartphones and computers. Many argue that the smartphone is having a greater effect on global society than the PC revolution.

0.3 An Outline of Our Study

This text follows a bottom-up approach to the study of computer science, beginning with such hands-on topics as computer hardware and leading to the more abstract topics such as algorithm complexity and computability. The result is that our study follows a pattern of building larger and larger abstract tools as our understanding of the subject expands.

We begin by considering topics dealing with the design and construction of machines for executing algorithms. In Chapter 1 (Data Storage), we look at how information is encoded and stored within modern computers, and in Chapter 2 (Data Manipulation), we investigate the basic internal operation of a simple computer. Although part of this study involves technology, the general theme is technology independent. That is, such topics as digital circuit design, data encoding and compression systems, and computer architecture are relevant over a wide range of technology and promise to remain relevant regardless of the direction of future technology.

In Chapter 3 (Operating Systems), we study the software that controls the overall operation of a computer. This software is called an operating system. It is a computer's operating system that controls the interface between the machine and its outside world, protecting the machine and the data stored within from unauthorized access, allowing a computer user to request the execution of various programs, and coordinating the internal activities required to fulfill the user's requests.

In Chapter 4 (Networking and the Internet), we study how computers are connected to each other to form computer networks and how networks are connected to form internets. This study leads to topics such as network protocols, the Internet's structure and internal operation, the World Wide Web, and numerous issues of security.

Chapter 5 (Algorithms) introduces the study of algorithms from a more formal perspective. We investigate how algorithms are discovered, identify several fundamental algorithmic structures, develop elementary techniques for representing algorithms, and introduce the subjects of algorithm efficiency and correctness.

In Chapter 6 (Programming Languages), we consider the subject of algorithm representation and the program development process. Here we find that the search for better programming techniques has led to a variety of programming methodologies or paradigms, each with its own set of programming languages. We investigate these paradigms and languages as well as consider issues of grammar and language translation.

Chapter 7 (Software Engineering) introduces the branch of computer science known as software engineering, which deals with the problems encountered when developing large software systems. The underlying theme is that the design of large software systems is a complex task that embraces problems beyond those of traditional engineering. Thus, the subject of software engineering has become an important field of research within computer science, drawing from such diverse fields as engineering, project management, personnel management, programming language design, and even architecture.

In the next two chapters we look at ways data can be organized within a computer system. In Chapter 8 (Data Abstractions), we introduce techniques traditionally used for organizing data in a computer's main memory and then trace the evolution of data abstraction from the concept of primitives to today's object-oriented techniques. In Chapter 9 (Database Systems), we consider methods traditionally used for organizing data in a computer's mass storage and investigate how extremely large and complex database systems are implemented.

In Chapter 10 (Computer Graphics), we explore the subject of graphics and animation, a field that deals with creating and photographing virtual worlds. Based on advancements in the more traditional areas of computer science such as machine architecture, algorithm design, data structures, and software engineering, the discipline of graphics and animation has seen significant progress and has now blossomed into an exciting, dynamic subject. Moreover, the field exemplifies how various components of computer science combine with other disciplines such as physics, art, and photography to produce striking results.

In Chapter 11 (Artificial Intelligence), we learn that to develop more useful machines computer science has turned to the study of human intelligence for insight. The hope is that by understanding how our own minds reason and perceive, researchers will be able to design algorithms that mimic these processes and thus transfer comparable capabilities to machines. The result is the area of computer science known as artificial intelligence, which leans heavily on research in such areas as psychology, biology, and linguistics.

We close our study with Chapter 12 (Theory of Computation) by investigating the theoretical foundations of computer science—a subject that allows us to understand the limitations of algorithms (and thus machines). Here we identify some problems that cannot be solved algorithmically (and therefore lie beyond the capabilities of machines) as well as learn that the solutions to many other problems require such enormous time or space that they are also unsolvable from a practical perspective. Thus, it is through this study that we are able to grasp the scope and limitations of algorithmic systems.

In each chapter, our goal is to explore the subject deeply enough to enable true understanding. We want to develop a working knowledge of computer science—a knowledge that will allow you to understand the technical society in which you live and to provide a foundation from which you can learn on your own as science and technology advance.

0.4 The Overarching Themes of Computer Science

In addition to the main topics of each chapter as listed above, we also hope to broaden your understanding of computer science by incorporating several overarching themes.

The miniaturization of computers and their expanding capabilities have brought computer technology to the forefront of today's society, and computer technology is so prevalent that familiarity with it is fundamental to being a member of the modern world. Computing technology has altered the ability of governments to exert control; had enormous impact on global economics; led to startling advances in scientific research; revolutionized the role of data collection, storage, and applications; provided new means for people to communicate and interact; and has repeatedly challenged society's status quo. The result is a proliferation of subjects surrounding computer science, each of which is now a significant field of study in its own right. Moreover, as with mechanical engineering and physics, it is often difficult to draw a line between these fields and computer science itself. Thus, to gain a proper perspective, our study will not only cover topics central to the core of computer science but also will explore a variety of disciplines dealing with both applications and consequences of the science. Indeed, an introduction to computer science is an interdisciplinary undertaking.

As we set out to explore the breadth of the field of computing, it is helpful to keep in mind the main themes that unite computer science. While the codification of the "Seven Big Ideas of Computer Science"[1] postdates the first ten editions of this book, they closely parallel the themes of the chapters to come. The "Seven Big Ideas" are, briefly: Algorithms, Abstraction, Creativity, Data, Programming, Internet, and Impact. In the chapters that follow, we include a variety of topics, in each case introducing central ideas of the topic, current areas of research, and some of the techniques being applied to advance knowledge in that realm. Watch for the "Big Ideas" as we return to them again and again.

---

[1]www.csprinciples.org

Algorithms

Limited data storage capabilities and intricate, time-consuming programming procedures restricted the complexity of the algorithms used in the earliest computing machines. However, as these limitations began to disappear, machines were applied to increasingly larger and more complex tasks. As attempts to express the composition of these tasks in algorithmic form began to tax the abilities of the human mind, more and more research efforts were directed toward the study of algorithms and the programming process.

It was in this context that the theoretical work of mathematicians began to pay dividends. As a consequence of Gödel's incompleteness theorem, mathematicians had already been investigating those questions regarding algorithmic processes that advancing technology was now raising. With that, the stage was set for the emergence of a new discipline known as *computer science*.

Today, computer science has established itself as the science of algorithms. The scope of this science is broad, drawing from such diverse subjects as mathematics, engineering, psychology, biology, business administration, and linguistics. Indeed, researchers in different branches of computer science may have very distinct definitions of the science. For example, a researcher in the field of computer architecture may focus on the task of miniaturizing circuitry and thus view computer science as the advancement and application of technology. But, a researcher in the field of database systems may see computer science as seeking ways to make information systems more useful. And, a researcher in the field of artificial intelligence may regard computer science as the study of intelligence and intelligent behavior.

Nevertheless, all of these researchers are involved in aspects of the science of algorithms. Given the central role that algorithms play in computer science (see Figure 0.5), it is instructive to identify some questions that will provide focus for our study of this big idea.

- Which problems can be solved by algorithmic processes?
- How can the discovery of algorithms be made easier?

Figure 0.5   The central role of algorithms in computer science

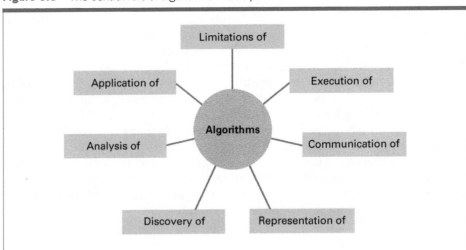

- How can the techniques of representing and communicating algorithms be improved?
- How can the characteristics of different algorithms be analyzed and compared?
- How can algorithms be used to manipulate information?
- How can algorithms be applied to produce intelligent behavior?
- How does the application of algorithms affect society?

Abstraction

The term **abstraction,** as we are using it here, refers to the distinction between the external properties of an entity and the details of the entity's internal composition. It is abstraction that allows us to ignore the internal details of a complex device such as a computer, automobile, or microwave oven and use it as a single, comprehensible unit. Moreover, it is by means of abstraction that such complex systems are designed and manufactured in the first place. Computers, automobiles, and microwave ovens are constructed from components, each of which represents a level of abstraction at which the use of the component is isolated from the details of the component's internal composition.

It is by applying abstraction that we are able to construct, analyze, and manage large, complex computer systems that would be overwhelming if viewed in their entirety at a detailed level. At each level of abstraction, we view the system in terms of components, called **abstract tools,** whose internal composition we ignore. This allows us to concentrate on how each component interacts with other components at the same level and how the collection as a whole forms a higher-level component. Thus we are able to comprehend the part of the system that is relevant to the task at hand rather than being lost in a sea of details.

We emphasize that abstraction is not limited to science and technology. It is an important simplification technique with which our society has created a lifestyle that would otherwise be impossible. Few of us understand how the various conveniences of daily life are actually implemented. We eat food and wear clothes that we cannot produce by ourselves. We use electrical devices and communication systems without understanding the underlying technology. We use the services of others without knowing the details of their professions. With each new advancement, a small part of society chooses to specialize in its implementation, while the rest of us learn to use the results as abstract tools. In this manner, society's warehouse of abstract tools expands, and society's ability to progress increases.

Abstraction is a recurring pillar of our study. We will learn that computing equipment is constructed in levels of abstract tools. We will also see that the development of large software systems is accomplished in a modular fashion in which each module is used as an abstract tool in larger modules. Moreover, abstraction plays an important role in the task of advancing computer science itself, allowing researchers to focus attention on particular areas within a complex field. In fact, the organization of this text reflects this characteristic of the science. Each chapter, which focuses on a particular area within the science, is often surprisingly independent of the others, yet together the chapters form a comprehensive overview of a vast field of study.

Creativity

While computers may merely be complex machines mechanically executing rote algorithmic instructions, we shall see that the field of computer science is an inherently creative one. Discovering and applying new algorithms is a human activity that depends on our innate desire to apply our tools to solve problems in the world around us. Computer science not only extends forms of expression spanning the visual, language and musical arts, but also enables new modes of digital expression that pervade the modern world.

Creating large software systems is much less like following a cookbook recipe than it is like conceiving of a grand new sculpture. Envisioning its form and function requires careful planning. Fabricating its components requires time, attention to detail, and practiced skill. The final product embodies the design aesthetics and sensibilities of its creators.

Data

Computers are capable of representing any information that can be discretized and digitized. Algorithms can process or transform such digitally represented information in a dizzying variety of ways. The result of this is not merely the shuffling of digital data from one part of the computer to another; computer algorithms enable us to search for patterns, to create simulations, and to correlate connections in ways that generate new knowledge and insight. Massive storage capacities, high-speed computer networks, and powerful computational tools are driving discoveries in many other disciplines of science, engineering and the humanities. Whether predicting the effects of a new drug by simulating complex protein folding, statistically analyzing the evolution of language across centuries of digitized books, or rendering 3D images of internal organs from a noninvasive medical scan, data is driving modern discovery across the breadth of human endeavors.

Some of the questions about data that we will explore in our study include:

- How do computers store data about common digital artifacts, such as numbers, text, images, sounds, and video?
- How do computers approximate data about analog artifacts in the real world?
- How do computers detect and prevent errors in data?
- What are the ramifications of an ever-growing and interconnected digital universe of data at our disposal?

Programming

Translating human intentions into executable computer algorithms is now broadly referred to as *programming*, although the proliferation of languages and tools available now bear little resemblance to the programmable computers of the 1950s and early 1960s. While computer science consists of much more than computer programming, the ability to solve problems by devising executable algorithms (programs) remains a foundational skill for all computer scientists.

Computer hardware is capable of executing only relatively simple algorithmic steps, but the abstractions provided by computer programming languages allow humans to reason about and encode solutions for far more complex problems. Several key questions will frame our discussion of this theme.

- How are programs built?
- What kinds of errors can occur in programs?
- How are errors in programs found and repaired?
- What are the effects of errors in modern programs?
- How are programs documented and evaluated?

Internet

The Internet connects computers and electronic devices around the world and has had a profound impact in the way that our technological society stores, retrieves, and shares information. Commerce, news, entertainment, and communication now depend increasingly on this interconnected web of smaller computer networks. Our discussion will not only describe the mechanisms of the Internet as an artifact, but will also touch on the many aspects of human society that are now intertwined with the global network.

The reach of the Internet also has profound implications for our privacy and the security of our personal information. Cyberspace harbors many dangers. Consequently, cryptography and cybersecurity are of growing importance in our connected world.

Impact

Computer science not only has profound impacts on the technologies we use to communicate, work, and play, it also has enormous social repercussions. Progress in computer science is blurring many distinctions on which our society has based decisions in the past and is challenging many of society's long-held principles. In law, it generates questions regarding the degree to which intellectual property can be owned and the rights and liabilities that accompany that ownership. In ethics, it generates numerous options that challenge the traditional principles on which social behavior is based. In government, it generates debates regarding the extent to which computer technology and its applications should be regulated. In philosophy, it generates contention between the presence of intelligent behavior and the presence of intelligence itself. And, throughout society, it generates disputes concerning whether new applications represent new freedoms or new controls.

Such topics are important for those contemplating careers in computing or computer-related fields. Revelations within science have sometimes found controversial applications, causing serious discontent for the researchers involved. Moreover, an otherwise successful career can quickly be derailed by an ethical misstep.

The ability to deal with the dilemmas posed by advancing computer technology is also important for those outside its immediate realm. Indeed, technology is infiltrating society so rapidly that few, if any, are independent of its effects.

This text provides the technical background needed to approach the dilemmas generated by computer science in a rational manner. However, technical knowledge of the science alone does not provide solutions to all the questions involved. With this in mind, this text includes several sections that are devoted to social, ethical, and legal impacts of computer science. These include security concerns, issues of software ownership and liability, the social impact of database technology, and the consequences of advances in artificial intelligence.

Moreover, there is often no definitive correct answer to a problem, and many valid solutions are compromises between opposing (and perhaps equally valid) views. Finding solutions in these cases often requires the ability to listen, to recognize other points of view, to carry on a rational debate, and to alter one's own opinion as new insights are gained. Thus, each chapter of this text ends with a collection of questions under the heading "Social Issues" that investigate the relationship between computer science and society. These are not necessarily questions to be answered. Instead, they are questions to be considered. In many cases, an answer that may appear obvious at first will cease to satisfy you as you explore alternatives. In short, the purpose of these questions is not to lead you to a "correct" answer, but rather to increase your awareness, including your awareness of the various stakeholders in an issue, your awareness of alternatives, and your awareness of both the short- and long-term consequences of those alternatives.

Philosophers have introduced many approaches to ethics in their search for fundamental theories that lead to principles for guiding decisions and behavior.

Character-based ethics (sometimes called virtue ethics) were promoted by Plato and Aristotle, who argued that "good behavior" is not the result of applying identifiable rules, but instead is a natural consequence of "good character." Whereas other ethical bases, such as consequence-based ethics, duty-based ethics, and contract-based ethics, propose that a person resolve an ethical dilemma by asking, "What are the consequences?", "What are my duties?", or "What contracts do I have?," character-based ethics proposes that dilemmas be resolved by asking, "Who do I want to be?" Thus, good behavior is obtained by building good character, which is typically the result of sound upbringing and the development of virtuous habits.

It is character-based ethics that underlies the approach normally taken when "teaching" ethics to professionals in various fields. Rather than presenting specific ethical theories, the approach is to introduce case studies that expose a variety of ethical questions in the professionals' area of expertise. Then, by discussing the pros and cons in these cases, the professionals become more aware, insightful, and sensitive to the perils lurking in their professional lives and thus grow in character. This is the spirit in which the questions regarding social issues at the end of each chapter are presented.

Social Issues

The following questions are intended as a guide to the ethical/social/legal issues associated with the field of computing. The goal is not merely to answer these questions. You should also consider why you answered as you did and whether your justifications are consistent from one question to the next.

1. The premise that our society is *different* from what it would have been without the computer revolution is generally accepted. Is our society *better* than it would have been without the revolution? Is our society worse? Would your answer differ if your position within society were different?

2. Is it acceptable to participate in today's technical society without making an effort to understand the basics of that technology? For instance, do members of a democracy, whose votes often determine how technology will be supported and used, have an obligation to try to understand that technology?

Does your answer depend on which technology is being considered? For example, is your answer the same when considering nuclear technology as when considering computer technology?

3. By using cash in financial transactions, individuals have traditionally had the option to manage their financial affairs without service charges. However, as more of our economy is becoming automated, financial institutions are implementing service charges for access to these automated systems. Is there a point at which these charges unfairly restrict an individual's access to the economy? For example, suppose an employer pays employees only by check, and all financial institutions were to place a service charge on check cashing and depositing. Would the employees be unfairly treated? What if an employer insists on paying only via direct deposit?

4. In the context of interactive television, to what extent should a company be allowed to retrieve information from children (perhaps via an interactive game format)? For example, should a company be allowed to obtain a child's report on his or her parents' buying patterns? What about information about the child?

5. To what extent should a government regulate computer technology and its applications? Consider, for example, the issues mentioned in questions 3 and 4. What justifies governmental regulation?

6. To what extent will our decisions regarding technology in general, and computer technology in particular, affect future generations?

7. As technology advances, our educational system is constantly challenged to reconsider the level of abstraction at which topics are presented. Many questions take the form of whether a skill is still necessary or whether students should be allowed to rely on an abstract tool. Students of trigonometry are no longer taught how to find the values of trigonometric functions using tables. Instead, they use calculators as abstract tools to find these values. Some argue that long division should also give way to abstraction. What other subjects are involved with similar controversies? Do modern word processors eliminate the need to develop spelling skills? Will the use of video technology someday remove the need to read?

8. The concept of public libraries is largely based on the premise that all citizens in a democracy must have access to information. As more information is stored and disseminated via computer technology, does access to this technology become a right of every individual? If so, should public libraries be the channel by which this access is provided?

9. What ethical concerns arise in a society that relies on the use of abstract tools? Are there cases in which it is unethical to use a product or service without understanding how it works? Without knowing how it is produced? Or, without understanding the byproducts of its use?

10. As our society becomes more automated, it becomes easier for governments to monitor their citizens' activities. Is that good or bad?

11. Which technologies that were imagined by George Orwell (Eric Blair) in his novel *1984* have become reality? Are they being used in the manner in which Orwell predicted?

12. If you had a time machine, in which period of history would you like to live? Are there current technologies that you would like to take with you? Could your choice of technologies be taken with you without taking others? To what

extent can one technology be separated from another? Is it consistent to protest against global warming yet accept modern medical treatment?

13. Suppose your job requires that you reside in another culture. Should you continue to practice the ethics of your native culture or adopt the ethics of your host culture? Does your answer depend on whether the issue involves dress code or human rights? Which ethical standards should prevail if you continue to reside in your native culture but conduct business with a foreign culture on the Internet?

14. Has society become too dependent on computer applications for commerce, communications, or social interactions? For example, what would be the consequences of a long-term interruption in Internet and/or cellular telephone service?

15. Most smartphones are able to identify the phone's location by means of GPS. This allows applications to provide location-specific information (such as the local news, local weather, or the presence of businesses in the immediate area) based on the phone's current location. However, such GPS capabilities may also allow other applications to broadcast the phone's location to other parties. Is this good? How could knowledge of the phone's location (thus your location) be abused?

Additional Reading

Goldstine, J. J. *The Computer from Pascal to von Neumann*. Princeton, NJ: Princeton University Press, 1972.

Kizza, J. M. *Ethical and Social Issues in the Information Age*, 3rd ed. London: Springer-Verlag, 2007.

Mollenhoff, C. R. *Atanasoff: Forgotten Father of the Computer*. Ames, IA: Iowa State University Press, 1988.

Neumann, P. G. *Computer Related Risks*. Boston, MA: Addison-Wesley, 1995.

Ni, L. *Smart Phone and Next Generation Mobile Computing*. San Francisco, CA: Morgan Kaufmann, 2006.

Quinn, M. J. *Ethics for the Information Age*, 5th ed. Boston, MA: AddisonWesley, 2012.

Randell, B. *The Origins of Digital Computers*, 3rd ed. New York: SpringerVerlag, 1982.

Spinello, R. A., and H. T. Tavani. *Readings in CyberEthics*, 2nd ed. Sudbury, MA: Jones and Bartlett, 2004.

Swade, D. *The Difference Engine*. New York: Viking, 2000.

Tavani, H. T. *Ethics and Technology: Ethical Issues in an Age of Information and Communication Technology*, 4th ed. New York: Wiley, 2012.

Woolley, B. *The Bride of Science: Romance, Reason, and Byron's Daughter*. New York: McGraw-Hill, 1999.

Data Storage

In this chapter, we consider topics associated with data representation and the storage of data within a computer. The types of data we will consider include text, numeric values, images, audio, and video. Much of the information in this chapter is also relevant to fields other than traditional computing, such as digital photography, audio/video recording and reproduction, and long-distance communication.

We begin our study of computer science by considering how information is encoded and stored inside computers. Our first step is to discuss the basics of a computer's data storage devices and then to consider how information is encoded for storage in these systems. We will explore the ramifications of today's data storage systems and how such techniques as data compression and error handling are used to overcome their shortfalls.

1.1 Bits and Their Storage

Inside today's computers information is encoded as patterns of 0s and 1s. These digits are called **bits** (short for *binary digits*). Although you may be inclined to associate bits with numeric values, they are really only symbols whose meaning depends on the application at hand. Sometimes patterns of bits are used to represent numeric values; sometimes they represent characters in an alphabet and punctuation marks; sometimes they represent images; and sometimes they represent sounds.

Boolean Operations

To understand how individual bits are stored and manipulated inside a computer, it is convenient to imagine that the bit 0 represents the value *false* and the bit 1 represents the value *true*. Operations that manipulate true/false values are called **Boolean operations,** in honor of the mathematician George Boole (1815–1864), who was a pioneer in the field of mathematics called logic. Three of the basic Boolean operations are AND, OR, and XOR (exclusive or) as summarized in Figure 1.1. (We capitalize these Boolean operation names to distinguish them from their English word counterparts.) These operations are similar to the arithmetic operations TIMES and PLUS because they combine a pair of values (the operation's input) to produce a third value (the output). In contrast to arithmetic operations, however, Boolean operations combine true/false values rather than numeric values.

The Boolean operation AND is designed to reflect the truth or falseness of a statement formed by combining two smaller, or simpler, statements with the conjunction *and*. Such statements have the generic form

   P AND *Q*

where *P* represents one statement, and *Q* represents another—for example,

   Kermit is a frog AND Miss Piggy is an actress.

The inputs to the AND operation represent the truth or falseness of the compound statement's components; the output represents the truth or falseness of the compound statement itself. Since a statement of the form *P* AND *Q* is true only when both of its components are true, we conclude that 1 AND 1 should be 1, whereas all other cases should produce an output of 0, in agreement with Figure 1.1.

In a similar manner, the OR operation is based on compound statements of the form

   P OR *Q*

where, again, *P* represents one statement and *Q* represents another. Such statements are true when at least one of their components is true, which agrees with the OR operation depicted in Figure 1.1.

Figure 1.1 The possible input and output values of Boolean operations AND, OR, and XOR (exclusive or)

The AND operation

0	0	1	1
AND 0	AND 1	AND 0	AND 1
0	0	0	1

The OR operation

0	0	1	1
OR 0	OR 1	OR 0	OR 1
0	1	1	1

The XOR operation

0	0	1	1
XOR 0	XOR 1	XOR 0	XOR 1
0	1	1	0

There is not a single conjunction in the English language that captures the meaning of the XOR operation. XOR produces an output of 1 (true) when one of its inputs is 1 (true) and the other is 0 (false). For example, a statement of the form P XOR Q means "either P or Q but not both." (In short, the XOR operation produces an output of 1 when its inputs are different.)

The operation NOT is another Boolean operation. It differs from AND, OR, and XOR because it has only one input. Its output is the opposite of that input; if the input of the operation NOT is true, then the output is false, and vice versa. Thus, if the input of the NOT operation is the truth or falseness of the statement

> Fozzie is a bear.

then the output would represent the truth or falseness of the statement

> Fozzie is not a bear.

Gates and Flip-Flops

A device that produces the output of a Boolean operation when given the operation's input values is called a **gate.** Gates can be constructed from a variety of technologies such as gears, relays, and optic devices. Inside today's computers, gates are usually implemented as small electronic circuits in which the digits 0 and 1 are represented as voltage levels. We need not concern ourselves with such details, however. For our purposes, it suffices to represent gates in their symbolic form, as shown in Figure 1.2. Note that the AND, OR, XOR, and NOT gates are represented by distinctively shaped symbols, with the input values entering on one side, and the output exiting on the other.

Gates provide the building blocks from which computers are constructed. One important step in this direction is depicted in the circuit in Figure 1.3. This is a particular example from a collection of circuits known as a **flip-flop.** A flip-flop

Figure 1.2   A pictorial representation of AND, OR, XOR, and NOT gates as well as their input and output values

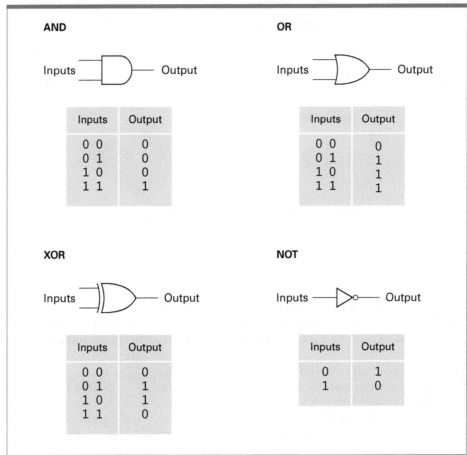

is a fundamental unit of computer memory. It is a circuit that produces an output value of 0 or 1, which remains constant until a pulse (a temporary change to a 1 that returns to 0) from another circuit causes it to shift to the other value. In other words, the output can be set to "remember" a zero or a one under control of external stimuli. As long as both inputs in the circuit in Figure 1.3 remain 0, the output (whether 0 or 1) will not change. However, temporarily placing a 1 on the upper input will force the output to be 1, whereas temporarily placing a 1 on the lower input will force the output to be 0.

Let us consider this claim in more detail. Without knowing the current output of the circuit in Figure 1.3, suppose that the upper input is changed to 1 while the lower input remains 0 (Figure 1.4a). This will cause the output of the OR gate to be 1, regardless of the other input to this gate. In turn, both inputs to the AND gate will now be 1, since the other input to this gate is already 1 (the output produced by the NOT gate whenever the lower input of the flip-flop is at 0). The output of the AND gate will then become 1, which means that the second input to the OR gate will now be 1 (Figure 1.4b). This guarantees that the output of the OR gate will remain 1, even when the upper input to the flip-flop is changed back to 0 (Figure 1.4c). In summary, the flip-flop's output has become 1, and this output value will remain after the upper input returns to 0.

Figure 1.3   A simple flip-flop circuit

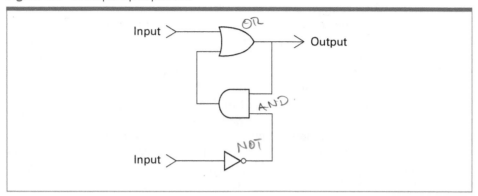

In a similar manner, temporarily placing the value 1 on the lower input will force the flip-flop's output to be 0, and this output will persist after the input value returns to 0.

Our purpose in introducing the flip-flop circuit in Figures 1.3 and 1.4 is threefold. First, it demonstrates how devices can be constructed from gates, a process known as digital circuit design, which is an important topic in computer

Figure 1.4   Setting the output of a flip-flop to 1

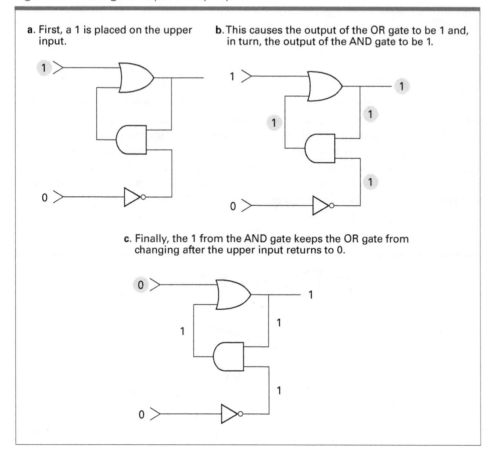

a. First, a 1 is placed on the upper input.

b. This causes the output of the OR gate to be 1 and, in turn, the output of the AND gate to be 1.

c. Finally, the 1 from the AND gate keeps the OR gate from changing after the upper input returns to 0.

engineering. Indeed, the flip-flop is only one of many circuits that are basic tools in computer engineering.

Second, the concept of a flip-flop provides an example of abstraction and the use of abstract tools. Actually, there are other ways to build a flip-flop. One alternative is shown in Figure 1.5. If you experiment with this circuit, you will find that, although it has a different internal structure, its external properties are the same as those of Figure 1.3. A computer engineer does not need to know which circuit is actually used within a flip-flop. Instead, only an understanding of the flip-flop's external properties is needed to use it as an abstract tool. A flip-flop, along with other well-defined circuits, forms a set of building blocks from which an engineer can construct more complex circuitry. In turn, the design of computer circuitry takes on a hierarchical structure, each level of which uses the lower level components as abstract tools.

The third purpose for introducing the flip-flop is that it is one means of storing a bit within a modern computer. More precisely, a flip-flop can be set to have the output value of either 0 or 1. Other circuits can adjust this value by sending pulses to the flip-flop's inputs, and still other circuits can respond to the stored value by using the flip-flop's output as their inputs. Thus, many flip-flops, constructed as very small electrical circuits, can be used inside a computer as a means of recording information that is encoded as patterns of 0s and 1s. Indeed, technology known as **very large-scale integration (VLSI),** which allows millions of electrical components to be constructed on a wafer (called a **chip**), is used to create miniature devices containing millions of flip-flops along with their controlling circuitry. Consequently, these chips are used as abstract tools in the construction of computer systems. In fact, in some cases VLSI is used to create an entire computer system on a single chip.

Hexadecimal Notation

When considering the internal activities of a computer, we must deal with patterns of bits, which we will refer to as a string of bits, some of which can be quite long. A long string of bits is often called a **stream.** Unfortunately, streams are difficult for the human mind to comprehend. Merely transcribing the pattern 101101010011 is tedious and error prone. To simplify the representation of such bit patterns, therefore, we usually use a shorthand notation called **hexadecimal notation,** which takes advantage of the fact that bit patterns within a machine

Figure 1.5   Another way of constructing a flip-flop

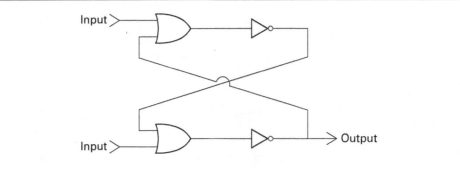

Figure 1.6 The hexadecimal encoding system

Bit pattern	Hexadecimal representation
0000	0
0001	1
0010	2
0011	3
0100	4
0101	5
0110	6
0111	7
1000	8
1001	9
1010	A
1011	B
1100	C
1101	D
1110	E
1111	F

tend to have lengths in multiples of four. In particular, hexadecimal notation uses a single symbol to represent a pattern of four bits. For example, a string of twelve bits can be represented by three hexadecimal symbols.

Figure 1.6 presents the hexadecimal encoding system. The left column displays all possible bit patterns of length four; the right column shows the symbol used in hexadecimal notation to represent the bit pattern to its left. Using this system, the bit pattern 10110101 is represented as B5. This is obtained by dividing the bit pattern into substrings of length four and then representing each substring by its hexadecimal equivalent—1011 is represented by B, and 0101 is represented by 5. In this manner, the 16-bit pattern 1010010011001000 can be reduced to the more palatable form A4C8.

We will use hexadecimal notation extensively in the next chapter. There you will come to appreciate its efficiency.

Questions & Exercises

1. What input bit patterns will cause the following circuit to produce an output of 1?

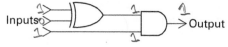

2. In the text, we claimed that placing a 1 on the lower input of the flip-flop in Figure 1.3 (while holding the upper input at 0) will force the flip-flop's output to be 0. Describe the sequence of events that occurs within the flip-flop in this case.

3. Assuming that both inputs to the flip-flop in Figure 1.5 begin as 0, describe the sequence of events that occurs when the upper input is temporarily set to 1.

4. **a.** If the output of an AND gate is passed through a NOT gate, the combination computes the Boolean operation called NAND, which has an output of 0 only when both its inputs are 1. The symbol for a NAND gate is the same as an AND gate except that it has a circle at its output. The following is a circuit containing a NAND gate. What Boolean operation does the circuit compute?

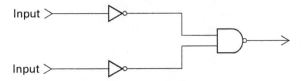

b. If the output of an OR gate is passed through a NOT gate, the combination computes the Boolean operation called NOR that has an output of 1 only when both its inputs are 0. The symbol for a NOR gate is the same as an OR gate except that it has a circle at its output. The following is a circuit containing an AND gate and two NOR gates. What Boolean operation does the circuit compute?

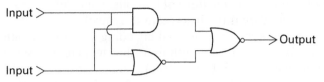

5. Use hexadecimal notation to represent the following bit patterns:

   a. 0110101011110010   **b.** 1110100001010100010111

   c. 01001000

6. What bit patterns are represented by the following hexadecimal patterns?

   a. 5FD97   **b.** 610A   **c.** ABCD   **d.** 0100

1.2 Main Memory

For the purpose of storing data, a computer contains a large collection of circuits (such as flip-flops), each capable of storing a single bit. This bit reservoir is known as the machine's **main memory.**

Memory Organization

A computer's main memory is organized in manageable units called **cells,** with a typical cell size being eight bits. (A string of eight bits is called a **byte.** Thus, a typical memory cell has a capacity of one byte.) Small computers embedded in such household devices as microwave ovens may have main memories consisting

Figure 1.7 The organization of a byte-size memory cell

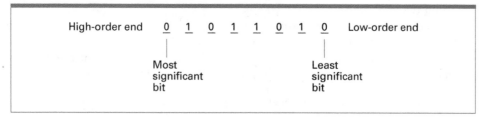

of only a few hundred cells, whereas large computers may have billions of cells in their main memories.

Although there is no left or right within a computer, we normally envision the bits within a memory cell as being arranged in a row. The left end of this row is called the **high-order end,** and the right end is called the **low-order end.** The leftmost bit is called either the high-order bit or the **most significant bit** in reference to the fact that if the contents of the cell were interpreted as representing a numeric value, this bit would be the most significant digit in the number. Similarly, the rightmost bit is referred to as the low-order bit or the **least significant bit.** Thus we may represent the contents of a byte-size memory cell as shown in Figure 1.7.

To identify individual cells in a computer's main memory, each cell is assigned a unique "name," called its **address.** The system is analogous to the technique of identifying houses in a city by addresses. In the case of memory cells, however, the addresses used are entirely numeric. To be more precise, we envision all the cells being placed in a single row and numbered in this order starting with the value zero. Such an addressing system not only gives us a way of uniquely identifying each cell but also associates an order to the cells (Figure 1.8), giving us phrases such as "the next cell" or "the previous cell."

An important consequence of assigning an order to both the cells in main memory and the bits within each cell is that the entire collection of bits within a computer's main memory is essentially ordered in one long row. Pieces of this long row can therefore be used to store bit patterns that may be longer than the

Figure 1.8 Memory cells arranged by address

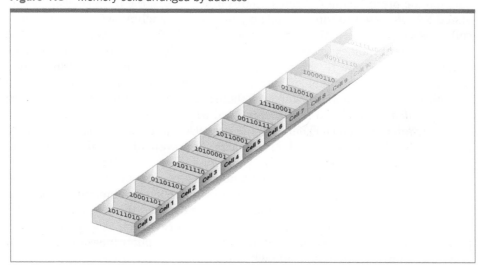

length of a single cell. In particular, we can still store a string of 16 bits merely by using two consecutive memory cells.

To complete the main memory of a computer, the circuitry that actually holds the bits is combined with the circuitry required to allow other circuits to store and retrieve data from the memory cells. In this way, other circuits can get data from the memory by electronically asking for the contents of a certain address (called a read operation), or they can record information in the memory by requesting that a certain bit pattern be placed in the cell at a particular address (called a write operation).

Because a computer's main memory is organized as individual, addressable cells, the cells can be accessed independently as required. To reflect the ability to access cells in any order, a computer's main memory is often called **random access memory (RAM).** This random access feature of main memory is in stark contrast to the mass storage systems that we will discuss in the next section, in which long strings of bits are manipulated as amalgamated blocks.

Although we have introduced flip-flops as a means of storing bits, the RAM in most modern computers is constructed using analogous, but more complex technologies that provide greater miniaturization and faster response time. Many of these technologies store bits as tiny electric charges that dissipate quickly. Thus these devices require additional circuitry, known as a refresh circuit, that repeatedly replenishes the charges many times a second. In recognition of this volatility, computer memory constructed from such technology is often called **dynamic memory,** leading to the term **DRAM** (pronounced "DEE–ram") meaning Dynamic RAM. Or, at times the term **SDRAM** (pronounced "ES-DEE-ram"), meaning Synchronous DRAM, is used in reference to DRAM that applies additional techniques to decrease the time needed to retrieve the contents from its memory cells.

Measuring Memory Capacity

As we will learn in the next chapter, it is convenient to design main memory systems in which the total number of cells is a power of two. In turn, the size of the memories in early computers were often measured in 1024 (which is 2^{10}) cell units. Since 1024 is close to the value 1000, the computing community adopted the prefix *kilo* in reference to this unit. That is, the term *kilobyte* (abbreviated KB) was used to refer to 1024 bytes. Thus, a machine with 4096 memory cells was said to have a 4KB memory ($4096 = 4 \times 1024$). As memories became larger, this terminology grew to include MB (megabyte), GB (gigabyte), and TB (terabyte). Unfortunately, this application of prefixes *kilo-, mega-,* and so on, represents a misuse of terminology because these are already used in other fields in reference to units that are powers of a thousand. For example, when measuring distance, *kilometer* refers to 1000 meters, and when measuring radio frequencies, *megahertz* refers to 1,000,000 hertz. In the late 1990s, international standards organizations developed specialized terminology for powers of two: *kibi-, mebi-, gibi-,* and *tebi*-bytes denote powers of 1024, rather than powers of a thousand. However, while this distinction is the law of the land in many parts of the world, both the general public and many computer scientists have been reluctant to abandon the more familiar, yet ambiguous "megabyte." Thus, a word of caution is in order when using this terminology. As a general rule, terms such as *kilo-, mega-,* etc. refer to powers of two when used in the context of computer measurements, but they refer to powers of a thousand when used in other contexts.

Questions & Exercises

1. If the memory cell whose address is 5 contains the value 8, what is the difference between writing the value 5 into cell number 6 and moving the contents of cell number 5 into cell number 6?

2. Suppose you want to interchange the values stored in memory cells 2 and 3. What is wrong with the following sequence of steps:

   Step 1. Move the contents of cell number 2 to cell number 3.

   Step 2. Move the contents of cell number 3 to cell number 2.

   Design a sequence of steps that correctly interchanges the contents of these cells. If needed, you may use additional cells.

3. How many bits would be in the memory of a computer with 4KB memory?

1.3 Mass Storage

Due to the volatility and limited size of a computer's main memory, most computers have additional memory devices called **mass storage** (or secondary storage) systems, including magnetic disks, CDs, DVDs, magnetic tapes, flash drives, and solid-state disks (all of which we will discuss shortly). The advantages of mass storage systems over main memory include less volatility, large storage capacities, low cost, and in many cases, the ability to remove the storage medium from the machine for archival purposes.

A major disadvantage of magnetic and optical mass storage systems is that they typically require mechanical motion and therefore require significantly more time to store and retrieve data than a machine's main memory, where all activities are performed electronically. Moreover, storage systems with moving parts are more prone to mechanical failures than solid state systems.

Magnetic Systems

For years, magnetic technology has dominated the mass storage arena. The most common example in use today is the **magnetic disk** or **hard disk drive (HDD),** in which a thin spinning disk with magnetic coating is used to hold data (Figure 1.9). Read/write heads are placed above and/or below the disk so that as the disk spins, each head traverses a circle, called a **track.** By repositioning the read/write heads, different concentric tracks can be accessed. In many cases, a disk storage system consists of several disks mounted on a common spindle, one on top of the other, with enough space for the read/write heads to slip between the platters. In such cases, the read/write heads move in unison. Each time the read/write heads are repositioned, a new set of tracks—which is called a **cylinder**—becomes accessible.

Since a track can contain more information than we would normally want to manipulate at any one time, each track is divided into small arcs called **sectors** on which information is recorded as a continuous string of bits. All sectors on a disk contain the same number of bits (typical capacities are in the range of 512 bytes to a few KB), and in the simplest disk storage systems each track contains the same

Figure 1.9 A disk storage system

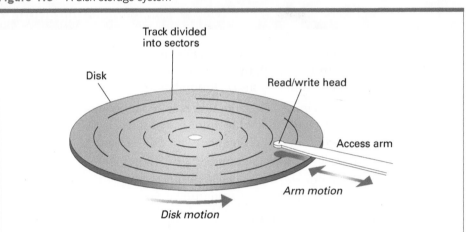

number of sectors. Thus, the bits within a sector on a track near the outer edge of the disk are less compactly stored than those on the tracks near the center, since the outer tracks are longer than the inner ones. In contrast, in high-capacity disk storage systems, the tracks near the outer edge are capable of containing significantly more sectors than those near the center, and this capability is often used by applying a technique called **zoned-bit recording.** Using zoned-bit recording, several adjacent tracks are collectively known as zones, with a typical disk containing approximately 10 zones. All tracks within a zone have the same number of sectors, but each zone has more sectors per track than the zone inside of it. In this manner, efficient use of the entire disk surface is achieved. Regardless of the details, a disk storage system consists of many individual sectors, each of which can be accessed as an independent string of bits.

The capacity of a disk storage system depends on the number of platters used and the density in which the tracks and sectors are placed. Lower-capacity systems may consist of a single platter. High-capacity disk systems, capable of holding many gigabytes, or even terabytes, consist of perhaps three to six platters mounted on a common spindle. Furthermore, data may be stored on both the upper and lower surfaces of each platter.

Several measurements are used to evaluate a disk system's performance: (1) **seek time** (the time required to move the read/write heads from one track to another); (2) **rotation delay** or **latency time** (half the time required for the disk to make a complete rotation, which is the average amount of time required for the desired data to rotate around to the read/write head once the head has been positioned over the desired track); (3) **access time** (the sum of seek time and rotation delay); and (4) **transfer rate** (the rate at which data can be transferred to or from the disk). (Note that in the case of zone-bit recording, the amount of data passing a read/write head in a single disk rotation is greater for tracks in an outer zone than for an inner zone, and therefore the data transfer rate varies depending on the portion of the disk being used.)

A factor limiting the access time and transfer rate is the speed at which a disk system rotates. To facilitate fast rotation speeds, the read/write heads in these systems do not touch the disk but instead "float" just off the surface. The spacing is so close that even a single particle of dust could become jammed between the head and disk surface, destroying both (a phenomenon known as a head crash). Thus, disk systems are typically housed in cases that are sealed at the factory. With this construction, disk systems are able to rotate at speeds of several hundred times per second, achieving transfer rates that are measured in MB per second.

Since disk systems require physical motion for their operation, these systems suffer when compared to speeds within electronic circuitry. Delay times within an electronic circuit are measured in units of nanoseconds (billionths of a second) or less, whereas seek times, latency times, and access times of disk systems are measured in milliseconds (thousandths of a second). Thus the time required to retrieve information from a disk system can seem like an eternity to an electronic circuit awaiting a result.

Magnetic storage technologies that are now less widely used include **magnetic tape,** in which information is recorded on the magnetic coating of a thin plastic tape wound on reels, and **floppy disk drives,** in which single platters with a magnetic coating are encased in a portable cartridge designed to be readily removed from the drive. Magnetic tape drives have extremely long seek times, just as their cousins, audio cassettes, suffer from long rewind and fast-forward times. Low cost and high data capacities still make magnetic tape suitable for applications where data is primarily read or written linearly, such as archival data backups. The removable nature of floppy disk platters came at the cost of much lower data densities and access speeds than hard disk platters, but their portability was extremely valuable in earlier decades, prior to the arrival of flash drives with larger capacity and higher durability.

Optical Systems

Another class of mass storage systems applies optical technology. An example is the **compact disk (CD).** These disks are 12 centimeters (approximately 5 inches) in diameter and consist of reflective material covered with a clear protective coating. Information is recorded on them by creating variations in their reflective surfaces. This information can then be retrieved by means of a laser that detects irregularities on the reflective surface of the CD as it spins.

CD technology was originally applied to audio recordings using a recording format known as **CD-DA (compact disk-digital audio),** and the CDs used today for computer data storage use essentially the same format. In particular, information on these CDs is stored on a single track that spirals around the CD like a groove in an old-fashioned phonograph record, however, unlike old-fashioned phonograph records, the track on a CD spirals from the inside out (Figure 1.10). This track is divided into units called sectors, each with its own identifying markings and a capacity of 2KB of data, which equates to 1/75 of a second of music in the case of audio recordings.

Note that the distance around the spiraled track is greater toward the outer edge of the disk than at the inner portion. To maximize the capacity of a CD, information is stored at a uniform linear density over the entire spiraled track, which means that more information is stored in a loop around the outer portion of the spiral than in a loop around the inner portion. In turn, more sectors will be read in a single revolution of the disk when the laser is scanning the outer portion of the spiraled track than when the laser is scanning the inner portion of the track. Thus, to obtain a uniform rate of data transfer, CD-DA players are designed

Figure 1.10   CD storage format

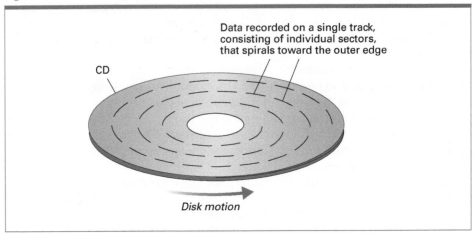

to vary the rotation speed depending on the location of the laser. However, most CD systems used for computer data storage spin at a faster, constant speed and thus must accommodate variations in data transfer rates.

As a consequence of such design decisions, CD storage systems perform best when dealing with long, continuous strings of data, as when reproducing music. In contrast, when an application requires access to items of data in a random manner, the approach used in magnetic disk storage (individual, concentric tracks divided into individually accessible sectors) outperforms the spiral approach used in CDs.

Traditional CDs have capacities in the range of 600 to 700MB. However, **DVDs (Digital Versatile Disks),** which are constructed from multiple, semitransparent layers that serve as distinct surfaces when viewed by a precisely focused laser, provide storage capacities of several GB. Such disks are capable of storing lengthy multimedia presentations, including entire motion pictures. Finally, Blu-ray technology, which uses a laser in the blue-violet spectrum of light (instead of red), is able to focus its laser beam with very fine precision. As a result, **BDs (Blu-ray Disks)** provides over five times the capacity of a DVD. This seemingly vast amount of storage is needed to meet the demands of high definition video.

Flash Drives

A common property of mass storage systems based on magnetic or optic technology is that physical motion, such as spinning disks, moving read/write heads, and aiming laser beams, is required to store and retrieve data. This means that data storage and retrieval is slow compared to the speed of electronic circuitry. **Flash memory** technology has the potential of alleviating this drawback. In a flash memory system, bits are stored by sending electronic signals directly to the storage medium where they cause electrons to be trapped in tiny chambers of silicon dioxide, thus altering the characteristics of small electronic circuits. Since these chambers are able to hold their captive electrons for many years without external power, this technology is excellent for portable, nonvolatile data storage.

Although data stored in flash memory systems can be accessed in small byte-size units as in RAM applications, current technology dictates that stored data be erased in large blocks. Moreover, repeated erasing slowly damages the silicon dioxide chambers, meaning that current flash memory technology is not suitable for general main memory applications where its contents might be altered many times a second. However, in those applications in which alterations can be controlled to a reasonable level, such as in digital cameras and smartphones, flash memory has become the mass storage technology of choice. Indeed, since flash memory is not sensitive to physical shock (in contrast to magnetic and optic systems), it is now replacing other mass storage technologies in portable applications such as laptop computers.

Flash memory devices called **flash drives,** with capacities of hundreds of GBs, are available for general mass storage applications. These units are packaged in ever smaller plastic cases with a removable cap on one end to protect the unit's electrical connector when the drive is offline. The high capacity of these portable units as well as the fact that they are easily connected to and disconnected from a computer make them ideal for portable data storage. However, the vulnerability of their tiny storage chambers dictates that they are not as reliable as optical disks for truly long-term applications.

Larger flash memory devices called **SSDs (solid-state disks)** are explicitly designed to take the place of magnetic hard disks. SSDs compare favorably to hard disks in their resilience to vibrations and physical shock, their quiet operation (due to no moving parts), and their lower access times. SSDs remain more expensive than hard disks of comparable size and thus are still considered a high-end option when buying a computer. SSD sectors suffer from the more limited lifetime of all flash memory technologies, but the use of **wear-leveling** techniques can reduce the impact of this by relocating frequently altered data blocks to fresh locations on the drive.

Another application of flash technology is found in **SD (Secure Digital) memory cards** (or just SD Card). These provide up to two GBs of storage and are packaged in a plastic rigged wafer about the size a postage stamp (SD cards are also available in smaller mini and micro sizes), **SDHC (High Capacity)** memory cards can provide up to 32 GBs and the next generation **SDXC (Extended Capacity) memory cards** may exceed a TB. Given their compact physical size, these cards conveniently slip into slots of small electronic devices. Thus, they are ideal for digital cameras, smartphones, music players, car navigation systems, and a host of other electronic appliances.

Questions & Exercises

1. What is gained by increasing the rotation speed of a disk or CD?
2. When recording data on a multiple-disk storage system, should we fill a complete disk surface before starting on another surface, or should we first fill an entire cylinder before starting on another cylinder?
3. Why should the data in a reservation system that is constantly being updated be stored on a magnetic disk instead of a CD or DVD?

4. What factors allow CD, DVD, and Blu-ray disks all to be read by the same drive?

5. What advantage do flash drives have over the other mass storage systems introduced in this section?

6. What advantages continue to make magnetic hard disk drives competitive?

1.4 Representing Information as Bit Patterns

Having considered techniques for storing bits, we now consider how information can be encoded as bit patterns. Our study focuses on popular methods for encoding text, numerical data, images, and sound. Each of these systems has repercussions that are often visible to a typical computer user. Our goal is to understand enough about these techniques so that we can recognize their consequences for what they are.

Representing Text

Information in the form of text is normally represented by means of a code in which each of the different symbols in the text (such as the letters of the alphabet and punctuation marks) is assigned a unique bit pattern. The text is then represented as a long string of bits in which the successive patterns represent the successive symbols in the original text.

In the 1940s and 1950s, many such codes were designed and used in connection with different pieces of equipment, producing a corresponding proliferation of communication problems. To alleviate this situation, the **American National Standards Institute (ANSI,** pronounced "AN–see") adopted the **American Standard Code for Information Interchange (ASCII,** pronounced "AS–kee"). This code uses bit patterns of length seven to represent the upper- and lowercase letters of the English alphabet, punctuation symbols, the digits 0 through 9, and certain control information such as line feeds, carriage returns, and tabs. ASCII is extended to an eight-bit-per-symbol format by adding a 0 at the most significant end of each of the seven-bit patterns. This technique not only produces a code in which each pattern fits conveniently into a typical byte-size memory cell but also provides 128 additional bit patterns (those obtained by assigning the extra bit the value 1) that can be used to represent symbols beyond the English alphabet and associated punctuation.

A portion of ASCII in its eight-bit-per-symbol format is shown in Appendix A. By referring to this appendix, we can decode the bit pattern

01001000　01100101　01101100　01101100　01101111　00101110

as the message "Hello." as demonstrated in Figure 1.11.

The **International Organization for Standardization** (also known as **ISO,** in reference to the Greek word *isos,* meaning equal) has developed a number of extensions to ASCII, each of which was designed to accommodate a major language group. For example, one standard provides the symbols needed to express the text of most Western European languages. Included in its 128 additional patterns are symbols for the British pound and the German vowels ä, ö, and ü.

Figure 1.11   The message "Hello." in ASCII or UTF-8 encoding

01001000	01100101	01101100	01101100	01101111	00101110
H	e	l	l	o	.

The ISO-extended ASCII standards made tremendous headway toward supporting all of the world's multilingual communication; however, two major obstacles surfaced. First, the number of extra bit patterns available in extended ASCII is simply insufficient to accommodate the alphabet of many Asian and some Eastern European languages. Second, because a given document was constrained to using symbols in just the one selected standard, documents containing text of languages from disparate language groups could not be supported. Both proved to be a significant detriment to international use. To address this deficiency, **Unicode** was developed through the cooperation of several of the leading manufacturers of hardware and software and has rapidly gained the support of the computing community. This code uses a unique pattern of up to 21 bits to represent each symbol. When the Unicode character set is combined with the **Unicode Transformation Format 8-bit (UTF-8)** encoding standard, the original ASCII characters can still be represented with 8 bits, while the thousands of additional characters from such languages as Chinese, Japanese, and Hebrew can be represented by 16 bits. Beyond the characters required for all of the world's commonly used languages, UTF-8 uses 24- or 32-bit patterns to represent more obscure Unicode symbols, leaving ample room for future expansion.

A file consisting of a long sequence of symbols encoded using ASCII or Unicode is often called a **text file.** It is important to distinguish between simple text files that are manipulated by utility programs called **text editors** (or often simply editors) and the more elaborate files produced by **word processors** such as Microsoft's Word. Both consist of textual material. However, a text file contains only a character-by-character encoding of the text, whereas a file produced by a word processor contains numerous proprietary codes representing changes in fonts, alignment information, and other parameters.

Representing Numeric Values

Storing information in terms of encoded characters is inefficient when the information being recorded is purely numeric. To see why, consider the problem of storing the value 25. If we insist on storing it as encoded symbols in ASCII using one byte per symbol, we need a total of 16 bits. Moreover, the largest number we could store using 16 bits is 99. However, as we will shortly see, by using **binary notation** we can store any integer in the range from 0 to 65535 in these 16 bits. Thus, binary notation (or variations of it) is used extensively for encoded numeric data for computer storage.

Binary notation is a way of representing numeric values using only the digits 0 and 1 rather than the digits 0, 1, 2, 3, 4, 5, 6, 7, 8, and 9 as in the traditional decimal, or base 10, system. We will study the binary system more thoroughly in Section 1.5. For now, all we need is an elementary understanding of the system. For this purpose consider an old-fashioned car odometer whose display wheels

The American National Standards Institute

The American National Standards Institute (ANSI) was founded in 1918 by a small consortium of engineering societies and government agencies as a nonprofit federation to coordinate the development of voluntary standards in the private sector. Today, ANSI membership includes more than 1300 businesses, professional organizations, trade associations, and government agencies. ANSI is headquartered in New York and represents the United States as a member body in the ISO. The website for the American National Standards Institute is at http://www.ansi.org.

Similar organizations in other countries include Standards Australia (Australia), Standards Council of Canada (Canada), China State Bureau of Quality and Technical Supervision (China), Deutsches Institut für Normung (Germany), Japanese Industrial Standards Committee (Japan), Dirección General de Normas (Mexico), State Committee of the Russian Federation for Standardization and Metrology (Russia), Swiss Association for Standardization (Switzerland), and British Standards Institution (United Kingdom).

contain only the digits 0 and 1 rather than the traditional digits 0 through 9. The odometer starts with a reading of all 0s, and as the car is driven for the first few miles, the rightmost wheel rotates from a 0 to a 1. Then, as that 1 rotates back to a 0, it causes a 1 to appear to its left, producing the pattern 10. The 0 on the right then rotates to a 1, producing 11. Now the rightmost wheel rotates from 1 back to 0, causing the 1 to its left to rotate to a 0 as well. This in turn causes another 1 to appear in the third column, producing the pattern 100. In short, as we drive the car we see the following sequence of odometer readings:

0000
0001
0010
0011
0100
0101
0110
0111
1000

This sequence consists of the binary representations of the integers zero through eight. Although tedious, we could extend this counting technique to discover that the bit pattern consisting of 16 1s represents the value 65535, which confirms our claim that any integer in the range from 0 to 65535 can be encoded using 16 bits.

Due to this efficiency, it is common to store numeric information in a form of binary notation rather than in encoded symbols. We say "a form of binary notation" because the straightforward binary system just described is only the basis for several numeric storage techniques used within machines. Some of these variations of the binary system are discussed later in this chapter. For now, we merely note that a system called **two's complement** notation (see Section 1.6) is common for storing whole numbers because it provides a convenient method for representing negative numbers as well as positive. For representing numbers with fractional parts such as 4-1/2 or 3/4, another technique, called **floating-point notation** (see Section 1.7), is used.

Representing Images

One means of representing an image is to interpret the image as a collection of dots, each of which is called a **pixel,** short for "picture element." The appearance of each pixel is then encoded and the entire image is represented as a collection of these encoded pixels. Such a collection is called a **bit map.** This approach is popular because many display devices, such as printers and display screens, operate on the pixel concept. In turn, images in bit map form are easily formatted for display.

The method of encoding the pixels in a bit map varies among applications. In the case of a simple black-and-white image, each pixel can be represented by a single bit whose value depends on whether the corresponding pixel is black or white. This is the approach used by most facsimile machines. For more elaborate black-and-white photographs, each pixel can be represented by a collection of bits (usually eight), which allows a variety of shades of grayness to be represented. In the case of color images, each pixel is encoded by more complex system. Two approaches are common. In one, which we will call RGB encoding, each pixel is represented as three color components—a red component, a green component, and a blue component—corresponding to the three primary colors of light. One byte is normally used to represent the intensity of each color component. In turn, three bytes of storage are required to represent a single pixel in the original image.

An alternative to simple RGB encoding is to use a "brightness" component and two color components. In this case the "brightness" component, which is called the pixel's luminance, is essentially the sum of the red, green, and blue components. (Actually, it is considered to be the amount of white light in the pixel, but these details need not concern us here.) The other two components, called the blue chrominance and the red chrominance, are determined by computing the difference between the pixel's luminance and the amount of blue or red light, respectively, in the pixel. Together these three components contain the information required to reproduce the pixel.

The popularity of encoding images using luminance and chrominance components originated in the field of color television broadcast because this approach provided a means of encoding color images that was also compatible with older black-and-white television receivers. Indeed, a gray-scale version of an image can be produced by using only the luminance components of the encoded color image.

ISO—The International Organization for Standardization

The International Organization for Standardization (more commonly called ISO) was established in 1947 as a worldwide federation of standardization bodies, one from each country. Today, it is headquartered in Geneva, Switzerland, and has more than 100 member bodies as well as numerous correspondent members. (A correspondent member is usually a standardization body from a country that does not have a nationally recognized standardization body. Such members cannot participate directly in the development of standards but are kept informed of ISO activities.) ISO maintains a website at http://www.iso.org.

A disadvantage of representing images as bit maps is that an image cannot be rescaled easily to any arbitrary size. Essentially, the only way to enlarge the image is to make the pixels bigger, which leads to a grainy appearance. (This is the technique called "digital zoom" used in digital cameras as opposed to "optical zoom" that is obtained by adjusting the camera lens.)

An alternate way of representing images that avoids this scaling problem is to describe the image as a collection of geometric structures, such as lines and curves, that can be encoded using techniques of analytic geometry. Such a description allows the device that ultimately displays the image to decide how the geometric structures should be displayed rather than insisting that the device reproduce a particular pixel pattern. This is the approach used to produce the scalable fonts that are available via today's word processing systems. For example, TrueType (developed by Microsoft and Apple) is a system for geometrically describing text symbols. Likewise, PostScript (developed by Adobe Systems) provides a means of describing characters as well as more general pictorial data. This geometric means of representing images is also popular in **computer-aided design (CAD)** systems in which drawings of three-dimensional objects are displayed and manipulated on computer display screens.

The distinction between representing an image in the form of geometric structures as opposed to bit maps is evident to users of many drawing software systems (such as Microsoft's Paint utility) that allow the user to draw pictures consisting of pre-established shapes such as rectangles, ovals, and elementary curves. The user simply selects the desired geometric shape from a menu and then directs the drawing of that shape via a mouse. During the drawing process, the software maintains a geometric description of the shape being drawn. As directions are given by the mouse, the internal geometric representation is modified, reconverted to bit map form, and displayed. This allows for easy scaling and shaping of the image. Once the drawing process is complete, however, the underlying geometric description is discarded and only the bit map is preserved, meaning that additional alterations require a tedious pixel-by-pixel modification process. On the other hand, some drawing systems preserve the description as geometric shapes that can be modified later. With these systems, the shapes can be easily resized, maintaining a crisp display at any dimension.

Representing Sound

The most generic method of encoding audio information for computer storage and manipulation is to sample the amplitude of the sound wave at regular intervals and record the series of values obtained. For instance, the series 0, 1.5, 2.0, 1.5, 2.0, 3.0, 4.0, 3.0, 0 would represent a sound wave that rises in amplitude, falls briefly, rises to a higher level, and then drops back to 0 (Figure 1.12). This technique, using a sample rate of 8000 samples per second, has been used for years in long-distance voice telephone communication. The voice at one end of the communication is encoded as numeric values representing the amplitude of the voice every eight-thousandth of a second. These numeric values are then transmitted over the communication line to the receiving end, where they are used to reproduce the sound of the voice.

Although 8000 samples per second may seem to be a rapid rate, it is not sufficient for high-fidelity music recordings. To obtain the quality sound reproduction obtained by today's musical CDs, a sample rate of 44,100 samples per second

Figure 1.12 The sound wave represented by the sequence 0, 1.5, 2.0, 1.5, 2.0, 3.0, 4.0, 3.0, 0

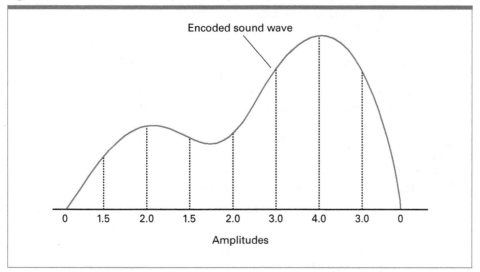

Encoded sound wave

| 0 | 1.5 | 2.0 | 1.5 | 2.0 | 3.0 | 4.0 | 3.0 | 0 |

Amplitudes

is used. The data obtained from each sample are represented in 16 bits (32 bits for stereo recordings). Consequently, each second of music recorded in stereo requires more than a million bits.

An alternative encoding system known as Musical Instrument Digital Interface (MIDI, pronounced "MID–ee") is widely used in the music synthesizers found in electronic keyboards, for video game sound, and for sound effects accompanying websites. By encoding directions for producing music on a synthesizer rather than encoding the sound itself, MIDI avoids the large storage requirements of the sampling technique. More precisely, MIDI encodes what instrument is to play which note for what duration of time, which means that a clarinet playing the note D for two seconds can be encoding in three bytes rather than more than two million bits when sampled at a rate of 44,100 samples per second.

In short, MIDI can be thought of as a way of encoding the sheet music read by a performer rather than the performance itself, and in turn, a MIDI "recording" can sound significantly different when performed on different synthesizers.

Questions & Exercises

1. Here is a message encoded in ASCII using 8 bits per symbol. What does it say? (See Appendix A)

   01000011 01101111 01101101 01110000 01110101 01110100 01100101
   01110010 00100000 01010011 01100011 01101001 01100101 01101110
   01100011 01100101

2. In the ASCII code, what is the relationship between the codes for an uppercase letter and the same letter in lowercase? (*See* Appendix A.)

3. Encode these sentences in ASCII:

    a. "Stop!" Cheryl shouted.   b. Does 2 + 3 = 5?

4. Describe a device from everyday life that can be in either of two states, such as a flag on a flagpole that is either up or down. Assign the symbol 1 to one of the states and 0 to the other, and show how the ASCII representation for the letter b would appear when stored with such bits.

5. Convert each of the following binary representations to its equivalent base 10 form:

    a. 0101   b. 1001   c. 1011
    d. 0110   e. 10000   f. 10010

6. Convert each of the following base 10 representations to its equivalent binary form:

    a. 6   b. 13   c. 11
    d. 18   e. 27   f. 4

7. What is the largest numeric value that could be represented with three bytes if each digit were encoded using one ASCII pattern per byte? What if binary notation were used?

8. An alternative to hexadecimal notation for representing bit patterns is **dotted decimal notation** in which each byte in the pattern is represented by its base 10 equivalent. In turn, these byte representations are separated by periods. For example, 12.5 represents the pattern 0000110000000101 (the byte 00001100 is represented by 12, and 00000101 is represented by 5), and the pattern 1000100000001000000000111 is represented by 136.16.7. Represent each of the following bit patterns in dotted decimal notation.

    a. 0000111100001111   b. 001100110000000010000000
    c. 0000101010100000

9. What is an advantage of representing images via geometric structures as opposed to bit maps? What about bit map techniques as opposed to geometric structures?

10. Suppose a stereo recording of one hour of music is encoded using a sample rate of 44,100 samples per second as discussed in the text. How does the size of the encoded version compare to the storage capacity of a CD?

1.5 The Binary System

In Section 1.4 we saw that binary notation is a means of representing numeric values using only the digits 0 and 1 rather than the 10 digits 0 through 9 that are used in the more common base 10 notational system. It is time now to look at binary notation more thoroughly.

Binary Notation

Recall that in the base 10 system, each position in a representation is associated with a quantity. In the representation 375, the 5 is in the position associated with the quantity one, the 7 is in the position associated with ten, and the 3 is in the position associated with the quantity one hundred (Figure 1.13a). Each quantity is 10 times that of the quantity to its right. The value represented by the entire expression is obtained by multiplying the value of each digit by the quantity associated with that digit's position and then adding those products. To illustrate, the pattern 375 represents $(3 \times \text{hundred}) + (7 \times \text{ten}) + (5 \times \text{one})$, which, in more technical notation, is $(3 \times 10^2) + (7 \times 10^1) + (5 \times 10^0)$.

The position of each digit in binary notation is also associated with a quantity, except that the quantity associated with each position is twice the quantity associated with the position to its right. More precisely, the rightmost digit in a binary representation is associated with the quantity one (2^0), the next position to the left is associated with two (2^1), the next is associated with four (2^2), the next with eight (23), and so on. For example, in the binary representation 1011, the rightmost 1 is in the position associated with the quantity one, the 1 next to it is in the position associated with two, the 0 is in the position associated with four, and the leftmost 1 is in the position associated with eight (Figure 1.13b).

To extract the value represented by a binary representation, we follow the same procedure as in base 10—we multiply the value of each digit by the quantity associated with its position and add the results. For example, the value represented by 100101 is 37, as shown in Figure 1.14. Note that since binary notation uses only the digits 0 and 1, this multiply-and-add process reduces merely to adding the quantities associated with the positions occupied by 1s. Thus the binary pattern 1011 represents the value eleven, because the 1s are found in the positions associated with the quantities one, two, and eight.

In Section 1.4 we learned how to count in binary notation, which allowed us to encode small integers. For finding binary representations of large values, you may prefer the approach described by the algorithm in Figure 1.15. Let us apply this algorithm to the value thirteen (Figure 1.16). We first divide thirteen by two, obtaining a quotient of six and a remainder of one. Since the quotient was not zero, Step 2 tells us to divide the quotient (six) by two, obtaining a new quotient of three and a remainder of zero. The newest quotient is still not zero, so we divide it by two, obtaining a quotient of one and a remainder of one. Once again, we divide the newest quotient (one) by two, this time obtaining a quotient of zero and a remainder of one. Since we have now acquired a quotient of zero, we move on to Step 3, where we learn that the binary representation of the original value (thirteen) is 1101, obtained from the list of remainders.

Figure 1.13 The base 10 and binary systems

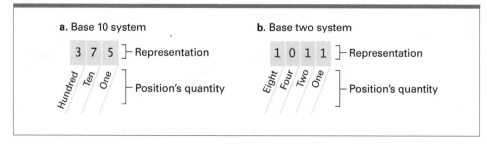

Figure 1.14   Decoding the binary representation 100101

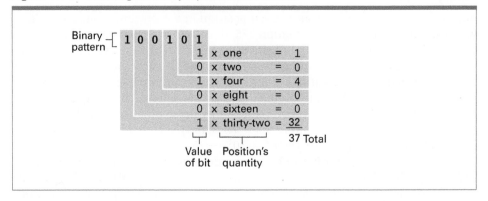

Figure 1.15   An algorithm for finding the binary representation of a positive integer

Step 1.   Divide the value by two and record the remainder.

Step 2.   As long as the quotient obtained is not zero, continue to divide
the newest quotient by two and record the remainder.

Step 3.   Now that a quotient of zero has been obtained, the binary
representation of the original value consists of the remainders
listed from right to left in the order they were recorded.

Figure 1.16   Applying the algorithm in Figure 1.15 to obtain the binary representation
of thirteen

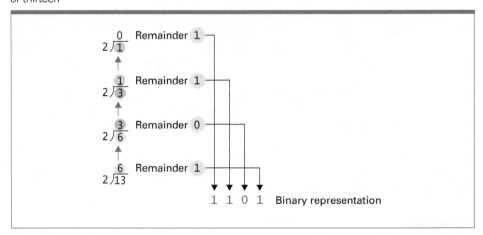

Binary Addition

To understand the process of adding two integers that are represented in binary,
let us first recall the process of adding values that are represented in traditional
base 10 notation. Consider, for example, the following problem:

$$\begin{array}{r} 58 \\ + \ 27 \\ \hline \end{array}$$

We begin by adding the 8 and the 7 in the rightmost column to obtain the sum 15. We record the 5 at the bottom of that column and carry the 1 to the next column, producing

```
  1
 58
+ 27
  5
```

We now add the 5 and 2 in the next column along with the 1 that was carried to obtain the sum 8, which we record at the bottom of the column. The result is as follows:

```
 58
+ 27
 85
```

In short, the procedure is to progress from right to left as we add the digits in each column, write the least significant digit of that sum under the column, and carry the more significant digit of the sum (if there is one) to the next column.

To add two integers represented in binary notation, we follow the same procedure except that all sums are computed using the addition facts shown in Figure 1.17 rather than the traditional base 10 facts that you learned in elementary school. For example, to solve the problem

```
  111010
+  11011
```

we begin by adding the rightmost 0 and 1; we obtain 1, which we write below the column. Now we add the 1 and 1 from the next column, obtaining 10. We write the 0 from this 10 under the column and carry the 1 to the top of the next column. At this point, our solution looks like this:

```
     1
  111010
+  11011
      01
```

We add the 1, 0, and 0 in the next column, obtain 1, and write the 1 under this column. The 1 and 1 from the next column total 10; we write the 0 under the column and carry the 1 to the next column. Now our solution looks like this:

```
    1
  111010
+  11011
     0101
```

Figure 1.17 The binary addition facts

```
  0     1     0     1
 +0    +0    +1    +1
  0     1     1    10
```

The 1, 1, and 1 in the next column total 11 (binary notation for the value three); we write the low-order 1 under the column and carry the other 1 to the top of the next column. We add that 1 to the 1 already in that column to obtain 10. Again, we record the low-order 0 and carry the 1 to the next column. We now have

```
    1
  111010
+  11011
  010101
```

The only entry in the next column is the 1 that we carried from the previous column so we record it in the answer. Our final solution is this:

```
  111010
+  11011
 1010101
```

Fractions in Binary

To extend binary notation to accommodate fractional values, we use a **radix point** in the same role as the decimal point in decimal notation. That is, the digits to the left of the point represent the integer part (whole part) of the value and are interpreted as in the binary system discussed previously. The digits to its right represent the fractional part of the value and are interpreted in a manner similar to the other bits, except their positions are assigned fractional quantities. That is, the first position to the right of the radix is assigned the quantity 1/2 (which is 2^{-1}), the next position the quantity 1/4 (which is 2^{-2}), the next 1/8 (which is 2^{-3}), and so on. Note that this is merely a continuation of the rule stated previously: Each position is assigned a quantity twice the size of the one to its right. With these quantities assigned to the bit positions, decoding a binary representation containing a radix point requires the same procedure as used without a radix point. More precisely, we multiply each bit value by the quantity assigned to that bit's position in the representation. To illustrate, the binary representation 101.101 decodes to 5-5/8, as shown in Figure 1.18.

For addition, the techniques applied in the base 10 system are also applicable in binary. That is, to add two binary representations having radix points, we

Figure 1.18 Decoding the binary representation 101.101

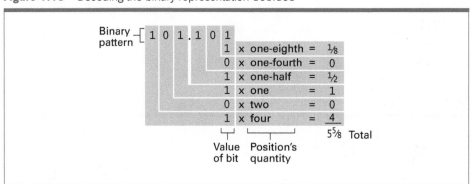

Analog versus Digital

Prior to the twenty-first century, many researchers debated the pros and cons of digital versus analog technology. In a digital system, a value is encoded as a series of digits and then stored using several devices, each representing one of the digits. In an analog system, each value is stored in a single device that can represent any value within a continuous range.

Let us compare the two approaches using buckets of water as the storage devices. To simulate a digital system, we could agree to let an empty bucket represent the digit 0 and a full bucket represent the digit 1. Then we could store a numeric value in a row of buckets using floating-point notation (see Section 1.7). In contrast, we could simulate an analog system by partially filling a single bucket to the point at which the water level represented the numeric value being represented. At first glance, the analog system may appear to be more accurate since it would not suffer from the truncation errors inherent in the digital system (again see Section 1.7). However, any movement of the bucket in the analog system could cause errors in detecting the water level, whereas a significant amount of sloshing would have to occur in the digital system before the distinction between a full bucket and an empty bucket would be blurred. Thus the digital system would be less sensitive to error than the analog system. This robustness is a major reason why many applications that were originally based on analog technology (such as telephone communication, audio recordings, and television) are shifting to digital technology.

merely align the radix points and apply the same addition process as before. For example, 10.011 added to 100.11 produces 111.001, as shown here:

```
   10.011
+ 100.110
  111.001
```

Questions & Exercises

1. Convert each of the following binary representations to its equivalent base 10 form:

   a. 101010   b. 100001   c. 10111   d. 0110   e. 11111

2. Convert each of the following base 10 representations to its equivalent binary form:

   a. 32   b. 64   c. 96   d. 15   e. 27

3. Convert each of the following binary representations to its equivalent base 10 form:

   a. 11.01   b. 101.111   c. 10.1   d. 110.011   e. 0.101

4. Express the following values in binary notation:

   a. $4\frac{1}{2}$ b. $2\frac{3}{4}$ c. $1\frac{1}{8}$ d. $\frac{5}{16}$ e. $5\frac{5}{8}$

5. Perform the following additions in binary notation:

a. 11011
    +1100

b. 1010.001
    +   1.101

c. 11111
    + 0001

d. 111.11
    + 00.01

1.6 Storing Integers

Mathematicians have long been interested in numeric notational systems, and many of their ideas have turned out to be very compatible with the design of digital circuitry. In this section we consider two of these notational systems, two's complement notation and excess notation, which are used for representing integer values in computing equipment. These systems are based on the binary system but have additional properties that make them more compatible with computer design. With these advantages, however, come disadvantages as well. Our goal is to understand these properties and how they affect computer usage.

Two's Complement Notation

The most popular system for representing integers within today's computers is **two's complement** notation. This system uses a fixed number of bits to represent each of the values in the system. In today's equipment, it is common to use a two's complement system in which each value is represented by a pattern of 32 bits. Such a large system allows a wide range of numbers to be represented but is awkward for demonstration purposes. Thus, to study the properties of two's complement systems, we will concentrate on smaller systems.   .

Figure 1.19 shows two complete two's complement systems—one based on bit patterns of length three, the other based on bit patterns of length four. Such a system is constructed by starting with a string of 0s of the appropriate length and then counting in binary until the pattern consisting of a single 0 followed by 1s is reached. These patterns represent the values 0, 1, 2, 3, ... The patterns representing negative values are obtained by starting with a string of 1s of the appropriate length and then counting backward in binary until the pattern consisting of a single 1 followed by 0s is reached. These patterns represent the values −1, −2, −3, ... (If counting backward in binary is difficult for you, merely start at the very bottom of the table with the pattern consisting of a single 1 followed by 0s, and count up to the pattern consisting of all 1s.)

Note that in a two's complement system, the leftmost bit of a bit pattern indicates the sign of the value represented. Thus, the leftmost bit is often called the **sign bit.** In a two's complement system, negative values are represented by the patterns whose sign bits are 1; nonnegative values are represented by patterns whose sign bits are 0.

In a two's complement system, there is a convenient relationship between the patterns representing positive and negative values of the same magnitude. They are identical when read from right to left, up to and including the first 1. From there on, the patterns are complements of one another. (The **complement** of a pattern is the pattern obtained by changing all the 0s to 1s and all the 1s to 0s; 0110 and 1001 are complements.) For example, in the 4-bit system in Figure 1.19

Figure 1.19 Two's complement notation systems

a. Using patterns of length three

Bit pattern	Value represented
011	3
010	2
001	1
000	0
111	-1
110	-2
101	-3
100	-4

b. Using patterns of length four

Bit pattern	Value represented
0111	7
0110	6
0101	5
0100	4
0011	3
0010	2
0001	1
0000	0
1111	-1
1110	-2
1101	-3
1100	-4
1011	-5
1010	-6
1001	-7
1000	-8

the patterns representing 2 and −2 both end with 10, but the pattern representing 2 begins with 00, whereas the pattern representing −2 begins with 11. This observation leads to an algorithm for converting back and forth between bit patterns representing positive and negative values of the same magnitude. We merely copy the original pattern from right to left until a 1 has been copied, then we complement the remaining bits as they are transferred to the final bit pattern (Figure 1.20).

Understanding these basic properties of two's complement systems also leads to an algorithm for decoding two's complement representations. If the pattern

Figure 1.20 Encoding the value—6 in two's complement notation using 4 bits

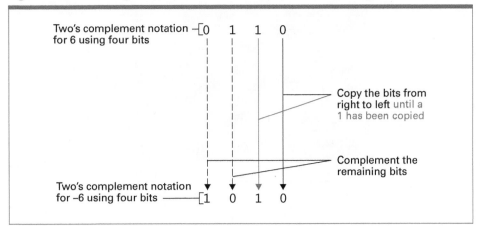

to be decoded has a sign bit of 0, we need merely read the value as though the pattern were a binary representation. For example, 0110 represents the value 6, because 110 is binary for 6. If the pattern to be decoded has a sign bit of 1, we know the value represented is negative, and all that remains is to find the magnitude of the value. We do this by applying the "copy and complement" procedure in Figure 1.20 and then decoding the pattern obtained as though it were a straightforward binary representation. For example, to decode the pattern 1010, we first recognize that since the sign bit is 1, the value represented is negative. Hence, we apply the "copy and complement" procedure to obtain the pattern 0110, recognize that this is the binary representation for 6, and conclude that the original pattern represents −6.

Addition in Two's Complement Notation To add values represented in two's complement notation, we apply the same algorithm that we used for binary addition, except that all bit patterns, including the answer, are the same length. This means that when adding in a two's complement system, any extra bit generated on the left of the answer by a final carry must be truncated. Thus "adding" 0101 and 0010 produces 0111, and "adding" 0111 and 1011 results in 0010 (0111 + 1011 = 10010, which is truncated to 0010).

   With this understanding, consider the three addition problems in Figure 1.21. In each case, we have translated the problem into two's complement notation (using bit patterns of length four), performed the addition process previously described, and decoded the result back into our usual base 10 notation.

   Observe that the third problem in Figure 1.21 involves the addition of a positive number to a negative number, which demonstrates a major benefit of two's complement notation: Addition of any combination of signed numbers can be accomplished using the same algorithm and thus the same circuitry. This is in stark contrast to how humans traditionally perform arithmetic computations. Whereas elementary school children are first taught to add and later taught to subtract, a machine using two's complement notation needs to know only how to add.

Figure 1.21   Addition problems converted to two's complement notation

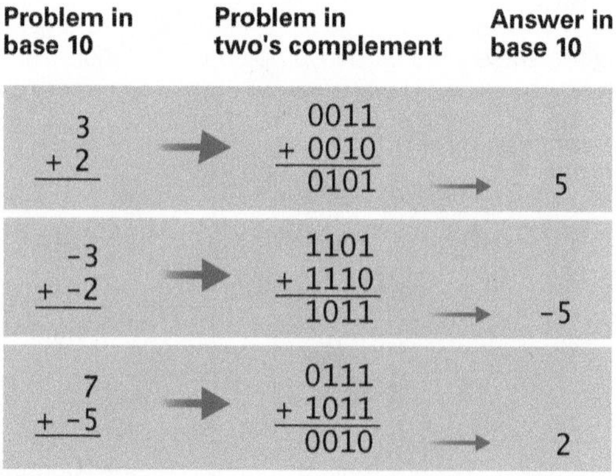

For example, the subtraction problem $7 - 5$ is the same as the addition problem $7 + (-5)$. Consequently, if a machine were asked to subtract 5 (stored as 0101) from 7 (stored as 0111), it would first change the 5 to -5 (represented as 1011) and then perform the addition process of $0111 + 1011$ to obtain 0010, which represents 2, as follows:

```
  7              0111            0111
 ⁻5       →     ⁻ 0101     →    + 1011
                                 0010      →       2
```

We see, then, that when two's complement notation is used to represent numeric values, a circuit for addition combined with a circuit for negating a value is sufficient for solving both addition and subtraction problems. (Such circuits are shown and explained in Appendix B.)

The Problem of Overflow One problem we have avoided in the preceding examples is that in any two's complement system there is a limit to the size of the values that can be represented. When using two's complement with patterns of 4 bits, the largest positive integer that can be represented is 7, and the most negative integer is -8. In particular, the value 9 cannot be represented, which means that we cannot hope to obtain the correct answer to the problem $5 + 4$. In fact, the result would appear as -7. This phenomenon is called **overflow.** That is, overflow is the problem that occurs when a computation produces a value that falls outside the range of values that can be represented. When using two's complement notation, this might occur when adding two positive values or when adding two negative values. In either case, the condition can be detected by checking the sign bit of the answer. An overflow is indicated if the addition of two positive values results in the pattern for a negative value or if the sum of two negative values appears to be positive.

Of course, because most computers use two's complement systems with longer bit patterns than we have used in our examples, larger values can be manipulated without causing an overflow. Today, it is common to use patterns of 32 bits for storing values in two's complement notation, allowing for positive values as large as 2,147,483,647 to accumulate before overflow occurs. If still larger values are needed, longer bit patterns can be used or perhaps the units of measure can be changed. For instance, finding a solution in terms of miles instead of inches results in smaller numbers being used and might still provide the accuracy required.

The point is that computers can make mistakes. So, the person using the machine must be aware of the dangers involved. One problem is that computer programmers and users become complacent and ignore the fact that small values can accumulate to produce large numbers. For example, in the past it was common to use patterns of 16 bits for representing values in two's complement notation, which meant that overflow would occur when values of $2^{15} = 32{,}768$ or larger were reached. On September 19, 1989, a hospital computer system malfunctioned after years of reliable service. Close inspection revealed that this date was 32,768 days after January 1, 1900, and the machine was programmed to compute dates based on that starting date. Thus, because of overflow, September 19, 1989, produced a negative value—a phenomenon the computer's program was not designed to handle.

Excess Notation

Another method of representing integer values is **excess notation.** As is the case with two's complement notation, each of the values in an excess notation system is represented by a bit pattern of the same length. To establish an excess system, we first select the pattern length to be used, then write down all the different bit patterns of that length in the order they would appear if we were counting in binary. Next, we observe that the first pattern with a 1 as its most significant bit appears approximately halfway through the list. We pick this pattern to represent zero; the patterns following this are used to represent 1, 2, 3, . . .; and the patterns preceding it are used for −1, −2, −3, ... The resulting code, when using patterns of length four, is shown in Figure 1.22. There we see that the value 5 is represented by the pattern 1101 and −5 is represented by 0011. (Note that one difference between an excess system and a two's complement system is that the sign bits are reversed.)

The system represented in Figure 1.22 is known as excess eight notation. To understand why, first interpret each of the patterns in the code using the traditional binary system and then compare these results to the values represented in the excess notation. In each case, you will find that the binary interpretation exceeds the excess notation interpretation by the value 8. For example, the pattern 1100 in binary notation represents the value 12, but in our excess system it represents 4; 0000 in binary notation represents 0, but in the excess system it represents negative 8. In a similar manner, an excess system based on patterns of length five would be called excess 16 notation, because the pattern 10000, for instance, would be used to represent zero rather than representing its usual value of 16. Likewise, you may want to confirm that the three-bit excess system would be known as excess four notation (Figure 1.23).

Figure 1.22   An excess eight conversion table

Bit pattern	Value represented
1111	7
1110	6
1101	5
1100	4
1011	3
1010	2
1001	1
1000	0
0111	−1
0110	−2
0101	−3
0100	−4
0011	−5
0010	−6
0001	−7
0000	−8

Figure 1.23 An excess notation system using bit patterns of length three

Bit pattern	Value represented
111	3
110	2
101	1
100	0
011	-1
010	-2
001	-3
000	-4

Questions & Exercises

1. Convert each of the following two's complement representations to its equivalent base 10 form:

   a. 00011   b. 01111   c. 11100

   d. 11010   e. 00000   f. 10000

2. Convert each of the following base 10 representations to its equivalent two's complement form using patterns of 8 bits:

   a. 6   b. −6   c. −17

   d. 13   e. −1   f. 0

3. Suppose the following bit patterns represent values stored in two's complement notation. Find the two's complement representation of the negative of each value:

   a. 00000001   b. 01010101   c. 11111100

   d. 11111110   e. 00000000   f. 01111111

4. Suppose a machine stores numbers in two's complement notation. What are the largest and smallest numbers that can be stored if the machine uses bit patterns of the following lengths?

   a. four   b. six   c. eight

5. In the following problems, each bit pattern represents a value stored in two's complement notation. Find the answer to each problem in two's complement notation by performing the addition process described in the text. Then check your work by translating the problem and your answer into base 10 notation.

   a. 0101 + 0010   b. 0011 + 0001   c. 0101 + 1010

   d. 1110 + 0011   e. 1010 + 1110

6. Solve each of the following problems in two's complement notation, but this time watch for overflow and indicate which answers are incorrect because of this phenomenon.

    a. 0100 + 0011   b. 0101 + 0110   c. 1010 + 1010
    d. 1010 + 0111   e. 0111 + 0001

7. Translate each of the following problems from base 10 notation into two's complement notation using bit patterns of length four, then convert each problem to an equivalent addition problem (as a machine might do), and perform the addition. Check your answers by converting them back to base 10 notation.

    a. 6 − (−1)   b. 3 − (−2)   c. 4 − 6
    d. 2 − (−4)   e. 1 − 5

8. Can overflow ever occur when values are added in two's complement notation with one value positive and the other negative? Explain your answer.

9. Convert each of the following excess eight representations to its equivalent base 10 form without referring to the table in the text:

    a. 1110   b. 0111   c. 1000
    d. 0010   e. 0000   f. 1001

10. Convert each of the following base 10 representations to its equivalent excess eight form without referring to the table in the text:

    a. 5   b. −5   c. 3
    d. 0   e. 7   f. −8

11. Can the value 9 be represented in excess eight notation? What about representing 6 in excess four notation? Explain your answer.

1.7 Storing Fractions

In contrast to the storage of integers, the storage of a value with a fractional part requires that we store not only the pattern of 0s and 1s representing its binary representation but also the position of the radix point. A popular way of doing this is based on scientific notation and is called **floating-point** notation.

Floating-Point Notation

Let us explain floating-point notation with an example using only one byte of storage. Although machines normally use much longer patterns, this 8-bit format is representative of actual systems and serves to demonstrate the important concepts without the clutter of long bit patterns.

We first designate the high-order bit of the byte as the sign bit. Once again, a 0 in the sign bit will mean that the value stored is nonnegative, and a 1 will mean that the value is negative. Next, we divide the remaining 7 bits of the byte into two groups, or fields: the **exponent field** and the **mantissa field.** Let us designate the 3 bits following the sign bit as the exponent field and the remaining 4 bits as the mantissa field. Figure 1.24 illustrates how the byte is divided.

We can explain the meaning of the fields by considering the following example. Suppose a byte consists of the bit pattern 01101011. Analyzing this pattern with the preceding format, we see that the sign bit is 0, the exponent is 110, and the mantissa is 1011. To decode the byte, we first extract the mantissa and place a radix point on its left side, obtaining

.1011

Next, we extract the contents of the exponent field (110) and interpret it as an integer stored using the 3-bit excess method (see again Figure 1.24). Thus the pattern in the exponent field in our example represents a positive 2. This tells us to move the radix in our solution to the right by 2 bits. (A negative exponent would mean to move the radix to the left.) Consequently, we obtain

10.11

which is the binary representation for $2\frac{3}{4}$. (Recall the representation of binary fractions from Figure 1.18.) Next, we note that the sign bit in our example is 0; the value represented is thus nonnegative. We conclude that the byte 01101011 represents $2\frac{3}{4}$. Had the pattern been 11101011 (which is the same as before except for the sign bit), the value represented would have been $2\frac{3}{4}$.

As another example, consider the byte 00111100. We extract the mantissa to obtain

.1100

and move the radix 1 bit to the left, since the exponent field (011) represents the value -1. We therefore have

.01100

which represents 3/8. Since the sign bit in the original pattern is 0, the value stored is nonnegative. We conclude that the pattern 00111100 represents $\frac{3}{8}$.

To store a value using floating-point notation, we reverse the preceding process. For example, to encode $1\frac{1}{8}$, first we express it in binary notation and obtain 1.001. Next, we copy the bit pattern into the mantissa field from left to right, starting with the leftmost 1 in the binary representation. At this point, the byte looks like this:

_ _ _ _ 1 0 0 1

Figure 1.24 Floating-point notation components

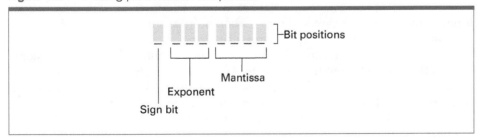

Bit positions

Mantissa

Exponent

Sign bit

We must now fill in the exponent field. To this end, we imagine the contents of the mantissa field with a radix point at its left and determine the number of bits and the direction the radix must be moved to obtain the original binary number. In our example, we see that the radix in .1001 must be moved 1 bit to the right to obtain 1.001. The exponent should therefore be a positive one, so we place 101 (which is positive one in excess four notation as shown in Figure 1.23) in the exponent field. Finally, we fill the sign bit with 0 because the value being stored is nonnegative. The finished byte looks like this:

$$\underline{0}\ \underline{1}\ \underline{0}\ \underline{1}\ \underline{1}\ \underline{0}\ \underline{0}\ \underline{1}$$

There is a subtle point you may have missed when filling in the mantissa field. The rule is to copy the bit pattern appearing in the binary representation from left to right, starting with the leftmost 1. To clarify, consider the process of storing the value ³⁄₈, which is .011 in binary notation. In this case the mantissa will be

$$\underline{\ }\ \underline{\ }\ \underline{\ }\ \underline{\ }\ \underline{1}\ \underline{1}\ \underline{0}\ \underline{0}$$

It will not be

$$\underline{\ }\ \underline{\ }\ \underline{\ }\ \underline{\ }\ \underline{0}\ \underline{1}\ \underline{1}\ \underline{0}$$

This is because we fill in the mantissa field starting with the leftmost 1 that appears in the binary representation. Representations that conform to this rule are said to be in **normalized form.**

Using normalized form eliminates the possibility of multiple representations for the same value. For example, both 00111100 and 01000110 would decode to the value ³⁄₈, but only the first pattern is in normalized form. Complying with normalized form also means that the representation for all nonzero values will have a mantissa that starts with 1. The value zero, however, is a special case; its floating-point representation is a bit pattern of all 0s.

Truncation Errors

Let us consider the annoying problem that occurs if we try to store the value 2⁵⁄₈ with our one-byte floating-point system. We first write 2⁵⁄₈ in binary, which gives us 10.101. But when we copy this into the mantissa field, we run out of room, and the rightmost 1 (which represents the last ¹⁄₈) is lost (Figure 1.25). If we ignore this problem for now and continue by filling in the exponent field and the sign bit, we end up with the bit pattern 01101010, which represents 2¹⁄₂ instead of 2⁵⁄₈. What has occurred is called a **truncation error,** or **round-off error**—meaning that part of the value being stored is lost because the mantissa field is not large enough.

The significance of such errors can be reduced by using a longer mantissa field. In fact, most computers manufactured today use at least 32 bits for storing values in floating-point notation instead of the 8 bits we have used here. This also allows for a longer exponent field at the same time. Even with these longer formats, however, there are still times when more accuracy is required.

Another source of truncation errors is a phenomenon that you are already accustomed to in base 10 notation: the problem of nonterminating expansions, such as those found when trying to express ¹⁄₃ in decimal form. Some values cannot be accurately expressed regardless of how many digits we use. The difference between our traditional base 10 notation and binary notation is that more values have nonterminating representations in binary than in decimal notation. For example, the value 1/10 is nonterminating when expressed in binary. Imagine the problems this might cause the unwary person using floating-point notation to

Figure 1.25 Encoding the value 2⅝

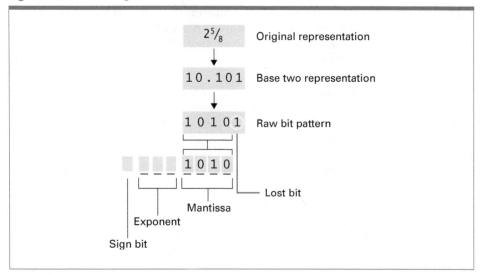

store and manipulate dollars and cents. In particular, if the dollar is used as the unit of measure, the value of a dime could not be stored accurately. A solution in this case is to manipulate the data in units of pennies so that all values are integers that can be accurately stored using a method such as two's complement.

Truncation errors and their related problems are an everyday concern for people working in the area of numerical analysis. This branch of mathematics deals with the problems involved when doing actual computations that are often massive and require significant accuracy.

The following is an example that would warm the heart of any numerical analyst. Suppose we are asked to add the following three values using our one-byte floating-point notation defined previously:

$2\frac{1}{2} + \frac{1}{8} + \frac{1}{8}$

Single Precision Floating Point

The floating-point notation introduced in this chapter (Section 1.7) is far too simplistic to be used in an actual computer. After all, with just 8 bits, only 256 numbers out of the set of all real numbers can be expressed. Our discussion has used 8 bits to keep the examples simple, yet still cover the important underlying concepts.

Many of today's computers support a 32-bit form of this notation called **Single Precision Floating Point.** This format uses 1 bit for the sign, 8 bits for the exponent (in an excess notation), and 23 bits for the mantissa. Thus, single precision floating point is capable of expressing very large numbers (order of 10^{38}) down to very small numbers (order of 10^{-37}) with the precision of 7 decimal digits. That is to say, the first 7 digits of a given decimal number can be stored with very good accuracy (a small amount of error may still be present). Any digits passed the first 7 will certainly be lost by truncation error (although the magnitude of the number is retained).

Another form, called **Double Precision Floating Point,** uses 64 bits and provides a precision of 15 decimal digits.

If we add the values in the order listed, we first add $2\frac{1}{2}$ to $\frac{1}{8}$ and obtain $2\frac{5}{8}$, which in binary is 10.101. Unfortunately, because this value cannot be stored accurately (as seen previously), the result of our first step ends up being stored as $2\frac{1}{2}$ (which is the same as one of the values we were adding). The next step is to add this result to the last 1/8. Here again a truncation error occurs, and our final result turns out to be the incorrect answer $2\frac{1}{2}$.

Now let us add the values in the opposite order. We first add $\frac{1}{8}$ to $\frac{1}{8}$ to obtain $\frac{1}{4}$. In binary this is .01; so the result of our first step is stored in a byte as 00111000, which is accurate. We now add this $\frac{1}{4}$ to the next value in the list, $2\frac{1}{2}$, and obtain $2\frac{3}{4}$, which we can accurately store in a byte as 01101011. The result this time is the correct answer.

To summarize, in adding numeric values represented in floating-point notation, the order in which they are added can be important. The problem is that if a very large number is added to a very small number, the small number may be truncated. Thus, the general rule for adding multiple values is to add the smaller values together first, in hopes that they will accumulate to a value that is significant when added to the larger values. This was the phenomenon experienced in the preceding example.

Designers of today's commercial software packages do a good job of shielding the uneducated user from problems such as this. In a typical spreadsheet system, correct answers will be obtained unless the values being added differ in size by a factor of 10^{16} or more. Thus, if you found it necessary to add one to the value

10,000,000,000,000,000

you might get the answer

10,000,000,000,000,000

rather than

10,000,000,000,000,001

Such problems are significant in applications (such as navigational systems) in which minor errors can be compounded in additional computations and ultimately produce significant consequences, but for the typical PC user the degree of accuracy offered by most commercial software is sufficient.

Questions & Exercises

1. Decode the following bit patterns using the floating-point format discussed in the text:

    a. 01001010 b. 01101101 c. 00111001 d. 11011100 e. 10101011

2. Encode the following values into the floating-point format discussed in the text. Indicate the occurrence of truncation errors.

    a. $2\frac{3}{4}$　　　b. $5\frac{1}{4}$　　　c. $\frac{3}{4}$　　　d. $-3\frac{1}{2}$　　　e. $-4\frac{3}{8}$

3. In terms of the floating-point format discussed in the text, which of the patterns 01001001 and 00111101 represents the larger value? Describe a simple procedure for determining which of two patterns represents the larger value.

4. When using the floating-point format discussed in the text, what is the largest value that can be represented? What is the smallest positive value that can be represented?

1.8 Data and Programming

While humans have devised the data representations and basic operations that comprise modern computers, few people are very good at working with computers directly at this level. People prefer to reason about computational problems at a higher level of abstraction, and they rely on the computer to handle the lowest levels of detail. A *programming language* is a computer system created to allow humans to precisely express algorithms to the computer using a higher level of abstraction.

In the twentieth century, programming computers was considered to be the province of a few highly trained experts; to be sure, there remain many problems in computing that require the attention of experienced computer scientists and software engineers. However, in the twenty-first century, as computers and computing have become increasingly intertwined in every aspect of our modern lives, it has grown steadily more difficult to identify career fields that do not require at least some degree of programming skill. Indeed, some have identified programming or *coding* to be the next foundational pillar of modern literacy, alongside reading, writing, and arithmetic.

In this section, and in programming supplement sections in subsequent chapters, we look at how a programming language reflects the main ideas of the chapter and allows humans to more easily solve problems involving computation.

Getting Started with Python

Python is a programming language that was created by Guido van Rossum in the late 1980s. Today it is one of the top ten most-used languages and remains popular in developing web applications, in scientific computation, and as an introductory language for students. Organizations that use Python range from Google to NASA, DropBox to Industrial Light & Magic, and across the spectrum of casual, scientific, and artistic computer users. Python emphasizes readability and includes elements of the imperative, object-oriented, and functional programming paradigms, which will be explored in Chapter 6.

The software for editing and running programs written in Python is freely available from **www.python.org**, as are many other resources for getting started. The Python language has evolved and continues to evolve over time. All of the examples in this book will use a version of the language called Python 3. Earlier versions of Python are capable of running very similar programs, but there have been many minor changes, such as punctuation, since Python 2.

Python is an *interpreted language,* which for beginners means that Python instructions can be typed into an interactive prompt or can be stored in a plain text file (called a "script") and run later. In the examples below, either mode can be used, but exercise and chapter review problems will generally ask for a Python script.

Hello Python

By longstanding tradition, the first program described in many programming language introductions is "Hello, World." This simple program outputs a nominal greeting, demonstrating how a particular language produces a result, and also how a language represents text. In Python[1], we write this program as

```
print('Hello, World!')
```

Type this statement into Python's interactive interpreter, or save it as a Python script and execute it. In either case, the result should be:

```
Hello, World!
```

Python parrots the text between the quotation marks back to the user.

There are several aspects to note even in this simple Python script. First, print is a built-in function, a predefined operation that Python scripts can use to produce *output,* a result of the program that will be made visible to the user. The print is followed by opening and closing parentheses; what comes between those parentheses is the value to be printed.

Second, Python can denote strings of text using single quotation marks. The quotation marks in front of the capital H and after the exclamation point denote the beginning and end of a string of characters that will be treated as a value in Python.

Programming languages carry out their instructions very precisely. If a user makes subtle changes to the message between the starting and finishing quotation marks within the print statement, the resultant printed text will change accordingly. Take a moment to try different capitalizations, punctuation, and even different words within the print statement to see that this is so.

Variables

Python allows the user to name values for later use, an important abstraction when constructing compact, understandable scripts. These named storage locations are termed *variables,* analogous to the mathematical variables often seen in algebra courses. Consider the slightly enhanced version of Hello World below:

```
message = 'Hello, World!'
print(message)
```

In this script, the first line is an *assignment statement.* The use of the = can be misleading to beginners, who are accustomed to the algebraic usage of the equal sign. This assignment statement should be read, "variable **message** is assigned

---

[1]This Python code is for version 3 of the language, which will be referred to only as "Python" for the remainder of the book. Earlier versions of Python do not always require the opening and closing parentheses.

the string value `'Hello, World!'`". In general, an assignment statement will have a variable name on the left side of the equal sign and a value to the right.

Python is a *dynamically typed* language, which means that our script need not establish ahead of time that there will be a variable called **message**, or what type of value should be stored in **message**. In the script, it is sufficient to state that our text string will be assigned to **message**, and then to refer to that variable **message** in the subsequent `print` statement.

The naming of variables is largely up to the user in Python. Python's simple rules are that variable names must begin with an alphabet letter and may consist of an arbitrary number of letters, digits, and the underscore character, _. While a variable named m may be sufficient for a two-line example script, experienced programmers strive to give meaningful, descriptive variable names in their scripts.

Python variable names are *case-sensitive,* meaning that capitalization matters. A variable named **size** is treated as distinct from variables named **Size** or **SIZE**. A small number of *keywords,* names that are reserved for special meaning in Python, cannot be used as variable names. You can view this list by accessing the built-in Python help system.

```
help('keywords')
```

Variables can be used to store all of the types of values that Python is able to represent.

```
my_integer = 5
my_floating_point = 26.2
my_Boolean = True
my_string = 'characters'
```

Observe that the types of values we see here correspond directly to the representations covered earlier in this chapter: Boolean trues and falses (Section 1.1), text (Section 1.4), integers (Section 1.6), and floating point numbers (Section 1.7). With additional Python code (beyond the scope of our simple introduction in this text) we could store image and sound data (Section 1.4) with Python variables, as well.

Python expresses hexadecimal values using a **0x** prefix, as in

```
my_integer = 0xFF
print(my_integer)
```

Specifying a value in hexadecimal does not alter the representation of that value in the computer's memory, which stores integer values as a collection of ones and zeros regardless of the numerical base used in the programmer's reasoning. Hexadecimal notation remains a shortcut for humans, used in situations where that representation may aid in understanding the script. The `print` statement above thus prints **255**, the base 10 interpretation of hexadecimal **0xFF**, because that is the default behavior for `print`. More complex adjustments to the `print` statement can be used to output values in other representations, but we confine our discussion here to the more familiar base 10.

Unicode characters, including those beyond the ubiquitous ASCII subset, can be included directly in strings when the text editor supports them,

```
print('₹1000')          # Prints ₹1000, one thousand Indian Rupees
```

or can be specified using four hexadecimal digits following a `'\u'` prefix.

```
print('\u00A31000')        # Prints £1000, one thousand British
                           # Pounds Sterling
```

The portion of the string `'\u00A3'` encodes the Unicode representation of the British pound symbol. The `'1000'` follows immediately so that there will be no space between the currency symbol and the amount in the final output: £1000.

These example statements introduce another language feature, in addition to Unicode text strings. The # symbol denotes the beginning of a *comment,* a human-readable notation to the Python code that will be ignored by the computer when executed. Experienced programmers use comments in their code to explain difficult segments of the algorithm, include history or authorship information, or just to note where a human should pay attention when reading the code. All of the characters to the right of the # until the end of the line are ignored by Python.

Operators and Expressions

Python's built-in operators allow values to be manipulated and combined in a variety of familiar ways.

```
print(3 + 4)      # Prints "7", which is 3 plus 4.
print(5 - 6)      # Prints "-1", which is 5 minus 6
print(7 * 8)      # Prints "56", which is 7 times 8
print(45 / 4)     # Prints "11.25", which is 45 divided by 4
print(2 ** 10)    # Prints "1024", which is 2 to the 10th power
```

When an operation such as forty-five divided by four produces a non-integer result, such as **11.25**, Python implicitly switches to a floating-point representation. When purely integer answers are desired, a different set of operators can be used.

```
print(45 // 4)    # Prints "11", which is 45 integer divided by 4
print(45 % 4)     # Prints "1", because 4 * 11 + 1 = 45
```

The double slash signifies the *integer floor division* operator, while the percentage symbol signifies the *modulus,* or remainder operator. Taken together, we can read these calculations as, "four goes into forty-five eleven times, with a remainder of one." In the earlier example, we used ** to signify exponentiation, which can be somewhat surprising given that the caret symbol, ∧, is often used for this purpose in typewritten text and even some other programming languages. In Python, the caret operator belongs to the group of *bitwise Boolean operations*, which will be discussed in the next chapter.

String values also can be combined and manipulated in some intuitive ways.

```
s = 'hello' + 'world'
t = s * 4

print(t)    # Prints "helloworldhelloworldhelloworldhelloworld"
```

The plus operator *concatenates* string values, while the multiplication operator *replicates* string values.

The multiple meanings of some of the built-in operators can lead to confusion. This script will produce an error:

```python
print('USD$' + 1000)      # TypeError: Can't convert 'int' to str implicitly
```

The error indicates that the string concatenation operator doesn't know what to do when the second operand is not also a string. Fortunately, Python provides functions that allow values to be converted from one type of representation to another. The int() function will convert a floating-point value back to an integer representation, discarding the fractional part. It will also convert a string of text digits into an integer representation, provided that the string correctly spells out a valid number. Likewise, the str() function can be used to convert numeric representations into UTF-8 encoded text strings. Thus, the following modification to the print statement above corrects the error.

```python
print('USD$' + str(1000))      # Prints "USD$1000"
```

Currency Conversion

The complete Python script example below demonstrates many of the concepts introduced in this section. Given a set number of U.S. dollars, the script produces monetary conversions to four other currencies.

```python
# A converter for international currency exchange.
USD_to_GBP = 0.66    # Today's rate, US dollars to British Pounds
USD_to_EUR = 0.77    # Today's rate, US dollars to Euros
USD_to_JPY = 99.18   # Today's rate, US dollars to Japanese Yen
USD_to_INR = 59.52   # Today's rate, US dollars to Indian Rupees

GBP_sign   = '\u00A3' # Unicode values for non-ASCII currency symbols.
EUR_sign   = '\u20AC'
JPY_sign   = '\u00A5'
INR_sign   = '\u20B9'

dollars    = 1000 # The number of dollars to convert

pounds     = dollars * USD_to_GBP    # Conversion calculations
euros      = dollars * USD_to_EUR
yen        = dollars * USD_to_JPY
rupees     = dollars * USD_to_INR

print('Today, $' + str(dollars))    # Printing the results
print('converts to ' + GBP_sign + str(pounds))
```

```
print('converts to ' + EUR_sign + str(euros))
print('converts to ' + JPY_sign + str(yen))
print('converts to ' + INR_sign + str(rupees))
```

When executed, this script outputs the following:

```
Today, $1000
converts to £660.0
converts to €770.0
converts to ¥99180.0
converts to ₹59520.0
```

Debugging

Programming languages are not very forgiving for beginners, and a great deal of time learning to write software can be spent trying to find **bugs,** or errors in the code. There are three major classes of bug that we create in software: **syntax errors** (mistakes in the symbols that have been typed), **semantic errors** (mistakes in the meaning of the program), and **runtime errors** (mistakes that occur when the program is executed.)

Syntax errors are the most common for novices and include simple errors such as forgetting one of the quote marks at the beginning or ending of a text string, failing to close open parentheses, or misspelling the function name print. The Python interpreter will generally try to point these errors out when it encounters them, displaying an offending line number and a description of the problem. With some practice, a beginner can quickly learn to recognize and interpret common error cases. As examples:

```
print(5 + )
SyntaxError: invalid syntax
```

This expression is missing a value between the addition operator and the closing parenthesis.

```
print(5.e)
SyntaxError: invalid token
```

Python expects digits to follow the decimal point, not a letter.

```
pront(5)
NameError: name 'pront' is not defined
```

Like calling someone by the wrong name, misspelling the name of a known function or variable can result in confusion and embarrassment.

Semantic errors are flaws in the algorithm, or flaws in the way the algorithm is expressed in a language. Examples might include using the wrong variable name in a calculation or getting the order of arithmetic operations wrong in a complex expression. Python follows the standard rules for operator precedence, so in an expression like `total_pay = 40 + extra_hours * pay_rate`, the multiplication will be performed before the addition, incorrectly calculating the total pay. (Unless your pay rate happens to be $1/hour.) Use parenthesis to properly specify the order of operations in complex expressions, thereby avoiding both semantic errors and code that may be harder to understand (e.g., `total_pay = (40 + extra_hours) * pay_rate`).

Finally, runtime errors at this level might include unintentionally dividing by zero or using a variable before you have defined it. Python reads statements from top to bottom; it and must see an assignment statement to a variable before that variable is used in an expression.

Testing is an integral part of writing Python scripts—or really any kind of program—effectively. Run your script frequently as you write it, perhaps as often as after you complete each line of code. This allows syntax errors to be identified and fixed early and helps focus the author's attention on what should be happening at each step of the script.

Questions & Exercises

1. What makes Python an *interpreted* programming language?
2. Write Python statements that print the following:

   a. The words "Computer Science Rocks", followed by an exclamation point
   b. The number 42
   c. An approximation of the value of Pi to 4 decimal places

3. Write Python statements to make the following assignments to variables:

   a. The word "programmer" to a variable called, `rockstar`
   b. The number of seconds in an hour to a variable called `seconds_per_hour`
   c. The average temperature of the human body to a variable called `bodyTemp`

4. Write a Python statement that given an existing variable called `bodyTemp` in degrees Fahrenheit stores the equivalent temperature in degrees Celsius to a new variable called `metricBodyTemp`.

1.9 Data Compression

For the purpose of storing or transferring data, it is often helpful (and sometimes mandatory) to reduce the size of the data involved while retaining the underlying information. The technique for accomplishing this is called **data compression.** We begin this section by considering some generic data compression methods and then look at some approaches designed for specific applications.

Generic Data Compression Techniques

Data compression schemes fall into two categories. Some are **lossless,** others are **lossy.** Lossless schemes are those that do not lose information in the compression process. Lossy schemes are those that may lead to the loss of information. Lossy techniques often provide more compression than lossless ones and are therefore popular in settings in which minor errors can be tolerated, as in the case of images and audio.

In cases where the data being compressed consist of long sequences of the same value, the compression technique called **run-length encoding,** which is a lossless method, is popular. It is the process of replacing sequences of identical data elements with a code indicating the element that is repeated and the number of times it occurs in the sequence. For example, less space is required to indicate that a bit pattern consists of 253 ones, followed by 118 zeros, followed by 87 ones than to actually list all 458 bits.

Another lossless data compression technique is **frequency-dependent encoding,** a system in which the length of the bit pattern used to represent a data item is inversely related to the frequency of the item's use. Such codes are examples of variable-length codes, meaning that items are represented by patterns of different lengths. David Huffman is credited with discovering an algorithm that is commonly used for developing frequency-dependent codes, and it is common practice to refer to codes developed in this manner as **Huffman codes.** In turn, most frequency-dependent codes in use today are Huffman codes.

As an example of frequency-dependent encoding, consider the task of encoded English language text. In the English language the letters *e, t, a,* and *i* are used more frequently than the letters *z, q,* and *x.* So, when constructing a code for text in the English language, space can be saved by using short bit patterns to represent the former letters and longer bit patterns to represent the latter ones. The result would be a code in which English text would have shorter representations than would be obtained with uniform-length codes.

In some cases, the stream of data to be compressed consists of units, each of which differs only slightly from the preceding one. An example would be consecutive frames of a motion picture. In these cases, techniques using **relative encoding,** also known as **differential encoding,** are helpful. These techniques record the differences between consecutive data units rather than entire units; that is, each unit is encoded in terms of its relationship to the previous unit. Relative encoding can be implemented in either lossless or lossy form depending on whether the differences between consecutive data units are encoded precisely or approximated.

Still other popular compression systems are based on **dictionary encoding** techniques. Here the term *dictionary* refers to a collection of building blocks from which the message being compressed is constructed, and the message itself is encoded as a sequence of references to the dictionary. We normally think of dictionary encoding systems as lossless systems, but as we will see in our discussion of image compression, there are times when the entries in the dictionary are only approximations of the correct data elements, resulting in a lossy compression system.

Dictionary encoding can be used by word processors to compress text documents because the dictionaries already contained in these processors for the purpose of spell checking make excellent compression dictionaries. In particular, an entire word can be encoded as a single reference to this dictionary rather than as a sequence of individual characters encoded using a system such as UTF-8. A typical dictionary in a word processor contains approximately 25,000 entries, which means an individual entry can be identified by an integer in the range of 0 to 24,999. This means that a particular entry in the dictionary can be identified by a pattern of only 15 bits. In contrast, if the word being referenced consisted of six letters, its character-by-character encoding would require 48 bits using UTF-8.

A variation of dictionary encoding is **adaptive dictionary encoding** (also known as dynamic dictionary encoding). In an adaptive dictionary encoding system, the dictionary is allowed to change during the encoding process. A popular example is **Lempel-Ziv-Welsh (LZW) encoding** (named after its creators, Abraham Lempel, Jacob Ziv, and Terry Welsh). To encode a message using LZW, one starts with a dictionary containing the basic building blocks from which the message is constructed, but as larger units are found in the message, they are added to the dictionary—meaning that future occurrences of those units can be encoded as single, rather than multiple, dictionary references. For example, when encoding English text, one could start with a dictionary containing individual characters, digits, and punctuation marks. But as words in the message are identified, they could be added to the dictionary. Thus, the dictionary would grow as the message is encoded, and as the dictionary grows, more words (or recurring patterns of words) in the message could be encoded as single references to the dictionary.

The result would be a message encoded in terms of a rather large dictionary that is unique to that particular message. But this large dictionary would not have to be present to decode the message. Only the original small dictionary would be needed. Indeed, the decoding process could begin with the same small dictionary with which the encoding process started. Then, as the decoding process continues, it would encounter the same units found during the encoding process, and thus be able to add them to the dictionary for future reference just as in the encoding process.

To clarify, consider applying LZW encoding to the message

xyx xyx xyx xyx

starting with a dictionary with three entries, the first being x, the second being y, and the third being a space. We would begin by encoding xyx as 121, meaning that the message starts with the pattern consisting of the first dictionary entry, followed by the second, followed by the first. Then the space is encoded to produce 1213. But, having reached a space, we know that the preceding string of characters forms a word, and so we add the pattern xyx to the dictionary as the fourth entry. Continuing in this manner, the entire message would be encoded as 121343434.

If we were now asked to decode this message, starting with the original three-entry dictionary, we would begin by decoding the initial string 1213 as xyx followed by a space. At this point we would recognize that the string xyx forms a word and add it to the dictionary as the fourth entry, just as we did during the encoding process. We would then continue decoding the message by recognizing that the 4 in the message refers to this new fourth entry and decode it as the word xyx, producing the pattern

xyx xyx

Continuing in this manner we would ultimately decode the string 121343434 as

xyx xyx xyx xyx

which is the original message.

Compressing Images

In Section 1.4, we saw how images are encoded using bit map techniques. Unfortunately, the bit maps produced are often very large. In turn, numerous compression schemes have been developed specifically for image representations.

One system known as **GIF** (short for **Graphic Interchange Format** and pronounced "Giff" by some and "Jiff" by others) is a dictionary encoding system that was developed by CompuServe. It approaches the compression problem by reducing the number of colors that can be assigned to a pixel to only 256. The red-green-blue combination for each of these colors is encoded using three bytes, and these 256 encodings are stored in a table (a dictionary) called the palette. Each pixel in an image can then be represented by a single byte whose value indicates which of the 256 palette entries represents the pixel's color. (Recall that a single byte can contain any one of 256 different bit patterns.) Note that GIF is a lossy compression system when applied to arbitrary images because the colors in the palette may not be identical to the colors in the original image.

GIF can obtain additional compression by extending this simple dictionary system to an adaptive dictionary system using LZW techniques. In particular, as patterns of pixels are encountered during the encoding process, they are added to the dictionary so that future occurrences of these patterns can be encoded more efficiently. Thus, the final dictionary consists of the original palette and a collection of pixel patterns.

One of the colors in a GIF palette is normally assigned the value "transparent," which means that the background is allowed to show through each region assigned that "color." This option, combined with the relative simplicity of the GIF system, makes GIF a logical choice in simple animation applications in which multiple images must move around on a computer screen. On the other hand, its ability to encode only 256 colors renders it unsuitable for applications in which higher precision is required, as in the field of photography.

Another popular compression system for images is **JPEG** (pronounced "JAY-peg"). It is a standard developed by the **Joint Photographic Experts Group** (hence the standard's name) within ISO. JPEG has proved to be an effective standard for compressing color photographs and is widely used in the photography industry, as witnessed by the fact that most digital cameras use JPEG as their default compression technique.

The JPEG standard actually encompasses several methods of image compression, each with its own goals. In those situations that require the utmost in precision, JPEG provides a lossless mode. However, JPEG's lossless mode does not produce high levels of compression when compared to other JPEG options. Moreover, other JPEG options have proven very successful, meaning that JPEG's lossless mode is rarely used. Instead, the option known as JPEG's baseline standard (also known as JPEG's lossy sequential mode) has become the standard of choice in many applications.

Image compression using the JPEG baseline standard requires a sequence of steps, some of which are designed to take advantage of a human eye's limitations. In particular, the human eye is more sensitive to changes in brightness than to changes in color. So, starting from an image that is encoded in terms of luminance and chrominance components, the first step is to average the chrominance values over two-by-two pixel squares. This reduces the size of the chrominance information by a factor of four while preserving all the original brightness information. The result is a significant degree of compression without a noticeable loss of image quality.

The next step is to divide the image into eight-by-eight pixel blocks and to compress the information in each block as a unit. This is done by applying a mathematical technique known as the discrete cosine transform, whose details need not concern us here. The important point is that this transformation converts the original eight-by-eight block into another block whose entries reflect how the pixels in the original block relate to each other rather than the actual pixel values. Within this new block, values below a predetermined threshold are then replaced by zeros, reflecting the fact that the changes represented by these values are too subtle to be detected by the human eye. For example, if the original block contained a checkerboard pattern, the new block might reflect a uniform average color. (A typical eight-by-eight pixel block would represent a very small square within the image so the human eye would not identify the checkerboard appearance anyway.)

At this point, more traditional run-length encoding, relative encoding, and variable-length encoding techniques are applied to obtain additional compression. All together, JPEG's baseline standard normally compresses color images by a factor of at least 10, and often by as much as 30, without noticeable loss of quality.

Still another data compression system associated with images is **TIFF** (short for **Tagged Image File Format**). However, the most popular use of TIFF is not as a means of data compression but instead as a standardized format for storing photographs along with related information such as date, time, and camera settings. In this context, the image itself is normally stored as red, green, and blue pixel components without compression.

The TIFF collection of standards does include data compression techniques, most of which are designed for compressing images of text documents in facsimile applications. These use variations of run-length encoding to take advantage of the fact that text documents consist of long strings of white pixels. The color image compression option included in the TIFF standards is based on techniques similar to those used by GIF and are therefore not widely used in the photography community.

Compressing Audio and Video

The most commonly used standards for encoding and compressing audio and video were developed by the **Motion Picture Experts Group (MPEG)** under the leadership of ISO. In turn, these standards themselves are called MPEG.

MPEG encompasses a variety of standards for different applications. For example, the demands for high definition television (HDTV) broadcast are distinct from those for video conferencing, in which the broadcast signal must find its way over a variety of communication paths that may have limited capabilities. Both of these applications differ from that of storing video in such a manner that sections can be replayed or skipped over.

The techniques employed by MPEG are well beyond the scope of this text, but in general, video compression techniques are based on video being constructed as a sequence of pictures in much the same way that motion pictures are recorded on film. To compress such sequences, only some of the pictures, called I-frames, are encoded in their entirety. The pictures between the I-frames are encoded using relative encoding techniques. That is, rather than encode the entire picture, only its distinctions from the prior image are recorded. The I-frames themselves are usually compressed with techniques similar to JPEG.

The best known system for compressing audio is **MP3,** which was developed within the MPEG standards. In fact, the acronym *MP3* is short for

MPEG layer 3. Among other compression techniques, MP3 takes advantage of the properties of the human ear, removing those details that the human ear cannot perceive. One such property, called **temporal masking,** is that for a short period after a loud sound, the human ear cannot detect softer sounds that would otherwise be audible. Another, called **frequency masking,** is that a sound at one frequency tends to mask softer sounds at nearby frequencies. By taking advantage of such characteristics, MP3 can be used to obtain significant compression of audio while maintaining near CD quality sound.

Using MPEG and MP3 compression techniques, video cameras are able to record as much as an hour's worth of video within 128MB of storage, and portable music players can store as many as 400 popular songs in a single GB. But, in contrast to the goals of compression in other settings, the goal of compressing audio and video is not necessarily to save storage space. Just as important is the goal of obtaining encodings that allow information to be transmitted over today's communication systems fast enough to provide timely presentation. If each video frame required a MB of storage and the frames had to be transmitted over a communication path that could relay only one KB per second, there would be no hope of successful video conferencing. Thus, in addition to the quality of reproduction allowed, audio and video compression systems are often judged by the transmission speeds required for timely data communication. These speeds are normally measured in **bits per second (bps).** Common units include **Kbps** (kilo-bps, equal to one thousand bps), **Mbps** (mega-bps, equal to one million bps), and **Gbps** (giga-bps, equal to one billion bps). Using MPEG techniques, video presentations can be successfully relayed over communication paths that provide transfer rates of 40 Mbps. MP3 recordings generally require transfer rates of no more than 64 Kbps.

Questions & Exercises

1. List four generic compression techniques.
2. What would be the encoded version of the message

   xyx yxxxy xyx yxxxy yxxxy

   if LZW compression, starting with the dictionary containing *x, y,* and a space (as described in the text), were used?
3. Why would GIF be better than JPEG when encoding color cartoons?
4. Suppose you were part of a team designing a spacecraft that will travel to other planets and send back photographs. Would it be a good idea to compress the photographs using GIF or JPEG's baseline standard to reduce the resources required to store and transmit the images?
5. What characteristic of the human eye does JPEG's baseline standard exploit?
6. What characteristic of the human ear does MP3 exploit?
7. Identify a troubling phenomenon that is common when encoding numeric information, images, and sound as bit patterns.

1.10 Communication Errors

When information is transferred back and forth among the various parts of a computer, or transmitted from the earth to the moon and back, or, for that matter, merely left in storage, a chance exists that the bit pattern ultimately retrieved may not be identical to the original one. Particles of dirt or grease on a magnetic recording surface or a malfunctioning circuit may cause data to be incorrectly recorded or read. Static on a transmission path may corrupt portions of the data. In the case of some technologies, normal background radiation can alter patterns stored in a machine's main memory.

To resolve such problems, a variety of encoding techniques have been developed to allow the detection and even the correction of errors. Today, because these techniques are largely built into the internal components of a computer system, they are not apparent to the personnel using the machine. Nonetheless, their presence is important and represents a significant contribution to scientific research. It is fitting, therefore, that we investigate some of these techniques that lie behind the reliability of today's equipment.

Parity Bits

A simple method of detecting errors is based on the principle that if each bit pattern being manipulated has an odd number of 1s and a pattern with an even number of 1s is encountered, an error must have occurred. To use this principle, we need an encoding system in which each pattern contains an odd number of 1s. This is easily obtained by first adding an additional bit, called a **parity bit,** to each pattern in an encoding system already available (perhaps at the high-order end). In each case, we assign the value 1 or 0 to this new bit so that the entire resulting pattern has an odd number of 1s. Once our encoding system has been modified in this way, a pattern with an even number of 1s indicates that an error has occurred and that the pattern being manipulated is incorrect.

Figure 1.26 demonstrates how parity bits could be added to the ASCII codes for the letters A and F. Note that the code for A becomes 101000001 (parity bit 1) and the ASCII for F becomes 001000110 (parity bit 0). Although the original 8-bit pattern for A has an even number of 1s and the original 8-bit pattern for F has an odd number of 1s, both the 9-bit patterns have an odd number of 1s. If this technique were applied to all the 8-bit ASCII patterns, we would obtain a 9-bit encoding system in which an error would be indicated by any 9-bit pattern with an even number of 1s.

Figure 1.26   The ASCII codes for the letters A and F adjusted for odd parity

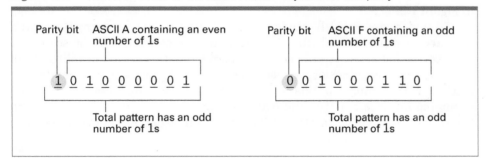

The parity system just described is called **odd parity,** because we designed our system so that each correct pattern contains an odd number of 1s. Another technique is called **even parity.** In an even parity system, each pattern is designed to contain an even number of 1s, and thus an error is signaled by the occurrence of a pattern with an odd number of 1s.

Today it is not unusual to find parity bits being used in a computer's main memory. Although we envision these machines as having memory cells of 8-bit capacity, in reality each has a capacity of 9 bits, 1 bit of which is used as a parity bit. Each time an 8-bit pattern is given to the memory circuitry for storage, the circuitry adds a parity bit and stores the resulting 9-bit pattern. When the pattern is later retrieved, the circuitry checks the parity of the 9-bit pattern. If this does not indicate an error, then the memory removes the parity bit and confidently returns the remaining 8-bit pattern. Otherwise, the memory returns the 8 data bits with a warning that the pattern being returned may not be the same pattern that was originally entrusted to memory.

The straightforward use of parity bits is simple, but it has its limitations. If a pattern originally has an odd number of 1s and suffers two errors, it will still have an odd number of 1s, and thus the parity system will not detect the errors. In fact, straightforward applications of parity bits fail to detect any even number of errors within a pattern.

One means of minimizing this problem is sometimes applied to long bit patterns, such as the string of bits recorded in a sector on a magnetic disk. In this case the pattern is accompanied by a collection of parity bits making up a **checkbyte.** Each bit within the checkbyte is a parity bit associated with a particular collection of bits scattered throughout the pattern. For instance, one parity bit may be associated with every eighth bit in the pattern starting with the first bit, while another may be associated with every eighth bit starting with the second bit. In this manner, a collection of errors concentrated in one area of the original pattern is more likely to be detected, since it will be in the scope of several parity bits. Variations of this checkbyte concept lead to error detection schemes known as **checksums** and **cyclic redundancy checks (CRC).**

Error-Correcting Codes

Although the use of a parity bit allows the detection of an error, it does not provide the information needed to correct the error. Many people are surprised that **error-correcting codes** can be designed so that errors can be not only detected but also corrected. After all, intuition says that we cannot correct errors in a received message unless we already know the information in the message. However, a simple code with such a corrective property is presented in Figure 1.27.

To understand how this code works, we first define the term **Hamming distance,** which is named after R. W. Hamming, who pioneered the search for error-correcting codes after becoming frustrated with the lack of reliability of the early relay machines of the 1940s. The Hamming distance between two bit patterns is the number of bits in which the patterns differ. For example, the Hamming distance between the patterns representing A and B in the code in Figure 1.27 is four, and the Hamming distance between B and C is three. The

Figure 1.27 An error-correcting code

Symbol	Code
A	000000
B	001111
C	010011
D	011100
E	100110
F	101001
G	110101
H	111010

important feature of the code in Figure 1.27 is that any two patterns are separated by a Hamming distance of at least three.

If a single bit is modified in a pattern from Figure 1.27, the error can be detected since the result will not be a legal pattern. (We must change at least 3 bits in any pattern before it will look like another legal pattern.) Moreover, we can also figure out what the original pattern was. After all, the modified pattern will be a Hamming distance of only one from its original form but at least two from any of the other legal patterns.

Thus, to decode a message that was originally encoded using Figure 1.27, we simply compare each received pattern with the patterns in the code until we find one that is within a distance of one from the received pattern. We consider this to be the correct symbol for decoding. For example, if we received the bit pattern 010100 and compared this pattern to the patterns in the code, we would obtain the table in Figure 1.28. Thus, we would conclude that the character transmitted must have been a D because this is the closest match.

Figure 1.28 Decoding the pattern 010100 using the code in Figure 1.27

Character	Code	Pattern received	Distance between received pattern and code
A	0 0 0 0 0 0	0 1 0 1 0 0	2
B	0 0 1 1 1 1	0 1 0 1 0 0	4
C	0 1 0 0 1 1	0 1 0 1 0 0	3
D	0 1 1 1 0 0	0 1 0 1 0 0	1 ——— Smallest distance
E	1 0 0 1 1 0	0 1 0 1 0 0	3
F	1 0 1 0 0 1	0 1 0 1 0 0	5
G	1 1 0 1 0 1	0 1 0 1 0 0	2
H	1 1 1 0 1 0	0 1 0 1 0 0	4

You will observe that using this technique with the code in Figure 1.27 actually allows us to detect up to two errors per pattern and to correct one error. If we designed the code so that each pattern was a Hamming distance of at least five from each of the others, we would be able to detect up to four errors per pattern and correct up to two. Of course, the design of efficient codes associated with large Hamming distances is not a straightforward task. In fact, it constitutes a part of the branch of mathematics called algebraic coding theory, which is a subject within the fields of linear algebra and matrix theory.

Error-correcting techniques are used extensively to increase the reliability of computing equipment. For example, they are often used in high-capacity magnetic disk drives to reduce the possibility that flaws in the magnetic surface will corrupt data. Moreover, a major distinction between the original CD format used for audio disks and the later format used for computer data storage is in the degree of error correction involved. CD-DA format incorporates error-correcting features that reduce the error rate to only one error for two CDs. This is quite adequate for audio recordings, but a company using CDs to supply software to customers would find that flaws in 50 percent of the disks would be intolerable. Thus, additional error-correcting features are employed in CDs used for data storage, reducing the probability of error to one in 20,000 disks.

Questions & Exercises

1. The following bytes were originally encoded using odd parity. In which of them do you know that an error has occurred?

   a. 100101101   b. 100000001   c. 000000000
   d. 111000000   e. 011111111

2. Could errors have occurred in a byte from question 1 without your knowing it? Explain your answer.

3. How would your answers to questions 1 and 2 change if you were told that even parity had been used instead of odd?

4. Encode these sentences in ASCII using odd parity by adding a parity bit at the high-order end of each character code:

   a. "Stop!" Cheryl shouted.   b. Does 2 + 3 = 5?

5. Using the error-correcting code presented in Figure 1.27, decode the following messages:

   a. 001111 100100 001100   b. 010001 000000 001011
   c. 011010 110110 100000 011100

6. Construct a code for the characters A, B, C, and D using bit patterns of length five so that the Hamming distance between any two patterns is at least three.

Chapter Review Problems

(Asterisked problems are associated with optional sections.)

1. Determine the output of each of the following circuits, assuming that the upper input is 1 and the lower input is 0. What would be the output when upper input is 0 and the lower input is 1?

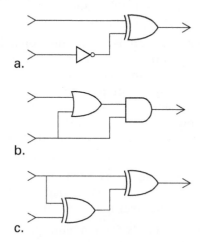

a.

b.

c.

2. a. What Boolean operation does the circuit compute?

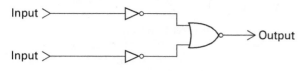

b. What Boolean operation does the circuit compute?

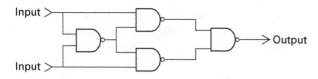

*3. a. If we were to purchase a flip-flop circuit from an electronic component store, we may find that it has an additional input called *flip*. When this input changes from a 0 to 1, the output flips state (if it was 0 it is now 1 and vice versa). However, when the flip input changes from 1 to a 0, nothing happens. Even though we may not know the details of the circuitry needed to accomplish this behavior, we could still use this device as an abstract tool in other circuits. Consider the circuitry using two of the following flip-flops. If a pulse were sent on the circuit's input, the bottom flip-flop would change state. However, the second flip-flop would not change, since its input (received from the output of the NOT gate) went from a 1 to a 0. As a result, this circuit would now produce the outputs 0 and 1. A second pulse would flip the state of both flip-flops, producing an output of 1 and 0. What would be the output after a third pulse? After a fourth pulse?

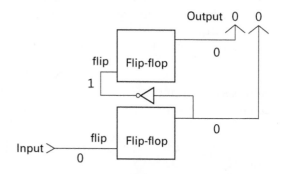

b. It is often necessary to coordinate activities of various components within a computer. This is accomplished by connecting a pulsating signal (called a clock) to circuitry similar to part a. Additional gates (as shown) send signals in a coordinated fashion to other connected circuits. On studying this circuit, you should be able to confirm that on the 1st, 5th, 9th ... pulses of the clock, a 1 will be sent on output A. On what pulses of the clock will a 1 be sent on output B? On what pulses of the clock will a 1 be sent on output C? On which output is a 1 sent on the 4th pulse of the clock?

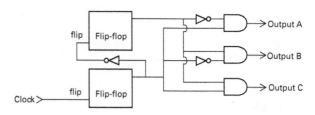

4. Assume that both of the inputs in the following circuit are 1. Describe what would happen if the upper input were temporarily changed to 0. Describe what would happen if the lower input were temporarily changed to 0. Redraw the circuit using NAND gates.

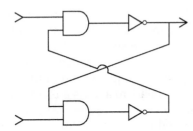

5. The following table represents the addresses and contents (using hexadecimal notation) of some cells in a machine's main memory. Starting with this memory arrangement, follow the sequence of instructions and record the final contents of each of these memory cells:

Address	Contents
00	AB
01	53
02	D6
03	02

Step 1. Move the contents of the cell whose address is 03 to the cell at address 00.

Step 2. Move the value 01 into the cell at address 02.

Step 3. Move the value stored at address 01 into the cell at address 03.

6. How many cells can be in a computer's main memory if each cell's address can be represented by two hexadecimal digits? What if four hexadecimal digits are used?

7. What bit patterns are represented by the following hexadecimal notations?
   a. CD   b. 67   c. 9A
   d. FF   e. 10

8. What is the value of the most significant bit in the bit patterns represented by the following hexadecimal notations?
   a. 8F   b. FF
   c. 6F   d. 1F

9. Express the following bit patterns in hexadecimal notation:
   a. 101000001010
   b. 110001111011
   c. 000010111110

10. Suppose a digital camera has a storage capacity of 256MB. How many photographs could be stored in the camera if each consisted of 1024 pixels per row and 1024 pixels per column if each pixel required three bytes of storage?

11. Suppose a picture is represented on a display screen by a rectangular array containing 1024 columns and 768 rows of pixels. If for each pixel, 8 bits are required to encode the color and another 8 bits to encode the intensity, how many byte-size memory cells are required to hold the entire picture?

12. a. Identify two advantages that main memory has over magnetic disk storage.
    b. Identify two advantages that magnetic disk storage has over main memory.

13. Suppose that only 50GB of your personal computer's 120GB hard-disk drive is empty. Would it be reasonable to use CDs to store all the material you have on the drive as a backup? What about DVDs?

14. If each sector on a magnetic disk contains 1024 bytes, how many sectors are required to store a single page of text (perhaps 50 lines of 100 characters) in a foreign language if each character is represented in two bytes of Unicode?

15. How many bytes of storage space would be required to store a 400-page novel in which each page contains 3500 characters if ASCII were used? How many bytes would be required if two byte Unicode characters were used?

16. How long is the latency time of a typical hard-disk drive spinning at 3600 revolutions per minute?

17. What is the average access time for a hard disk spinning at 360 revolutions per second with a seek time of 10 milliseconds?

18. Suppose a typist could type 60 words per minute continuously day after day. How long

would it take the typist to fill a CD whose capacity is 640MB? Assume one word is five characters and each character requires one byte of storage.

19. Here is a message in ASCII. What does it say?
01010111 01101000 01100001 01110100
00100000 01100100 01101111 01100101
01110011 00100000 01101001 01110100
00100000 01110011 01100001 01111001
00111111

20. The following is a message encoded in ASCII using one byte per character and then represented in hexadecimal notation. What is the message?

686578206E6F746174696F6E

21. Encode the following sentences in ASCII using one byte per character.
a. Does 100/5 = 20?
b. The total cost is $7.25.

22. Express your answers to the previous problem in hexadecimal notation.

23. List the binary representations of the integers from 8 to 18.

24. a. Write the number 23 by representing the 2 and 3 in ASCII.
b. Write the number 23 in binary representation.

25. What values have binary representations in which only one of the bits is 1? List the binary representations for the smallest six values with this property.

*26. Convert each of the following binary representations to its equivalent base 10 representation:
a. 1111   b. 0001   c. 10101
d. 1000   e. 10011   f. 000000
g. 1001   h. 10001   i. 100001
j. 11001   k. 11010   l. 11011

*27. Convert each of the following base 10 representations to its equivalent binary representation:
a. 7   b. 11   c. 16
d. 17   e. 31

*28. Convert each of the following excess 16 representations to its equivalent base 10 representation:
a. 10001   b. 10101   c. 01101
d. 01111   e. 11111

*29. Convert each of the following base 10 representations to its equivalent excess four representation:
a. 0   b. 3   c. −2
d. −1   e. 2

*30. Convert each of the following two's complement representations to its equivalent base 10 representation:
a. 01111   b. 10100   c. 01100
d. 10000   e. 10110

*31. Convert each of the following base 10 representations to its equivalent two's complement representation in which each value is represented in 7 bits:
a. 13   b. −13   c. −1
d. 0   e. 16

*32. Perform each of the following additions assuming the bit strings represent values in two's complement notation. Identify each case in which the answer is incorrect because of overflow.
a. 00101 + 01000   b. 11111 + 00001
c. 01111 + 00001   d. 10111 + 11010
e. 11111 + 11111   f. 00111 + 01100

*33. Solve each of the following problems by translating the values into two's complement notation (using patterns of 5 bits), converting any subtraction problem to an equivalent addition problem, and performing that addition. Check your work by converting your answer to base 10 notation. (Watch out for overflow.)
a. 5 + 1   b. 5 − 1   c. 12 − 5
d. 8 − 7   e. 12 + 5   f. 5 − 11

*34. Convert each of the following binary representations into its equivalent base 10 representation:
a. 11.11   b. 100.0101   c. 0.1101
d. 1.0   e. 10.01

*35. Express each of the following values in binary notation:
a. $5\frac{3}{4}$ b. $15\frac{15}{16}$ c. $5\frac{3}{8}$
d. $1\frac{1}{4}$ e. $6\frac{5}{8}$

*36. Decode the following bit patterns using the floating-point format described in Figure 1.24:
a. 01011001   b. 11001000
c. 10101100   d. 00111001

*37. Encode the following values using the 8-bit floating-point format described in Figure 1.24. Indicate each case in which a truncation error occurs.
   a. $-7\frac{1}{2}$ b. $\frac{1}{2}$ c. $-3\frac{3}{4}$
   d. $\frac{7}{32}$ e. $\frac{31}{32}$

*38. Assuming you are not restricted to using normalized form, list all the bit patterns that could be used to represent the value 3/8 using the floating-point format described in Figure 1.24.

*39. What is the best approximation to the square root of 2 that can be expressed in the 8-bit floating-point format described in Figure 1.24? What value is actually obtained if this approximation is squared by a machine using this floating-point format?

*40. What is the best approximation to the value one-tenth that can be represented using the 8-bit floating-point format described in Figure 1.24?

*41. Explain how errors can occur when measurements using the metric system are recorded in floating-point notation. For example, what if 110 cm was recorded in units of meters?

*42. One of the bit patterns 01011 and 11011 represents a value stored in excess 16 notation and the other represents the same value stored in two's complement notation.
   a. What can be determined about this common value?
   b. What is the relationship between a pattern representing a value stored in two's complement notation and the pattern representing the same value stored in excess notation when both systems use the same bit pattern length?

*43. The three bit patterns 10000010, 01101000, and 00000010 are representations of the same value in two's complement, excess, and the 8-bit floating-point format presented in Figure 1.24, but not necessarily in that order. What is the common value, and which pattern is in which notation?

*44. Which of the following values cannot be represented accurately in the floating-point format introduced in Figure 1.24?
   a. $6\frac{1}{2}$ b. $\frac{13}{16}$ c. 9
   d. $\frac{17}{32}$ e. $\frac{15}{16}$

*45. If you changed the length of the bit strings being used to represent integers in binary from 4 bits to 6 bits, what change would be made in the value of the largest integer you could represent? What if you were using two's complement notation?

*46. What would be the hexadecimal representation of the largest memory address in a memory consisting of 4MB if each cell had a one-byte capacity?

*47. What would be the encoded version of the message
   xxy yyx xxy xxy yyx
   if LZW compression, starting with the dictionary containing x, y, and a space (as described in Section 1.8), were used?

*48. The following message was compressed using LZW compression with a dictionary whose first, second, and third entries are x, y, and space, respectively. What is the decompressed message?
   22123113431213536

*49. If the message
   xxy yyx xxy xxyy
   were compressed using LZW with a starting dictionary whose first, second, and third entries were x, y, and space, respectively, what would be the entries in the final dictionary?

*50. As we will learn in the next chapter, one means of transmitting bits over traditional telephone systems is to convert the bit patterns into sound, transfer the sound over the telephone lines, and then convert the sound back into bit patterns. Such techniques are limited to transfer rates of 57.6 Kbps. Is this sufficient for teleconferencing if the video is compressed using MPEG?

*51. Encode the following sentences in ASCII using even parity by adding a parity bit at the high-order end of each character code:
   a. Does $100/5 = 20$?
   b. The total cost is $7.25.

*52. The following message was originally transmitted with odd parity in each short bit string. In which strings have errors definitely occurred?
   11001 11011 10110 00000 11111 10001
   10101 00100 01110

*53. Suppose a 24-bit code is generated by representing each symbol by three consecutive copies of its ASCII representation (for example, the symbol A is represented by the bit string 010000010100000101000001). What error-correcting properties does this new code have?

*54. Using the error-correcting code described in Figure 1.28, decode the following words:
   a. 111010 110110
   b. 101000 100110 001100
   c. 011101 000110 000000 010100
   d. 010010 001000 001110 101111
      000000 110111 100110
   e. 010011 000000 101001 100110

*55. International currency exchange rates change frequently. Investigate current exchange rates, and update the currency converter script from Section 1.8 accordingly.

*56. Find another currency not already included in the currency converter from Section 1.8. Acquire its current conversion rate and find its Unicode currency symbol on the web. Extend the script to convert this new currency.

*57. If your web browser and text editor properly support Unicode and UTF-8, copy/paste the actual international currency symbols into the converter script of Section 1.8, in place of the cumbersome codes like, '\u00A3'. (If your software has trouble handling Unicode, you may get strange symbols in your text editor when you try to do this.)

*58. The currency converter script of Section 1.8 uses the variable **dollars** to store the amount of money to be converted before performing each of the multiplications. This made the script one line longer than simply typing the integer quantity 1000 directly into each of the multiplication calculations. Why is it advantageous to create this extra variable ahead of time?

*59. Write and test a Python script that given a number of bytes outputs the equivalent number of kilobytes, megabytes, gigabytes, and terabytes. Write and test a complementary script that given a number of terabytes outputs the equivalent number of GB, MB, KB, and bytes.

*60. Write and test a Python script that given a number of minutes and seconds for a recording calculates the number of bits used to encode uncompressed, CD-quality stereo audio data of that length. (Review Section 1.4 for the necessary parameters and equations.)

*61. Identify the error(s) in this Python script.
```
days_per_week = 7
weeks_per_year = 52
days_per_year = days_per_week **
                weeks_per_year
PRINT(days_per_year)
```

Social Issues

The following questions are intended as a guide to the ethical/social/legal issues associated with the field of computing. The goal is not merely to answer these questions. You should also consider why you answered as you did and whether your justifications are consistent from one question to the next.

1. A truncation error has occurred in a critical situation, causing extensive damage and loss of life. Who is liable, if anyone? The designer of the hardware? The designer of the software? The programmer who actually wrote that part of the program? The person who decided to use the software in that particular application? What if the software had been corrected by the company that originally developed it, but that update had not been purchased and applied in the critical application? What if the software had been pirated?

2. Is it acceptable for an individual to ignore the possibility of truncation errors and their consequences when developing his or her own applications?

3. Was it ethical to develop software in the 1970s using only two digits to represent the year (such as using 76 to represent the year 1976), ignoring the fact that the software would be flawed as the turn of the century approached? Is it ethical today to use only three digits to represent the year (such as 982 for 1982 and 015 for 2015)? What about using only four digits?

4. Many argue that encoding information often dilutes or otherwise distorts the information, since it essentially forces the information to be quantified. They argue that a questionnaire in which subjects are required to record their opinions by responding within a scale from one to five is inherently flawed. To what extent is information quantifiable? Can the pros and cons of different locations for a waste disposal plant be quantified? Is the debate over nuclear power and nuclear waste quantifiable? Is it dangerous to base decisions on averages and other statistical analysis? Is it ethical for news agencies to report polling results without including the exact wording of the questions? Is it possible to quantify the value of a human life? Is it acceptable for a company to stop investing in the improvement of a product, even though additional investment could lower the possibility of a fatality relating to the product's use?

5. Should there be a distinction in the rights to collect and disseminate data depending on the form of the data? That is, should the right to collect and disseminate photographs, audio, or video be the same as the right to collect and disseminate text?

6. Whether intentional or not, a report submitted by a journalist usually reflects that journalist's bias. Often by changing only a few words, a story can be given either a positive or negative connotation. (Compare, "The majority of those surveyed opposed the referendum." to "A significant portion of those surveyed supported the referendum.") Is there a difference between altering a story (by leaving out certain points or carefully selecting words) and altering a photograph?

7. Suppose that the use of a data compression system results in the loss of subtle but significant items of information. What liability issues might be raised? How should they be resolved?

Additional Reading

Drew, M., and Z. Li. *Fundamentals of Multimedia.* Upper Saddle River, NJ: Prentice-Hall, 2004.

Halsall, F. *Multimedia Communications.* Boston, MA: Addison-Wesley, 2001.

Hamacher, V. C., Z. G. Vranesic, and S. G. Zaky. *Computer Organization,* 5th ed. New York: McGraw-Hill, 2002.

Knuth, D. E. *The Art of Computer Programming,* Vol. 2, 3rd ed. Boston, MA: Addison-Wesley, 1998.

Long, B. *Complete Digital Photography,* 3rd ed. Hingham, MA: Charles River Media, 2005.

Miano, J. *Compressed Image File Formats.* New York: ACM Press, 1999.

Petzold, C. *CODE: The Hidden Language of Computer Hardware and Software.* Redman, WA: Microsoft Press, 2000.

Salomon, D. *Data Compression: The Complete Reference,* 4th ed. New York: Springer, 2007.

Sayood, K. *Introduction to Data Compression,* 3rd ed. San Francisco, CA: Morgan Kaufmann, 2005.

CHAPTER

Data Manipulation 2

In this chapter we will learn how a computer manipulates data and communicates with peripheral devices such as printers and keyboards. In doing so, we will explore the basics of computer architecture and learn how computers are programmed by means of encoded instructions, called machine language instructions.

In Chapter 1 we studied topics relating to the storage of data inside a computer. In this chapter we will see how a computer manipulates that data. This manipulation consists of moving data from one location to another as well as performing operations such as arithmetic calculations, text editing, and image manipulation. We begin by extending our understanding of computer architecture beyond that of data storage systems.

2.1 Computer Architecture

The circuitry in a computer that controls the manipulation of data is called the **central processing unit,** or **CPU** (often referred to as merely the processor). In the machines of the mid-twentieth century, CPUs were large units comprised of perhaps several racks of electronic circuitry that reflected the significance of the unit. However, technology has shrunk these devices drastically. The CPUs found in today's desktop computers and notebooks are packaged as small flat squares (approximately two inches by two inches) whose connecting pins plug into a socket mounted on the machine's main circuit board (called the **motherboard**). In smartphones, mini-notebooks, and other **Mobile Internet Devices (MID),** CPUs are around half the size of a postage stamp. Due to their small size, these processors are called **microprocessors.**

CPU Basics

A CPU consists of three parts (Figure 2.1): the **arithmetic/logic unit,** which contains the circuitry that performs operations on data (such as addition and subtraction); the **control unit,** which contains the circuitry for coordinating the machine's activities; and the **register unit,** which contains data storage cells (similar to main memory cells), called **registers,** that are used for temporary storage of information within the CPU.

Some of the registers within the register unit are considered **general-purpose registers,** whereas others are **special-purpose registers.** We will discuss some of the special-purpose registers in Section 2.3. For now, we are concerned only with the general-purpose registers.

Figure 2.1   CPU and main memory connected via a bus

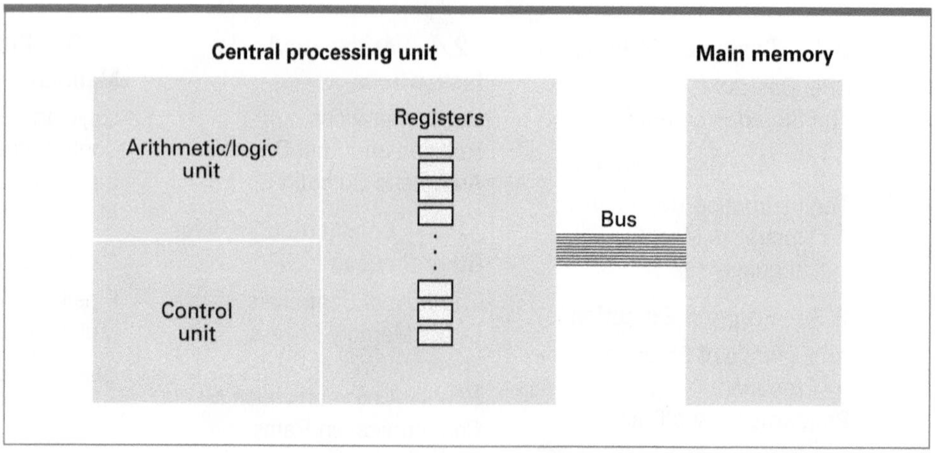

General-purpose registers serve as temporary holding places for data being manipulated by the CPU. These registers hold the inputs to the arithmetic/logic unit's circuitry and provide storage space for results produced by that unit. To perform an operation on data stored in main memory, the control unit transfers the data from memory into the general-purpose registers, informs the arithmetic/logic unit which registers hold the data, activates the appropriate circuitry within the arithmetic/logic unit, and tells the arithmetic/logic unit which register should receive the result.

For the purpose of transferring bit patterns, a machine's CPU and main memory are connected by a collection of wires called a **bus** (see again Figure 2.1). Through this bus, the CPU extracts (reads) data from main memory by supplying the address of the pertinent memory cell along with an electronic signal telling the memory circuitry that it is supposed to retrieve the data in the indicated cell. In a similar manner, the CPU places (writes) data in memory by providing the address of the destination cell and the data to be stored together with the appropriate electronic signal telling main memory that it is supposed to store the data being sent to it.

Based on this design, the task of adding two values stored in main memory involves more than the mere execution of the addition operation. The data must be transferred from main memory to registers within the CPU, the values must be added with the result being placed in a register, and the result must then be stored in a memory cell. The entire process is summarized by the five steps listed in Figure 2.2.

The Stored-Program Concept

Early computers were not known for their flexibility—the steps that each device executed were built into the control unit as a part of the machine. To gain more flexibility, some of the early electronic computers were designed so that the CPU could be conveniently rewired. This flexibility was accomplished by means of a pegboard arrangement similar to old telephone switchboards in which the ends of jumper wires were plugged into holes.

Figure 2.2   Adding values stored in memory

Step 1. Get one of the values to be added from memory and place it in a register.

Step 2. Get the other value to be added from memory and place it in another register.

Step 3. Activate the addition circuitry with the registers used in Steps 1 and 2 as inputs and another register designated to hold the result.

Step 4. Store the result in memory.

Step 5. Stop.

Cache Memory

It is instructive to compare the memory facilities within a computer in relation to their functionality. Registers are used to hold the data immediately applicable to the operation at hand; main memory is used to hold data that will be needed in the near future; and mass storage is used to hold data that will likely not be needed in the immediate future. Many machines are designed with an additional memory level, called cache memory. **Cache memory** is a portion (perhaps several hundred KB) of high-speed memory located within the CPU itself. In this special memory area, the machine attempts to keep a copy of that portion of main memory that is of current interest. In this setting, data transfers that normally would be made between registers and main memory are made between registers and cache memory. Any changes made to cache memory are then transferred collectively to main memory at a more opportune time. The result is a CPU that can execute its machine cycle more rapidly because it is not delayed by main memory communication.

A breakthrough (credited, apparently incorrectly, to John von Neumann) came with the realization that a program, just like data, can be encoded and stored in main memory. If the control unit is designed to extract the program from memory, decode the instructions, and execute them, the program that the machine follows can be changed merely by changing the contents of the computer's memory instead of rewiring the CPU.

The idea of storing a computer's program in its main memory is called the **stored-program concept** and has become the standard approach used today—so standard, in fact, that it seems obvious. What made it difficult originally was that everyone thought of programs and data as different entities: Data were stored in memory; programs were part of the CPU. The result was a prime example of not seeing the forest for the trees. It is easy to be caught in such ruts, and the development of computer science might still be in many of them today without our knowing it. Indeed, part of the excitement of the science is that new insights are constantly opening doors to new theories and applications.

Questions & Exercises

1. What sequence of events do you think would be required to move the contents of one memory cell in a computer to another memory cell?

2. What information must the CPU supply to the main memory circuitry to write a value into a memory cell?

3. Mass storage, main memory, and general-purpose registers are all storage systems. What is the difference in their use?

2.2 Machine Language

To apply the stored-program concept, CPUs are designed to recognize instructions encoded as bit patterns. This collection of instructions along with the encoding system is called the **machine language.** An instruction expressed in this language is called a machine-level instruction or, more commonly, a **machine instruction.**

The Instruction Repertoire

The list of machine instructions that a typical CPU must be able to decode and execute is quite short. In fact, once a machine can perform certain elementary but well-chosen tasks, adding more features does not increase the machine's theoretical capabilities. In other words, beyond a certain point, additional features may increase such things as convenience but add nothing to the machine's fundamental capabilities.

The degree to which machine designs should take advantage of this fact has led to two philosophies of CPU architecture. One is that a CPU should be designed to execute a minimal set of machine instructions. This approach leads to what is called a **reduced instruction set computer (RISC).** The argument in favor of RISC architecture is that such a machine is efficient, fast, and less expensive to manufacture. On the other hand, others argue in favor of CPUs with the ability to execute a large number of complex instructions, even though many of them are technically redundant. The result of this approach is known as a **complex instruction set computer (CISC).** The argument in favor of CISC architecture is that the more complex CPU can better cope with the ever-increasing complexities

Who Invented What?

Awarding a single individual credit for an invention is always a dubious undertaking. Thomas Edison is credited with inventing the incandescent lamp, but other researchers were developing similar lamps, and in a sense Edison was lucky to be the one to obtain the patent. The Wright brothers are credited with inventing the airplane, but they were competing with and benefited from the work of many contemporaries, all of whom were preempted to some degree by Leonardo da Vinci, who toyed with the idea of flying machines in the fifteenth century. Even Leonardo's designs were apparently based on earlier ideas. Of course, in these cases the designated inventor still has legitimate claims to the credit bestowed. In other cases, history seems to have awarded credit inappropriately—an example is the stored-program concept. Without a doubt, John von Neumann was a brilliant scientist who deserves credit for numerous contributions. But one of the contributions for which popular history has chosen to credit him, the stored-program concept, was apparently developed by researchers led by J. P. Eckert at the Moore School of Electrical Engineering at the University of Pennsylvania. John von Neumann was merely the first to publish work reporting the idea and thus computing lore has selected him as the inventor.

of today's software. With CISC, programs can exploit a powerful rich set of instructions, many of which would require a multi-instruction sequence in a RISC design.

In the 1990s and into the millennium, commercially available CISC and RISC processors were actively competing for dominance in desktop computing. Intel processors, used in PCs, are examples of CISC architecture; PowerPC processors (developed by an alliance between Apple, IBM, and Motorola) are examples of RISC architecture and were used in the Apple Macintosh. As time progressed, the manufacturing cost of CISC was drastically reduced; thus Intel's processors (or their equivalent from AMD—Advanced Micro Devices, Inc.) are now found in virtually all desktop and laptop computers (even Apple is now building computers based on Intel products).

While CISC secured its place in desktop computers, it has an insatiable thirst for electrical power. In contrast, the company Advanced RISC Machine (ARM) has designed a RISC architecture specifically for low power consumption. (Advanced RISC Machine was originally Acorn Computers and is now ARM Holdings.) Thus, ARM-based processors, manufactured by a host of vendors including Qualcomm and Texas Instruments, are readily found in game controllers, digital TVs, navigation systems, automotive modules, cellular telephones, smartphones, and other consumer electronics.

Regardless of the choice between RISC and CISC, a machine's instructions can be categorized into three groupings: (1) the data transfer group, (2) the arithmetic/logic group, and (3) the control group.

Data Transfer The data transfer group consists of instructions that request the movement of data from one location to another. Steps 1, 2, and 4 in Figure 2.2 fall into this category. We should note that using terms such as *transfer* or *move* to identify this group of instructions is actually a misnomer. It is rare that the data being transferred is erased from its original location. The process involved in a transfer instruction is more like copying the data rather than moving it. Thus terms such as *copy* or *clone* better describe the actions of this group of instructions.

While on the subject of terminology, we should mention that special terms are used when referring to the transfer of data between the CPU and main memory. A request to fill a general-purpose register with the contents of a memory cell is

Variable-Length Instructions

To simplify explanations in the text, the machine language used for examples in this chapter (and described in Appendix C) uses a fixed size (two bytes) for all instructions. Thus, to fetch an instruction, the CPU always retrieves the contents of two consecutive memory cells and increments its program counter by two. This consistency streamlines the task of fetching instructions and is characteristic of RISC machines. CISC machines, however, have machine languages whose instructions vary in length. Today's Intel processors, for example, have instructions that range from single-byte instructions to multiple-byte instructions whose length depends on the exact use of the instruction. CPUs with such machine languages determine the length of the incoming instruction by the instruction's op-code. That is, the CPU first fetches the op-code of the instruction and then, based on the bit pattern received, knows how many more bytes to fetch from memory to obtain the rest of the instruction.

commonly referred to as a LOAD instruction; conversely, a request to transfer the contents of a register to a memory cell is called a STORE instruction. In Figure 2.2, Steps 1 and 2 are LOAD instructions, and Step 4 is a STORE instruction.

An important group of instructions within the data transfer category consists of the commands for communicating with devices outside the CPU-main memory context (printers, keyboards, display screens, disk drives, etc.). Since these instructions handle the input/output (I/O) activities of the machine, they are called **I/O instructions** and are sometimes considered as a category in their own right. On the other hand, Section 2.5 describes how these I/O activities can be handled by the same instructions that request data transfers between the CPU and main memory. Thus, we shall consider the I/O instructions to be a part of the data transfer group.

Arithmetic/Logic The arithmetic/logic group consists of the instructions that tell the control unit to request an activity within the arithmetic/logic unit. Step 3 in Figure 2.2 falls into this group. As its name suggests, the arithmetic/logic unit is capable of performing operations other than the basic arithmetic operations. Some of these additional operations are the Boolean operations AND, OR, and XOR, introduced in Chapter 1, which we will discuss in more detail later in this chapter.

Another collection of operations available within most arithmetic/logic units allows the contents of registers to be moved to the right or the left within the register. These operations are known as either SHIFT or ROTATE operations, depending on whether the bits that "fall off the end" of the register are merely discarded (SHIFT) or are used to fill the holes left at the other end (ROTATE).

Control The control group consists of those instructions that direct the execution of the program rather than the manipulation of data. Step 5 in Figure 2.2 falls into this category, although it is an extremely elementary example. This group contains many of the more interesting instructions in a machine's repertoire, such as the family of JUMP (or BRANCH) instructions used to direct the CPU to execute an instruction other than the next one in the list. These JUMP instructions appear in two varieties: **unconditional jumps** and **conditional jumps.** An example of the former would be the instruction "Skip to Step 5"; an example of the latter would be, "If the value obtained is 0, then skip to Step 5." The distinction is that a conditional jump results in a "change of venue" only if a certain condition is satisfied. As an example, the sequence of instructions in Figure 2.3 represents an algorithm for dividing two values where Step 3 is a conditional jump that protects against the possibility of division by zero.

An Illustrative Machine Language

Let us now consider how the instructions of a typical computer are encoded. The machine that we will use for our discussion is described in Appendix C and summarized in Figure 2.4. It has 16 general-purpose registers and 256 main memory cells, each with a capacity of 8 bits. For referencing purposes, we label the registers with the values 0 through 15 and address the memory cells with the values 0 through 255. For convenience we think of these labels and addresses as values represented in base two and compress the resulting bit patterns using hexadecimal notation. Thus, the registers are labeled 0 through F, and the memory cells are addressed 00 through FF.

Figure 2.3   Dividing values stored in memory

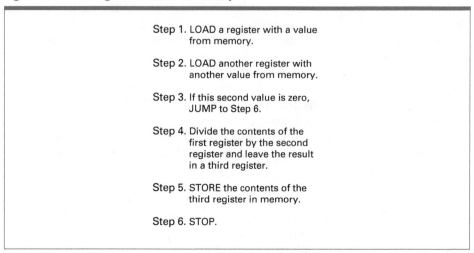

Step 1. LOAD a register with a value from memory.

Step 2. LOAD another register with another value from memory.

Step 3. If this second value is zero, JUMP to Step 6.

Step 4. Divide the contents of the first register by the second register and leave the result in a third register.

Step 5. STORE the contents of the third register in memory.

Step 6. STOP.

The encoded version of a machine instruction consists of two parts: the **op-code** (short for operation code) field and the **operand** field. The bit pattern appearing in the op-code field indicates which of the elementary operations, such as STORE, SHIFT, XOR, and JUMP, is requested by the instruction. The bit patterns found in the operand field provide more detailed information about the operation specified by the op-code. For example, in the case of a STORE operation, the information in the operand field indicates which register contains the data to be stored and which memory cell is to receive the data.

The entire machine language of our illustrative machine (Appendix C) consists of only twelve basic instructions. Each of these instructions is encoded using a total of 16 bits, represented by four hexadecimal digits (Figure 2.5). The op-code for each instruction consists of the first 4 bits or, equivalently, the first hexadecimal digit. Note (Appendix C) that these op-codes are represented by the hexadecimal digits 1 through C. In particular, the table in Appendix C

Figure 2.4   The architecture of the machine described in Appendix C

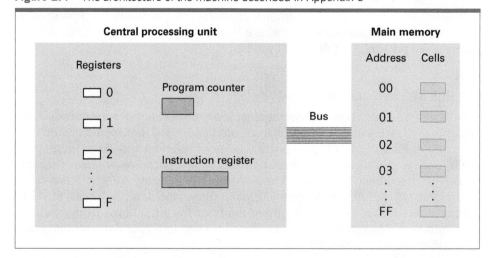

Figure 2.5 The composition of an instruction for the machine in Appendix C

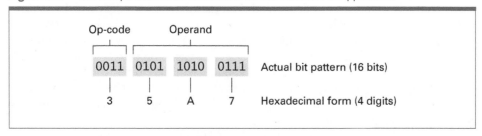

shows us that an instruction beginning with the hexadecimal digit 3 refers to a STORE instruction, and an instruction beginning with hexadecimal A refers to a ROTATE instruction.

The operand field of each instruction in our illustrative machine consists of three hexadecimal digits (12 bits), and in each case (except for the HALT instruction, which needs no further refinement) clarifies the general instruction given by the op-code. For example (Figure 2.6), if the first hexadecimal digit of an instruction were 3 (the op-code for storing the contents of a register), the next hexadecimal digit of the instruction would indicate which register is to be stored, and the last two hexadecimal digits would indicate which memory cell is to receive the data. Thus the instruction 35A7 (hexadecimal) translates to the statement "STORE the bit pattern found in register 5 in the memory cell whose address is A7." (Note how the use of hexadecimal notation simplifies our discussion. In reality, the instruction 35A7 is the bit pattern 0011010110100111.)

The instruction 35A7 also provides an explicit example of why main memory capacities are measured in powers of two. Because 8 bits in the instruction are reserved for specifying the memory cell utilized by this instruction, it is possible to reference exactly 2^8 different memory cells. It behooves us therefore to build main memory with this many cells—addressed from 0 to 255. If main memory had more cells, we would not be able to write instructions that distinguished between them; if main memory had fewer cells, we would be able to write instructions that referenced nonexisting cells.

Figure 2.6 Decoding the instruction 35A7

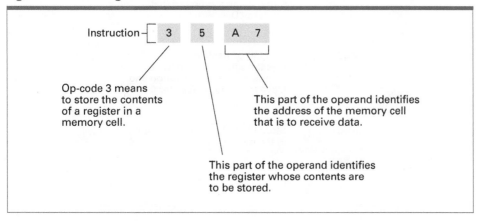

As another example of how the operand field is used to clarify the general instruction given by an op-code, consider an instruction with the op-code 7 (hexadecimal), which requests that the contents of two registers be ORed. (We will see what it means to OR two registers in Section 2.4. For now we are interested merely in how instructions are encoded.) In this case, the next hexadecimal digit indicates the register in which the result should be placed, while the last two hexadecimal digits indicate which two registers are to be ORed. Thus the instruction 70C5 translates to the statement "OR the contents of register C with the contents of register 5 and leave the result in register 0."

A subtle distinction exists between our machine's two LOAD instructions. Here we see that the op-code 1 (hexadecimal) identifies an instruction that loads a register with the contents of a memory cell, whereas the op-code 2 (hexadecimal) identifies an instruction that loads a register with a particular value. The difference is that the operand field in an instruction of the first type contains an address, whereas in the second type the operand field contains the actual bit pattern to be loaded.

Note that the machine has two ADD instructions: one for adding two's complement representations and one for adding floating-point representations. This distinction is a consequence of the fact that adding bit patterns that represent values encoded in two's complement notation requires different activities within the arithmetic/logic unit from adding values encoded in floating-point notation. We close this section with Figure 2.7, which contains an encoded version of the instructions in Figure 2.2. We have assumed that the values to be added are stored in two's complement notation at memory addresses 6C and 6D and the sum is to be placed in the memory cell at address 6E.

Figure 2.7   An encoded version of the instructions in Figure 2.2

Encoded instructions	Translation
156C	Load register 5 with the bit pattern found in the memory cell at address 6C.
166D	Load register 6 with the bit pattern found in the memory cell at address 6D.
5056	Add the contents of register 5 and 6 as though they were two's complement representation and leave the result in register 0.
306E	Store the contents of register 0 in the memory cell at address 6E.
C000	Halt.

Questions & Exercises

1. Why might the term *move* be considered an incorrect name for the operation of moving data from one location in a machine to another?

2. In the text, JUMP instructions were expressed by identifying the destination explicitly by stating the name (or step number) of the destination within the JUMP instruction (for example, "Jump to Step 6"). A drawback of this technique is that if an instruction name (number) is later changed, we must be sure to find all jumps to that instruction and change that name also. Describe another way of expressing a JUMP instruction so that the name of the destination is not explicitly stated.

3. Is the instruction "If 0 equals 0, then jump to Step 7" a conditional or unconditional jump? Explain your answer.

4. Write the example program in Figure 2.7 in actual bit patterns.

5. The following are instructions written in the machine language described in Appendix C. Rewrite them in English.

   a. 368A   b. BADE   c. 803C   d. 40F4

6. What is the difference between the instructions 15AB and 25AB in the machine language of Appendix C?

7. Here are some instructions in English. Translate each of them into the machine language of Appendix C.

   a. LOAD register number 3 with the hexadecimal value 56.
   b. ROTATE register number 5 three bits to the right.
   c. AND the contents of register A with the contents of register 5 and leave the result in register 0.

2.3 Program Execution

A computer follows a program stored in its memory by copying the instructions from memory into the CPU as needed. Once in the CPU, each instruction is decoded and obeyed. The order in which the instructions are fetched from memory corresponds to the order in which the instructions are stored in memory unless otherwise altered by a JUMP instruction.

To understand how the overall execution process takes place, it is necessary to consider two of the special purpose registers within the CPU: the **instruction register** and the **program counter** (see again Figure 2.4). The instruction register is used to hold the instruction being executed. The program counter contains the address of the next instruction to be executed, thereby serving as the machine's way of keeping track of where it is in the program.

The CPU performs its job by continually repeating an algorithm that guides it through a three-step process known as the **machine cycle.** The steps in the machine cycle are fetch, decode, and execute (Figure 2.8). During the fetch step, the CPU requests that main memory provide it with the instruction that is stored at the address indicated by the program counter. Since each instruction in our machine is two bytes long, this fetch process involves retrieving the contents of two memory cells from main memory. The CPU places the instruction received from memory in its instruction register and then increments the program counter by two so that the counter contains the address of the next instruction stored in memory. Thus the program counter will be ready for the next fetch.

With the instruction now in the instruction register, the CPU decodes the instruction, which involves breaking the operand field into its proper components based on the instruction's op-code.

The CPU then executes the instruction by activating the appropriate circuitry to perform the requested task. For example, if the instruction is a load from memory, the CPU sends the appropriate signals to main memory, waits for main memory to send the data, and then places the data in the requested register. If the instruction is for an arithmetic operation, the CPU activates the appropriate circuitry in the arithmetic/logic unit with the correct registers as inputs and waits for the arithmetic/logic unit to compute the answer and place it in the appropriate register.

Once the instruction in the instruction register has been executed, the CPU again begins the machine cycle with the fetch step. Observe that since the program counter was incremented at the end of the previous fetch, it again provides the CPU with the correct address.

A somewhat special case is the execution of a JUMP instruction. Consider, for example, the instruction B258 (Figure 2.9), which means "JUMP to the instruction at address 58 (hexadecimal) if the contents of register 2 is the same as that of register 0." In this case, the execute step of the machine cycle begins with the comparison of registers 2 and 0. If they contain different bit patterns, the execute

Figure 2.8 The machine cycle

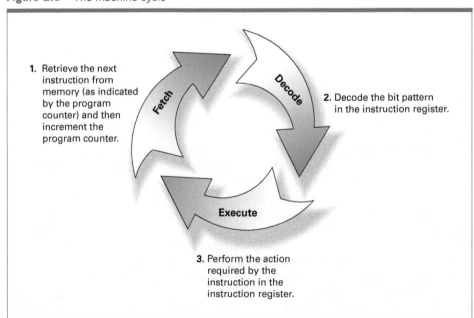

1. Retrieve the next instruction from memory (as indicated by the program counter) and then increment the program counter.

Fetch

Decode

2. Decode the bit pattern in the instruction register.

Execute

3. Perform the action required by the instruction in the instruction register.

Comparing Computer Power

When shopping for a personal computer, you will find that clock speeds are often used to compare machines. A computer's **clock** is a circuit, called an oscillator, that generates pulses that are used to coordinate the machine's activities—the faster this oscillating circuit generates pulses, the faster the machine performs its machine cycle. Clock speeds are measured in hertz (abbreviated as Hz) with one Hz equal to one cycle (or pulse) per second. Typical clock speeds in desktop computers are in the range of a few hundred MHz (older models) to several GHz. (MHz is short for megahertz, which is a million Hz. GHz is short for gigahertz, which is 1000 MHz.)

Unfortunately, different CPU designs might perform different amounts of work in one clock cycle, and thus clock speed alone fails to be relevant in comparing machines with different CPUs. If you are comparing a machine based on an Intel processor to one based on ARM, it would be more meaningful to compare performance by means of **benchmarking,** which is the process of comparing the performance of different machines when executing the same program, known as a benchmark. By selecting benchmarks representing different types of applications, you get meaningful comparisons for various market segments.

step terminates and the next machine cycle begins. If, however, the contents of these registers are equal, the machine places the value 58 (hexadecimal) in its program counter during the execute step. In this case, then, the next fetch step finds 58 in the program counter, so the instruction at that address will be the next instruction to be fetched and executed.

Note that if the instruction had been B058, then the decision of whether the program counter should be changed would depend on whether the contents of register 0 was equal to that of register 0. But these are the same registers and thus must have equal content. In turn, any instruction of the form B0XY will cause a jump to be executed to the memory location XY regardless of the contents of register 0.

Figure 2.9 Decoding the instruction B258

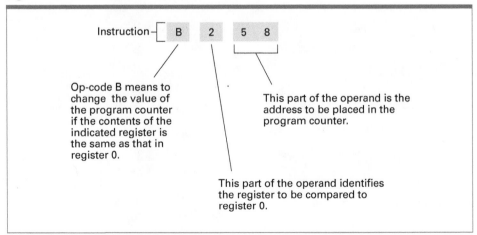

Instruction— B 2 5 8

Op-code B means to change the value of the program counter if the contents of the indicated register is the same as that in register 0.

This part of the operand is the address to be placed in the program counter.

This part of the operand identifies the register to be compared to register 0.

An Example of Program Execution

Let us follow the machine cycle applied to the program presented in Figure 2.7, which retrieves two values from main memory, computes their sum, and stores that total in a main memory cell. We first need to put the program somewhere in memory. For our example, suppose the program is stored in consecutive addresses, starting at address A0 (hexadecimal). With the program stored in this manner, we can cause the machine to execute it by placing the address (A0) of the first instruction in the program counter and starting the machine (Figure 2.10).

The CPU begins the fetch step of the machine cycle by extracting the instruction stored in main memory at location A0 and placing this instruction (156C) in its instruction register (Figure 2.11a). Notice that, in our machine, instructions are 16 bits (two bytes) long. Thus the entire instruction to be fetched occupies the memory cells at both address A0 and A1. The CPU is designed to take this into account so it retrieves the contents of both cells and places the bit patterns received in the instruction register, which is 16 bits long. The CPU then adds two to the program counter so that this register contains the address of the next instruction (Figure 2.11b). At the end of the fetch step of the first machine cycle, the program counter and instruction register contain the following data:

```
Program Counter: A2
Instruction Register: 156C
```

Next, the CPU analyzes the instruction in its instruction register and concludes that it is to load register 5 with the contents of the memory cell at address 6C. This load activity is performed during the execution step of the machine cycle, and the CPU then begins the next cycle.

This cycle begins by fetching the instruction 166D from the two memory cells starting at address A2. The CPU places this instruction in the instruction register

Figure 2.10   The program from Figure 2.7 stored in main memory ready for execution

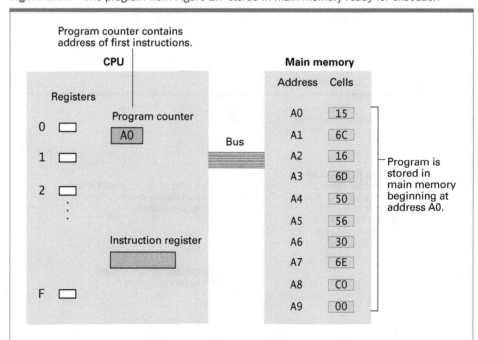

Figure 2.11   Performing the fetch step of the machine cycle

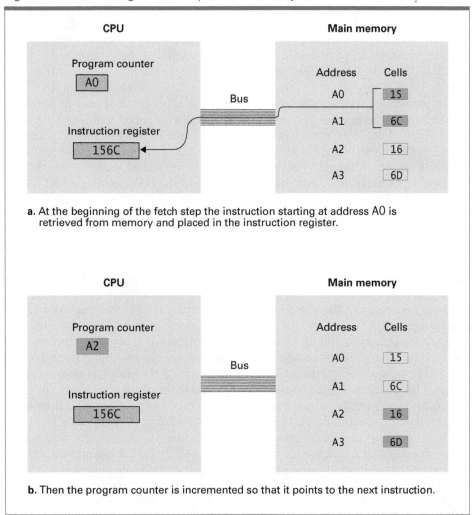

a. At the beginning of the fetch step the instruction starting at address A0 is retrieved from memory and placed in the instruction register.

b. Then the program counter is incremented so that it points to the next instruction.

and increments the program counter to A4. The values in the program counter and instruction register therefore become the following:

```
Program Counter: A4
Instruction Register: 166D
```

Now the CPU decodes the instruction 166D and determines that it is to load register 6 with the contents of memory address 6D. It then executes the instruction. It is at this time that register 6 is actually loaded.

Since the program counter now contains A4, the CPU extracts the next instruction starting at this address. The result is that 5056 is placed in the instruction register, and the program counter is incremented to A6. The CPU now decodes the contents of its instruction register and executes it by activating the two's complement addition circuitry with inputs being registers 5 and 6.

During this execution step, the arithmetic/logic unit performs the requested addition, leaves the result in register 0 (as requested by the control unit), and reports to the control unit that it has finished. The CPU then begins another machine cycle. Once again, with the aid of the program counter, it fetches the next instruction (306E) from the two memory cells starting at memory location A6 and increments the program counter to A8. This instruction is then decoded and executed. At this point, the sum is placed in memory location 6E.

The next instruction is fetched starting from memory location A8, and the program counter is incremented to AA. The contents of the instruction register (C000) are now decoded as the halt instruction. Consequently, the machine stops during the execute step of the machine cycle, and the program is completed.

In summary, we see that the execution of a program stored in memory involves the same process you and I might use if we needed to follow a detailed list of instructions. Whereas we might keep our place by marking the instructions as we perform them, the CPU keeps its place by using the program counter. After determining which instruction to execute next, we would read the instruction and extract its meaning. Then, we would perform the task requested and return to the list for the next instruction in the same manner that the CPU executes the instruction in its instruction register and then continues with another fetch.

Programs Versus Data

Many programs can be stored simultaneously in a computer's main memory, as long as they occupy different locations. Which program will be run when the machine is started can then be determined merely by setting the program counter appropriately.

One must keep in mind, however, that because data are also contained in main memory and encoded in terms of 0s and 1s, the machine alone has no way of knowing what is data and what is program. If the program counter were assigned the address of data instead of the address of the desired program, the CPU, not knowing any better, would extract the data bit patterns as though they were instructions and execute them. The final result would depend on the data involved.

We should not conclude, however, that providing programs and data with a common appearance in a machine's memory is bad. In fact, it has proved a useful attribute because it allows one program to manipulate other programs (or even itself) the same as it would data. Imagine, for example, a program that modifies itself in response to its interaction with its environment and thus exhibits the ability to learn, or perhaps a program that writes and executes other programs in order to solve problems presented to it.

Questions & Exercises

1. Suppose the memory cells from addresses 00 to 05 in the machine described in Appendix C contain the (hexadecimal) bit patterns given in the following table:

Address	Contents
00	14
01	02
02	34
03	17
04	C0
05	00

If we start the machine with its program counter containing 00, what bit pattern is in the memory cell whose address is hexadecimal 17 when the machine halts?

2. Suppose the memory cells at addresses B0 to B8 in the machine described in Appendix C contain the (hexadecimal) bit patterns given in the following table:

Address	Contents
B0	13
B1	B8
B2	A3
B3	02
B4	33
B5	B8
B6	C0
B7	00
B8	0F

a. If the program counter starts at B0, what bit pattern is in register number 3 after the first instruction has been executed?

b. What bit pattern is in memory cell B8 when the halt instruction is executed?

3. Suppose the memory cells at addresses A4 to B1 in the machine described in Appendix C contain the (hexadecimal) bit patterns given in the following table:

Address	Contents
A4	20
A5	00
A6	21
A7	03
A8	22
A9	01
AA	B1
AB	B0
AC	50
AD	02
AE	B0
AF	AA
B0	C0
B1	00

When answering the following questions, assume that the machine is started with its program counter containing A4.

a. What is in register 0 the first time the instruction at address AA is executed?

b. What is in register 0 the second time the instruction at address AA is executed?

c. How many times is the instruction at address AA executed before the machine halts?

4. Suppose the memory cells at addresses F0 to F9 in the machine described in Appendix C contain the (hexadecimal) bit patterns described in the following table:

Address	Contents
F0	20
F1	C0
F2	30
F3	F8
F4	20
F5	00
F6	30
F7	F9
F8	FF
F9	FF

If we start the machine with its program counter containing F0, what does the machine do when it reaches the instruction at address F8?

2.4 Arithmetic/Logic Instructions

As indicated earlier, the arithmetic/logic group of instructions consists of instructions requesting arithmetic, logic, and shift operations. In this section, we look at these operations more closely.

Logic Operations

We introduced the logic operations AND, OR, and XOR (exclusive or, often pronounced, "ex-or") in Chapter 1 as operations that combine two input bits to produce a single output bit. These operations can be extended to **bitwise operations** that combine two strings of bits to produce a single output string by applying the basic operation to individual columns. For example, the result of ANDing the patterns 10011010 and 11001001 results in

```
    10011010
AND 11001001
    10001000
```

where we have merely written the result of ANDing the two bits in each column at the bottom of the column. Likewise, ORing and XORing these patterns would produce

```
    10011010            10011010
OR  11001001        XOR 11001001
    11011011            01010011
```

One of the major uses of the AND operation is for placing 0s in one part of a bit pattern while not disturbing the other part. There are many applications for this in practice, such as filtering certain colors out of a digital image represented in the RGB format, as described in the previous chapter. Consider, for example, what happens if the byte 00001111 is the first operand of an AND operation.

Without knowing the contents of the second operand, we still can conclude that the four most significant bits of the result will be 0s. Moreover, the four least significant bits of the result will be a copy of that part of the second operand, as shown in the following example:

```
    00001111
AND 10101010
    00001010
```

This use of the AND operation is an example of the process called **masking.** Here one operand, called a **mask,** determines which part of the other operand will affect the result. In the case of the AND operation, masking produces a result that is a partial replica of one of the operands, with 0s occupying the nonduplicated positions. One trivial use of the AND operation in this context would be to mask off all of the bits associated with the red component of the pixels in an image, leaving only the blue and green components. This transformation is frequently available as an option in image manipulation software.

AND operations are useful when manipulating other types of **bit map** besides images, whenever a string of bits is used in which each bit represents the presence or absence of a particular object. As a non-graphical example, a string of 52 bits, in which each bit is associated with a particular playing card, can be used to represent a poker hand by assigning 1s to those five bits associated with the cards in the hand and 0s to all the others. Likewise, a bit map of 52 bits, of which thirteen are 1s, can be used to represent a hand of bridge, or a bit map of 32 bits can be used to represent which of thirty-two ice cream flavors are available.

Suppose, then, that the eight bits in a memory cell are being used as a bit map, and we want to find out whether the object associated with the third bit from the high-order end is present. We merely need to AND the entire byte with the mask 00100000, which produces a byte of all 0s if and only if the third bit from the high-order end of the bit map is itself 0. A program can then act accordingly by following the AND operation with a conditional branch instruction. Moreover, if the third bit from the high-order end of the bit map is a 1, and we want to change it to a 0 without disturbing the other bits, we can AND the bit map with the mask 11011111 and then store the result in place of the original bit map.

Where the AND operation can be used to duplicate a part of a bit string while placing 0s in the nonduplicated part, the OR operation can be used to duplicate a part of a string while putting 1s in the nonduplicated part. For this we again use a mask, but this time we indicate the bit positions to be duplicated with 0s and use 1s to indicate the nonduplicated positions. For example, ORing any byte with 11110000 produces a result with 1s in its most significant four bits while its remaining bits are a copy of the least significant four bits of the other operand, as demonstrated by the following example:

```
   11110000
OR 10101010
   11111010
```

Consequently, whereas the mask 11011111 can be used with the AND operation to force a 0 in the third bit from the high-order end of a byte, the mask 00100000 can be used with the OR operation to force a 1 in that position.

A major use of the XOR operation is in forming the complement of a bit string. XORing any byte with a mask of all 1s produces the complement of the byte. For example, note the relationship between the second operand and the result in the following example:

```
      11111111
XOR  10101010
      01010101
```

The XOR operation can be used to invert all of the bits of an RGB bitmap image, resulting in an "inverted" color image in which light colors have been replaced by dark colors, and vice versa.

In the machine language described in Appendix C, op-codes 7, 8, and 9 are used for the logic operations OR, AND, and XOR, respectively. Each requests that the corresponding logic operation be performed between the contents of two designated registers and that the result be placed in another designated register. For example, the instruction 7ABC requests that the result of ORing the contents of registers B and C be placed in register A.

Rotation and Shift Operations

The operations in the class of rotation and shift operations provide a means for moving bits within a register and are often used in solving alignment problems. These operations are classified by the direction of motion (right or left) and whether the process is circular. Within these classification guidelines are numerous variations with mixed terminology. Let us take a quick look at the ideas involved.

Consider a register containing a byte of bits. If we shift its contents one bit to the right, we imagine the rightmost bit falling off the edge and a hole appearing at the leftmost end. What happens with this extra bit and the hole is the distinguishing feature among the various shift operations. One technique is to place the bit that fell off the right end in the hole at the left end. The result is a **circular shift,** also called a **rotation.** Thus, if we perform a right circular shift on a byte-size bit pattern eight times, we obtain the same bit pattern we started with.

Another technique is to discard the bit that falls off the edge and always fill the hole with a 0. The term **logical shift** is often used to refer to these operations. Such shifts to the left can be used for multiplying two's complement representations by two. After all, shifting binary digits to the left corresponds to multiplication by two, just as a similar shift of decimal digits corresponds to multiplication by ten. Moreover, division by two can be accomplished by shifting the binary string to the right. In either shift, care must be taken to preserve the sign bit when using certain notational systems. Thus, we often find right shifts that always fill the hole (which occurs at the sign bit position) with its original value. Shifts that leave the sign bit unchanged are sometimes called **arithmetic shifts.**

Among the variety of shift and rotate instructions possible, the machine language described in Appendix C contains only a right circular shift, designated by op-code A. In this case the first hexadecimal digit in the operand specifies the register to be rotated, and the rest of the operand specifies the number of bits to be rotated. Thus the instruction A501 means "Rotate the contents of register

5 to the right by 1 bit." In particular, if register 5 originally contained the bit pattern 65 (hexadecimal), then it would contain B2 after this instruction is executed (Figure 2.12). (You may wish to experiment with how other shift and rotate instructions can be produced with combinations of the instructions provided in the machine language of Appendix C. For example, since a register is eight bits long, a right circular shift of three bits produces the same result as a left circular shift of five bits.)

Arithmetic Operations

Although we have already mentioned the arithmetic operations of add, subtract, multiply, and divide, a few loose ends should still be connected. First, we have already seen that subtraction can be simulated by means of addition and negation. Moreover, multiplication is merely repeated addition and division is repeated subtraction. (Six divided by two is three because three twos can be subtracted from six.) For this reason, some small CPUs are designed with only the add or perhaps only the add and subtract instructions.

We should also mention that numerous variations exist for each arithmetic operation. We have already alluded to this in relation to the add operations available on our machine in Appendix C. In the case of addition, for example, if the values to be added are stored in two's complement notation, the addition process must be performed as a straightforward column by column addition. However, if the operands are stored as floating-point values, the addition process must extract the mantissa of each, shift them right or left according to the exponent fields, check the sign bits, perform the addition, and translate the result into floating-point notation. Thus, although both operations are considered addition, the action of the machine is not the same.

Figure 2.12 Rotating the bit pattern 65 (hexadecimal) one bit to the right

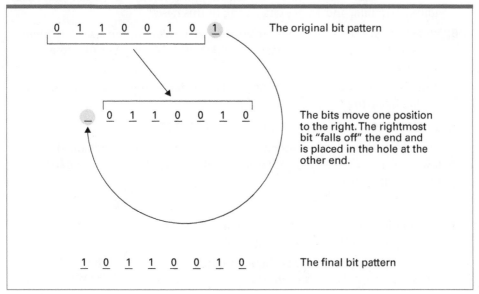

Questions & Exercises

1. Perform the indicated operations.

   a.   01001011   b.   100000011   c.   11111111
      AND 10101011   AND 11101100   AND 00101101

   d.   01001011   e.   10000011   f.   11111111
      OR   10101011   OR   11101100   OR   00101101

   g.   01001011   h.   100000011   i.   11111111
      XOR 10101011   XOR 11101100   XOR 00101101

2. Suppose you want to isolate the middle four bits of a byte by placing 0s in the other four bits without disturbing the middle four bits. What mask must you use together with what operation?

3. Suppose you want to complement the four middle bits of a byte while leaving the other four bits undisturbed. What mask must you use together with what operation?

4. a. Suppose you XOR the first two bits of a string of bits and then continue down the string by successively XORing each result with the next bit in the string. How is your result related to the number of 1s appearing in the string?

   b. How does this problem relate to determining what the appropriate parity bit should be when encoding a message?

5. It is often convenient to use a logical operation in place of a numeric one. For example, the logical operation AND combines two bits in the same manner as multiplication. Which logical operation is almost the same as adding two bits, and what goes wrong in this case?

6. What logical operation together with what mask can you use to change ASCII codes of lowercase letters to uppercase? What about uppercase to lowercase?

7. What is the result of performing a three-bit right circular shift on the following bit strings:

   a. 01101010   b. 00001111   c. 01111111

8. What is the result of performing a one-bit left circular shift on the following bytes represented in hexadecimal notation? Give your answer in hexadecimal form.

   a. AB   b. 5C   c. B7   d. 35

9. A right circular shift of three bits on a string of eight bits is equivalent to a left circular shift of how many bits?

10. What bit pattern represents the sum of 01101010 and 11001100 if the patterns represent values stored in two's complement notation? What if the

patterns represent values stored in the floating-point format discussed in Chapter 1?

11. Using the machine language of Appendix C, write a program that places a 1 in the most significant bit of the memory cell whose address is A7 without modifying the remaining bits in the cell.

12. Using the machine language of Appendix C, write a program that copies the middle four bits from memory cell E0 into the least significant four bits of memory cell E1, while placing 0s in the most significant four bits of the cell at location E1.

2.5 Communicating with Other Devices

Main memory and the CPU form the core of a computer. In this section, we investigate how this core, which we will refer to as the computer, communicates with peripheral devices such as mass storage systems, printers, keyboards, mice, display screens, digital cameras, and even other computers.

The Role of Controllers

Communication between a computer and other devices is normally handled through an intermediary apparatus known as a **controller.** In the case of a personal computer, a controller may consist of circuitry permanently mounted on the computer's motherboard or, for flexibility, it may take the form of a circuit board that plugs into a slot on the motherboard. In either case, the controller connects via cables to peripheral devices within the computer case or perhaps to a connector, called a **port,** on the back of the computer where external devices can be attached. These controllers are sometimes small computers themselves, each with its own memory circuitry and simple CPU that performs a program directing the activities of the controller.

A controller translates messages and data back and forth between forms compatible with the internal characteristics of the computer and those of the peripheral device to which it is attached. Originally, each controller was designed for a particular type of device; thus, purchasing a new peripheral device often required the purchase of a new controller as well.

Recently, steps have been taken within the personal computer arena to develop standards, such as the **universal serial bus (USB)** and **FireWire,** by which a single controller is able to handle a variety of devices. For example, a single USB controller can be used as the interface between a computer and any collection of USB-compatible devices. The list of devices on the market today that can communicate with a USB controller includes mice, printers, scanners, mass storage devices, digital cameras, and smartphones.

Each controller communicates with the computer itself by means of connections to the same bus that connects the computer's CPU and main memory (Figure 2.13). From this position it is able to monitor the signals being sent between the CPU and main memory as well as to inject its own signals onto the bus.

Figure 2.13   Controllers attached to a machine's bus

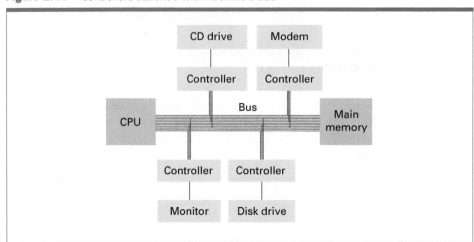

With this arrangement, the CPU is able to communicate with the controllers attached to the bus in the same manner that it communicates with main memory. To send a bit pattern to a controller, the bit pattern is first constructed in one of the CPU's general-purpose registers. Then an instruction similar to a STORE instruction is executed by the CPU to "store" the bit pattern in the controller. Likewise, to receive a bit pattern from a controller, an instruction similar to a LOAD instruction is used.

In some computer designs the transfer of data to and from controllers is directed by the same LOAD and STORE op-codes that are already provided for communication with main memory. In these cases, each controller is designed to respond to references to a unique set of addresses while main memory is designed to ignore references to these locations. Thus when the CPU sends a message on the bus to store a bit pattern at a memory location that is assigned to a controller, the bit pattern is actually "stored" in the controller rather than main memory. Likewise, if the CPU tries to read data from such a memory location, as in a LOAD instruction, it will receive a bit pattern from the controller rather than from memory. Such a communication system is called **memory-mapped I/O** because the computer's input/output devices appear to be in various memory locations (Figure 2.14).

An alternative to memory-mapped I/O is to provide special op-codes in the machine language to direct transfers to and from controllers. Instructions with these op-codes are called I/O instructions. As an example, if the language

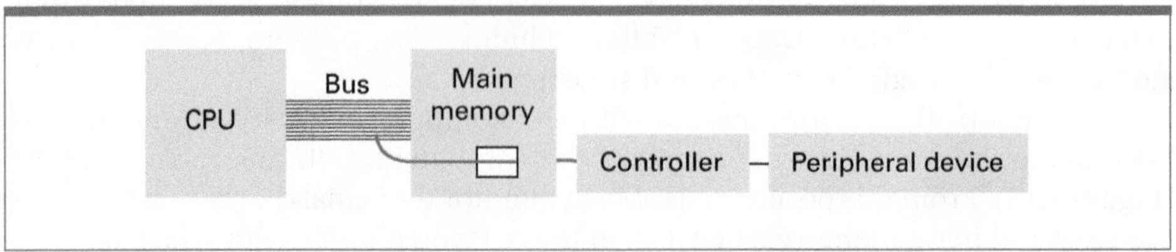

Figure 2.14   A conceptual representation of memory-mapped I/O

described in Appendix C followed this approach, it might include an instruction such as F5A3 to mean "STORE the contents of register 5 in the controller identified by the bit pattern A3."

Direct Memory Access

Since a controller is attached to a computer's bus, it can carry on its own communication with main memory during those nanoseconds in which the CPU is not using the bus. This ability of a controller to access main memory is known as **direct memory access (DMA),** and it is a significant asset to a computer's performance. For instance, to retrieve data from a sector of a disk, the CPU can send requests encoded as bit patterns to the controller attached to the disk asking the controller to read the sector and place the data in a specified area of main memory. The CPU can then continue with other tasks while the controller performs the read operation and deposits the data in main memory via DMA. Thus two activities will be performed at the same time. The CPU will be executing a program and the controller will be overseeing the transfer of data between the disk and main memory. In this manner, the computing resources of the CPU are not wasted during the relatively slow data transfer.

The use of DMA also has the detrimental effect of complicating the communication taking place over a computer's bus. Bit patterns must move between the CPU and main memory, between the CPU and each controller, and between each controller and main memory. Coordination of all this activity on the bus is a major design issue. Even with excellent designs, the central bus can become an impediment as the CPU and the controllers compete for bus access. This impediment

USB and FireWire

The universal serial bus (USB) and FireWire are standardized serial communication systems that simplify the process of adding new peripheral devices to a personal computer. USB was developed under the lead of Intel. The development of FireWire was led by Apple. In both cases the underlying theme is for a single controller to provide external ports at which a variety of peripheral devices can be attached. In this setting, the controller translates the internal signal characteristics of the computer to the appropriate USB or FireWire standard signals. In turn, each device connected to the controller converts its internal idiosyncrasies to the same USB or FireWire standard, allowing communication with the controller. The result is that attaching a new device to a PC does not require the insertion of a new controller. Instead, one merely plugs any USB compatible device into a USB port or a FireWire compatible device into a FireWire port.

Of the two, FireWire provides a faster transfer rate, but the lower cost of USB 2.0 technology has made it the leader in the lower-cost mass market arena. A new, faster version of the USB standard, version 3.0, has also begun to appear on the market. USB-compatible devices on the market today include mice, keyboards, printers, scanners, digital cameras, smartphones, and mass storage systems designed for backup applications. FireWire applications tend to focus on devices that require higher transfer rates such as video recorders and online mass storage systems.

is known as the **von Neumann bottleneck** because it is a consequence of the underlying **von Neumann architecture** in which a CPU fetches its instructions from memory over a central bus.

Handshaking

The transfer of data between two computer components is rarely a one-way affair. Even though we may think of a printer as a device that receives data, the truth is that a printer also sends data back to the computer. After all, a computer can produce and send characters to a printer much faster than the printer can print them. If a computer blindly sent data to a printer, the printer would quickly fall behind, resulting in lost data. Thus a process such as printing a document involves a constant two-way dialogue, known as **handshaking,** in which the computer and the peripheral device exchange information about the device's status and coordinate their activities.

Handshaking often involves a **status word,** which is a bit pattern that is generated by the peripheral device and sent to the controller. The status word is a bit map in which the bits reflect the conditions of the device. For example, in the case of a printer, the value of the least significant bit of the status word may indicate whether the printer is out of paper, while the next bit may indicate whether the printer is ready for additional data. Still another bit may be used to indicate the presence of a paper jam. Depending on the system, the controller may respond to this status information itself or make it available to the CPU. In either case, the status word provides the mechanism by which communication with a peripheral device can be coordinated.

Popular Communication Media

Communication between computing devices is handled over two types of paths: parallel and serial. These terms refer to the manner in which signals are transferred with respect to each other. In the case of **parallel communication,** several signals are transferred at the same time, each on a separate "line." Such a technique is capable of transferring data rapidly but requires a relatively complex communication path. Examples include a computer's internal bus where multiple wires are used to allow large blocks of data and other signals to be transferred simultaneously.

In contrast, **serial communication** is based on transferring signals one after the other over a single line. Thus serial communication requires a simpler data path than parallel communication, which is the reason for its popularity. USB and FireWire, which offer relatively high-speed data transfer over short distances of only a few meters, are examples of serial communication systems. For slightly longer distances (within a home or office building), serial communication over Ethernet connections (Section 4.1), either by wire or radio broadcast, are popular.

For communication over greater distances, traditional voice telephone lines dominated the personal computer arena for many years. These communication paths, consisting of a single wire over which tones are transferred one after the other, are inherently serial systems. The transfer of digital data over these lines is accomplished by first converting bit patterns into audible tones by means of a **modem** (short for *modulator-demodulator*), transferring these tones serially over the telephone system, and then converting the tones back into bits by another modem at the destination.

For faster long-distance communication over traditional telephone lines, telephone companies offer a service known as **DSL (Digital Subscriber Line),** which takes advantage of the fact that existing telephone lines are capable of handling a wider frequency range than that used by traditional voice communication. More precisely, DSL uses frequencies above the audible range to transfer digital data while leaving the lower-frequency spectrum for voice communication. Although DSL has been highly successful, telephone companies are rapidly upgrading their systems to fiber-optic lines, which support digital communication more readily than traditional telephone lines.

Cable modems are a competing technology that modulate and demodulate bit patterns to be transmitted over cable television systems. Many cable providers now make use of both fiber-optic lines and traditional coaxial cable to provide both high definition television signals and computer network access.

Satellite links via high-frequency radio broadcast make computer network access possible even in some remote locations far from high speed telephone and cable television networks.

Communication Rates

The rate at which bits are transferred from one computing component to another is measured in **bits per second (bps).** Common units include **Kbps** (kilo-bps, equal to one thousand bps), **Mbps** (mega-bps, equal to one million bps), and **Gbps** (giga-bps, equal to one billion bps). (Note the distinction between bits and bytes—that is, 8 Kbps is equal to 1 KB per second. In abbreviations, a lowercase b usually means *bit* whereas an uppercase B means *byte.*)

For short distance communication, USB 2.0 and FireWire provide transfer rates of several hundred Mbps, which is sufficient for most multimedia applications. This, combined with their convenience and relatively low cost, is why they are popular for communication between home computers and local peripherals such as printers, external disk drives, and cameras.

By combining **multiplexing** (the encoding or interweaving of data so that a single communication path serves the purpose of multiple paths) and data compression techniques, traditional voice telephone systems were able to support transfer rates of 57.6 Kbps. This falls short of the needs of today's multimedia and Internet applications, such as high definition video streaming from sites like Netflix or YouTube. To play MP3 music recordings requires a transfer rate of about 64 Kbps, and to play even low quality video clips requires transfer rates measured in units of Mbps. This is why alternatives such as DSL, cable, and satellite links, which provide transfer rates well into the Mbps range, have replaced traditional audio telephone systems. (For example, DSL offers transfer rates on the order of 54 Mbps.)

The maximum rate available in a particular setting depends on the type of the communication path and the technology used in its implementation. This maximum rate is often loosely equated to the communication path's **bandwidth,** although the term *bandwidth* also has connotations of capacity rather than transfer rate. That is, to say that a communication path has a high bandwidth (or provides **broadband** service) means that the communication path has the ability to transfer bits at a high rate as well as the capacity to carry large amounts of information simultaneously.

Questions & Exercises

1. Assume that the machine described in Appendix C uses memory-mapped I/O and that the address B5 is the location within the printer port to which data to be printed should be sent.

   a. If register 7 contains the ASCII code for the letter A, what machine language instruction should be used to cause that letter to be printed at the printer?

   b. If the machine executes a million instructions per second, how many times can this character be sent to the printer in one second?

   c. If the printer is capable of printing five traditional pages of text per minute, will it be able to keep up with the characters being sent to it in (b)?

2. Suppose that the hard disk on your personal computer rotates at 3000 revolutions a minute, that each track contains 16 sectors, and that each sector contains 1024 bytes. Approximately what communication rate is required between the disk drive and the disk controller if the controller is going to receive bits from the disk drive as they are read from the spinning disk?

3. Estimate how long it would take to transfer a 300-page novel encoded in 16-bit Unicode characters at a transfer rate of 54 Mbps.

2.6 Programming Data Manipulation

One of the essential features of computer programming languages such as Python is that they shield users from the tedious details of working with the lowest levels of the machine. Having just completed much of a chapter on the lowest levels of data manipulation in computer processors, it is instructive to review some of the major details that Python scripts shield the programmer from needing to worry about.

As we will explore in greater detail in Chapter 6, high-level programming language statements are mapped down to low-level machine instructions in order to be executed. A single Python statement might map to a single machine instruction, or to many tens or even hundreds of machine instructions, depending on the complexity of the statement and the efficiency of the machine language. Different implementations of the Python language interpreter, in concert with other elements of the computer's operating system software, take care of this mapping process for each particular computer processor. As a result, the Python programmer does not need to know whether she is executing her Python script on a RISC processor or a CISC processor.

We can recognize many Python operations that correspond closely to the basic machine instructions for modern computers or for the simple machine described in Appendix C. Addition of Python integers and floating-point numbers clearly resembles the ADD op-codes of our simple machine. Assigning values to variables surely involves the LOAD, STORE, and MOVE op-codes in some arrangement. Python shields us from worrying about which processor registers are in use, but leverages the op-codes of the machine to carry out our instructions. We cannot see the instruction register, program counter, or memory cell addresses, but the Python script executes sequentially, one statement after the other, in the same way as the simple machine language programs.

Logic and Shift Operations

Logic and shift operations can be executed on any kind of numerical data, but because they often deal with individual bits of data, it is easiest to illustrate these operations with binary values. Just as Python uses the 0x prefix to specify values in hexadecimal, the 0b prefix can be used to specify values in binary[1].

```
x    = 0b00110011
mask = 0b00001111
```

Note that this is effectively no different from assigning x the value 51, (which is 110011 in binary), or 0x33 (which is 51 expressed in hexadecimal), or from assigning mask the value 15, (which is 1111 in binary), or 0x0F (15 in hexadecimal). The representation we use to spell out the integer value in the Python assignment statement does not change how it is represented in the computer, only how human readers understand it.

Built-in Python operators exist for each of the bitwise logical operators described in Section 2.4.

```
print(0b00000101 ^ 0b00000100)    # Prints 5 XOR 4, which is 1
print(0b00000101 | 0b00000100)    # Prints 5 OR  4, which is 5
print(0b00000101 & 0b00000100)    # Prints 5 AND 4, which is 4
```

As a result, we can replicate each of the example problems of Section 2.4 as Python code.

```
                                  #         10011010
print(0b10011010 & 0b11001001)    #     AND 11001001
                                  #         10001000


                                  #         10011010
print(0b10011010 | 0b11001001)    #     OR  11001001
                                  #         11011011


                                  #         10011010
print(0b10011010 ^ 0b11001001)    #     XOR 11001001
                                  #         01010011
```

For all of these examples, Python will print the result in its default output representation, which is base-10. If the user would also like the output to be displayed in binary notation, a built-in function exists to convert any integer value into the string of zero and one characters for the corresponding binary representation.

---

[1]This syntax is another recent addition to the evolving Python language. Make sure that you are using at least Python 3 to replicate these examples.

```
print(bin(0b10011010 & 0b11001001))   # Prints "0b10001000"
print(bin(0b10011010 | 0b11001001))   # Prints "0b11011011"
print(bin(0b10011010 ^ 0b11001001))   # Prints "0b1010011"
```

Because newer versions of Python can use an arbitrary number of digits for representing numbers, leading zeros are not printed. Thus, the third line above prints only seven digits, rather than eight.

Python's built-in operators for performing logical shift operations consist of dual greater-than and less-than symbols, visually suggesting the direction of shift. The operand on the right of the operator indicates the number of bit positions to shift.

```
print(0b00111100 >> 2)   # Prints  "15", which is 0b00001111
print(0b00111100 << 2)   # Prints "240", which is 0b11110000
```

In addition to shifting bit masks left or right, bit shift operators are also an efficient way to multiply (left shift) or divide (right shift) by powers of 2.

Control Structures

The control group of machine language instructions presented earlier in this chapter affords us a mechanism for jumping from one part of a program to another. In higher-level languages like Python, this enables what are called **control structures,** syntax patterns that allow us to express algorithms more powerfully. One example of this is the if-statement, which allows a segment of code to be conditionally skipped if a Boolean value in the script is not true.

```
if (water_temp > 140):
  print('Bath water too hot!')
```

Intuitively, this Python snippet will be mapped to machine instructions that make the comparison between the **water_temp** variable and the integer value 140, probably both previously loaded into registers. A conditional jump instruction will skip over the machine instructions for the print() built-in if the **water_temp** value was not 140 or larger.

Another control structure is the looping construct while, which allows a segment of code to be executed multiple times, often subject to some condition.

```
while (n < 10):
  print(n)
  n = n + 1
```

Assuming the variable **n** starts with a value less than 10, this loop will continue printing and incrementing **n** until it becomes greater than or equal to 10.

We will spend more time examining these and other control structures in Chapter 5 and beyond. For now, we focus on a mechanism that allows us to jump to another part of the program, carry out a desired task, and then return to the program point we came from.

Functions We have already seen three built-in Python operations that do not follow the same syntactic form as the arithmetic and logic operators. The print(), str() and bin() operations are invoked using given names instead of symbols, and also involve parentheses wrapped around their operands.

Both of these are examples of a Python language feature called **functions.** The term *function* in mathematics is often used to describe algebraic relationships, such as "f(x) = x^2 + 3x + 4." Upon seeing such a function definition, we understand that in subsequent lines the expression "f(5)" is taken to mean that the value 5 should be plugged in wherever the parameter x occurs in the expression defining f(). Thus, f(5) = 5^2 + 3*5 + 4 = 25 + 15 + 4 = 44. Programming language functions are quite similar in that they allow us to use a name for a series of operations that should be performed on the given parameter or parameters. Due to the way that this language feature is mapped to lower level machine languages, the appearance of a function in an expression or statement is known as a **function call,** or sometimes **calling** a function.

The occurrences of print() and bin() in the examples above are two such function calls; they indicate that the Python interpreter will go execute the definition of the named function, and then return to continue with its work. The syntax is to follow the name of the function immediately with an opening parenthesis, and then to give the function **argument value** that will be plugged in for the parameter when the function definition is evaluated, followed by a closing parenthesis. It is important to match opening and closing parentheses—not doing so will cause a Python syntax error and is a common mistake for beginners.

From now on, we will follow the convention of including the parentheses when talking about Python functions, such as print(), so as to clearly denote them as distinct from variables or other items.

Functions come in many varieties beyond what we have already seen. Some functions take more than one argument, such as the max() function:

```
x = 1034
y = 1056
z = 2078
biggest = max(x, y, z)
print(biggest)                    # Prints "2078"
```

Multiple arguments are separated by commas within the parentheses. Some functions **return** a value, which is to say that the function call itself can appear as part of a more complex expression, or as the right-hand side of an assignment statement. These are sometimes called **fruitful functions.** This is the case for both max() (as above) and bin(), which takes an integer value as an argument and returns the corresponding string of zeros and ones. Other functions do not return a value, and usually are used as standalone statements, as is the case for print(). Functions that do not return a value are sometimes called **void functions,** or **procedures,** although Python makes no distinction in its syntax rules. It makes no sense to assign the result of a void function to a variable, as in

```
x = print('hello world!')    # x is assigned None
```

although this is not an error in Python, per se, and is subtly different from not assigning a value to x at all.

Each of the functions we have seen so far is one of the few dozen built-in functions that Python knows about, but there are extensive libraries of additional functions that a more advanced script can refer to. The Python library modules contain many useful functions that may not normally be required, but that can be called upon when needed.

```python
# Calculates the hypotenuse of a right triangle
import math

sideA = 3.0
sideB = 4.0
# Calculate third side via Pythagorean Theorem
hypotenuse = math.sqrt(sideA**2 + sideB**2)

print(hypotenuse)
```

In this example, the import statement forewarns the Python interpreter that the script refers to the library called "math," which happens to be one of the standard set of library modules that Python comes equipped with. The sqrt() function defined within the math library module provides the square root of the argument, which in this case was the expression of sideA squared plus sideB squared. Note that the library function call includes both the module name ("math") and the function name ("sqrt"), joined by a period.

The Python math module includes dozens of useful mathematical functions, including logorithmic, trigonometric, and hyperbolic functions, as well as some familiar constant values such as math.pi.

Beyond the built-in and library module functions, Python provides syntax for a script to define its own functions. We will define a few very simple examples at the end of this section, and explore more elaborate variations in a later chapter.

Input and Output

The previous example snippets and scripts have used the built-in Python print() function to output results. Many programming languages provide similar mechanisms for achieving input and output, providing programmers with a convenient abstraction to move data in or out of the computer processor. In fact, these I/O built-ins communicate with the hardware controllers and peripheral devices discussed in the previous section.

None of our example scripts thus far have required any input from the user. Simple user input can be accomplished with the built-in Python input() function.

```python
echo = input('Please enter a string to echo: ')
print(echo * 3)
```

The input() function takes as an optional argument a prompt string to present to the user when waiting for input. When run, this script will pause after displaying "Please enter a string to echo: ", and wait for the user to type something. When the user hits the enter key, the script assigns the string of characters typed (not including the enter key,) to the variable echo. The second line of the script then outputs the string repeated three times. (Recall that the * operator replicates string operands.)

Armed with the ability to acquire input, let's rewrite our hypotenuse script to prompt a user for the side lengths rather than hardcode the values into assignment statements.

```
# Calculates the hypotenuse of a right triangle
import math

# Inputting the side lengths, first try
sideA = input('Length of side A? ')
sideB = input('Length of side B? ')
# Calculate third side via Pythagorean Theorem
hypotenuse = math.sqrt(sideA**2 + sideB**2)

print(hypotenuse)
```

When run, this script prompts the user with, "Length of side A? ", and awaits input. Let us suppose that the user types "3" and enter. The script prompts the user with "Length of side B? ", and awaits input. Let us suppose that the user types "4" and enter. At this point, the Python interpreter aborts the script, printing out:

```
hypotenuse = math.sqrt(sideA**2 + sideB**2)
TypeError: unsupported operand type(s) for ** or pow(): 'str' and 'int'
```

This type of error can be easy to create in a dynamically typed language like Python. Our hypotenuse calculation, which worked in the earlier version of the script, now causes an error when the values have been read as input from the user instead. The problem is indeed a "TypeError," stemming from the fact that Python no longer knows how to take the square of variable sideA, because sideA is now a character string in this version of the script, rather than an integer as before. The problem comes not from the line that calculates the hypotenuse, but from earlier in the script, when the values of sideA and sideB are returned from input(). This, too, is common when encountering errors with programming languages. The Python interpreter attempts to provide the line of script responsible for the problem, but the real culprit is actually earlier in the script.

In the string echoing snippet above, it was clear that the value assigned to **echo** should be the string of characters typed in by the user. The input() function behaves in the same way in the hypotenuse program, even though the programmer's intent is now to enter integer values. The representation of the ASCII- or UTF-8-encoded string "4" differs from the two's complement representation of the integer 4, and the Python script must explicitly make the conversion from one representation to the other before proceeding to calculations with integers.

Fortunately, another built-in function provides the capability. The int() function attempts to convert its argument into an integer representation. If it cannot, an appropriate error message is produced.

There are at least three places that we can use the int() function to remove the bug in this script. We can call it before even assigning the result of input() to the variable. We can add new lines of script that are only for calling the conversion function. Or, we can make the conversion just before squaring the variable within the call to the math.sqrt() function. The revised script below uses the first option; the other two are left as an exercise for the reader.

```
# Calculates the hypotenuse of a right triangle
import math
```

```
# Inputting the side lengths, with integer conversion
sideA = int(input('Length of side A? '))
sideB = int(input('Length of side B? '))
# Calculate third side via Pythagorean Theorem
hypotenuse = math.sqrt(sideA**2 + sideB**2)

print(hypotenuse)
```

The revised script operates as intended and can be used for many right triangles without having to edit the script, as in the pre-input version.

As a final note, the int() function performs its conversion by carefully examining the string argument and interpreting it as a number. If the input string is a number, but not an integer, as for example, "3.14," the int() function discards the fractional portion and returns only the integer value. This operation is a truncation and will not "round up" as a human might expect. Similar conversion functions exist in Python for all of the other standard value types.

Marathon Training Assistant

The complete Python script below demonstrates many of the concepts introduced in this section. As the popularity of recreational distance running has increased, many participants find themselves pursuing complex training schedules to prepare their bodies for the rigors of running a marathon. This script assists a runner who wishes to calculate how long her training workout will take, based upon the distance and pace she wishes to run. Given a *pace* (number of minutes and seconds to run a single mile), and a total mileage, this script calculates the projected elapsed time to run the workout, as well as a user-friendly speed calculation in miles per hour. Figure 2.15 gives some example data points; in each row, given the first three columns as input, the last three columns would be the expected results. Note that different implementations of Python may print a different number of decimal places from Figure 2.15 for speed values that don't work out to round numbers.

Figure 2.15 Example marathon training data

Time Per Mile				Total Elapsed Time	
Minutes	Seconds	Miles	Speed (mph)	Minutes	Seconds
9	14	5	6.49819494584	46	10
8	0	3	7.5	24	0
7	45	6	7.74193548387	46	30
7	25	1	8.08988764044	7	25

```
# Marathon training assistant.
import math

# This function converts a number of minutes and seconds into just seconds.
def total_seconds(min, sec):
  return min * 60 + sec

# This function calculates a speed in miles per hour given
# a time (in seconds) to run a single mile.
def speed(time):
  return 3600 / time

# Prompt user for pace and mileage.
pace_minutes = int(input('Minutes per mile? '))
pace_seconds = int(input('Seconds per mile? '))
miles = int(input('Total miles? '))

# Calculate and print speed.
mph = speed(total_seconds(pace_minutes, pace_seconds))
print('Your speed is')
print(mph)

# Calculate elapsed time for planned workout.
total = miles * total_seconds(pace_minutes, pace_seconds)
elapsed_minutes = total // 60
elapsed_seconds = total % 60

print('Your total elapsed time is')
print(elapsed_minutes)
print(elapsed_seconds)
```

The script above uses both built-in functions—input(), int(), and print()—as well as user-defined functions—speed() and total_seconds(). The keyword def precedes a user function definition and is followed by the name for the function and a list of parameters to be provided when the function is called. The indented line that follows is called the **body** of a function and expresses the steps that define the function. In a later chapter, we will see examples of functions with more than one statement in their body. The keyword return highlights the expression that will be calculated to find the result of the function.

The user-defined functions are defined at the top of the script, but are not actually invoked until the script reaches the lines where they are called as part of a larger expression. Note also the way in which function calls are stacked in this script. The results of the calls to input() are immediately passed as arguments to the int() function, and the result of the int() function is then assigned to a variable. Similarly, the result of total_seconds() is immediately passed as an argument to the speed() function, whose result is then assigned to the variable mph. In each of these cases, it would be permissible to make the function calls one at a time, assign the result to a new variable, and then call the next function that relies on the first result. However, this more compact form is more succinct and does not require a proliferation of temporary variables to hold intermediate results of the calculation.

Given inputs of 7 minutes and 45 seconds per mile, for 6 miles, this script outputs:

```
Your speed is
7.74193548387
Your total elapsed time is
46
30
```

The format of this output remains quite primitive. It lacks proper units (**7.74193548387 mph**, and **46 minutes, 30 seconds**), prints an inappropriate number of decimal places for a simple calculation, and breaks lines in too many places. Cleaner output is left as an exercise for the reader.

Questions & Exercises

1. The hypotenuse example script truncates the sides to integers, but outputs a floating-point number. Why? Adapt the script to output an integer.

2. Adapt the hypotenuse script to use floating-point numbers as input, without truncating them. Which is more appropriate, the integer version from the previous question, or the floating-point version?

3. The Python built-in function str() will convert a numerical argument into a character string representation, and the '+' can be used to concatenate strings together. Use these to modify the marathon script to produce cleaner output, for example:

   ```
   Your speed is 7.74193548387 mph
   Your total elapsed time is 46 minutes, 30 seconds
   ```

4. Use the Python built-in bin() to write a script that reads a base-10 integers as input and outputs the corresponding binary representation of that integer in ones and zeros.

5. The XOR operation is often used both for efficiently calculating checksums (see Section 1.9) and encryption (see Section 4.5). Write a simple Python script that reads in a number and outputs that number XORed with a pattern of ones and zeros, such as 0x55555555. The same script will "encrypt" a number into a seemingly unrelated number, but when run again and given the encrypted number as input will return the original number.

6. Explore some of the error conditions that you can create with unexpected inputs to the example scripts from this section. What happens if you enter all zeros for the hypotenuse script or the marathon script? What about negative numbers? Strings of characters instead of numbers?

2.7 Other Architectures

To broaden our perspective, let us consider some alternatives to the traditional machine architecture we have discussed so far.

Pipelining

Electric pulses travel through a wire no faster than the speed of light. Since light travels approximately 1 foot in a nanosecond (one billionth of a second), it requires at least 2 nanoseconds for the CPU to fetch an instruction from a memory cell that is 1 foot away. (The read request must be sent to memory, requiring at least 1 nanosecond, and the instruction must be sent back to the CPU, requiring at least another nanosecond.) Consequently, to fetch and execute an instruction in such a machine requires several nanoseconds—which means that increasing the execution speed of a machine ultimately becomes a miniaturization problem.

However, increasing execution speed is not the only way to improve a computer's performance. The real goal is to improve the machine's **throughput,** which refers to the total amount of work the machine can accomplish in a given amount of time.

An example of how a computer's throughput can be increased without requiring an increase in execution speed involves **pipelining,** which is the technique of allowing the steps in the machine cycle to overlap. In particular, while one instruction is being executed, the next instruction can be fetched, which means that more than one instruction can be in "the pipe" at any one time, each at a different stage of being processed. In turn, the total throughput of the machine is increased even though the time required to fetch and execute each individual instruction remains the same. (Of course, when a JUMP instruction is reached, any gain that would have been obtained by prefetching is not realized because the instructions in "the pipe" are not the ones needed after all.)

Modern machine designs push the pipelining concept beyond our simple example. They are often capable of fetching several instructions at the same time and actually executing more than one instruction at a time when those instructions do not rely on each other.

The Multi-Core CPU

As technology provides ways of placing more and more circuitry on a silicon chip, the physical distinction between a computer's components diminishes. For instance, a single chip might contain a CPU and main memory. This is an example of the "system-on-a-chip (SoC)" approach in which the goal is to provide a complete apparatus in a single device that can be used as an abstract tool in higher level designs. In other cases, multiple copies of the same circuit are provided within a single device. This latter tactic originally appeared in the form of chips containing several independent gates or perhaps multiple flip-flops. Today's state of the art allows for more than one entire CPU to be placed on a single chip. This is the underlying architecture of devices known as multi-core CPUs, which consist of two or more CPUs residing on the same chip along with shared cache memory. (Multi-core CPUs containing two processing units are typically called dual-core CPUs.) Such devices simplify the construction of MIMD systems and are readily available for use in home computers.

Multiprocessor Machines

Pipelining can be viewed as a first step toward **parallel processing,** which is the performance of several activities at the same time. However, true parallel processing requires more than one processing unit, resulting in computers known as multiprocessor or **multi-core** machines.

Most computers today are designed with this idea in mind. One strategy is to attach several processing units, each resembling the CPU in a single-processor machine, to the same main memory. In this configuration, the processors can proceed independently yet coordinate their efforts by leaving messages to one another in the common memory cells. For instance, when one processor is faced with a large task, it can store a program for part of that task in the common memory and then request another processor to execute it. The result is a machine in which different instruction sequences are performed on different sets of data, which is called a **MIMD** (**multiple-instruction stream, multiple-data stream**) architecture, as opposed to the more traditional **SISD** (**single-instruction stream, single-data stream**) architecture.

A variation of multiple-processor architecture is to link the processors together so that they execute the same sequence of instructions in unison, each with its own set of data. This leads to a **SIMD** (**single-instruction stream, multiple-data stream**) architecture. Such machines are useful in applications in which the same task must be applied to each set of similar items within a large block of data. Another approach to parallel processing is to construct large computers as conglomerates of smaller machines, each with its own memory and CPU. Within such an architecture, each of the small machines is coupled to its neighbors so that tasks assigned to the whole system can be divided among the individual machines. Thus if a task assigned to one of the internal machines can be broken into independent subtasks, that machine can ask its neighbors to perform these subtasks concurrently. The original task can then be completed in much less time than would be required by a single-processor machine.

Questions & Exercises

1. Referring back to question 3 of Section 2.3, if the machine used the pipeline technique discussed in the text, what will be in "the pipe" when the instruction at address AA is executed? Under what conditions would pipelining not prove beneficial at this point in the program?

2. What conflicts must be resolved in running the program in question 4 of Section 2.3 on a pipeline machine?

3. Suppose there were two "central" processing units attached to the same memory and executing different programs. Furthermore, suppose that one of these processors needs to add one to the contents of a memory cell at roughly the same time that the other needs to subtract one from the same cell. (The net effect should be that the cell ends up with the same value with which it started.)

   a. Describe a sequence in which these activities would result in the cell ending up with a value one less than its starting value.

   b. Describe a sequence in which these activities would result in the cell ending up with a value one greater than its starting value.

Chapter Review Problems

(Asterisked problems are associated with optional sections.)

1. a. In what way are general-purpose registers and main memory cells similar?
   b. In what way do general-purpose registers and main memory cells differ?

2. Answer the following questions in terms of the machine language described in Appendix C.
   a. Write the instruction 2304 (hexadecimal) as a string of 16 bits.
   b. Write the op-code of the instruction B2A5 (hexadecimal) as a string of 4 bits.
   c. Write the operand field of the instruction B2A5 (hexadecimal) as a string of 12 bits.

3. Suppose a block of data is stored in the memory cells of the machine described in Appendix C from address 98 to A2, inclusive. How many memory cells are in this block? List their addresses.

4. What is the value of the program counter in the machine described in Appendix C immediately after executing the instruction B0CD?

5. Suppose the memory cells at addresses 00 through 05 in the machine described in Appendix C contain the following bit patterns:

Address	Contents
00	22
01	11
02	32
03	02
04	C0
05	00

   Assuming that the program counter initially contained 00, record the contents of the program counter, instruction register, and memory cell at address 02 at the end of each fetch phase of the machine cycle until the machine halts.

6. Suppose three values x, y, and z are stored in a machine's memory. Describe the sequence of events (loading registers from memory, saving values in memory, and so on) that leads to the computation of x + y + z. How about (2x) + y?

7. The following are instructions written in the machine language described in Appendix C. Translate them into English.

   a. 7123   b. 40E1   c. A304
   d. B100   e. 2BCD

8. Suppose a machine language is designed with an op-code field of 4 bits. How many different instruction types can the language contain? What if the op-code field is increased to 6 bits?

9. Translate the following instructions from English into the machine language described in Appendix C.
   a. LOAD register 6 with the hexadecimal value 77.
   b. LOAD register 7 with the contents of memory cell 77.
   c. JUMP to the instruction at memory location 24 if the contents of register 0 equals the value in register A.
   d. ROTATE register 4 three bits to the right.
   e. AND the contents of registers E and 2 leaving the result in register 1.

10. Rewrite the program in Figure 2.7 assuming that the values to be added are encoded using floating-point notation rather than two's complement notation.

11. Classify each of the following instructions (in the machine language of Appendix C) in terms of whether its execution changes the contents of the memory cell at location 3B, retrieves the contents of the memory cell at location 3C, or is independent of the contents of the memory cell at location 3C.
    a. 353C   b. 253C   c. 153C
    d. 3C3C   e. 403C

12. Suppose the memory cells at addresses 00 through 03 in the machine described in Appendix C contain the following bit patterns:

Address	Contents
00	26
01	55
02	C0
03	00

    a. Translate the first instruction into English.
    b. If the machine is started with its program counter containing 00, what bit pattern is in register 6 when the machine halts?

13. Suppose the memory cells at addresses 00 through 02 in the machine described in Appendix C contain the following bit patterns:

Address	Contents
00	12
01	21
02	34

a. What would be the first instruction executed if we started the machine with its program counter containing 00?
b. What would be the first instruction executed if we started the machine with its program counter containing 01?

14. Suppose the memory cells at addresses 00 through 05 in the machine described in Appendix C contain the following bit patterns:

Address	Contents
00	12
01	02
02	32
03	42
04	C0
05	00

When answering the following questions, assume that the machine starts with its program counter equal to 00.
a. Translate the instructions that are executed into English.
b. What bit pattern is in the memory cell at address 42 when the machine halts?
c. What bit pattern is in the program counter when the machine halts?

15. Suppose the memory cells at addresses 00 through 09 in the machine described in Appendix C contain the following bit patterns:

Address	Contents
00	1C
01	03
02	2B
03	03
04	5A
05	BC
06	3A
07	00
08	C0
09	00

Assume that the machine starts with its program counter containing 00.
a. What will be in the memory cell at address 00 when the machine halts?
b. What bit pattern will be in the program counter when the machine halts?

16. Suppose the memory cells at addresses 00 through 07 in the machine described in Appendix C contain the following bit patterns:

Address	Contents
00	2B
01	07
02	3B
03	06
04	C0
05	00
06	00
07	23

a. List the addresses of the memory cells that contain the program that will be executed if we start the machine with its program counter containing 00.
b. List the addresses of the memory cells that are used to hold data.

17. Suppose the memory cells at addresses 00 through 0D in the machine described in Appendix C contain the following bit patterns:

Address	Contents
00	20
01	04
02	21
03	01
04	40
05	12
06	51
07	12
08	B1
09	0C
0A	B0
0B	06
0C	C0
0D	00

Assume that the machine starts with its program counter containing 00.
a. What bit pattern will be in register 0 when the machine halts?

b. What bit pattern will be in register 1 when the machine halts?

c. What bit pattern is in the program counter when the machine halts?

18. Suppose the memory cells at addresses F0 through FD in the machine described in Appendix C contain the following (hexadecimal) bit patterns:

Address	Contents
F0	20
F1	00
F2	22
F3	02
F4	23
F5	04
F6	B3
F7	FC
F8	50
F9	02
FA	B0
FB	F6
FC	C0
FD	00

If we start the machine with its program counter containing F0, what is the value in register 0 when the machine finally executes the halt instruction at location FC?

19. If the machine in Appendix C executes an instruction every microsecond (a millionth of a second), how long does it take to complete the program in Problem 18?

20. Suppose the memory cells at addresses 20 through 28 in the machine described in Appendix C contain the following bit patterns:

Address	Contents
20	12
21	20
22	32
23	30
24	B0
25	21
26	24
27	C0
28	00

Assume that the machine starts with its program counter containing 20.

a. What bit patterns will be in registers 0, 1, and 2 when the machine halts?

b. What bit pattern will be in the memory cell at address 30 when the machine halts?

c. What bit pattern will be in the memory cell at address B0 when the machine halts?

21. Suppose the memory cells at addresses AF through B1 in the machine described in Appendix C contain the following bit patterns:

Address	Contents
AF	B0
B0	B0
B1	AF

What would happen if we started the machine with its program counter containing AF?

22. Suppose the memory cells at addresses 00 through 05 in the machine described in Appendix C contain the following (hexadecimal) bit patterns:

Address	Contents
00	25
01	B0
02	35
03	04
04	C0
05	00

If we start the machine with its program counter containing 00, when does the machine halt?

23. In each of the following cases, write a short program in the machine language described in Appendix C to perform the requested activities. Assume that each of your programs is placed in memory starting at address 00.

a. Move the value at memory location D8 to memory location B3.

b. Interchange the values stored at memory locations D8 and B3.

c. If the value stored in memory location 44 is 00, then place the value 01 in memory location 46; otherwise, put the value FF in memory location 46.

24. A game that used to be popular among computer hobbyists is core wars—a variation of battleship. (The term *core* originates from an early memory technology in which 0s and 1s were represented as magnetic fields in little rings of magnetic material. The rings were called cores.) The game is played between two opposing programs, each stored in different locations of the same computer's memory. The computer is assumed to alternate between the two programs, executing an instruction from one followed by an instruction from the other. The goal of each program is to cause the other to malfunction by writing extraneous data on top of it; however, neither program knows the location of the other.
    a. Write a program in the machine language of Appendix C that approaches the game in a defensive manner by being as small as possible.
    b. Write a program in the language of Appendix C that tries to avoid any attacks from the opposing program by moving to different locations. More precisely, beginning at location 00, write a program that will copy itself to location 70 and then jump to location 70.
    c. Extend the program in (b) to continue relocating to new memory locations. In particular, make your program move to location 70, then to E0 (= 70 + 70) then to 60 (= 70 + 70 + 70) etc.

25. Write a program in the machine language of Appendix C to compute the sum of floating-point values stored at memory locations A0, A1, A2, and A3. Your program should store the total at memory location A4.

26. Suppose the memory cells at addresses 00 through 05 in the machine described in Appendix C contain the following (hexadecimal) bit patterns:

Address	Contents
00	20
01	C0
02	30
03	04
04	00
05	00

What happens if we start the machine with its program counter containing 00?

27. What happens if the memory cells at addresses 08 and 09 of the machine described in Appendix C contain the bit patterns B0 and 08, respectively, and the machine is started with its program counter containing the value 08?

28. Suppose the following program, written in the machine language of Appendix C, is stored in main memory beginning at address 30 (hexadecimal). What task will the program perform when executed?

```
2003
2101
2200
2310
1400
3410
5221
5331
3239
333B
B248
B038
C000
```

29. Summarize the steps involved when the machine described in Appendix C performs an instruction with op-code B. Express your answer as a set of directions as though you were telling the CPU what to do.

*30. Summarize the steps involved when the machine described in Appendix C performs an instruction with op-code 5. Express your answer as a set of directions as though you were telling the CPU what to do.

*31. Summarize the steps involved when the machine described in Appendix C performs an instruction with op-code 6. Express your answer as a set of directions as though you were telling the CPU what to do.

*32. Suppose the registers 4 and 5 in the machine described in Appendix C contain the bit patterns 3A and C8, respectively. What bit pattern is left in register 0 after executing each of the following instructions:
    a. 5045 b. 6045 c. 7045
    d. 8045 e. 9045

*33. Using the machine language described in Appendix C, write programs to perform each of the following tasks:

    a. Copy the bit pattern stored in memory location 44 into memory location AA.

    b. Change the least significant 4 bits in the memory cell at location 34 to 0s while leaving the other bits unchanged.

    c. Copy the least significant 4 bits from memory location A5 into the least significant 4 bits of location A6 while leaving the other bits at location A6 unchanged.

    d. Copy the least significant 4 bits from memory location A5 into the most significant 4 bits of A5. (Thus, the first 4 bits in A5 will be the same as the last 4 bits.)

*34. Perform the indicated operations:

```
a.      111001      b.      000101
    AND 101001          AND 101010

c.      001110      d.      111011
    AND 010101          AND 110111

e.      111001      f.      010100
    OR  101001          OR  101010

g.      000100      h.      101010
    OR  010101          OR  110101

i.      111001      j.      000111
    XOR 101001          XOR 101010

k.      010000      l.      111111
    XOR 010101          XOR 110101
```

*35. Identify both the mask and the logical operation needed to accomplish each of the following objectives:

    a. Put 1s in the upper 4 bits of an 8-bit pattern without disturbing the other bits.

    b. Complement the most significant bit of an 8-bit pattern without changing the other bits.

    c. Complement a pattern of 8 bits.

    d. Put a 0 in the least significant bit of an 8-bit pattern without disturbing the other bits.

    e. Put 1s in all but the most significant bit of an 8-bit pattern without disturbing the most significant bit.

    f. Filter out all of the green color component from an RGB bitmap image pixel in which the middle 8 bits of a 24-bit pattern store the green information.

    g. Invert all of the bits in a 24-bit RGB bitmap pixel.

    h. Set all the bits in a 24-bit RGB bitmap pixel to 1, indicating the color "white".

*36. Write and test short Python scripts to implement each of the parts of the previous question.

*37. Identify a logical operation (along with a corresponding mask) that, when applied to an input string of 8 bits, produces an output string of all 0s if and only if the input string is 10000001.

*38. Write and test a short Python script to implement the previous question.

*39. Describe a sequence of logical operations (along with their corresponding masks) that, when applied to an input string of 8 bits, produces an output byte of all 0s if the input string both begins and ends with 1s. Otherwise, the output should contain at least one 1.

*40. Write and test a short Python script to implement the previous question.

*41. What would be the result of performing a 4-bit left circular shift on the following bit patterns?

    a. 10101   b. 11110000   c. 001
    d. 101000   e. 00001

*42. What would be the result of performing a 2-bit right circular shift on the following bytes represented in hexadecimal notation (give your answers in hexadecimal notation)?

    a. 3F   b. 0D
    c. FF   d. 77

*43. a. What single instruction in the machine language of Appendix C could be used to accomplish a 5-bit right circular shift of register B?

    b. What single instruction in the machine language of Appendix C could be used to accomplish a 2-bit left circular shift of register B?

*44. Write a program in the machine language of Appendix C that reverses the contents of the memory cell at address 8C. (That is, the final bit pattern at address 8C when read from left to right should agree with the original pattern when read from right to left.)

*45. Write a program in the machine language of Appendix C that subtracts the value stored at A1 from the value stored at address A2 and places the result at address A0. Assume that the values are encoded in two's complement notation.

*46. High definition video can be delivered at a rate of 30 frames per second (fps) where each frame has a resolution of 1920 x 1080 pixels using 24 bits per pixel. Can an uncompressed video stream of this format be sent over a USB 1.1 serial port? USB 2.0 serial port? USB 3.0 serial port? (Note: The maximum speeds of USB 1.1, USB 2.0, and USB 3.0 serial ports are 12Mbps, 480Mbps, and 5Gbps respectively.)

*47. Suppose a person is typing forty words per minute at a keyboard. (A word is considered to be five characters.) If a machine executes 500 instructions every microsecond (millionth of a second), how many instructions does the machine execute during the time between the typing of two consecutive characters?

*48. How many bits per second must a keyboard transmit to keep up with a typist typing forty words per minute? (Assume each character is encoded in ASCII and each word consists of six characters.)

*49. Suppose the machine described in Appendix C communicates with a printer using the technique of memory-mapped I/O. Suppose also that address FF is used to send characters to the printer, and address FE is used to receive information about the printer's status. In particular, suppose the least significant bit at the address FE indicates whether the printer is ready to receive another character (with a 0 indicating "not ready" and a 1 indicating "ready"). Starting at address 00, write a machine language routine that waits until the printer is ready for another character and then sends the

character represented by the bit pattern in register 5 to the printer.

*50. Write a program in the machine language described in Appendix C that places 0s in all the memory cells from address A0 through C0 but is small enough to fit in the memory cells from address 00 through 13 (hexadecimal).

*51. Suppose a machine has 200 GB of storage space available on a hard disk and receives data over a broadband connection at the rate of 15 Mbps. At this rate, how long will it take to fill the available storage space?

*52. Suppose a satellite system is being used to receive a serial data stream at 250 Kbps. If a burst of atmospheric interference lasts 6.96 seconds, how many data bits will be affected?

*53. Suppose you are given 32 processors, each capable of finding the sum of two multidigit numbers in a millionth of a second. Describe how parallel processing techniques can be applied to find the sum of 64 numbers in only six-millionths of a second. How much time does a single processor require to find this same sum?

*54. Summarize the difference between a CISC architecture and a RISC architecture.

*55. Identify two approaches to increasing throughput.

*56. Describe how the average of a collection of numbers can be computed more rapidly with a multiprocessor machine than a single processor machine.

*57. Write and test a Python script that reads in a floating-point radius of a circle and outputs the circumference and area of the circle.

*58. Write and test a Python script that reads in a character string and an integer and outputs the character string repeated the number of times given by the integer.

*59. Write and test a Python script that reads in two floating-point side lengths of a right triangle and outputs the hypotenuse length, perimeter, and area.

Social Issues

The following questions are intended as a guide to the ethical/social/legal issues associated with the field of computing. The goal is not merely to answer these questions. You should also consider why you answered as you did and whether your justifications are consistent from one question to the next.

1. Suppose a computer manufacturer develops a new machine architecture. To what extent should the company be allowed to own that architecture? What policy would be best for society?

2. In a sense, the year 1923 marked the birth of what many now call *planned obsolescence*. This was the year that General Motors, led by Alfred Sloan, introduced the automobile industry to the concept of model years. The idea was to increase sales by changing styling rather than necessarily introducing a better automobile. Sloan is quoted as saying, "We want to make you dissatisfied with your current car so you will buy a new one." To what extent is this marketing ploy used today in the computer industry?

3. We often think in terms of how computer technology has changed our society. Many argue, however, that this technology has often kept changes from occurring by allowing old systems to survive and, in some cases, become more entrenched. For example, would a central government's role in society have survived without computer technology? To what extent would centralized authority be present today had computer technology not been available? To what extent would we be better or worse off without computer technology?

4. Is it ethical for an individual to take the attitude that he or she does not need to know anything about the internal details of a machine because someone else will build it, maintain it, and fix any problems that arise? Does your answer depend on whether the machine is a computer, automobile, nuclear power plant, or toaster?

5. Suppose a manufacturer produces a computer chip and later discovers a flaw in its design. Suppose further that the manufacturer corrects the flaw in future production but decides to keep the original flaw a secret and does not recall the chips already shipped, reasoning that none of the chips already in use are being used in an application in which the flaw will have consequences. Is anyone hurt by the manufacturer's decision? Is the manufacturer's decision justified if no one is hurt and the decision keeps the manufacturer from losing money and possibly having to lay off employees?

6. Does advancing technology provide cures for heart disease or is it a source of a sedentary life style that contributes to heart disease?

7. It is easy to imagine financial or navigational disasters that may occur as the result of arithmetic errors due to overflow and truncation problems. What consequences could result from errors in image storage systems due to loss of image details (perhaps in fields such as reconnaissance or medical diagnosis)?

8. ARM Holdings is a small company that designs the processors for a wide variety of consumer electronic devices. It does not manufacture any of the processors; instead the designs are licensed to semiconductor vendors (such as Qualcomm, Samsung, and Texas Instruments) who pay a royalty for each unit produced. This business model spreads the high cost of research and

development of computer processors across the entire consumer electronic market. Today, over 95 percent of all cellular phones (not just smartphones), over 40 percent of all digital cameras, and 25 percent of digital TVs use an ARM processor. Furthermore, ARM processors are found in mini-notebooks, MP3 players, game controllers, electronic book readers, navigation systems, and the list goes on. Given this, do you consider this company to be a monopoly? Why or why not? Because consumer devices play an ever-increasing role in today's society, is the dependency on this little-known company good, or does it raise concerns?

Additional Reading

Carpinelli, J. D. *Computer Systems Organization and Architecture.* Boston, MA: Addison-Wesley, 2001.

Comer, D. E. *Essentials of Computer Architecture.* Upper Saddle River, NJ: Prentice-Hall, 2005.

Dandamudi, S P. *Guide to RISC Processors for Programmers and Engineers.* New York: Springer, 2005.

Furber, S. *ARM System-on-Chip Architecture,* 2nd ed. Boston, MA: Addison Wesley, 2000.

Hamacher, V. C., Z. G. Vranesic, and S. G. Zaky. *Computer Organization,* 5th ed. New York: McGraw-Hill, 2002.

Knuth, D. E. *The Art of Computer Programming, Vol. 1,* 3rd ed. Boston, MA: Addison-Wesley, 1998.

Murdocca, M. J., and V. P. Heuring. *Computer Architecture and Organization: An Integrated Approach.* New York: Wiley, 2007.

Stallings, W. *Computer Organization and Architecture,* 9th ed. Upper Saddle River, NJ: Prentice-Hall, 2012.

Tanenbaum, A. S. *Structured Computer Organization,* 6th ed. Upper Saddle River, NJ: Prentice-Hall, 2012.

Algorithms

In the introductory chapter we learned that the central theme of computer science is the study of algorithms. It is time now for us to focus on this core topic. Our goal is to explore enough of this foundational material so that we can truly understand and appreciate the science of computing.

We have seen that before a computer can perform a task, it must be given an algorithm telling it precisely what to do; consequently, the study of algorithms is the cornerstone of computer science. In this chapter we introduce many of the fundamental concepts of this study, including the issues of algorithm discovery and representation as well as the major control concepts of iteration and recursion. In so doing we also present a few well-known algorithms for searching and sorting. We begin by reviewing the concept of an algorithm.

5.1 The Concept of an Algorithm

In the introductory chapter we informally defined an algorithm as a set of steps that define how a task is performed. In this section we look more closely at this fundamental concept.

An Informal Review

We have encountered a multitude of algorithms in our study. We have found algorithms for converting numeric representations from one form to another, detecting and correcting errors in data, compressing and decompressing data files, controlling multiprogramming in a multitasking environment, and many more. Moreover, we have seen that the machine cycle that is followed by a CPU is nothing more than the simple algorithm

```
As long as the halt instruction has not been executed continue to
execute the following steps:
    a. Fetch an instruction.
    b. Decode the instruction.
    c. Execute the instruction.
```

As demonstrated by the algorithm describing a magic trick in Figure 0.1, algorithms are not restricted to technical activities. Indeed, they underlie even such mundane activities as shelling peas:

```
Obtain a basket of unshelled peas and an empty bowl. As long as
there are unshelled peas in the basket continue to execute the
following steps:
    a. Take a pea from the basket.
    b. Break open the pea pod.
    c. Dump the peas from the pod into the bowl.
    d. Discard the pod.
```

In fact, many researchers believe that every activity of the human mind, including imagination, creativity, and decision making, is actually the result of algorithm execution—a conjecture we will revisit in our study of artificial intelligence (Chapter 11).

But before we proceed further, let us consider the formal definition of an algorithm.

The Formal Definition of an Algorithm

Informal, loosely defined concepts are acceptable and common in everyday life, but a science must be based on well-defined terminology. Consider, then, the formal definition of an algorithm stated in Figure 5.1.

Figure 5.1   The definition of an algorithm

An algorithm is an ordered set
of unambiguous, executable steps
that defines a terminating process.

Note that the definition requires that the set of steps in an algorithm be ordered. This means that the steps in an algorithm must have a well-established structure in terms of the order of their execution. This does not mean, however, that the steps must be executed in a sequence consisting of a first step, followed by a second, and so on. Some algorithms, known as parallel algorithms, contain more than one sequence of steps, each designed to be executed by different processors in a multiprocessor machine. In such cases the overall algorithm does not possess a single thread of steps that conforms to the first-step, second-step scenario. Instead, the algorithm's structure is that of multiple threads that branch and reconnect as different processors perform different parts of the overall task. (We will revisit this concept in Chapter 6.) Other examples include algorithms executed by circuits such as the flip-flop in Chapter 1, in which each gate performs a single step of the overall algorithm. Here the steps are ordered by cause and effect, as the action of each gate propagates throughout the circuit.

Next, consider the requirement that an algorithm must consist of executable steps. To appreciate this condition, consider the instruction

`Make a list of all the positive integers`

which would be impossible to perform because there are infinitely many positive integers. Thus any set of instructions involving this instruction would not be an algorithm. Computer scientists use the term *effective* to capture the concept of being executable. That is, to say that a step is effective means that it is doable.

Another requirement imposed by the definition in Figure 5.1 is that the steps in an algorithm be unambiguous. This means that during execution of an algorithm, the information in the state of the process must be sufficient to determine uniquely and completely the actions required by each step. In other words, the execution of each step in an algorithm does not require creative skills. Rather, it requires only the ability to follow directions. (In Chapter 12 we will learn that "algorithms," called nondeterministic algorithms, that do not conform to this restriction are an important topic of research.)

The definition in Figure 5.1 also requires that an algorithm define a terminating process, which means that the execution of an algorithm must lead to an end. The origin of this requirement is in theoretical computer science, where the goal is to answer such questions as "What are the ultimate limitations of algorithms and machines?" Here computer science seeks to distinguish between problems whose answers can be obtained algorithmically and problems whose answers lie beyond the capabilities of algorithmic systems. In this context, a line is drawn between processes that culminate with an answer and those that merely proceed forever without producing a result.

There are, however, meaningful applications for nonterminating processes, including monitoring the vital signs of a hospital patient and maintaining an aircraft's altitude in flight. Some would argue that these applications involve merely the repetition of algorithms, each of which reaches an end and then automatically repeats. Others would counter that such arguments are simply attempts to cling to an overly restrictive formal definition. In any case, the result is that the term *algorithm* is often used in applied, or informal, settings in reference to sets of steps that do not necessarily define terminating processes. An example is the long-division "algorithm" that does not define a terminating process for dividing 1 by 3. Technically, such instances represent misuses of the term.

The Abstract Nature of Algorithms

It is important to emphasize the distinction between an algorithm and its representation—a distinction that is analogous to that between a story and a book. A story is abstract, or conceptual, in nature; a book is a physical representation of a story. If a book is translated into another language or republished in a different format, it is merely the representation of the story that changes—the story itself remains the same.

In the same manner, an algorithm is abstract and distinct from its representation. A single algorithm can be represented in many ways. As an example, the algorithm for converting temperature readings from Celsius to Fahrenheit is traditionally represented as the algebraic formula

$$F = (\%)C + 32$$

But it could be represented by the instruction

Multiply the temperature reading in Celsius by $\%$
and then add 32 to the product

or even in the form of an electronic circuit. In each case the underlying algorithm is the same; only the representations differ.

The distinction between an algorithm and its representation presents a problem when we try to communicate algorithms. A common example involves the level of detail at which an algorithm must be described. Among meteorologists, the instruction "Convert the Celsius reading to its Fahrenheit equivalent" suffices, but a layperson, requiring a more detailed description, might argue that the instruction is ambiguous. The problem, however, is not with the underlying algorithm but that the algorithm is not represented in enough detail for the layperson. In the next section we will see how the concept of primitives can be used to eliminate such ambiguity problems in an algorithm's representation.

Finally, while on the subject of algorithms and their representations, we should clarify the distinction between two other related concepts—programs and processes. A *program* is a representation of an algorithm. (Here we are using the term *algorithm* in its less formal sense in that many programs are representations of nonterminating "algorithms.") In fact, within the computing community the term *program* usually refers to a formal representation of an algorithm designed for computer application. We defined a *process* in Chapter 3 to be the activity of executing a program. Note, however, that to execute a program is to execute the algorithm represented by the program, so a process could equivalently be defined as the activity of executing an algorithm. We conclude that programs, algorithms, and processes are distinct, yet related, entities. A program is the representation of an algorithm, whereas a process is the activity of executing an algorithm.

Questions & Exercises

1. Summarize the distinctions between a process, an algorithm, and a program.

2. Give some examples of algorithms with which you are familiar. Are they really algorithms in the precise sense?

3. Identify some points of vagueness in our informal definition of an algorithm introduced in Section 0.1 of the introductory chapter.

4. In what sense do the steps described by the following list of instructions fail to constitute an algorithm?

   Step 1. Take a coin out of your pocket and put it on the table.
   Step 2. Return to Step 1.

5.2 Algorithm Representation

In this section we consider issues relating to an algorithm's representation. Our goal is to introduce the basic concepts of primitives and pseudocode as well as to establish a representation system for our own use.

Primitives

The representation of an algorithm requires some form of language. In the case of humans this might be a traditional natural language (English, Spanish, Russian, Japanese) or perhaps the language of pictures, as demonstrated in Figure 5.2, which describes an algorithm for folding a bird from a square piece of paper. Often, however, such natural channels of communication lead to misunderstandings, sometimes because the terminology used has more than one meaning. (The sentence, "Visiting grandchildren can be nerve-racking," could mean either that the grandchildren cause problems when they come to visit or that going to see them is problematic.) Problems also arise over misunderstandings regarding the level of detail required. Few readers could successfully fold a bird from the directions given in Figure 5.2, yet a student of origami would probably have little difficulty. In short, communication problems arise when the language used for an algorithm's representation is not precisely defined or when information is not given in adequate detail.

Computer science approaches these problems by establishing a well-defined set of building blocks from which algorithm representations can be constructed. Such a building block is called a **primitive.** Assigning precise definitions to these primitives removes many problems of ambiguity, and requiring algorithms to be described in terms of these primitives establishes a uniform level of detail. A collection of primitives along with a collection of rules stating how the primitives can be combined to represent more complex ideas constitutes a **programming language.**

Each primitive has its own syntax and semantics. Syntax refers to the primitive's symbolic representation; semantics refers to the meaning of the primitive. The syntax of *air* consists of three symbols, whereas the semantics is a gaseous substance that surrounds the world. As an example, Figure 5.3 presents some of the primitives used in origami.

Figure 5.2   Folding a bird from a square piece of paper

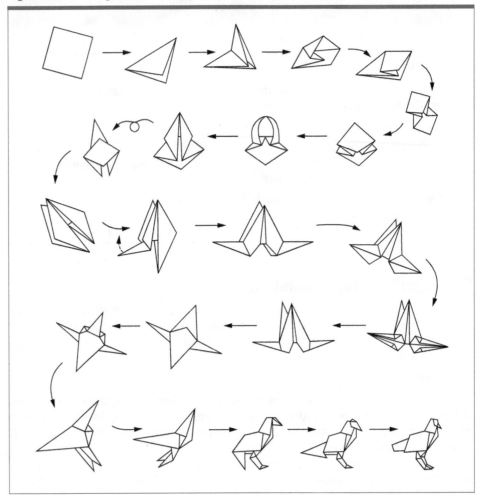

To obtain a collection of primitives to use in representing algorithms for computer execution, we could turn to the individual instructions that the machine is designed to execute. If an algorithm is expressed at this level of detail, we will certainly have a program suitable for machine execution. However, expressing algorithms at this level is tedious, and so one normally uses a collection of "higher-level" primitives, each being an abstract tool constructed from the lower-level primitives provided in the machine's language. The result is a formal programming language in which algorithms can be expressed at a conceptually higher level than in machine language. We will discuss such programming languages in the next chapter.

Pseudocode

For now, we forgo the introduction of a formal programming language in favor of a less formal, more intuitive notational system known as pseudocode. In general, a **pseudocode** is a notational system in which ideas can be expressed informally during the algorithm development process.

Figure 5.3 Origami primitives

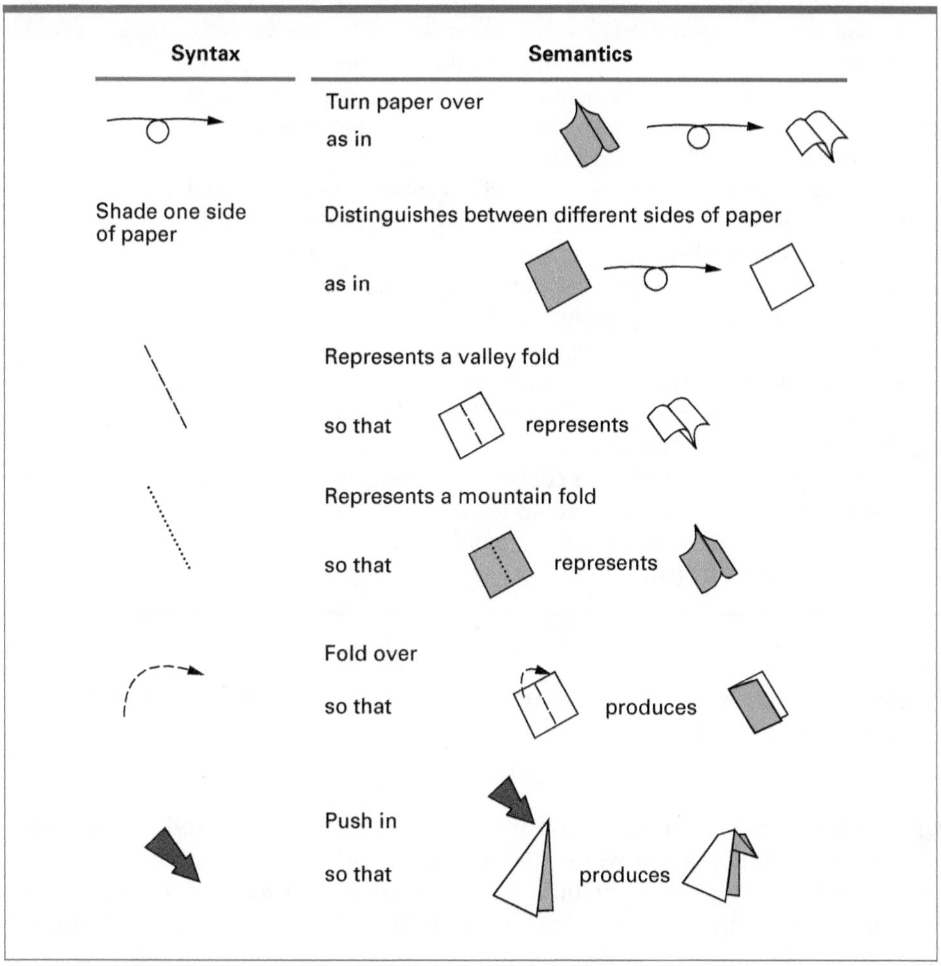

One way to obtain a pseudocode is simply to loosen the rules of a formal programming language, borrowing the syntax-semantic structures of the language, intermixed with less formal consructs. There are many such pseudocode variants, because there are many programming languages in existence. Two particularly popular choices are loose versions of the languages Algol and Pascal, largely because these were widely used in textbooks and academic papers for decades. More recently, pseudocode reminiscent of the Java and C languages has proliferated, again because most programmers will have at least a reading knowledge of these languages. Regardless of where a pseudocode borrows its syntax from, one essential property is required for it to serve its purpose in expressing algorithms: A pseudocode must have a consistent, concise notation for representing recurring semantic structures. For our purposes, we will use a Python-like syntax to express pseudocode throughout the remainder of the book. Some of our pseudocode semantic structures will borrow from language constructs presented in previous chapters, while others will look ahead to constructs to be formally covered in future chapters.

One such recurring semantic structure is the saving of a computed value. For example, if we have computed the sum of our checking and savings account

Algorithm Representation During Algorithm Design

The task of designing a complex algorithm requires that the designer keep track of numerous interrelated concepts—a requirement that can exceed the capabilities of the human mind. Thus the designer of complex algorithms needs a way to record and recall portions of an evolving algorithm as his or her concentration requires.

During the 1950s and 1960s, flowcharts (by which algorithms are represented by geometric shapes connected by arrows) were the state-of-the-art design tool. However, flowcharts often became tangled webs of crisscrossing arrows that made understanding the structure of the underlying algorithm difficult. Thus the use of flowcharts as design tools has given way to other representation techniques. An example is the pseudocode used in this text, by which algorithms are represented with well-defined textual structures. Flowcharts are still beneficial when the goal is presentation rather than design. For example, Figures 5.8 and 5.9 apply flowchart notation to demonstrate the algorithmic structure represented by popular control statements.

The search for better design notations is a continuing process. In Chapter 7 we will see that the trend is to use graphical techniques to assist in the global design of large software systems, while pseudocode remains popular for designing the smaller procedural components within a system.

balances, we may want to save the result so we can refer to it later. In such cases we will use the form

```
name = expression
```

where name is the name by which we will refer to the result and **expression** describes the computation whose result is to be saved. This pseudocode structure directly follows the equivalent Python **assignment statement,** which we introduced in Chapter 1 for storing a value into a Python variable. For example, the statement

```
RemainingFunds = CheckingBalance + SavingsBalance
```

is an assignment statement that assigns the sum of **CheckingBalance** and **SavingsBalance** to the name **RemainingFunds**. Thus, the term **RemainingFunds** can be used in future statements to refer to that sum.

Another recurring semantic structure is the selection of one of two possible activities depending on the truth or falseness of some condition. Examples include:

> If the gross domestic product has increased, buy common stock; otherwise, sell common stock.
>
> Buy common stock if the gross domestic product has increased and sell it otherwise.
>
> Buy or sell common stock depending on whether the gross domestic product has increased or decreased, respectively.

Each of these statements could be rewritten to conform to the structure

```
if (condition):
  activity
else:
  activity
```

From Pseudocode to Python

Our pseudocode in this chapter closely mirrors actual Python syntax for the `if` and `while` structures, as well as function definition and calling syntax.

```
if (condition):
    activity
else:
    activity
```

Our pseudocode `if` and `while` structures can be converted to Python simply by being more precise with the **condition** and **activity** portions. For example, rather than the English phrase, "sales have decreased" as a condition, we would need a proper Python comparison expression, such as

```
if (sales_current < sales_previous):
```

where the sales variables had already been assigned in previous lines of the script. Similarly, informal English sentences or phrases used as the **activity** in our pseudocode would need to be replaced with Python statements and expressions such as those we have already seen in earlier chapters.

How can you tell the difference between pseudocode and actual Python code in this book? As a rule, real Python code uses operators (like "<", "=", or "+") to string together multiple named variables into more complex expressions, or commas to separate a list of parameters being sent to a function. Articles like "the" and "a," or prepositions like "from" appear in pseudocode. We use periods at the end of sentences in pseudocode; Python statements do not have punctuation at the end.

where we have used the keywords `if` and `else` to announce the different substructures within the main structure and have used colons and indentation to delineate the boundaries of these substructures. The **condition** and the `else` will always be followed immediately by a colon. The corresponding **activity** will be indented. If an **activity** consists of multiple steps, they will all be similarly indented. By adopting this syntactic structure for our pseudocode, we acquire a uniform way in which to express this common semantic structure. Thus, whereas the statement

> Depending on whether the year is a leap year, divide the total by 366 or 365, respectively

might possess a more creative literary style, we will consistently opt for the straightforward

```
if (year is leap year):
    daily total = total / 366
else:
    daily total = total / 365
```

We also adopt the shorter syntax

```
if (condition):
    Activity
```

for those cases not involving an `else` activity. Using this notation, the statement

> Should it be the case that sales have decreased, lower the price by 5%.

will be reduced to

```
if (sales have decreased):
  lower the price by 5%
```

Still another common semantic structure is the repeated execution of a statement or sequence of statements as long as some condition remains true. Informal examples include

> As long as there are tickets to sell, continue selling tickets.

and

> While there are tickets to sell, keep selling tickets.

For such cases, we adopt the uniform pattern

```
while (condition):
  Activity
```

for our pseudocode. In short, such a statement means to check the **condition** and, if it is true, perform the **activity** and return to check the **condition** again. If, however, the **condition** is found to be false, move on to the next instruction following the `while` structure. Thus both of the preceding statements are reduced to

```
while (tickets remain to be sold):
  sell a ticket
```

In many programming languages, indentation often enhances the readability of a program. In Python, and thus also in our Python-derived pseudocode, indentation is essential to the notation. For example, in the statement

```
if (not raining):
  if (temperature == hot):
    go swimming
  else:
    play golf
else:
  watch television
```

indentation tells us that the question of whether **temperature** equals **hot** will not even be asked unless it is **not raining**. Note the use of double equal signs, "==" to differentiate between assignment (=) and comparison (==). The question about the temperature is **nested** inside the if-statement, and is, in effect, the activity to be performed if the outer if-statement condition holds true. Similarly, indentation tells us that `else:` **play golf** belongs to the inner if-statement, rather than to the outer if-statement. Thus we will adopt the use of indentation in our pseudocode.

We want to use our pseudocode to describe activities that can be used as abstract tools in other applications. Computer science has a variety of terms for such program units, including subprogram, subroutine, procedure, method, and function, each with its own variation of meaning. We will follow Python convention, using the term **function** for our pseudocode and using the Python keyword def to announce the title by which the pseudocode unit will be known. More precisely, we will begin a pseudocode unit with a statement of the form

def name():

where name is the particular name of the unit. We will then follow this introductory statement with the statements that define the unit's action. For example, Figure 5.4 is a pseudocode representation of a function called Greetings that prints the message "Hello" three times.

When the task performed by a function is required elsewhere in our pseudocode, we will merely request it by name. For example, if two functions were named ProcessLoan and RejectApplication, then we could request their services within an if-else structure by writing

```
if (. . .):
  ProcessLoan()
else:
  RejectApplication()
```

which would result in the execution of the function ProcessLoan if the tested condition were true or in the execution of RejectApplication if the condition were false.

If functions are to be used in different situations, they should be designed to be as generic as possible. A function for sorting lists of names should be designed to sort any list—not a particular list—so it should be written in such a way that the list to be sorted is not specified in the function itself. Instead, the list should be referred to by a generic name within the function's representation.

In our pseudocode, we will adopt the convention of listing these generic names (which are called **parameters**) in parentheses on the same line on which we identify the function's name. In particular, a function named Sort, which is designed to sort any list of names, would begin with the statement

def Sort (List):

Later in the representation where a reference to the list being sorted is required, the generic name List would be used. In turn, when the services of Sort are required, we will identify which list is to be substituted for List in the function Sort. Thus we will write something such as

Sort(the organization's membership list)

and

Sort(the wedding guest list)

depending on our needs.

Figure 5.4 The function Greetings in pseudocode

```
def Greetings():
  Count = 3
  while (Count > 0):
    print('Hello')
    Count = Count - 1
```

Naming Items in Programs

In a natural language, items often have multiword names such as "cost of producing a widget" or "estimated arrival time." Experience has shown that use of such multiword names in the representation of an algorithm can complicate the algorithm's description. It is better to have each item identified by a single contiguous block of text. Over the years many techniques have been used to compress multiple words into a single lexical unit to obtain descriptive names for items in programs. One is to use underlines to connect words, producing names such as `estimated_arrival_time`. Another is to use uppercase letters to help a reader comprehend a compressed multiword name. For example, one could start each word with an uppercase letter to obtain names such as `EstimatedArrivalTime`. This technique is called **Pascal casing,** because it was popularized by users of the Pascal programming language. A variation of Pascal casing is called **camel casing,** which is identical to Pascal casing except that the first letter remains in lowercase as in `estimatedArrivalTime`. In this text we lean toward Pascal casing, but the choice is largely a matter of taste.

Questions & Exercises

1. A primitive in one context might turn out to be a composite of primitives in another. For instance, our `while` statement is a primitive in our pseudocode, yet it is ultimately implemented as a composite of machine-language instructions. Give two examples of this phenomenon in a non-computer setting.

2. In what sense is the construction of functions the construction of primitives?

3. The Euclidean algorithm finds the greatest common divisor of two positive integers X and Y by the following process:

   As long as the value of neither X nor Y is zero, assign the larger the remainder of dividing the larger by the smaller. The greatest common divisor, if it exists, will be the remaining non-zero value.

   Express this algorithm in our pseudocode.

4. Describe a collection of primitives that are used in a subject other than computer programming.

5.3 Algorithm Discovery

The development of a program consists of two activities—discovering the underlying algorithm and representing that algorithm as a program. Up to this point we have been concerned with the issues of algorithm representation without considering the question of how algorithms are discovered in the first place. Yet algorithm discovery is usually the more challenging step in the software development process. After all, discovering an algorithm to solve a problem requires finding a method of solving that problem. Thus, to understand how algorithms are discovered is to understand the problem-solving process.

The Art of Problem Solving

The techniques of problem solving and the need to learn more about them are not unique to computer science but rather are topics pertinent to almost any field. The close association between the process of algorithm discovery and that of general problem solving has caused computer scientists to join with those of other disciplines in the search for better problem-solving techniques. Ultimately, one would like to reduce the process of problem solving to an algorithm in itself, but this has been shown to be impossible. (This is a result of the material in Chapter 12, where we will show that there are problems that do not have algorithmic solutions.) Thus the ability to solve problems remains more of an artistic skill to be developed than a precise science to be learned.

As evidence of the elusive, artistic nature of problem solving, the following loosely defined problem-solving phases presented by the mathematician G. Polya in 1945 remain the basic principles on which many attempts to teach problem-solving skills are based today.

Phase 1. Understand the problem.

Phase 2. Devise a plan for solving the problem.

Phase 3. Carry out the plan.

Phase 4. Evaluate the solution for accuracy and for its potential as a tool for solving other problems.

Translated into the context of program development, these phases become

Phase 1. Understand the problem.

Phase 2. Get an idea of how an algorithmic function might solve the problem.

Phase 3. Formulate the algorithm and represent it as a program.

Phase 4. Evaluate the program for accuracy and for its potential as a tool for solving other problems.

Having presented Polya's list, we should emphasize that these phases are not steps to be followed when trying to solve a problem but rather phases that will be completed sometime during the solution process. The key word here is *followed*. You do not solve problems by following. Rather, to solve a problem, you must take the initiative and lead. If you approach the task of solving a problem in the frame of mind depicted by "Now I've finished Phase 1, it's time to move on to Phase 2," you are not likely to be successful. However, if you become involved with the problem and ultimately solve it, you most likely can look back at what you did and realize that you performed Polya's phases.

Another important observation is that Polya's phases are not necessarily completed in sequence. Successful problem solvers often start formulating strategies for solving a problem (Phase 2) before the problem itself is entirely understood (Phase 1). Then, if these strategies fail (during Phases 3 or 4), the potential problem solver gains a deeper understanding of the intricacies of the problem and, with this deeper understanding, can return to form other and hopefully more successful strategies.

Keep in mind that we are discussing how problems are solved—not how we would like them to be solved. Ideally, we would like to eliminate the waste inherent in the trial-and-error process just described. In the case of developing large software systems, discovering a misunderstanding as late as Phase 4 can represent a tremendous loss in resources. Avoiding such catastrophes is a major goal of software engineers (Chapter 7), who have traditionally insisted on a thorough understanding of a problem before proceeding with a solution. One could argue, however, that a true understanding of a problem is not obtained until a solution has been found. The mere fact that a problem is unsolved implies a lack of understanding. To insist on a complete understanding of the problem before proposing any solutions is therefore somewhat idealistic.

As an example, consider the following problem:

> Person A is charged with the task of determining the ages of person B's three children. B tells A that the product of the children's ages is 36. After considering this clue, A replies that another clue is required, so B tells A the sum of the children's ages. Again, A replies that another clue is needed, so B tells A that the oldest child plays the piano. After hearing this clue, A tells B the ages of the three children.
>
> How old are the three children?

At first glance the last clue seems to be totally unrelated to the problem, yet it is apparently this clue that allows A to finally determine the ages of the children. How can this be? Let us proceed by formulating a plan of attack and following this plan, even though we still have many questions about the problem. Our plan will be to trace the steps described by the problem statement while keeping track of the information available to person A as the story progresses.

The first clue given A is that the product of the children's ages is 36. This means that the triple representing the three ages is one of those listed in Figure 5.5(a). The next clue is the sum of the desired triple. We are not told what this sum is, but we are told that this information is not enough for A to isolate the correct triple; therefore the desired triple must be one whose sum appears at least twice in the table of Figure 5.5(b). But the only triples appearing in Figure 5.5(b) with identical sums are (1,6,6) and (2,2,9), both of which produce the sum 13. This is the information available to A at the time the last clue is given. It is at this point that we finally understand the significance of the last clue. It has nothing to do with playing the piano; rather it is the fact that there is an oldest child. This rules out the triple (1,6,6) and thus allows us to conclude that the children's ages are 2, 2, and 9.

In this case, then, it is not until we attempt to implement our plan for solving the problem (Phase 3) that we gain a complete understanding of the problem (Phase 1). Had we insisted on completing Phase 1 before proceeding, we would probably never have found the children's ages. Such irregularities in the problem-solving process are fundamental to the difficulties in developing systematic approaches to problem solving.

Figure 5.5　Analyzing the possibilities

a. Triples whose product is 36		b. Sums of triples from part (a)	
(1,1,36)	(1,6,6)	1 + 1 + 36 = 38	1 + 6 + 6 = 13
(1,2,18)	(2,2,9)	1 + 2 + 18 = 21	2 + 2 + 9 = 13
(1,3,12)	(2,3,6)	1 + 3 + 12 = 16	2 + 3 + 6 = 11
(1,4,9)	(3,3,4)	1 + 4 + 9 = 14	3 + 3 + 4 = 10

Another irregularity is the mysterious inspiration that might come to a potential problem solver who, having worked on a problem without apparent success, at a later time suddenly sees the solution while doing another task. This phenomenon was identified by H. von Helmholtz as early as 1896 and was discussed by the mathematician Henri Poincaré in a lecture before the Psychological Society in Paris. There, Poincaré described his experiences of realizing the solution to a problem he had worked on after he had set it aside and begun other projects. The phenomenon reflects a process in which a subconscious part of the mind appears to continue working and, if successful, forces the solution into the conscious mind. Today, the period between conscious work on a problem and the sudden inspiration is known as an incubation period, and its understanding remains a goal of current research.

Getting a Foot in the Door

We have been discussing problem solving from a somewhat philosophical point of view while avoiding a direct confrontation with the question of how we should go about trying to solve a problem. There are, of course, numerous problem-solving approaches, each of which can be successful in certain settings. We will identify some of them shortly. For now, we note that there seems to be a common thread running through these techniques, which simply stated is "get your foot in the door." As an example, let us consider the following simple problem:

Before A, B, C, and D ran a race they made the following predictions:

A predicted that B would win.
B predicted that D would be last.
C predicted that A would be third.
D predicted that A's prediction would be correct.

Only one of these predictions was true, and this was the prediction made by the winner. In what order did A, B, C, and D finish the race?

After reading the problem and analyzing the data, it should not take long to realize that since the predictions of A and D were equivalent and only one prediction was true, the predictions of both A and D must be false. Thus neither A nor D were winners. At this point we have our foot in the door, and obtaining the complete solution to our problem is merely a matter of extending our knowledge from here. If A's prediction was false, then B did not win either. The only remaining choice for the winner is C. Thus, C won the race, and C's prediction was true. Consequently, we know that A came in third. That means that the finishing order was either CBAD or CDAB. But the former is ruled out because B's prediction must be false. Therefore the finishing order was CDAB.

Of course, being told to get our foot in the door is not the same as being told how to do it. Obtaining this toehold, as well as realizing how to expand this initial thrust into a complete solution to the problem, requires creative input from the would-be problem solver. There are, however, several general approaches that have been proposed by Polya and others for how one might go about getting a foot in the door. One is to try working the problem backward. For instance, if the problem is to find a way of producing a particular output from a given input, one might start with that output and attempt to back up to the given input. This approach is typical of people trying to discover the bird-folding algorithm in the previous section. They tend to unfold a completed bird in an attempt to see how it is constructed.

Another general problem-solving approach is to look for a related problem that is either easier to solve or has been solved before and then try to apply its solution to the current problem. This technique is of particular value in the context of program development. Generally, program development is not the process of solving a particular instance of a problem but rather of finding a general algorithm that can be used to solve all instances of the problem. More precisely, if we were faced with the task of developing a program for alphabetizing lists of names, our task would not be to sort a particular list but to find a general algorithm that could be used to sort any list of names. Thus, although the instructions

```
Interchange the names David and Alice.
Move the name Carol to the position between Alice and David.
Move the name Bob to the position between Alice and Carol.
```

correctly sort the list David, Alice, Carol, and Bob, they do not constitute the general-purpose algorithm we desire. What we need is an algorithm that can sort this list as well as other lists we might encounter. This is not to say that our solution for sorting a particular list is totally worthless in our search for a general-purpose algorithm. We might, for instance, get our foot in the door by considering such special cases in an attempt to find general principles that can in turn be used to develop the desired general-purpose algorithm. In this case, then, our solution is obtained by the technique of solving a collection of related problems.

Still another approach to getting a foot in the door is to apply **stepwise refinement,** which is essentially the technique of not trying to conquer an entire task (in all its detail) at once. Rather, stepwise refinement proposes that one first view the problem at hand in terms of several subproblems. The idea is that by breaking the original problem into subproblems, one is able to approach the overall solution in terms of steps, each of which is easier to solve than the entire original problem. In turn, stepwise refinement proposes that these steps be decomposed into smaller steps and these smaller steps be broken into still smaller ones until the entire problem has been reduced to a collection of easily solved subproblems.

In this light, stepwise refinement is a **top-down methodology** in that it progresses from the general to the specific. In contrast, a **bottom-up methodology** progresses from the specific to the general. Although contrasting in theory, the two approaches often complement each other in creative problem solving. The decomposition of a problem proposed by the top-down methodology of stepwise refinement is often guided by the problem solver's intuition, which might be working in a bottom-up mode.

The top-down methodology of stepwise refinement is essentially an organizational tool whose problem-solving attributes are consequences of this organization. It has long been an important design methodology in the data processing community, where the development of large software systems encompasses a significant organizational component. But, as we will learn in Chapter 7, large software systems are increasingly being constructed by combining prefabricated components—an approach that is inherently bottom-up. Thus, both top-down and bottom-up methodologies remain important tools in computer science.

The importance of maintaining such a broad perspective is exemplified by the fact that bringing preconceived notions and preselected tools to the problem-solving task can sometimes mask a problem's simplicity. The ages-of-the-children problem discussed earlier in this section is an excellent example of this phenomenon. Students of algebra invariably approach the problem as a system of simultaneous equations, an approach that leads to a dead end and often traps the would-be problem solver into believing that the information given is not sufficient to solve the problem.

Another example is the following:

> As you step from a pier into a boat, your hat falls into the water, unbeknownst to you. The river is flowing at 2.5 miles per hour so your hat begins to float downstream. In the meantime, you begin traveling upstream in the boat at a speed of 4.75 miles per hour relative to the water. After 10 minutes you realize that your hat is missing, turn the boat around, and begin to chase your hat down the river. How long will it take to catch up with your hat?

Most algebra students as well as calculator enthusiasts approach this problem by first determining how far upstream the boat will have traveled in 10 minutes as well as how far downstream the hat will have traveled during that same time. Then, they determine how long it will take for the boat to travel downstream to this position. But, when the boat reaches this position, the hat will have floated farther downstream. Thus, the problem solver either begins to apply techniques of calculus or becomes trapped in a cycle of computing where the hat will be each time the boat goes to where the hat was.

The problem is much simpler than this, however. The trick is to resist the urge to begin writing formulas and making calculations. Instead, we need to put these skills aside and adjust our perspective. The entire problem takes place in the river. The fact that the water is moving in relation to the shore is irrelevant. Think of the same problem posed on a large conveyor belt instead of a river. First, solve the problem with the conveyor belt at rest. If you place your hat at your feet while standing on the belt and then walk away from your hat for 10 minutes, it will take 10 minutes to return to your hat. Now turn on the conveyor belt. This means that the scenery will begin to move past the belt, but, because you are on the belt, this does not change your relationship to the belt or your hat. It will still take 10 minutes to return to your hat.

We conclude that algorithm discovery remains a challenging art that must be developed over a period of time rather than taught as a subject consisting of well-defined methodologies. Indeed, to train a potential problem solver to follow certain methodologies is to quash those creative skills that should instead be nurtured.

Questions & Exercises

1. a. Find an algorithm for solving the following problem: Given a positive integer n, find the list of positive integers whose product is the largest among all the lists of positive integers whose sum is n. For example, if n is 4, the desired list is 2, 2 because 2×2 is larger than $1 \times 1 \times 1 \times 1$, $2 \times 1 \times 1$, and 3×1. If n is 5, the desired list is 2, 3.

   b. What is the desired list if $n = 2001$?

   c. Explain how you got your foot in the door.

2. a. Suppose we are given a checkerboard consisting of 2^n rows and 2^n columns of squares, for some positive integer n, and a box of L-shaped tiles, each of which can cover exactly three squares on the board. If any single square is cut out of the board, can we cover the remaining board with tiles such that tiles do not overlap or hang off the edge of the board?

   b. Explain how your solution to (a) can be used to show that $2^{2n} - 1$ is divisible by 3 for all positive integers n.

   c. How are (a) and (b) related to Polya's phases of problem solving?

3. Decode the following message, then explain how you got your foot in the door. *Pdeo eo pda yknnayp wjosan.*

4. Would you be following a top-down methodology if you attempted to solve a picture puzzle merely by pouring the pieces out on a table and trying to piece them together? Would your answer change if you looked at the puzzle box to see what the entire picture was supposed to look like?

5.4 Iterative Structures

Our goal now is to study some of the repetitive structures used in describing algorithmic processes. In this section we discuss **iterative structures** in which a collection of instructions is repeated in a looping manner. In the next section we will introduce the technique of recursion. As a side effect, we will introduce some popular algorithms—the sequential search, the binary search, and the insertion sort. We begin by introducing the sequential search algorithm.

The Sequential Search Algorithm

Consider the problem of searching within a list for the occurrence of a particular target value. We want to develop an algorithm that determines whether that value is in the list. If the value is in the list, we consider the search a success; otherwise we consider it a failure. We assume that the list is sorted according to some rule for ordering its entries. For example, if the list is a list of names, we assume the names appear in alphabetical order, or if the list consists of numeric values, we assume its entries appear in order of increasing magnitude.

To get our foot in the door, we imagine how we might search a guest list of perhaps 20 entries for a particular name. In this setting we might scan the list from its beginning, comparing each entry with the target name. If we find the target name, the search terminates as a success. However, if we reach the end of the list without finding the target value, our search terminates as a failure. In fact, if we reach a name greater than (alphabetically) the target name without finding the target, our search terminates as a failure. (Remember, the list is arranged in alphabetical order, so reaching a name greater than the target name indicates that the target does not appear in the list.) In summary, our rough idea is to continue searching down the list as long as there are more names to be investigated and the target name is greater than the name currently being considered.

In our pseudocode, this process can be represented as

```
Select the first entry in the list as TestEntry.
while (TargetValue > TestEntry and entries remain):
  Select the next entry in the list as TestEntry.
```

Upon terminating this **while** structure, one of two conditions will be true: Either the target value has been found or the target value is not in the list. In either case we can detect a successful search by comparing the test entry to the target value. If they are equal, the search has been successful. Thus we add the statement

```
if (TargetValue == TestEntry):
  Declare the search a success.
else:
  Declare the search a failure.
```

to the end of our pseudocode routine.

Finally, we observe that the first statement in our routine, which selects the first entry in the list as the test entry, is based on the assumption that the list in question contains at least one entry. We might reason that this is a safe guess, but just to be sure, we can position our routine as the else option of the statement

```
if (List is empty):
  Declare search a failure.
else:
    . . .
```

This produces the function shown in Figure 5.6. Note that this function can be used from within other functions by using statements such as

```
Search() the passenger list using Darrel Baker as the target value.
```

to find out if Darrel Baker is a passenger and

```
Search() the list of ingredients using nutmeg as the target value.
```

to find out if nutmeg appears in the list of ingredients.

Figure 5.6   The sequential search algorithm in pseudocode

```
def Search(List, TargetValue):
  if (List is empty):
    Declare search a failure.
  else:
    Select the first entry in List to be TestEntry.
    while (TargetValue > TestEntry and
        there remain entries to be considered):
      Select the next entry in List as TestEntry.
    if (TargetValue == TestEntry):
      Declare search a success.
    else:
      Declare search a failure.
```

In summary, the algorithm represented by Figure 5.6 considers the entries in the sequential order in which they occur in the list. For this reason, the algorithm is called the **sequential search** algorithm. Because of its simplicity, it is often used for short lists or when other concerns dictate its use. However, in the case of long lists, sequential searches are not as efficient as other techniques (as we shall soon see).

Loop Control

The repetitive use of an instruction or sequence of instructions is an important algorithmic concept. One method of implementing such repetition is the iterative structure known as the **loop**, in which a collection of instructions, called the **body** of the loop, is executed in a repetitive fashion under the direction of some control process. A typical example is found in the sequential search algorithm represented in Figure 5.6. Here we use a while statement to control the repetition of the single statement `Select the next entry in List as the TestEntry`. Indeed, the while statement

```
while (condition):
  Body
```

exemplifies the concept of a loop structure in that its execution traces the cyclic pattern

```
check the condition.
execute the body.
check the condition.
execute the body.
      .
      .
      .
check the condition.
```

until the condition fails.

As a general rule, the use of a loop structure produces a higher degree of flexibility than would be obtained merely by explicitly writing the body several times. For example, to execute the statement

```
Add a drop of sulfuric acid.
```

three times, we could write:

```
Add a drop of sulfuric acid.
Add a drop of sulfuric acid.
Add a drop of sulfuric acid.
```

But we cannot produce a similar sequence that is equivalent to the loop structure

```
while (the pH level is greater than 4):
  add a drop of sulfuric acid
```

because we do not know in advance how many drops of acid will be required.

Let us now take a closer look at the composition of loop control. You might be tempted to view this part of a loop structure as having minor importance. After all, it is typically the body of the loop that actually performs the task at hand (for example, adding drops of acid)—the control activities appear merely as the overhead involved because we chose to execute the body in a repetitive fashion. However, experience has shown that the control of a loop is the more error-prone part of the structure and therefore deserves our attention.

The control of a loop consists of the three activities initialize, test, and modify (Figure 5.7), with the presence of each being required for successful loop control. The test activity has the obligation of causing the termination of the looping process by watching for a condition that indicates termination should take place. This condition is known as the **termination condition.** It is for the purpose of this test activity that we provide a condition within each while statement of our pseudocode. In the case of the while statement, however, the condition stated is the condition under which the body of the loop should be executed—the termination condition is the negation of the condition appearing in the while structure. Thus, in the statement

while (the pH level is greater than 4):
  add a drop of sulfuric acid

the termination condition is "the pH level is *not* greater than 4," and in the while statement of Figure 5.6, the termination condition could be stated as

(TargetValue <= TestEntry) or (there are no more entries to be considered)

The other two activities in the loop control ensure that the termination condition will ultimately occur. The initialization step establishes a starting condition, and the modification step moves this condition toward the termination condition. For instance, in Figure 5.6, initialization takes place in the statement preceding the while statement, where the current test entry is established as the first list entry. The modification step in this case is actually accomplished within the loop body, where our position of interest (identified by the test entry) is moved toward the end of the list. Thus, having executed the initialization step, repeated application of the modification step results in the termination condition being reached. (Either we will reach a test entry that is greater than or equal to the target value or we ultimately reach the end of the list.)

We should emphasize that the initialization and modification steps must lead to the appropriate termination condition. This characteristic is critical for proper loop control, and thus one should always double-check for its presence when designing a loop structure. Failure to make such an evaluation can

Figure 5.7 Components of repetitive control

Initialize:	Establish an initial state that will be modified toward the termination condition
Test:	Compare the current state to the termination condition and terminate the repetition if equal
Modify:	Change the state in such a way that it moves toward the termination condition

lead to errors even in the simplest cases. A typical example is found in the statements

```
Number = 1
while (Number != 6):
   Number = Number + 2
```

Note the use of the Python "!=" operator, which we read as, "not equal". Here the termination condition is "Number == 6." But the value of Number is initialized at 1 and then incremented by 2 in the modification step. Thus, as the loop cycles, the values assigned to Number will be 1, 3, 5, 7, 9, and so on, but never the value 6. As a result, this loop will never terminate.

The order in which the components of loop control are executed can have subtle consequences. In fact, there are two common loop structures that differ merely in this regard. The first is exemplified by our pseudocode statement

```
while (condition):
   Activity
```

whose semantics are represented in Figure 5.8 in the form of a **flowchart.** (Such charts use various shapes to represent individual steps and use arrows to indicate the order of the steps. The distinction between the shapes indicates the type of action involved in the associated step. A diamond indicates a decision and a rectangle indicates an arbitrary statement or sequence of statements.) Note that the test for termination in the while structure occurs before the loop's body is executed.

In contrast, the structure in Figure 5.9 requests that the body of the loop be executed before the test for termination is performed. In this case, the loop's body is always performed at least once, whereas in the while structure, the body is never executed if the termination condition is satisfied the first time it is tested.

Python does not have a built-in structure for this second kind of loop, although it is easy enough to build an equivalent using the existing while structure with an if-statement and a break at the end of the loop body. For our pseudocode,

Figure 5.8 The while loop structure

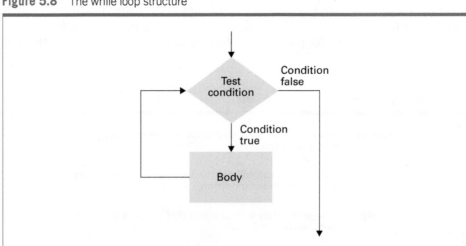

Figure 5.9   The repeat loop structure

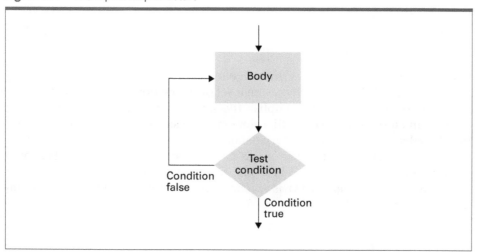

we will borrow keywords that exists in several other languages, using the syntactic form

```
repeat:
  activity
until (condition)
```

to represent the structure shown in Figure 5.9. Thus, the statement

```
repeat:
  take a coin from your pocket
until (there are no coins in your pocket)
```

assumes there is a coin in your pocket at the beginning, but

```
while (there is a coin in your pocket):
  take a coin from your pocket
```

does not.

Following the terminology of our pseudocode, we will usually refer to these structures as the while loop structure or the **repeat** loop structure. In a more generic context you might hear the while loop structure referred to as a **pretest loop** (since the test for termination is performed before the body is executed) and the **repeat** loop structure referred to as a **posttest loop** (since the test for termination is performed after the body is executed).

While many algorithms require careful consideration of the initialization, test, and modify activities when controlling loops, others follow some very common patterns. Particularly when working with lists of data, the most common pattern is to start with the first element in a list and consider each element in the list until the end is reached. Returning briefly to our sequential search example, we saw the pattern similar to

```
Select the first entry in the list
while (there remain entries to be considered):
    . . .
  Select the next entry in the list
```

Because this structure occurs so frequently in algorithms, we will use the syntactic form

```
for Item in List:
   . . .
```

to describe a loop that iterates through each element of a list. Notice that this pseudocode primitive is effectively one level of abstraction higher than the while structure, because we can accomplish the same effect with separate initialize, modify, and test structures, but this version more succinctly conveys the meaning of the loop without unnecessary detail.

Each time through the body of this for loop structure, the value Item will become the next element in List. The termination condition of this loop is implicitly when the end of List is reached. As an example, to total up the numbers in a list we could use

```
Sum = 0
for Number in List:
  Sum = Sum + Number
```

This type of loop is often called a **for-each** loop in languages other than Python and is a special case of the pretest loop. The for structure is best suited to situations in which the algorithm will perform the same steps on each element in a list, and it is not necessary to separately keep track of a loop counting variable.

The Insertion Sort Algorithm

As an additional example of using iterative structures, let us consider the problem of sorting a list of names into alphabetical order. But before proceeding, we should identify the constraints under which we will work. Simply stated, our goal is to sort the list "within itself." In other words, we want to sort the list by shuffling its entries as opposed to moving the list to another location. Our situation is analogous to the problem of sorting a list whose entries are recorded on separate index cards spread out on a crowded desktop. We have cleared off enough space for the cards but are not allowed to push additional materials back to make more room. This restriction is typical in computer applications, not because the workspace within the machine is necessarily crowded like our desktop, but simply because we want to use the storage space available in an efficient manner.

Let us get a foot in the door by considering how we might sort the names on the desktop. Consider the list of names

> Fred
> Alex
> Diana
> Byron
> Carol

One approach to sorting this list is to note that the sublist consisting of only the top name, Fred, is sorted but the sublist consisting of the top two names, Fred and Alex, is not. Thus we might pick up the card containing the name Alex, slide the name Fred down into the space where Alex was, and then place the name Alex in the hole at the top of the list, as represented by the first row in Figure 5.10. At this point our list would be

Alex
Fred
Diana
Byron
Carol

Now the top two names form a sorted sublist, but the top three do not. Thus we might pick up the third name, Diana, slide the name Fred down into the hole

Figure 5.10   Sorting the list Fred, Alex, Diana, Byron, and Carol alphabetically

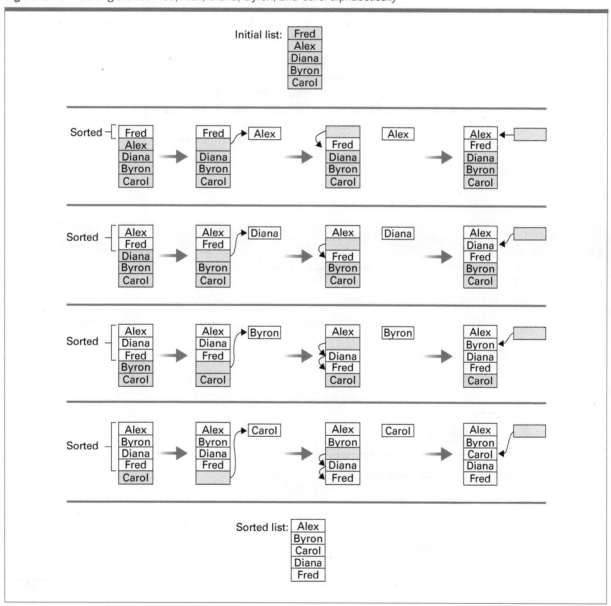

where Diana was, and then insert Diana in the hole left by Fred, as summarized in the second row of Figure 5.10. The top three entries in the list would now be sorted. Continuing in this fashion, we could obtain a list in which the top four entries are sorted by picking up the fourth name, Byron, sliding the names Fred and Diana down, and then inserting Byron in the hole (see the third row of Figure 5.10). Finally, we can complete the sorting process by picking up Carol, sliding Fred and Diana down, and then inserting Carol in the remaining hole (see the fourth row of Figure 5.10).

Having analyzed the process of sorting a particular list, our task now is to generalize this process to obtain an algorithm for sorting general lists. To this end, we observe that each row of Figure 5.10 represents the same general process: Pick up the first name in the unsorted portion of the list, slide the names greater than the extracted name down, and insert the extracted name back in the list where the hole appears. If we identify the extracted name as the pivot entry, this process can be expressed in our pseudocode as

```
Move the pivot entry to a temporary location leaving a hole in List
while (there is a name above the hole and
    that name is greater than the pivot):
    move the name above the hole down into the hole
        leaving a hole above the name
Move the pivot entry into the hole in List.
```

Iterative Structures in Music

Musicians were using and programming iterative structures centuries before computer scientists. Indeed, the structure of a song (being composed of multiple verses, each followed by the chorus) is exemplified by the **while** statement

```
while (there is a verse remaining):
    sing the next verse
    sing the chorus
```

Moreover, the notation

is merely a composer's way of expressing the structure

```
N = 1
while (N < 3):
    play the passage
    play the Nth ending
    N = N + 1
```

Next, we observe that this process should be executed repeatedly. To begin the sorting process, the pivot should be the second entry in the list and then, before each additional execution, the pivot selection should be one more entry down the list until the last entry has been positioned. That is, as the preceding routine is repeated, the initial position of the pivot entry should advance from the second entry to the third, then to the fourth, etc., until the routine has positioned the last entry in the list. Following this lead we can control the required repetition with the statements

```
N = 2
while (the value of N does not exceed the length of List):
  Select the Nth entry in List as the pivot entry
    .
    .
    .
  N = N + 1
```

where N represents the position to use for the pivot entry, **the length of List** refers to the number of entries in the list, and the dots indicate the location where the previous routine should be placed.

Our complete pseudocode program is shown in Figure 5.11. In short, the program sorts a list by repeatedly removing an entry and inserting it into its proper place. It is because of this repeated insertion process that the underlying algorithm is called the **insertion sort.**

Note that the structure of Figure 5.11 is that of a loop within a loop, the outer loop being expressed by the first while statement and the inner loop represented by the second while statement. Each execution of the body of the outer loop results in the inner loop being initialized and executed until its termination condition is obtained. Thus, a single execution of the outer loop's body will result in several executions of the inner loop's body.

The initialization component of the outer loop's control consists of establishing the initial value of N with the statement

```
N = 2
```

Figure 5.11   The insertion sort algorithm expressed in pseudocode

```
def Sort (List):
  N = 2
  while (the value of N does not exceed the length of List):
    Select the Nth entry in List as the pivot entry.
    Move the pivot entry to a temporary location leaving
      a hole in List.
    while (there is a name above the hole and that name
        is greater than the pivot):
      Move the name above the hole down into the hole
        leaving a hole above the name.
    Move the pivot entry into the hole in List.
    N = N + 1
```

The modification component is handled by incrementing the value of N at the end of the loop's body with the statement

N = N + 1

The termination condition occurs when the value of N exceeds the length of the list.

    The inner loop's control is initialized by removing the pivot entry from the list and thus creating a hole. The loop's modification step is accomplished by moving entries down into the hole, thus causing the hole to move up. The termination condition consists of the hole being immediately below a name that is not greater than the pivot or of the hole reaching the top of the list.

Questions & Exercises

1. Modify the sequential search function in Figure 5.6 to allow for lists that are not sorted.

2. Convert the pseudocode routine

   ```
   Z = 0
   X = 1
   while (X < 6):
      Z = Z + X
      X = X + 1
   ```

   to an equivalent routine using a **repeat** statement.

3. Some of the popular programming languages today use the syntax

   while (. . .) do (. . .)

   to represent a pretest loop and the syntax

   do (. . .) while (. . .)

   to represent a posttest loop. Although elegant in design, what problems could result from such similarities?

4. Suppose the insertion sort as presented in Figure 5.11 was applied to the list Gene, Cheryl, Alice, and Brenda. Describe the organization of the list at the end of each execution of the body of the outer while structure.

5. Why would we not want to change the phrase "greater than" in the while statement in Figure 5.11 to "greater than or equal to"?

6. A variation of the insertion sort algorithm is the **selection sort.** It begins by selecting the smallest entry in the list and moving it to the front. It then selects the smallest entry from the remaining entries in the list and moves it to the second position in the list. By repeatedly selecting the smallest entry from the remaining portion of the list and moving that entry forward, the sorted version of the list grows from the front of the list, while the back portion of the list consisting of the remaining unsorted entries shrinks. Use our pseudocode to express a function similar to that in Figure 5.11 for sorting a list using the selection sort algorithm.

7. Another well-known sorting algorithm is the **bubble sort.** It is based on the process of repeatedly comparing two adjacent names and interchanging them if they are not in the correct order relative to each other. Let us suppose that the list in question has n entries. The bubble sort would begin by comparing (and possibly interchanging) the entries in positions n and $n - 1$. Then, it would consider the entries in positions $n - 1$ and $n - 2$, and continue moving forward in the list until the first and second entries in the list had been compared (and possibly interchanged). Observe that this pass through the list will pull the smallest entry to the front of the list. Likewise, another such pass will ensure that the next to the smallest entry will be pulled to the second position in the list. Thus, by making a total of $n - 1$ passes through the list, the entire list will be sorted. (If one watches the algorithm at work, one sees the small entries bubble to the top of the list—an observation from which the algorithm gets its name.) Use our pseudocode to express a function similar to that in Figure 5.11 for sorting a list using the bubble sort algorithm.

5.5 Recursive Structures

Recursive structures provide an alternative to the loop paradigm for implementing the repetition of activities. Whereas a loop involves repeating a set of instructions in a manner in which the set is completed and then repeated, recursion involves repeating the set of instructions as a subtask of itself. As an analogy, consider the process of conducting telephone conversations with the call waiting feature. There, an incomplete telephone conversation is set aside while another incoming call is processed. The result is that two conversations take place. However, they are not performed one-after-the-other as in a loop structure, but instead one is performed within the other.

The Binary Search Algorithm

As a way of introducing recursion, let us again tackle the problem of searching to see whether a particular entry is in a sorted list, but this time we get our foot in the door by considering the procedure we follow when searching a dictionary. In this case we do not perform a sequential entry-by-entry or even a page-by-page procedure. Rather, we begin by opening the directory to a page in the area where we believe the target entry is located. If we are lucky, we will find the target value there; otherwise, we must continue searching. But at this point we will have narrowed our search considerably.

Of course, in the case of searching a dictionary, we have prior knowledge of where words are likely to be found. If we are looking for the word *somnambulism*, we would start by opening to the latter portion of the dictionary. In the case of generic lists, however, we do not have this advantage, so let us agree to always start our search with the "middle" entry in the list. Here we write the word *middle* in quotation marks because the list might have an even number of entries and thus no middle entry in the exact sense. In this case, let us agree that the "middle" entry refers to the first entry in the second half of the list.

If the middle entry in the list is the target value, we can declare the search a success. Otherwise, we can at least restrict the search process to the first or last half of the list depending on whether the target value is less than or greater than the entry we have considered. (Remember that the list is sorted.)

To search the remaining portion of the list, we could apply the sequential search, but instead let us apply the same approach to this portion of the list that we used for the whole list. That is, we select the middle entry in the remaining portion of the list as the next entry to consider. As before, if that entry is the target value, we are finished. Otherwise we can restrict our search to an even smaller portion of the list.

This approach to the searching process is summarized in Figure 5.12, where we consider the task of searching the list on the left of the figure for the entry John. We first consider the middle entry Harry. Since our target belongs after this entry, the search continues by considering the lower half of the original list. The middle of this sublist is found to be Larry. Since our target should precede Larry, we turn our attention to the first half of the current sublist. When we interrogate the middle of that secondary sublist, we find our target John and declare the search a success. In short, our strategy is to successively divide the list in question into smaller segments until the target is found or the search is narrowed to an empty segment.

We need to emphasize this last point. If the target value is not in the original list, our approach to searching the list will proceed by dividing the list into smaller segments until the segment under consideration is empty. At this point our algorithm should recognize that the search is a failure.

Figure 5.13 is a first draft of our thoughts using our pseudocode. It directs us to begin a search by testing to see if the list is empty. If so, we are told to report that the search is a failure. Otherwise, we are told to consider the middle entry in the list. If this entry is not the target value, we are told to search either the front half or the back half of the list. Both of these possibilities require a secondary search. It would be nice to perform these searches by calling on the services of

Figure 5.12 Applying our strategy to search a list for the entry John

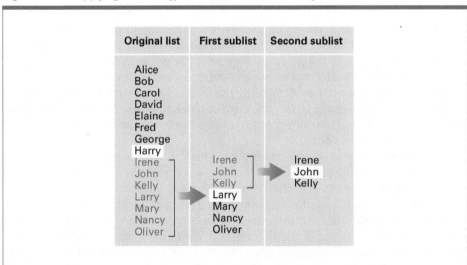

Figure 5.13   A first draft of the binary search technique

```
if (List is empty):
  Report that the search failed.
else:
  TestEntry = the "middle" entry in the List
  if (TargetValue == TestEntry):
    Report that the search succeeded.
  if (TargetValue < TestEntry):
    Search() the portion of List preceding TestEntry for TargetValue,
      and report the result of that search.
  if (TargetValue > TestEntry):
    Search() the portion of List following TestEntry for TargetValue,
      and report the result of that search.
```

an abstract tool. In particular, our approach is to apply a function named Search to carry out these secondary searches. To complete our program, therefore, we must provide such a function.

But this function should perform the same task that is expressed by the pseudocode we have already written. It should first check to see if the list it is given is empty, and if it is not, it should proceed by considering the middle entry of that list. Thus we can supply the function we need merely by identifying the current routine as being the function named Search and inserting references to that function where the secondary searches are required. The result is shown in Figure 5.14.

Note that this function contains a reference to itself. If we were following this function and came to the instruction

```
Search(. . . )
```

we would apply the same function to the smaller list that we were applying to the original one. If that search succeeded, we would return to declare our original search successful; if this secondary search failed, we would declare our original search a failure.

Searching and Sorting

The sequential and binary search algorithms are only two of many algorithms for performing the search process. Likewise, the insertion sort is only one of many sorting algorithms. Other classic algorithms for sorting include the merge sort (discussed in Chapter 12), the selection sort (question 6 in Section 5.4), the bubble sort (question 7 in Section 5.4), the quick sort (which applies a divide-and-conquer approach to the sorting process), and the heap sort (which uses a clever technique for finding the entries that should be moved forward in the list). You will find discussions of these algorithms in the books listed under Additional Reading at the end of this chapter.

Figure 5.14   The binary search algorithm in pseudocode

```
def Search(List, TargetValue):
  if (List is empty):
    Report that the search failed.
  else:
    TestEntry = the "middle" entry in List
    if (TargetValue == TestEntry):
      Report that the search succeeded.
    if (TargetValue < TestEntry):
      Sublist = portion of List preceding
        TestEntry
      Search(Sublist, TargetValue)
    if (TargetValue > TestEntry):
      Sublist = portion of List following
        TestEntry
      Search(Sublist, TargetValue)
```

To see how the function in Figure 5.14 performs its task, let us follow it as it searches the list Alice, Bill, Carol, David, Evelyn, Fred, and George, for the target value Bill. Our search begins by selecting David (the middle entry) as the test entry under consideration. Since the target value (Bill) is less than this test entry, we are instructed to apply the function Search to the list of entries preceding David—that is, the list Alice, Bill, and Carol. In so doing, we create a second copy of the search function and assign it to this secondary task.

We now have two copies of our search function being executed, as summarized in Figure 5.15. Progress in the original copy is temporarily suspended at the instruction

Search(Sublist, TargetValue)

while we apply the second copy to the task of searching the list Alice, Bill, and Carol. When we complete this secondary search, we will discard the second copy of the function, report its findings to the original copy, and continue progress in the original. In this way, the second copy of the function executes as a subordinate to the original, performing the task requested by the original module and then disappearing.

The secondary search selects Bill as its test entry because that is the middle entry in the list Alice, Bill, and Carol. Since this is the same as the target value, it declares its search to be a success and terminates.

At this point, we have completed the secondary search as requested by the original copy of the function, so we are able to continue the execution of that original copy. Here we are told that the result of the secondary search should be reported as the result of the original search. Thus we report that the original search has succeeded. Our process has correctly determined that Bill is a member of the list Alice, Bill, Carol, David, Evelyn, Fred, and George.

Let us now consider what happens if we ask the function in Figure 5.14 to search the list Alice, Carol, Evelyn, Fred, and George for the entry David. This time the original copy of the function selects Evelyn as its test entry and concludes that the target value must reside in the preceding portion of the list. It therefore

Figure 5.15   Recursively Searching

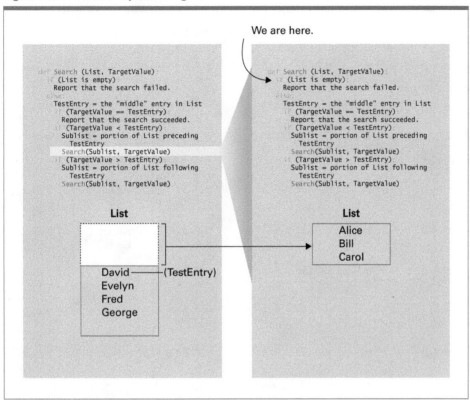

requests another copy of the function to search the list of entries appearing in front of Evelyn—that is, the two-entry list consisting of Alice and Carol. At this stage our situation is as represented in Figure 5.16.

The second copy of the function selects Carol as its current entry and concludes that the target value must lie in the latter portion of its list. It then requests a third copy of the function to search the list of names following Carol in the list Alice and Carol. This sublist is empty, so the third copy of the function has the task of searching the empty list for the target value David. Our situation at this point is represented by Figure 5.17. The original copy of the function is charged with the task of searching the list Alice, Carol, Evelyn, Fred, and George, with the test entry being Evelyn; the second copy is charged with searching the list Alice and Carol, with its test entry being Carol; and the third copy is about to begin searching the empty list.

Of course, the third copy of the function quickly declares its search to be a failure and terminates. The completion of the third copy's task allows the second copy to continue its task. It notes that the search it requested was unsuccessful, declares its own task to be a failure, and terminates. This report is what the original copy of the function has been waiting for, so it can now proceed. Since the search it requested failed, it declares its own search to have failed and terminates. Our routine has correctly concluded that David is not contained in the list Alice, Carol, Evelyn, Fred, and George.

In summary, if we were to look back at the previous examples, we could see that the process employed by the algorithm represented in Figure 5.14 is to

Figure 5.16   Second Recursive Search, First Snapshot

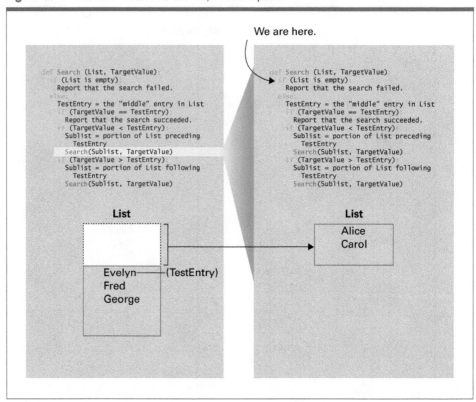

repeatedly divide the list in question into two smaller pieces in such a way that the remaining search can be restricted to only one of these pieces. This divide-by-two approach is the reason why the algorithm is known as the **binary search.**

Recursive Control

The binary search algorithm is similar to the sequential search in that each algorithm requests the execution of a repetitive process. However, the implementation of this repetition is significantly different. Whereas the sequential search involves a circular form of repetition, the binary search executes each stage of the repetition as a subtask of the previous stage. This technique is known as **recursion.**

As we have seen, the illusion created by the execution of a recursive function is the existence of multiple copies of the function, each of which is called an activation of the function. These activations are created dynamically in a telescoping manner and ultimately disappear as the algorithm advances. Of those activations existing at any given time, only one is actively progressing. The others are effectively in limbo, each waiting for another activation to terminate before it can continue.

Being a repetitive process, recursive systems are just as dependent on proper control as are loop structures. Just as in loop control, recursive systems are dependent on testing for a termination condition and on a design that ensures

Figure 5.17 Second Recursive Search, Second Snapshot

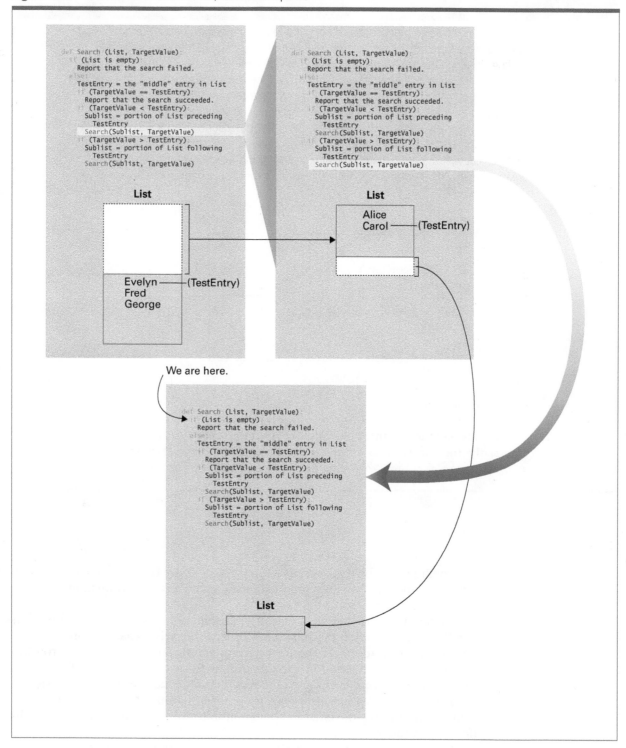

Recursive Structures in Art

The following recursive function can be applied to a rectangular canvas to produce drawings of the style of the Dutch painter Piet Mondrian (1872–1944), who produced paintings in which the rectangular canvas was divided into successively smaller rectangles. Try following the function yourself to produce drawings similar to the one shown. Begin by applying the function to a rectangle representing the canvas on which you are working. (If you are wondering whether the algorithm represented by this function is an algorithm according to the definition in Section 5.1, your suspicions are well-founded. It is, in fact, an example of a nondeterministic algorithm since there are places at which the person or machine following the function is asked to make "creative" decisions. Perhaps this is why Mondrian's results are considered art while ours are not.)

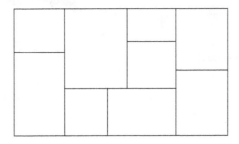

```
def Mondrian (Rectangle):
    if (the size of Rectangle is too large for your artistic taste):
        divide Rectangle into two smaller rectangles.
        apply the function Mondrian to one of the smaller rectangles.
        apply the function Mondrian to the other smaller rectangle.
```

this condition will be reached. In fact, proper recursive control involves the same three ingredients—initialization, modification, and test for termination—that are required in loop control.

In general, a recursive function is designed to test for the termination condition (often called the **base case** or **degenerative case**) before requesting further activations. If the termination condition is not met, the routine creates another activation of the function and assigns it the task of solving a revised problem that is closer to the termination condition than that assigned to the current activation. However, if the termination condition is met, a path is taken that causes the current activation to terminate without creating additional activations.

Let us see how the initialization and modification phases of repetitive control are implemented in our binary search function of Figure 5.14. In this case, the creation of additional activations is terminated once the target value is found or the task is reduced to that of searching an empty list. The process is initialized implicitly by being given an initial list and a target value. From this initial configuration the function modifies its assigned task to that of searching a smaller list. Since the original list is of finite length and each modification step reduces the length of the list in question, we are assured that the target value ultimately is found or the task is reduced to that of searching the empty list. We can therefore conclude that the repetitive process is guaranteed to cease.

Finally, since both loop and recursive control structures are ways to cause the repetition of a set of instructions, we might ask whether they are equivalent in power. That is, if an algorithm were designed using a loop structure, could another algorithm using only recursive techniques be designed that would solve the same problem and vice versa? Such questions are important in computer science because their answers ultimately tell us what features should be provided in a programming language in order to obtain the most powerful programming system possible. We will return to these ideas in Chapter 12 where we consider some of the more theoretical aspects of computer science and its mathematical foundations. With this background, we will then be able to prove the equivalence of iterative and recursive structures in Appendix E.

Questions & Exercises

1. What names are interrogated by the binary search (Figure 5.14) when searching for the name Joe in the list Alice, Brenda, Carol, Duane, Evelyn, Fred, George, Henry, Irene, Joe, Karl, Larry, Mary, Nancy, and Oliver?

2. What is the maximum number of entries that must be interrogated when applying the binary search to a list of 200 entries? What about a list of 100,000 entries?

3. What sequence of numbers would be printed by the following recursive function if we started it with N assigned the value 1?

```
def Exercise (N):
  print(N)
  if (N < 3):
    Exercise(N + 1)
  print(N)
```

4. What is the termination condition in the recursive function of question 3?

5.6 Efficiency and Correctness

In this section we introduce two topics that constitute important research areas within computer science. The first of these is algorithm efficiency, and the second is algorithm correctness.

Algorithm Efficiency

Even though today's machines are capable of executing millions or billions of instructions each second, efficiency remains a major concern in algorithm design. Often the choice between efficient and inefficient algorithms can make the difference between a practical solution to a problem and an impractical one.

Let us consider the problem of a university registrar faced with the task of retrieving and updating student records. Although the university has an actual enrollment of approximately 10,000 students during any one semester, its "current student" file contains the records of more than 30,000 students who are considered current in the sense that they have registered for at least one course in the past few years but have not completed a degree. For now, let us assume that these records are stored in the registrar's computer as a list ordered by student identification numbers. To find any student record, the registrar would therefore search this list for a particular identification number.

We have presented two algorithms for searching such a list: the sequential search and the binary search. Our question now is whether the choice between these two algorithms makes any difference in the case of the registrar. We consider the sequential search first.

Given a student identification number, the sequential search algorithm starts at the beginning of the list and compares the entries found to the identification number desired. Not knowing anything about the source of the target value, we cannot conclude how far into the list this search must go. We can say, though, that after many searches we expect the average depth of the searches to be halfway through the list; some will be shorter, but others will be longer. Thus, we estimate that over a period of time, the sequential search will investigate roughly 15,000 records per search. If retrieving and checking each record for its identification number requires 10 milliseconds (10 one-thousandths of a second), such a search would require an average of 150 seconds or 2.5 minutes—an unbearably long time for the registrar to wait for a student's record to appear on a computer screen. Even if the time required to retrieve and check each record were reduced to only 1 millisecond, the search would still require an average of 15 seconds, which is still a long time to wait.

In contrast, the binary search proceeds by comparing the target value to the middle entry in the list. If this is not the desired entry, then at least the remaining search is restricted to only half of the original list. Thus, after interrogating the middle entry in the list of 30,000 student records, the binary search has at most 15,000 records still to consider. After the second inquiry, at most 7,500 remain, and after the third retrieval, the list in question has dropped to no more than 3,750 entries. Continuing in this fashion, we see that the target record will be found after retrieving at most 15 entries from the list of 30,000 records. Thus, if each of these retrievals can be performed in 10 milliseconds, the process of searching for a particular record requires only 0.15 of a second—meaning that access to any particular student record will appear to be instantaneous from the registrar's point of view. We conclude that the choice between the sequential search algorithm and the binary search algorithm would have a significant impact in this application.

This example indicates the importance of the area of computer science known as algorithm analysis that encompasses the study of the resources, such as time or storage space, that algorithms require. A major application of such studies is the evaluation of the relative merits of alternative algorithms. Algorithm analysis often involves best-case, worst-case, and average-case scenarios. In our example, we performed an average-case analysis of the sequential search algorithm and a worst-case analysis of the binary search algorithm in order to estimate the time required to search through a list of 30,000 entries. In general such analysis is performed in a more generic context. That is, when considering algorithms for searching lists, we do not focus on a list of a particular length, but instead try to identify a formula that would indicate the algorithm's performance for lists of arbitrary lengths. It is not difficult to generalize our previous reasoning to lists of arbitrary lengths. In particular, when applied to a list with n entries, the sequential search algorithm will interrogate an average of $n/2$ entries, whereas the binary search algorithm will interrogate at most $log_2 n$ entries in its worst-case scenario. ($log_2 n$ represents the base two logarithm of n. Unless otherwise stated, computer scientists usually mean base two when talking about logorithms.)

Let us analyze the insertion sort algorithm (summarized in Figure 5.11) in a similar manner. Recall that this algorithm involves selecting a list entry, called the pivot entry, comparing this entry to those preceding it until the proper place for the pivot is found, and then inserting the pivot entry in this place. Since the activity of comparing two entries dominates the algorithm, our approach will be to count the number of such comparisons that are performed when sorting a list whose length is n.

The algorithm begins by selecting the second list entry to be the pivot. It then progresses by picking successive entries as the pivot until it has reached the end of the list. In the best possible case, each pivot is already in its proper place, and thus it needs to be compared to only a single entry before this is discovered. Thus, in the best case, applying the insertion sort to a list with n entries requires $n - 1$ comparisons. (The second entry is compared to one entry, the third entry to one entry, and so on.)

In contrast, the worst-case scenario is that each pivot must be compared to all the preceding entries before its proper location can be found. This occurs if the original list is in reverse order. In this case the first pivot (the second list entry) is compared to one entry, the second pivot (the third list entry) is compared to two entries, and so on (Figure 5.18). Thus the total number of comparisons when sorting a list of n entries is $1 + 2 + 3 + \ldots + (n - 1)$, which is equivalent to $(1/2)(n^2 - n)$. In particular, if the list contained 10 entries, the worst-case scenario of the insertion sort algorithm would require 45 comparisons.

Figure 5.18 Applying the insertion sort in a worst-case situation.

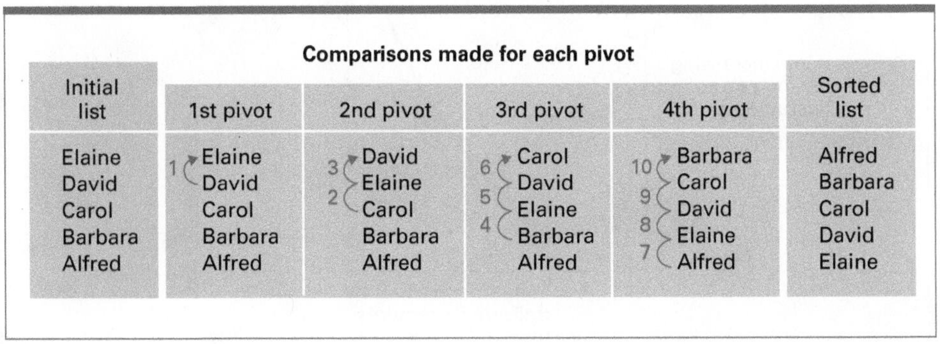

In the average case of the insertion sort, we would expect each pivot to be compared to half of the entries preceding it. This results in half as many comparisons as were performed in the worst case, or a total of $(1/4)(n^2 - n)$ comparisons to sort a list of n entries. If, for example, we use the insertion sort to sort a variety of lists of length 10, we expect the average number of comparisons per sort to be 22.5.

The significance of these results is that the number of comparisons made during the execution of the insertion sort algorithm gives an approximation of the amount of time required to execute the algorithm. Using this approximation, Figure 5.19 shows a graph indicating how the time required to execute the insertion sort algorithm increases as the length of the list increases. This graph is based on our worst-case analysis of the algorithm, where we concluded that sorting a list of length n would require at most $(1/2)(n^2 - n)$ comparisons between list entries. On the graph, we have marked several list lengths and indicated the time required in each case. Notice that as the list lengths increase by uniform increments, the time required to sort the list increases by increasingly greater amounts. Thus the algorithm becomes less efficient as the size of the list increases.

Let us apply a similar analysis to the binary search algorithm. Recall that we concluded that searching a list with n entries using this algorithm would require interrogating at most $log_2 n$ entries, which again gives an approximation to the amount of time required to execute the algorithm for various list sizes. Figure 5.20 shows a graph based on this analysis on which we have again marked several list lengths of uniformly increasing size and identified the time required by the algorithm in each case. Note that the time required by the algorithm increases by decreasing increments. That is, the binary search algorithm becomes more efficient as the size of the list increases.

Figure 5.19 Graph of the worst-case analysis of the insertion sort algorithm

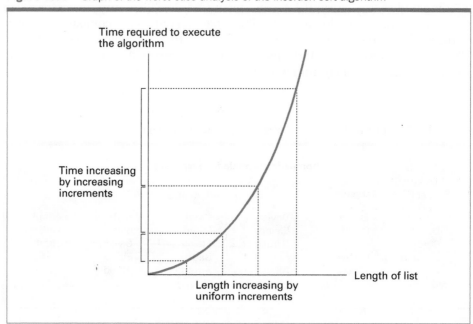

Figure 5.20   Graph of the worst-case analysis of the binary search algorithm

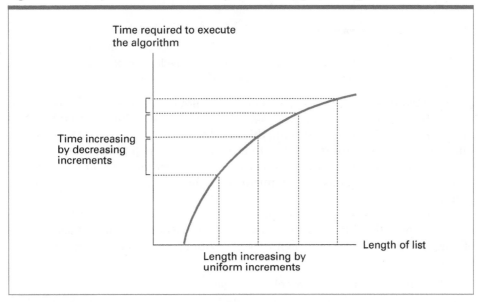

The distinguishing factor between Figures 5.19 and 5.20 is the general shape of the graphs involved. This general shape reveals how well an algorithm should be expected to perform for larger and larger inputs. Moreover, the general shape of a graph is determined by the type of the expression being represented rather than the specifics of the expression—all linear expressions produce a straight line; all quadratic expressions produce a parabolic curve; all logarithmic expressions produce the logarithmic shape shown in Figure 5.20. It is customary to identify a shape with the simplest expression that produces that shape. In particular, we identify the parabolic shape with the expression n^2 and the logarithmic shape with the expression $log_2 n$.

Since the shape of the graph obtained by comparing the time required for an algorithm to perform its task to the size of the input data reflects the efficiency characteristics of the algorithm, it is common to classify algorithms according to the shapes of these graphs—normally based on the algorithm's worst-case analysis. The notation used to identify these classes is sometimes called **big-theta notation.** All algorithms whose graphs have the shape of a parabola, such as the insertion sort, are put in the class represented by $\Theta(n^2)$ (read "big theta of n squared"); all algorithms whose graphs have the shape of a logarithmic expression, such as the binary search, fall in the class represented by $\Theta(log_2 n)$ (read "big theta of $log n$"). Knowing the class in which a particular algorithm falls allows us to predict its performance and to compare it against other algorithms that solve the same problem. Two algorithms in $\Theta(n^2)$ will exhibit similar changes in time requirements as the size of the inputs increases. Moreover, the time requirements of an algorithm in $\Theta(log_2 n)$ will not expand as rapidly as that of an algorithm in $\Theta(n^2)$.

Software Verification

Recall that the fourth phase in Polya's analysis of problem solving (Section 5.3) is to evaluate the solution for accuracy and for its potential as a tool for solving other problems. The significance of the first part of this phase is exemplified by the following example:

> A traveler with a gold chain of seven links must stay in an isolated hotel for seven nights. The rent each night consists of one link from the chain. What is the fewest number of links that must be cut so that the traveler can pay the hotel one link of the chain each morning without paying for lodging in advance?

To solve this problem we first realize that not every link in the chain must be cut. If we cut only the second link, we could free both the first and second links from the other five. Following this insight, we are led to the solution of cutting only the second, fourth, and sixth links in the chain, a process that releases each link while cutting only three (Figure 5.21). Furthermore, any fewer cuts leaves two links connected, so we might conclude that the correct answer to our problem is three.

Upon reconsidering the problem, however, we might make the observation that when only the third link in the chain is cut, we obtain three pieces of chain of lengths one, two, and four (Figure 5.22). With these pieces we can proceed as follows:

> First morning: Give the hotel the single link.
>
> Second morning: Retrieve the single link and give the hotel the two-link piece.
>
> Third morning: Give the hotel the single link.
>
> Fourth morning: Retrieve the three links held by the hotel and give the hotel the four-link piece.
>
> Fifth morning: Give the hotel the single link.
>
> Sixth morning: Retrieve the single link and give the hotel the double-link piece.
>
> Seventh morning: Give the hotel the single link.

Consequently, our first answer, which we thought was correct, is incorrect. How, then, can we be sure that our new solution is correct? We might argue as follows: Since a single link must be given to the hotel on the first morning, at least one link of the chain must be cut, and since our new solution requires only one cut, it must be optimal.

Translated into the programming environment, this example emphasizes the distinction between a program that is believed to be correct and a program that is

Figure 5.21 Separating the chain using only three cuts

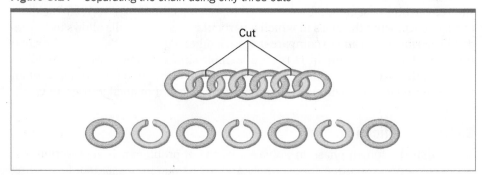

Figure 5.22   Solving the problem with only one cut

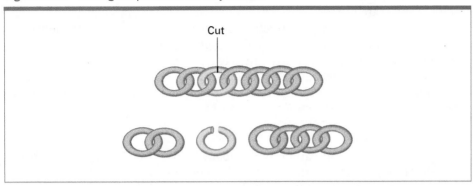

correct. The two are not necessarily the same. The data processing community is rich in horror stories involving software that although "known" to be correct, still failed at a critical moment because of some unforeseen situation. Verification of software is therefore an important undertaking, and the search for efficient verification techniques constitutes an active field of research in computer science.

A major line of research in this area attempts to apply the techniques of formal logic to prove the correctness of a program. That is, the goal is to apply formal logic to prove that the algorithm represented by a program does what it is intended to do. The underlying thesis is that by reducing the verification process to a formal procedure, one is protected from the inaccurate conclusions that might be associated with intuitive arguments, as was the case in the gold chain problem. Let us consider this approach to program verification in more detail.

Just as a formal mathematical proof is based on axioms (geometric proofs are often founded on the axioms of Euclidean geometry, whereas other proofs are based on the axioms of set theory), a formal proof of a program's correctness is based on the specifications under which the program was designed. To prove that a program correctly sorts lists of names, we are allowed to begin with the assumption that the program's input is a list of names, or if the program is designed to compute the average of one or more positive numbers, we assume that the input does, in fact, consist of one or more positive numbers. In short, a

Beyond Verification of Software

Verification problems, as discussed in the text, are not unique to software. Equally important is the problem of confirming that the hardware that executes a program is free of flaws. This involves the verification of circuit designs as well as machine construction. Again, the state of the art relies heavily on testing, which, as in the case of software, means that subtle errors can find their way into finished products. Records indicate that the Mark I, constructed at Harvard University in the 1940s, contained wiring errors that were not detected for many years. In the 1990s, a flaw was discovered in the floating- point portion of the early Pentium microprocessors that caused it to calculate the wrong answer when certain numbers were divided. In both of these cases, the error was detected before serious consequences developed.

proof of correctness begins with the assumption that certain conditions, called **preconditions,** are satisfied at the beginning of the program's execution.

The next step in a proof of correctness is to consider how the consequences of these preconditions propagate through the program. For this purpose, researchers have analyzed various program structures to determine how a statement, known to be true before the structure is executed, is affected by executing the structure. As a simple example, if a certain statement about the value of Y is known to hold prior to executing the instruction

```
X = Y
```

then that same statement can be made about X after the instruction has been executed. More precisely, if the value of Y is not 0 before the instruction is executed, then we can conclude that the value of X will not be 0 after the instruction is executed.

A slightly more involved example occurs in the case of an if-else structure such as

```
if (condition):
    instruction A
else:
    instruction B
```

Here, if some statement is known to hold before execution of the structure, then immediately before executing **instruction A**, we know that both that statement and the condition tested are true, whereas if **instruction B** is to be executed, we know the statement and the negation of the condition tested must hold.

Following rules such as these, a proof of correctness proceeds by identifying statements, called **assertions,** that can be established at various points in the program. The result is a collection of assertions, each being a consequence of the program's preconditions and the sequence of instructions that lead to the point in the program at which the assertion is established. If the assertion so established at the end of the program corresponds to the desired output specifications (which are called **postconditions**), we conclude that the program is correct.

As an example, consider the typical `while` loop structure represented in Figure 5.23. Suppose, as a consequence of the preconditions given at point A, we can establish that a particular assertion is true each time the test for termination is performed (point B) during the repetitive process. (An assertion at a point in a loop that is true every time that point in the loop is reached is known as a **loop invariant.**) Then, if the repetition ever terminates, execution moves to point C, where we can conclude that both the loop invariant and the termination condition hold. (The loop invariant still holds because the test for termination does not alter any values in the program, and the termination condition holds because otherwise the loop does not terminate.) If these combined statements imply the desired postconditions, our proof of correctness can be completed merely by showing that the initialization and modification components of the loop ultimately lead to the termination condition.

You should compare this analysis to our example of the insertion sort shown in Figure 5.11. The outer loop in that program is based on the loop invariant

> Each time the test for termination is performed, the entries in the list from position 1 through position $N - 1$ are sorted

Figure 5.23   The assertions associated with a typical while structure

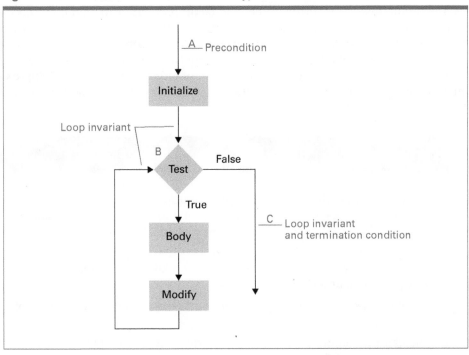

and the termination condition is

The value of N is greater than the length of the list.

Thus, if the loop ever terminates, we know that both conditions must be satisfied, which implies that the entire list would be sorted.

Progress in the development of program verification techniques continues to be challenging. However, advancements are being made. One of the more significant is found in the programming language SPARK, which is closely related to the more popular language Ada. (Ada is one of the languages from which we will draw examples in the next chapter.) In addition to allowing programs to be expressed in a high-level form such as our pseudocode, SPARK gives programmers a means of including assertions such as preconditions, postconditions, and loop invariants within the program. Thus, a program written in SPARK contains not only the algorithm to be applied but also the information required for the application of formal proof-of-correctness techniques. To date, SPARK has been used successfully in numerous software development projects involving critical software applications, including secure software for the U.S. National Security Agency, internal control software used in Lockheed Martin's C130J Hercules aircraft, and critical rail transportation control systems.

In spite of successes such as SPARK, formal program verification techniques have not yet found widespread usage, and thus most of today's software is "verified" by testing—a process that is shaky at best. After all, verification by testing proves nothing more than that the program performs correctly for the cases under which it was tested. Any additional conclusions are merely projections. The errors contained in a program are often consequences of subtle oversights that are easily overlooked during testing as well as development. Consequently errors in a program, just as our error in the gold chain problem, can, and often do, go undetected, even though significant effort may be exerted to avoid it. A dramatic example occurred at AT&T: An error in the software controlling 114 switching stations went undetected from the software's installation in December 1989 until January 15, 1990, at which time a unique set of circumstances caused approximately five million calls to be unnecessarily blocked over a nine-hour period.

Questions & Exercises

1. Suppose we find that a machine programmed with our insertion sort algorithm requires an average of one second to sort a list of 100 names. How long do you estimate it takes to sort a list of 1,000 names? How about 10,000 names?

2. Give an example of an algorithm in each of the following classes: $\Theta(log_2 n)$, $\Theta(n)$, and $\Theta(n^2)$.

3. List the classes $\Theta(n^2)$, $\Theta(log_2 n)$, $\Theta(n)$, and $\Theta(n^3)$ in decreasing order of efficiency.

4. Consider the following problem and a proposed answer. Is the proposed answer correct? Why or why not?

   Problem:—Suppose a box contains three cards. One of three cards is painted black on both sides, one is painted red on both sides, and the third is painted red on one side and black on the other. One of the cards is drawn from the box, and you are allowed to see one side of it. What is the probability that the other side of the card is the same color as the side you see?

   Proposed answer:—One-half. Suppose the side of the card you can see is red. (The argument would be symmetric with this one if the side were black.) Only two cards among the three have a red side. Thus the card you see must be one of these two. One of these two cards is red on the other side, while the other is black. Thus the card you can see is just as likely to be red on the other side as it is to be black.

5. The following program segment is an attempt to compute the quotient (forgetting any remainder) of two positive integers (a dividend and a divisor) by counting the number of times the divisor can be subtracted from the dividend before what is left becomes less than the divisor. For instance, 7/3 should produce 2 because 3 can be subtracted from 7 twice. Is the program correct? Justify your answer.

```
Count = 0
Remainder = Dividend
repeat:
   Remainder = Remainder - Divisor
   Count = Count + 1
   until (Remainder < Divisor)
Quotient = Count.
```

6. The following program segment is designed to compute the product of two nonnegative integers X and Y by accumulating the sum of X copies of Y— that is, 3 times 4 is computed by accumulating the sum of three 4s. Is the program correct? Justify your answer.

```
Product = Y
Count = 1
while (Count < X):
   Product = Product + Y
   Count = Count + 1
```

7. Assuming the precondition that the value associated with N is a positive integer, establish a loop invariant that leads to the conclusion that if the following routine terminates, then Sum is assigned the value $0 + 1 + \ldots + N$.

```
Sum = 0
K = 0
while (K < N):
   K = K + 1
   Sum = Sum + K
```

Provide an argument to the effect that the routine does in fact terminate.

8. Suppose that both a program and the hardware that executes it have been formally verified to be accurate. Does this ensure accuracy?

Chapter Review Problems

(Asterisked problems are associated with optional sections.)

1. Give an example of a set of steps that conforms to the informal definition of an algorithm given in the opening paragraph of Section 5.1 but does not conform to the formal definition given in Figure 5.1.

2. Explain the distinction between an ambiguity in a proposed algorithm and an ambiguity in the representation of an algorithm.

3. Describe how the use of primitives helps remove ambiguities in an algorithm's representation.

4. Select a subject with which you are familiar and design a pseudocode for giving directions in that subject. In particular, describe the primitives you would use and the syntax you would use to represent them. (If you are having trouble thinking of a subject, try sports, arts, or crafts.)

5. Does the following program represent an algorithm in the strict sense? Why or why not?

```
Count = 0
while (Count != 5):
   Count = Count + 2
```

6. In what sense do the following three steps not constitute an algorithm?

Step 1: Draw a straight line segment between the points with rectangular coordinates (2,5) and (6,11).

Step 2: Draw a straight line segment between the points with rectangular coordinates (1,3) and (3,6).

Step 3: Draw a circle whose center is at the intersection of the previous line segments and whose radius is two.

7. Rewrite the following program segment using a **repeat** structure rather than a while structure. Be sure the new version prints the same values as the original.

```
Count = 2
while (Count < 7):
    print(Count)
    Count = Count + 1
```

8. Rewrite the following program segment using a while structure rather than a **repeat** structure. Be sure the new version prints the same values as the original.

```
Count = 1
repeat:
    print(Count)
    Count = Count + 1
until (Count == 5)
```

9. What must be done to translate a posttest loop expressed in the form

```
repeat:
    (. . .)
until (. . .)
```

into an equivalent posttest loop expressed in the form

```
do:
    (. . .)
while (. . .)
```

10. Design an algorithm that, when given an arrangement of the digits 0, 1, 2, 3, 4, 5, 6, 7, 8, 9, rearranges the digits so that the new arrangement represents the next larger value that can be represented by these digits (or reports that no such rearrangement exists if no rearrangement produces a larger value). Thus 5647382901 would produce 5647382910.

11. Design an algorithm for finding all the factors of a positive integer. For example, in the case of the integer 12, your algorithm should report the values 1, 2, 3, 4, 6, and 12.

12. Design an algorithm for determining the day of the week of any date since January 1, 1700. For example, August 17, 2001 was a Friday.

13. What is the difference between a formal programming language and a pseudocode?

14. What is the difference between syntax and semantics?

15. The following is an addition problem in traditional base 10 notation. Each letter represents a different digit. What digit does each letter represent? How did you get your foot in the door?

```
  XYZ
+ YWY
 ZYZW
```

16. The following is a multiplication problem in traditional base 10 notation. Each letter represents a different digit. What digit does each letter represent? How did you get your foot in the door?

```
   XY
 × YX
   XY
  YZ
  WVY
```

17. The following is an addition problem in binary notation. Each letter represents a unique binary digit. Which letter represents 1 and which represents 0? Design an algorithm for solving problems like this.

```
  YXX
+ XYX
 XYYY
```

18. Four prospectors with only one lantern must walk through a mine shaft. At most, two prospectors can travel together and any prospector in the shaft must be with the lantern. The prospectors, named Andrews, Blake, Johnson, and Kelly, can walk through the shaft in one minute, two minutes, four minutes, and eight minutes, respectively. When two walk together they travel at the speed of the slower prospector. How can all four prospectors get through the mine shaft in only 15 minutes? After you have solved this problem, explain how you got your foot in the door.

19. Starting with a large wine glass and a small wine glass, fill the small glass with wine and then pour that wine into the large glass. Next, fill the small glass with water and pour some

of that water into the large glass. Mix the contents of the large glass, and then pour the mixture back into the small glass until the small glass is full. Will there be more water in the large glass than there is wine in the small glass? After you have solved this problem, explain how you got your foot in the door.

20. Two bees, named Romeo and Juliet, live in different hives but have met and fallen in love. On a windless spring morning, they simultaneously leave their respective hives to visit each other. Their routes meet at a point 50 meters from the closest hive, but they fail to see each other and continue on to their destinations. At their destinations, they spend the same amount of time to discover that the other is not home and begin their return trips. On their return trips, they meet at a point that is 20 meters from the closest hive. This time they see each other and have a picnic lunch before returning home. How far apart are the two hives? After you have solved this problem, explain how you got your foot in the door.

21. Design an algorithm that, given two strings of characters, tests whether the first string appears as a substring somewhere in the second.

22. The following algorithm is designed to print the beginning of what is known as the Fibonacci sequence. Identify the body of the loop. Where is the initialization step for the loop control? The modification step? The test step? What list of numbers is produced?

```
Last = 0
Current = 1
while (Current < 100):
   print(Current)
   Temp = Last
   Last = Current
   Current = Last + Temp
```

23. What sequence of numbers is printed by the following algorithm if it is started with input values 0 and 1?

```
def MysteryWrite (Last, Current):
   if (Current < 100):
      print(Current)
      Temp = Current + Last
      MysteryWrite(Current, Temp)
```

24. Modify the function MysteryWrite in the preceding problem so that the values are printed in reverse order.

25. What letters are interrogated by the binary search (Figure 5.14) if it is applied to the list A, B, C, D, E, F, G, H, I, J, K, L, M, N, O when searching for the value J? What about searching for the value Z?

26. After performing many sequential searches on a list of 6,000 entries, what would you expect to be the average number of times that the target value would have been compared to a list entry? What if the search algorithm was the binary search?

27. Identify the termination condition in each of the following iterative statements.

a. while (Count < 5):
   . . .
b. repeat:
   . . .
   until (Count == 1)
c. while ((Count < 5) and (Total < 56)):
   . . .

28. Identify the body of the following loop structure and count the number of times it will be executed. What happens if the test is changed to read "(Count != 6)"?

```
Count = 1
while (Count != 7):
   print(Count)
   Count = Count + 3
```

29. What problems do you expect to arise if the following program is implemented on a computer? (Hint: Remember the problem of round-off errors associated with floating-point arithmetic.)

```
Count = one_tenth
repeat:
   print(Count)
   Count = Count + one_tenth
   until (Count == 1)
```

30. Design a recursive version of the Euclidean algorithm (question 3 of Section 5.2).

31. Suppose we apply both Test1 and Test2 (defined next) to the input value 1. What is the difference in the printed output of the two routines?

```
def Test1 (Count):
  if (Count != 5):
    print(Count)
    Test1(Count + 1)
def Test2(Count):
  if (Count != 5):
    Test2(Count + 1)
    print(Count)
```

32. Identify the important constituents of the control mechanism in the routines of the previous problem. In particular, what condition causes the process to terminate? Where is the state of the process modified toward this termination condition? Where is the state of the control process initialized?

33. Identify the termination condition in the following recursive function.

```
def XXX (N):
  if (N == 5):
    XXX(N + 1)
```

34. Call the function MysteryPrint (defined below) with the value 3 and record the values that are printed.

```
def MysteryPrint (N):
  if (N > 0):
    print(N)
    MysteryPrint(N - 2)
  print(N + 1)
```

35. Call the function MysteryPrint (defined below) with the value 2 and record the values that are printed.

```
def MysteryPrint (N):
  if (N > 0):
    print(N)
    MysteryPrint(N - 2)
  else:
    print(N)
    if (N > -1):
      MysteryPrint(N + 1)
```

36. Design an algorithm to generate the sequence of positive integers (in increasing order) whose only prime divisors are 2 and 3; that is, your program should produce the sequence 2, 3, 4, 6, 8, 9, 12, 16, 18, 24, 27, ... Does your program represent an algorithm in the strict sense?

37. Answer the following questions in terms of the list: Alice, Byron, Carol, Duane, Elaine, Floyd, Gene, Henry, Iris.

a. Which search algorithm (sequential or binary) will find the name Gene more quickly?

b. Which search algorithm (sequential or binary) will find the name Alice more quickly?

c. Which search algorithm (sequential or binary) will detect the absence of the name Bruce more quickly?

d. Which search algorithm (sequential or binary) will detect the absence of the name Sue more quickly?

e. How many entries will be interrogated when searching for the name Elaine when using the sequential search? How many will be interrogated when using the binary search?

38. The factorial of 0 is defined to be 1. The factorial of a positive integer is defined to be the product of that integer times the factorial of the next smaller nonnegative integer. We use the notation n! to express the factorial of the integer n. Thus the factorial of 3 (written 3!) is $3 \times (2!) = 3 \times (2 \times (1!)) = 3 \times (2 \times (1 \times (0!))) = 3 \times (2 \times (1 \times (1))) = 6$. Design a recursive algorithm that computes the factorial of a given value.

39. a. Suppose you must sort a list of five names, and you have already designed an algorithm that sorts a list of four names. Design an algorithm to sort the list of five names by taking advantage of the previously designed algorithm.

b. Design a recursive algorithm to sort arbitrary lists of names based on the technique used in (a).

40. The puzzle called the Towers of Hanoi consists of three pegs, one of which contains several rings stacked in order of descending diameter from bottom to top. The problem is to move the stack of rings to another peg. You are allowed to move only one ring at a time, and at no time is a ring to be placed on top of a smaller one. Observe that if the puzzle involved only one ring, it would be extremely easy. Moreover, when faced with the problem of moving several rings, if you could move all but the largest ring to another peg, the largest ring could then be placed on the third peg, and then the problem would be to move the remaining rings on top of it. Using this observation, develop a recursive algorithm

for solving the Towers of Hanoi puzzle for an arbitrary number of rings.

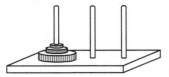

41. Another approach to solving the Towers of Hanoi puzzle (question 40) is to imagine the pegs arranged on a circular stand with a peg mounted at each of the positions of 4, 8, and 12 o'clock. The rings, which begin on one of the pegs, are numbered 1, 2, 3, and so on, starting with the smallest ring being 1. Odd-numbered rings, when on top of a stack, are allowed to move clockwise to the next peg; likewise, even-numbered rings are allowed to move counterclockwise (as long as that move does not place a ring on a smaller one). Under this restriction, always move the largest-numbered ring that can be moved. Based on this observation, develop a nonrecursive algorithm for solving the Towers of Hanoi puzzle.

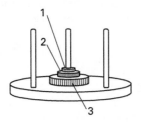

42. Develop two algorithms, one based on a loop structure and the other on a recursive structure, to print the daily salary of a worker who each day is paid twice the previous day's salary (starting with one penny for the first day's work) for a 30-day period. What problems relating to number storage are you likely to encounter if you implement your solutions on an actual machine?

43. Design an algorithm to find the square root of a positive number by starting with the number itself as the first guess and repeatedly producing a new guess from the previous one by averaging the previous guess with the result of dividing the original number by the previous guess. Analyze the control of this repetitive process. In particular, what condition should terminate the repetition?

44. Design an algorithm that lists all possible rearrangements of the symbols in a string of five distinct characters.

45. Design an algorithm that, given a list of names, finds the longest name in the list. Use the for loop structure. Determine what your solution does if there are several "longest" names in the list. In particular, what would your algorithm do if all the names had the same length?

46. Design an algorithm that, given a list of five or more numbers, finds the five smallest and five largest numbers in the list without sorting the entire list.

47. Arrange the names Brenda, Doris, Raymond, Steve, Timothy, and William in an order that requires the least number of comparisons when sorted by the insertion sort algorithm (Figure 5.11).

48. What is the largest number of entries that are interrogated if the binary search algorithm (Figure 5.14) is applied to a list of 4,000 names? How does this compare to the sequential search (Figure 5.6)?

49. Use big-theta notation to classify the traditional grade school algorithms for addition and multiplication. That is, if asked to add two numbers each having n digits, how many individual additions must be performed? If requested to multiply two n-digit numbers, how many individual multiplications are required?

50. Sometimes a slight change in a problem can significantly alter the form of its solution. For example, find a simple algorithm for solving the following problem and classify it using big-theta notation:

> Divide a group of people into two disjoint subgroups (of arbitrary size) such that the difference in the total ages of the members of the two subgroups is as large as possible.

Now change the problem so that the desired difference is as small as possible and classify your approach to the problem.

51. From the following list, extract a collection of numbers whose sum is 3,165. How efficient is your approach to the problem?

26, 39, 104, 195, 403, 504, 793, 995, 1156, 1677

52. Does the loop in the following routine terminate? Explain your answer. Explain what might happen if this routine is actually executed by a computer (refer to Section 1.7).

```
X = 1
Y = 1 / 2
while (X != 0):
   X = X - Y
   Y = Y / 2
```

53. The following program segment is designed to compute the product of two nonnegative integers X and Y by accumulating the sum of X copies of Y; that is, 3 times 4 is computed by accumulating the sum of three 4s. Is the program segment correct? Explain your answer.

```
Product = 0
Count = 0
repeat:
   Product = Product + Y
   Count = Count + 1
   until (Count == X)
```

54. The following program segment is designed to report which of the positive integers X and Y is larger. Is the program segment correct? Explain your answer.

```
Difference = X - Y
if (Difference is positive):
   print('X is bigger than Y')
else:
   print('Y is bigger than X')
```

55. The following program segment is designed to find the largest entry in a nonempty list of integers. Is it correct? Explain your answer.

```
TestValue = first list entry
CurrentEntry = first list entry
while (CurrentEntry is not the
       last entry):
   if (CurrentEntry > TestValue):
      TestValue = CurrentEntry
   CurrentEntry = the next list entry
```

56. a. Identify the preconditions for the sequential search as represented in Figure 5.6. Establish a loop invariant for the while structure in that program that, when combined with the termination condition, implies that upon termination of the loop, the algorithm will report success or failure correctly.

b. Give an argument showing that the while loop in Figure 5.6 does in fact terminate.

57. Based on the preconditions that X and Y are assigned nonnegative integers, identify a loop invariant for the following while structure that, when combined with the termination condition, implies that the value associated with Z upon loop termination must be X – Y.

```
Z = X
J = 0
while (J < Y):
   Z = Z - 1
   J = J + 1
```

Social Issues

The following questions are intended as a guide to the ethical/social/legal issues associated with the field of computing. The goal is not merely to answer these questions. You should also consider why you answered as you did and whether your justifications are consistent from one question to the next.

1. Because it is currently impossible to verify completely the accuracy of complex programs, under what circumstances, if any, should the creator of a program be liable for errors?

2. Suppose you have an idea and develop it into a product that many people can use. Moreover, it has required a year of work and an investment of $50,000 to develop your idea into a form that is useful to the general public. In its

final form, however, the product can be used by most people without buying anything from you. What right do you have for compensation? Is it ethical to pirate computer software? What about music and motion pictures?

3. Suppose a software package is so expensive that it is totally out of your price range. Is it ethical to copy it for your own use? (After all, you are not cheating the supplier out of a sale because you would not have bought the package anyway.)

4. Ownership of rivers, forests, oceans, and so on has long been an issue of debate. In what sense should someone or some institution be given ownership of an algorithm?

5. Some people feel that new algorithms are discovered, whereas others feel that new algorithms are created. To which philosophy do you subscribe? Would the different points of view lead to different conclusions regarding ownership of algorithms and ownership rights?

6. Is it ethical to design an algorithm for performing an illegal act? Does it matter whether the algorithm is ever executed? Should the person who creates such an algorithm have ownership rights to that algorithm? If so, what should those rights be? Should algorithm ownership rights be dependent on the purpose of the algorithm? Is it ethical to advertise and circulate techniques for breaking security? Does it matter what is being broken into?

7. An author is paid for the motion picture rights to a novel even though the story is often altered in the film version. How much of a story has to change before it becomes a different story? What alterations must be made to an algorithm for it to become a different algorithm?

8. Educational software is now being marketed for children in the 18 months or younger age group. Proponents argue that such software provides sights and sounds that would otherwise not be available to many children. Opponents argue that it is a poor substitute for personal parent/child interaction. What is your opinion? Should you take any action based on your opinion without knowing more about the software? If so, what action?

Additional Reading

Aho, A. V., J. E. Hopcroft, and J. D. Ullman. *The Design and Analysis of Computer Algorithms.* Boston, MA: Addison-Wesley, 1974.

Baase, S., and A. Van Gelder. *Computer Algorithms: Introduction to Design and Analysis,* 3rd ed. Boston, MA: Addison-Wesley, 2000.

Barnes, J. *High Integrity Software: The SPARK Approach to Safety and Security.* Boston, MA: Addison-Wesley, 2003.

Gries, D. *The Science of Programming.* New York: Springer-Verlag, 1998.

Harbin, R. *Origami—the Art of Paper Folding.* London: Hodder Paperbacks, 1973.

Johnsonbaugh, R., and M. Schaefer. *Algorithms.* Upper Saddle River, NJ: Prentice-Hall, 2004.

Kleinberg, *Algorithm Design*, 2nd ed. Boston, MA: Addison-Wesley, 2014.

Knuth, D. E. *The Art of Computer Programming, Vol. 3,* 2nd ed. Boston, MA: Addison-Wesley, 1998.

Levitin, A. V. *Introduction to the Design and Analysis of Algorithms,* 3rd ed. Boston, MA: Addison-Wesley, 2011.

Polya, G. *How to Solve It.* Princeton, NJ: Princeton University Press, 1973.

Roberts, E. S. *Thinking Recursively.* New York: Wiley, 1986.

CHAPTER

Data Abstractions

In this chapter we investigate how data arrangements other than the cell-by-cell organization provided by a computer's main memory can be simulated—a subject known as data structures. The goal is to allow the data's user to access collections of data as abstract tools rather than force the user to think in terms of the computer's main memory organization. Our study will show how the desire to construct such abstract tools leads to the concept of objects and object-oriented programming.

We introduced the concept of data structure in Chapter 6, where we learned that high-level programming languages provide techniques by which programmers can express algorithms as though the data being manipulated were stored in ways other than the cell-by-cell arrangement provided by a computer's main memory. We also learned that the data structures supported by a programming language are known as primitive structures. In this chapter we will explore techniques by which data structures other than a language's primitive structures can be constructed and manipulated—a study that will lead us from traditional data structures to the object-oriented paradigm. An underlying theme throughout this progression is the construction of abstract tools.

8.1 Basic Data Structures

We begin our study by introducing some basic data structures that will serve as examples in future sections.

Arrays and Aggregates

In Section 6.2, we learned about the data structures known as arrays and aggregate types. Recall that an **array** is a "rectangular" block of data whose entries are of the same type. The simplest form of array is the one-dimensional array, a single row of elements with each position identified by an index. A one-dimensional array with 26 elements could be used to store the number of times each alphabet letter occurs in a page of text, for example. A two-dimensional array consists of multiple rows and columns in which positions are identified by pairs of indices—the first index identifies the row associated with the position, the second index identifies the column. An example would be a rectangular array of numbers representing the monthly sales made by members of a sales force—the entries across each row representing the monthly sales made by a particular member and the entries down each column representing the sales by each member for a particular month. Thus, the entry in the third row and first column would represent the sales made by the third salesperson in January.

In contrast to an array, recall that an **aggregate type** is a block of data items that might be of different types and sizes. The items within the block are usually called **fields.** An example of an aggregate type would be the block of data relating to a single employee, the fields of which might be the employee's name (an array of type character), age (of type integer), and skill rating (of type float). Fields in an aggregate type are usually accessed by field name, rather than by a numerical index number.

Lists, Stacks, and Queues

Another basic data structure is a **list,** which is a collection whose entries are arranged sequentially (Figure 8.1a). The beginning of a list is called the **head** of the list. The other end of a list is called the **tail.**

Almost any collection of data can be envisioned as a list. For example, text can be envisioned as a list of symbols, a two-dimensional array can be envisioned as a list of rows, and music recorded on a CD can be envisioned as a list of sounds. More traditional examples include guest lists, shopping lists, class enrollment lists, and inventory lists. Activities associated with a list vary depending on the situation.

Figure 8.1   Lists, stacks, and queues

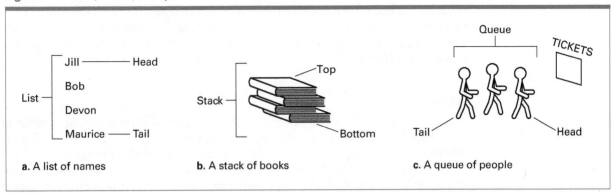

a. A list of names   **b.** A stack of books   **c.** A queue of people

In some cases we may need to remove entries from a list, add new entries to a list, "process" the entries in a list one at a time, change the arrangement of the entries in a list, or perhaps search to see if a particular item is in a list. We will investigate such operations later in this chapter.

By restricting the manner in which the entries of a list are accessed, we obtain two special types of lists known as stacks and queues. A **stack** is a list in which entries are inserted and removed only at the head. An example is a stack of books where physical restrictions dictate that all additions and deletions occur at the top (Figure 8.1b). Following colloquial terminology, the head of a stack is called the **top** of the stack. The tail of a stack is called its **bottom** or **base.** Inserting a new entry at the top of a stack is called **pushing** an entry. Removing an entry from the top of a stack is called **popping** an entry. Note that the last entry placed on a stack will always be the first entry removed—an observation that leads to a stack being known as a **last-in, first-out,** or **LIFO** (pronounced "LIE-foe") structure.

This LIFO characteristic means that a stack is ideal for storing items that must be retrieved in the reverse order from which they were stored, and thus a stack is often used as the underpinning of backtracking activities. (The term **backtracking** refers to the process of backing out of a system in the opposite order from which the system was entered. A classic example is the process of retracing one's steps in order to find one's way out of a forest.) For instance, consider the underlying structure required to support a recursive process. As each new activation is started, the previous activation must be set aside. Moreover, as each activation is completed, the last activation that was set aside must be retrieved. Thus, if the activations are pushed on a stack as they are set aside, then the proper activation will be on the top of the stack each time an activation needs to be retrieved.

A **queue** is a list in which the entries are removed only at the head and new entries are inserted only at the tail. An example is a line, or queue, of people waiting to buy tickets at a theater (Figure 8.1c)—the person at the head of the queue is served while new arrivals step to the rear (or tail) of the queue. We have already met the queue structure in Chapter 3 where we saw that a batch processing operating system stores the jobs waiting to be executed in a queue called the job queue. There we also learned that a queue is a **first-in, first-out,** or **FIFO** (pronounced "FIE-foe") structure, meaning that the entries are removed from a queue in the order in which they were stored.

Queues are often used as the underlying structure of a buffer, introduced in Chapter 1, which is a storage area for the temporary placement of data being transferred from one location to another. As the items of data arrive at the buffer, they are placed at the tail of the queue. Then, when it comes time to forward items to their final destination, they are forwarded in the order in which they appear at the head of the queue. Thus, items are forwarded in the same order in which they arrived.

Trees

A **tree** is a collection whose entries have a hierarchical organization similar to that of an organization chart of a typical company (Figure 8.2). The president is represented at the top, with lines branching down to the vice presidents, who are followed by regional managers, and so on. To this intuitive definition of a tree structure we impose one additional constraint, which (in terms of an organization chart) is that no individual in the company reports to two different superiors. That is, different branches of the organization do not merge at a lower level. (We have already seen examples of trees in Chapter 6 where they appeared in the form of parse trees.)

Each position in a tree is called a **node** (Figure 8.3). The node at the top is called the **root node** (if we turned the drawing upside down, this node would represent the base or root of the tree). The nodes at the other extreme are called **terminal nodes** (or sometimes **leaf nodes**). We often refer to the number of nodes in the longest path from the root to a leaf as the **depth** of the tree. In other words, the depth of a tree is the number of horizontal layers within it.

At times we refer to tree structures as though each node gives birth to those nodes immediately below it. In this sense, we often speak of a node's ancestors or descendants. We refer to its immediate descendants as its **children** and its immediate ancestor as its **parent.** Moreover, we speak of nodes with the same parent as being **siblings.** A tree in which each parent has no more than two children is called a **binary tree.**

If we select any node in a tree, we find that that node together with the nodes below it also have the structure of a tree. We call these smaller structures **subtrees.** Thus, each child node is the root of a subtree below the child's parent. Each such subtree is called a **branch** from the parent. In a binary tree, we often speak of a node's left branch or right branch in reference to the way the tree is displayed.

Figure 8.2   An example of an organization chart

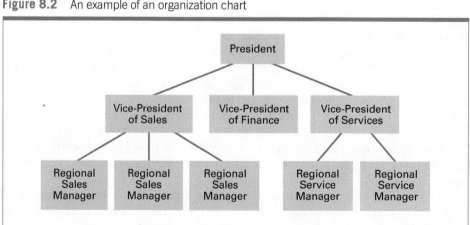

Figure 8.3   Tree terminology

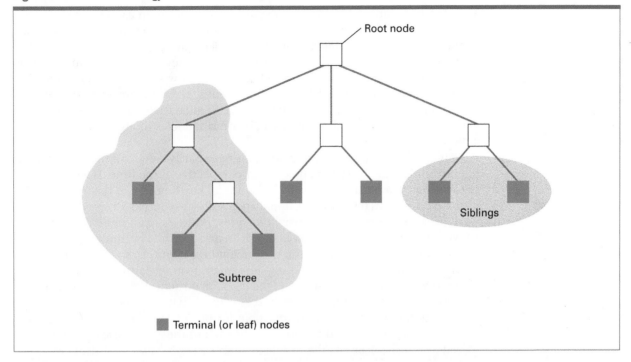

Root node

Subtree

Siblings

Terminal (or leaf) nodes

Questions & Exercises

1. Give examples (outside of computer science) of each of the following structures: list, stack, queue, and tree.

2. Summarize the distinction between lists, stacks, and queues.

3. Suppose the letter A is pushed onto an empty stack, followed by the letters B and C, in that order. Then suppose that a letter is popped off the stack and the letters D and E are pushed on. List the letters that would be on the stack in the order they would appear from top to bottom. If a letter is popped off the stack, which letter will be retrieved?

4. Suppose the letter A is placed in an empty queue, followed by the letters B and C, in that order. Then suppose that a letter is removed from the queue and the letters D and E are inserted. List the letters that would be in the queue in the order they would appear from head to tail. If a letter is now removed from the queue, which letter will it be?

5. Suppose a tree has four nodes A, B, C, and D. If A and C are siblings and D's parent is A, which nodes are leaf nodes? Which node is the root?

8.2 Related Concepts

In this section we isolate three topics that are closely associated with the subject of data structures: abstraction, the distinction between static and dynamic structures, and the concept of a pointer.

Abstraction Again

The structures presented in the previous section are often associated with data. However, a computer's main memory is not organized as arrays, lists, stacks, queues, and trees but is instead organized as a sequence of addressable memory cells. Thus, all other structures must be simulated. How this simulation is accomplished is the subject of this chapter. For now we merely point out that organizations such as arrays, lists, stacks, queues, and trees are abstract tools that are created so that users of the data can be shielded from the details of actual data storage and can be allowed to access information as though it were stored in a more convenient form.

The term *user* in this context does not necessarily refer to a human. Instead, the meaning of the word depends on our perspective at the time. If we are thinking in terms of a person using a PC to maintain bowling league records, then the user is a human. In this case, the application software (perhaps a spreadsheet software package) would be responsible for presenting the data in an abstract form convenient to the human—most likely as an array. If we are thinking in terms of a server on the Internet, then the user might be a client. In this case, the server would be responsible for presenting data in an abstract form convenient to the client. If we are thinking in terms of the modular structure of a program, then the user would be any module requiring access to the data. In this case, the module containing the data would be responsible for presenting the data in an abstract form convenient to the other modules. In each of these scenarios, the common thread is that the user has the privilege of accessing data as an abstract tool.

Static Versus Dynamic Structures

An important distinction in constructing abstract data structures is whether the structure being simulated is static or dynamic, that is, whether the shape or size of the structure changes over time. For example, if the abstract tool is a list of names, it is important to consider whether the list will remain a fixed size throughout its existence or expand and shrink as names are added and deleted.

As a general rule, static structures are more easily managed than dynamic ones. If a structure is static, we need merely to provide a means of accessing the various data items in the structure and perhaps a means of changing the values at designated locations. But, if the structure is dynamic, we must also deal with the problems of adding and deleting entries as well as finding the memory space required by a growing data structure. In the case of a poorly designed structure, adding a single new entry could result in a massive rearrangement of the structure, and excessive growth could dictate that the entire structure be transferred to another memory area where more space is available.

Pointers

Recall that the various cells in a machine's main memory are identified by numeric addresses. Being numeric values, these addresses themselves can be encoded and stored in memory cells. A **pointer** is a storage area that contains such an encoded address. In the case of data structures, pointers are used to record the location where data items are stored. For example, if we must repeatedly move an item of data from one location to another, we might designate a fixed location to serve as a pointer. Then, each time we move the item, we can

Figure 8.4 Novels arranged by title but linked according to authorship

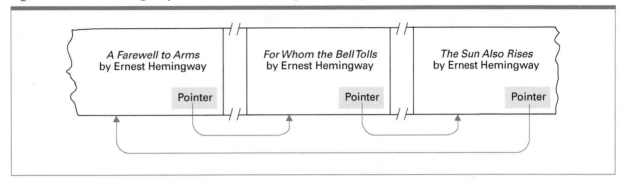

update the pointer to reflect the new address of the data. Later, when we need to access the item of data, we can find it by means of the pointer. Indeed, the pointer will always "point" to the data.

We have already encountered the concept of a pointer in our study of CPUs in Chapter 2. There we found that a register called a program counter is used to hold the address of the next instruction to be executed. Thus, the program counter plays the role of a pointer. In fact, another name for a program counter is **instruction pointer.**

As an example of the application of pointers, suppose we have a list of novels stored in a computer's memory alphabetically by title. Although convenient in many applications, this arrangement makes it difficult to find all the novels by a particular author—they are scattered throughout the list. To solve this problem, we can reserve an additional memory cell within each block of cells representing a novel and use this cell as a pointer to another block representing a book by the same author. In this manner the novels with common authorship can be linked in a loop (Figure 8.4). Once we find one novel by a given author, we can find all the others by following the pointers from one book to another.

Many modern programming languages include pointers as a primitive data type. That is, they allow the declaration, allocation, and manipulation of pointers in ways reminiscent of integers and character strings. Using such a language, a programmer can design elaborate networks of data within a machine's memory where pointers are used to link related items to each other.

Questions & Exercises

1. In what sense are data structures such as arrays, lists, stacks, queues, and trees abstractions?

2. Describe an application that you would expect to involve a static data structure. Then describe an application that you would expect to involve a dynamic data structure.

3. Describe contexts outside of computer science in which the pointer concept occurs.

8.3 Implementing Data Structures

Let us now consider ways in which the data structures discussed in the previous section can be stored in a computer's main memory. As we saw in Chapter 6, these structures are often provided as primitive structures in high-level programming languages. Our goal here is to understand how programs that deal with such structures are translated into machine-language programs that manipulate data stored in main memory.

Storing Arrays

We begin with techniques for storing arrays.

Suppose we want to store a sequence of 24 hourly temperature readings, each of which requires one memory cell of storage space. Moreover, suppose we want to identify these readings by their positions in the sequence. That is, we want to be able to access the first reading or the fifth reading. In short, we want to manipulate the sequence as though it were a one-dimensional array.

We can obtain this goal merely by storing the readings in a sequence of 24 memory cells with consecutive addresses. Then, if the address of the first cell in the sequence is x, the location of any particular temperature reading can be computed by subtracting one from the index of the desired reading and then adding the result to x. In particular, the fourth reading would be located at address $x + (4 - 1)$, as shown in Figure 8.5.

This technique is used by most translators of high-level programming languages to implement one-dimensional arrays. When the translator encounters a declaration statement such as

`int Readings[24];`

declaring that the term `Readings` is to refer to a one-dimensional array of 24 integer values, the translator arranges for 24 consecutive memory cells to be set aside. Later in the program, if it encounters the assignment statement

`Readings[4] = 67;`

requesting that the value 67 be placed in the fourth entry of the array **Readings**, the translator builds the sequence of machine instructions required to place the

Figure 8.5   The array of temperature readings stored in memory starting at address x

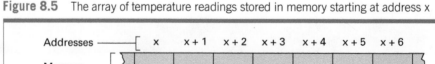
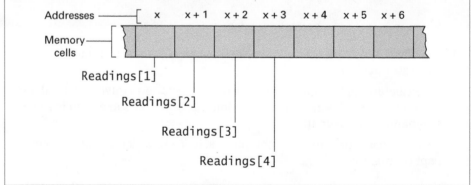

value 67 in the memory cell at address $x + (4 - 1)$, where x is the address of the first cell in the block associated with the array Readings. In this manner, the programmer is allowed to write the program as though the temperature readings were actually stored in a one-dimensional array. (Caution: In the languages Python, C, C++, C#, and Java, array indices start at 0 rather than 1, so the fourth reading would be referenced by Readings[3]. See question 3 at the end of this section.)

Now suppose we want to record the sales made by a company's sales force during a one-week period. In this case, we might envision the data arranged in a two-dimensional array, where the values across each row indicate the sales made by a particular employee, and the values down a column represent all the sales made during a particular day.

To accommodate this need, we first recognize that the array is static in the sense that its size does not vary as updates are made. We can therefore calculate the amount of storage area needed for the entire array and reserve a block of contiguous memory cells of that size. Next, we store the data in the array row by row. Starting at the first cell of the reserved block, we store the values from the first row of the array into consecutive memory locations; following this, we store the next row, then the next, and so on (Figure 8.6). Such a storage system is said to use **row major order** in contrast to **column major order** in which the array is stored column by column.

With the data stored in this manner, let us consider how we could find the value in the third row and fourth column of the array. Envision that we are at the first location in the reserved block of the machine's memory. Starting at this location, we find the data in the first row of the array followed by the second, then the third, and so on. To get to the third row, we must move beyond both the first and second rows. Since each row contains five entries (one for each day of the week from Monday through Friday), we must move beyond a total of 10 entries to reach the first entry of the third row. From there, we must move beyond another three entries to reach the entry in the fourth column of the row. Altogether, to reach the entry in the third row and fourth column, we must move beyond 13 entries from the beginning of the block.

Figure 8.6 A two-dimensional array with four rows and five columns stored in row major order

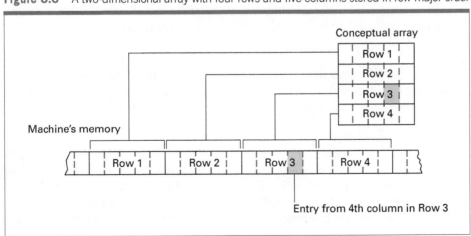

Implementing Contiguous Lists

The primitives for constructing and manipulating arrays that are provided in most high-level programming languages are convenient tools for constructing and manipulating contiguous lists. If the entries of the list are all the same primitive data type, then the list is nothing more than a one-dimensional array. A slightly more involved example is a list of ten names, each of which is no longer than eight characters, as discussed in the text. In this case, a programmer could construct the contiguous list as a two-dimensional array of characters with ten rows and eight columns, which would produce the structure represented in Figure 8.6 (assuming that the array is stored in row major order).

Many high-level languages incorporate features that encourage such implementations of lists. For example, suppose the two-dimensional array of characters proposed above was called MemberList. Then in addition to the traditional notation in which the expression MemberList[3,5] refers to the single character in the third row and fifth column, some languages adopt the expression MemberList[3] to refer to the entire third row, which would be the third entry in the list.

The preceding calculation can be generalized to obtain a formula for converting references in terms of row and column positions into actual memory addresses. In particular, if we let c represent the number of columns in an array (which is the number of entries in each row), then the address of the entry in the ith row and jth column will be

$$x + (c \times (i - 1)) + (j - 1)$$

where x is the address of the cell containing the entry in the first row and first column. That is, we must move beyond $i - 1$ rows, each of which contains c entries, to reach the ith row and then $j - 1$ more entries to reach the jth entry in this row. In our prior example $c = 5$, $i = 3$, and $j = 4$, so if the array were stored starting at address x, then the entry in the third row, fourth column would be at address $x + (5 \times (3 - 1)) + (4 - 1) = x + 13$. The expression $(c \times (i - 1)) + (j - 1)$ is sometimes called the **address polynomial.**

Once again, this is the technique used by most translators of high-level programming languages. When faced with the declaration statement

```
int Sales[8, 5];
```

declaring that the term Sales is to refer to a two-dimensional array of integer values with 8 rows and 5 columns, the translator arranges for 40 consecutive memory cells to be set aside. Later, if it encounters the assignment statement

```
Sales[3, 4] = 5;
```

requesting that the value 5 be placed in the entry at the third row and fourth column of the array Sales, it builds the sequence of machine instructions required to place the value 5 in the memory cell whose address is $x + 5 \times (3 - 1) + (4 - 1)$, where x is the address of the first cell in the block associated with the array Sales. In this manner, the programmer is allowed to write the program as though the sales were actually stored in a two-dimensional array.

Storing Aggregates

Now suppose we want to store an aggregate called **Employee** consisting of the three fields: **Name** of type character array, **Age** of type integer, and **SkillRating** of type float. If the number of memory cells required by each field is fixed, then we can store the aggregate in a block of contiguous cells. For example, suppose the field **Name** required at most 25 cells, **Age** required only one cell, and **SkillRating** required only one cell. Then, we could set aside a block of 27 contiguous cells, store the name in the first 25 cells, store the age in the 26th cell, and store the skill rating in the last cell (Figure 8.7a).

With this arrangement, it would be easy to access the different fields within the aggregate. A reference to a field can be translated to a memory cell by knowing the address where the aggregate begins, and the offset of the desired field within that aggregate. If the address of the first cell were x, then any reference to **Employee.Name** (meaning the **Name** field within the aggregate **Employee**) would translate to the 25 cells starting at address x and a reference to **Employee.Age** (the **Age** field within **Employee**) would translate to the cell at address $x + 25$. In particular, if a translator found a statement such as

Employee.Age = 22;

in a high-level program, then it would merely build the machine language instructions required to place the value 22 in the memory cell whose address is $x + 25$.

Figure 8.7   Storing the aggregate type **Employee**

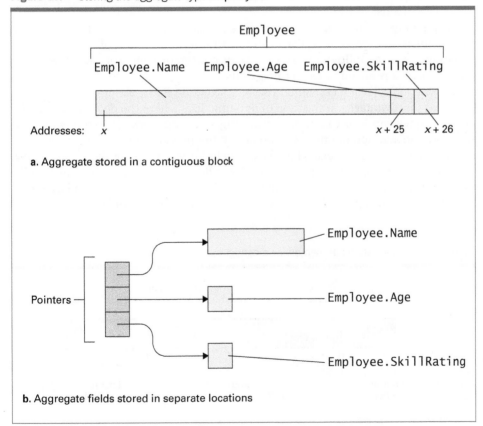

a. Aggregate stored in a contiguous block

b. Aggregate fields stored in separate locations

An alternative to storing an aggregate in a block of contiguous memory cells is to store each field in a separate location and then link them together by means of pointers. More precisely, if the aggregate contains three fields, then we find a place in memory to store three pointers, each of which points to one of the fields (Figure 8.7b). If these pointers are stored in a block starting at address x, then the first field can be found by following the pointer stored at location x, the second field can be found by following the pointer at location $x + 1$, and so forth.

This arrangement is especially useful in those cases in which the size of the aggregate's fields is dynamic. For instance, by using the pointer system the size of the first field can be increased merely by finding an area in memory to hold the larger field and then adjusting the appropriate pointer to point to the new location. But if the aggregate were stored in a contiguous block, the entire structure would have to be altered.

Storing Lists

Let us now consider techniques for storing a list of names in a computer's main memory. One strategy is to store the entire list in a single block of memory cells with consecutive addresses. Assuming that each name is no longer than eight letters, we can divide the large block of cells into a collection of subblocks, each containing eight cells. Into each subblock we can store a name by recording its ASCII code using one cell per letter. If the name alone does not fill all the cells in the subblock allocated to it, we can merely fill the remaining cells with the ASCII code for a space. Using this system requires a block of 80 consecutive memory cells to store a list of 10 names.

The storage system just described is summarized in Figure 8.8. The significant point is that the entire list is stored in one large block of memory, with successive entries following each other in contiguous memory cells. Such an organization is referred to as a **contiguous list.**

A contiguous list is a convenient storage structure for implementing static lists, but it has disadvantages in the case of dynamic lists where the deletion and insertion of names can lead to a time-consuming shuffling of entries. In a worst-case scenario, the addition of entries could create the need to move the entire list to a new location to obtain an available block of cells large enough for the expanded list.

These problems can be simplified if we allow the individual entries in a list to be stored in different areas of memory rather than together in one large, contiguous block. To explain, let us reconsider our example of storing a list of names

Figure 8.8 Names stored in memory as a contiguous list

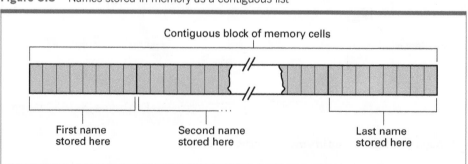

(where each name is no more than eight characters long). This time we store each name in a block of nine contiguous memory cells. The first eight of these cells are used to hold the name itself, and the last cell is used as a pointer to the next name in the list. Following this lead, the list can be scattered among several small nine-cell blocks linked together by pointers. Because of this linkage system, such an organization is called a **linked list.**

To keep track of the beginning of a linked list, we set aside another pointer in which we save the address of the first entry. Since this pointer points to the beginning, or head, of the list, it is called the **head pointer.**

To mark the end of a linked list, we use a **null pointer** (also known as a **NIL pointer** in some languages, or the None object in Python), which is merely a special bit pattern placed in the pointer cell of the last entry to indicate that no further entries are in the list. For example, if we agree never to store a list entry at address 0, the value zero will never appear as a legitimate pointer value and can therefore be used as the null pointer.

The final linked list structure is represented by the diagram in Figure 8.9, in which we depict the scattered blocks of memory used for the list by individual rectangles. Each rectangle is labeled to indicate its composition. Each pointer is represented by an arrow that leads from the pointer itself to the pointer's addressee. Traversing the list involves following the head pointer to find the first entry. From there, we follow the pointers stored with the entries to hop from one entry to the next until the null pointer is reached.

To appreciate the advantages of a linked list over a contiguous one, consider the task of deleting an entry. In a contiguous list this would create a hole, meaning that those entries following the deleted one would have to be moved forward to keep the list contiguous. However, in the case of a linked list, an entry can be deleted by changing a single pointer. This is done by changing the pointer that formerly pointed to the deleted entry so that it points to the entry following the deleted entry (Figure 8.10). From then on, when the list is traversed, the deleted entry is passed by because it no longer is part of the chain.

Inserting a new entry in a linked list is only a little more involved. We first find an unused block of memory cells large enough to hold the new entry and a pointer. Here we store the new entry and fill in the pointer with the address of the entry in the list that should follow the new entry. Finally, we change the pointer associated with the entry that should precede the new entry so that it points to

Figure 8.9   The structure of a linked list

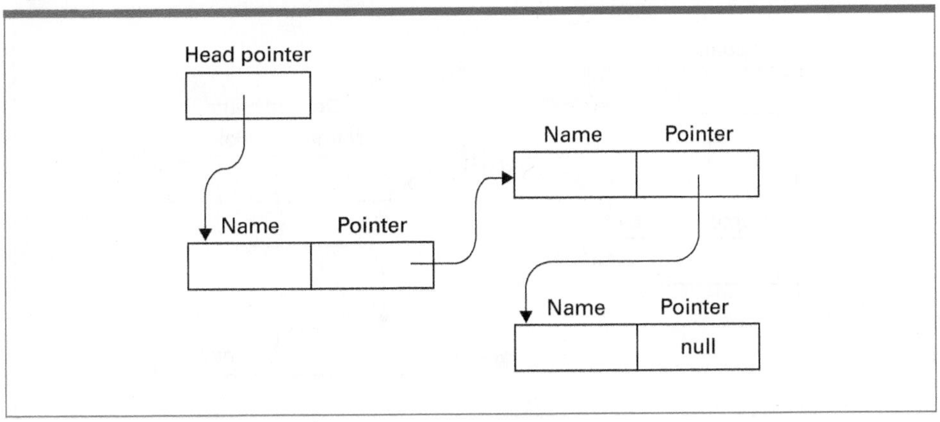

A Problem with Pointers

Just as the use of flowcharts led to tangled algorithm designs (Chapter 5), and the haphazard use of **goto** statements led to poorly designed programs (Chapter 6), undisciplined use of pointers has been found to produce needlessly complex and error-prone data structures. To bring order to this chaos, many programming languages restrict the flexibility of pointers. For example, Java does not allow pointers in their general form. Instead, it allows only a restricted form of pointers called references. One distinction is that a reference cannot be modified by an arithmetic operation. For example, if a Java programmer wanted to advance the reference **Next** to the next entry in a contiguous list, he or she would use a statement equivalent to

```
redirect Next to the next list entry
```

whereas a C programmer would use a statement equivalent to

```
assign Next the value Next + 1
```

Note that the Java statement better reflects the underlying goal. Moreover, to execute the Java statement, there must be another list entry, but if **Next** already pointed to the last entry in the list, the C statement would result in **Next** pointing to something outside the list—a common error for beginning, and even seasoned, C programmers.

the new entry (Figure 8.11). After we make this change, the new entry will be found in the proper place each time the list is traversed.

Storing Stacks and Queues

For storing stacks and queues, an organization similar to a contiguous list is often used. In the case of a stack, a block of memory, large enough to accommodate the stack at its maximum size, is reserved. (Determining the size of this block can often be a critical design decision. If too little room is reserved, the stack will ultimately exceed the allotted storage space; however, if too much room is reserved, memory space will be wasted.) One end of this block is designated as

Figure 8.10 Deleting an entry from a linked list

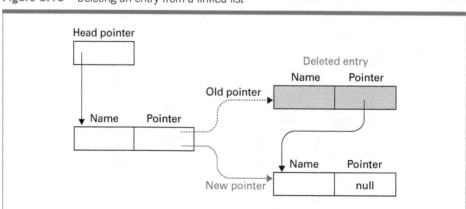

Figure 8.11   Inserting an entry into a linked list

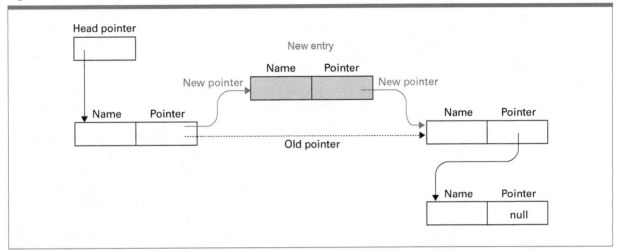

the stack's base. It is here that the first entry to be pushed onto the stack is stored. Then each additional entry is placed next to its predecessor as the stack grows toward the other end of the reserved block.

Observe that as entries are pushed and popped, the location of the top of the stack will move back and forth within the reserved block of memory cells. To keep track of this location, its address is stored in an additional memory cell known as the **stack pointer.** That is, the stack pointer is a pointer to the top of the stack.

The complete system, as illustrated in Figure 8.12, works as follows: To push a new entry on the stack, we first adjust the stack pointer to point to the vacancy just beyond the top of the stack and then place the new entry at this location. To pop an entry from the stack, we read the data pointed to by the stack pointer and then adjust the stack pointer to point to the next entry down on the stack.

The traditional implementation of a queue is similar to that of a stack. Again we reserve a block of contiguous cells in main memory large enough to hold the queue at its projected maximum size. However, in the case of a queue we need to perform operations at both ends of the structure, so we set aside two memory cells to use as pointers instead of only one as we did for a stack. One of these

Figure 8.12   A stack in memory

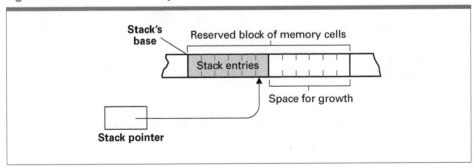

pointers, called the **head pointer,** keeps track of the head of the queue; the other, called the **tail pointer,** keeps track of the tail. When the queue is empty, both of these pointers point to the same location (Figure 8.13). Each time an entry is inserted into the queue, it is placed in the location pointed to by the tail pointer, and then the tail pointer is adjusted to point to the next unused location. In this manner, the tail pointer is always pointing to the first vacancy at the tail of the queue. Removing an entry from the queue involves extracting the entry pointed to by the head pointer and then adjusting the head pointer to point to the next entry in the queue.

A problem with the storage system as described thus far is that, as entries are inserted and removed, the queue crawls through memory like a glacier (see again Figure 8.13). Thus we need a mechanism for confining the queue to its reserved block of memory. The solution is simple. We let the queue migrate through the block. Then, when the tail of the queue reaches the end of the block, we start inserting additional entries back at the original end of the block, which by this time is vacant. Likewise, when the last entry in the block finally becomes the head of the queue and this entry is removed, the head pointer is adjusted back to the beginning of the block where other entries are, by this time, waiting. In this manner, the queue chases itself around within the block as though the ends of the

Figure 8.13   A queue implementation with head and tail pointers. Note how the queue crawls through memory as entries are inserted and removed

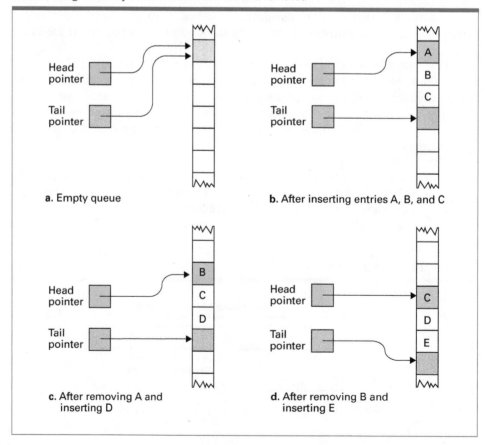

a. Empty queue

b. After inserting entries A, B, and C

c. After removing A and inserting D

d. After removing B and inserting E

Figure 8.14   A circular queue containing the letters P through V

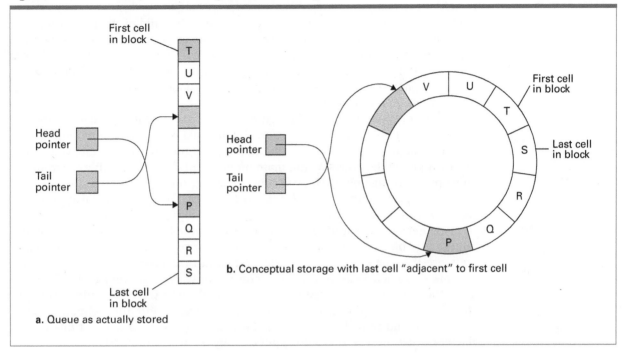

a. Queue as actually stored

b. Conceptual storage with last cell "adjacent" to first cell

block were connected to form a loop (Figure 8.14). The result is an implementation called a **circular queue.**

Storing Binary Trees

For the purpose of discussing tree storage techniques, we restrict our attention to binary trees, which we recall are trees in which each node has at most two children. Such trees normally are stored in memory using a linked structure similar to that of linked lists. However, rather than each entry consisting of two components (the data followed by a next-entry pointer), each entry (or node) of the binary tree contains three components: (1) the data, (2) a pointer to the node's first child, and (3) a pointer to the node's second child. Although there is no left or right inside a machine, it is helpful to refer to the first pointer as the **left child pointer** and the other pointer as the **right child pointer** in reference to the way we would draw the tree on paper. Thus each node of the tree is represented by a short, contiguous block of memory cells with the format shown in Figure 8.15.

Figure 8.15   The structure of a node in a binary tree

Cells containing the data	Left child pointer	Right child pointer

Storing the tree in memory involves finding available blocks of memory cells to hold the nodes and linking these nodes according to the desired tree structure. Each pointer must be set to point to the left or right child of the pertinent node or assigned the null value if there are no more nodes in that direction of the tree. (This means that a terminal node is characterized by having both of its pointers assigned null.) Finally, we set aside a special memory location, called a **root pointer,** where we store the address of the root node. It is this root pointer that provides initial access to the tree.

An example of this linked storage system is presented in Figure 8.16, where a conceptual binary tree structure is exhibited along with a representation of how that tree might actually appear in a computer's memory. Note that the actual arrangement of the nodes within main memory might be quite different from the conceptual arrangement. However, by following the root pointer, one can find the root node and then trace any path down the tree by following the appropriate pointers from node to node.

An alternative to storing a binary tree as a linked structure is to use a single, contiguous block of memory cells for the entire tree. Using this approach, we store the tree's root node in the first cell of the block. (For simplicity, we assume that each node of the tree requires only one memory cell.) Then we store the left child of the root in the second cell, store the right child of the root in the third cell, and in general, continue to store the left and right children of the node found in cell n in the cells $2n$ and $2n + 1$, respectively. Cells within the block that represent locations not used by the tree are marked with a unique bit pattern that indicates the absence of data. Using this technique, the same tree shown in Figure 8.16 would be stored as shown in Figure 8.17. Note that the system is essentially that of storing the nodes across successively lower

Figure 8.16 The conceptual and actual organization of a binary tree using a linked storage system

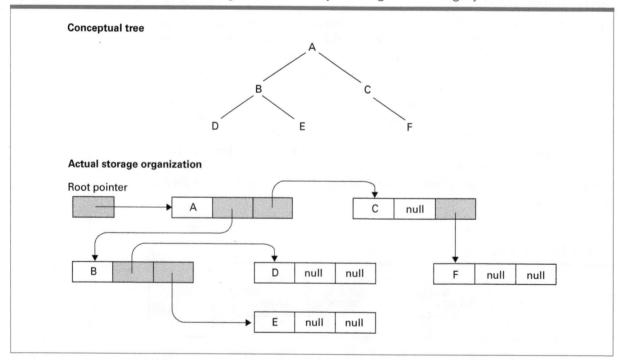

Figure 8.17   A tree stored without pointers

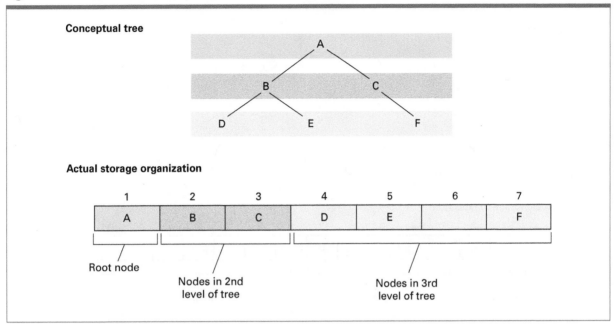

levels of the tree as segments, one after the other. That is, the first entry in the block is the root node, followed by the root's children, followed by the root's grandchildren, and so on.

In contrast to the linked structure described earlier, this alternative storage system provides an efficient method for finding the parent or sibling of any node. The location of a node's parent can be found by dividing the node's position in the block by 2 while discarding any remainder (the parent of the node in position 7 would be the node in position 3). The location of a node's sibling can be found by adding 1 to the location of a node in an even-numbered position or subtracting 1 from the location of a node in an odd-numbered position. For example, the sibling of the node in position 4 is the node in position 5, while the sibling of the node in position 3 is the node in position 2. Moreover, this storage system makes efficient use of space when the binary tree is approximately balanced (in the sense that both subtrees below the root node have the same depth) and full (in the sense that it does not have long, thin branches). For trees without these characteristics, though, the system can become quite inefficient, as shown in Figure 8.18.

Manipulating Data Structures

We have seen that the way data structures are actually stored in a computer's memory is not the same as the conceptual structure envisioned by the user. A two-dimensional array is not actually stored as a two-dimensional rectangular block, and a list or a tree might actually consist of small pieces scattered over a large area of memory.

Hence, to allow the user to access the structure as an abstract tool, we must shield the user from the complexities of the actual storage system. This means that instructions given by the user (and stated in terms of the abstract tool) must be converted into steps that are appropriate for the actual storage system. In the

Figure 8.18   A sparse, unbalanced tree shown in its conceptual form and as it would be stored without pointers

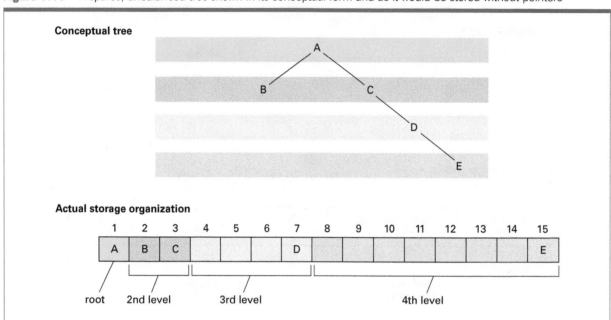

case of arrays, we have seen how this can be done by using an address polynomial to convert row and column indices into memory cell addresses. In particular, we have seen how the statement

```
Sales[3, 4] = 5;
```

written by a programmer who is thinking in terms of an abstract array can be converted into steps that perform the correct modifications to main memory. Likewise, we have seen how statements such as

```
Employee.Age = 22;
```

referring to an abstract aggregate type can be translated into appropriate actions depending on how the aggregate is actually stored.

In the case of lists, stacks, queues, and trees, instructions stated in terms of the abstract structure are usually converted into the appropriate actions by means of functions that perform the required task while shielding the user from the details of the underlying storage system. For example, if the function insert were provided for inserting new entries into a linked list, then J. W. Brown could be inserted in the list of students enrolled in Physics 208 merely by executing a function call such as

```
insert("Brown, J.W.", Physics208)
```

Note that the function call is stated entirely in terms of the abstract structure—the manner in which the list is actually implemented is hidden.

As a more detailed example, Figure 8.19 presents a function named printList for printing a linked list of values. This function assumes that the first entry of the list is pointed to by a field called **Head** within the aggregate called **List**, and that each entry in the list consists of two pieces: a value ("**Value**") and a pointer

Figure 8.19   A function for printing a linked list

```
def PrintList(List):
  CurrentPointer = List.Head
  while (CurrentPointer != None):
    print(CurrentPointer.Value)
    CurrentPointer = CurrentPointer.Next
```

to the next entry ("**Next**"). In the figure, the special Python value None is used as the null pointer. Once this function has been developed, it can be used to print a linked list as an abstract tool without being concerned for the steps actually required to print the list. For example, to obtain a printed class list for Economics 301, a user need only perform the function call

printList(Economics301ClassList)

to obtain the desired results. Moreover, if we should later decide to change the manner in which the list is actually stored, then only the internal actions of the function printList must be changed—the user would continue to request the printing of the list with the same function call as before.

Questions & Exercises

1. Show how the array below would be arranged in main memory when stored in row major order.

5	3	7
4	2	8
1	9	6

2. Give a formula for finding the entry in the ith row and jth column of a two-dimensional array if it is stored in column major order rather than row major order.

3. In the Python, C, C++, Java, and C# programming languages, indices of arrays start at 0 rather than at 1. Thus the entry in the first row, fourth column of an array named **Array** is referenced by **Array[0][3]**. In this case, what address polynomial is used by the translator to convert references of the form **Array[i][j]** into memory addresses?

4. What condition indicates that a linked list is empty?

5. Modify the function in Figure 8.19 so that it stops printing once a particular name has been printed.

6. Based on the technique of this section for implementing a stack in a contiguous block of cells, what condition indicates that the stack is empty?

7. Describe how a stack can be implemented in a high-level language in terms of a one-dimensional array.

8. When a queue is implemented in a circular fashion as described in this section, what is the relationship between the head and tail pointers when the queue is empty? What about when the queue is full? How can one detect whether a queue is full or empty?

9. Draw a diagram representing how the tree below appears in memory when stored using the left and right child pointers, as described in this section. Then, draw another diagram showing how the tree would appear in contiguous storage using the alternative storage system described in this section.

8.4 A Short Case Study

Let us consider the task of storing a list of names in alphabetical order. We assume that the operations to be performed on this list are the following:

> *search* for the presence of an entry,
>
> *print* the list in alphabetical order, and
>
> *insert* a new entry

Our goal is to develop a storage system along with a collection of functions to perform these operations—thus producing a complete abstract tool.

We begin by considering options for storing the list. If the list were stored according to the linked list model, we would need to search the list in a sequential fashion, a process that, as we discussed in Chapter 5, could be very inefficient if the list becomes long. We will therefore seek an implementation that allows us to use the binary search algorithm (Section 5.5) for our search procedure. To apply this algorithm, our storage system must allow us to find the middle entry of successively smaller portions of the list. Our solution is to store the list as a binary tree. We make the middle list entry the root node. Then we make the middle of the remaining first half of the list the root's left child, and we make the middle of the remaining second half the root's right child. The middle entries of each remaining fourth of the list become the children of the root's children and so forth. For example, the tree in Figure 8.20 represents the list of letters A, B, C, D, E, F, G, H, I, J, K, L, and M. (We consider the larger of the middle two entries as the middle when the part of the list in question contains an even number of entries.)

Figure 8.20 The letters A through M arranged in an ordered tree

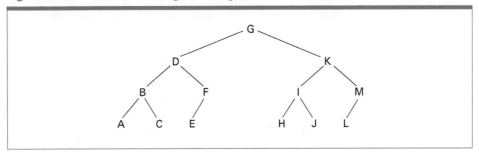

To search the list stored in this manner, we compare the target value to the root node. If the two are equal, our search has succeeded. If they are not equal, we move to the left or right child of the root, depending on whether the target is less than or greater than the root, respectively. There we find the middle of the portion of the list that is necessary to continue the search. This process of comparing and moving to a child continues until we find the target value (meaning that our search was successful) or we reach a null pointer (None) without finding the target value (meaning that our search was a failure).

Figure 8.21 shows how this search process can be expressed in the case of a linked tree structure. The Python elif keyword is a shortcut for "else: if ...". Note that this function is merely a refinement of the function in Figure 5.14, which is our original statement of the binary search. The distinction is largely cosmetic. Instead of stating the algorithm in terms of searching successively smaller segments of the list, we now state the algorithm in terms of searching successively smaller subtrees (Figure 8.22).

Having stored our "list" as a binary tree, you might think that the process of printing the list in alphabetical order would now be difficult. However, to print the list in alphabetical order, we merely need to print the left subtree in alphabetical order, print the root node, and then print the right subtree in alphabetical

Figure 8.21 The binary search as it would appear if the list were implemented as a linked binary tree

```
def Search(Tree, TargetValue):
  if (Tree is None):
    return None            # Search failed
  elif (TargetValue == Tree.Value):
    return Tree            # Search succeeded
  elif (TargetValue < Tree.Value):
    # Continue search in left subtree.
    return Search(Tree.Left, TargetValue)
  elif (TargetValue > Tree.Value):
    # Continue search in right subtree.
    return Search(Tree.Right, TargetValue)
```

Garbage Collection

As dynamic data structures grow and shrink, storage space is used and released. The process of reclaiming unused storage space for future use is known as **garbage collection.** Garbage collection is required in numerous settings. The memory manager within an operating system must perform garbage collection as it allocates and retrieves memory space. The file manager performs garbage collection as files are stored in and deleted from the machine's mass storage. Moreover, any process running under the control of the dispatcher might need to perform garbage collection within its own allotted memory space.

Garbage collection involves some subtle problems. In the case of linked structures, each time a pointer to a data item is changed, the garbage collector must decide whether to reclaim the storage space to which the pointer originally pointed. The problem becomes especially complex in intertwined data structures involving multiple paths of pointers. Inaccurate garbage collection routines can lead to loss of data or to inefficient use of storage space. For example, if garbage collection fails to reclaim storage space, the available space will slowly dwindle away, a phenomenon known as a **memory leak.**

order (Figure 8.23). After all, the left subtree contains all the elements that are less than the root node, while the right subtree contains all the elements that are greater than the root. A sketch of our logic so far looks like this:

```
if (tree not empty):
  print the left subtree in alphabetical order
  print the root node
  print the right subtree in alphabetical order
```

Figure 8.22   The successively smaller trees considered by the function in Figure 8.21 when searching for the letter J

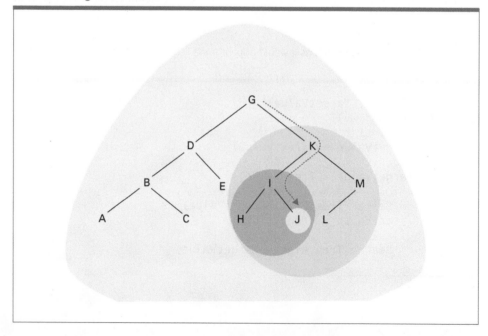

Figure 8.23   Printing a search tree in alphabetical order

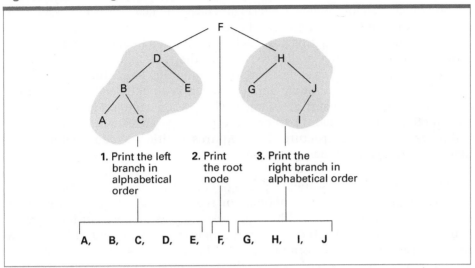

This outline involves the tasks of printing the left subtree and the right subtree in alphabetical order, both of which are essentially smaller versions of our original task. That is, solving the problem of printing a tree involves the smaller task of printing subtrees, which suggests a recursive approach to our tree printing problem.

Following this lead, we can expand our initial idea into a complete Python function for printing our tree as shown in Figure 8.24. We have assigned the function the name PrintTree and then requested the services of PrintTree for printing the left and right subtrees. Note that the termination condition of the recursive process (reaching a null subtree, "**None**") is guaranteed to be reached, because each successive activation of the function operates on a smaller tree than the one causing the activation.

The task of inserting a new entry in the tree is also easier than it might appear at first. Your intuition might lead you to believe that insertions might require cutting the tree open to allow room for new entries, but actually the node being added can always be attached as a new leaf, regardless of the value involved. To find the proper place for a new entry, we move down the tree along the path that we would follow if we were searching for that entry. Since the entry is not in

Figure 8.24   A function for printing the data in a binary tree

```
def PrintTree(Tree):
    if (Tree != None):
        PrintTree(Tree.Left)
        print(Tree.Value)
        PrintTree(Tree.Right)
```

the tree, our search will lead to a null pointer. At this point we will have found the proper location for the new node (Figure 8.25). Indeed, this is the location to which a search for the new entry would lead.

A function expressing this process in the case of a linked tree structure is shown in Figure 8.26. It searches the tree for the value being inserted (called NewValue) and then places a new leaf node containing NewValue at the proper location. Note that if the entry being inserted is actually found in the tree during the search, no insertion is made. The Python code in Figure 8.26 uses the function call TreeNode() to create a new aggregate to serve as a fresh leaf in the linked tree structure. This requires additional code outside of the figure to identify TreeNode as user-defined type, as we will see in the next section.

We conclude that a software package consisting of a linked binary tree structure together with our functions for searching, printing, and inserting provides a complete package that could be used as an abstract tool by our hypothetical application. Indeed, when properly implemented, this package could be used without concern for the actual underlying storage structure. By using the procedures in the package, the user could envision a list of names stored in alphabetical order, whereas the reality would be that the "list" entries are actually scattered among blocks of memory cells that are linked as a binary tree.

Figure 8.25 Inserting the entry M into the list B, E, G, H, J, K, N, P stored as a tree

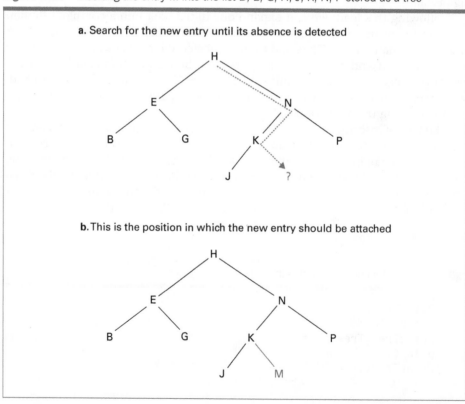

Figure 8.26 A function for inserting a new entry in a list stored as a binary tree

```
def Insert(Tree, NewValue):
  if (Tree is None):
    # Create a new leaf with NewValue
    Tree = TreeNode()
    Tree.Value = NewValue
  elif (NewValue < Tree.Value):
    # Insert NewValue into the left subtree
    Tree.Left = Insert(Tree.Left, NewValue)
  elif (NewValue > Tree.Value):
    # Insert NewValue into the right subtree
    Tree.Right = Insert(Tree.Right, NewValue)
  else:
    # Make no change.
  return Tree
```

Questions & Exercises

1. Draw a binary tree that you could use to store the list R, S, T, U, V, W, X, Y, and Z for future searching.

2. Indicate the path traversed by the binary search algorithm in Figure 8.21 when applied to the tree in Figure 8.20 in searching for the entry J. What about the entry P?

3. Draw a diagram representing the status of activations of the recursive tree-printing algorithm in Figure 8.24 at the time node K is printed within the ordered tree in Figure 8.20.

4. Describe how a tree structure in which each node has as many as 26 children could be used to encode the correct spelling of words in the English language.

8.5 Customized Data Types

In Chapter 6 we introduced the concept of a data type and discussed such elementary types as integer, float, character, and Boolean. These data types are provided in most programming languages as primitive data types. In this section we consider ways in which a programmer can define his or her own data types to fit more closely the needs of a particular application.

User-Defined Data Types

Expressing an algorithm is often easier if data types other than those provided as primitives in the programming language are available. For this reason, many modern programming languages allow programmers to define additional data types, using the primitive types as building blocks. The most elementary examples of such "home-made" data types are known as **user-defined data types,** which are essentially conglomerates of primitive types collected under a single name.

To explain, suppose we wanted to develop a program involving numerous variables, each with the same aggregate structure consisting of a name, age, and skill rating. One approach would be to define each variable separately as an aggregate type (Section 6.2). A better approach, however, would be to define the aggregate to be a new (user-defined) data type and then to use that new type as though it were a primitive.

Recalling the example from Section 6.2, in C the statement

```
struct
{
  char  Name[25];
  int   Age;
  float SkillRating;
} Employee;
```

defines a new aggregate, called **Employee**, containing fields called **Name** (of type character), **Age** (of type integer), and **SkillRating** (of type float).

In contrast, the C statement

```
struct EmployeeType
{
  char  Name[25];
  int   Age;
  float SkillRating;
};
```

does not define a new aggregate variable, but defines a new aggregate type, **EmployeeType**. This new data type could then be used to declare variables in the same way as a primitive data type. That is, in the same way that C allows the variable x to be declared as an integer using the statement

```
int x;
```

the variable **Employee1** could be declared to be of the type **Employee** with the statement

```
struct EmployeeType Employee1;
```

Then, later in the program, the variable **Employee1** would refer to an entire block of memory cells containing the name, age, and skill rating of an employee. Individual items within the block could be referenced by expressions such as **Employee1.Name** and **Employee1.Age**. Thus, a statement such as

```
Employee1.Age = 26;
```

might be used to assign the value 26 to the **Age** field within the block known as **Employee1**. Moreover, the statement

```
struct EmployeeType DistManager, SalesRep1, SalesRep2;
```

could be used to declare the three variables **DistManager**, **SalesRep1**, and **SalesRep2** to be of type **EmployeeType** just as a statement of the form

```
float Sleeve, Waist, Neck;
```

is normally used to declare the variables Sleeve, Waist, and Neck to be of the primitive type float.

It is important to distinguish between a user-defined data type and an actual item of that type. The latter is referred to as an **instance** of the type. A user-defined data type is essentially a template that is used in constructing instances of the type. It describes the properties that all instances of that type have but does not itself constitute an occurrence of that type (just as a cookie-cutter is a template from which cookies are made but is not itself a cookie). In the preceding example, the user-defined data type EmployeeType was used to construct three instances of that type, known as DistManager, SalesRep1, and SalesRep2.

Abstract Data Types

User-defined data types such as C's structs and Pascal's records play an important role in many programming languages, helping the software designer to tailor the representation of data to the needs for a particular program. Traditional user-defined data types, however, merely allow programmers to define new storage systems. They do not also provide operations to be performed on data with these structures.

An **abstract data type (ADT)** is a user-defined data type that can include both data (representation) and functions (behavior). Programming languages that support creation of ADTs generally provide two features: (1) syntax for defining the ADT as single unit, and (2) a mechanism for hiding the internal structure of the ADT from other parts of the program that will make use of it. The first feature is an important organizational tool for keeping the data and functions of an ADT together, which simplifies maintenance and debugging. The second feature provides reliability, by preventing other code outside of the ADT from accessing its data without going through the functions that have been provided for that purpose.

To clarify, suppose we wanted to create and use several stacks of integer values within a program. Our approach might be to implement each stack as an array of 20 integer values. The bottom entry in the stack would be placed (pushed) into the first array position, and additional stack entries would be placed (pushed) into successively higher entries in the array (see question 7 in Section 8.3). An additional integer variable would be used as the stack pointer. It would hold the index of the array entry into which the next stack entry should be pushed. Thus each stack would consist of an array containing the stack itself and an integer playing the role of the stack pointer.

To implement this plan, we could first establish a user-defined type called StackType with a C statement of the form

```
struct StackType
{
  int StackEntries[20];
  int StackPointer = 0;
};
```

(Recall that in languages such as C, C++, C#, and Java, indices for the array StackEntries range from 0 to 19, so we have initialized StackPointer to the value 0.) Having made this declaration, we could then declare stacks called StackOne, StackTwo, and StackThree via the statement

```
struct StackType StackOne, StackTwo, StackThree;
```

At this point, each of the variables StackOne, StackTwo, and StackThree would reference a unique block of memory cells used to implement an individual stack. But what if we now want to push the value 25 onto StackOne? We would like to avoid the details of the array structure underlying the stack's implementation and merely use the stack as an abstract tool—perhaps by using a function call similar to

```
push(25, StackOne);
```

But such a statement would not be available unless we also defined an appropriate function named push. Other operations we would like to perform on variables of type StackType would include popping entries off the stack, checking to see if the stack is empty, and checking to see if the stack is full—all of which would require definitions of additional functions. In short, our definition of the data type StackType has not included all the properties we would like to have associated with the type. Moreover, any function in the program can potentially access the StackPointer and StackEntries fields of our StackType variables, bypassing the careful checks we would design into our push and pop functions. A sloppy assignment statement in another part of the program could overwrite a data element stored in the middle of the stack data structure, or even destroy the LIFO behavior that is characteristic of all stacks.

What is needed is a mechanism for defining the operations that are allowed on our StackType, as well as for protecting the internal variables from outside interference. One such mechanism is the Java language's interface syntax. For example, in Java, we could write

```
interface StackType
{
  public int pop(); /* Return the item at top of stack */
  public void push(int item); /* Add a new item to stack */
  public boolean isEmpty(); /* Check if stack is emtpy */
  public boolean isFull(); /* Check if stack is full */

}
```

Alone, this abstract data type does not specify how the stack will be stored, or what algorithms will be used to execute the push, pop, isEmpty, and isFull functions. Those details (which have been *abstracted* away in this interface) will be specified in other Java code elsewhere. However, like our user-defined data type before, programmers are able to declare variables or function parameters to be of type StackType.

We could declare StackOne, StackTwo, and StackThree to be stacks with the statement

```
StackType StackOne, StackTwo, StackThree;
```

Later in the program (these three variables start out as null references and must be instantiated with concrete Java classes before use—but we are not concerned with those details here), we could push entries onto these stacks with statements such as

```
StackOne.push(25);
```

which means to execute the push function associated with **StackOne** using the value 25 as the actual parameter.

As opposed to the more elementary user-defined data types, abstract data types are complete data types, and their appearance in such languages as Ada in the 1980s represented a significant step forward in programming language design. Today, object-oriented languages provide for extended versions of abstract data types called classes, as we will see in the next section.

Questions & Exercises

1. What is the difference between a data type and an instance of that type?
2. What is the difference between a user-defined data type and an abstract data type?
3. Describe an abstract data type for implementing a list.
4. Describe an abstract data type for implementing checking accounts.

8.6 Classes and Objects

As we learned in Chapter 6, the object-oriented paradigm leads to systems composed of units called objects that interact with each other to accomplish tasks. Each object is an entity that responds to messages received from other objects. Objects are described by templates known as classes.

In many respects, these classes are actually descriptions of abstract data types (whose instances are called objects). For example, Figure 8.27 shows how a class known as StackOfIntegers can be defined in the languages Java and C#. (The equivalent class definition in C + + has the same structure but slightly different syntax.) Note that this class provides a body for each of the functions declared in the abstract data type StackType. In addition, this class contains an array of integers called **StackEntries**, and an integer used to identify the top of the stack within the array called **StackPointer**.

Using this class as a template, an object named **StackOne** can be created in a Java or C# program by the statement

StackType StackOne = new StackOfIntegers();

or in a C + + program by the statement

StackOfIntegers StackOne();

Later in the programs, the value 106 can be pushed onto **StackOne** using the statement

StackOne.push(106);

or the top entry from **StackOne** can be retrieved and placed in the variable OldValue using the statement

OldValue = StackOne.pop();

Figure 8.27   A stack of integers implemented in Java and C#

```
class StackOfIntegers implements StackType
{
  private int[] StackEntries = new int[20];
  private int StackPointer = 0;

  public void push(int NewEntry)
  {  if (StackPointer < 20)
       StackEntries[StackPointer++] = NewEntry;
  }

  public int pop()
  {  if (StackPointer > 0) return StackEntries[--StackPointer];
     else return 0;
  }

  public boolean isEmpty()
  {      return (StackPointer == 0);    }

  public boolean isFull()
  {      return (StackPointer >= MAX);    }
}
```

These features are essentially the same as those associated with abstract data types. There are, however, distinctions between classes and abstract data types. The former is an extension of the latter. For instance, as we learned in Section 6.5, object-oriented languages allow classes to inherit properties from other classes and to contain special methods called constructors that customize individual objects when they are created. Moreover, classes can be associated with varying degrees of encapsulation (Section 6.5), allowing the internal properties of their instances to be protected from misguided shortcuts, while exposing other fields to be available externally.

We conclude that the concepts of classes and objects represent another step in the evolution of techniques for representing data abstractions in programs. It is, in fact, the ability to define and use abstractions in a convenient manner that has led to the popularity of the object-oriented programming paradigm.

The Standard Template Library

The data structures discussed in this chapter have become standard programming structures—so standard, in fact, that many programming environments treat them very much like primitives. One example is found in the C++ programming environment, which is enhanced by the Standard Template Library (STL). The STL contains a collection of predefined classes that describe popular data structures. Consequently, by incorporating the STL into a C++ program, the programmer is relieved from the task of describing these structures in detail. Instead, he or she needs merely to declare identifiers to be of these types in the same manner that we declared StackOne to be of type StackOfIntegers in Section 8.6.

1. In what ways are abstract data types and classes similar? In what ways are they different?

2. What is the difference between a class and an object?

3. Describe a class that would be used as a template for constructing objects of type queue-of-integers.

8.7 Pointers in Machine Language

In this chapter we have introduced pointers and have shown how they are used in constructing data structures. In this section we consider how pointers are handled in machine language.

Suppose that we want to write a program in the machine language described in Appendix C to pop an entry off the stack as described in Figure 8.12 and place that entry in a general-purpose register. In other words, we want to load a register with the contents of the memory cell that contains the entry on top of the stack. Our machine language provides two instructions for loading registers: one with op-code 2, the other with op-code 1. Recall that in the case of op-code 2, the operand field contains the data to be loaded, and in the case of op-code 1, the operand field contains the address of the data to be loaded.

We do not know what the contents will be, so we cannot use op-code 2 to obtain our goal. Moreover, we cannot use op-code 1, because we do not know what the address will be. After all, the address of the top of the stack will vary as the program is executed. However, we do know the address of the stack pointer. That is, we know the location of the address of the data we want to load. What we need, then, is a third op-code for loading a register, in which the operand contains the address of a pointer to the data to be loaded.

To accomplish this goal we could extend the language in Appendix C to include an op-code D. An instruction with this op-code could have the form DRXY, which would mean to load register R with the contents of the memory cell whose address is found at address XY (Figure 8.28). Thus if the stack pointer is in the memory cell at address AA, then the instruction D5AA would cause the data at the top of the stack to be loaded into register 5.

This instruction, however, does not complete the pop operation. We must also subtract one from the stack pointer so that it points to the new top of the stack. This means that, following the load instruction, our machine language program would have to load the stack pointer into a register, subtract one from it, and store the result back in memory.

By using one of the registers as the stack pointer instead of a memory cell, we could reduce this movement of the stack pointer back and forth between registers and memory. But this would mean that we must redesign the load instruction so that it expects the pointer to be in a register rather than in main memory. Thus, instead of the earlier approach, we might define an instruction with op-code D to have the form DR0S, which would mean to load register R

Figure 8.28 Our first attempt at expanding the machine language in Appendix C to take advantage of pointers

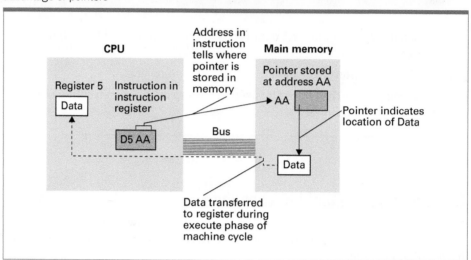

with the contents of the memory cell pointed to by register S (Figure 8.29). Then, a complete pop operation could be performed by following this instruction with an instruction (or instructions) to subtract one from the value stored in register S.

Note that a similar instruction is needed to implement a push operation. We might therefore extend the language described in Appendix C further by introducing the op-code E so that an instruction of the form ER0S would mean to store the contents of register R in the memory cell pointed to by register S. Again, to complete the push operation, this instruction would be followed by an instruction (or instructions) to add one to the value in register S.

Figure 8.29 Loading a register from a memory cell that is located by means of a pointer stored in a register

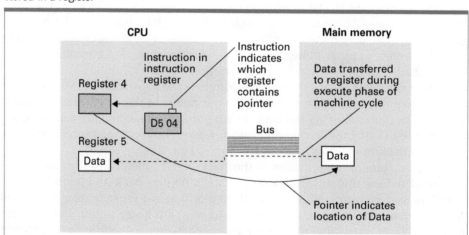

These new op-codes D and E that we have proposed not only demonstrate how machine languages are designed to manipulate pointers, they also demonstrate an addressing technique that was not present in the original machine language. As presented in Appendix C, the machine language uses two means of identifying the data involved in an instruction. The first of these is demonstrated by an instruction whose op-code is 2. Here, the operand field contains the data involved explicitly. This is called **immediate addressing.** The second means of identifying data is demonstrated by instructions with op-codes 1 and 3. Here the operand fields contain the address of the data involved. This is called **direct addressing.** However, our proposed new op-codes D and E demonstrate yet another form of identifying data. The operand fields of these instructions contain the address of the address of the data. This is called **indirect addressing.** All three are common in today's machine languages.

Questions & Exercises

1. Suppose the machine language described in Appendix C has been extended as suggested at the end of this section. Moreover, suppose register 8 contains the pattern DB, the memory cell at address DB contains the pattern CA, and the cell at address CA contains the pattern A5. What bit pattern will be in register 5 immediately after executing each of the following instructions?

   a. 25A5

   b. 15CA

   c. D508

2. Using the extensions described at the end of this section, write a complete machine language routine to perform a pop operation. Assume that the stack is implemented as shown in Figure 8.12, the stack pointer is in register F, and the top of the stack is to be popped into register 5.

3. Using the extensions described at the end of this section, write a program to copy the contents of five contiguous memory cells starting at address A0 to the five cells starting at address B0. Assume your program starts at address 00.

4. In the chapter, we introduced a machine instruction of the form DR0S. Suppose we extended this form to DRXS, meaning "Load register R with the data pointed to by the value in register S plus the value X." Thus the pointer to the data is obtained by retrieving the value in register S and then incrementing that value by X. The value in register S is not altered. (If register F contained 04, then the instruction DE2F would load register E with the contents of the memory cell at address 06. The value of register F would remain 04.) What advantages would this instruction have? What about an instruction of the form DRTS—meaning "Load register R with the data pointed to by the value in register S incremented by the value in register T"?

Chapter Review Problems

(Asterisked problems are associated with optional sections.)

1. Draw pictures showing how the array below appears in a machine's memory when stored in row major order and in column major order:

A	B	C	D
E	F	G	H
I	J	K	L

2. Suppose an array with six rows and eight columns is stored in row major order starting at address 20 (base 10). If each entry in the array requires only one memory cell, what is the address of the entry in the third row and fourth column? What if each entry requires two memory cells?

3. Rework question 2 assuming column major order rather than row major order.

4. What complications are imposed if one tries to implement a dynamic list using a traditional one-dimensional array?

5. Describe a method for storing three-dimensional arrays. What address polynomial would be used to locate the entry in the ith plane, jth row, and the kth column?

6. Suppose the list of letters A, B, C, E, F, and G is stored in a contiguous block of memory cells. What activities are required to insert the letter D in the list, assuming that the list's alphabetical order is to be maintained?

7. The following table represents the contents of some cells in a computer's main memory along with the address of each cell represented. Note that some of the cells contain letters of the alphabet, and each such cell is followed by an empty cell. Place addresses in these empty cells so that each cell containing a letter together with the following cell form an entry in a linked list in which the letters appear in alphabetical order. (Use zero for the null pointer.) What address should the head pointer contain?

Address	Contents
11	C
12	
13	G
14	
15	E
16	
17	B
18	
19	U
20	
21	F
22	

8. The following table represents a portion of a linked list in a computer's main memory. Each entry in the list consists of two cells: The first contains a letter of the alphabet; the second contains a pointer to the next list entry. Alter the pointers so that the letter N is no longer in the list. Then replace the letter N with the letter G and alter the pointers so that the new letter appears in the list in its proper place in alphabetical order.

Address	Contents
30	J
31	38
32	B
33	30
34	X
35	46
36	N
37	40
38	K
39	36
40	P
41	34

9. The following table represents a linked list using the same format as in the preceding problems. If the head pointer contains the value 44, what name is represented by

the list? Change the pointers so that the list contains the name Jean.

Address	Contents
40	N
41	46
42	I
43	40
44	J
45	50
46	E
47	00
48	M
49	42
50	A
51	40

10. Which of the following routines correctly inserts NewEntry immediately after the entry called PreviousEntry in a linked list? What is wrong with the other routine?

Routine 1:

1. Copy the value in the pointer field of PreviousEntry into the pointer field of NewEntry.
2. Change the value in the pointer field of PreviousEntry to the address of NewEntry.

Routine 2:

1. Change the value in the pointer field of PreviousEntry to the address of NewEntry.
2. Copy the value in the pointer field of PreviousEntry into the pointer field of NewEntry.

11. Design a function for concatenating two linked lists (that is, placing one before the other to form a single list).

12. Design a function for combining two sorted contiguous lists into a single sorted contiguous list. What if the lists are linked?

13. Design a function for reversing the order of a linked list.

14. a. Design an algorithm for printing a linked list in reverse order using a stack as an auxiliary storage structure.

b. Design a recursive function to perform this same task without making explicit use of a stack. In what form is a stack still involved in your recursive solution?

15. Sometimes a single linked list is given two different orders by attaching two pointers to each entry rather than one. Fill in the table below so that by following the first pointer after each letter one finds the name Carol, but by following the second pointer after each letter one finds the letters in alphabetical order. What values belong in the head pointer of each of the two lists represented?

Address	Contents
60	O
61	
62	
63	C
64	
65	
66	A
67	
68	
69	L
70	
71	
72	R
73	
74	

16. The table below represents a stack stored in a contiguous block of memory cells, as discussed in the text. If the base of the stack is at address 10 and the stack pointer contains the value 12, what value is retrieved by a pop instruction? What value is in the stack pointer after the pop operation?

Address	Contents
10	F
11	C
12	A
13	B
14	E

17. Draw a table showing the final contents of the memory cells if the instruction in question 16 had been to push the letter D on the stack rather than to pop a letter. What would the value in the stack pointer be after the push instruction?

18. Design a function to remove the bottom entry from a stack so that the rest of the stack is retained. You should access the stack using only push and pop operations. What auxiliary storage structure should be used to solve this problem?

19. Design a function to compare the contents of two stacks.

20. Suppose you were given two stacks. If you were only allowed to move entries one at a time from one stack to another, what rearrangements of the original data would be possible? What arrangements would be possible if you were given three stacks?

21. Suppose you were given three stacks and you were only allowed to move entries one at a time from one stack to another. Design an algorithm for reversing two adjacent entries on one of the stacks.

22. Suppose we want to create a stack of names that vary in length. Why is it advantageous to store the names in separate areas of memory and then build the stack out of pointers to these names rather than allowing the stack to contain the names themselves?

23. Does a queue crawl through memory in the direction of its head or its tail?

24. Suppose you wanted to implement a "queue" in which new entries had priorities associated with them. Thus a new entry should be placed in front of those entries with lower priorities. Describe a storage system for implementing such a "queue" and justify your decisions.

25. Suppose the entries in a queue require one memory cell each, the head pointer contains the value 11, and the tail pointer contains the value 17. What are the values of these pointers after one entry is inserted and two are removed?

26. a. Suppose a queue implemented in a circular fashion is in the state shown in the following diagram. Draw a diagram showing the structure after the letters G and R are

inserted, three letters are removed, and the letters D and P are inserted.

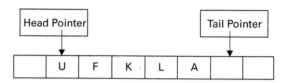

b. What error occurs in part (a) if the letters G, R, D, and P are inserted before any letters are removed?

27. Describe how an array could be used to implement a queue in a program written in a high-level language.

28. Suppose you were given two queues and you were only allowed to move one entry at a time from the head of a queue to the tail of either. Design an algorithm for reversing two adjacent entries in one of the queues.

29. The table below represents a tree stored in a machine's memory. Each node of the tree consists of three cells. The first cell contains the data (a letter), the second contains a pointer to the node's left child, and the third contains a pointer to the node's right child. A value of 0 represents a null pointer. If the value of the root pointer is 55, draw a picture of the tree.

Address	Contents
40	G
41	0
42	0
43	X
44	0
45	0
46	J
47	49
48	0
49	M
50	0
51	0
52	F
53	43
54	40
55	W
56	46
57	52

30. The table below represents the contents of a block of cells in a computer's main memory. Note that some of the cells contain letters of the alphabet, and each of those cells is followed by two blank cells. Fill in the blank cells so that the memory block represents the tree that follows. Use the first cell following a letter as the pointer to that node's left child and the next cell as the pointer to the right child. Use 0 for null pointers. What value should be in the root pointer?

Address	Contents
30	C
31	
32	
33	H
34	
35	
36	K
37	
38	
39	E
40	
41	
42	G
43	
44	
45	P
46	
47	

```
        G
      /   \
     C     K
      \   / \
       E H   P
```

31. Design a nonrecursive algorithm to replace the recursive one represented in Figure 8.21.

32. Design a nonrecursive algorithm to replace the recursive one represented in Figure 8.24. Use a stack to control any backtracking that might be necessary.

33. Apply the recursive tree-printing algorithm of Figure 8.24. Draw a diagram representing the nested activations of the algorithm (and the current position in each) at the time node X is printed.

34. While keeping the root node the same and without changing the physical location of the data elements, change the pointers in the tree of question 29 so the tree-printing algorithm of Figure 8.24 prints the nodes alphabetically.

35. Draw a diagram showing how the binary tree below appears in memory when stored without pointers using a block of contiguous memory cells as described in Section 8.3.

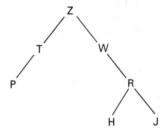

36. Suppose the contiguous cells representing a binary tree as described in Section 8.3 contained the values A, B, C, D, E, F, and F, respectively. Draw a picture of the tree.

37. Give an example in which you might want to implement a list (the conceptual structure) as a tree (the actual underlying structure). Give an example in which you might want to implement a tree (the conceptual structure) as a list (the actual underlying structure).

38. The linked tree structures discussed in the text contained pointers that allowed one to move down the tree from parents to children. Describe a pointer system that would allow movement up the tree from children to parents. What about movement among siblings?

39. Describe a data structure suitable for representing a board configuration during a chess game.

40. Identify the trees below whose nodes would be printed in alphabetical order by the algorithm in Figure 8.24.

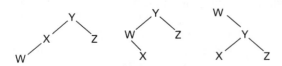

41. Modify the function in Figure 8.24 to print the "list" in reverse order.

42. Describe a tree structure that can be used to store the genealogical history of a family. What operations are performed on the tree? If the tree is implemented as a linked structure, what pointers should be associated with each node? Design procedures to perform the operations you identified above, assuming that the tree is implemented as a linked structure with the pointers you just described. Using your storage system, explain how one could find all the siblings of a person.

43. Design a procedure for finding and deleting a given value from a tree stored in the fashion of Figure 8.20.

44. In the traditional implementation of a tree, each node is constructed with a separate pointer for each possible child. The number of such pointers is a design decision and represents the maximum number of children any node can have. If a node has fewer children than pointers, some of its pointers are simply set to null. But such a node can never have more children than pointers. Describe how a tree could be implemented without limiting the number of children a node could have.

45. Using pseudocode modeled on the C struct statement introduced in Section 8.5, define a user-defined data type representing data regarding an employee of a company (such as name, address, job assignment, pay scale, and so on).

46. Using pseudocode similar to the Java class syntax of Figure 8.27, sketch a definition of an abstract data type representing a list of names. In particular, what structure would contain the list and what functions would be provided to manipulate the list? (You do not need to include detailed descriptions of the functions.)

47. Using pseudocode similar to the Java class syntax of Figure 8.27, sketch a definition of an abstract data type representing a queue. Then give pseudocode statements showing how instances of that type could be created and how entries could be inserted in and deleted from those instances.

48. a. What is the difference between a user-defined data type and a primitive data type?
    b. What is the difference between an abstract data type and a user-defined data type?

49. Identify the data structures and procedures that might appear in an abstract data type representing an address book.

50. Identify the data structures and procedures that might appear in an abstract data type representing a simple spacecraft in a video game.

51. Modify Figure 8.27 and the StackType interface from Section 8.5 so that the class defines a queue rather than a stack.

52. In what way is a class more general than a traditional abstract data type?

*53. Using instructions of the form DR0S and ER0S as described at the end of Section 8.7, write a complete machine language routine to push an entry onto a stack implemented as shown in Figure 8.12. Assume that the stack pointer is in register F and that the entry to be pushed is in register 5.

*54. Suppose each entry in a linked list consists of one memory cell of data followed by a pointer to the next list entry. Moreover, suppose that a new entry located at memory address A0 is to be inserted between the entries at locations B5 and C4. Using the language described in Appendix C and the additional op-codes D and E as described at the end of Section 8.7, write a machine-language routine to perform the insertion.

*55. What advantages does an instruction of the form DR0S as described in Section 8.7 have over an instruction of the form DRXY? What advantage does the form DRXS as described in question 4 of Section 8.7 have over the form DR0S?

Social Issues

The following questions are intended as a guide to the ethical/social/legal issues associated with the field of computing. The goal is not merely to answer these questions. You should also consider why you answered as you did and whether your justifications are consistent from one question to the next.

1. Suppose a software analyst designs a data organization that allows for efficient manipulation of data in a particular application. How can the rights to that data structure be protected? Is a data structure the expression of an idea (like a poem) and therefore protected by copyright or do data structures fall through the same legal loopholes as algorithms? What about patent law?

2. To what extent is incorrect data worse than no data?

3. In many application programs, the size to which a stack can grow is determined by the amount of memory available. If the available space is consumed, then the software is designed to produce a message such as "stack overflow" and terminate. In most cases this error never occurs, and the user is never aware of it. Who is liable if such an error occurs and sensitive information is lost? How could the software developer minimize his or her liability?

4. In a data structure based on a pointer system, the deletion of an item usually consists of changing a pointer rather than erasing memory cells. Thus when an entry in a linked list is deleted, the deleted entry actually remains in memory until its memory space is required by other data. What ethical and security issues result from this persistence of deleted data?

5. It is easy to transfer data and programs from one computer to another. Thus it is easy to transfer the knowledge held by one machine to many machines. In contrast, it sometimes takes a long time for a human to transfer knowledge to another human. For example, it takes time for a human to teach another human a new language. What implications could this contrast in knowledge transfer rate have if the capabilities of machines begin to challenge the capabilities of humans?

6. The use of pointers allows related data to be linked in a computer's memory in a manner reminiscent of the way many believe information is associated in the human mind. How are such links in a computer's memory similar to links in a brain? How are they different? Is it ethical to attempt to build computers that more closely mimic the human mind?

7. Has the popularization of computer technology produced new ethical issues or simply provided a new context in which previous ethical theories are applicable?

8. Suppose the author of an introductory computer science textbook wants to include program examples to demonstrate concepts in the text. However, to obtain clarity, many of the examples must be simplified versions of what would actually be used in professional-quality software. The author knows that the examples could be used by unsuspecting readers and ultimately could find their way into significant software applications in which more robust techniques would be more appropriate. Should the author use the simplified examples, insist that all examples be robust even if doing so decreases their demonstrative value, or refuse to use such examples unless clarity and robustness can both be obtained?

Additional Reading

Carrano, F. M., and T. Henry. *Data Abstraction and Problem Solving with C++: Walls and Mirrors,* 6th ed. Boston, MA: Addison-Wesley, 2012.

Gray, S. *Data Structures in Java: From Abstract Data Types to the Java Collections Framework.* Boston, MA: Addison-Wesley, 2007.

Main, M. *Data Structures and Other Objects Using Java,* 4th ed. Boston, MA: Addison-Wesley, 2011.

Main, M., and W. Savitch. *Data Structures and Other Objects Using C++,* 4th ed. Boston, MA: Addison-Wesley, 2010.

Prichard, J., and F.M. Carrano. *Data Abstraction and Problem Solving with Java: Walls and Mirrors,* 3rd ed. Boston, MA: Addison-Wesley, 2010.

Shaffer, C. A. *Practical Introduction to Data Structures and Algorithm Analysis,* 2nd ed. Upper Saddle River, NJ: Prentice Hall, 2001.

Weiss, M. A. *Data Structures and Problem Solving Using Java,* 4th ed. Boston, MA: Addison-Wesley, 2011.

Weiss, M. A. *Data Structures and Algorithm Analysis in C++,* 4th ed. Boston, MA: Addison-Wesley, 2013.

Weiss, M. A. *Data Structures and Algorithm Analysis in Java,* 3rd ed. Boston, MA: Addison-Wesley, 2011.

Appendixes

appendix

A

ASCII

The following is a partial listing of ASCII code, in which each bit pattern has been extended with a 0 on its left to produce the 8-bit pattern commonly used today. The hexadecimal value of each 8-bit pattern is given in the third column.

Symbol	ASCII	Hex	Symbol	ASCII	Hex	Symbol	ASCII	Hex
line feed	00001010	0A	>	00111110	3E	^	01011110	5E
carriage return	00001011	0B	?	00111111	3F	_	01011111	5F
space	00100000	20	@	01000000	40	`	01100000	60
!	00100001	21	A	01000001	41	a	01100001	61
"	00100010	22	B	01000010	42	b	01100010	62
#	00100011	23	C	01000011	43	c	01100011	63
$	00100100	24	D	01000100	44	d	01100100	64
%	00100101	25	E	01000101	45	e	01100101	65
&	00100110	26	F	01000110	46	f	01100110	66
'	00100111	27	G	01000111	47	g	01100111	67
(	00101000	28	H	01001000	48	h	01101000	68
)	00101001	29	I	01001001	49	i	01101001	69
*	00101010	2A	J	01001010	4A	j	01101010	6A
+	00101011	2B	K	01001011	4B	k	01101011	6B
'	00101100	2C	L	01001100	4C	l	01101100	6C
	00101101	2D	M	01001101	4D	m	01101101	6D
.	00101110	2E	N	01001110	4E	n	01101110	6E
/	00101111	2F	O	01001111	4F	o	01101111	6F
0	00110000	30	P	01010000	50	p	01110000	70
1	00110001	31	Q	01010001	51	q	01110001	71
2	00110010	32	R	01010010	52	r	01110010	72
3	00110011	33	S	01010011	53	s	01110011	73
4	00110100	34	T	01010100	54	t	01110100	74
5	00110101	35	U	01010101	55	u	01110101	75
6	00110110	36	V	01010110	56	v	01110110	76
7	00110111	37	W	01010111	57	w	01110111	77
8	00111000	38	X	01011000	58	x	01111000	78
9	00111001	39	Y	01011001	59	y	01111001	79
:	00111010	3A	Z	01011010	5A	z	01111010	7A
;	00111011	3B	[	01011011	5B	{	01111011	7B
<	00111100	3C	\	01011100	5C	|	01111100	7C
=	00111101	3D	]	01011101	5D	}	01111101	7D

appendix

B

Circuits to Manipulate Two's Complement Representations

This appendix presents circuits for negating and adding values represented in two's complement notation. We begin with the circuit in Figure B.1 that converts a four-bit two's complement representation to the representation for the negative of that value. For example, given the two's complement representation of 3, the circuit produces the representation for −3. It does this by following the same algorithm as presented in the text. That is, it copies the pattern from right to left until a 1 has been copied and then complements each remaining bit as it is moved from the input to the output. Because one input of the rightmost XOR gate is fixed at 0, this gate will merely pass its other input to the output. However, this output is also passed to the left as one of the inputs to the next XOR gate. If this output is 1, the next XOR gate will complement its input bit as it passes to the output. Moreover, this 1 will also be passed to the left through the OR gate to affect the next gate as well. In this manner, the first 1 that is copied to the output will also be passed to the left, where it will cause all the remaining bits to be complemented as they are moved to the output.

Figure B.1   A circuit that negates a two's complement pattern

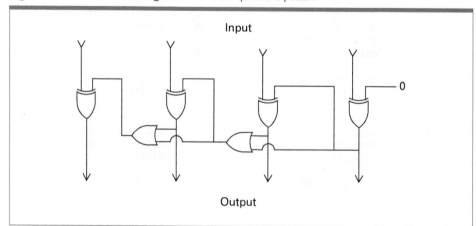

Next, let us consider the process of adding two values represented in two's complement notation. In particular, when solving the problem

```
+ 0110
+ 1011
```

we proceed from right to left in a column-by-column manner, executing the same algorithm for each column. Thus once we obtain a circuit for adding one column of such a problem, we can construct a circuit for adding many columns merely by repeating the single-column circuit.

The algorithm for adding a single column in a multiple-column addition problem is to add the two values in the current column, add that sum to any carry from the previous column, write the least significant bit of this sum in the answer, and transfer any carry to the next column. The circuit in Figure B.2 follows this same algorithm. The upper XOR gate determines the sum of the two input bits. The lower XOR gate adds this sum to the value carried from the previous column. The two AND gates together with the OR gate pass any carry to the left. In particular, a carry of 1 will be produced if the original two input bits in this column were 1 or if the sum of these bits and the carry were both 1.

Figure B.2   A circuit to add a single column in a multiple-column addition problem

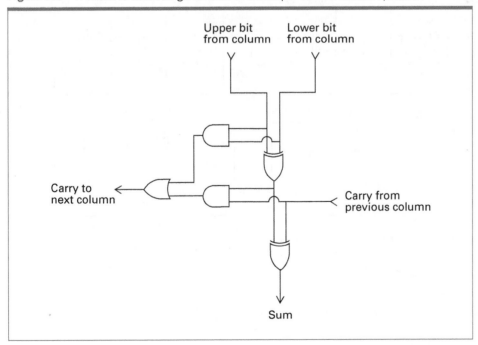

Figure B.3 shows how copies of this single-column circuit can be used to produce a circuit that computes the sum of two values represented in a four-bit two's complement system. Each rectangle represents a copy of the single-column addition circuit. Note that the carry value given to the rightmost rectangle is always 0 because there is no carry from a previous column. In a similar manner, the carry produced from the leftmost rectangle is ignored.

The circuit in Figure B.3 is known as a *ripple adder* because the carry information must propagate, or ripple, from the rightmost to the leftmost column. Although simple in composition, such circuits are slower to perform their functions than more clever versions, such as the lookahead carry adder, which minimize this column-to-column propagation. Thus the circuit in Figure B.3, although sufficient for our purposes, is not the circuit that is used in today's machines.

Figure B.3 A circuit for adding two values in a two's complement notation using four copies of the circuit in Figure B.2

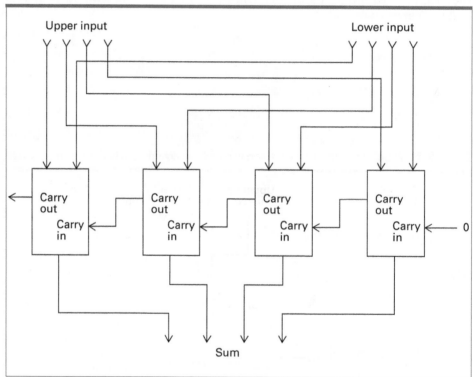

appendix

C

A Simple Machine Language

In this appendix we present a simple but representative machine language. We begin by explaining the architecture of the machine itself.

The Machine's Architecture

The machine has 16 general-purpose registers numbered 0 through F (in hexadecimal). Each register is one byte (eight bits) long. For identifying registers within instructions, each register is assigned the unique four-bit pattern that represents its register number. Thus register 0 is identified by 0000 (hexadecimal 0), and register 4 is identified by 0100 (hexadecimal 4).

There are 256 cells in the machine's main memory. Each cell is assigned a unique address consisting of an integer in the range of 0 to 255. An address can therefore be represented by a pattern of eight bits ranging from 00000000 to 11111111 (or a hexadecimal value in the range of 00 to FF).

Floating-point values are assumed to be stored in an eight-bit format discussed in Section 1.7 and summarized in Figure 1.24.

The Machine's Language

Each machine instruction is two bytes long. The first 4 bits provide the op-code; the last 12 bits make up the operand field. The table that follows lists the instructions in hexadecimal notation together with a short description of each. The letters R, S, and T are used in place of hexadecimal digits in those fields representing a register identifier that varies depending on the particular application of the instruction. The letters X and Y are used in lieu of hexadecimal digits in variable fields not representing a register.

Op-code	Operand	Description
1	RXY	LOAD the register R with the bit pattern found in the memory cell whose address is XY. *Example:* 14A3 would cause the contents of the memory cell located at address A3 to be placed in register 4.
2	RXY	LOAD the register R with the bit pattern XY. *Example:* 20A3 would cause the value A3 to be placed in register 0.

Op-code	Operand	Description
3	RXY	STORE the bit pattern found in register R in the memory cell whose address is XY. *Example:* 35B1 would cause the contents of register 5 to be placed in the memory cell whose address is B1.
4	ORS	MOVE the bit pattern found in register R to register S. *Example:* 40A4 would cause the contents of register A to be copied into register 4.
5	RST	ADD the bit patterns in registers S and T as though they were two's complement representations and leave the result in register R. *Example:* 5726 would cause the binary values in registers 2 and 6 to be added and the sum placed in register 7.
6	RST	ADD the bit patterns in registers S and T as though they represented values in floating-point notation and leave the floating-point result in register R. *Example:* 634E would cause the values in registers 4 and E to be added as floating-point values and the result to be placed in register 3.
7	RST	OR the bit patterns in registers S and T and place the result in register R. *Example:* 7CB4 would cause the result of ORing the contents of registers B and 4 to be placed in register C.
8	RST	AND the bit patterns in registers S and T and place the result in register R. *Example:* 8045 would cause the result of ANDing the contents of registers 4 and 5 to be placed in register 0.
9	RST	EXCLUSIVE OR the bit patterns in registers S and T and place the result in register R. *Example:* 95F3 would cause the result of EXCLUSIVE ORing the contents of registers F and 3 to be placed in register 5.
A	ROX	ROTATE the bit pattern in register R one bit to the right X times. Each time place the bit that started at the low-order end at the high-order end. *Example:* A403 would cause the contents of register 4 to be rotated 3 bits to the right in a circular fashion.
B	RXY	JUMP to the instruction located in the memory cell at address XY if the bit pattern in register R is equal to the bit pattern in register number 0. Otherwise, continue with the normal sequence of execution. (The jump is implemented by copying XY into the program counter during the execute phase.) *Example:* B43C would first compare the contents of register 4 with the contents of register 0. If the two were equal, the pattern 3C would be placed in the program counter so that the next instruction executed would be the one located at that memory address. Otherwise, nothing would be done and program execution would continue in its normal sequence.
C	000	HALT execution. *Example:* C000 would cause program execution to stop.

appendix

D

High-Level Programming Languages

This appendix contains a brief background of each of the languages used as examples in Chapter 6.

Ada

The language Ada, named after Augusta Ada Byron (1815–1851), who was an advocate of Charles Babbage and the daughter of poet Lord Byron, was developed at the initiative of the U.S. Department of Defense in an attempt to obtain a single, general-purpose language for all its software development needs. A major emphasis during Ada's design was to incorporate features for programming real-time computer systems used as a part of larger machines such as missile guidance systems, environmental control systems within buildings, and control systems in automobiles and small home appliances. Ada thus contains features for expressing activities in parallel processing environments as well as convenient techniques for handling special cases (called exceptions) that might arise in the application environment. Although originally designed as an imperative language, newer versions of Ada have embraced the object-oriented paradigm.

The design of the Ada language has consistently emphasized features that lead to the efficient development of reliable software, a characteristic exemplified by the fact that all of the internal control software in the Boeing 777 aircraft was written in Ada. This is also a major reason that Ada was used as a starting point in the development of the language SPARK, as indicated in Chapter 5.

C

The language C was developed by Dennis Ritchie at Bell Laboratories in the early 1970s. Although originally designed as a language for developing system software, C has achieved popularity throughout the programming community and has been standardized by the American National Standards Institute.

C was originally envisioned as merely a step up from machine language. Consequently, its syntax is terse compared with other high-level languages that use complete English words to express some primitives that are represented by special symbols in C. This terseness allows for efficient representations of complex algorithms, which is a major reason for C's popularity. (Often a concise representation is more readable than a lengthy one.)

C++

The language C++ was developed by Bjarne Stroustrup at Bell Laboratories as an enhanced version of the language C. The goal was to produce a language compatible with the object-oriented paradigm. Today, C++ is not only a prominent object-oriented language in its own right but it has served as a starting point for the development of two other leading object-oriented languages: Java and C#.

C#

The language C# was developed by Microsoft to be a tool in the .NET Framework, which is a comprehensive system for developing application software for machines running Microsoft system software. The C# language is very similar to C++ and Java. Indeed, the reason Microsoft introduced C# as a different language was not that it is truly new in the language sense, but that, as a different language, Microsoft could customize specific features of the language without concern for standards that were already associated with other languages or for proprietary rights of other corporations. Thus the novelty of C# is in its role as a prominent language for developing software utilizing the .NET Framework. With Microsoft's backing, C# and the .NET Framework promise to be prominent players in the world of software development for years to come.

FORTRAN

FORTRAN is an acronym for FORmula TRANslator. This language was one of the first high-level languages developed (it was announced in 1957) and one of the first to gain wide acceptance within the computing community. Over the years its official description has undergone numerous extensions, meaning that today's FORTRAN language is much different from the original. Indeed, by studying the evolution of FORTRAN, one would witness the effects of research in programming language design. Although originally designed as an imperative language, newer versions of FORTRAN now encompass many object-oriented features. FORTRAN continues to be a popular language within the scientific community. In particular, many numerical analysis and statistical packages are, and will probably continue to be, written in FORTRAN.

Java

Java is an object-oriented language developed by Sun Microsystems in the early 1990s. Its designers borrowed heavily from C and C++. The excitement over Java is due, not to the language itself, but to the language's universal implementation and the vast number of predesigned templates that are available in the Java programming environment. The universal implementation means that a program written in Java can be executed efficiently over a wide range of machines; and the availability of templates means that complex software can be developed with relative ease. For example, templates such as applet and servlet streamline the development of software for the World Wide Web.

The Equivalence of Iterative and Recursive Structures

In this appendix, we use our Bare Bones language of Chapter 12 as a tool to answer the question posed in Chapter 5 regarding the relative power of iterative and recursive structures. Recall that Bare Bones contains only three assignment statements (clear, incr, and decr) and one control structure (constructed from a while statement). This simple language has the same computing power as a Turing machine; thus, if we accept the Church-Turing thesis, we might conclude that any problem with an algorithmic solution has a solution expressible in Bare Bones.

The first step in the comparison of iterative and recursive structures is to replace the iterative structure of Bare Bones with a recursive structure. We do this by removing the while statement from the language and in its place providing the ability to divide a Bare Bones program into units along with the ability to call one of these units from another location in the program. More precisely, we propose that each program in the modified language consist of a number of syntactically disjoint program units. We suppose that each program must contain exactly one unit called MAIN having the syntactic structure of

```
def MAIN():
    .
    .
    .
```

(where the dots represent other indented Bare Bones statements) and perhaps other units (semantically subordinate to MAIN) that have the structure

```
def unit():
    .
    .
    .
```

(where unit represents the unit's name that has the same syntax as variable names). The semantics of this partitioned structure is that the program always begins execution at the beginning of the unit MAIN and halts when that unit's indented body is completed. Program units other than MAIN can be called as functions by means of the conditional statement

```
if name not 0:
    unit()
```

(where **name** represents any variable name and unit represents any of the program unit names other than MAIN). Moreover, we allow the units other than MAIN to call themselves recursively.

With these added features, we can simulate the while structure found in the original Bare Bones. For example, a Bare Bones program of the form

```
while X not 0:
  S
```

(where **S** represents any sequence of Bare Bones statements) can be replaced by the unit structure

```
def MAIN():
  if X not 0:
    unitA()
def unitA():
  S
  if X not 0:
    unitA()
```

Consequently, we conclude that the modified language has all the capabilities of the original Bare Bones.

It can also be shown that any problem that can be solved using the modified language can be solved using Bare Bones. One method of doing this is to show how any algorithm expressed in the modified language could be written in the original Bare Bones. However, this involves an explicit description of how recursive structures can be simulated with the while structure of Bare Bones.

For our purpose, it is simpler to rely on the Church-Turing thesis as presented in Chapter 12. In particular, the Church-Turing thesis, combined with the fact that Bare Bones has the same power as Turing machines, dictates that no language can be more powerful than our original Bare Bones. Therefore, any problem solvable in our modified language can also be solved using Bare Bones.

We conclude that the power of the modified language is the same as that of the original Bare Bones. The only distinction between the two languages is that one provides an iterative control structure and the other provides recursion. Thus the two control structures are in fact equivalent in terms of computing power.

appendix

F

Answers to Questions & Exercises

Chapter 1

Section 1.1

1. One and only one of the upper two inputs must be 1, and the lowest input must be 1.

2. The 1 on the lower input is negated to 0 by the NOT gate, causing the output of the AND gate to become 0. Thus both inputs to the OR gate are 0 (remember that the upper input to the flip-flop is held at 0) so the output of the OR gate becomes 0. This means that the output of the AND gate will remain 0 after the lower input to the flip-flop returns to 0.

3. The output of the upper OR gate will become 1, causing the upper NOT gate to produce an output of 0. This will cause the lower OR gate to produce a 0, causing the lower NOT gate to produce a 1. This 1 is seen as the output of the flip-flop as well as being fed back to the upper OR gate, where it holds the output of that gate at 1, even after the flip-flop's input has returned to 0.

4. a. The entire circuit is equivalent to a single OR gate.
   b. This entire circuit is also equivalent to a single XOR gate.

5. a. 6AF2   b. E85517   c. 48

6. a. 0101111111101100010111
   b. 0110000100001010
   c. 101010 1111001101
   d. 0000000100000000

Section 1.2

1. In the first case, memory cell number 6 ends up containing the value 5. In the second case, it ends up with the value 8.

2. Step 1 erases the original value in cell number 3 when the new value is written there. Consequently, Step 2 does not place the original value from cell number 3 in cell number 2. The result is that both cells end up with

the value that was originally in cell number 2. A correct procedure is the following:

Step 1. Move the contents of cell number 2 to cell number 1.

Step 2. Move the contents of cell number 3 to cell number 2.

Step 3. Move the contents of cell number 1 to cell number 3.

3. 32768 bits

Section 1.3

1. Faster retrieval of data and higher transfer rates

2. The point to remember here is that the slowness of mechanical motion compared with the speed of the internal functioning of the computer dictates that we minimize the number of times we must move the read/write heads. If we fill a complete surface before starting the next, we must move the read/write head each time we finish with a track. The number of moves therefore is approximately the same as the total number of tracks on the two surfaces. If, however, we alternate between surfaces by electronically switching between the read/write heads, we must move the read/write heads only after each cylinder has been filled.

3. In this application, information must be retrieved from mass storage in a random manner, which would be time consuming in the context of the spiral system used on CDs and DVDs. (Moreover, current technology does not allow individual portions of data to be updated on a CD or DVD.)

4. CD, DVD, and Blu-ray disks are all the same physical size and use the same spiral track layout for placing data on the platter. A player equipped with multiple lasers is able to read all three types of optical disk.

5. Flash drives do not require physical motion so they have shorter response times and do not suffer from physical wear.

6. Magnetic hard disks are faster and have higher capacities than other forms of magnetic media, such as floppy disks and magnetic tape. Speed, capacity, and rewriting ability compare favorably to optical media. Price per units of storage on magnetic disks continues to be lower than solid-state disks, although this advantage has steadily eroded in recent years.

Section 1.4

1. Computer Science

2. The two patterns are the same, except that the sixth bit from the low-order end is always 0 for uppercase and 1 for lowercase.

3. a.
00100010	01010011	01110100	01101111
01110000	00100001	00100010	00100000
01000011	01101000	01100101	01110010
01111001	01101100	00100000	01110011
01101000	01101111	01110101	01110100
01100101	01110100	00101110	

b. 01000100   01101111   01100101   01110011
   00100000   00110010   00100000   00101011
   00100000   00110011   00100000   00111101
   00100000   00110101   00111111

4.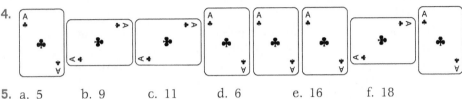

5. a. 5   b. 9   c. 11   d. 6   e. 16   f. 18
6. a. 110   b. 1101   c. 1011   d. 10010   e. 11011   f. 100

7. In 24 bits, we can store three symbols using ASCII. Thus we can store values as large as 999. However, if we use the bits as binary digits, we can store values up to 16,777,215.

8. a. 15.15   b. 51.0.128   c. 10.160

9. Geometric representations are more conducive to changes in scale than images encoded as bit maps. However, geometric representations do not typically provide the same photographic quality that bit maps produce. Indeed, as discussed in Section 1.9, JPEG representations of bit maps are very popular in photography.

10. With a sample rate of 44,100 samples per second, one hour of stereo music would require 635,040,000 bytes of storage. Thus, it would just about fill a CD whose capacity is slightly more than 600MB.

Section 1.5

1. a. 42   b. 33   c. 23   d. 6   e. 31
2. a. 100000   b. 1000000 c. 1100000 d. 1111   e. 11011
3. a. $3\frac{1}{4}$ b. $5\frac{7}{8}$ c. $2\frac{1}{2}$ d. $6\frac{3}{8}$ e. $\frac{5}{8}$
4. a. 100.1   b. 10.11   c. 1.001   d. 0.0101   e. 101.101
5. a. 100111   b. 1011.110 c. 100000   d. 1000.00

Section 1.6

1. a. 3   b. 15   c. −4   d. −6   e. 0   f. −16
2. a. 00000110   b. 11111010   c. 11101111
   d. 00001101   e. 11111111   f. 00000000
3. a. 11111111   b. 10101011   c. 00000100
   d. 00000010   e. 00000000   f. 10000001
4. a. With 4 bits the largest value is 7 and the smallest is −8.
   b. With 6 bits the largest value is 31 and the smallest is −32.
   c. With 8 bits the largest value is 127 and the smallest is −128.
5. a. 0111 (5 + 2 = 7)   b. 0100 (3 + 1 = 4)   c. 1111 (5 + (−6) = −1)
   d. 0001 (−2 + 3 = 1)   e. 1000 (−6 + (−2) = −8)

6. a. 0111　　　b. 1011 (overflow)　　　c. 0100 (overflow)
　d. 0001　　　e. 1000 (overflow)

7.
a. 0110	b. 0011	c. 0100	d. 0010	e. 0001
+ 0001	+ 1110	+ 1010	+ 0100	+1011
0111	0001	1110	0110	1100

8. No. Overflow occurs when an attempt is made to store a number that is too large for the system being used. When adding a positive value to a negative value, the result must be between the values being added. Therefore the result will be small enough to be stored without error.

9. a. 6 because $1110 \rightarrow 14 - 8$
　b. -1 because $0111 \rightarrow 7 - 8$
　c. 0 because $1000 \rightarrow 8 - 8$
　d. -6 because $0010 \rightarrow 2 - 8$
　e. -8 because $0000 \rightarrow 0 - 8$
　f. 1 because $1001 \rightarrow 9 - 8$

10. a. 1101 because $5 + 8 = 13 \rightarrow 1101$
　b. 0011 because $-5 + 8 = 3 \rightarrow 0011$
　c. 1011 because $3 + 8 = 11 \rightarrow 1011$
　d. 1000 because $0 + 8 = 8 \rightarrow 1000$
　e. 1111 because $7 + 8 = 15 \rightarrow 1111$
　f. 0000 because $-8 + 8 = 0 \rightarrow 0000$

11. No. The largest value that can be stored in excess eight notation is 7, represented by 1111. To represent a larger value, at least excess 16 (which uses patterns of 5 bits) must be used. Similarly, 6 cannot be represented in excess four notation. (The largest value that can be represented in excess four notation is 3.)

Section 1.7

1. a. $\frac{5}{8}$　　b. $3\frac{1}{4}$　　c. $\frac{9}{32}$　　d. $-1\frac{1}{2}$　　e. $-\left(\frac{11}{64}\right)$

2. a. 01101011　　b. 01111010 (truncation error)
　c. 01001100　　d. 11101110　　e. 11111000 (truncation error)

3. 01001001 ($\frac{9}{16}$) is larger than 00111101 ($\frac{13}{32}$). The following is a simple way of determining which of two patterns represents the larger value:

Case 1. If the sign bits are different, the larger is the one with 0 sign bit.

Case 2. If the sign bits are both 0, scan the remaining portions of the patterns from left to right until a bit position is found where the two patterns differ. The pattern containing the 1 in this position represents the larger value.

Case 3. If the sign bits are both 1, scan the remaining portions of the patterns from left to right until a bit position is found where the two patterns differ. The pattern containing the 0 in this position represents the larger value. The simplicity of this comparison process is one of the reasons for representing the exponent in floating-point systems with an excess notation rather than with two's complement.

4. The largest value would be 7½, which is represented by the pattern 01111111. As for the smallest positive value, you could argue that there are two "correct" answers. First, if you stick to the coding process described in the text, which requires the most significant bit of the mantissa to be 1 (called normalized form), the answer is ½₂, which is represented by the pattern 00001000. However, most machines do not impose this restriction for values close to 0. For such a machine, the correct answer is ½₅₆ represented by 00000001.

Section 1.8

1. Python is considered an *interpreted language* because users can type program fragments interactively at a prompt, rather than having to save the script, invoke a compiler, and then execute the program.

2. a. `print('Computer Science Rocks' + '!')`
   b. `print(42)`
   c. `print(3.1416)`

3. a. `rockstar = 'programmer'`
   b. `seconds_per_hour = 60 * 60`
      or
      `seconds_per_hour = 3600`
   c. `bodyTemp = 98.6`

4. `metricBodyTemp = (bodyTemp - 32)/1.8`

Section 1.9

1. Run-length encoding, frequency-dependent encoding, relative encoding, and dictionary encoding

2. 121321112343535

3. Color cartoons consist of blocks of solid color with sharp edges. Moreover, the number of colors involved is limited.

4. No. Both GIF and JPEG are lossy compression systems, meaning that details in the image will be lost.

5. JPEG's baseline standard takes advantage of the fact that the human eye is not as sensitive to changes in color as it is to changes in brightness. Thus it reduces the number of bits used to represent color information without noticeable loss in image quality.

6. Temporal masking and frequency masking

7. When encoding information, approximations are made. In the case of numeric data, these approximations are compounded when computations are performed, which can lead to erroneous results. Approximations are not as critical in the cases of images and sound because the encoded data are normally only stored, transferred, and reproduced. If, however, images or sound were repeatedly reproduced, rerecorded, and then reencoded, these approximations could compound and ultimately lead to worthless data.

Section 1.10

1. b, c, and e

2. Yes. If an even number of errors occurs in one byte, the parity technique does not detect them.

3. In this case, errors occur in bytes a and d of Question 1. The answer to Question 2 remains the same.

4. a. 100100010   101010011   101110100
101101111   001110000   100100001
100100010   000100000   001000011
001101000   101100101   101110010
001111001   101101100   000100000
001110011   001101000   101101111
001110101   101110100   101100101
001100100   100101110
 b. 101000100   101101111   101100101
001110011   100100000   000110010
000100000   100101011   000100000
100110011   000100000   000111101
000100000   100110101   100111111

5. a. BED   b. CAB   c. HEAD

6. One solution is the following:
   A 00000
   B 11100
   C 01111
   D 10011

Chapter 2

Section 2.1

1. On some machines this is a two-step process consisting of first reading the contents from the first cell into a register and then writing it from the register into the destination cell. On most machines, this is accomplished as one activity without using an intermediate register.

2. The value to be written, the address of the cell in which to write, and the command to write

3. General-purpose registers are used to hold the data immediately applicable to the operation at hand; main memory is used to hold data that will be needed in the near future; and mass storage is used to hold data that will likely not be needed in the near future.

Section 2.2

1. The term *move* often carries the connotation of removing from one location and placing in another, thus leaving a hole behind. In most cases within a machine, this removal does not take place. Rather, the object being moved is most often copied (or cloned) into the new location.

2. A common technique, called relative addressing, is to state how far rather than where to jump. For example, an instruction might be to jump forward three instructions or jump backward two instructions. You should note, however, that such statements must be altered if additional instructions are later inserted between the origin and the destination of the jump.

3. This could be argued either way. The instruction is stated in the form of a conditional jump. However, because the condition that 0 be equal to 0 is always satisfied, the jump will always be made as if there were no condition stated at all. You will often find machines with such instructions in their repertoires because they provide an efficient design. For example, if a machine is designed to execute an instruction with a structure such as "If . . . jump to. . . " this instruction form can be used to express both conditional and unconditional jumps.

4. 156C = 0001010101101100
   166D = 0001011001101101
   5056 = 0101000001010110
   306E = 0011000001101110
   C000 = 1100000000000000

5. a. STORE the contents of register 6 in memory cell number 8A.
   b. JUMP to location DE if the contents of register A equals that of register 0.
   c. AND the contents of registers 3 and C, leaving the result in register 0.
   d. MOVE the contents of register F to register 4.

6. The instruction 15AB requires that the CPU query the memory circuitry for the contents of the memory cell at address AB. This value, when obtained from memory, is then placed in register 5. The instruction 25AB does not require such a request of memory. Rather, the value AB is placed in register 5.

7. a. 2356   b. A503   c. 80A5

Section 2.3

1. Hexadecimal 34

2. a. 0F   b. C3

3. a. 00   b. 01   c. four times

4. It halts. This is an example of what is often called self-modifying code. That is, the program modifies itself. Note that the first two instructions place hexadecimal C0 at memory location F8, and the next two instructions place 00 at location F9. Thus, by the time the machine reaches the instruction at F8, the halt instruction (C000) has been placed there.

Section 2.4

1. a. 00001011   b. 10000000   c. 00101101
   d. 11101011   e. 11101111   f. 11111111
   g. 11100000   h. 01101111   i. 11010010

2. 00111100 with the AND operation

3. 00111100 with the XOR operation

4. a. The final result is 0 if the string contained an even number of 1s. Otherwise it is 1.
   b. The result is the value of the parity bit for even parity.

5. The logical XOR operation mirrors addition except for the case where both operands are 1, in which case the XOR produces a 0, whereas the sum is 10. (Thus the XOR operation can be considered an addition operation with no carry.)

6. Use AND with the mask 11011111 to change lowercase to uppercase. Use OR with 00100000 to change uppercase to lowercase.

7. a. 01001101   b. 11100001   c. 11101111

8. a. 57   b. B8   c. 6F   d. 6A

9. 5

10. 00110110 in two's complement; 01011110 in floating-point. The point here is that the procedure used to add the values is different depending on the interpretation given the bit patterns.

11. One solution is as follows:

    12A7 (LOAD register 2 with the contents of memory cell A7.)
    2380 (LOAD register 3 with the value 80.)
    7023 (OR registers 2 and 3 leaving the result in register 0.)
    30A7 (STORE contents of register 0 in memory cell A7.)
    C000 (HALT.)

12. One solution is as follows:

    15E0 (LOAD register 5 with the contents of memory cell E0.)
    A502 (ROTATE the contents of register 5 to the left by 2 bits.)
    260F (LOAD register 6 with the value 0F.)
    8056 (AND registers 5 and 6, leaving the result in register 0.)
    30E1 (STORE the contents of register 0 in memory cell E1.)
    C000 (HALT.)

Section 2.5

1. a. 37B5
   b. One million times
   c. No. A typical page of text contains less than 4000 characters. Thus the ability to print five pages in a minute indicates a printing rate of no more than 20,000 characters per minute, which is much less than one million characters per second. (The point is that a computer can send characters to a printer much faster than the printer can print them; thus the printer needs a way of telling the computer to wait.)

2. The disk will make 50 revolutions in one second, meaning that 800 sectors will pass under the read/write head in a second. Because each sector contains 1024 bytes, bits will pass under the read/write head at approximately 6.5 Mbps. Thus communication between the controller and the disk drive will have to be at least this fast if the controller is going to keep up with the data being read from the disk.

3. A 300-page novel represented in Unicode consists of about 2MB or 16,000,000 bits. Thus approximately 0.3 seconds would be required to transfer the entire novel at 54 Mbps.

Section 2.6

1. The int() function calls used when inputting the side lengths will truncate any floating-point values entered to integer values. However, the math.sqrt() function returns a floating-point value, regardless of whether its parameters were integers or floats. To output an integer instead, the final line of the script can be replaced with

   ```
   print(int(hypotenuse))
   ```

   or the assignment statement for hypotenuse can be replaced with

   ```
   hypotenuse = int(math.sqrt(sideA**2 + sideB**2))
   ```

2. Replacing both int() calls in the original script with float() produces a script that works with floating-point values.

3. One example of Python code that would produce cleaner output is:

   ```
   print('Your speed is ' + str(mph) + ' mph')
   . . .
   print('Your total elapsed time is ' + str(elapsed_minutes) +
         ' minutes, ' + str(elapsed_seconds) + ' seconds')
   ```

4. One example would be:

   ```
   number = int(input('Enter a base-10 number: '))
   print('Binary representation is: ' + str(bin(number)))
   ```

5. One example would be:

   ```
   number = int(input('Enter a number to encrypt or decrypt: '))
   number = number ^ 0x55555555
   print('Result is: ' + str(number))
   ```

6. Unexpected inputs in simple scripts such as these will generally cause errors or unexpected behavior. More complex scripts would check the input for suitability before trying to convert it to an integer, or would include conditionals to check for negative side lengths, etc.

Section 2.7

1. The pipe would contain the instructions B1B0 (being executed), 5002, and perhaps even B0AA. If the value in register 1 is equal to the value in register 0, the jump to location B0 is executed, and the effort already expended on the instructions in the pipe is wasted. On the other hand, no time is wasted because the effort expended on these instructions did not require extra time.

2. If no precautions are taken, the information at memory locations F8 and F9 is fetched as an instruction before the previous part of the program has had a chance to modify these cells.

3. a. The CPU that is trying to add 1 to the cell can first read the value in the cell. Following this the other CPU reads the cell's value. (Note that at this point both CPUs have retrieved the same value.) If the first CPU now finishes its addition and writes its result back in the cell before the second finishes its subtraction and writes its result, the final value in the cell reflects only the activity of the second CPU.

   b. The CPUs might read the data from the cell as before, but this time the second CPU might write its result before the first. Thus only the activity of the first CPU is reflected in the cell's final value.

Chapter 3

Section 3.1

1. A traditional example is the line of people waiting to buy tickets to an event. In this case there might be someone who tries to "break in line," which would violate the FIFO structure.

2. Options (b), (c), and (e)

3. Embedded systems often focus on dedicated tasks, whereas PCs are general-purpose computers. Embedded systems frequently have more limited resources than PCs of comparable age, but may face strict deadlines with minimal human intervention.

4. Time-sharing refers to more than one user accessing a machine at the same time. Multitasking refers to a user performing more than one task at the same time.

Section 3.2

1. *Shell:* Communicates with the machine's environment.

   File manager: Coordinates the use of the machine's mass storage.

   Device drivers: Handle communication with the machine's peripheral devices.

   Memory manager: Coordinates the use of the machine's main memory.

   Scheduler: Coordinates the processes in the system.

   Dispatcher: Controls the assignment of processes to CPU time.

2. The line is vague, and the distinction is often in the eye of the beholder. Roughly speaking, utility software performs basic, universal tasks, whereas application software performs tasks unique to the machine's application.

3. Virtual memory is the imaginary memory space whose apparent presence is created by the process of swapping data and programs back and forth between main memory and mass storage.

4. When the machine is turned on, the CPU begins executing the bootstrap, which resides in ROM. This bootstrap directs the CPU through the process of transferring the operating system from mass storage into the volatile area of main memory. When this transfer is complete, the bootstrap directs the CPU to jump to the operating system.

Section 3.3

1. A program is a set of directions. A process is the action of following those directions.

2. The CPU completes its current machine cycle, saves the state of the current process, and sets its program counter to a predetermined value (which is the location of the interrupt handler). Thus the next instruction executed will be the first instruction within the interrupt handler.

3. They could be given higher priorities so that they would be given preference by the dispatcher. Another option would be to give the higher-priority processes longer time slices.

4. If each process consumed its entire time slice, the machine could provide a complete slice to almost 20 processes in one second. If processes did not consume their entire time slices, this value could be much higher, but then the time required to perform a context switch might become more significant (see Question 5).

5. A total of $^{5000}/_{5001}$ of the machine's time would be spent actually performing processes. However, when a process requests an I/O activity, its time slice is terminated while the controller performs the request. Thus if each process made such a request after only one microsecond of its time slice, the efficiency of the machine would drop to 1/2. That is, the machine would spend as much time performing context switches as it would executing processes.

Section 3.4

1. This system guarantees that the resource is not used by more than one process at a time; however, it dictates that the resource be allocated in a strictly alternating fashion. Once a process has used and relinquished the resource, it must wait for the other process to use the resource before the original process can access it again. This is true even if the first process needs the resource right away and the other process will not need it for some time.

2. If two cars enter opposite ends of the tunnel at the same time, they will not be aware of the other's presence. The process of entering and turning on the lights is another example of a critical region, or in this case we might call it a critical process. In this terminology, we could summarize the flaw by saying that cars at opposite ends of the tunnel could execute the critical process at the same time.

3. a. This guarantees that the nonsharable resource is not required and allocated on a partial basis; that is, a car is given the whole bridge or nothing at all.
   b. This means that the nonsharable resource can be forcibly retrieved.
   c. This makes the nonsharable resource shareable, which removes the competition.

4. A sequence of arrows that forms a closed loop in the directed graph. It is on this observation that techniques have been developed that allow some operating systems to recognize the existence of deadlock and consequently to take appropriate corrective action.

Section 3.5

1. Names and dates are considered poor candidates because they are common choices and therefore represent easy targets for password guessers. The use of complete words is also considered poor because password guessers can easily write a program to try the words found in a dictionary. Moreover, passwords containing only characters are discouraged because they are formed from a limited character set.

2. Four is the number of different bit patterns that can be formed using 2 bits. If more privilege levels were required, the designers would need at least 3 bits to represent the different levels and would therefore probably choose to use a total of 8 levels. In the same manner, the natural choice for fewer than 4 privilege levels would be 2, which is the number of patterns that can be represented with 1 bit.

3. The process could alter the operating system program so that the dispatcher gave every time slice to that process.

Chapter 4

Section 4.1

1. An open network is one whose specifications and protocols are public, allowing different vendors to produce compatible products.

2. Both connect two buses to form a larger bus network. However, a bridge forwards only those messages destined for the other side of the bridge, whereas a switch has multiple connections that each may act as a bridge.

3. A router is a device that directs messages between networks in an internet.

4. How about a mail-order business and its clients, a bank teller and the bank's customers, or a pharmacist and his or her customers?

5. There are numerous protocols involved in traffic flow, verbal telephone communication, and etiquette.

6. Cluster computing typically involves multiple, dedicated computers to provide high-availability or load-balanced distributed computing. Grid computing is more loosely coupled than cluster computing, and could involve machines that join the distributed computation when they are otherwise idle.

Section 4.2

1. Tier-1 and tier-2 ISPs provide the Internet's communication "core," whereas access ISPs provide access to that core to their customers.

2. The DNS (Domain Name System) is the Internet-wide collection of name servers that allow translation from mnemonic addresses to IP addresses (and in the other direction as well).

3. The expression 3.6.9 represents the three-byte pattern 000000110000011000001001. The bit pattern 0001010100011100 would be represented as 21.28 in dotted decimal notation.

4. There could be several answers to this. One is that both progress from the specific to the general. Internet addresses in mnemonic form begin with the name of a particular machine and progress to the name of the TLD. Postal addresses begin with the name of an individual and progress to increasingly larger regions such as city, state, and country. This order is reversed in IP addresses, which start with the bit pattern identifying the domain.

5. Name servers help translate mnemonic addresses into IP addresses. Mail servers send, receive, and store email messages. FTP servers provide file transfer service.

6. Protocols can describe the format of messages that are exchanged, the proper ordering of messages in an exchange, and the meaning of messages.

7. They relieve the initial server from the burden of sending individual messages to each client. The P2P approach shifts this burden to the clients (peers) themselves, whereas multicast shifts this burden to the Internet routers.

8. Criteria to consider may include cost, portability, the practicality of using your computer as your phone, the need to preserve any existing analog phones, emergency 911 service, and the reliability and service areas of the various providers involved.

Section 4.3

1. A URL is essentially the address of a document in the World Wide Web. A browser is a program that assists a user in accessing hypertext.

2. A markup language is a system for inserting explanatory information in a document.

3. HTML is a particular markup language. XML is a standard for producing markup languages.

4. a. < html > marks the beginning of an HTML document.
   b. < head > marks the beginning of a document's head.
   c. < /p > marks the end of a paragraph.
   d. < /a > marks the end of an item that is linked to another document.

5. Client side and server side are terms used to identify whether an activity is performed at the client's computer or the server's computer.

Section 4.4

1. The link layer receives the message and hands it to the network layer. The network layer determines the direction in which the message should be forwarded and gives the message back to the link layer to be forwarded. The higher layers are not required for routing, although advanced routers may use the transport or application layers to provide additional services such as selective filtering or tiered quality of service.

2. Unlike TCP, UDP is a connectionless protocol that does not confirm that the message was received at the destination.

3. The transport layer uses transport protocol port numbers to determine which unit within the application layer should receive an incoming message.

4. Nothing really. A programmer at any host could modify the software at that host to keep such records. This is why sensitive data should be encrypted.

Section 4.5

1. Phishing is a technique for obtaining sensitive information by asking users for their passwords, credit card numbers, etc., through email while masquerading as a legitimate entity such as the user's bank or the campus IT department. Computers are not secured against phishing; users must rely on sound judgment when revealing sensitive data to others without proper verification.

2. A region's gateway is a router that merely forwards packets (parts of messages) as they pass through. Thus a firewall at the gateway cannot filter traffic by its content but merely by its address information.

3. The use of passwords protects data (and therefore information as well). The use of encryption protects information.

4. In the case of a public-key encryption system, knowing how messages are encrypted does not allow messages to be decrypted.

5. The problems are international in nature and therefore not subject to the laws of a single government. Moreover, legal remedies merely provide recourse to injured parties rather than preventing the injuries.

Chapter 5

Section 5.1

1. A process is the activity of executing an algorithm. A program is a representation of an algorithm.

2. In the introductory chapter we cited algorithms for playing music, operating washing machines, constructing models, and performing magic tricks, as well as the Euclidean algorithm. Many of the "algorithms" you meet in everyday life fail to be algorithms according to our formal definition. The example of the long-division algorithm was cited in the text. Another is the algorithm executed by a clock that continues to advance its hands and ring its chimes day after day.

3. The informal definition fails to require that the steps be ordered and unambiguous. It merely hints at the requirements that the steps be executable and lead to an end.

4. There are two points here. The first is that the instructions define a nonterminating process. In reality, however, the process will ultimately reach the state in which there are no coins in your pocket. In fact, this might be the starting state. At this point the problem is that of ambiguity. The algorithm, as represented, does not tell us what to do in this situation.

Section 5.2

1. One example is found in the composition of matter. At one level, the primitives are considered molecules, yet these particles are actually composites made up of atoms, which in turn are composed of electrons, protons, and neutrons. Today, we know that even these "primitives" are composites.

2. Once a function is correctly constructed, it can be used as a building block for larger program structures without reconsidering the function's internal composition.

3.
```
X = the larger input
Y = the smaller input
while (Y not zero):
   Remainder = remainder after dividing X by Y
   X = Y
   Y = Remainder
GCD = X
```

4. All other colors of light can be produced by combining red, blue, and green. Thus a television picture tube is designed to produce these three basic colors.

Section 5.3

1. a.
```
if (n == 1 or n == 2):
    the answer is the list containing the single value n
else:
    Divide n by 3, obtaining a quotient q and a remainder r
    if (r == 0):
       the answer is the list containing q 3s
    if (r == 1):
       the answer is the list containing (q - 1) 3s and two 2s
    if (r == 2):
       the answer is the list containing q 3s and one 2
```

   b. The result would be the list containing 667 threes.
   c. You probably experimented with small input values until you began to see a pattern.

2. a. Yes. Hint: Place the first tile in the center so that it avoids the quadrant containing the hole while covering one square from each of the other quadrants. Each quadrant then represents a smaller version of the original problem.
   b. The board with a single hole contains $2^{2n} - 1$ squares, and each tile covers exactly three squares.
   c. Parts (a) and (b) of this question provide an excellent example of how knowing a solution to one problem helps solve another. See Polya's fourth phase.

3. It says, "This is the correct answer."

4. Simply trying to assemble the pieces would be a bottom-up approach. However, by looking at the puzzle box to see what the picture is supposed to look like adds a top-down component to your approach.

Section 5.4

1. Change the test in the `while` statement to read "target value != current entry and there remain entries to be considered."

2.
```
Z = 0
X = 1
repeat:
  Z = Z + X
  X = X + 1
until (X == 6)
```

3. This has proven to be a problem with the C language. When the `do` and `while` key words are separated by several lines, readers of a program often stumble over the proper interpretation of a `while` clause. In particular, the `while` at the end of a `do` statement is often interpreted as the beginning of a `while` statement. Thus experience would say that it is better to use different key words to represent pretest and posttest loop structures.

4.

Cheryl	Alice	Alice
Gene	Cheryl	Brenda
Alice	Gene	Cheryl
Brenda	Brenda	Gene

5. It is a waste of time to insist on placing the pivot above an identical entry in the list. For instance, make the proposed change and then try the new program on a list in which all entries are the same.

6.
```
def sort (List):
  N = 1
  while (N is less than the length of List):
    J = N + 1
    while (J is not greater than length of List):
      if (the entry in position J is less than the entry in
          position N):
        interchange the two entries
      J = J + 1
    N = N + 1
```

7. The following is an inefficient solution. Can you make it more efficient?

```
def sort (List):
  N = the length of List
  while (N > 1):
    J = the length of List
    while (J > 1):
      if (the entry in position J < the entry in
          position J - 1):
        interchange the two entries
      J = J - 1
    N = N - 1
```

Section 5.5

1. The first name considered would be Henry, the next would be Larry, and the last would be Joe.

2. 8, 17

3. 1, 2, 3, 3, 2, 1

4. The termination condition is "N is bigger than or equal to 3" (or "N is not less than 3"). This is the condition under which no additional activations are created.

Section 5.6

1. If the machine can sort 100 names in one second, it can perform $\frac{1}{4}(10,000 - 100)$ comparisons in one second. This means that each comparison takes approximately 0.0004 second. Consequently, sorting 1000 names [which requires an average of $\frac{1}{4}(1,000,000 - 1000)$ comparisons] requires roughly 100 seconds or $1\frac{2}{3}$ minutes.

2. The binary search belongs to $\Theta(\log_2 n)$, the sequential search belongs to $\Theta(n)$, and the insertion sort belongs to $\Theta(n^2)$.

3. The class $\Theta(\log_2 n)$ is most efficient, followed by $\Theta(n)$, $\Theta(n^2)$, and $\Theta(n^3)$.

4. No. The answer is not correct, although it might sound right. The truth is that two of the three cards are the same on both sides. Thus the probability of picking such a card is two-thirds.

5. No. If the dividend is less than the divisor, such as in $\frac{3}{7}$, the answer given is 1, although it should be 0.

6. No. If the value of X is zero and the value of Y is nonzero, the answer given will not be correct.

7. Each time the test for termination is conducted, the statement "Sum $= 1 + 2 + \ldots + K$ and K less than or equal to N" is true. Combining this with the termination condition "K greater than or equal to N" produces the desired conclusion "Sum $= 1 + 2 + \ldots + N$." Because K is initialized at zero and incremented by one each time through the loop, its value must ultimately reach that of N.

8. Unfortunately, no. Problems beyond the control of hardware and software design, such as mechanical malfunctions and electrical problems, can affect computations.

Chapter 6

Section 6.1

1. A program in a third-generation language is machine independent in the sense that its steps are not stated in terms of the machine's attributes such as registers and memory cell addresses. On the other hand, it is machine dependent in the sense that arithmetic overflow and truncation errors will still occur.

2. The major distinction is that an assembler translates each instruction in the source program into a single machine instruction, whereas a compiler often produces many machine-language instructions to obtain the equivalent of a single source program instruction.

3. The declarative paradigm is based on developing a description of the problem to be solved. The functional paradigm forces the programmer to describe the problem's solution in terms of solutions to smaller problems. The object-oriented paradigm places emphasis on describing the components in the problem's environment.

4. The third-generation languages allow the program to be expressed more in terms of the problem's environment and less in terms of computer gibberish than do the earlier-generation languages.

Section 6.2

1. Using a descriptive constant can improve the accessibility of the program.

2. A declarative statement describes terminology; an imperative statement describes steps in an algorithm.

3. Integer, float, character, and Boolean

4. The `if-else` and `while` loop structures are very common.

5. All components of an array have the same type.

Section 6.3

1. The scope of a variable is the range of the program in which that variable is accessible.

2. A fruitful function is a function that returns a value associated with the function's name.

3. Because that is what they are. I/O operations are actually calls to routines within the machine's operating system.

4. A formal parameter is an identifier within a function. It serves as a place holder for the value, the actual parameter, that is passed to the function when the function is called.

5. A function that passes parameters call-by-reference can potentially make changes to the parameters that will be visible to the caller; call-by-value parameters are copies, and changes made to them within the function will not be visible from outside.

Section 6.4

1. Lexical analysis: the process of identifying tokens.
   Parsing: the process of recognizing the grammatical structure of the program.
   Code generation: the process of producing the instructions in the object program.

2. A symbol table is the record of information the parser has obtained from the program's declarative statements.

3. In the syntax diagrams, terms that appear in ovals are terminals. Terms that require further description are in rectangles, and are called "nonterminals."

4.

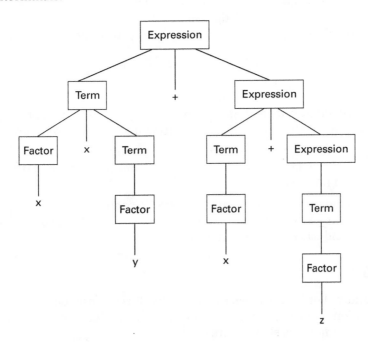

5. The strings that conform to the structure Chacha consist of one or more of the following substrings:
forward backward cha cha cha
backward forward cha cha cha
swing right cha cha cha
swing left cha cha cha

6. Python keywords appear in this color. Module names, functions and classes appear in this color, as do first time variable assignments. String constants and comments appear in this color. All other Python code appears in this color.

Section 6.5

1. A class is the description of an object.

2. One would probably be MeteorClass from which the various meteors would be constructed. Within the class LaserClass one might find an instance variable named AimDirection indicating the direction in which the laser is aimed. This variable would probably be used by the fire, turnRight, and turnLeft methods.

3. The Employee class might contain features relating to an employee's name, address, years in service, etc. The FullTimeEmployee class might contain features relating to retirement benefits. The PartTimeEmployee class might contain features relating to hours worked per week, hourly wage, etc.

4. A constructor is a special method in a class that is executed when an instance of the class is created.

5. Some items in a class are designated as private to keep other program units from gaining direct access to those items. If an item is private, then the repercussions of modifying that item should be restricted to the interior of the class.

Section 6.6

1. The list would include techniques for initiating the execution of concurrent processes and techniques for implementing interprocess communication.

2. One is to place the burden on the processes, another is to place the burden on the data. The latter has the advantage of concentrating the task at a single point in the program.

3. These include weather forecasting, air traffic control, simulation of complex systems (from nuclear reactions to pedestrian traffic), computer networking, and database maintenance.

Section 6.7

1. R, T, and V. For instance, we can show that R is a consequence by adding its negation to the collection and showing that resolution can lead to the empty statement, as shown here:

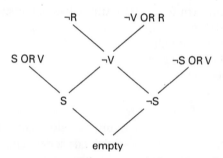

2. No. The collection is inconsistent, because resolution can lead to the empty statement, as shown here:

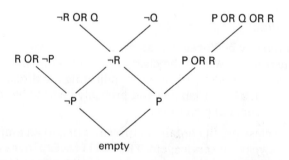

3. `mother(X, Y) :- parent(X, Y), female(X).`
   `father(X, Y) :- parent(X, Y), male(X).`

4. Prolog will conclude that **carol** is her own sibling. To solve this problem, the rule needs to include the fact that X cannot be equal to Y, which in Prolog is written X \ = Y. Thus an improved version of the rule would be

```
sibling (X, Y) :-X \= Y, parent(Z, X), parent(Z, Y).
```

which says that X is Y's sibling if X and Y are not equal and have a common parent. The following version would insist that X and Y are siblings only if they have both parents in common:

```
sibling (X, Y) :- X \= Y, Z \= W
parent (Z, X), parent (Z, Y),
parent (W, X), parent (W, Y).
```

Chapter 7

Section 7.1

1. A long sequence of assignment statements is not as complex in the context of program design as a few nested `if` statements.

2. How about the number of errors found after a fixed period of use? One problem here is that this value cannot be measured in advance.

3. The point here is to think about how software properties can be measured. One approach for estimating the number of errors in a piece of software is to intentionally place some errors in the software when it is designed. Then, after the software has supposedly been debugged, check to see how many of the original errors are still present. For example, if you intentionally place seven errors in the software and find that five have been removed after debugging, then you might conjecture that only $5/7$ of the total errors in the software have been removed.

4. Possible answers include the discovery of metrics, the development of prefabricated components, the development of CASE tools, the move toward standards. Another, which is covered later in Section 7.5, is the development of modeling and notational systems such as UML.

Section 7.2

1. Small efforts made during development can pay enormous dividends during maintenance.

2. The requirements analysis phase concentrates on what the proposed system must accomplish. The design phase concentrates on how the system accomplishes its goals. The implementation phase concentrates on the actual construction of the system. The testing phase concentrates on making sure that the system does what it is intended to do.

3. A software requirements specification is a written agreement between a client and a software engineering firm stating the requirements and specifications of the software to be developed.

Section 7.3

1. The traditional waterfall approach dictates that the requirements analysis, design, implementation, and testing phases be performed in a linear manner. The newer models allow for a more relaxed trial-and-error approach.

2. How about the incremental model, the iterative model, and XP?

3. Traditional evolutionary prototyping is performed within the organization developing the software, whereas open-source development is not restricted to an organization. In the case of open-source development the person overseeing the development does not necessarily determine what enhancements will be reported, whereas in the case of traditional evolutionary prototyping the person managing the software development assigns personnel to specific enhancement tasks.

4. This is one for you to think about. If you were an administrator in a software development company, would you be able to adopt the open-source methodology for the development of software to be sold by your company?

Section 7.4

1. The chapters of a novel build on one another, whereas the sections in an encyclopedia are largely independent. Hence, a novel has more coupling between its chapters than an encyclopedia has between its sections. However, the sections within an encyclopedia probably have a higher level of cohesion than the chapters in a novel.

2. The accumulated score would be an example of data coupling. Other "couplings" that might exist would include fatigue, momentum, knowledge gained about an opponent's strategy, and perhaps self-confidence. In many sports the cohesion of the units is increased by terminating the action and restarting the next unit from a fresh beginning. For example, in baseball each inning starts without any base runners, even though the team might have finished the previous inning with the bases loaded. In other cases the units are scored separately as in tennis where each set is won or lost without regard for the other sets.

3. This is a tough one. From one point of view, we could start by placing everything in a single module. This would result in little cohesion and no coupling at all. If we then begin to divide this single module into smaller ones, the result would be an increase in coupling. We might therefore conclude that increasing cohesion tends to increase coupling. On the other hand, suppose the problem at hand naturally divides into three very cohesive modules, which we will call A, B, and C. If our original design did not observe this natural division (for example, half of task A might be placed with half of task B, and so on), we would expect the cohesion to be low and the coupling high. In this case, redesigning the system by isolating tasks A, B, and C into separate modules would most likely decrease intermodule coupling as intramodule cohesion increases.

4. Coupling is linking between modules. Cohesion is the connectedness within a module. Information hiding is the restriction of information sharing.

5. You should probably add an arrow indicating that `ControlGame` must tell `UpdateScore` who won the volley and another arrow in the other direction indicating that `UpdateScore` will report the current status (such as "set over" or "match over") when it returns control to `ControlGame`.

6. Delete all the horizontal arrows in Figure 7.5 except for the first and last. That is, the judge should evaluate **Player A's** serve and directly send the **updateScore** message to **Score**. (This, of course, ignores the chance for a second serve. How could you modify the program design to allow for double faults?)

7. A traditional programmer writes programs in terms of statements such as those introduced in Chapter 6. A component assembler builds programs by linking prefabricated blocks called components.

8. There are many answers to this question. One combination is to have the calendar automatically set an alarm in a clock to notifying the user of an upcoming appointment. Furthermore, the calendar application could use the components of a map application to provide the directions to the address of the appointment.

Section 7.5

1. Make sure that your diagram deals with the flow of data (not the movement of books). The following diagram indicates that book identifications (from patrons) and patron records (from the library files) are combined to form loan records that are stored in the library files.

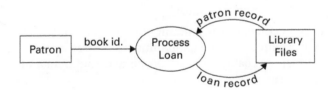

2.

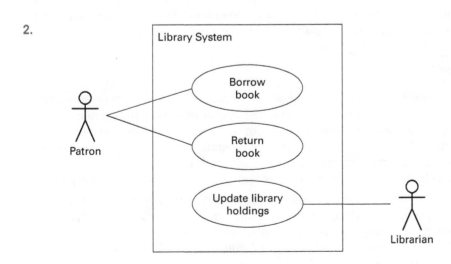

3.

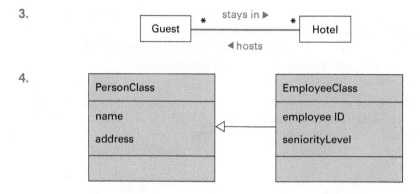

4.

5. Simply draw a rectangle around the figure and add a "sd" label in the upper left-hand corner as in Figure 7.13.

6. Design patterns provide standardized, well-developed approaches for implementing recurring software themes.

Section 7.6

1. The SQA (software quality assurance) group oversees and enforces the quality control systems adopted by the organization.

2. Humans have a tendency not to record the steps (decisions, actions, etc.) that they take during a project. (There are also issues of personality conflicts, jealousies, and ego clashes.)

3. Record keeping and reviewing.

4. The purpose of testing software is to find errors. In a sense, then, a test that does not reveal an error is a failure.

5. One would be to consider the amount of branching in the modules. For instance, a procedural module containing numerous loops and if-else statements would probably be more prone to errors than a module with a simple logical structure.

6. Boundary value analysis would suggest that you test the software on a list with 100 entries as well as a list with no entries. You might also perform a test with a list that is already in the correct order.

Section 7.7

1. Documentation takes the form of user documentation, system documentation, and technical documentation. It might appear in accompanying manuals, within the source program in the form of comments and well-written code, through interactive messages that the program itself writes at a terminal, through data dictionaries, and in the form of design documents such as structure charts, class diagrams, dataflow diagrams, and entity-relationship diagrams.

2. In both the development and modification phases. The point is that modifications must be documented as thoroughly as the original program. (It is also true that software is documented while in its use phase. For example, a user of the system might discover problems, which, rather than being fixed, are merely reported in future editions of the system user's manual.

Moreover, "how to" books are often produced after the software has been in use for an extended period.)

3. Different people will have different opinions on this one. Some will argue that the program is the point of the whole project and thus is naturally the more important. Others will argue that a program is worth nothing if it is not documented, because if you cannot understand a program, you cannot use it or modify it. Moreover, with good documentation, the task of creating the program can be "easily" re-created.

Section 7.8

1. a. How about the ability to adjust the tilt of a display or the shape of a mouse? On smartphones, how about the use of touch screens instead of a mouse, or tilting the phone to provide input?
   b. How about the layout of a window on the display including the design of toolbars, scroll elevators, and pull-down menus? On a smartphone, isn't titling the camera to point at the items of interest in line with the way humans think?

2. a. It would be impractical and inconvenient to use a mouse (or even a stylus) on a smartphone. Furthermore, the reduced size of the display screen requires that nonessential elements of the display be constrained to limited space. For this reason, scrollbars are often omitted. If present, scrollbars are shown as thin lines.
   b. A sliding touch on the display screen is a natural gesture to the way we think. We may move papers or other items by sliding them around on a desk. An augment can be made that this is more natural than the use of scrollbars on a desktop computer. While indeed the scrollbar moves as expected, the area being scrolled moves in the opposite direction. For a user who has never used a computer, this behavior may seem counterintuitive.

3. You could answer "the role of human characteristics." Another good answer would be that interface design focuses on the external, rather than the internal, characteristics of a software system.

4. The three that are discussed in the text are the formation of habits, the narrowness of attention, and limited multiprocessing capabilities. Can you imagine others? How about the tendency to make assumptions?

Section 7.9

1. The copyright notice asserts ownership of the work and identifies personnel authorized to use the work. All works including requirements specifications, design documents, source code, and the final product usually involve a considerable investment to produce. An individual or corporation should take the steps to insure that their ownership rights are reserved and that all intellectual property is not used by undesired parties.

2. Copyright and patent laws benefit society because they encourage creators of new products to make them available to the public. Without such protection, companies would hesitate to make major investments in new products.

3. A disclaimer does not protect a company against negligence.

Chapter 8

Section 8.1

1. List: A listing of the members of a sports team.
   Stack: The stack of trays in a cafeteria.
   Queue: The line at a cafeteria.
   Tree: The organization chart of many governments.

2. Stacks and queues can be thought of as special types of lists. In the case of a general list, entries can be inserted and removed at any location. In the case of a stack, entries can be inserted and removed only at the head. In the case of a queue, entries can be inserted only at the tail, and entries can be removed only at the head.

3. The letters on the stack from top to bottom would be E, D, B, and A. If a letter were popped off the stack, it would be the letter E.

4. The letters in the queue from head to tail would be B, C, D, and E. If a letter were removed from the queue, it would be the letter B.

5. The leaf (or terminal) nodes are D and C. B must be the root node because all the other nodes have parents.

Section 8.2

1. Data within a computer's main memory is actually stored in individually addressable memory cells. Structures such as arrays, lists, and trees are simulated to make the data more accessible to the data's users.

2. If you were to write a program for playing a game of checkers, the data structure representing the checkerboard would probably be a static structure because the size of the board does not change during the game. However, if you were to write a program for playing a game of dominoes, the data structure representing the pattern of dominoes constructed on the table would probably be a dynamic structure because this pattern varies in size and cannot be predetermined.

3. A telephone directory is essentially a collection of pointers (telephone numbers) to people. The clues left at the scene of a crime are (perhaps encrypted) pointers to the perpetrator.

Section 8.3

1. 5 3 7 4 2 8 1 9 6

2. If R is the number of rows in the matrix, the formula is $R(J - 1) + (I - 1)$.

3. $(c - i) + j$

4. The head pointer contains the NIL value.

5. ```
   def PrintList (List):
       Last = the last name to be printed
       Finished = False
       CurrentPointer = List.Head
   ```
   ```

```
while ((CurrentPointer != None) and (Finished != False)):
    print(CurrentPointer.Value)
    if (name just printed == Last):
        Finished = True
    CurrentPointer = CurrentPointer.Next
```

6. The stack pointer points to the cell immediately below the base of the stack.

7. Represent the stack as a one-dimensional array and the stack pointer as a variable of integer type. Then use this stack pointer to maintain a record of the position of the stack's top within the array rather than of the exact memory address.

8. Both empty and full conditions are indicated by the equal head and tail pointers. Thus additional information is required to distinguish between the two conditions.

9.

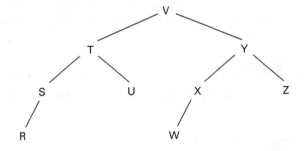

Section 8.4

1.

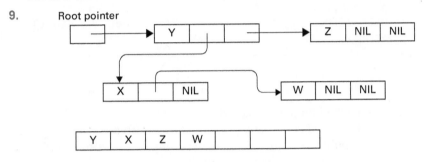

2. When searching for J:

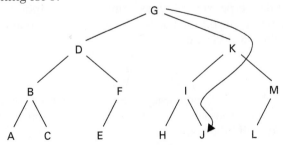

When searching for P:

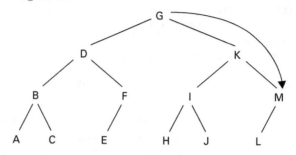

3.

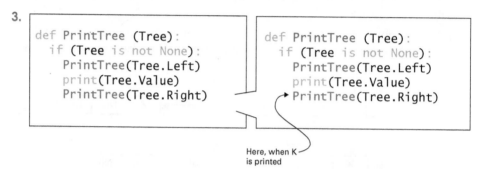

Here, when K
is printed

4. At each node, each child pointer could be used to represent a unique letter in the alphabet. A word could be represented by a path down the tree along the sequence of pointers representing the spelling of the word. A node could be marked in a special way if it represented the end of a correctly spelled word.

Section 8.5

1. A type is a template; an instance of that type is an actual entity built from that template. As an analogy, dog is a type of animal, whereas Lassie and Rex are instances of that type.

2. A user-defined data type is a description of data organization, whereas an abstract data type includes operations for manipulating the data.

3. A point to be made here is that you have a choice between implementing the list as a contiguous list or a linked list. The choice you make will affect the structure of the functions for inserting new entries, deleting old ones, and finding entries of interest. However, this choice should not be visible to a user of an instance of the abstract data type.

4. The abstract data type would at least contain a description of a data structure for storing the account balance and functions for making a deposit and making a withdrawal via a check.

Section 8.6

1. Both abstract data types and classes are templates for constructing instances of a type. Classes, however, are more general in that they are associated with inheritance and might describe a collection of only functions.

2. A class is a template from which objects are constructed.

3. The class might contain a circular queue along with functions for adding entries, removing entries, testing to see if the queue is full, and testing to see if the queue is empty.

Section 8.7

1. a. A5   b. A5   c. CA

2. D50F, 2EFF, 5FFE

3. 2EA0, 2FB0, 2101, 20B5, D50E, E50F, 5EE1, 5FF1, BF14, B008, C000

4. When traversing a linked list in which each entry consists of two memory cells (a data cell followed by a pointer to the next entry), an instruction of the form DR0S could be used to retrieve the data and DR1S could be used to retrieve the pointer to the next entry. If the form DRTS were used, then the exact memory cell being referenced could be adjusted by modifying the value in register T.

Chapter 9

Section 9.1

1. The purchasing department would be interested in inventory records to place orders for more raw goods, whereas the accounting department would need the information to balance the books.

2. A database model provides an organizational perspective of a database that is more compatible with applications than the actual organization. Thus defining a database model is the first step toward allowing the database to be used as an abstract tool.

3. The application software translates the user's requests from the terminology of the application into terminology compatible with the database model that is supported by the database management system. The database management system in turn converts these requests into actions on the actual database.

Section 9.2

1. a. Jerry Smith   b. Cheryl H. Clark   c. S26Z

2. One solution is

```
TEMP  ←  SELECT from JOB
    where Dept = "PERSONNEL"
LIST  ←  PROJECT JobTitle from TEMP
```

In some systems this results in a list with a job title repeated, depending on how many times it occurred in the personnel department. That is, our list might contain numerous occurrences of the title secretary. It is more common, however, to design the PROJECT operation so that it removes duplicate tuples from the resulting relation.

3. One solution is

```
TEMP1 ← JOIN JOB and ASSIGNMENT
                  where JOB.JobId = ASSIGNMENT.JobId
TEMP2 ← SELECT from TEMP1
                  where TermDate = '*'
TEMP3 ← JOIN EMPLOYEE and TEMP2
                  where EMPLOYEE.EmplId = TEMP2.EmplId
RESULT ← PROJECT Name, Dept from TEMP3
```

4. ```
   SELECT JobTitle
     FROM Job
     WHERE Dept = 'PERSONNEL';
   ```

   ```
   SELECT Employee.Name, Job.Dept
     FROM Job, Assignment, and Employee
     WHERE (Job.Job = Assignment.JobId) and
         (Assignment.EmplId = Employee.EmplID)
           and (Assignment.TermDate = '*');
   ```

5. The model itself does not provide data independence. This is a property of the data management system. Data independence is achieved by providing the data management system the ability to present a consistent relational organization to the application software even though the actual organization might change.

6. Through common attributes. For instance, the **EMPLOYEE** relation in this section is tied to the **ASSIGNMENT** relation via the attribute **EmplId**, and the **ASSIGNMENT** relation is tied to the **JOB** relation by the attribute **JobId**. Attributes used to connect relations like this are sometimes called connection attributes.

Section 9.3

1. There might be methods for assigning and retrieving the **StartDate** as well as the **TermDate**. Another method might be provided for reporting the total time in service.

2. A persistent object is an object that is stored indefinitely.

3. One approach is to establish an object for each type of product in inventory. Each of these objects could maintain the total inventory of its product, the cost of the product, and links to the outstanding orders for the product.

4. As indicated at the beginning of this section, object-oriented databases appear to handle composite data types more easily than relational databases. Moreover, the fact that objects can contain methods that take an active role in answering questions promises to give object-oriented databases an advantage over relational databases whose relations merely hold the data.

Section 9.4

1. Once a transaction has reached its commit point, the database management system accepts the responsibility of seeing that the complete transaction is performed on the database. A transaction that has not reached its commit
   ```

point does not have such assurance. If problems arise, it might have to be resubmitted.

2. One approach would be to stop interweaving transactions for an instant so that all current transactions can be completed in full. This would establish a point at which a future cascading rollback would terminate.

3. A balance of $100 would result if the transactions were executed one at a time. A balance of $200 would result if the first transaction were executed after the second transaction retrieved the original balance and before that second transaction stored its new balance. A balance of $300 would result if the second transaction were executed after the first retrieved the original balance and before the first transaction stored its new balance.

4. a. If no other transaction has exclusive access, the shared access will be granted.
   b. If another transaction already has some form of access, the database management system will normally make the new transaction wait, or it could roll back the other transactions and give access to the new transaction.

5. Deadlock would occur if each of two transactions acquired exclusive access to different items and then required access to the other.

6. The preceding deadlock could be removed by rolling back one of the transactions (using the log) and giving the other transaction access to the data item previously held by the first.

Section 9.5

1. You should be led through these initial stages:

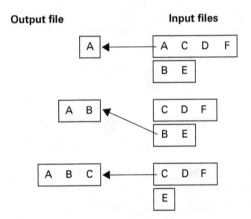

2. The idea is to first divide the file to be stored into many separate files containing one record each. Next, group the one-record files into pairs, and apply the merge algorithm to each pair. This results in half as many files, each with two records. Furthermore, each of these two-record files is sorted. We can group them into pairs and again apply the merge algorithm to the pairs. Again we find ourselves with fewer but larger files, each of which is sorted. Continuing in this fashion, we are ultimately left with only one file that consists of all the original records but in sorted order. (If an odd

number of files occurs at any stage of this process, we need merely to set the odd one aside and pair it with one of the larger files in the next stage.)

3. If the file is stored on tape or CD, its physical organization is most likely sequential. However, if the file is stored on magnetic disk, then it is most likely scattered over various sectors on the disk and the sequential nature of the file is a conceptual property that is supported by a pointer system or some form of a list in which the sectors on which the file is stored are recorded.

4. First find the target key in the file's index. From there, obtain the location of the target record. Then retrieve the record at that location.

5. A poorly chosen hash algorithm results in more clustering than normal and thus in more overflow. Because the overflow from each section of mass storage is organized as a linked list, searching through the overflow records is essentially searching a sequential file.

6. The section assignments are as follows:

   a. 0   b. 0   c. 3   d. 0   e. 3
   f. 3   g. 3   h. 3   i. 3   j. 0

   Thus all the records hash into buckets 0 and 3, leaving buckets 1, 2, 4, and 5 empty. The problem here is that the number of buckets being used (6) and the key values have the common factor of 3. (You might try rehashing these key values using 7 buckets and see what improvement you find.)

7. The point here is that we are essentially applying a hash algorithm to place the people in the group into one of 365 categories. The hash algorithm, of course, is the calculation of one's birthday. The amazing thing is that only twenty-three people are required before the probability is in favor of at least two of the birthdays being the same. In terms of a hashed file, this indicates that when hashing records into 365 available buckets of mass storage, clustering is likely to be present after only twenty-three records have been entered.

Section 9.6

1. Searching for patterns in dynamic data is problematic.

2. Class description—Identify characteristics of subscribers to a certain magazine.
   Class discrimination—Identify features that distinguish between subscribers of two magazines.
   Cluster analysis—Identify magazines that tend to attract similar subscribers.
   Association analysis—Identify links between subscribers to various magazines and different purchasing habits.
   Outlier analysis—Identify subscribers to a magazine who do not conform to the profile of normal subscribers.
   Sequential pattern analysis—Identify trends in magazine subscription.

3. The data cube might allow sales data to be viewed as sales by month, sales by geographic region, sales by product class, etc.

4. Traditional database inquiries retrieve facts stored in the database. Data mining looks for patterns among the facts.

Section 9.7

1. The point here is to compare your answer to this question with that of the next. The two raise essentially the same question but in different contexts.

2. See previous problem.

3. You might receive announcements or advertisements for opportunities that you would not have otherwise received, but you might also become the subject of solicitation or the target of crime.

4. The point here is that a free press can alert the public to abuses or potential abuses and thus bring public opinion into play. In most of the cases cited in the text, it was a free press that initiated corrective action by alerting the public.

Chapter 10

Section 10.1

1. Image processing deals with analyzing two-dimensional images, 2D graphics deals with converting two-dimensional shapes into images, and 3D graphics deals with converting three-dimensional scenes into images.

2. Traditional photography produces images of actual scenes, whereas 3D graphics produces images of virtual scenes.

3. The first is "building" the virtual scene. The second is capturing the image.

Section 10.2

1. The steps are modeling (building the scene), rendering (producing a picture), and displaying (displaying the picture).

2. The image window is the portion of the projection plane that constitutes the image.

3. A frame buffer is a memory area that contains an encoded version of an image.

Section 10.3

1. It is a rhombus (a squashed square).

2. A procedural model is a program segment that directs the construction of an object.

3. The list could include the grass-covered ground, a stone walkway, a gazebo, trees, shrubbery, clouds, sun, and actors. The point here is to emphasize the scope of a scene graph—it can contain a lot of detail.

4. Representing all objects by polygonal meshes provides a uniform approach to the rendering process. (In most cases, rendering is approached as the task of rendering planar patches rather than rendering objects.)

5. Texture mapping is a means of associating a two-dimensional image with the surface of an object.

Section 10.4

1. Specular light is light that is "directly" reflected off a surface. Diffuse light is light that is "scattered" off a surface. Ambient light is light that does not have a precise source.

2. Clipping is the process of discarding those objects (and parts of objects) that do not lie within the view volume.

3. Suppose a highlight should appear in the middle of a patch. That highlight is caused by a specific surface orientation at that point of the patch. Because Gouraud shading considers only the surface orientations along the boundaries of the patch, it will miss the highlight. But, because Phong shading attempts to determine the surface orientations within the patch interior, it may detect the highlight.

4. The rendering pipeline provides a standardized approach to rendering, which ultimately leads to more efficient rendering systems. In particular, the rendering pipeline can be implemented in firmware, meaning that the rendering process can be performed more quickly than if the task were implemented via traditional software.

5. The purpose of this question is to get you to think about the distinctions between local and global lighting models rather than to produce a specific predetermined answer. Potential solutions that you might propose include placing appropriately modified copies of the objects to be reflected behind the mirror while considering the mirror transparent or trying to handle images in the mirror as a form of drop shadows.

Section 10.5

1. We are interested only in the rays that ultimately reach the image window. If we started at the light source, we would not know which rays to follow.

2. Distributed ray tracing tries to avoid the inherent shiny appearance produced by traditional ray tracing by tracing multiple rays.

3. Radiosity is time consuming and fails to capture specular affects.

4. Both ray tracing and radiosity implement a global lighting model, and both are computationally intense. However, ray tracing tends to produce shiny-appearing surfaces, whereas radiosity leads to dull-appearing surfaces.

Section 10.6

1. There is not an exact answer. If an image lingers for 200 milliseconds and we projected five frames per second, each frame would have just faded away by the time the next frame was projected. This would probably result in a pulsating image that would be uncomfortable to watch for an extended time but still produce an animated effect. (In fact, slower rates can produce rough animation.) Note that the rate of five frames per second is well below the motion picture standard of twenty-four frames per second.

2. A storyboard is a "pictorial outline" of the desired animation sequence.

3. In-betweening is the process of creating frames that fill in the gaps between key frames.

4. Dynamics is the branch of mechanics that analyzes motion as the consequence of forces. Kinematics is the branch of mechanics that analyzes motion without regard for the forces that cause the motion.

Chapter 11

Section 11.1

1. Those introduced in the chapter include reflex actions, actions based on real-world knowledge, goal seeking actions, learning, and perception.

2. Our purpose here is not to give a decisive answer to this issue but to use it to show how delicate the argument over the existence of intelligence really is.

3. Although most of us would probably say no, we would probably claim that if a human dispensed the same products in a similar atmosphere, awareness would be present even though we might not be able to explain the distinction.

4. There is not a right or wrong answer. Most would agree that the machine at least appears to be intelligent.

5. There is not a right or wrong answer. It should be noted that chat bots, programs designed to emulate a person chatting, have difficulty carrying on a meaningful conversation for even a short period of time. Chat bots are easily identified as machines.

Section 11.2

1. In the remote control case, the system needs only to relay the picture, whereas to use the picture for maneuvering, the robot must be able to "understand" the meaning of the picture.

2. The possible interpretations for one section of the drawing do not match any of those of another section. To embed this insight into a program, you might isolate the interpretations allowable for various line junctions and then write a program that tries to find a set of compatible interpretations (one for each junction). In fact, if you stop and think about it, this is probably what your own senses did in trying to evaluate the drawing. Did you detect your eyes scanning back and forth between the two ends of the drawing as your senses tried to piece possible interpretations together? (If this subject interests you, you will want to read about the work of people such as D. A. Huffman, M. B. Clowes, and D. Waltz.)

3. There are four blocks in the stack but only three are visible. The point is that understanding this apparently simple concept requires a significant amount of "intelligence."

4. Interesting, isn't it? Such subtle distinctions in meaning present significant problems in the field of natural language understanding.

5. Is the sentence describing what kind of horses they are, or is it telling what some people are doing?

6. The parsing process produces identical structures, but the semantic analysis recognizes that the prepositional phrase in the first sentence tells where the fence was built, whereas the phrase in the second sentence tells when the fence was built.

7. They are brother and sister.

Section 11.3

1. Production systems provide a uniform approach to a variety of problems. That is, although apparently different in their original form, all problems reformulated into terms of production systems become the problem of finding a path through a state graph.

2.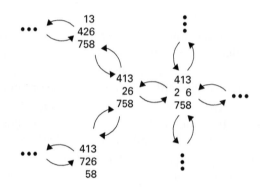

3. The tree is four moves deep. The upper portion appears as follows:

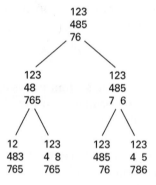

4. The task requires too much paper as well as too much time.

5. Our heuristic system for solving the eight-puzzle is based on an analysis of the immediate situation, just as that of the mountain climber. This short-sightedness is what allowed our algorithm to proceed initially along the wrong path in the example of this section just as a mountain climber can be led into trouble by always plotting a course based only on the local terrain. (This analogy often causes heuristic systems based on local or immediate information to be called hill-climbing systems.)

6. The system rotates the 5, 6, and 8 tiles either clockwise or counterclockwise until the goal state is reached.

7. The problem here is that our heuristic scheme ignores the value of keeping the hole adjacent to the tiles that are out of place. If the hole is surrounded by tiles in their correct position, some of these tiles must be moved before those tiles still seeking their correct place can be moved. Thus it is incorrect to consider all those tiles surrounding the hole as actually being correct. To fix this flaw, we might first observe that a tile in its correct position but blocking the hole from incorrectly positioned tiles must be moved away from its correct position and later moved back. Thus each correctly positioned tile on a path between the hole and the nearest incorrectly

positioned tile accounts for at least two moves in the remaining solution. We can therefore modify our projected cost calculation as follows:

First, calculate the projected cost as before. However, if the hole is totally isolated from the incorrectly positioned tiles, find a shortest path between the hole and an incorrectly positioned tile, multiply the number of tiles on this path by two, and add the resulting value to the previous projected cost.

With this system, the leaf nodes in Figure 11.10 have projected costs of 6, 6, and 4 (from left to right), and thus the correct branch is pursued initially.

Our new system is not foolproof. For example, consider the following configuration. The solution is to slide the 5 tile down, rotate the top two rows clockwise until those tiles are correct, move the 5 tile back up, and finally move the 8 tile to its correct position. However, our new heuristic system wants us to start by moving the 8 tile, because the state obtained by this initial move has a projected cost of only 6 compared with the other options that have costs of 8.

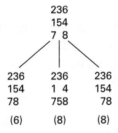

8. The solution found by the best fit algorithm is the path from Leesburg to Dayton and then to Bedford. This path is not the shortest route.

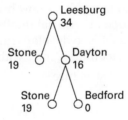

9. The solution found is the path from Leesburg to Stone, and then to Bedford. This path is the shortest route.

```
                    o Leesburg
                    0 + 34 = 34
                   /\
                  /  \
     Stone         o   o Dayton
     16 + 19 = 35      37 +16 = 53
                /\
               /  \
   Bedford      o  o Dayton
   35 + 0 = 35     44 + 16 = 60
```

Section 11.4

1. Real-world knowledge is the information about the environment that a human uses to understand and reason. Developing methods for representing, storing, and recalling this information is a major goal of research in artificial intelligence.

2. It uses the closed-world assumption.

3. The frame problem is the problem of correctly updating a machine's store of knowledge as events occur. The task is complicated by the fact that many events have indirect consequences.

4. Imitation, supervised training, and reinforcement. Reinforcement does not involve direct human intervention.

5. Traditional techniques derive a single computer system. Evolutionary techniques involve multiple generations of trial systems from which a "good" system may be discovered.

Section 11.5

1. All patterns produce an output of 0 except for the pattern 1, 0, which produces an output of 1.

2. Assign a weight of 1 to each input, and assign the unit a threshold value of 1.5.

3. A major problem identified in the text is that the training process might oscillate, repeating the same adjustments over and over.

4. The network will wander to the configuration in which the center neuron is excited and all others are inhibited.

Section 11.6

1. Rather than developing a complete plan of action, the reactive approach is to wait and make decisions as options arise.

2. The point here is for you to think about how broad the field of robotics is. It encompasses the entire scope of artificial intelligence as well as numerous topics in other fields. The goal is to develop truly autonomous machines that can move about and react intelligently with their environments.

3. Internal control and physical structure.

Section 11.7

1. There is no right or wrong answer.

2. There is no right or wrong answer.

3. There is no right or wrong answer.

Chapter 12

Section 12.1

1. How about the boolean operations AND, OR, and XOR. In fact, we used tables in Chapter 1 when introducing these functions.

2. The computation of a loan payment, the area of a circle, or a car's mileage.

3. Mathematicians call such functions transcendental functions. Examples include the logarithmic and trigonometric functions. These particular

examples can still be computed but not by algebraic means. For example, the trigonometric functions can be calculated by actually drawing the triangle involved, measuring its sides, and only then turning to the algebraic operation of dividing.

4. One example is the problem of trisecting an angle. That is, they were unable to construct an angle that was one-third the size of a given angle. The point is that the Greeks' straight-edge and compass computational system is another example of a system with limitations.

Section 12.2

1. The result is the following diagram:

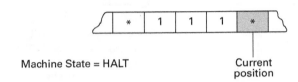

Machine State = HALT   Current position

2.

Current state	Current cell content	Value to write	Direction to move	New state to enter
START	*	*	left	STATE 1
STATE 1	0	0	left	STATE 2
STATE 1	1	0	left	STATE 2
STATE 1	*	0	left	STATE 2
STATE 2	0	*	right	STATE 3
STATE 2	1	*	right	STATE 3
STATE 2	*	*	right	STATE 3
STATE 3	0	0	right	HALT
STATE 3	1	0	right	HALT

3.

Current state	Current cell content	Value to write	Direction to move	New state to enter
START	*	*	left	SUBTRACT
SUBTRACT	0	1	left	BORROW
SUBTRACT	1	0	left	NO BORROW
BORROW	0	1	left	BORROW
BORROW	1	0	left	NO BORROW
BORROW	*	*	right	ZERO
NO BORROW	0	0	left	NO BORROW
NO BORROW	1	1	left	NO BORROW
NO BORROW	*	*	right	RETURN
ZERO	0	0	right	ZERO
ZERO	1	0	right	ZERO
ZERO	*	*	no move	HALT
RETURN	0	0	right	RETURN
RETURN	1	1	right	RETURN
RETURN	*	*	no move	HALT

4. The point here is that the concept of a Turing machine is supposed to capture the meaning of "to compute." That is, any time a situation occurs in
which computing is taking place, the components and activities of a Turing
machine should be present. For example, a person figuring income tax is
doing a certain degree of computing. The computing machine is the person
and the tape is represented by the paper on which values are recorded.

5. The machine described by the following table halts if started with an even
input but never halts if started with an odd input:

Current state	Cell content	Value to write	Direction to move	New state to enter
START	*	*	left	STATE 1
STATE 1	0	0	right	HALT
STATE 1	1	1	no move	STATE 1
STATE 1	*	*	no move	STATE 1

Section 12.3

1. ```
clear AUX
incr AUX
while X not 0:
   clear X
   clear AUX
while AUX not 0:
   incr X
   clear AUX
```

2. ```
while X not 0:
   decr X
```

3. ```
copy X to AUX
while AUX not 0:
   S1
   clear AUX
copy X to AUX
invert AUX (See Question #1)
while AUX not 0:
   S2
   clear AUX
while X not 0:
   clear AUX
   clear X
```

4. If we assume that X refers to the memory cell at address 40 and that each program segment starts at location 00, we have the following conversion table:

```
clear X
incr X
decr X
```
```

```
while X not 0:
        .
        .
        .
```

5. Just as in a real machine, negative numbers could be dealt with via a coding system. For example, the rightmost bit in each string can be used as a sign but with the remaining bits used to represent the magnitude of the value.

6. The function is multiplication by 2.

Section 12.4

1. Yes. In fact, this program halts regardless of the initial values of its variables, and therefore it must halt if its variables are initialized to the program's encoded representation.

2. The program halts only if the initial value of X ends in a 1. Because the ASCII representation of a semicolon is 00111011, the encoded version of the program must end in a 1. Therefore the program is self-terminating.

3. The point here is that the logic is the same as in our argument that the halting problem does not have an algorithmic solution. If the house painter paints his or her own house, then he or she does not and vice versa.

Section 12.5

1. We could conclude only that the problem has complexity $\Theta(2^n)$. If we could show that the "best algorithm" for solving the problem belongs to $\Theta(2^n)$, we could conclude that the problem belongs to $\Theta(2^n)$.

2. No. As a general rule, the algorithm in $\Theta(n^2)$ will outperform the one in $\Theta(2^n)$, but for small input values an exponential algorithm often outperforms a polynomial algorithm. In fact, it is true that exponential algorithms are sometimes preferred to polynomial ones when the application involves only small inputs.

3. The point is that the number of subcommittees is growing exponentially, and from this point on, the job of listing all the possibilities becomes a laborious task.

4. Within the class of polynomial problems is the sorting problem, which can be solved by polynomial algorithms such as the insertion sort. Within the class of nonpolynomial problems is the task of listing all the subcommittees that could be formed from a given parent committee. Any polynomial problem is an NP problem. The Traveling Salesman problem is an example of an NP problem that has not been shown to be a polynomial problem.

5. No. Our use of the term *complexity* refers to the time required to execute an algorithm—not to how hard the algorithm might be to understand.

Section 12.6

1. $211 - 313 = 66043$

2. The message 101 is the binary representation for 5. $5^e = 5^5 = 15625$. 15625 (mod 91) = 64, which is 1000000 in binary notation. Thus, 1000000 is the encrypted version of the message.

3. The message 10 is the binary representation for 2. $2^d = 2^{29} = 536870912$. 536870912 (mod 91) = 32, which is 100000 in binary notation. Thus, 100000 is the decrypted version of the message.

4. $n = p - q = 7 - 19 = 133$. To find d we need a positive integer value k such that $k(p - 1)(q - 1) + 1 = k(6 - 18) + 1 = 108k + 1$ is evenly divisible by $e = 5$. The values $k = 1$ and $k = 2$ are not satisfactory, but $k = 3$ produces $108k + 1 = 325$, which is divisible by 5. The quotient 65 is the value of d.

Taken from:
Building Java Programs: A Back to Basics Approach, Fourth Edition
by Stuart Reges and Marty Stepp

Introduction to
Java Programming

Introduction

This chapter begins with a review of some basic terminology about computers and computer programming. Many of these concepts will come up in later chapters, so it will be useful to review them before we start delving into the details of how to program in Java.

We will begin our exploration of Java by looking at simple programs that produce output. This discussion will allow us to explore many elements that are common to all Java programs, while working with programs that are fairly simple in structure.

After we have reviewed the basic elements of Java programs, we will explore the technique of procedural decomposition by learning how to break up a Java program into several methods. Using this technique, we can break up complex tasks into smaller subtasks that are easier to manage and we can avoid redundancy in our program solutions.

1.1 Basic Computing Concepts

Computers are pervasive in our daily lives, and, thanks to the Internet, they give us access to nearly limitless information. Some of this information is essential news, like the headlines at cnn.com. Computers let us share photos with our families and map directions to the nearest pizza place for dinner.

Lots of real-world problems are being solved by computers, some of which don't much resemble the one on your desk or lap. Computers allow us to sequence the human genome and search for DNA patterns within it. Computers in recently manufactured cars monitor each vehicle's status and motion. Digital music players such as Apple's iPod actually have computers inside their small casings. Even the Roomba vacuum-cleaning robot houses a computer with complex instructions about how to dodge furniture while cleaning your floors.

But what makes a computer a computer? Is a calculator a computer? Is a human being with a paper and pencil a computer? The next several sections attempt to address this question while introducing some basic terminology that will help prepare you to study programming.

Why Programming?

At most universities, the first course in computer science is a programming course. Many computer scientists are bothered by this because it leaves people with the impression that computer science is programming. While it is true that many trained computer scientists spend time programming, there is a lot more to the discipline. So why do we study programming first?

A Stanford computer scientist named Don Knuth answers this question by saying that the common thread for most computer scientists is that we all in some way work with *algorithms*.

> **Algorithm**
> A step-by-step description of how to accomplish a task.

Knuth is an expert in algorithms, so he is naturally biased toward thinking of them as the center of computer science. Still, he claims that what is most important is not the algorithms themselves, but rather the thought process that computer scientists employ to develop them. According to Knuth,

> It has often been said that a person does not really understand something
> until after teaching it to someone else. Actually a person does not *really*
> understand something until after teaching it to a *computer*, i.e., expressing
> it as an algorithm.[1]

---

[1]Knuth, Don. *Selected Papers on Computer Science*. Stanford, CA: Center for the Study of Language and Information, 1996.

Knuth is describing a thought process that is common to most of computer science, which he refers to as *algorithmic thinking*. We study programming not because it is the most important aspect of computer science, but because it is the best way to explain the approach that computer scientists take to solving problems.

The concept of algorithms is helpful in understanding what a computer is and what computer science is all about. The Merriam-Webster dictionary defines the word "computer" as "one that computes." Using that definition, all sorts of devices qualify as computers, including calculators, GPS navigation systems, and children's toys like the Furby. Prior to the invention of electronic computers, it was common to refer to humans as computers. The nineteenth-century mathematician Charles Peirce, for example, was originally hired to work for the U.S. government as an "Assistant Computer" because his job involved performing mathematical computations.

In a broad sense, then, the word "computer" can be applied to many devices. But when computer scientists refer to a computer, we are usually thinking of a universal computation device that can be programmed to execute any algorithm. Computer science, then, is the study of computational devices and the study of computation itself, including algorithms.

Algorithms are expressed as computer programs, and that is what this book is all about. But before we look at how to program, it will be useful to review some basic concepts about computers.

Hardware and Software

A computer is a machine that manipulates data and executes lists of instructions known as *programs*.

> **Program**
> A list of instructions to be carried out by a computer.

One key feature that differentiates a computer from a simpler machine like a calculator is its versatility. The same computer can perform many different tasks (playing games, computing income taxes, connecting to other computers around the world), depending on what program it is running at a given moment. A computer can run not only the programs that exist on it currently, but also new programs that haven't even been written yet.

The physical components that make up a computer are collectively called *hardware*. One of the most important pieces of hardware is the central processing unit, or *CPU*. The CPU is the "brain" of the computer: It is what executes the instructions. Also important is the computer's *memory* (often called random access memory, or *RAM*, because the computer can access any part of that memory at any time). The computer uses its memory to store programs that are being executed, along with their data. RAM is limited in size and does not retain its contents when the computer is turned off. Therefore, computers generally also use a *hard disk* as a larger permanent storage area.

Computer programs are collectively called *software*. The primary piece of software running on a computer is its operating system. An *operating system* provides an environment in which many programs may be run at the same time; it also provides a bridge between those programs, the hardware, and the *user* (the person using the computer). The programs that run inside the operating system are often called *applications*.

When the user selects a program for the operating system to run (e.g., by double-clicking the program's icon on the desktop), several things happen: The instructions for that program are loaded into the computer's memory from the hard disk, the operating system allocates memory for that program to use, and the instructions to run the program are fed from memory to the CPU and executed sequentially.

The Digital Realm

In the last section, we saw that a computer is a general-purpose device that can be programmed. You will often hear people refer to modern computers as *digital* computers because of the way they operate.

> **Digital**
>
> Based on numbers that increase in discrete increments, such as the integers 0, 1, 2, 3, etc.

Because computers are digital, everything that is stored on a computer is stored as a sequence of integers. This includes every program and every piece of data. An MP3 file, for example, is simply a long sequence of integers that stores audio information. Today we're used to digital music, digital pictures, and digital movies, but in the 1940s, when the first computers were built, the idea of storing complex data in integer form was fairly unusual.

Not only are computers digital, storing all information as integers, but they are also *binary*, which means they store integers as *binary numbers*.

> **Binary Number**
>
> A number composed of just 0s and 1s, also known as a base-2 number.

Humans generally work with *decimal* or base-10 numbers, which match our physiology (10 fingers and 10 toes). However, when we were designing the first computers, we wanted systems that would be easy to create and very reliable. It turned out to be simpler to build these systems on top of binary phenomena (e.g., a circuit being open or closed) rather than having 10 different states that would have to be distinguished from one another (e.g., 10 different voltage levels).

From a mathematical point of view, you can store things just as easily using binary numbers as you can using base-10 numbers. But since it is easier to construct a physical device that uses binary numbers, that's what computers use.

This does mean, however, that people who aren't used to computers find their conventions unfamiliar. As a result, it is worth spending a little time reviewing how binary numbers work. To count with binary numbers, as with base-10 numbers, you start with 0 and count up, but you run out of digits much faster. So, counting in binary, you say

```
0
1
```

And already you've run out of digits. This is like reaching 9 when you count in base-10. After you run out of digits, you carry over to the next digit. So, the next two binary numbers are

```
10
11
```

And again, you've run out of digits. This is like reaching 99 in base-10. Again, you carry over to the next digit to form the three-digit number 100. In binary, whenever you see a series of ones, such as 111111, you know you're just one away from the digits all flipping to 0s with a 1 added in front, the same way that, in base-10, when you see a number like 999999, you know that you are one away from all those digits turning to 0s with a 1 added in front.

Table 1.1 shows how to count up to the base-10 number 8 using binary.

Table 1.1 Decimal vs. Binary

Decimal	Binary
0	0
1	1
2	10
3	11
4	100
5	101
6	110
7	111
8	1000

We can make several useful observations about binary numbers. Notice in the table that the binary numbers 1, 10, 100, and 1000 are all perfect powers of 2 (2^0, 2^1, 2^2, 2^3). In the same way that in base-10 we talk about a ones digit, tens digit, hundreds digit, and so on, we can think in binary of a ones digit, twos digit, fours digit, eights digit, sixteens digit, and so on.

Computer scientists quickly found themselves needing to refer to the sizes of different binary quantities, so they invented the term *bit* to refer to a single binary digit and the term *byte* to refer to 8 bits. To talk about large amounts of memory, they invented the terms "kilobytes" (KB), "megabytes" (MB), "gigabytes" (GB), and so on. Many people think that these correspond to the metric system, where "kilo" means 1000, but that is only approximately true. We use the fact that 2^{10} is approximately equal to 1000 (it actually equals 1024). Table 1.2 shows some common units of memory storage:

Table 1.2   Units of Memory Storage

Measurement	Power of 2	Actual Value	Example
kilobyte (KB)	2^{10}	1024	500-word paper (3 KB)
megabyte (MB)	2^{20}	1,048,576	typical book (1 MB) or song (5 MB)
gigabyte (GB)	2^{30}	1,073,741,824	typical movie (4.7 GB)
terabyte (TB)	2^{40}	1,099,511,627,776	20 million books in the Library of Congress (20 TB)
petabyte (PB)	2^{50}	1,125,899,906,842,624	10 billion photos on Facebook (1.5 PB)

The Process of Programming

The word *code* describes program fragments ("these four lines of code") or the act of programming ("Let's code this into Java"). Once a program has been written, you can *execute* it.

> **Program Execution**
>
> The act of carrying out the instructions contained in a program.

The process of execution is often called *running*. This term can also be used as a verb ("When my program runs it does something strange") or as a noun ("The last run of my program produced these results").

A computer program is stored internally as a series of binary numbers known as the *machine language* of the computer. In the early days, programmers entered numbers like these directly into the computer. Obviously, this is a tedious and confusing way to program a computer, and we have invented all sorts of mechanisms to simplify this process.

Modern programmers write in what are known as high-level programming languages, such as Java. Such programs cannot be run directly on a computer: They first have to be translated into a different form by a special program known as a *compiler*.

> **Compiler**
>
> A program that translates a computer program written in one language into an equivalent program in another language (often, but not always, translating from a high-level language into machine language).

A compiler that translates directly into machine language creates a program that can be executed directly on the computer, known as an *executable*. We refer to such compilers as *native compilers* because they compile code to the lowest possible level (the native machine language of the computer).

This approach works well when you know exactly what computer you want to use to run your program. But what if you want to execute a program on many different computers? You'd need a compiler that generates different machine language output for each of them. The designers of Java decided to use a different approach. They cared a lot about their programs being able to run on many different computers, because they wanted to create a language that worked well for the Web.

Instead of compiling into machine language, Java programs compile into what are known as *Java bytecodes*. One set of bytecodes can execute on many different machines. These bytecodes represent an intermediate level: They aren't quite as high-level as Java or as low-level as machine language. In fact, they are the machine language of a theoretical computer known as the *Java Virtual Machine (JVM)*.

> ### Java Virtual Machine
> A theoretical computer whose machine language is the set of Java bytecodes.

A JVM isn't an actual machine, but it's similar to one. When we compile programs to this level, there isn't much work remaining to turn the Java bytecodes into actual machine instructions.

To actually execute a Java program, you need another program that will execute the Java bytecodes. Such programs are known generically as *Java runtimes*, and the standard environment distributed by Oracle Corporation is known as the *Java Runtime Environment (JRE)*.

> ### Java Runtime
> A program that executes compiled Java bytecodes.

Most people have Java runtimes on their computers, even if they don't know about them. For example, Apple's Mac OS X includes a Java runtime, and many Windows applications install a Java runtime.

Why Java?

When Sun Microsystems released Java in 1995, it published a document called a "white paper" describing its new programming language. Perhaps the key sentence from that paper is the following:

> Java: A simple, object-oriented, network-savvy, interpreted, robust, secure, architecture neutral, portable, high-performance, multithreaded, dynamic language.[2]

This sentence covers many of the reasons why Java is a good introductory programming language. For starters, Java is reasonably simple for beginners to learn, and it embraces object-oriented programming, a style of writing programs that has been shown to be very successful for creating large and complex software systems.

---

[2]http://www.oracle.com/technetwork/java/langenv-140151.html

Java also includes a large amount of prewritten software that programmers can utilize to enhance their programs. Such off-the-shelf software components are often called *libraries*. For example, if you wish to write a program that connects to a site on the Internet, Java contains a library to simplify the connection for you. Java contains libraries to draw graphical user interfaces (GUIs), retrieve data from databases, and perform complex mathematical computations, among many other things. These libraries collectively are called the *Java class libraries*.

> **Java Class Libraries**
>
> The collection of preexisting Java code that provides solutions to common programming problems.

The richness of the Java class libraries has been an extremely important factor in the rise of Java as a popular language. The Java class libraries in version 1.7 include over 4000 entries.

Another reason to use Java is that it has a vibrant programmer community. Extensive online documentation and tutorials are available to help programmers learn new skills. Many of these documents are written by Oracle, including an extensive reference to the Java class libraries called the *API Specification* (API stands for Application Programming Interface).

Java is extremely platform independent; unlike programs written in many other languages, the same Java program can be executed on many different operating systems, such as Windows, Linux, and Mac OS X.

Java is used extensively for both research and business applications, which means that a large number of programming jobs exist in the marketplace today for skilled Java programmers. A sample Google search for the phrase "Java jobs" returned around 180,000,000 hits at the time of this writing.

The Java Programming Environment

You must become familiar with your computer setup before you start programming. Each computer provides a different environment for program development, but there are some common elements that deserve comment. No matter what environment you use, you will follow the same basic three steps:

1. Type in a program as a Java class.
2. Compile the program file.
3. Run the compiled version of the program.

The basic unit of storage on most computers is a *file*. Every file has a name. A file name ends with an *extension*, which is the part of a file's name that follows the period. A file's extension indicates the type of data contained in the file. For example, files with the extension .doc are Microsoft Word documents, and files with the extension .mp3 are MP3 audio files.

The Java program files that you create must use the extension .java. When you compile a Java program, the resulting Java bytecodes are stored in a file with the same name and the extension .class.

Most Java programmers use what are known as Integrated Development Environments, or IDEs, which provide an all-in-one environment for creating, editing, compiling, and executing program files. Some of the more popular choices for introductory computer science classes are Eclipse, jGRASP, DrJava, BlueJ, and TextPad. Your instructor will tell you what environment you should use.

Try typing the following simple program in your IDE (the line numbers are not part of the program but are used as an aid):

```
1   public class Hello {
2       public static void main(String[] args) {
3           System.out.println("Hello, world!");
4       }
5   }
```

Don't worry about the details of this program right now. We will explore those in the next section.

Once you have created your program file, move to step 2 and compile it. The command to compile will be different in each development environment, but the process is the same (typical commands are "compile" or "build"). If any errors are reported, go back to the editor, fix them, and try to compile the program again. (We'll discuss errors in more detail later in this chapter.)

Once you have successfully compiled your program, you are ready to move to step 3, running the program. Again, the command to do this will differ from one environment to the next, but the process is similar (the typical command is "run"). The diagram in Figure 1.1 summarizes the steps you would follow in creating a program called Hello.java.

In some IDEs (most notably Eclipse), the first two steps are combined. In these environments the process of compiling is more incremental; the compiler will warn you about errors as you type in code. It is generally not necessary to formally ask such an environment to compile your program because it is compiling as you type.

When your program is executed, it will typically interact with the user in some way. The Hello.java program involves an onscreen window known as the *console*.

> **Console Window**
>
> A special text-only window in which Java programs interact with the user.

The console window is a classic interaction mechanism wherein the computer displays text on the screen and sometimes waits for the user to type responses. This is known as *console* or *terminal interaction*. The text the computer prints to the console window is known as the *output* of the program. Anything typed by the user is known as the console *input*.

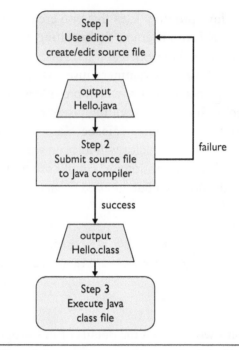

Figure I.I   Creation and execution of a Java program

To keep things simple, most of the sample programs in this book involve console interaction. Keeping the interaction simple will allow you to focus your attention and effort on other aspects of programming.

1.2 And Now—Java

It's time to look at a complete Java program. In the Java programming language, nothing can exist outside of a *class*.

> **Class**
>
> A unit of code that is the basic building block of Java programs.

The notion of a class is much richer than this, as you'll see when we get to Chapter 8, but for now all you need to know is that each of your Java programs will be stored in a class.

It is a tradition in computer science that when you describe a new programming language, you should start with a program that produces a single line of output with the words, "Hello, world!" The "hello world" tradition has been broken by many authors of Java books because the program turns out not to be as short and simple when it is written in Java as when it is written in other languages, but we'll use it here anyway.

Here is our "hello world" program:

```
1   public class Hello {
2       public static void main(String[] args) {
3           System.out.println("Hello, world!");
4       }
5   }
```

This program defines a class called `Hello`. Oracle has established the convention that class names always begin with a capital letter, which makes it easy to recognize them. Java requires that the class name and the file name match, so this program must be stored in a file called `Hello.java`. You don't have to understand all the details of this program just yet, but you do need to understand the basic structure.

The basic form of a Java class is as follows:

```
public class <name> {
    <method>
    <method>
    ...
    <method>
}
```

This type of description is known as a *syntax template* because it describes the basic form of a Java construct. Java has rules that determine its legal *syntax* or grammar. Each time we introduce a new element of Java, we'll begin by looking at its syntax template. By convention, we use the less-than (<) and greater-than (>) characters in a syntax template to indicate items that need to be filled in (in this case, the name of the class and the methods). When we write "..." in a list of elements, we're indicating that any number of those elements may be included.

The first line of the class is known as the *class header*. The word `public` in the header indicates that this class is available to anyone to use. Notice that the program code in a class is enclosed in curly brace characters (`{ }`). These characters are used in Java to group together related bits of code. In this case, the curly braces are indicating that everything defined within them is part of this public class.

So what exactly can appear inside the curly braces? What can be contained in a class? All sorts of things, but for now, we'll limit ourselves to *methods*. Methods are the next-smallest unit of code in Java, after classes. A method represents a single action or calculation to be performed.

> **Method**
>
> A program unit that represents a particular action or computation.

Simple methods are like verbs: They command the computer to perform some action. Inside the curly braces for a class, you can define several different methods.

At a minimum, a complete program requires a special method that is known as the `main` method. It has the following syntax:

```
public static void main(String[] args) {
    <statement>;
    <statement>;
    ...
    <statement>;
}
```

Just as the first line of a class is known as a class header, the first line of a method is known as a *method header*. The header for `main` is rather complicated. Most people memorize this as a kind of magical incantation. You want to open the door to Ali Baba's cave? You say, "Open Sesame!" You want to create an executable Java program? You say, `public static void main(String[] args)`. A group of Java teachers make fun of this with a website called publicstaticvoidmain.com.

Just memorizing magical incantations is never satisfying, especially for computer scientists who like to know everything that is going on in their programs. But this is a place where Java shows its ugly side, and you'll just have to live with it. New programmers, like new drivers, must learn to use something complex without fully understanding how it works. Fortunately, by the time you finish this book, you'll understand every part of the incantation.

Notice that the `main` method has a set of curly braces of its own. They are again used for grouping, indicating that everything that appears between them is part of the `main` method. The lines in between the curly braces specify the series of actions the computer should perform when it executes the method. We refer to these as the *statements* of the method. Just as you put together an essay by stringing together complete sentences, you put together a method by stringing together statements.

> **Statement**
>
> An executable snippet of code that represents a complete command.

Each statement is terminated by a semicolon. The sample "hello world" program has just a single statement that is known as a `println` statement:

```
System.out.println("Hello, world!");
```

Notice that this statement ends with a semicolon. The semicolon has a special status in Java; it is used to terminate statements in the same way that periods terminate sentences in English.

In the basic "hello world" program there is just a single command to produce a line of output, but consider the following variation (called `Hello2`), which has four lines of code to be executed in the `main` method:

```
1   public class Hello2 {
2       public static void main(String[] args) {
3           System.out.println("Hello, world!");
4           System.out.println();
5           System.out.println("This program produces four");
6           System.out.println("lines of output.");
7       }
8   }
```

Notice that there are four semicolons in the `main` method, one at the end of each of the four `println` statements. The statements are executed in the order in which they appear, from first to last, so the `Hello2` program produces the following output:

```
Hello, world!

This program produces four
lines of output.
```

Let's summarize the different levels we just looked at:

- A Java program is stored in a class.
- Within the class, there are methods. At a minimum, a complete program requires a special method called `main`.
- Inside a method like `main`, there is a series of statements, each of which represents a single command for the computer to execute.

It may seem odd to put the opening curly brace at the end of a line rather than on a line by itself. Some people would use this style of indentation for the program instead:

```
1   public class Hello3
2   {
3       public static void main(String[] args)
4       {
5           System.out.println("Hello, world!");
6       }
7   }
```

Different people will make different choices about the placement of curly braces. The style we use follows Oracle's official Java coding conventions, but the other style has its advocates too. Often people will passionately argue that one way is much better than the other, but it's really a matter of personal taste because each choice has some advantages and some disadvantages. Your instructor may require a particular style; if not, you should choose a style that you are comfortable with and then use it consistently.

Now that you've seen an overview of the structure, let's examine some of the details of Java programs.

Did You Know?

Hello, World!

The "hello world" tradition was started by Brian Kernighan and Dennis Ritchie. Ritchie invented a programming language known as C in the 1970s and, together with Kernighan, coauthored the first book describing C, published in 1978. The first complete program in their book was a "hello world" program. Kernighan and Ritchie, as well as their book *The C Programming Language*, have been affectionately referred to as "K & R" ever since.

Many major programming languages have borrowed the basic C syntax as a way to leverage the popularity of C and to encourage programmers to switch to it. The languages C++ and Java both borrow a great deal of their core syntax from C.

Kernighan and Ritchie also had a distinctive style for the placement of curly braces and the indentation of programs that has become known as "K & R style." This is the style that Oracle recommends and that we use in this book.

String Literals (Strings)

When you are writing Java programs (such as the preceding "hello world" program), you'll often want to include some literal text to send to the console window as output. Programmers have traditionally referred to such text as a *string* because it is composed of a sequence of characters that we string together. The Java language specification uses the term *string literals*.

In Java you specify a string literal by surrounding the literal text in quotation marks, as in

```
"This is a bunch of text surrounded by quotation marks."
```

You must use double quotation marks, not single quotation marks. The following is not a valid string literal:

```
'Bad stuff here.'
```

The following is a valid string literal:

```
"This is a string even with 'these' quotes inside."
```

String literals must not span more than one line of a program. The following is not a valid string literal:

```
"This is really
bad stuff
right here."
```

System.out.println

As you have seen, the `main` method of a Java program contains a series of statements for the computer to carry out. They are executed sequentially, starting with the first statement, then the second, then the third, and so on until the final statement has been executed. One of the simplest and most common statements is `System.out.println`, which is used to produce a line of output. This is another "magical incantation" that you should commit to memory. As of this writing, Google lists around 8,000,000 web pages that mention `System.out.println`. The key thing to remember about this statement is that it's used to produce a line of output that is sent to the console window.

The simplest form of the `println` statement has nothing inside its parentheses and produces a blank line of output:

```
System.out.println();
```

You need to include the parentheses even if you don't have anything to put inside them. Notice the semicolon at the end of the line. All statements in Java must be terminated with a semicolon.

More often, however, you use `println` to output a line of text:

```
System.out.println("This line uses the println method.");
```

The above statement commands the computer to produce the following line of output:

```
This line uses the println method.
```

Each `println` statement produces a different line of output. For example, consider the following three statements:

```
System.out.println("This is the first line of output.");
System.out.println();
System.out.println("This is the third, below a blank line.");
```

Executing these statements produces the following three lines of output (the second line is blank):

```
This is the first line of output.

This is the third, below a blank line.
```

Escape Sequences

Any system that involves quoting text will lead you to certain difficult situations. For example, string literals are contained inside quotation marks, so how can you include a quotation mark inside a string literal? String literals also aren't allowed to break across lines, so how can you include a line break inside a string literal?

The solution is to embed what are known as *escape sequences* in the string literals. Escape sequences are two-character sequences that are used to represent special characters. They all begin with the backslash character (\). Table 1.3 lists some of the more common escape sequences.

Table 1.3 **Common Escape Sequences**

Sequence	Represents
\t	tab character
\n	new line character
\"	quotation mark
\\	backslash character

Keep in mind that each of these two-character sequences actually stands for just a single character. For example, consider the following statement:

```
System.out.println("What \"characters\" does this \\ print?");
```

If you executed this statement, you would get the following output:

```
What "characters" does this \ print?
```

The string literal in the `println` has three escape sequences, each of which is two characters long and produces a single character of output.

While string literals themselves cannot span multiple lines (that is, you cannot use a carriage return within a string literal to force a line break), you can use the \n escape sequence to embed new line characters in a string. This leads to the odd situation where a single `println` statement can produce more than one line of output.

For example, consider this statement:

```
System.out.println("This\nproduces 3 lines\nof output.");
```

If you execute it, you will get the following output:

```
This
produces 3 lines
of output.
```

The `println` itself produces one line of output, but the string literal contains two new line characters that cause it to be broken up into a total of three lines of output. To produce the same output without new line characters, you would have to issue three separate `println` statements.

This is another programming habit that tends to vary according to taste. Some people (including the authors) find it hard to read string literals that contain \n escape sequences, but other people prefer to write fewer lines of code. Once again, you should make up your own mind about when to use the new line escape sequence.

print versus println

Java has a variation of the `println` command called `print` that allows you to produce output on the current line without going to a new line of output. The `println` command really does two different things: It sends output to the current line, and then it moves to the beginning of a new line. The `print` command does only the first of these. Thus, a series of `print` commands will generate output all on the same line. Only a `println` command will cause the current line to be completed and a new line to be started. For example, consider these six statements:

```
System.out.print("To be ");
System.out.print("or not to be.");
System.out.print("That is ");
System.out.println("the question.");
System.out.print("This is");
System.out.println(" for the whole family!");
```

These statements produce two lines of output. Remember that every `println` statement produces exactly one line of output; because there are two `println` statements here, there are two lines of output. After the first statement executes, the current line looks like this:

```
To be 
      ^
```

The arrow below the output line indicates the position where output will be sent next. We can simplify our discussion if we refer to the arrow as the *output cursor*. Notice that the output cursor is at the end of this line and that it appears after a space. The reason is that the command was a `print` (doesn't go to a new line) and the string literal in the `print` ended with a space. Java will not insert a space for you unless you specifically request it. After the next `print`, the line looks like this:

```
To be or not to be. 
                   ^
```

There's no space at the end now because the string literal in the second `print` command ends in a period, not a space. After the next `print`, the line looks like this:

```
To be or not to be.That is 
                          ^
```

There is no space between the period and the word "That" because there was no space in the `print` commands, but there is a space at the end of the string literal in the third statement. After the next statement executes, the output looks like this:

```
To be or not to be.That is the question.

^
```

Because this fourth statement is a `println` command, it finishes the output line and positions the cursor at the beginning of the second line. The next statement is another `print` that produces this:

```
To be or not to be.That is the question.
This is
       ^
```

The final `println` completes the second line and positions the output cursor at the beginning of a new line:

```
To be or not to be.That is the question.
This is for the whole family!


^
```

These six statements are equivalent to the following two single statements:

```
System.out.println("To be or not to be.That is the question.");
System.out.println("This is for the whole family!");
```

Using the `print` and `println` commands together to produce lines like these may seem a bit silly, but you will see that there are more interesting applications of `print` in the next chapter.

Remember that it is possible to have an empty `println` command:

```
System.out.println();
```

Because there is nothing inside the parentheses to be written to the output line, this command positions the output cursor at the beginning of the next line. If there are `print` commands before this empty `println`, it finishes out the line made by those `print` commands. If there are no previous `print` commands, it produces a blank line. An empty `print` command is meaningless and illegal.

Identifiers and Keywords

The words used to name parts of a Java program are called *identifiers*.

> **Identifier**
> A name given to an entity in a program, such as a class or method.

Identifiers must start with a letter, which can be followed by any number of letters or digits. The following are all legal identifiers:

```
first            hiThere      numStudents   TwoBy4
```

The Java language specification defines the set of letters to include the underscore and dollar-sign characters (_ and $), which means that the following are legal identifiers as well:

```
two_plus_two       _count       $2donuts       MAX_COUNT
```

The following are illegal identifiers:

```
two+two          hi there     hi-There     2by4
```

Java has conventions for capitalization that are followed fairly consistently by programmers. All class names should begin with a capital letter, as with the `Hello`, `Hello2`, and `Hello3` classes introduced earlier. The names of methods should begin with lowercase letters, as in the `main` method. When you are putting several words together to form a class or method name, capitalize the first letter of each word after the first. In the next chapter we'll discuss constants, which have yet another capitalization scheme, with all letters in uppercase and words separated by underscores. These different schemes might seem like tedious constraints, but using consistent capitalization in your code allows the reader to quickly identify the various code elements.

For example, suppose that you were going to put together the words "all my children" into an identifier. The result would be

- `AllMyChildren` for a class name (each word starts with a capital)
- `allMyChildren` for a method name (starts with a lowercase letter, subsequent words capitalized)
- `ALL_MY_CHILDREN` for a constant name (all uppercase, with words separated by underscores; described in Chapter 2)

Java is case sensitive, so the identifiers `class`, `Class`, `CLASS`, and `cLASs` are all considered different. Keep this in mind as you read error messages from the compiler. People are good at understanding what you write, even if you misspell words or make little mistakes like changing the capitalization of a word. However, mistakes like these cause the Java compiler to become hopelessly confused.

Don't hesitate to use long identifiers. The more descriptive your names are, the easier it will be for people (including you) to read your programs. Descriptive identifiers are worth the time they take to type. Java's `String` class, for example, has a method called `compareToIgnoreCase`.

Be aware, however, that Java has a set of predefined identifiers called *keywords* that are reserved for particular uses. As you read this book, you will learn many of these keywords and their uses. You can only use keywords for their intended purposes. You must be careful to avoid using these words in the names of identifiers. For example, if you name a method `short` or `try`, this will cause a problem, because `short` and `try` are reserved keywords. Table 1.4 shows the complete list of reserved keywords.

Table 1.4   List of Java Keywords

abstract	continue	for	new	switch
assert	default	goto	package	synchronized
boolean	do	if	private	this
break	double	implements	protected	throw
byte	else	import	public	throws
case	enum	instanceof	return	transient
catch	extends	int	short	try
char	final	interface	static	void
class	finally	long	strictfp	volatile
const	float	native	super	while

A Complex Example: DrawFigures1

The println statement can be used to draw text figures as output. Consider the following more complicated program example (notice that it uses two empty println statements to produce blank lines):

```
1  public class DrawFigures1 {
2      public static void main(String[] args) {
3          System.out.println("   /\\");
4          System.out.println("  /  \\");
5          System.out.println(" /    \\");
6          System.out.println(" \\    /");
7          System.out.println("  \\  /");
8          System.out.println("   \\/");
9          System.out.println();
10         System.out.println(" \\      /");
11         System.out.println("  \\  /");
12         System.out.println("   \\/");
13         System.out.println("   /\\");
14         System.out.println("  /  \\");
15         System.out.println(" /    \\");
16         System.out.println();
17         System.out.println("   /\\");
18         System.out.println("  /  \\");
19         System.out.println(" /    \\");
20         System.out.println("+------+");
21         System.out.println("|      |");
22         System.out.println("|      |");
23         System.out.println("+------+");
24         System.out.println("|United|");
25         System.out.println("|States|");
26         System.out.println("+------+");
27         System.out.println("|      |");
```

```
28          System.out.println("|        |");
29          System.out.println("+------+");
30          System.out.println("   /\\");
31          System.out.println("  /  \\");
32          System.out.println(" /    \\");
33      }
34  }
```

The following is the output the program generates. Notice that the program includes double backslash characters (\\), but the output has single backslash characters. This is an example of an escape sequence, as described previously.

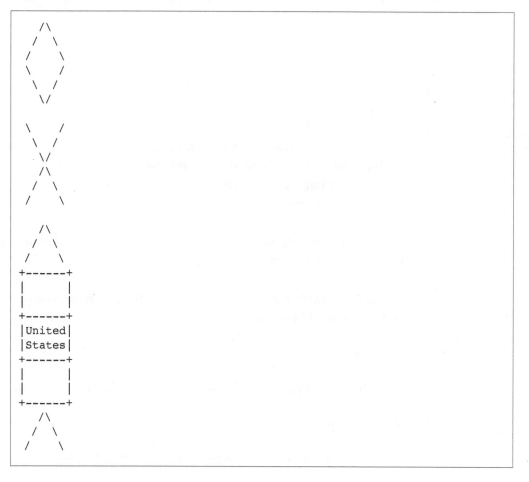

Comments and Readability

Java is a free-format language. This means you can put in as many or as few spaces and blank lines as you like, as long as you put at least one space or other punctuation mark between words. However, you should bear in mind that the layout of a program can enhance (or detract from) its readability. The following program is legal but hard to read:

```
1  public class Ugly{public static void main(String[] args)
2  {System.out.println("How short I am!");}}
```

Here are some simple rules to follow that will make your programs more readable:

- Put class and method headers on lines by themselves.
- Put no more than one statement on each line.
- Indent your program properly. When an opening brace appears, increase the indentation of the lines that follow it. When a closing brace appears, reduce the indentation. Indent statements inside curly braces by a consistent number of spaces (a common choice is four spaces per level of indentation).
- Use blank lines to separate parts of the program (e.g., methods).

Using these rules to rewrite the `Ugly` program yields the following code:

```
1  public class Ugly {
2      public static void main(String[] args) {
3          System.out.println("How short I am!");
4      }
5  }
```

Well-written Java programs can be quite readable, but often you will want to include some explanations that are not part of the program itself. You can annotate programs by putting notes called *comments* in them.

> **Comment**
>
> Text that programmers include in a program to explain their code. The compiler ignores comments.

There are two comment forms in Java. In the first form, you open the comment with a slash followed by an asterisk and you close it with an asterisk followed by a slash:

```
/* like this */
```

You must not put spaces between the slashes and the asterisks:

```
/ * this is bad * /
```

You can put almost any text you like, including multiple lines, inside the comment:

```
/* Thaddeus Martin
   Assignment #1
   Instructor: Professor Walingford
   Grader:    Bianca Montgomery        */
```

The only things you aren't allowed to put inside a comment are the comment end characters. The following code is not legal:

👎 `/* This comment has an asterisk/slash /*/ in it,`
`    which prematurely closes the comment. This is bad. */`

Java also provides a second comment form for shorter, single-line comments. You can use two slashes in a row to indicate that the rest of the current line (everything to the right of the two slashes) is a comment. For example, you can put a comment after a statement:

`System.out.println("You win!"); // Good job!`

Or you can create a comment on its own line:

`// give an introduction to the user`
`System.out.println("Welcome to the game of blackjack.");`
`System.out.println();`
`System.out.println("Let me explain the rules.");`

You can even create blocks of single-line comments:

`// Thaddeus Martin`
`// Assignment #1`
`// Instructor:  Professor Walingford`
`// Grader:      Bianca Montgomery`

Some people prefer to use the first comment form for comments that span multiple lines but it is safer to use the second form because you don't have to remember to close the comment. It also makes the comment stand out more. This is another case in which, if your instructor does not tell you to use a particular comment style, you should decide for yourself which style you prefer and use it consistently.

Don't confuse comments with the text of `println` statements. The text of your comments will not be displayed as output when the program executes. The comments are there only to help readers examine and understand the program.

It is a good idea to include comments at the beginning of each class file to indicate what the class does. You might also want to include information about who you are, what course you are taking, your instructor and/or grader's name, the date, and so on. You should also comment each method to indicate what it does.

Commenting becomes more useful in larger and more complicated programs, as well as in programs that will be viewed or modified by more than one programmer. Clear comments are extremely helpful to explain to another person, or to yourself at a later time, what your program is doing and why it is doing it.

In addition to the two comment forms already discussed, Java supports a particular style of comments known as *Javadoc comments*. Their format is more complex, but they have the advantage that you can use a program to extract the comments to make HTML files suitable for reading with a web browser. Javadoc comments are useful in more advanced programming and are discussed in more detail in Appendix B.

1.3 Program Errors

In 1949, Maurice Wilkes, an early pioneer of computing, expressed a sentiment that still rings true today:

> As soon as we started programming, we found out to our surprise that it wasn't as easy to get programs right as we had thought. Debugging had to be discovered. I can remember the exact instant when I realized that a large part of my life from then on was going to be spent in finding mistakes in my own programs.

You also will have to face this reality as you learn to program. You're going to make mistakes, just like every other programmer in history, and you're going to need strategies for eliminating those mistakes. Fortunately, the computer itself can help you with some of the work.

There are three kinds of errors that you'll encounter as you write programs:

- *Syntax errors* occur when you misuse Java. They are the programming equivalent of bad grammar and are caught by the Java compiler.
- *Logic errors* occur when you write code that doesn't perform the task it is intended to perform.
- *Runtime errors* are logic errors that are so severe that Java stops your program from executing.

Syntax Errors

Human beings tend to be fairly forgiving about minor mistakes in speech. For example, we might find it to be odd phrasing, but we generally understand Master Yoda when he says, "Unfortunate that you rushed to face him . . . that incomplete was your training. Not ready for the burden were you."

The Java compiler will be far less forgiving. The compiler reports syntax errors as it attempts to translate your program from Java into bytecodes if your program breaks any of Java's grammar rules. For example, if you misplace a single semicolon in your program, you can send the compiler into a tailspin of confusion. The compiler may report several error messages, depending on what it thinks is wrong with your program.

A program that generates compilation errors cannot be executed. If you submit your program to the compiler and the compiler reports errors, you must fix the errors and resubmit the program. You will not be able to proceed until your program is free of compilation errors.

Some development environments, such as Eclipse, help you along the way by underlining syntax errors as you write your program. This makes it easy to spot exactly where errors occur.

It's possible for you to introduce an error before you even start writing your program, if you choose the wrong name for its file.

Common Programming Error

File Name Does Not Match Class Name

As mentioned earlier, Java requires that a program's class name and file name match. For example, a program that begins with `public class Hello` must be stored in a file called `Hello.java`.

If you use the wrong file name (for example, saving it as `WrongFileName.java`), you'll get an error message like this:

```
WrongFileName.java:1: error: class Hello is public,
    should be declared in a file named Hello.java
public class Hello {
       ^
1 error
```

The file name is just the first hurdle. A number of other errors may exist in your Java program. One of the most common syntax errors is to misspell a word. You may have punctuation errors, such as missing semicolons. It's also easy to forget an entire word, such as a required keyword.

The error messages the compiler gives may or may not be helpful. If you don't understand the content of the error message, look for the caret marker (∧) below the line, which points at the position in the line where the compiler became confused. This can help you pinpoint the place where a required keyword might be missing.

Common Programming Error

Misspelled Words

Java (like most programming languages) is very picky about spelling. You need to spell each word correctly, including proper capitalization. Suppose, for example, that you were to replace the `println` statement in the "hello world" program with the following:

```
System.out.pruntln("Hello, world!");
```

When you try to compile this program, it will generate an error message similar to the following:

```
Hello.java:3: error: cannot find symbol
symbol  : method pruntln(java.lang.String)
```

Continued on next page

Continued from previous page

```
location: variable out of type PrintStream
        System.out.pruntln("Hello, world!");
            ^
1 error
```

The first line of this output indicates that the error occurs in the file `Hello.java` on line 3 and that the error is that the compiler cannot find a symbol. The second line indicates that the symbol it can't find is a method called `pruntln`. That's because there is no such method; the method is called `println`. The error message can take slightly different forms depending on what you have misspelled. For example, you might forget to capitalize the word `System`:

```
system.out.println("Hello, world!");
```

You will get the following error message:

```
Hello.java:3: error: package system does not exist
        system.out.println("Hello, world!");
            ^
1 error
```

Again, the first line indicates that the error occurs in line 3 of the file `Hello.java`. The error message is slightly different here, though, indicating that it can't find a package called `system`. The second and third lines of this error message include the original line of code with an arrow (caret) pointing to where the compiler got confused. The compiler errors are not always very clear, but if you pay attention to where the arrow is pointing, you'll have a pretty good sense of where the error occurs.

If you still can't figure out the error, try looking at the error's line number and comparing the contents of that line with similar lines in other programs. You can also ask someone else, such as an instructor or lab assistant, to examine your program.

Common Programming Error

Forgetting a Semicolon

All Java statements must end with semicolons, but it's easy to forget to put a semicolon at the end of a statement, as in the following program:

```
1  public class MissingSemicolon {
2      public static void main(String[] args) {
3          System.out.println("A rose by any other name")
```

Continued on next page

Continued from previous page

```
4            System.out.println("would smell as sweet");
5        }
6    }
```

In this case, the compiler produces output similar to the following:

```
MissingSemicolon.java:3: error: ';' expected
        System.out.println("would smell as sweet");
           ^
1 error
```

Some versions of the Java compiler list line 4 as the cause of the problem, not line 3, where the semicolon was actually forgotten. This is because the compiler is looking forward for a semicolon and isn't upset until it finds something that isn't a semicolon, which it does when it reaches line 4. Unfortunately, as this case demonstrates, compiler error messages don't always direct you to the correct line to be fixed.

Common Programming Error

Forgetting a Required Keyword

Another common syntax error is to forget a required keyword when you are typing your program, such as static or class. Double-check your programs against the examples in the textbook to make sure you haven't omitted an important keyword.

The compiler will give different error messages depending on which keyword is missing, but the messages can be hard to understand. For example, you might write a program called Bug4 and forget the keyword class when writing its class header. In this case, the compiler will provide the following error message:

```
Bug4.java:1: error: class, interface, or enum expected
public Bug4 {
       ^
1 error
```

However, if you forget the keyword void when declaring the main method, the compiler generates a different error message:

```
Bug5.java:2: error: invalid method declaration; return type required
    public static main(String[] args) {
                  ^
1 error
```

Yet another common syntax error is to forget to close a string literal.

A good rule of thumb to follow is that the first error reported by the compiler is the most important one. The rest might be the result of that first error. Many programmers don't even bother to look at errors beyond the first, because fixing that error and recompiling may cause the other errors to disappear.

Logic Errors (Bugs)

Logic errors are also called *bugs*. Computer programmers use words like "bug-ridden" and "buggy" to describe poorly written programs, and the process of finding and eliminating bugs from programs is called *debugging*.

The word "bug" is an old engineering term that predates computers; early computing bugs sometimes occurred in hardware as well as software. Admiral Grace Hopper, an early pioneer of computing, is largely credited with popularizing the use of the term in the context of computer programming. She often told the true story of a group of programmers at Harvard University in the mid-1940s who couldn't figure out what was wrong with their programs until they opened up the computer and found an actual moth trapped inside.

The form that a bug takes may vary. Sometimes your program will simply behave improperly. For example, it might produce the wrong output. Other times it will ask the computer to perform some task that is clearly a mistake, in which case your program will have a runtime error that stops it from executing. In this chapter, since your knowledge of Java is limited, generally the only type of logic error you will see is a mistake in program output from an incorrect `println` statement or method call.

We'll look at an example of a runtime error in the next section.

1.4 Procedural Decomposition

Brian Kernighan, coauthor of *The C Programming Language*, has said, "Controlling complexity is the essence of computer programming." People have only a modest capacity for detail. We can't solve complex problems all at once. Instead, we structure our problem solving by dividing the problem into manageable pieces and conquering each piece individually. We often use the term *decomposition* to describe this principle as applied to programming.

> **Decomposition**
> A separation into discernible parts, each of which is simpler than the whole.

With procedural programming languages like C, decomposition involves dividing a complex task into a set of subtasks. This is a very verb- or action-oriented approach, involving dividing up the overall action into a series of smaller actions. This technique is called *procedural decomposition*.

Common Programming Error

Not Closing a String Literal or Comment

Every string literal has to have an opening quote and a closing quote, but it's easy to forget the closing quotation mark. For example, you might say:

```
System.out.println("Hello, world!);
```

This produces three different error messages, even though there is only one underlying syntax error:

```
Hello.java:3: error: unclosed string literal
        System.out.println("hello world);
                           ^
Hello.java:3: error: ';' expected
        System.out.println("hello world);
                                        ^
Hello.java:5: error: reached end of file while parsing

    }
    ^
3 errors
```

In this case, the first error message is quite clear, including an arrow pointing at the beginning of the string literal that wasn't closed. The second error message was caused by the first. Because the string literal was not closed, the compiler didn't notice the right parenthesis and semicolon that appear at the end of the line.

A similar problem occurs when you forget to close a multiline comment by writing */, as in the first line of the following program:

```
/* This is a bad program.

public class Bad {
    public static void main(String[] args){
        System.out.println("Hi there.");
    }
} /* end of program */
```

The preceding file is not a program; it is one long comment. Because the comment on the first line is not closed, the entire program is swallowed up.

Luckily, many Java editor programs color the parts of a program to help you identify them visually. Usually, if you forget to close a string literal or comment, the rest of your program will turn the wrong color, which can help you spot the mistake.

Java was designed for a different kind of decomposition that is more noun- or object-oriented. Instead of thinking of the problem as a series of actions to be performed, we think of it as a collection of objects that have to interact.

As a computer scientist, you should be familiar with both types of problem solving. This book begins with procedural decomposition and devotes many chapters to mastering various aspects of the procedural approach. Only after you have thoroughly practiced procedural programming will we turn our attention back to object decomposition and object-oriented programming.

As an example of procedural decomposition, consider the problem of baking a cake. You can divide this problem into the following subproblems:

- Make the batter.
- Bake the cake.
- Make the frosting.
- Frost the cake.

Each of these four tasks has details associated with it. To make the batter, for example, you follow these steps:

- Mix the dry ingredients.
- Cream the butter and sugar.
- Beat in the eggs.
- Stir in the dry ingredients.

Thus, you divide the overall task into subtasks, which you further divide into even smaller subtasks. Eventually, you reach descriptions that are so simple they require no further explanation (i.e., primitives).

A partial diagram of this decomposition is shown in Figure 1.2. "Make cake" is the highest-level operation. It is defined in terms of four lower-level operations called "Make batter," "Bake," "Make frosting," and "Frost cake." The "Make batter" operation is defined in terms of even lower-level operations, and the same could be done for the other three operations. This diagram is called a structure diagram and is intended to show how a problem is broken down into subproblems. In this diagram, you can also tell in what order operations are performed by reading from left to right. That is not true of most structure diagrams. To determine the actual order in which subprograms are performed, you usually have to refer to the program itself.

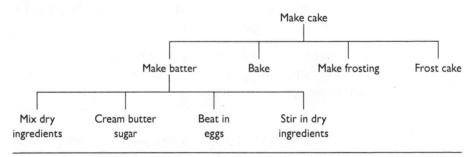

Figure 1.2 Decomposition of "Make cake" task

One final problem-solving term has to do with the process of programming. Professional programmers develop programs in stages. Instead of trying to produce a complete working program all at once, they choose some piece of the problem to implement first. Then they add another piece, and another, and another. The overall program is built up slowly, piece by piece. This process is known as *iterative enhancement* or *stepwise refinement*.

> **Iterative Enhancement**
>
> The process of producing a program in stages, adding new functionality at each stage. A key feature of each iterative step is that you can test it to make sure that piece works before moving on.

Now, let's look at a construct that will allow you to iteratively enhance your Java programs to improve their structure and reduce their redundancy: static methods.

Static Methods

VideoNote

Java is designed for objects, and programming in Java usually involves decomposing a problem into various objects, each with methods that perform particular tasks. You will see how this works in later chapters, but for now, we are going to explore procedural decomposition. We will postpone examining some of Java's details while we discuss programming in general.

Consider the following program, which draws two text boxes on the console:

```
1   public class DrawBoxes {
2       public static void main(String[] args) {
3           System.out.println("+------+");
4           System.out.println("|      |");
5           System.out.println("|      |");
6           System.out.println("+------+");
7           System.out.println();
8           System.out.println("+------+");
9           System.out.println("|      |");
10          System.out.println("|      |");
11          System.out.println("+------+");
12      }
13   }
```

The program works correctly, but the four lines used to draw the box appear twice. This redundancy is undesirable for several reasons. For example, you might wish to change the appearance of the boxes, in which case you'll have to make all of the edits twice. Also, you might wish to draw additional boxes, which would require you to type additional copies of (or copy and paste) the redundant lines.

A preferable program would include a Java command that specifies how to draw the box and then executes that command twice. Java doesn't have a "draw a box" command, but you can create one. Such a named command is called a *static method*.

> **Static Method**
>
> A block of Java statements that is given a name.

Static methods are units of procedural decomposition. We typically break a class into several static methods, each of which solves some piece of the overall problem. For example, here is a static method to draw a box:

```java
public static void drawBox() {
    System.out.println("+------+");
    System.out.println("|      |");
    System.out.println("|      |");
    System.out.println("+------+");
}
```

You have already seen a static method called `main` in earlier programs. Recall that the `main` method has the following form:

```java
public static void main(String[] args) {
    <statement>;
    <statement>;
    ...
    <statement>;
}
```

The static methods you'll write have a similar structure:

```java
public static void <name>() {
    <statement>;
    <statement>;
    ...
    <statement>;
}
```

The first line is known as the method header. You don't yet need to fully understand what each part of this header means in Java; for now, just remember that you'll need to write `public static void`, followed by the name you wish to give the method, followed by a set of parentheses. Briefly, here is what the words in the header mean:

- The keyword `public` indicates that this method is available to be used by all parts of your program. All methods you write will be public.

- The keyword `static` indicates that this is a static (procedural-style, not object-oriented) method. For now, all methods you write will be static, until you learn about defining objects in Chapter 8.

- The keyword `void` indicates that this method executes statements but does not produce any value. (Other methods you'll see later compute and return values.)

- `<name>` (e.g., `drawBox`) is the name of the method.

- The empty parentheses specify a list (in this case, an empty list) of values that are sent to your method as input; such values are called *parameters* and will not be included in your methods until Chapter 3.

Including the keyword `static` for each method you define may seem cumbersome. Other Java textbooks often do not discuss static methods as early as we do here; instead, they show other techniques for decomposing problems. But even though static methods require a bit of work to create, they are powerful and useful tools for improving basic Java programs.

After the header in our sample method, a series of `println` statements makes up the body of this static method. As in the `main` method, the statements of this method are executed in order from first to last.

By defining the method `drawBox`, you have given a simple name to this sequence of `println` statements. It's like saying to the Java compiler, "Whenever I tell you to 'drawBox,' I really mean that you should execute the `println` statements in the `drawBox` method." But the command won't actually be executed unless our `main` method explicitly says that it wants to do so. The act of executing a static method is called a *method call*.

> **Method Call**
>
> A command to execute another method, which causes all of the statements inside that method to be executed.

To execute the `drawBox` command, include this line in your program's `main` method:

```
drawBox();
```

Since we want to execute the `drawBox` command twice (to draw two boxes), the `main` method should contain two calls to the `drawBox` method. The following program uses the `drawBox` method to produce the same output as the original `DrawBoxes` program:

```
1   public class DrawBoxes2 {
2       public static void main(String[] args) {
3           drawBox();
4           System.out.println();
5           drawBox();
6       }
7
8       public static void drawBox() {
9           System.out.println("+------+");
10          System.out.println("|      |");
11          System.out.println("|      |");
12          System.out.println("+------+");
13      }
14  }
```

Flow of Control

The most confusing thing about static methods is that programs with static methods do not execute sequentially from top to bottom. Rather, each time the program encounters a static method call, the execution of the program "jumps" to that static method, executes each statement in that method in order, and then "jumps" back to the point where the call began and resumes executing. The order in which the statements of a program are executed is called the program's *flow of control*.

> **Flow of Control**
>
> The order in which the statements of a Java program are executed.

Let's look at the control flow of the `DrawBoxes2` program shown previously. It has two methods. The first method is the familiar `main` method, and the second is `drawBox`. As in any Java program, execution starts with the `main` method:

```
public static void main(String[] args) {
    drawBox();
    System.out.println();
    drawBox();
}
```

In a sense, the execution of this program is sequential: Each statement listed in the `main` method is executed in turn, from first to last.

But this `main` method includes two different calls on the `drawBox` method. This program will do three different things: execute `drawBox`, execute a `println`, then execute `drawBox` again.

The diagram below indicates the flow of control produced by this program.

```
public static void main(String[] args) {
    drawBox();
```

```
public static void drawBox() {
    System.out.println("+------+");
    System.out.println("|      |");
    System.out.println("|      |");
    System.out.println("+------+");
}
```

```
    System.out.println();
    drawBox();
```

```
public static void drawBox() {
    System.out.println("+------+");
    System.out.println("|      |");
    System.out.println("|      |");
    System.out.println("+------+");
}
```

```
}
```

Following the diagram, you can see that nine println statements are executed. First you transfer control to the drawBox method and execute its four statements. Then you return to main and execute its println statement. Then you transfer control a second time to drawBox and once again execute its four statements. Making these method calls is almost like copying and pasting the code of the method into the main method. As a result, this program has the exact same behavior as the nine-line main method of the DrawBoxes program:

```
public static void main(String[] args) {
    System.out.println("+------+");
    System.out.println("|      |");
    System.out.println("|      |");
    System.out.println("+------+");
    System.out.println();
    System.out.println("+------+");
    System.out.println("|      |");
    System.out.println("|      |");
    System.out.println("+------+");
}
```

This version is simpler in terms of its flow of control, but the first version avoids the redundancy of having the same println statements appear multiple times. It also gives a better sense of the structure of the solution. In the original version, it is clear that there is a subtask called drawBox that is being performed twice. Also, while the last version of the `main` method contains fewer lines of code than the `DrawBoxes2` program, consider what would happen if you wanted to add a third box to the output. You would have to add the five requisite `println` statements again, whereas in the programs that use the `drawBox` method you can simply add one more `println` and a third method call.

Java allows you to define methods in any order you like. It is a common convention to put the `main` method as either the first or last method in the class. In this textbook we will generally put `main` first, but the programs would behave the same if we switched the order. For example, the following modified program behaves identically to the previous `DrawBoxes2` program:

```
1   public class DrawBoxes3 {
2       public static void drawBox() {
3           System.out.println("+------+");
4           System.out.println("|      |");
5           System.out.println("|      |");
6           System.out.println("+------+");
7       }
8
9       public static void main(String[] args) {
10          drawBox();
11          System.out.println();
12          drawBox();
13      }
14  }
```

The `main` method is always the starting point for program execution, and from that starting point you can determine the order in which other methods are called.

Methods That Call Other Methods

The `main` method is not the only place where you can call another method. In fact, any method may call any other method. As a result, the flow of control can get quite complicated. Consider, for example, the following rather strange program. We use nonsense words ("foo," "bar," "baz," and "mumble") on purpose because the program is not intended to make sense.

```
1   public class FooBarBazMumble {
2       public static void main(String[] args) {
3           foo();
4           bar();
5           System.out.println("mumble");
6       }
7
8       public static void foo() {
9           System.out.println("foo");
10      }
```

```
11
12      public static void bar() {
13          baz();
14          System.out.println("bar");
15      }
16
17      public static void baz() {
18          System.out.println("baz");
19      }
20  }
```

You can't tell easily what output this program produces, so let's explore in detail what the program is doing. Remember that Java always begins with the method called main. In this program, the main method calls the foo method and the bar method and then executes a println statement:

```
public static void main(String[] args) {
    foo();
    bar();
    System.out.println("mumble");
}
```

Each of these two method calls will expand into more statements. Let's first expand the calls on the foo and bar methods:

```
public static void main(String[] args) {
    foo();

        public static void foo() {
            System.out.println("foo");
        }

    bar();

        public static void bar() {
            baz();
            System.out.println("bar");
        }

    System.out.println("mumble");
}
```

This helps to make our picture of the flow of control more complete, but notice that bar calls the baz method, so we have to expand that as well.

```
public static void main(String[] args) {
    foo();
```

```
public static void foo() {
    System.out.println("foo");
}
```

```
bar();
```

```
public static void bar() {
    baz();
```

```
public static void baz() {
    System.out.println("baz");
}
```

```
    System.out.println("bar");
}
```

```
    System.out.println("mumble");
}
```

Finally, we have finished our picture of the flow of control of this program. It should make sense, then, that the program produces the following output:

```
foo
baz
bar
mumble
```

We will see a much more useful example of methods calling methods when we go through the case study at the end of the chapter.

Did You Know?

The New Hacker's Dictionary

Computer scientists and computer programmers use a lot of jargon that can be confusing to novices. A group of software professionals spearheaded by Eric Raymond have collected together many of the jargon terms in a book called *The New Hacker's Dictionary*. You can buy the book, or you can browse it online at Eric's website: http://catb.org/esr/jargon/html/frames.html.

For example, if you look up *foo*, you'll find this definition: "Used very generally as a sample name for absolutely anything, esp. programs and files." In

Continued on next page

Continued from previous page

other words, when we find ourselves looking for a nonsense word, we use "foo."

The New Hacker's Dictionary contains a great deal of historical information about the origins of jargon terms. The entry for *foo* includes a lengthy discussion of the combined term *foobar* and how it came into common usage among engineers.

If you want to get a flavor of what is there, check out the entries for *bug*, *hacker*, *bogosity,* and *bogo-sort*.

An Example Runtime Error

Runtime errors occur when a bug causes your program to be unable to continue executing. What could cause such a thing to happen? One example is if you asked the computer to calculate an invalid value, such as 1 divided by 0. Another example would be if your program tries to read data from a file that does not exist.

We haven't discussed how to compute values or read files yet, but there is a way you can "accidentally" cause a runtime error. The way to do this is to write a static method that calls itself. If you do this, your program will not stop running, because the method will keep calling itself indefinitely, until the computer runs out of memory. When this happens, the program prints a large number of lines of output, and then eventually stops executing with an error message called a `StackOverflowError`. Here's an example:

```
1   public class Infinite {
2       public static void main(String[] args) {
3           oops();
4       }
5
6       public static void oops() {
7           System.out.println("Make it stop!");
8           oops();
9       }
10  }
```

This ill-fated program produces the following output (with large groups of identical lines represented by "..."):

```
Make it stop!
Make it stop!
Make it stop!
Make it stop!
Make it stop!
Make it stop!
Make it stop!
```

```
Make it stop!
Make it stop!
...
Make it stop!
Exception in thread "main" java.lang.StackOverflowError
        at sun.nio.cs.SingleByteEncoder.encodeArrayLoop(Unknown Source)
        at sun.nio.cs.SingleByteEncoder.encodeLoop(Unknown Source)
        at java.nio.charset.CharsetEncoder.encode(Unknown Source)
        at sun.nio.cs.StreamEncoder$CharsetSE.implWrite(Unknown Source)
        at sun.nio.cs.StreamEncoder.write(Unknown Source)
        at java.io.OutputStreamWriter.write(Unknown Source)
        at java.io.BufferedWriter.flushBuffer(Unknown Source)
        at java.io.PrintStream.newLine(Unknown Source)
        at java.io.PrintStream.println(Unknown Source)
        at Infinite.oops(Infinite.java:7)
        at Infinite.oops(Infinite.java:8)
        at Infinite.oops(Infinite.java:8)
        at Infinite.oops(Infinite.java:8)
        at ...
```

Runtime errors are, unfortunately, something you'll have to live with as you learn to program. You will have to carefully ensure that your programs not only compile successfully, but do not contain any bugs that will cause a runtime error. The most common way to catch and fix runtime errors is to run the program several times to test its behavior.

1.5 Case Study: `DrawFigures`

VideoNote

Earlier in the chapter, you saw a program called `DrawFigures1` that produced the following output:

It did so with a long sequence of `println` statements in the `main` method. In this section you'll improve the program by using static methods for procedural decomposition to capture structure and eliminate redundancy. The redundancy might be more obvious, but let's start by improving the way the program captures the structure of the overall task.

Structured Version

If you look closely at the output, you'll see that it has a structure that would be desirable to capture in the program structure. The output is divided into three subfigures: the diamond, the X, and the rocket.

You can better indicate the structure of the program by dividing it into static methods. Since there are three subfigures, you can create three methods, one for each subfigure. The following program produces the same output as `DrawFigures1`:

```
1   public class DrawFigures2 {
2       public static void main(String[] args) {
3           drawDiamond();
4           drawX();
5           drawRocket();
6       }
7
8       public static void drawDiamond() {
9           System.out.println("    /\\");
10          System.out.println("   /  \\");
11          System.out.println("  /    \\");
12          System.out.println("  \\    /");
13          System.out.println("   \\  /");
14          System.out.println("    \\/");
15          System.out.println();
16      }
17
```

```
18        public static void drawX() {
19            System.out.println(" \\     /");
20            System.out.println("  \\   /");
21            System.out.println("   \\ /");
22            System.out.println("   /\\");
23            System.out.println("  /   \\");
24            System.out.println(" /     \\");
25            System.out.println();
26        }
27
28        public static void drawRocket() {
29            System.out.println("    /\\");
30            System.out.println("   /  \\");
31            System.out.println("  /    \\");
32            System.out.println("+------+");
33            System.out.println("|      |");
34            System.out.println("|      |");
35            System.out.println("+------+");
36            System.out.println("|United|");
37            System.out.println("|States|");
38            System.out.println("+------+");
39            System.out.println("|      |");
40            System.out.println("|      |");
41            System.out.println("+------+");
42            System.out.println("    /\\");
43            System.out.println("   /  \\");
44            System.out.println("  /    \\");
45        }
46 }
```

The program appears in a class called `DrawFigures2` and has four static methods defined within it. The first static method is the usual `main` method, which calls three methods. The three methods called by `main` appear next.

Figure 1.3 is a structure diagram for this version of the program. Notice that it has two levels of structure. The overall problem is broken down into three subtasks.

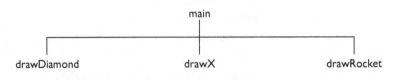

Figure 1.3   Decomposition of `DrawFigures2`

Final Version without Redundancy

The program can still be improved. Each of the three subfigures has individual elements, and some of those elements appear in more than one of the three subfigures. The program prints the following redundant group of lines several times:

A better version of the preceding program adds an additional method for each redundant section of output. The redundant sections are the top and bottom halves of the diamond shape and the box used in the rocket. Here is the improved program:

```
1   public class DrawFigures3 {
2       public static void main(String[] args) {
3           drawDiamond();
4           drawX();
5           drawRocket();
6       }
7
8       public static void drawDiamond() {
9           drawCone();
10          drawV();
11          System.out.println();
12      }
13
14      public static void drawX() {
15          drawV();
16          drawCone();
17          System.out.println();
18      }
19
20      public static void drawRocket() {
21          drawCone();
22          drawBox();
23          System.out.println("|United|");
24          System.out.println("|States|");
25          drawBox();
26          drawCone();
27          System.out.println();
28      }
29
```

```
30       public static void drawBox() {
31            System.out.println("+------+");
32            System.out.println("|      |");
33            System.out.println("|      |");
34            System.out.println("+------+");
35       }
36
37       public static void drawCone() {
38            System.out.println("   /\\");
39            System.out.println("  /  \\");
40            System.out.println(" /    \\");
41       }
42
43       public static void drawV() {
44            System.out.println(" \\    /");
45            System.out.println("  \\  /");
46            System.out.println("   \\/");
47       }
48  }
```

This program, now called `DrawFigures3`, has seven static methods defined within it. The first static method is the usual `main` method, which calls three methods. These three methods in turn call three other methods, which appear next.

Analysis of Flow of Execution

The structure diagram in Figure 1.4 shows which static methods `main` calls and which static methods each of them calls. As you can see, this program has three levels of structure and two levels of decomposition. The overall task is split into three subtasks, each of which has two subtasks.

A program with methods has a more complex flow of control than one without them, but the rules are still fairly simple. Remember that when a method is called, the computer executes the statements in the body of that method. Then the computer proceeds to the next statement after the method call. Also remember that the computer always starts with the `main` method, executing its statements from first to last.

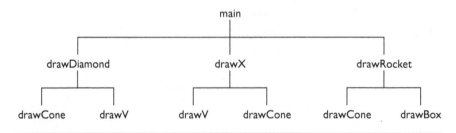

Figure 1.4   Decomposition of `DrawFigures3`

So, to execute the `DrawFigures3` program, the computer first executes its `main` method. That, in turn, first executes the body of the method `drawDiamond`. `drawDiamond` executes the methods `drawCone` and `drawV` (in that order). When `drawDiamond` finishes executing, control shifts to the next statement in the body of the `main` method: the call to the `drawX` method.

A complete breakdown of the flow of control from static method to static method in `DrawFigures3` follows:

1st	`main`
2nd	`drawDiamond`
3rd	`drawCone`
4th	`drawV`
5th	`drawX`
6th	`drawV`
7th	`drawCone`
8th	`drawRocket`
9th	`drawCone`
10th	`drawBox`
11th	`drawBox`
12th	`drawCone`

Recall that the order in which you define methods does not have to parallel the order in which they are executed. The order of execution is determined by the body of the `main` method and by the bodies of methods called from `main`. A static method declaration is like a dictionary entry—it defines a word, but it does not specify how the word will be used. The body of this program's `main` method says to first execute `drawDiamond`, then `drawX`, then `drawRocket`. This is the order of execution, regardless of the order in which the methods are defined.

Java allows you to define methods in any order you like. Starting with `main` at the top and working down to lower and lower-level methods is a popular approach to take, but many people prefer the opposite, placing the low-level methods first and `main` at the end. Java doesn't care what order you use, so you can decide for yourself and do what you think is best. Consistency is important, though, so that you can easily find a method later in a large program.

It is important to note that the programs `DrawFigures1`, `DrawFigures2`, and `DrawFigures3` produce exactly the same output to the console. While `DrawFigures1` may be the easiest program for a novice to read, `DrawFigures2` and particularly `DrawFigures3` have many advantages over it. For one, a well-structured solution is easier to comprehend, and the methods themselves become a means of explaining the program. Also, programs with methods are more flexible and can more easily be adapted to similar but different tasks. You can take the seven methods defined in `DrawFigures3` and write a new program to produce a larger and more complex output. Building static methods to create new commands increases your flexibility without adding unnecessary complication. For example, you could replace the `main` method with a version that calls the other methods in the following new order. What output would it produce?

```java
public static void main(String[] args) {
    drawCone();
    drawCone();
    drawRocket();
    drawX();
    drawRocket();
    drawDiamond();
    drawBox();
    drawDiamond();
    drawX();
    drawRocket();
}
```

Chapter Summary

Computers execute sets of instructions called programs. Computers store information internally as sequences of 0s and 1s (binary numbers).

Programming and computer science deal with algorithms, which are step-by-step descriptions for solving problems.

Java is a modern object-oriented programming language developed by Sun Microsystems, now owned by Oracle Corporation, that has a large set of libraries you can use to build complex programs.

A program is translated from text into computer instructions by another program called a compiler. Java's compiler turns Java programs into a special format called Java bytecodes, which are executed using a special program called the Java Runtime Environment.

Java programmers typically complete their work using an editor called an Integrated Development Environment (IDE). The commands may vary from environment to

environment, but the same three-step process is always involved:

1. Type in a program as a Java class.
2. Compile the program file.
3. Run the compiled version of the program.

Java uses a command called `System.out.println` to display text on the console screen.

Written words in a program can take different meanings. Keywords are special reserved words that are part of the language. Identifiers are words defined by the programmer to name entities in the program. Words can also be put into strings, which are pieces of text that can be printed to the console.

Java programs that use proper spacing and layout are more readable to programmers. Readability is also improved by writing notes called comments inside the program.

The Java language has a syntax, or a legal set of commands that can be used. A Java program that does not follow the proper syntax will not compile. A program that does compile but that is written incorrectly may still contain errors called exceptions that occur when the program runs. A third kind of error is a logic or intent error. This kind of error occurs when the program runs but does not do what the programmer intended.

—————————

Commands in programs are called statements. A class can group statements into larger commands called static methods. Static methods help the programmer group code into

reusable pieces. An important static method that must be part of every program is called `main`.

—————————

Iterative enhancement is the process of building a program piece by piece, testing the program at each step before advancing to the next.

—————————

Complex programming tasks should be broken down into the major tasks the computer must perform. This process is called procedural decomposition. Correct use of static methods aids procedural decomposition.

—————————

Self-Check Problems

Section 1.1: Basic Computing Concepts

1. Why do computers use binary numbers?

2. Convert each of the following decimal numbers into its equivalent binary number:

   a. 6
   b. 44
   c. 72
   d. 131

3. What is the decimal equivalent of each of the following binary numbers?

   a. 100
   b. 1011
   c. 101010
   d. 1001110

4. In your own words, describe an algorithm for baking cookies. Assume that you have a large number of hungry friends, so you'll want to produce several batches of cookies!

5. What is the difference between the file `MyProgram.java` and the file `MyProgram.class`?

Section 1.2: And Now—Java

6. Which of the following can be used in a Java program as identifiers?

```
println          first-name    AnnualSalary    "hello"     ABC
42isTheAnswer    for           sum_of_data     _average    B4
```

7. Which of the following is the correct syntax to output a message?

   a. `System.println(Hello, world!);`
   b. `System.println.out('Hello, world!');`
   c. `System.println("Hello, world!");`

d. `System.out.println("Hello, world!");`

e. `Out.system.println"(Hello, world!)";`

8. What is the output produced from the following statements?

```
System.out.println("\"Quotes\"");
System.out.println("Slashes \\//");
System.out.println("How '\"confounding' \"\\\" it is!");
```

9. What is the output produced from the following statements?

```
System.out.println("name\tage\theight");
System.out.println("Archie\t17\t5'9\"");
System.out.println("Betty\t17\t5'6\"");
System.out.println("Jughead\t16\t6'");
```

10. What is the output produced from the following statements?

```
System.out.println("Shaq is 7'1");
System.out.println("The string \"\" is an empty message.");
System.out.println("\\'\"\"");
```

11. What is the output produced from the following statements?

```
System.out.println("\ta\tb\tc");
System.out.println("\\\\");
System.out.println("'");
System.out.println("\"\"\"");
System.out.println("C:\nin\the downward spiral");
```

12. What is the output produced from the following statements?

```
System.out.println("Dear \"DoubleSlash\" magazine,");
System.out.println();
System.out.println("\tYour publication confuses me. Is it");
System.out.println("a \\\\ slash or a //// slash?");
System.out.println("\nSincerely,");
System.out.println("Susan \"Suzy\" Smith");
```

13. What series of `println` statements would produce the following output?

```
"Several slashes are sometimes seen,"
said Sally. "I've said so." See?
\ / \\ // \\\ ///
```

14. What series of `println` statements would produce the following output?

```
This is a test of your
knowledge of "quotes" used
in 'string literals.'

You're bound to "get it right"
if you read the section on
''quotes.''
```

15. Write a `println` statement that produces the following output:

```
/ \ // \\ /// \\\
```

16. Rewrite the following code as a series of equivalent `System.out.println` statements (i.e., without any `System.out.print` statements):

```
System.out.print("Twas ");
System.out.print("brillig and the");
System.out.println(" ");
System.out.print(" slithy toves did");
System.out.print(" ");
System.out.println("gyre and");
System.out.println("gimble");
System.out.println();
System.out.println( "in the wabe.");
```

17. What is the output of the following program? Note that the program contains several comments.

```
 1  public class Commentary {
 2      public static void main(String[] args) {
 3          System.out.println("some lines of code");
 4          System.out.println("have // characters on them");
 5          System.out.println("which means ");  // that they are comments
 6          // System.out.println("written by the programmer.");
 7
 8          System.out.println("lines can also");
 9          System.out.println("have /* and */ characters");
10          /* System.out.println("which represents");
11          System.out.println("a multi-line style");
12          */ System.out.println("of comment.");
13      }
14  }
```

Section 1.3: Program Errors

18. Name the three errors in the following program:

```
 1  public MyProgram {
 2      public static void main(String[] args) {
 3          System.out.println("This is a test of the")
 4          System.out.Println("emergency broadcast system.");
 5      }
 6  }
```

19. Name the four errors in the following program:

```
 1  public class SecretMessage {
 2      public static main(string[] args) {
 3          System.out.println("Speak friend");
```

```
4          System.out.println("and enter);
5
6  }
```

20. Name the four errors in the following program:

```
1   public class FamousSpeech
2       public static void main(String[]) {
3           System.out.println("Four score and seven years ago,");
4           System.out.println("our fathers brought forth on");
5           System.out.println("this continent a new nation");
6           System.out.println("conceived in liberty,");
7           System.out.println("and dedicated to the proposition");
8           System.out.println("that");    /* this part should
9           System.out.println("all");        really say,
10          System.out.println("men");        "all PEOPLE!" */
11          System.out.println("are";
12          System.out.println("created");
13          System.out.println("equal");
14      }
15  }
```

Section 1.4: Procedural Decomposition

21. Which of the following method headers uses the correct syntax?

a. public static example() {
b. public static void example() {
c. public void static example() {
d. public static example void[] {
e. public void static example{} (

22. What is the output of the following program? (You may wish to draw a structure diagram first.)

```
1   public class Tricky {
2       public static void main(String[] args) {
3           message1();
4           message2();
5           System.out.println("Done with main.");
6       }
7
8       public static void message1() {
9           System.out.println("This is message1.");
10      }
11
12      public static void message2() {
13          System.out.println("This is message2.");
14          message1();
```

```
15            System.out.println("Done with message2.");
16      }
17  }
```

23. What is the output of the following program? (You may wish to draw a structure diagram first.)

```
1  public class Strange {
2      public static void first() {
3          System.out.println("Inside first method");
4      }
5
6      public static void second() {
7          System.out.println("Inside second method");
8          first();
9      }
10
11      public static void third() {
12          System.out.println("Inside third method");
13          first();
14          second();
15      }
16
17      public static void main(String[] args) {
18          first();
19          third();
20          second();
21          third();
22      }
23  }
```

24. What would have been the output of the preceding program if the `third` method had contained the following statements?

```
public static void third() {
    first();
    second();
    System.out.println("Inside third method");
}
```

25. What would have been the output of the `Strange` program if the `main` method had contained the following statements? (Use the original version of `third`, not the modified version from the most recent exercise.)

```
public static void main(String[] args) {
    second();
    first();
    second();
    third();
}
```

26. What is the output of the following program? (You may wish to draw a structure diagram first.)

```
1   public class Confusing {
2       public static void method2() {
3           method1();
4           System.out.println("I am method 2.");
5       }
6
7       public static void method3() {
8           method2();
9           System.out.println("I am method 3.");
10          method1();
11      }
12
13      public static void method1() {
14          System.out.println("I am method 1.");
15      }
16
17      public static void main(String[] args) {
18          method1();
19          method3();
20          method2();
21          method3();
22      }
23  }
```

27. What would have been the output of the preceding program if the method3 method had contained the following statements?

```
public static void method3() {
    method1();
    method2();
    System.out.println("I am method 3.");
}
```

28. What would have been the output of the Confusing program if the main method had contained the following statements? (Use the original version of method3, not the modified version from the most recent exercise.)

```
public static void main(String[] args) {
    method2();
    method1();
    method3();
    method2();
}
```

29. The following program contains at least 10 syntax errors. What are they?

```
1   public class LotsOf Errors {
2       public static main(String args) {
3           System.println(Hello, world!);
```

```
 4          message()
 5      }
 6
 7      public static void message {
 8          System.out println("This program surely cannot ";
 9          System.out.println("have any "errors" in it");
10      }
```

30. Consider the following program, saved into a file named `Example.java`:

```
 1  public class Example {
 2      public static void displayRule() {
 3          System.out.println("The first rule ");
 4          System.out.println("of Java Club is,");
 5          System.out.println();
 6          System.out.println("you do not talk about Java Club.");
 7      }
 8
 9      public static void main(String[] args) {
10          System.out.println("The rules of Java Club.");
11          displayRule();
12          displayRule();
13      }
14  }
```

What would happen if each of the following changes were made to the `Example` program? For example, would there be no effect, a syntax error, or a different program output? Treat each change independently of the others.

a. Change line 1 to: `public class Demonstration`
b. Change line 9 to: `public static void MAIN(String[] args) {`
c. Insert a new line after line 11 that reads: `System.out.println();`
d. Change line 2 to: `public static void printMessage() {`
e. Change line 2 to: `public static void showMessage() {` and change lines 11 and 12 to: `showMessage();`
f. Replace lines 3–4 with: `System.out.println("The first rule of Java Club is,");`

31. The following program is legal under Java's syntax rules, but it is difficult to read because of its layout and lack of comments. Reformat it using the rules given in this chapter, and add a comment header at the top of the program.

```
 1      public
 2  class GiveAdvice{ public static
 3  void main (String[]args){ System.out.println (
 4
 5  "Programs can be easy or");  System.out.println(
 6    "difficult to read, depending"
 7  );  System.out.println("upon their format.")
 8          ;System.out.println();System.out.println(
 9  "Everyone, including yourself,");
10  System.out.println
11  ("will be happier if you choose");
```

```
12              System.out.println("to format your programs."
13  );   }
14      }
```

32. The following program is legal under Java's syntax rules, but it is difficult to read because of its layout and lack of comments. Reformat it using the rules given in this chapter, and add a comment header at the top of the program.

```
1   public
2   class Messy{public
3   static void main(String[]args){message ()
4     ;System.out.println()     ; message ( );}    public static void
5   message() { System.out.println(
6       "I really wish that"
7       );System.out.println
8   ("I had formatted my source")
9   ;System.out.println("code correctly!");}}
```

Exercises

1. Write a complete Java program called `Stewie` that prints the following output:

```
///////////////////////
|| Victory is mine! ||
\\\\\\\\\\\\\\\\\\\\\\\
```

2. Write a complete Java program called `Spikey` that prints the following output:

```
  \/
 \\//
\\\///
///\\\
 //\\
  /\
```

3. Write a complete Java program called `WellFormed` that prints the following output:

```
A well-formed Java program has
a main method with { and }
braces.

A System.out.println statement
has ( and ) and usually a
String that starts and ends
with a " character.
(But we type \" instead!)
```

4. Write a complete Java program called `Difference` that prints the following output:

```
What is the difference between
a ' and a "? Or between a " and a \"?

One is what we see when we're typing our program.
The other is what appears on the "console."
```

5. Write a complete Java program called `MuchBetter` that prints the following output:

```
A "quoted" String is
'much' better if you learn
the rules of "escape sequences."
Also, "" represents an empty String.
Don't forget: use \" instead of " !
'' is not the same as "
```

6. Write a complete Java program called `Meta` whose output is the text that would be the source code of a Java program that prints "Hello, world!" as its output.

7. Write a complete Java program called `Mantra` that prints the following output. Use at least one static method besides `main`.

```
There's one thing every coder must understand:
The System.out.println command.

There's one thing every coder must understand:
The System.out.println command.
```

8. Write a complete Java program called `Stewie2` that prints the following output. Use at least one static method besides `main`.

```
////////////////////////
|| Victory is mine! ||
\\\\\\\\\\\\\\\\\\\\\\\\
|| Victory is mine! ||
\\\\\\\\\\\\\\\\\\\\\\\\
|| Victory is mine! ||
\\\\\\\\\\\\\\\\\\\\\\\\
|| Victory is mine! ||
\\\\\\\\\\\\\\\\\\\\\\\\
|| Victory is mine! ||
\\\\\\\\\\\\\\\\\\\\\\\\
```

9. Write a program called `Egg` that displays the following output:

10. Modify the program from the previous exercise to become a new program `Egg2` that displays the following output. Use static methods as appropriate.

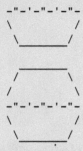

11. Write a Java program called `TwoRockets` that generates the following output. Use static methods to show structure and eliminate redundancy in your solution. Note that there are two rocket ships next to each other. What redundancy can you eliminate using static methods? What redundancy cannot be eliminated?

12. Write a program called `FightSong` that produces this output. Use at least two static methods to show structure and eliminate redundancy in your solution.

```
Go, team, go!
You can do it.

Go, team, go!
You can do it.
You're the best,
In the West.
Go, team, go!
You can do it.

Go, team, go!
You can do it.
You're the best,
in the West.
Go, team, go!
You can do it.

Go, team, go!
You can do it.
```

13. Write a Java program called `StarFigures` that generates the following output. Use static methods to show structure and eliminate redundancy in your solution.

```
*****
*****
 * *
  *
 * *


*****
*****
 * *
  *
 * *
*****
*****


    *
    *
    *
*****
*****
 * *
  *
 * *
```

14. Write a Java program called `Lanterns` that generates the following output. Use static methods to show structure and eliminate redundancy in your solution.

```
     *****
    *********
  *************


     *****
    *********
  *************
 *  |  |  |  |  *
  *************
     *****
    *********
  *************


     *****
    *********
  *************
     *****
 *  |  |  |  |  *
 *  |  |  |  |  *
     *****
     *****
```

15. Write a Java program called `EggStop` that generates the following output. Use static methods to show structure and eliminate redundancy in your solution.

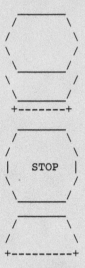

```
      _____
    /          \
   /            \
   \            /
    \          /
    _____/
    +-------+

      _____
    /          \
   /            \
   |   STOP   |
   \            /
    _____/

      _____
    /          \
   /            \
   +---------+
```

16. Write a program called `Shining` that prints the following line of output 1000 times:

```
All work and no play makes Jack a dull boy.
```

You should not write a program that uses 1000 lines of source code; use methods to shorten the program. What is the shortest program you can write that will produce the 1000 lines of output, using only the material from this chapter?

Programming Projects

1. Write a program to spell out MISSISSIPPI using block letters like the following (one per line):

```
M      M    IIIII    SSSSS    PPPPPP
MM    MM      I     S     S    P     P
M M  M M      I     S          P     P
M  M   M      I      SSSSS     PPPPP
M      M      I           S    P
M      M      I     S     S    P
M      M    IIIII    SSSSS     P
```

2. Sometimes we write similar letters to different people. For example, you might write to your parents to tell them about your classes and your friends and to ask for money; you might write to a friend about your love life, your classes, and your hobbies; and you might write to your brother about your hobbies and your friends and to ask for money. Write a program that prints similar letters such as these to three people of your choice. Each letter should have at least one paragraph in common with each of the other letters. Your main program should have three method calls, one for each of the people to whom you are writing. Try to isolate repeated tasks into methods.

3. Write a program that produces as output the following lyrics, which are similar to the song, "There Was an Old Lady Who Swallowed a Fly," by Simms Taback. Use methods for each verse and the refrain. Here are the complete lyrics to print:

```
There was an old lady who swallowed a fly.
I don't know why she swallowed that fly,
Perhaps she'll die.
```

```
There was an old lady who swallowed a spider,
That wriggled and iggled and jiggled inside her.
She swallowed the spider to catch the fly,
I don't know why she swallowed that fly,
Perhaps she'll die.

There was an old lady who swallowed a bird,
How absurd to swallow a bird.
She swallowed the bird to catch the spider,
She swallowed the spider to catch the fly,
I don't know why she swallowed that fly,
Perhaps she'll die.

There was an old lady who swallowed a cat,
Imagine that to swallow a cat.
She swallowed the cat to catch the bird,
She swallowed the bird to catch the spider,
She swallowed the spider to catch the fly,
I don't know why she swallowed that fly,
Perhaps she'll die.

There was an old lady who swallowed a dog,
What a hog to swallow a dog.
She swallowed the dog to catch the cat,
She swallowed the cat to catch the bird,
She swallowed the bird to catch the spider,
She swallowed the spider to catch the fly,
I don't know why she swallowed that fly,
Perhaps she'll die.

There was an old lady who swallowed a horse,
She died of course.
```

4. Write a program that produces as output the words of "The Twelve Days of Christmas." (Static methods simplify this task.) Here are the first two verses and the last verse of the song:

```
On the first day of Christmas,
my true love sent to me
a partridge in a pear tree.

On the second day of Christmas,
my true love sent to me
two turtle doves, and
a partridge in a pear tree.
...

On the twelfth day of Christmas,
my true love sent to me
Twelve drummers drumming,
eleven pipers piping,
ten lords a-leaping,
nine ladies dancing,
eight maids a-milking,
seven swans a-swimming,
six geese a-laying,
```

```
five golden rings,
four calling birds,
three French hens,
two turtle doves, and
a partridge in a pear tree.
```

5. Write a program that produces as output the words of "The House That Jack Built." Use methods for each verse and for repeated text. Here are lyrics to use:

```
This is the house that Jack built.

This is the malt
That lay in the house that Jack built.

This is the rat,
That ate the malt
That lay in the house that Jack built.

This is the cat,
That killed the rat,
That ate the malt
That lay in the house that Jack built.

This is the dog,
That worried the cat,
That killed the rat,
That ate the malt
That lay in the house that Jack built.

This is the cow with the crumpled horn,
That tossed the dog,
That worried the cat,
That killed the rat,
That ate the malt
That lay in the house that Jack built.

This is the maiden all forlorn
That milked the cow with the crumpled horn,
That tossed the dog,
That worried the cat,
That killed the rat,
That ate the malt
That lay in the house that Jack built.
```

6. Write a program that produces as output the words of "Bought Me a Cat." Use methods for each verse and for repeated text. Here are the song's complete lyrics:

```
Bought me a cat and the cat pleased me,
I fed my cat under yonder tree.
Cat goes fiddle-i-fee.

Bought me a hen and the hen pleased me,
I fed my hen under yonder tree.
```

```
Hen goes chimmy-chuck, chimmy-chuck,
Cat goes fiddle-i-fee.

Bought me a duck and the duck pleased me,
I fed my duck under yonder tree.
Duck goes quack, quack,
Hen goes chimmy-chuck, chimmy-chuck,
Cat goes fiddle-i-fee.

Bought me a goose and the goose pleased me,
I fed my goose under yonder tree.
Goose goes hissy, hissy,
Duck goes quack, quack,
Hen goes chimmy-chuck, chimmy-chuck,
Cat goes fiddle-i-fee.

Bought me a sheep and the sheep pleased me,
I fed my sheep under yonder tree.
Sheep goes baa, baa,
Goose goes hissy, hissy,
Duck goes quack, quack,
Hen goes chimmy-chuck, chimmy-chuck,
Cat goes fiddle-i-fee.
```

7. Write a program that produces as output the words of the following silly song. Use methods for each verse and for repeated text. Here are the song's complete lyrics:

```
I once wrote a program that wouldn't compile
I don't know why it wouldn't compile,
My TA just smiled.

My program did nothing
So I started typing.
I added System.out.println("I <3 coding"),
I don't know why it wouldn't compile,
My TA just smiled.

"Parse error," cried the compiler
Luckily I'm such a code baller.
I added a backslash to escape the quotes,
I added System.out.println("I <3 coding"),
I don't know why it wouldn't compile,
My TA just smiled.

Now the compiler wanted an identifier
And I thought the situation was getting dire.
I added a main method with its String[] args,
I added a backslash to escape the quotes,
I added System.out.println("I <3 coding"),
I don't know why it wouldn't compile,
My TA just smiled.
```

```
Java complained it expected an enum
Boy, these computers really are dumb!
I added a public class and called it Scum,
I added a main method with its String[] args,
I added a backslash to escape the quotes,
I added System.out.println("I <3 coding"),
I don't know why it wouldn't compile,
My TA just smiled.
```

Primitive Data and Definite Loops

Introduction

Now that you know something about the basic structure of Java programs, you are ready to learn how to solve more complex problems. For the time being we will still concentrate on programs that produce output, but we will begin to explore some of the aspects of programming that require problem-solving skills.

The first half of this chapter fills in two important areas. First, it examines expressions, which are used to perform simple computations in Java, particularly those involving numeric data. Second, it discusses program elements called variables that can change in value as the program executes.

The second half of the chapter introduces your first control structure: the for loop. You use this structure to repeat actions in a program. This is useful whenever you find a pattern in a task such as the creation of a complex figure, because you can use a for loop to repeat the action to create that particular pattern. The challenge is finding each pattern and figuring out what repeated actions will reproduce it.

The for loop is a flexible control structure that can be used for many tasks. In this chapter we use it for *definite loops*, where you know exactly how many times you want to perform a particular task. In Chapter 5 we will discuss how to write *indefinite loops*, where you don't know in advance how many times to perform a task.

2.1 Basic Data Concepts

Programs manipulate information, and information comes in many forms. Java is a *type-safe* language, which means that it requires you to be explicit about what kind of information you intend to manipulate and it guarantees that you manipulate the data in a reasonable manner. Everything that you manipulate in a Java program will be of a certain *type,* and you will constantly find yourself telling Java what types of data you intend to use.

> **Data Type**
>
> A name for a category of data values that are all related, as in type `int` in Java, which is used to represent integer values.

A decision was made early in the design of Java to support two different kinds of data: primitive data and objects. The designers made this decision purely on the basis of performance, to make Java programs run faster. Unfortunately, it means that you have to learn two sets of rules about how data works, but this is one of those times when you simply have to pay the price if you want to use an industrial-strength programming language. To make things a little easier, we will study the primitive data types first, in this chapter; in the next chapter, we will turn our attention to objects.

Primitive Types

There are eight primitive data types in Java: `boolean`, `byte`, `char`, `double`, `float`, `int`, `long`, and `short`. Four of these are considered fundamental: `boolean`, `char`, `double`, and `int`. The other four types are variations that exist for programs that have special requirements. The four fundamental types that we will explore are listed in Table 2.1.

The type names (`int`, `double`, `char`, and `boolean`) are Java keywords that you will use in your programs to let the compiler know that you intend to use that type of data.

It may seem odd to use one type for integers and another type for real numbers. Isn't every integer a real number? The answer is yes, but these are fundamentally different types of numbers. The difference is so great that we make this distinction even in English. We don't ask, "How much sisters do you have?" or "How many do you weigh?" We realize that sisters come in discrete integer quantities (0 sisters, 1 sister, 2 sisters, 3 sisters, and so on), and we use the word "many" for integer quantities ("How

Table 2.1   Commonly Used Primitive Types in Java

Type	Description	Examples
`int`	integers (whole numbers)	`42, -3, 18, 20493, 0`
`double`	real numbers	`7.35, 14.9, -19.83423`
`char`	single characters	`'a', 'X', '!'`
`boolean`	logical values	`true, false`

many sisters do you have?"). Similarly, we realize that weight can vary by tiny amounts (175 pounds versus 175.5 pounds versus 175.25 pounds, and so on), and we use the word "much" for these real-number quantities ("How much do you weigh?").

In programming, this distinction is even more important, because integers and reals are represented in different ways in the computer's memory: Integers are stored exactly, while reals are stored as approximations with a limited number of digits of accuracy. You will see that storing values as approximations can lead to round-off errors when you use real values.

The name `double` for real values is not very intuitive. It's an accident of history in much the same way that we still talk about "dialing" a number on our telephones even though modern telephones don't have dials. The C programming language introduced a type called `float` (short for "floating-point number") for storing real numbers. But `float`s had limited accuracy, so another type was introduced, called `double` (short for "double precision," meaning that it had double the precision of a simple `float`). As memory became cheaper, people began using `double` as the default for floating-point values. In hindsight, it might have been better to use the word `float` for what is now called `double` and a word like "half" for the values with less accuracy, but it's tough to change habits that are so ingrained. So, programming languages will continue to use the word `double` for floating-point numbers, and people will still talk about "dialing" people on the phone even if they've never touched a telephone dial.

Expressions

VideoNote

When you write programs, you will often need to include values and calculations. The technical term for these elements is *expressions*.

> **Expression**
>
> A simple value or a set of operations that produces a value.

The simplest expression is a specific value, like 42 or 28.9. We call these "literal values," or *literals*. More complex expressions involve combining simple values. Suppose, for example, that you want to know how many bottles of water you have. If you have two 6-packs, four 4-packs, and two individual bottles, you can compute the total number of bottles with the following expression:

```
(2 * 6) + (4 * 4) + 2
```

Notice that we use an asterisk to represent multiplication and that we use parentheses to group parts of the expression. The computer determines the value of an expression by *evaluating* it.

> **Evaluation**
>
> The process of obtaining the value of an expression.

The value obtained when an expression is evaluated is called the *result*. Complex expressions are formed using *operators*.

> **Operator**
>
> A special symbol (like + or *) that is used to indicate an operation to be performed on one or more values.

The values used in the expression are called *operands*. For example, consider the following simple expressions:

```
3 + 29
4 * 5
```

The operators here are the + and *, and the operands are simple numbers.

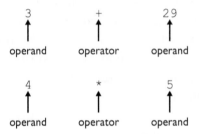

When you form complex expressions, these simpler expressions can in turn become operands for other operators. For example, the expression

```
(3 + 29) - (4 * 5)
```

has two levels of operators.

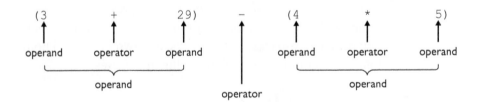

The addition operator has simple operands of 3 and 29 and the multiplication operator has simple operands of 4 and 5, but the subtraction operator has operands that are each parenthesized expressions with operators of their own. Thus, complex expressions can be built from smaller expressions. At the lowest level, you have simple numbers. These are used as operands to make more complex expressions, which in turn can be used as operands in even more complex expressions.

There are many things you can do with expressions. One of the simplest things you can do is to print the value of an expression using a `println` statement. For example, if you say:

```
System.out.println(42);
System.out.println(2 + 2);
```

you will get the following two lines of output:

```
42
4
```

Notice that for the second `println`, the computer evaluates the expression (adding 2 and 2) and prints the result (in this case, 4).

You will see many different operators as you progress through this book, all of which can be used to form expressions. Expressions can be arbitrarily complex, with as many operators as you like. For that reason, when we tell you, "An expression can be used here," we mean that you can use arbitrary expressions that include complex expressions as well as simple values.

Literals

The simplest expressions refer to values directly using what are known as *literals*. An integer literal (considered to be of type `int`) is a sequence of digits with or without a leading sign:

```
3     482     −29434     0     92348     +9812
```

A floating-point literal (considered to be of type `double`) includes a decimal point:

```
298.4    0.284    207.    .2843    −17.452    −.98
```

Notice that `207.` is considered a `double` even though it coincides with an integer, because of the decimal point. Literals of type `double` can also be expressed in scientific notation (a number followed by e followed by an integer):

```
2.3e4    1e-5    3.84e92    2.458e12
```

The first of these numbers represents 2.3 times 10 to the 4th power, which equals 23,000. Even though this value happens to coincide with an integer, it is considered to be of type `double` because it is expressed in scientific notation. The second number represents 1 times 10 to the −5th power, which is equal to 0.00001. The third number represents 3.84 times 10 to the 92nd power. The fourth number represents 2.458 times 10 to the 12th power.

We have seen that textual information can be stored in literal strings that store a sequence of characters. In later chapters we will explore how to process a string character by character. Each such character is of type `char`. A character literal is enclosed in single quotation marks and includes just one character:

```
'a'    'm'    'X'    '!'    '3'    '\\'
```

All of these examples are of type `char`. Notice that the last example uses an escape sequence to represent the backslash character. You can even refer to the single quotation character using an escape sequence:

```
'\''
```

Finally, the primitive type `boolean` stores logical information. We won't be exploring the use of type `boolean` until we reach Chapter 4 and see how to introduce logical tests into our programs, but for completeness, we include the `boolean` literal values here. Logic deals with just two possibilities: true and false. These two Java keywords are the two literal values of type `boolean`:

```
true    false
```

Arithmetic Operators

The basic arithmetic operators are shown in Table 2.2. The addition and subtraction operators will, of course, look familiar to you, as should the asterisk as a multiplication operator and the forward slash as a division operator. However, as you'll see, Java has two different division operations. The remainder or mod operation may be unfamiliar.

Division presents a problem when the operands are integers. When you divide 119 by 5, for example, you do not get an integer result. Therefore, the results of integer division are expressed as two different integers, a quotient and a remainder:

$$\frac{119}{5} = 23 \text{ (quotient) with 4 (remainder)}$$

In terms of the arithmetic operators:

`119 / 5` evaluates to `23`
`119 % 5` evaluates to `4`

Table 2.2   Arithmetic Operators in Java

Operator	Meaning	Example	Result
+	addition	2 + 2	4
−	subtraction	53 − 18	35
*	multiplication	3 * 8	24
/	division	4.8 / 2.0	2.4
%	remainder or mod	19 % 5	4

These two division operators should be familiar if you recall how long-division calculations are performed:

```
       31
34)1079
   102
    59
    34
    25
```

Here, dividing 1079 by 34 yields 31 with a remainder of 25. Using arithmetic operators, the problem would be described like this:

```
1079 / 34 evaluates to 31
1079 % 34 evaluates to 25
```

It takes a while to get used to integer division in Java. When you are using the division operator (/), the key thing to keep in mind is that it truncates anything after the decimal point. So, if you imagine computing an answer on a calculator, just think of ignoring anything after the decimal point:

- `19/5` is `3.8` on a calculator, so `19/5` evaluates to `3`
- `207/10` is `20.7` on a calculator, so `207/10` evaluates to `20`
- `3/8` is `0.375` on a calculator, so `3/8` evaluates to `0`

The remainder operator (%) is usually referred to as the "mod operator," or simply "mod." The mod operator lets you know how much was left unaccounted for by the truncating division operator. For example, given the previous examples, you'd compute the mod results as shown in Table 2.3.

In each case, you figure out how much of the number is accounted for by the truncating division operator. The mod operator gives you any excess (the remainder). When you put this into a formula, you can think of the mod operator as behaving as follows:

```
x % y = x   (x / y) * y
```

Table 2.3 Examples of Mod Operator

Mod problem	First divide	What does division account for?	How much is left over?	Answer
19 % 5	19/5 is 3	3 * 5 is 15	19 − 15 is 4	4
207 % 10	207/10 is 20	20 * 10 is 200	207 − 200 is 7	7
3 % 8	3/8 is 0	0 * 8 is 0	3 − 0 is 3	3

It is possible to get a result of 0 for the mod operator. This happens when one number divides evenly into another. For example, each of the following expressions evaluates to 0 because the second number goes evenly into the first number:

```
28 % 7
95 % 5
44 % 2
```

A few special cases are worth noting because they are not always immediately obvious to novice programmers:

- **Numerator smaller than denominator:** In this case division produces 0 and mod produces the original number. For example, `7 / 10` is 0 and `7 % 10` is 7.
- **Numerator of 0:** In this case both division and mod return 0. For example, both `0 / 10` and `0 % 10` evaluate to 0.
- **Denominator of 0:** In this case, both division and mod are undefined and produce a runtime error. For example, a program that attempts to evaluate either `7 / 0` or `7 % 0` will throw an `ArithmeticException` error.

The mod operator has many useful applications in computer programs. Here are just a few ideas:

- Testing whether a number is even or odd (`number % 2` is 0 for evens, `number % 2` is 1 for odds).
- Finding individual digits of a number (e.g., `number % 10` is the final digit).
- Finding the last four digits of a social security number (`number % 10000`).

The remainder operator can be used with `doubles` as well as with integers, and it works similarly: You consider how much is left over when you take away as many "whole" values as you can. For example, the expression `10.2 % 2.4` evaluates to `0.6` because you can take away four `2.4`s from `10.2`, leaving you with `0.6` left over.

For floating-point values (values of type `double`), the division operator does what we consider "normal" division. So, even though the expression `119 / 5` evaluates to `23`, the expression `119.0 / 5.0` evaluates to `23.8`.

Precedence

Java expressions are like complex noun phrases in English. Such phrases are subject to ambiguity. For example, consider the phrase "the man on the hill by the river with the telescope." Is the river by the hill or by the man? Is the man holding the telescope, or is the telescope on the hill, or is the telescope in the river? We don't know how to group the various parts together.

You can get the same kind of ambiguity if parentheses aren't used to group the parts of a Java expression. For example, the expression `2 + 3 * 4` has two operators. Which operation is performed first? You could interpret this two ways:

The first of these evaluates to 20 while the second evaluates to 14. To deal with the ambiguity, Java has rules of *precedence* that determine how to group together the various parts.

> **Precedence**
>
> The binding power of an operator, which determines how to group parts of an expression.

The computer applies rules of precedence when the grouping of operators in an expression is ambiguous. An operator with high precedence is evaluated first, followed by operators of lower precedence. Within a given level of precedence the operators are evaluated in one direction, usually left to right.

For arithmetic expressions, there are two levels of precedence. The multiplicative operators (*, /, %) have a higher level of precedence than the additive operators (+, −). Thus, the expression 2 + 3 * 4 is interpreted as

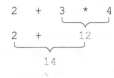

Within the same level of precedence, arithmetic operators are evaluated from left to right. This often doesn't make a difference in the final result, but occasionally it does. Consider, for example, the expression

40 − 25 − 9

which evaluates as follows:

$$40 \;\underbrace{-\; 25}\; -\; 9$$
$$\underbrace{15 \qquad -\; 9}$$
$$6$$

You would get a different result if the second subtraction were evaluated first.

You can always override precedence with parentheses. For example, if you really want the second subtraction to be evaluated first, you can force that to happen by introducing parentheses:

40 − (25 − 9)

Table 2.4   Java Operator Precedence

Description	Operators
unary operators	+, −
multiplicative operators	*, /, %
additive operators	+, −

The expression now evaluates as follows:

```
40  -  (25  -  9)
              16
40  -
         24
```

Another concept in arithmetic is *unary* plus and minus, which take a single operand, as opposed to the binary operators we have seen thus far (e.g., *, /, and even binary + and −), all of which take two operands. For example, we can find the negation of 8 by asking for −8. These unary operators have a higher level of precedence than the multiplicative operators. Consequently, we can form expressions like the following:

```
12 * −8
```

which evaluates to −96.

We will see many types of operators in the next few chapters. Table 2.4 is a precedence table that includes the arithmetic operators. As we introduce more operators, we'll update this table to include them as well. The table is ordered from highest precedence to lowest precedence and indicates that Java will first group parts of an expression using the unary operators, then using the multiplicative operators, and finally using the additive operators.

Before we leave this topic, let's look at a complex expression and see how it is evaluated step by step. Consider the following expression:

```
13 * 2 + 239 / 10 % 5 − 2 * 2
```

It has a total of six operators: two multiplications, one division, one mod, one subtraction, and one addition. The multiplication, division, and mod operations will be performed first, because they have higher precedence, and they will be performed from left to right because they are all at the same level of precedence:

```
13  *  2  +  239  /  10  %  5  -  2  *  2
    26     +  239  /  10  %  5  -  2  *  2
    26     +      23      %  5  -  2  *  2
    26     +              3      -  2  *  2
    26     +              3      -      4
```

Now we evaluate the additive operators from left to right:

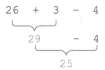

Mixing Types and Casting

You'll often find yourself mixing values of different types and wanting to convert from one type to another. Java has simple rules to avoid confusion and provides a mechanism for requesting that a value be converted from one type to another.

Two types that are frequently mixed are `int`s and `double`s. You might, for example, ask Java to compute `2 * 3.6`. This expression includes the `int` literal `2` and the `double` literal `3.6`. In this case, Java converts the `int` into a `double` and performs the computation entirely with `double` values; this is always the rule when Java encounters an `int` where it was expecting a `double`.

This becomes particularly important when you form expressions that involve division. If the two operands are both of type `int`, Java will use integer (truncating) division. If either of the two operands is of type `double`, however, it will do real-valued (normal) division. For example, `23 / 4` evaluates to `5`, but all of the following evaluate to `5.75`:

```
23.0 / 4
23. / 4
23 / 4.0
23 / 4.
23. / 4.
23.0 / 4.0
```

Sometimes you want Java to go the other way, converting a `double` into an `int`. You can ask Java for this conversion with a *cast*. Think of it as "casting a value in a different light." You request a cast by putting the name of the type you want to cast to in parentheses in front of the value you want to cast. For example,

```
(int) 4.75
```

will produce the `int` value `4`. When you cast a `double` value to an `int`, it simply truncates anything after the decimal point.

If you want to cast the result of an expression, you have to be careful to use parentheses. For example, suppose that you have some books that are each 0.15 feet wide and you want to know how many of them will fit in a bookshelf that is 2.5 feet wide. You could do a straight division of `2.5 / 0.15`, but that evaluates to a `double` result that is between 16 and 17. Americans use the phrase "16 and change" as a way to express the idea that a value is larger than 16 but not as big as 17. In this case, we don't care about the "change"; we only want to compute the 16 part. You might form the following expression:

```
(int) 2.5 / 0.15
```

Unfortunately, this expression evaluates to the wrong answer because the cast is applied to whatever comes right after it (here, the value 2.5). This casts 2.5 into the integer 2, divides by 0.15, and evaluates to 13 and change, which isn't an integer and isn't the right answer. Instead, you want to form this expression:

```
(int) (2.5 / 0.15)
```

This expression first performs the division to get 16 and change, and then casts that value to an int by truncating it. It thus evaluates to the int value 16, which is the answer you're looking for.

2.2 Variables

VideoNote

Primitive data can be stored in the computer's memory in a *variable*.

> **Variable**
>
> A memory location with a name and a type that stores a value.

Think of the computer's memory as being like a giant spreadsheet that has many cells where data can be stored. When you create a variable in Java, you are asking it to set aside one of those cells for this new variable. Initially the cell will be empty, but you will have the option to store a value in the cell. And as with a spreadsheet, you will have the option to change the value in that cell later.

Java is a little more picky than a spreadsheet, though, in that it requires you to tell it exactly what kind of data you are going to store in the cell. For example, if you want to store an integer, you need to tell Java that you intend to use type int. If you want to store a real value, you need to tell Java that you intend to use a double. You also have to decide on a name to use when you want to refer to this memory location. The normal rules of Java identifiers apply (the name must start with a letter, which can be followed by any combination of letters and digits). The standard convention in Java is to start variable names with a lowercase letter, as in number or digits, and to capitalize any subsequent words, as in numberOfDigits.

To explore the basic use of variables, let's examine a program that computes an individual's *body mass index* (BMI). Health professionals use this number to advise people about whether or not they are overweight. Given an individual's height and weight, we can compute that person's BMI. A simple BMI program, then, would naturally have three variables for these three pieces of information. There are several details that we need to discuss about variables, but it can be helpful to look at a complete program first to see the overall picture. The following program computes and prints the BMI for an individual who is 5 feet 10 inches tall and weighs 195 pounds:

```java
1  public class BMICalculator {
2      public static void main(String[] args) {
3          // declare variables
4          double height;
5          double weight;
6          double bmi;
7
8          // compute BMI
9          height = 70;
10         weight = 195;
11         bmi = weight / (height * height) * 703;
12
13         // print results
14         System.out.println("Current BMI:");
15         System.out.println(bmi);
16     }
17  }
```

Notice that the program includes blank lines to separate the sections and comments to indicate what the different parts of the program do. It produces the following output:

```
Current BMI:
27.976530612244897
```

Let's now examine the details of this program to understand how variables work. Before variables can be used in a Java program, they must be declared. The line of code that declares the variable is known as a variable *declaration*.

> **Declaration**
> A request to set aside a new variable with a given name and type.

Each variable is declared just once. If you declare a variable more than once, you will get an error message from the Java compiler. Simple variable declarations are of the form

```
<type> <name>;
```

as in the three declarations at the beginning of our sample program:

```
double height;
double weight;
double bmi;
```

Notice that a variable declaration, like a statement, ends with a semicolon. These declarations can appear anywhere a statement can occur. The declaration indicates the type and the name of the variable. Remember that the name of each primitive type is a keyword in Java (`int`, `double`, `char`, `boolean`). We've used the keyword `double` to define the type of these three variables.

Once a variable is declared, Java sets aside a memory location to store its value. However, with the simple form of variable declaration used in our program, Java does not store initial values in these memory locations. We refer to these as *uninitialized* variables, and they are similar to blank cells in a spreadsheet:

So how do we get values into those cells? The easiest way to do so is using an *assignment statement.* The general syntax of the assignment statement is

```
<variable> = <expression>;
```

as in

```
height = 70;
```

This statement stores the value `70` in the memory location for the variable `height`, indicating that this person is 70 inches tall (5 feet 10 inches). We often use the phrase "gets" or "is assigned" when reading a statement like this, as in "`height` gets `70`" or "`height` is assigned `70`."

When the statement executes, the computer first evaluates the expression on the right side; then, it stores the result in the memory location for the given variable. In this case the expression is just a simple literal value, so after the computer executes this statement, the memory looks like this:

height 70.0   weight ?   bmi ?

Notice that the value is stored as `70.0` because the variable is of type `double`. The variable `height` has now been initialized, but the variables `weight` and `bmi` are still uninitialized. The second assignment statement gives a value to `weight`:

```
weight = 195;
```

After executing this statement, the memory looks like this:

height 70.0   weight 195.0   bmi ?

The third assignment statement includes a formula (an expression to be evaluated):

```
bmi = weight / (height * height) * 703;
```

To calculate the value of this expression, the computer divides the weight by the square of the height and then multiplies the result of that operation by the literal value 703. The result is stored in the variable bmi. So, after the computer has executed the third assignment statement, the memory looks like this:

height 70.0   weight 195.0   bmi 27.976530612244897

The last two lines of the program report the BMI result using println statements:

```
System.out.println("Current BMI:");
System.out.println(bmi);
```

Notice that we can include a variable in a println statement the same way that we include literal values and other expressions to be printed.

As its name implies, a variable can take on different values at different times. For example, consider the following variation of the BMI program, which computes a new BMI assuming the person lost 15 pounds (going from 195 pounds to 180 pounds).

```
1   public class BMICalculator2 {
2       public static void main(String[] args) {
3           // declare variables
4           double height;
5           double weight;
6           double bmi;
7
8           // compute BMI
9           height = 70;
10          weight = 195;
11          bmi = weight / (height * height) * 703;
12
13          // print results
14          System.out.println("Previous BMI:");
15          System.out.println(bmi);
16
17          // recompute BMI
18          weight = 180;
19          bmi = weight / (height * height) * 703;
20
21          // report new results
22          System.out.println("Current BMI:");
23          System.out.println(bmi);
24      }
25  }
```

The program begins the same way, setting the three variables to the following values and reporting this initial value for BMI:

height `70.0`   weight `195.0`   bmi `27.976530612244897`

But the new program then includes the following assignment statement:

```
weight = 180;
```

This changes the value of the `weight` variable:

height `70.0`   weight `180.0`   bmi `27.976530612244897`

You might think that this would also change the value of the `bmi` variable. After all, earlier in the program we said that the following should be true:

```
bmi = weight / (height * height) * 703;
```

This is a place where the spreadsheet analogy is not as accurate. A spreadsheet can store formulas in its cells and when you update one cell it can cause the values in other cells to be updated. The same is not true in Java.

You might also be misled by the use of an equals sign for assignment. Don't confuse this statement with a statement of equality. The assignment statement does not represent an algebraic relationship. In algebra, you might say

$$x = y + 2$$

In mathematics you state definitively that x is equal to y plus two, a fact that is true now and forever. If x changes, y will change accordingly, and vice versa. Java's assignment statement is very different.

The assignment statement is a command to perform an action at a particular point in time. It does not represent a lasting relationship between variables. That's why we usually say "gets" or "is assigned" rather than saying "equals" when we read assignment statements.

Getting back to the program, resetting the variable called `weight` does not reset the variable called `bmi`. To recompute `bmi` based on the new value for `weight`, we must include the second assignment statement:

```
weight = 180;
bmi = weight / (height * height) * 703;
```

Otherwise, the variable `bmi` would store the same value as before. That would be a rather depressing outcome to report to someone who's just lost 15 pounds. By including both of these statements, we reset both the `weight` and `bmi` variables so that memory looks like this:

height `70.0`   weight `180.0`   bmi `25.82448979591837`

The output of the new version of the program is

```
Previous BMI:
27.976530612244897
Current BMI:
25.82448979591837
```

One very common assignment statement that points out the difference between algebraic relationships and program statements is:

```
x = x + 1;
```

Remember not to think of this as "x equals x + 1." There are no numbers that satisfy that equation. We use a word like "gets" to read this as "x gets the value of x plus one." This may seem a rather odd statement, but you should be able to decipher it given the rules outlined earlier. Suppose that the current value of x is 19. To execute the statement, you first evaluate the expression to obtain the result 20. The computer stores this value in the variable named on the left, x. Thus, this statement adds one to the value of the variable. We refer to this as *incrementing* the value of x. It is a fundamental programming operation because it is the programming equivalent of counting (1, 2, 3, 4, and so on). The following statement is a variation that counts down, which we call *decrementing* a variable:

```
x = x - 1;
```

We will discuss incrementing and decrementing in more detail later in this chapter.

Assignment/Declaration Variations

Java is a complex language that provides a lot of flexibility to programmers. In the last section we saw the simplest form of variable declaration and assignment, but there are many variations on this theme. It wouldn't be a bad idea to stick with the simplest form while you are learning, but you'll come across other forms as you read other people's programs, so you'll want to understand what they mean.

The first variation is that Java allows you to provide an initial value for a variable at the time that you declare it. The syntax is as follows:

```
<type> <name> = <expression>;
```

as in

```
double height = 70;
double weight = 195;
double bmi = weight / (height * height) * 703;
```

This variation combines declaration and assignment in one line of code. The first two assignments have simple numbers after the equals sign, but the third has a complex expression after the equals sign. These three assignments have the same effect as providing three declarations followed by three assignment statements:

```
double height;
double weight;
double bmi;
height = 70;
weight = 195;
bmi = weight / (height * height) * 703;
```

Another variation is to declare several variables that are all of the same type in a single statement. The syntax is

```
<type> <name>, <name>, <name>, ..., <name>;
```

as in

```
double height, weight;
```

This example declares two different variables, both of type `double`. Notice that the type appears just once, at the beginning of the declaration.

The final variation is a mixture of the previous two forms. You can declare multiple variables all of the same type, and you can initialize them at the same time. For example, you could say

```
double height = 70, weight = 195;
```

This statement declares the two `double` variables `height` and `weight` and gives them initial values (`70` and `195`, respectively). Java even allows you to mix initializing and not initializing, as in

```
double height = 70, weight = 195, bmi;
```

This statement declares three `double` variables called `height`, `weight`, and `bmi` and provides initial values to two of them (`height` and `weight`). The variable `bmi` is uninitialized.

Common Programming Error

Declaring the Same Variable Twice

One of the things to keep in mind as you learn is that you can declare any given variable just once. You can assign it as many times as you like once you've declared it, but the declaration should appear just once. Think of variable declaration as being like checking into a hotel and assignment as being like going in

Continued on next page

Continued from previous page

and out of your room. You have to check in first to get your room key, but then you can come and go as often as you like. If you tried to check in a second time, the hotel would be likely to ask you if you really want to pay for a second room.

If you declare a variable more than once, Java generates a compiler error. For example, say your program contains the following lines:

```
int x = 13;
System.out.println(x);
int x = 2;           // this line does not compile
System.out.println(x);
```

The first line is okay. It declares an integer variable called x and initializes it to 13. The second line is also okay, because it simply prints the value of x. But the third line will generate an error message indicating that "x is already defined." If you want to change the value of x you need to use a simple assignment statement instead of a variable declaration:

```
int x = 13;
System.out.println(x);
x = 2;
System.out.println(x);
```

We have been referring to the "assignment statement," but in fact assignment is an operator, not a statement. When you assign a value to a variable, the overall expression evaluates to the value just assigned. That means that you can form expressions that have assignment operators embedded within them. Unlike most other operators, the assignment operator evaluates from right to left, which allows programmers to write statements like the following:

```
int x, y, z;
x = y = z = 2 * 5 + 4;
```

Because the assignment operator evaluates from right to left, this statement is equivalent to:

```
x = (y = (z = 2 * 5 + 4));
```

The expression 2 * 5 + 4 evaluates to 14. This value is assigned to z. The assignment is itself an expression that evaluates to 14, which is then assigned to y. The assignment to y evaluates to 14 as well, which is then assigned to x. The result is that all three variables are assigned the value 14.

String Concatenation

You saw in Chapter 1 that you can output string literals using `System.out.println`. You can also output numeric expressions using `System.out.println`:

```
System.out.println(12 + 3 - 1);
```

This statement causes the computer first to evaluate the expression, which yields the value 14, and then to write that value to the console window. You'll often want to output more than one value on a line, but unfortunately, you can pass only one value to `println`. To get around this limitation, Java provides a simple mechanism called *concatenation* for putting together several pieces into one long string literal.

> **String Concatenation**
>
> Combining several strings into a single string, or combining a string with other data into a new, longer string.

The addition (+) operator concatenates the pieces together. Doing so forms an expression that can be evaluated. Even if the expression includes both numbers and text, it can be evaluated just like the numeric expressions we have been exploring. Consider, for example, the following:

```
"I have " + 3 + " things to concatenate"
```

You have to pay close attention to the quotation marks in an expression like this to keep track of which parts are "inside" a string literal and which are outside. This expression begins with the text `"I have "` (including a space at the end), followed by a plus sign and the integer literal 3. Java converts the integer into a textual form (`"3"`) and concatenates the two pieces together to form `"I have 3"`. Following the 3 is another plus and another string literal, `"things to concatenate"` (which starts with a space). This piece is glued onto the end of the previous string to form the string `"I have 3 things to concatenate"`.

Because this expression produces a single concatenated string, we can include it in a `println` statement:

```
System.out.println("I have " + 3 + " things to concatenate");
```

This statement produces a single line of output:

```
I have 3 things to concatenate
```

String concatenation is often used to report the value of a variable. Consider, for example, the following program that computes the number of hours, minutes, and seconds in a standard year:

```
1   public class Time {
2       public static void main(String[] args) {
3           int hours = 365 * 24;
```

```
4              int minutes = hours * 60;
5              int seconds = minutes * 60;
6              System.out.println("Hours in a year = " + hours);
7              System.out.println("Minutes in a year = " + minutes);
8              System.out.println("Seconds in a year = " + seconds);
9        }
10   }
```

Notice that the three `println` commands at the end each have a string literal concatenated with a variable. The program produces the following output:

```
Hours in a year = 8760
Minutes in a year = 525600
Seconds in a year = 31536000
```

You can use concatenation to form arbitrarily complex expressions. For example, if you had variables x, y, and z and you wanted to write out their values in coordinate format with parentheses and commas, you could say:

```
System.out.println("(" + x + ", " + y + ", " + z + ")");
```

If x, y, and z had the values 8, 19, and 23, respectively, this statement would output the string `"(8, 19, 23)"`.

The + used for concatenation has the same level of precedence as the normal arithmetic + operator, which can lead to some confusion. Consider, for example, the following expression:

```
2 + 3 + " hello " + 7 + 2 * 3
```

This expression has four addition operators and one multiplication operator. Because of precedence, we evaluate the multiplication first:

$$2 \ + \ 3 \ + \ \text{" hello "} \ + \ 7 \ + \ \underbrace{2 \ * \ 3}$$
$$2 \ + \ 3 \ + \ \text{" hello "} \ + \ 7 \ + \ \quad 6$$

This grouping might seem odd, but that's what the precedence rule says to do: We don't evaluate any additive operators until we've first evaluated all of the multiplicative operators. Once we've taken care of the multiplication, we're left with the four addition operators. These will be evaluated from left to right.

The first addition involves two integer values. Even though the overall expression involves a string, because this little subexpression has just two integers we perform integer addition:

$$\underbrace{2 \ + \ 3} \ + \ \text{" hello "} \ + \ 7 \ + \ 6$$
$$\quad 5 \quad + \ \text{" hello "} \ + \ 7 \ + \ 6$$

The next addition involves adding the integer 5 to the string literal " hello ". If either of the two operands is a string, we perform concatenation. So, in this case, we convert the integer into a text equivalent ("5") and glue the pieces together to form a new string value:

```
5   +   " hello "   +   7   +   6

    "5 hello "        +   7   +   6
```

You might think that Java would add together the 7 and 6 the same way it added the 2 and 3 to make 5. But it doesn't work that way. The rules of precedence are simple, and Java follows them with simple-minded consistency. Precedence tells us that addition operators are evaluated from left to right, so first we add the string "5 hello " to 7. That is another combination of a string and an integer, so Java converts the integer to its textual equivalent ("7") and concatenates the two parts together to form a new string:

```
"5 hello "   +   7   +   6

    "5 hello 7"        +   6
```

Now there is just a single remaining addition to perform, which again involves a string/integer combination. We convert the integer to its textual equivalent ("6") and concatenate the two parts together to form a new string:

```
"5 hello 7"   +   6

    "5 hello 76"
```

Clearly, such expressions can be confusing, but you wouldn't want the Java compiler to have to try to guess what you mean. Our job as programmers is easier if we know that the compiler is going to follow simple rules consistently. You can make the expression clearer, and specify how it is evaluated, by adding parentheses. For example, if we really did want Java to add together the 7 and 6 instead of concatenating them separately, we could have written the original expression in the following much clearer way:

```
(2 + 3) + " hello " + (7 + 2 * 3)
```

Because of the parentheses, Java will evaluate the two numeric parts of this expression first and then concatenate the results with the string in the middle. This expression evaluates to "5 hello 13".

Increment/Decrement Operators

In addition to the standard assignment operator, Java has several special operators that are useful for a particular family of operations that are common in programming. As we mentioned earlier, you will often find yourself increasing the value of a variable by a particular amount, an operation called *incrementing*. You will also often find yourself decreasing the value of a variable by a particular amount, an operation called *decrementing*. To accomplish this, you write statements like the following:

```
x = x + 1;
y = y - 1;
z = z + 2;
```

Likewise, you'll frequently find yourself wanting to double or triple the value of a variable or to reduce its value by a factor of 2, in which case you might write code like the following:

```
x = x * 2;
y = y * 3;
z = z / 2;
```

Java has a shorthand for these situations. You glue together the operator character (+, −, *, etc.) with the equals sign to get a special assignment operator (+=, −=, *=, etc.). This variation allows you to rewrite assignment statements like the previous ones as follows:

```
x += 1;
y -= 1;
z += 2;

x *= 2;
y *= 3;
z /= 2;
```

This convention is yet another detail to learn about Java, but it can make the code easier to read. Think of a statement like x += 2 as saying, "add 2 to x." That's more concise than saying x = x + 2.

Java has an even more concise way of expressing the particular case in which you want to increment by 1 or decrement by 1. In this case, you can use the increment and decrement operators (++ and −−). For example, you can say

```
x++;
y--;
```

There are actually two different forms of each of these operators, because you can also put the operator in front of the variable:

```
++x;
--y;
```

The two versions of ++ are known as the preincrement (++x) and postincrement (x++) operators. The two versions of −− are similarly known as the predecrement

Table 2.5   Java Operator Precedence

Description	Operators
unary operators	`++, --, +, -`
multiplicative operators	`*, /, %`
additive operators	`+, -`
assignment operators	`=, +=, -=, *=, /=, %=`

(--x) and postdecrement (x--) operators. The pre- versus post- distinction doesn't matter when you include them as statements by themselves, as in these two examples. The difference comes up only when you embed these statements inside more complex expressions, which we don't recommend.

Now that we've seen a number of new operators, it is worth revisiting the issue of precedence. Table 2.5 shows an updated version of the Java operator precedence table that includes the assignment operators and the increment and decrement operators. Notice that the increment and decrement operators are grouped with the unary operators and have the highest precedence.

Did You Know?

++ and --

The ++ and -- operators were first introduced in the C programming language. Java has them because the designers of the language decided to use the syntax of C as the basis for Java syntax. Many languages have made the same choice, including C++ and C#. There is almost a sense of pride among C programmers that these operators allow you to write extremely concise code, but many other people feel that they can make code unnecessarily complex. In this book we always use these operators as separate statements so that it is obvious what is going on, but in the interest of completeness we will look at the other option here.

The pre- and post- variations both have the same overall effect—the two increment operators increment a variable and the two decrement operators decrement a variable—but they differ in terms of what they evaluate to. When you increment or decrement, there are really two values involved: the original value that the variable had before the increment or decrement operation, and the final value that the variable has after the increment or decrement operation. The post- versions evaluate to the original (older) value and the pre- versions evaluate to the final (later) value.

Consider, for example, the following code fragment:

```java
int x = 10;
int y = 20;
int z = ++x * y--;
```

Continued on next page

Continued from previous page

What value is z assigned? The answer is 220. The third assignment increments x to 11 and decrements y to 19, but in computing the value of z, it uses the new value of x (++x) times the old value of y (y--), which is 11 times 20, or 220.

There is a simple mnemonic to remember this: When you see x++, read it as "give me x, then increment," and when you see ++x, read it as "increment, then give me x." Another memory device that might help is to remember that C++ is a bad name for a programming language. The expression "C++" would be interpreted as "evaluate to the old value of C and then increment C." In other words, even though you're trying to come up with something new and different, you're really stuck with the old awful language. The language you want is ++C, which would be a new and improved language rather than the old one. Some people have suggested that perhaps Java is ++C.

Variables and Mixing Types

You already know that when you declare a variable, you must tell Java what type of value it will be storing. For example, you might declare a variable of type int for integer values or of type double for real values. The situation is fairly clear when you have just integers or just reals, but what happens when you start mixing the types? For example, the following code is clearly okay:

```
int x;
double y;
x = 2 + 3;
y = 3.4 * 2.9;
```

Here, we have an integer variable that we assign an integer value and a double variable that we assign a double value. But what if we try to do it the other way around?

```
int x;
double y;
x = 3.4 * 2.9; // illegal
y = 2 + 3;     // okay
```

As the comments indicate, you can't assign an integer variable a double value, but you can assign a double variable an integer value. Let's consider the second case first. The expression 2 + 3 evaluates to the integer 5. This value isn't a double, but every integer is a real value, so it is easy enough for Java to convert the integer into a double. The technical term is that Java *promotes* the integer into a double.

The first case is more problematic. The expression 3.4 * 2.9 evaluates to the double value 9.86. This value can't be stored in an integer because it isn't an integer. If you want to perform this kind of operation, you'll have to tell Java to convert this value into an integer. As described earlier, you can cast a `double` to an `int`, which will truncate anything after the decimal point:

```
x = (int) (3.4 * 2.9);  // now legal
```

This statement first evaluates `3.4 * 2.9` to get `9.86` and then truncates that value to get the integer `9`.

Common Programming Error

Forgetting to Cast

We often write programs that involve a mixture of `int`s and `double`s, so it is easy to make mistakes when it comes to combinations of the two. For example, suppose that you want to compute the percentage of correctly answered questions on a student's test, given the total number of questions on the test and the number of questions the student got right. You might declare the following variables:

```
int totalQuestions;
int numRight;
double percent;
```

Suppose the first two are initialized as follows:

```
totalQuestions = 73;
numRight = 59;
```

How do you compute the percentage of questions that the student got right? You divide the number right by the total number of questions and multiply by 100 to turn it into a percentage:

```
percent = numRight / totalQuestions * 100; // incorrect
```

Unfortunately, if you print out the value of the variable `percent` after executing this line of code, you will find that it has the value `0.0`. But obviously the student got more than 0% correct.

The problem comes from integer division. The expression you are using begins with two `int` values:

```
numRight / totalQuestions
```

which means you are computing

```
59 / 73
```

Continued on next page

Continued from previous page

This evaluates to 0 with integer division. Some students fix this by changing the types of all the variables to double. That will solve the immediate problem, but it's not a good choice from a stylistic point of view. It is best to use the most appropriate type for data, and the number of questions on the test will definitely be an integer. You could try to fix this by changing the value 100 to 100.0:

```
percent = numRight / totalQuestions * 100.0; // incorrect
```

but this doesn't help because the division is done first. However, it does work if you put the 100.0 first:

```
percent = 100.0 * numRight / totalQuestions;
```

Now the multiplication is computed before the division, which means that everything is converted to double.

Sometimes you can fix a problem like this through a clever rearrangement of the formula, but you don't want to count on cleverness. This is a good place to use a cast. For example, returning to the original formula, you can cast each of the int variables to double:

```
percent = (double) numRight / (double) totalQuestions * 100.0;
```

You can also take advantage of the fact that once you have cast one of these two variables to double, the division will be done with doubles. So you could, for example, cast just the first value to double:

```
percent = (double) numRight / totalQuestions * 100.0;
```

2.3 The for Loop

VideoNote

Programming often involves specifying redundant tasks. The for loop helps to avoid such redundancy by repeatedly executing a sequence of statements over a particular range of values. Suppose you want to write out the squares of the first five integers. You could write a program like this:

```
1  public class WriteSquares {
2      public static void main(String[] args) {
3          System.out.println(1 + " squared = " + (1 * 1));
4          System.out.println(2 + " squared = " + (2 * 2));
5          System.out.println(3 + " squared = " + (3 * 3));
6          System.out.println(4 + " squared = " + (4 * 4));
7          System.out.println(5 + " squared = " + (5 * 5));
8      }
9  }
```

which would produce the following output:

```
1 squared = 1
2 squared = 4
3 squared = 9
4 squared = 16
5 squared = 25
```

But this approach is tedious. The program has five statements that are very similar. They are all of the form:

```
System.out.println(number + " squared = " + (number * number));
```

where number is either 1, 2, 3, 4, or 5. The for loop avoids such redundancy. Here is an equivalent program using a for loop:

```
1   public class WriteSquares2 {
2       public static void main(String[] args) {
3           for (int i = 1; i <= 5; i++) {
4               System.out.println(i + " squared = " + (i * i));
5           }
6       }
7   }
```

This program initializes a variable called i to the value 1. Then it repeatedly executes the println statement as long as the variable i is less than or equal to 5. After each println, it evaluates the expression i++ to increment i.

The general syntax of the for loop is as follows:

```
for (<initialization>; <continuation test>; <update>) {
    <statement>;
    <statement>;
    ...
    <statement>;
}
```

You always include the keyword for and the parentheses. Inside the parentheses are three different parts, separated by semicolons: the initialization, the continuation test, and the update. Then there is a set of curly braces that encloses a set of statements. The for loop controls the statements inside the curly braces. We refer to the controlled statements as the *body* of the loop. The idea is that we execute the body multiple times, as determined by the combination of the other three parts.

The diagram in Figure 2.1 indicates the steps that Java follows to execute a for loop. It performs whatever initialization you have requested once before the loop begins executing. Then it repeatedly performs the continuation test you have provided.

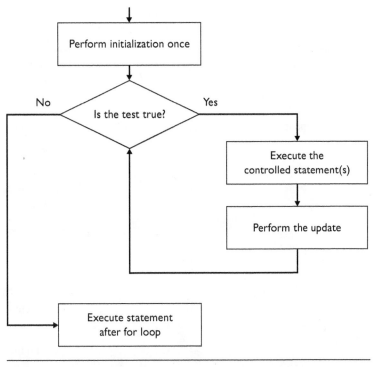

Figure 2.1 Flow of for loop

If the continuation test evaluates to true, it executes the controlled statements once and executes the update part. Then it performs the test again. If it again evaluates to true, it executes the statements again and executes the update again. Notice that the update is performed after the controlled statements are executed. When the test evaluates to false, Java is done executing the loop and moves on to whatever statement comes after the loop.

The for loop is the first example of a *control structure* that we will study.

> **Control Structure**
>
> A syntactic structure that controls other statements.

You should be careful to use indentation to indicate controlled statements. In the case of the for loop, all of the statements in the body of the loop are indented as a way to indicate that they are "inside" the loop.

Tracing for Loops

Let's examine the for loop of the WriteSquares2 program in detail:

```
for (int i = 1; i <= 5; i++) {
    System.out.println(i + " squared = " + (i * i));
}
```

Table 2.6 Trace of for (int i = 1; i <= 5; i++)

Step	Code	Description
initialization	int i = 1;	variable i is created and initialized to 1
test	i <= 5	true because 1 <= 5, so we enter the loop
body	{. . .}	execute the println with i equal to 1
update	i++	increment i, which becomes 2
test	i <= 5	true because 2 <= 5, so we enter the loop
body	{. . .}	execute the println with i equal to 2
update	i++	increment i, which becomes 3
test	i <= 5	true because 3 <= 5, so we enter the loop
body	{. . .}	execute the println with i equal to 3
update	i++	increment i, which becomes 4
test	i <= 5	true because 4 <= 5, so we enter the loop
body	{. . .}	execute the println with i equal to 4
update	i++	increment i, which becomes 5
test	i <= 5	true because 5 <= 5, so we enter the loop
body	{. . .}	execute the println with i equal to 5
update	i++	increment i, which becomes 6
test	i <= 5	false because 6 > 5, so we are finished

In this loop, the initialization (int i = 1) declares an integer variable i that is initialized to 1. The continuation test (i <= 5) indicates that we should keep executing as long as i is less than or equal to 5. That means that once i is greater than 5, we will stop executing the body of the loop. The update (i++) will increment the value of i by one each time, bringing i closer to being larger than 5. After five executions of the body and the accompanying five updates, i will be larger than 5 and the loop will finish executing. Table 2.6 traces this process in detail.

Java allows great flexibility in deciding what to include in the initialization part and the update, so we can use the for loop to solve all sorts of programming tasks. For now, though, we will restrict ourselves to a particular kind of loop that declares and initializes a single variable that is used to control the loop. This variable is often referred to as the *control variable* of the loop. In the test we compare the control variable against some final desired value, and in the update we change the value of the control variable, most often incrementing it by 1. Such loops are very common in programming. By convention, we often use names like i, j, and k for the control variables.

Each execution of the controlled statement of a loop is called an *iteration* of the loop (as in, "The loop finished executing after four iterations"). Iteration also refers to looping in general (as in, "I solved the problem using iteration").

Consider another for loop:

```
for (int i = 100; i <= 100; i++) {
    System.out.println(i + " squared = " + (i * i));
}
```

This loop executes a total of 201 times, producing the squares of all the integers between −100 and +100 inclusive. The values used in the initialization and the test, then, can be any integers. They can, in fact, be arbitrary integer expressions:

```java
for (int i = (2 + 2); i <= (17 * 3); i++) {
    System.out.println(i + " squared = " + (i * i));
}
```

This loop will generate the squares of all the integers between 4 and 51 inclusive. The parentheses around the expressions are not necessary but improve readability. Consider the following loop:

```java
for (int i = 1; i <= 30; i++) {
    System.out.println("+--------+");
}
```

This loop generates 30 lines of output, all exactly the same. It is slightly different from the previous one because the statement controlled by the for loop makes no reference to the control variable. Thus,

```java
for (int i = -30; i <= -1; i++) {
    System.out.println("+--------+");
}
```

generates exactly the same output. The behavior of such a loop is determined solely by the number of iterations it performs. The number of iterations is given by

```
<ending value> - <starting value> + 1
```

It is much simpler to see that the first of these loops iterates 30 times, so it is better to use that loop.

Now let's look at some borderline cases. Consider this loop:

```java
for (int i = 1; i <= 1; i++) {
    System.out.println("+--------+");
}
```

According to our rule it should iterate once, and it does. It initializes the variable i to 1 and tests to see if this is less than or equal to 1, which it is. So it executes the println, increments i, and tests again. The second time it tests, it finds that i is no longer less than or equal to 1, so it stops executing. Now consider this loop:

```java
for (int i = 1; i <= 0; i++) {
    System.out.println("+--------+"); // never executes
}
```

This loop performs no iterations at all. It will not cause an execution error; it just won't execute the body. It initializes the variable to 1 and tests to see if this is less than or equal to 0. It isn't, so rather than executing the statements in the body, it stops there.

When you construct a `for` loop, you can include more than one statement inside the curly braces. Consider, for example, the following code:

```java
for (int i = 1; i <= 20; i++) {
    System.out.println("Hi!");
    System.out.println("Ho!");
}
```

This will produce 20 pairs of lines, the first of which has the word "Hi!" on it and the second of which has the word "Ho!"

When a `for` loop controls a single statement, you don't have to include the curly braces. The curly braces are required only for situations like the previous one, where you have more than one statement that you want the loop to control. However, the Java coding convention includes the curly braces even for a single statement, and we follow this convention in this book. There are two advantages to this convention:

- Including the curly braces prevents future errors. Even if you need only one statement in the body of your loop now, your code is likely to change over time. Having the curly braces there ensures that, if you add an extra statement to the body later, you won't accidentally forget to include them. In general, including curly braces in advance is cheaper than locating obscure bugs later.

- Always including the curly braces reduces the level of detail you have to consider as you learn new control structures. It takes time to master the details of any new control structure, and it will be easier to master those details if you don't have to also be thinking about when to include and when not to include the braces.

Common Programming Error

Forgetting Curly Braces

You should use indentation to indicate the body of a `for` loop, but indentation alone is not enough. Java ignores indentation when it is deciding how different statements are grouped. Suppose, for example, that you were to write the following code:

```java
for (int i = 1; i <= 20; i++)
    System.out.println("Hi!");
    System.out.println("Ho!");
```

The indentation indicates to the reader that both of the `println` statements are in the body of the `for` loop, but there aren't any curly braces to indicate that to Java. As a result, this code is interpreted as follows:

Continued on next page

Continued from previous page

```java
for (int i = 1; i <= 20; i++) {
    System.out.println("Hi!");
}
System.out.println("Ho!");
```

Only the first `println` is considered to be in the body of the `for` loop. The second `println` is considered to be outside the loop. So, this code would produce 20 lines of output that all say "Hi!" followed by one line of output that says "Ho!" To include both `println`s in the body, you need curly braces around them:

```java
for (int i = 1; i <= 20; i++) {
    System.out.println("Hi!");
    System.out.println("Ho!");
}
```

for Loop Patterns

In general, if you want a loop to iterate exactly *n* times, you will use one of two standard loops. The first standard form looks like the ones you have already seen:

```java
for (int <variable> = 1; <variable> <= n; i++) {
    <statement>;
    <statement>;
    ...
    <statement>;
}
```

It's pretty clear that this loop executes *n* times, because it starts at 1 and continues as long as it is less than or equal to *n*. For example, this loop prints the numbers 1 through 10:

```java
for (int i = 1; i <= 10; i++) {
    System.out.print(i + " ");
}
```

Because it uses a `print` instead of a `println` statement, it produces a single line of output:

```
1 2 3 4 5 6 7 8 9 10
```

Often, however, it is more convenient to start our counting at 0 instead of 1. That requires a change in the loop test to allow you to stop when *n* is one less:

```
for (int <variable> = 0; <variable> < n; i++) {
    <statement>;
    <statement>;
    ...
    <statement>;
}
```

Notice that in this form when you initialize the variable to 0, you test whether it is strictly less than *n*. Either form will execute exactly *n* times, although there are some situations where the zero-based loop works better. For example, this loop executes 10 times just like the previous loop:

```
for (int i = 0; i < 10; i++) {
    System.out.print(i + " ");
}
```

Because it starts at 0 instead of starting at 1, it produces a different sequence of 10 values:

```
0 1 2 3 4 5 6 7 8 9
```

Most often you will use the loop that starts at 0 or 1 to perform some operation a fixed number of times. But there is a slight variation that is also sometimes useful. Instead of running the loop in a forward direction, we can run it backward. Instead of starting at 1 and executing until you reach *n*, you instead start at *n* and keep executing until you reach 1. You can accomplish this by using a decrement rather than an increment, so we sometimes refer to this as a decrementing loop.

Here is the general form of a decrementing loop:

```
for (int <variable> = n; <variable> >= 1; <variable>--) {
    <statement>;
    <statement>;
    ...
    <statement>;
}
```

For example, here is a decrementing loop that executes 10 times:

```
for (int i = 10; i >= 1; i--) {
    System.out.print(i + " ");
}
```

Because it runs backward, it prints the values in reverse order:

```
10 9 8 7 6 5 4 3 2 1
```

Nested for Loops

VideoNote

The for loop controls a statement, and the for loop is itself a statement, which means that one for loop can control another for loop. For example, you can write code like the following:

```
for (int i = 1; i <= 10; i++) {
    for (int j = 1; j <= 5; j++) {
        System.out.println("Hi there.");
    }
}
```

This code is probably easier to read from the inside out. The println statement produces a single line of output. The inner j loop executes this statement five times, producing five lines of output. The outer i loop executes the inner loop 10 times, which produces 10 sets of 5 lines, or 50 lines of output. The preceding code, then, is equivalent to

```
for (int i = 1; i <= 50; i++) {
    System.out.println("Hi there.");
}
```

This example shows that a for loop can be controlled by another for loop. Such a loop is called a *nested loop.* This example wasn't very interesting, though, because the nested loop can be eliminated.

Now that you know how to write for loops, you will want to be able to produce complex lines of output piece by piece using the print command. Recall from Chapter 1 that the print command prints on the current line of output without going to a new line of output. For example, if you want to produce a line of output that has 80 stars on it, you can use a print command to print one star at a time and have it execute 80 times rather than using a single println.

Let's look at a more interesting nested loop that uses a print command:

```
for (int i = 1; i <= 6; i++) {
    for (int j = 1; j <= 3; j++) {
        System.out.print(j + " ");
    }
}
```

We can once again read this from the inside out. The inner loop prints the value of its control variable j as it varies from 1 to 3. The outer loop executes this six different times. As a result, we get six occurrences of the sequence 1 2 3 as output:

```
1 2 3 1 2 3 1 2 3 1 2 3 1 2 3 1 2 3
```

This code prints all of its output on a single line of output. Let's look at some code that includes a combination of `print` and `println` to produce several lines of output:

```
for (int i = 1; i <= 6; i++) {
    for (int j = 1; j <= 10; j++) {
        System.out.print("*");
    }
    System.out.println();
}
```

When you write code that involves nested loops, you have to be careful to indent the code correctly to make the structure clear. At the outermost level, the preceding code is a simple `for` loop that executes six times:

```
for (int i = 1; i <= 6; i++) {
    ...
}
```

We use indentation for the statements inside this `for` loop to make it clear that they are the body of this loop. Inside, we find two statements: another `for` loop and a `println`. Let's look at the inner `for` loop:

```
for (int j = 1; j <= 10; j++) {
    System.out.print("*");
}
```

This loop is controlled by the outer `for` loop, which is why it is indented, but it itself controls a statement (the `print` statement), so we end up with another level of indentation. The indentation thus indicates that the `print` statement is controlled by the inner `for` loop, which in turn is controlled by the outer `for` loop. So what does this inner loop do? It prints 10 stars on the current line of output. They all appear on the same line because we are using a `print` instead of a `println`. Notice that after this loop we perform a `println`:

```
System.out.println();
```

The net effect of the `for` loop followed by the `println` is that we get a line of output with 10 stars on it. But remember that these statements are contained in an outer loop that executes six times, so we end up getting six lines of output, each with 10 stars:

```
**********
**********
**********
**********
**********
**********
```

Let's examine one more variation. In the code above, the inner `for` loop always does exactly the same thing: It prints exactly 10 stars on a line of output. But what happens if we change the test for the inner `for` loop to make use of the outer `for` loop's control variable (`i`)?

```java
for (int i = 1; i <= 6; i++) {
    for (int j = 1; j <= i; j++) {
        System.out.print("*");
    }
    System.out.println();
}
```

In the old version the inner loop always executes 10 times, producing 10 stars on each line of output. With the new test (`j <= i`), the inner loop will execute i times with each iteration. But i is changing: It takes on the values 1, 2, 3, 4, 5, and 6. On the first iteration of the outer loop, when i is 1, the test `j <= i` is effectively testing `j <= 1`, and it generates a line with one star on it. On the second iteration of the outer loop, when i is 2, the test is effectively testing `j <= 2`, and it generates a line with two stars on it. On the third iteration of the outer loop, when i is 3, the test is effectively testing `j <= 3`, and it generates a line with three stars on it. This continues through the sixth iteration.

In other words, this code produces a triangle as output:

```
*
**
***
****
*****
******
```

2.4 Managing Complexity

You've learned about several new programming constructs in this chapter, and it's time to put the pieces together to solve some complex tasks. As we pointed out in Chapter 1, Brian Kernighan, one of the coauthors of *The C Programming Language*, has said that "Controlling complexity is the essence of computer programming." In this section we will examine several techniques that computer scientists use to solve complex problems without being overwhelmed by complexity.

Scope

As programs get longer, it is increasingly likely that different parts of the program will interfere with each other. Java helps us to manage this potential problem by enforcing rules of *scope*.

> **Scope**
>
> The part of a program in which a particular declaration is valid.

As you've seen, when it comes to declaring static methods, you can put them in any order whatsoever. The scope of a static method is the entire class in which it appears. Variables work differently. The simple rule is that the scope of a variable declaration extends from the point where it is declared to the right curly brace that encloses it. In other words, find the pair of curly braces that directly encloses the variable declaration. The scope of the variable is from the point where it is declared to the closing curly brace.

This scope rule has several implications. Consider first what it means for different methods. Each method has its own set of curly braces to indicate the statements to be executed when the method is called. Any variables declared inside a method's curly braces won't be available outside the method. We refer to such variables as *local variables,* and we refer to the process of limiting their scope as *localizing* variables.

> **Local Variable**
>
> A variable declared inside a method that is accessible only in that method.

> **Localizing Variables**
>
> Declaring variables in the innermost (most local) scope possible.

In general, you will want to declare variables in the most local scope possible. You might wonder why we would want to localize variables to just one method. Why not just declare everything in one outer scope? That certainly seems simpler, but there are some important drawbacks. Localizing variables leads to some duplication (and possibly confusion) but provides more security. As an analogy, consider the use of refrigerators in dormitories. Every dorm room can have its own refrigerator, but if you are outside a room, you don't know whether it has a refrigerator in it. The contents of the room are hidden from you.

Java programs use variables to store values just as students use refrigerators to store beer, ice cream, and other valuables. The last time we were in a dorm we noticed that most of the individual rooms had refrigerators in them. This seems terribly redundant, but the reason is obvious. If you want to guarantee the security of something, you put it where nobody else can get it. You will use local variables in your programs in much the same way. If each individual method has its own local variables to use, you don't have to consider possible interference from other parts of the program.

Let's look at a simple example involving two methods:

```
1   // This program does not compile.
2   public class ScopeExample {
3       public static void main(String[] args) {
```

```
4              int x = 3;
5              int y = 7;
6              computeSum();
7          }
8
9      public static void computeSum() {
10             int sum = x + y; // illegal, x/y are not in scope
11             System.out.println("sum = " + sum);
12         }
13     }
```

In this example, the `main` method declares local variables x and y and gives them initial values. Then it calls the method `computeSum`. Inside this method, we try to use the values of x and y to compute a sum. However, because the variables x and y are local to the `main` method and are not visible inside of the `computeSum` method, this doesn't work. (In the next chapter, we will see a technique for allowing one method to pass a value to another.)

The program produces error messages like the following:

```
ScopeExample.java:10: error: cannot find symbol
symbol  : variable x
location: class ScopeExample
        int sum = x + y;  // illegal, x/y are not in scope
                  ^
ScopeExample.java:10: error: cannot find symbol
symbol  : variable y
location: class ScopeExample
        int sum = x + y;  // illegal, x/y are not in scope
                      ^
```

It's important to understand scope in discussing the local variables of one method versus another. Scope also has implications for what happens inside a single method. You have seen that curly braces are used to group together a series of statements. But you can have curly braces inside curly braces, and this leads to some scope issues. For example, consider the following code:

```
for (int i = 1; i <= 5; i++) {
    int squared = i * i;
    System.out.println(i + " squared = " + squared);
}
```

This is a variation of the code we looked at earlier in the chapter to print out the squares of the first five integers. In this version, a variable called `squared` is used to keep track of the square of the `for` loop control variable. This code works fine, but consider this variation:

```
for (int i = 1; i <= 5; i++) {
    int squared = i * i;
    System.out.println(i + " squared = " + squared);
}
System.out.println("Last square = " + squared); // illegal
```

This code generates a compiler error. The variable `squared` is declared inside the `for` loop. In other words, the curly braces that contain it are the curly braces for the loop. It can't be used outside this scope, so when you attempt to refer to it outside the loop, you'll get a compiler error.

If for some reason you need to write code like this that accesses the variable after the loop, you have to declare the variable in the outer scope before the loop:

```
int squared = 0;   // declaration is now in outer scope
for (int i = 1; i <= 5; i++) {
    squared = i * i;   // change this to an assignment statement
    System.out.println(i + " squared = " + squared);
}
System.out.println("Last square = " + squared); // now legal
```

There are a few special cases for scope, and the `for` loop is one of them. When a variable is declared in the initialization part of a `for` loop, its scope is just the `for` loop itself (the three parts in the `for` loop header and the statements controlled by the `for` loop). That means you can use the same variable name in multiple `for` loops:

```
for (int i = 1; i <= 10; i++) {
    System.out.println(i + " squared = " + (i * i));
}
for (int i = 1; i <= 10; i++) {
    System.out.println(i + " cubed = " + (i * i * i));
}
```

The variable `i` is declared twice in the preceding code, but because the scope of each variable is just the `for` loop in which it is declared, this isn't a problem. (It's like having two dorm rooms, each with its own refrigerator.) Of course, you can't do this with nested `for` loops. The following code, for example, will not compile:

```
for (int i = 1; i <= 5; i++) {
    for (int i = 1; i <= 10; i++) { // illegal
        System.out.println("hi there.");
    }
}
```

When Java encounters the inner `for` loop, it will complain that the variable `i` has already been declared within this scope. You can't declare the same variable twice within the same scope. You have to come up with two different names to distinguish between them, just as when there are two Carls in the same family they tend to be called "Carl Junior" and "Carl Senior" to avoid any potential confusion.

A control variable that is used in a `for` loop doesn't have to be declared in the initialization part of the loop. You can separate the declaration of the `for` loop control variable from the initialization of the variable, as in the following code:

```
int i;
for (i = 1; i <= 5; i++) {
    System.out.println(i + " squared = " + (i * i));
}
```

Doing so extends the variable's scope to the end of the enclosing set of curly braces. One advantage of this approach is that it enables you to refer to the final value of the control variable after the loop. Normally you wouldn't be able to do this, because the control variable's scope would be limited to the loop itself. However, declaring the control variable outside the loop is a dangerous practice, and it provides a good example of the problems you can encounter when you don't localize variables. Consider the following code, for example:

```
int i;
for (i = 1; i <= 5; i++) {
    for (i = 1; i <= 10; i++) {
        System.out.println("hi there.");
    }
}
```

As noted earlier, you shouldn't use the same control variable when you have nested loops. But unlike the previous example, this code compiles, because here the variable declaration is outside the outer `for` loop. So, instead of getting a helpful error message from the Java compiler, you get a program with a bug in it. You'd think from reading these loops that the code will produce 50 lines of output, but it actually produces just 10 lines of output. The inner loop increments the variable `i` until it becomes `11`, and that causes the outer loop to terminate after just one iteration. It can be even worse if you reverse the order of these loops:

```
int i;
for (i = 1; i <= 10; i++) {
    for (i = 1; i <= 5; i++) {
        System.out.println("hi there.");
    }
}
```

This code has an *infinite loop*.

> **Infinite Loop**
>
> A loop that never terminates.

This loop is infinite because no matter what the outer loop does to the variable `i`, the inner loop always sets it back to `1` and iterates until it becomes `6`. The outer loop then increments the variable to `7` and finds that `7` is less than or equal to `10`, so it always goes back to the inner loop, which once again sets the variable back to `1` and iterates up to `6`. This process goes on indefinitely. These are the kinds of interference problems you can get when you fail to localize variables.

Common Programming Error

Referring to the Wrong Loop Variable

The following code is intended to print a triangle of stars. However, it has a subtle bug that causes it to print stars infinitely:

```java
for (int i = 1; i <= 6; i++) {
    for (int j = 1; j <= i; i++){
        System.out.print("*");
    }
    System.out.println();
}
```

The problem is in the second line, in the inner `for` loop header's update statement. The programmer meant to write `j++` but instead accidentally wrote `i++`. A trace of the code is shown in Table 2.7.

Table 2.7   Trace of Nested `for` Loop

Step	Code	Description
initialization	`int i = 1;`	variable i is created and initialized to 1
initialization	`int j = 1;`	variable j is created and initialized to 1
test	`j <= i`	true because 1 <= 1, so we enter the inner loop
body	`{...}`	execute the print with j equal to 1
update	`i++`	increment i, which becomes 2
test	`j <= i`	true because 1 <= 2, so we enter the inner loop
body	`{...}`	execute the print with j equal to 1
update	`i++`	increment i, which becomes 3
...	...	...

The variable `j` should be increasing, but instead `i` is increasing. The effect of this mistake is that the variable `j` is never incremented in the inner loop, and therefore the test of `j <= i` never fails, so the inner loop doesn't terminate.

Continued on next page

Continued from previous page

Here's another broken piece of code. This one tries to print a 6 × 4 box of stars, but it also prints infinitely:

```
for (int i = 1; i <= 6; i++) {
    for (int j = 1; i <= 4; j++) {
        System.out.print("*");
    }
    System.out.println();
}
```

The problem is on the second line, this time in the inner `for` loop header's test. The programmer meant to write `j <= 4` but instead accidentally wrote `i <= 4`. Since the value of `i` is never incremented in the inner loop, the test of `i <= 4` never fails, so the inner loop again doesn't terminate.

Pseudocode

As you write more complex algorithms, you will find that you can't just write the entire algorithm immediately. Instead, you will increasingly make use of the technique of writing *pseudocode*.

> **Pseudocode**
>
> English-like descriptions of algorithms. Programming with pseudocode involves successively refining an informal description until it is easily translated into Java.

For example, you can describe the problem of drawing a box as

draw a box with 50 lines and 30 columns of asterisks.

While this statement describes the figure, it does not give specific instructions about how to draw it (that is, what algorithm to use). Do you draw the figure line by line or column by column? In Java, figures like these must be generated line by line, because once a `println` has been performed on a line of output, that line cannot be changed. There is no command for going back to a previous line in the output. Therefore, you must output the first line in its entirety, then the second line in its entirety, and so on. As a result, your decompositions for figures such as these will be line-oriented at the top level. Thus, a version of the statement that is closer to Java is

```
for (each of 50 lines) {
    draw a line of 30 asterisks.
}
```

This instruction can be made more specific by introducing the idea of repeatedly writing a single character on the output line and then moving to a new line of output:

```
for (each of 50 lines) {
    for (each of 30 columns) {
        write one asterisk on the output line.
    }
    go to a new output line.
}
```

Using pseudocode, you can gradually convert an English description into something that is easily translated into a Java program. The simple examples we've looked at so far are hardly worth the application of pseudocode, so we will now examine the problem of generating a more complex figure:

```
* * * * * * * *
 * * * * * * *
  * * * * *
   * * *
    *
```

This figure must also be generated line by line:

```
for (each of 5 lines) {
    draw one line of the triangle.
}
```

Unfortunately, each line is different. Therefore, you must come up with a general rule that fits all the lines. The first line of this figure has a series of asterisks on it with no leading spaces. Each of the subsequent lines has a series of spaces followed by a series of asterisks. Using your imagination a bit, you can say that the first line has 0 spaces on it followed by a series of asterisks. This allows you to write a general rule for making this figure:

```
for (each of 5 lines) {
    write some spaces (possibly 0) on the output line.
    write some asterisks on the output line.
    go to a new output line.
}
```

In order to proceed, you must determine a rule for the number of spaces and a rule for the number of asterisks. Assuming that the lines are numbered 1 through 5, looking at the figure, you can fill in Table 2.8.

You want to find a relationship between line number and the other two columns. This is simple algebra, because these columns are related in a linear way. The second

Table 2.8 Analysis of Figure

Line	Spaces	Asterisks
1	0	9
2	1	7
3	2	5
4	3	3
5	4	1

column is easy to get from the line number. It equals (`line − 1`). The third column is a little tougher. Because it goes down by 2 every time and the first column goes up by 1 every time, you need a multiplier of −2. Then you need an appropriate constant. The number 11 seems to do the trick, so you can make the third column equal (`11 − 2 * line`). You can improve your pseudocode, then, as follows:

```
for (line going 1 to 5) {
    write (line − 1) spaces on the output line.
    write (11 − 2 * line) asterisks on the output line.
    go to a new output line.
}
```

This pseudocode is simple to turn into a program:

```
1   public class DrawV {
2       public static void main(String[] args) {
3           for (int line = 1; line <= 5; line++) {
4               for (int i = 1; i <= (line − 1); i++) {
5                   System.out.print(" ");
6               }
7               for (int i = 1; i <= (11 − 2 * line); i++) {
8                   System.out.print("*");
9               }
10              System.out.println();
11          }
12      }
13  }
```

Sometimes we manage complexity by taking advantage of work that we have already done. For example, how would you produce this figure?

```
    *
   ***
  *****
 *******
*********
```

You could follow the same process you did before and find new expressions that produce the appropriate number of spaces and asterisks. However, there is an easier way. This figure is the same as the previous one, except the lines appear in reverse order. This is a good place to use a decrementing loop to run the `for` loop backward: Instead of starting at 1 and going up to 5 with a ++ update, you can start at 5 and go down to 1 using a −− update.

The simple way to produce the upward-pointing triangle, then, is with the following code:

```
1   public class DrawCone {
2       public static void main(String[] args) {
3           for (int line = 5; line >= 1; line--) {
4               for (int i = 1; i <= (line - 1); i++) {
5                   System.out.print(" ");
6               }
7               for (int i = 1; i <= (11 - 2 * line); i++) {
8                   System.out.print("*");
9               }
10              System.out.println();
11          }
12      }
13  }
```

Class Constants

The `DrawCone` program in the last section draws a cone with five lines. How would you modify it to produce a cone with three lines? Your first thought might be to simply change the 5 in the code to a 3. However, that would cause the program to produce the following output:

```
    *****
   *******
  *********
```

which is obviously wrong. If you work through the geometry of the figure, you will discover that the problem is with the use of the number 11 in the expression that calculates the number of asterisks to print. The number 11 comes from this formula:

```
2 * (number of lines) + 1
```

Thus, when the number of lines is five, the appropriate value is 11, but when the number of lines is three, the appropriate value is 7. Programmers call numbers like these *magic numbers.* They are magic in the sense that they seem to make the program work, but their definition is not always obvious. Glancing at the DrawCone program, one is apt to ask, "Why 5? Why 11? Why 3? Why 7? Why me?"

To make programs more readable and more adaptable, you should try to avoid magic numbers whenever possible. You do so by storing the magic numbers. You can use variables to store these values, but that is misleading, given that you are trying to represent values that don't change. Fortunately, Java offers an alternative: You can declare values that are similar to variables but that are guaranteed to have constant values. Not surprisingly, they are called *constants.* We most often define *class constants,* which can be accessed throughout the entire class.

> **Class Constant**
>
> A named value that cannot be changed. A class constant can be accessed anywhere in the class (i.e., its scope is the entire class).

You can choose a descriptive name for a constant that explains what it represents. You can then use that name instead of referring to the specific value to make your programs more readable and adaptable. For example, in the DrawCone program, you might want to introduce a constant called LINES that represents the number of lines (recall from Chapter 1 that we use all uppercase letters for constant names). You can use that constant in place of the magic number 5 and as part of an expression to calculate a value. This approach allows you to replace the magic number 11 with the formula from which it is derived (2 * LINES + 1).

Constants are declared with the keyword final, which indicates the fact that their values cannot be changed once assigned, as in

```
final int LINES = 5;
```

You can declare a constant anywhere you can declare a variable, but because constants are often used by several different methods, we generally declare them outside methods. This causes another run-in with our old pal, the static keyword. If you want your static methods to be able to access your constants, the constants themselves must be static. Likewise, just as we declare our methods to be public, we usually declare our constants to be public. The following is the general syntax for constant definitions:

```
public static final <type> <name> = <expression>;
```

For example, here are definitions for two constants:

```
public static final int HEIGHT = 10;
public static final int WIDTH = 20;
```

These definitions create constants called HEIGHT and WIDTH that will always have the values 10 and 20, respectively. These are known as class constants, because we declare them in the outermost scope of the class, along with the methods of the class. That way, they are visible in each method of the class.

We've already mentioned that we can avoid using a magic number in the DrawCone program by introducing a constant for the number of lines. Here's what the constant definition looks like:

```
public static final int LINES = 5;
```

We can now replace the 5 in the outer loop with this constant and replace the 11 in the second inner loop with the expression 2 * LINES + 1. The result is the following program:

```
1  public class DrawCone2 {
2      public static final int LINES = 5;
3
4      public static void main(String[] args) {
5          for (int line = LINES; line >= 1; line--) {
6              for (int i = 1; i <= (line - 1); i++) {
7                  System.out.print(" ");
8              }
9              int stars = 2 * LINES + 1 - 2 * line;
10             for (int i = 1; i <= stars; i++) {
11                 System.out.print("*");
12             }
13             System.out.println();
14         }
15     }
16 }
```

Notice that in this program the expression for the number of stars has become sufficiently complex that we've introduced a local variable called stars to store the value. The advantage of this program is that it is more readable and more adaptable. A simple change to the constant LINES will make it produce a figure with a different number of lines.

2.5 Case Study: Hourglass Figure

VideoNote

Now we'll consider an example that is even more complex. To solve it, we will follow three basic steps:

1. Decompose the task into subtasks, each of which will become a static method.

2. For each subtask, make a table for the figure and compute formulas for each column of the table in terms of the line number.

3. Convert the tables into actual for loop code for each method.

The output we want to produce is the following:

```
+------+
|\..../|
| \../ |
|  \/  |
|  /\  |
| /..\ |
|/....\|
+------+
```

Problem Decomposition and Pseudocode

To generate this figure, you have to first break it down into subfigures. In doing so, you should look for lines that are similar in one way or another. The first and last lines are exactly the same. The three lines after the first line all fit one pattern, and the three lines after that fit another:

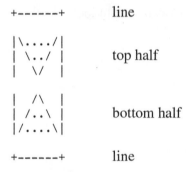

```
+------+          line

|\..../|
| \../ |          top half
|  \/  |

|  /\  |
| /..\ |          bottom half
|/....\|

+------+          line
```

Thus, you can break down the overall problem as follows:

draw a solid line.
draw the top half of the hourglass.
draw the bottom half of the hourglass.
draw a solid line.

You should solve each subproblem independently. Eventually you'll want to incorporate a class constant to make the program more flexible, but let's first solve the problem without worrying about the use of a constant.

The solid line task can be further specified as

write a plus on the output line.
write 6 dashes on the output line.
write a plus on the output line.
go to a new output line.

This set of instructions translates easily into a static method:

```
public static void drawLine() {
    System.out.print("+");
    for (int i = 1; i <= 6; i++) {
        System.out.print("-");
    }
    System.out.println("+");
}
```

The top half of the hourglass is more complex. Here is a typical line:

```
| \../ |
```

There are four individual characters, separated by spaces and dots.

$$| \qquad \backslash \qquad . . \qquad / \qquad |$$
bar   spaces   backslash   dots   slash   spaces   bar

Thus, a first approximation in pseudocode might look like this:

```
for (each of 3 lines) {
    write a bar on the output line.
    write some spaces on the output line.
    write a backslash on the output line.
    write some dots on the output line.
    write a slash on the output line.
    write some spaces on the output line.
    write a bar on the output line.
    go to a new line of output.
}
```

Again, you can make a table to figure out the required expressions. Writing the individual characters will be easy enough to translate into Java, but you need to be more specific about the spaces and dots. Each line in this group contains two sets of spaces and one set of dots. Table 2.9 shows how many to use.

The two sets of spaces fit the rule (line − 1), and the number of dots is (6 − 2 * line). Therefore, the pseudocode should read

```
for (line going 1 to 3) {
    write a bar on the output line.
    write (line − 1) spaces on the output line.
    write a backslash on the output line.
    write (6 − 2 * line) dots on the output line.
    write a slash on the output line.
    write (line − 1) spaces on the output line.
    write a bar on the output line.
    go to a new line of output.
}
```

Table 2.9 Analysis of Figure

Line	Spaces	Dots	Spaces
1	0	4	0
2	1	2	1
3	2	0	2

Initial Structured Version

The pseudocode for the top half of the hourglass is easily translated into a static method called drawTop. A similar solution exists for the bottom half of the hourglass. Put together, the program looks like this:

```
1   public class DrawFigure {
2       public static void main(String[] args) {
3           drawLine();
4           drawTop();
5           drawBottom();
6           drawLine();
7       }
8
9       // produces a solid line
10      public static void drawLine() {
11          System.out.print("+");
12          for (int i = 1; i <= 6; i++) {
13              System.out.print("—");
14          }
15          System.out.println("+");
16      }
17
18      // produces the top half of the hourglass figure
19      public static void drawTop() {
20          for (int line = 1; line <= 3; line++) {
21              System.out.print("|");
22              for (int i = 1; i <= (line − 1); i++) {
23                  System.out.print(" ");
24              }
25              System.out.print("\\");
26              for (int i = 1; i <= (6 − 2 * line); i++) {
27                  System.out.print(".");
28              }
29              System.out.print("/");
30              for (int i = 1; i <= (line − 1); i++) {
31                  System.out.print(" ");
32              }
```

```
33              System.out.println("|");
34          }
35      }
36
37      // produces the bottom half of the hourglass figure
38      public static void drawBottom() {
39          for (int line = 1; line <= 3; line++) {
40              System.out.print("|");
41              for (int i = 1; i <= (3  line); i++) {
42                  System.out.print(" ");
43              }
44              System.out.print("/");
45              for (int i = 1; i <= 2 * (line  1); i++) {
46                  System.out.print(".");
47              }
48              System.out.print("\\");
49              for (int i = 1; i <= (3  line); i++) {
50                  System.out.print(" ");
51              }
52              System.out.println("|");
53          }
54      }
55  }
```

Adding a Class Constant

The DrawFigure program produces the desired output, but it is not very flexible. What if we wanted to produce a similar figure of a different size? The original problem involved an hourglass figure that had three lines in the top half and three lines in the bottom half. What if we wanted the following output, with four lines in the top half and four lines in the bottom half?

```
+--------+
|\......./|
| \..../ |
|  \../  |
|   \/   |
|   /\   |
|  /..\  |
| /....\ |
|/......\|
+--------+
```

Obviously the program would be more useful if we could make it flexible enough to produce either output. We do so by eliminating the magic numbers with the introduction of a class constant. You might think that we need to introduce two constants—one for the height and one for the width—but because of the regularity of this

Table 2.10 **Analysis of Different Height Figures**

Subheight	Dashes in `drawLine`	Spaces in `drawTop`	Dots in `drawTop`	Spaces in `drawBottom`	Dots in `drawBottom`
3	6	line - 1	6 - 2 * line	3 - line	2 * (line - 1)
4	8	line - 1	8 - 2 * line	4 - line	2 * (line - 1)

figure, the height is determined by the width and vice versa. Consequently, we only need to introduce a single class constant. Let's use the height of the hourglass halves:

```
public static final int SUB_HEIGHT = 4;
```

We've called the constant `SUB_HEIGHT` rather than `HEIGHT` because it refers to the height of each of the two halves, rather than the figure as a whole. Notice how we use the underscore character to separate the different words in the name of the constant.

So, how do we modify the original program to incorporate this constant? We look through the program for any magic numbers and insert the constant or an expression involving the constant where appropriate. For example, both the `drawTop` and `draw-Bottom` methods have a `for` loop that executes 3 times to produce 3 lines of output. We change this to 4 to produce 4 lines of output, and more generally, we change it to `SUB_HEIGHT` to produce `SUB_HEIGHT` lines of output.

In other parts of the program we have to update our formulas for the number of dashes, spaces, and dots. Sometimes we can use educated guesses to figure out how to adjust such a formula to use the constant. If you can't guess a proper formula, you can use the table technique to find the appropriate formula. Using this new output with a subheight of 4, you can update the various formulas in the program. Table 2.10 shows the various formulas.

We then go through each formula and figure out how to replace it with a new formula involving the constant. The number of dashes increases by 2 when the subheight increases by 1, so we need a multiplier of 2. The expression 2 * `SUB_HEIGHT` produces the correct values. The number of spaces in `drawTop` does not change with the subheight, so the expression does not need to be altered. The number of dots in `drawTop` involves the number 6 for a subheight of 3 and the number 8 for a subheight of 4. Once again we need a multiplier of 2, so we use the expression 2 * `SUB_HEIGHT` - 2 * `line`. The number of spaces in `drawBottom` involves the value 3 for a subheight of 3 and the value 4 for a subheight of 4, so the generalized expression is `SUB_HEIGHT` - `line`. The number of dots in `drawBottom` does not change when subheight changes.

Here is the new version of the program with a class constant for the subheight. It uses a `SUB_HEIGHT` value of 4, but we could change this to 3 to produce the smaller version or to some other value to produce yet another version of the figure.

```
1   public class DrawFigure2 {
2       public static final int SUB_HEIGHT = 4;
3
4       public static void main(String[] args) {
5           drawLine();
```

```
 6            drawTop();
 7            drawBottom();
 8            drawLine();
 9        }
10    '

11        // produces a solid line
12        public static void drawLine() {
13            System.out.print("+");
14            for (int i = 1; i <= (2 * SUB_HEIGHT); i++) {
15                System.out.print("-");
16            }
17            System.out.println("+");
18        }

19
20        // produces the top half of the hourglass figure
21        public static void drawTop() {
22            for (int line = 1; line <= SUB_HEIGHT; line++) {
23                System.out.print("|");
24                for (int i = 1; i <= (line - 1); i++) {
25                    System.out.print(" ");
26                }
27                System.out.print("\\");
28                int dots = 2 * SUB_HEIGHT - 2 * line;
29                for (int i = 1; i <= dots; i++) {
30                    System.out.print(".");
31                }
32                System.out.print("/");
33                for (int i = 1; i <= (line - 1); i++) {
34                    System.out.print(" ");
35                }
36                System.out.println("|");
37            }
38        }

39
40        // produces the bottom half of the hourglass figure
41        public static void drawBottom() {
42            for (int line = 1; line <= SUB_HEIGHT; line++) {
43                System.out.print("|");
44                for (int i = 1; i <= (SUB_HEIGHT - line); i++) {
45                    System.out.print(" ");
46                }
47                System.out.print("/");
48                for (int i = 1; i <= 2 * (line - 1); i++) {
49                    System.out.print(".");
50                }
```

```
51              System.out.print("\\");
52              for (int i = 1; i <= (SUB_HEIGHT  line); i++) {
53                  System.out.print(" ");
54              }
55              System.out.println("|");
56          }
57      }
58  }
```

Notice that the SUB_HEIGHT constant is declared with class-wide scope, rather than locally in the individual methods. While localizing variables is a good idea, the same is not true for constants. We localize variables to avoid potential interference, but that argument doesn't hold for constants, since they are guaranteed not to change. Another argument for using local variables is that it makes static methods more independent. That argument has some merit when applied to constants, but not enough. It is true that class constants introduce dependencies between methods, but often that is what you want. For example, the three methods in DrawFigure2 should not be independent of each other when it comes to the size of the figure. Each subfigure has to use the same size constant. Imagine the potential disaster if each method had its own SUB_HEIGHT, each with a different value—none of the pieces would fit together.

Further Variations

The solution we have arrived at may seem cumbersome, but it adapts more easily to a new task than does our original program. For example, suppose that you want to generate the following output:

```
+----------+
|\......../|
| \....../ |
|  \..../  |
|   \../   |
|    \/    |
|    /\    |
|   /..\   |
|  /....\  |
| /......\ |
|/........\|
+----------+
|    /\    |
|   /..\   |
|  /....\  |
| /......\ |
|/........\|
|\......../|
| \....../ |
|  \..../  |
|   \../   |
|    \/    |
+----------+
```

This output uses a subheight of 5 and includes both a diamond pattern and an X pattern. You can produce this output by changing the SUB_HEIGHT constant to 5:

```java
public static final int SUB_HEIGHT = 5;
```

and rewriting the main method as follows to produce both the original X pattern and the new diamond pattern, which you get simply by reversing the order of the calls on the two halves:

```java
public static void main(String[] args) {
    drawLine();
    drawTop();
    drawBottom();
    drawLine();
    drawBottom();
    drawTop();
    drawLine();
}
```

Chapter Summary

Java groups data into types. There are two major categories of data types: primitive data and objects. Primitive types include int (integers), double (real numbers), char (individual text characters), and boolean (logical values).

Values and computations are called expressions. The simplest expressions are individual values, also called literals. Some example literals are: 42, 3.14, 'Q', and false. Expressions may contain operators, as in (3 + 29) − 4 * 5. The division operation is odd in that it's split into quotient (/) and remainder (%) operations.

Rules of precedence determine the order in which multiple operators are evaluated in complex expressions. Multiplication and division are performed before addition and subtraction. Parentheses can be used to force a particular order of evaluation.

Data can be converted from one type to another by an operation called a cast.

Variables are memory locations in which values can be stored. A variable is declared with a name and a type. Any data value with a compatible type can be stored in the variable's memory and used later in the program.

Primitive data can be printed on the console using the System.out.println method, just like text strings. A string can be connected to another value (concatenated) with the + operator to produce a larger string. This feature allows you to print complex expressions including numbers and text on the console.

A loop is used to execute a group of statements several times. The for loop is one kind of loop that can be used to apply the same statements over a range of numbers or to repeat statements a specified number of times. A loop can contain another loop, called a nested loop.

_____

A variable exists from the line where it is declared to the right curly brace that encloses it. This range, also called the scope of the variable, constitutes the part of the program where the variable can legally be used. A variable declared inside a method or loop is called a local variable. A local variable can only be used inside its method or loop.

_____

An algorithm can be easier to write if you first write an English description of it. Such a description is also called pseudocode.

_____

Important constant values written into a program should be declared as class constants, both to explain their names and values and to make it easier to change their values later.

_____

Self-Check Problems

Section 2.1: Basic Data Concepts

1. Which of the following are legal `int` literals?

```
22     1.5     −1     2.3     10.0     5.     −6875309     '7'
```

2. What is the result of the following expression?

```
1 + 2 * 3 + 7 * 2 % 5
```
a. 1   b. 2   c. 5   d. 11   e. 21

3. Trace the evaluation of the following expressions, and give their resulting values:

```
a. 2 + 3 * 4 − 6
b. 14 / 7 * 2 + 30 / 5 + 1
c. (12 + 3) / 4 * 2
d. (238 % 10 + 3) % 7
e. (18 − 7) * (43 % 10)
f. 2 + 19 % 5 − (11 * (5 / 2))
g. 813 % 100 / 3 + 2.4
h. 26 % 10 % 4 * 3
i. 22 + 4 * 2
j. 23 % 8 % 3
k. 12 − 2 − 3
l. 6/2 + 7/3
m. 6 * 7 % 4
n. 3 * 4 + 2 * 3
o. 177 % 100 % 10 / 2
p. 89 % (5 + 5) % 5
q. 392 / 10 % 10 / 2
r. 8 * 2 − 7 / 4
s. 37 % 20 % 3 * 4
t. 17 % 10 / 4
```

4. Trace the evaluation of the following expressions, and give their resulting values:

```
a. 4.0 / 2 * 9 / 2
b. 2.5 * 2 + 8 / 5.0 + 10 / 3
c. 12 / 7 * 4.4 * 2 / 4
d. 4 * 3 / 8 + 2.5 * 2
e. (5 * 7.0 / 2 - 2.5) / 5 * 2
f. 41 % 7 * 3 / 5 + 5 / 2 * 2.5
g. 10.0 / 2 / 4
h. 8 / 5 + 13 / 2 / 3.0
i. (2.5 + 3.5) / 2
j. 9 / 4 * 2.0 - 5 / 4
k. 9 / 2.0 + 7 / 3 - 3.0 / 2
l. 813 % 100 / 3 + 2.4
m. 27 / 2 / 2.0 * (4.3 + 1.7) - 8 / 3
n. 53 / 5 / (0.6 + 1.4) / 2 + 13 / 2
o. 2 * 3 / 4 * 2 / 4.0 + 4.5 - 1
p. 89 % 10 / 4 * 2.0 / 5 + (1.5 + 1.0 / 2) * 2
```

5. Trace the evaluation of the following expressions, and give their resulting values:

```
a. 2 + 2 + 3 + 4
b. "2 + 2" + 3 + 4
c. 2 + " 2 + 3 " + 4
d. 3 + 4 + " 2 + 2"
e. "2 + 2 " + (3 + 4)
f. "(2 + 2) " + (3 + 4)
g. "hello 34 " + 2 * 4
h. 2 + "(int) 2.0" + 2 * 2 + 2
i. 4 + 1 + 9 + "." + (-3 + 10) + 11 / 3
j. 8 + 6 * -2 + 4 + "0" + (2 + 5)
k. 1 + 1 + "8 - 2" + (8 - 2) + 1 + 1
l. 5 + 2 + "(1 + 1)" + 4 + 2 * 3
m. "1" + 2 + 3 + "4" + 5 * 6 + "7" + (8 + 9)
```

Section 2.2: Variables

6. Which of the following choices is the correct syntax for declaring a real number variable named grade and initializing its value to 4.0?

```
a. int grade : 4.0;
b. grade = double 4.0;
c. double grade = 4.0;
d. grade = 4;
e. 4.0 = grade;
```

7. Imagine you are writing a personal fitness program that stores the user's age, gender, height (in feet or meters), and weight (to the nearest pound or kilogram). Declare variables with the appropriate names and types to hold this information.

8. Imagine you are writing a program that stores a student's year (Freshman, Sophomore, Junior, or Senior), the number of courses the student is taking, and his or her GPA on a 4.0 scale. Declare variables with the appropriate names and types to hold this information.

9. Suppose you have an `int` variable called `number`. What Java expression produces the last digit of the number (the 1s place)?

10. The following program contains 9 mistakes! What are they?

```
1   public class Oops2 {
2       public static void main(String[] args) {
3           int x;
4           System.out.println("x is" x);
5
6           int x = 15.2;    // set x to 15.2
7           System.out.println("x is now + x");
8
9           int y;           // set y to 1 more than x
10          y = int x + 1;
11          System.out.println("x and y are " + x + and + y);
12      }
13  }
```

11. Suppose you have an `int` variable called `number`. What Java expression produces the second-to-last digit of the number (the 10s place)? What expression produces the third-to-last digit of the number (the 100s place)?

12. What is the value of variable x after the following code executes?

```
int x = 3;
x = x + 2;
x = x + x;
```

a. 3   b. 5   c. 7   d. 10   e. 12

13. What are the values of a, b, and c after the following statements?

```
int a = 5;
int b = 10;
int c = b;

a = a + 1;
b = b - 1;
c = c + a;
```

14. What are the values of `first` and `second` at the end of the following code? How would you describe the net effect of the code statements in this exercise?

```
int first = 8;
int second = 19;
first = first + second;
second = first - second;
first = first - second;
```

15. Rewrite the code from the previous exercise to be shorter, by declaring the variables together and by using the special assignment operators (e.g., += , −=, *=, and /=) as appropriate.

16. What are the values of i, j, and k after the following statements?

```
int i = 2;
int j = 3;
int k = 4;
int x = i + j + k;


i = x - i - j;
j = x - j - k;
k = x - i - k;
```

17. What is the output from the following code?

```
int max;
int min = 10;
max = 17 - 4 / 10;
max = max + 6;
min = max - min;
System.out.println(max * 2);
System.out.println(max + min);
System.out.println(max);
System.out.println(min);
```

18. Suppose you have a real number variable x. Write a Java expression that computes the following value y while using the * operator only four times:

$$y = 12.3x^4 - 9.1x^3 + 19.3x^2 - 4.6x + 34.2$$

19. The following program redundantly repeats the same expressions many times. Modify the program to remove all redundant expressions using variables of appropriate types.

```
1   public class ComputePay {
2       public static void main(String[] args) {
3           // Calculate pay at work based on hours worked each day
4           System.out.println("My total hours worked:");
5           System.out.println(4 + 5 + 8 + 4);
6
7           System.out.println("My hourly salary:");
8           System.out.println("$8.75");
9
10          System.out.println("My total pay:");
11          System.out.println((4 + 5 + 8 + 4) * 8.75);
```

```
12
13            System.out.println("My taxes owed:");  // 20% tax
14            System.out.println((4 + 5 + 8 + 4) * 8.75 * 0.20);
15      }
16 }
```

20. The following program redundantly repeats the same expressions many times. Modify the program to remove all redundant expressions using variables of appropriate types.

```
// This program computes the total amount owed for a meal,
// assuming 8% tax and a 15% tip.
public class Receipt {
    public static void main(String[] args) {
        System.out.println("Subtotal:");
        System.out.println(38 + 40 + 30);
        System.out.println("Tax:");
        System.out.println((38 + 40 + 30) * .08);
        System.out.println("Tip:");
        System.out.println((38 + 40 + 30) * .15);
        System.out.println("Total:");
        System.out.println(38 + 40 + 30 +
                           (38 + 40 + 30) * .08 +
                           (38 + 40 + 30) * .15);
    }
}
```

Section 2.3: The for Loop

21. Complete the following code, replacing the "FINISH ME" parts with your own code:

```
public class Count2 {
    public static void main(String[] args) {
        for (int i = /* FINISH ME */) {
            System.out.println(/* FINISH ME */);
        }
    }
}
```

to produce the following output:

```
2 times 1 = 2
2 times 2 = 4
2 times 3 = 6
2 times 4 = 8
```

22. Assume that you have a variable called `count` that will take on the values 1, 2, 3, 4, and so on. You are going to formulate expressions in terms of `count` that will yield different sequences. For example, to get the sequence 2, 4, 6, 8, 10, 12, ..., you would use the expression (2 * count). Fill in the following table, indicating an expression that will generate each sequence.

Sequence	Expression
a. 2, 4, 6, 8, 10, 12, . . .	
b. 4, 19, 34, 49, 64, 79, . . .	
c. 30, 20, 10, 0, 10, 20, . . .	
d. 7, 3, 1, 5, 9, 13, . . .	
e. 97, 94, 91, 88, 85, 82, . . .	

23. Complete the code for the following `for` loop:

```
for (int i = 1; i <= 6; i++) {
    // your code here
}
```

so that it prints the following numbers, one per line:

```
-4
14
32
50
68
86
```

24. What is the output of the following `oddStuff` method?

```
public static void oddStuff() {
    int number = 4;
    for (int count = 1; count <= number; count++) {
        System.out.println(number);
        number = number / 2;
    }
}
```

25. What is the output of the following loop?

```
int total = 25;
for (int number = 1; number <= (total / 2); number++) {
    total = total — number;
    System.out.println(total + " " + number);
}
```

26. What is the output of the following loop?

```
System.out.println("+---+");
for (int i = 1; i <= 3; i++) {
    System.out.println("\\    /");
    System.out.println("/    \\");
}
System.out.println("+---+");
```

27. What is the output of the following loop?

```
for (int i = 1; i <= 3; i++)
    System.out.println("How many lines");
    System.out.println("are printed?");
```

28. What is the output of the following loop?

```
System.out.print("T-minus ");
for (int i = 5; i >= 1; i--) {
    System.out.print(i + ", ");
}
System.out.println("Blastoff!");
```

29. What is the output of the following sequence of loops?

```
for (int i = 1; i <= 5; i++) {
    for (int j = 1; j <= 10; j++) {
        System.out.print((i * j) + " ");
    }
    System.out.println();
}
```

30. What is the output of the following sequence of loops?

```
for (int i = 1; i <= 10; i++) {
    for (int j = 1; j <= 10 — i; j++) {
        System.out.print(" ");
    }
    for (int j = 1; j <= 2 * i — 1; j++) {
        System.out.print("*");
    }
    System.out.println();
}
```

31. What is the output of the following sequence of loops?

```
for (int i = 1; i <= 2; i++) {
    for (int j = 1; j <= 3; j++) {
        for (int k = 1; k <= 4; k++) {
            System.out.print("*");
        }
        System.out.print("!");
    }
    System.out.println();
}
```

32. What is the output of the following sequence of loops? Notice that the code is the same as that in the previous exercise, except that the placement of the braces has changed.

```
for (int i = 1; i <= 2; i++) {
    for (int j = 1; j <= 3; j++) {
        for (int k = 1; k <= 4; k++) {
            System.out.print("*");
        }
    }
    System.out.print("!");
    System.out.println();
}
```

33. What is the output of the following sequence of loops? Notice that the code is the same as that in the previous exercise, except that the placement of the braces has changed.

```
for (int i = 1; i <= 2; i++) {
    for (int j = 1; j <= 3; j++) {
        for (int k = 1; k <= 4; k++) {
            System.out.print("*");
            System.out.print("!");
        }
        System.out.println();
    }
}
```

Section 2.4: Managing Complexity

34. Suppose that you are trying to write a program that produces the following output:

```
1 3 5 7 9 11 13 15 17 19 21

1 3 5 7 9 11
```

The following program is an attempt at a solution, but it contains four major errors. Identify them all.

```
1  public class BadNews {
2      public static final int MAX_ODD = 21;
3
4      public static void writeOdds() {
```

```
 5              // print each odd number
 6              for (int count = 1; count <= (MAX_ODD  2); count++) {
 7                  System.out.print(count + " ");
 8                  count = count + 2;
 9              }
10
11              // print the last odd number
12              System.out.print(count + 2);
13          }
14
15      public static void main(String[] args) {
16              // write all odds up to 21
17              writeOdds();
18
19              // now, write all odds up to 11
20              MAX_ODD = 11;
21              writeOdds();
22          }
23  }
```

35. What is the output of the following unknown method?

```
 1  public class Strange {
 2      public static final int MAX = 5;
 3
 4      public static void unknown() {
 5          int number = 0;
 6
 7          for (int count = MAX; count >= 1; count--) {
 8              number += (count * count);
 9          }
10
11          System.out.println("The result is: " + number);
12      }
13
14      public static void main(String[] args) {
15          unknown();
16      }
17  }
```

36. Suppose that you have a variable called line that will take on the values 1, 2, 3, 4, and so on, and a class constant named SIZE that takes one of two values. You are going to formulate expressions in terms of line and SIZE that will yield different sequences of numbers of characters. Fill in the table below, indicating an expression that will generate each sequence.

line value	constant SIZE value	Number of characters	Expression
a. 1, 2, 3, 4, 5, 6, ...	1	4, 6, 8, 10, 12, 14, ...	
1, 2, 3, 4, 5, 6, ...	2	6, 8, 10, 12, 14, 16, ...	
b. 1, 2, 3, 4, 5, 6, ...	3	13, 17, 21, 25, 29, 33, ...	
1, 2, 3, 4, 5, 6, ...	5	19, 23, 27, 31, 35, 39, ...	
c. 1, 2, 3, 4, 5, 6, ...	4	10, 9, 8, 7, 6, 5, ...	
1, 2, 3, 4, 5, 6, ...	9	20, 19, 18, 17, 16, 15, ...	

37. Write a table that determines the expressions for the number of each type of character on each of the 6 lines in the following output.

```
!!!!!!!!!!!!!!!!!!!!!!!!!
\\!!!!!!!!!!!!!!!!!!!!!//
\\\\!!!!!!!!!!!!!!!!!////
\\\\\\!!!!!!!!!!!!!//////
\\\\\\\\!!!!!!!!////////
\\\\\\\\\\!!!!!//////////
```

38. Suppose that a program has been written that produces the output shown in the previous problem. Now the author wants the program to be scalable using a class constant called SIZE. The previous output used a constant height of 6, since there were 6 lines. The following is the output for a constant height of 4. Create a new table that shows the expressions for the character counts at this new size of 4, and compare these tables to figure out the expressions for any size using the SIZE constant.

```
!!!!!!!!!!!!!!!!
\\!!!!!!!!!!!!//
\\\\!!!!!!!!////
\\\\\\!!!!!//////
```

Exercises

1. In physics, a common useful equation for finding the position s of a body in linear motion at a given time t, based on its initial position s_0, initial velocity v_0, and rate of acceleration a, is the following:

$$s = s_0 + v_0 t + \frac{1}{2} a t^2$$

Write code to declare variables for s_0, v_0, a, and t, and then write the code to compute s on the basis of these values.

2. Write a for loop that produces the following output:

```
1 4 9 16 25 36 49 64 81 100
```

For added challenge, try to modify your code so that it does not need to use the * multiplication operator. (It can be done! Hint: Look at the differences between adjacent numbers.)

3. The Fibonacci numbers are a sequence of integers in which the first two elements are 1, and each following element is the sum of the two preceding elements. The mathematical definition of each kth Fibonacci number is the following:

$$F(k) = \begin{cases} F(k-1) + F(k-2), k > 2 \\ \quad\quad 1, k \leq 2 \end{cases}$$

The first 12 Fibonacci numbers are

```
1 1 2 3 5 8 13 21 34 55 89 144
```

Write a `for` loop that computes and prints the first 12 Fibonacci numbers.

4. Write nested `for` loops to produce the following output:

```
*****
*****
*****
*****
```

5. Write nested `for` loops to produce the following output:

```
*
**
***
****
*****
```

6. Write nested `for` loops to produce the following output:

```
1
22
333
4444
55555
666666
7777777
```

7. Write nested `for` loops to produce the following output:

```
    1
   2
  3
 4
5
```

8. Write nested `for` loops to produce the following output:

```
    1
   22
  333
 4444
55555
```

9. Write nested `for` loops to produce the following output, with each line 40 characters wide:

```
----------------------------------------
_-^-_-^-_-^-_-^-_-^-_-^-_-^-_-^-_-^-_-^-
11223344556677889900112233445566778899 00
----------------------------------------
```

10. It's common to print a rotating, increasing list of single-digit numbers at the start of a program's output as a visual guide to number the columns of the output to follow. With this in mind, write nested `for` loops to produce the following output, with each line 60 characters wide:

```
        |           |           |           |           |           |
123456789012345678901234567890123456789012345678901234567890
```

11. Modify your code from the previous exercise so that it could easily be modified to display a different range of numbers (instead of `1234567890`) and a different number of repetitions of those numbers (instead of 60 total characters), with the vertical bars still matching up correctly. Use class constants instead of "magic numbers." Here are some example outputs that could be generated by changing your constants:

```
    |     |     |     |     |     |     |     |     |     |
12340123401234012340123401234012340123401234012340
      |         |         |         |         |         |         |
12345670123456701234567012345670123456701234567012345670
```

12. Write nested `for` loops that produce the following output:

```
000111222333444555666777888999
000111222333444555666777888999
000111222333444555666777888999
```

13. Modify the code so that it now produces the following output:

```
999998888877777666665555544444333332222211111100000
999998888877777666665555544444333332222211111100000
999998888877777666665555544444333332222211111100000
999998888877777666665555544444333332222211111100000
999998888877777666665555544444333332222211111100000
```

14. Modify the code so that it now produces the following output:

```
9999999999888888888777777766666665555554444333221
9999999999888888888777777766666665555554444333221
9999999999888888888777777766666665555554444333221
9999999999888888888777777766666665555554444333221
```

15. Write a method called `printDesign` that produces the following output. Use nested `for` loops to capture the structure of the figure.

```
-----1-----
----333----
---55555---
--7777777--
-999999999-
```

16. Write a Java program called `SlashFigure` that produces the following output. Use nested `for` loops to capture the structure of the figure. (See also Self-Check Problems 34 and 35.)

```
!!!!!!!!!!!!!!!!!!!!!!!!!
\\!!!!!!!!!!!!!!!!!!!!!//
\\\\!!!!!!!!!!!!!!!!////
\\\\\\!!!!!!!!!!!!//////
\\\\\\\\!!!!!!!!////////
\\\\\\\\\\!!!!//////////
```

17. Modify your `SlashFigure` program from the previous exercise to become a new program called `SlashFigure2` that uses a global constant for the figure's height. (You may want to make loop tables first.) The previous output used a constant height of 6. The following are the outputs for constant heights of 4 and 8:

Height 4	Height 8
`!!!!!!!!!!!!!!`	`!!!!!!!!!!!!!!!!!!!!!!!!!!!!!!`
`\\!!!!!!!!!!//`	`\\!!!!!!!!!!!!!!!!!!!!!!!!!!//`
`\\\\!!!!!!////`	`\\\\!!!!!!!!!!!!!!!!!!!!!!////`
`\\\\\\!!//////`	`\\\\\\!!!!!!!!!!!!!!!!!!//////`
	`\\\\\\\\!!!!!!!!!!!!!!!!////////`
	`\\\\\\\\\\!!!!!!!!!!!!!!//////////`
	`\\\\\\\\\\\\!!!!!!!!!!//////////`
	`\\\\\\\\\\\\\\!!//////////////`

18. Write a pseudocode algorithm that will produce the following figure as output:

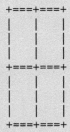

19. Use your pseudocode from the previous exercise to write a Java program called `Window` that produces the preceding figure as output. Use nested `for` loops to print the repeated parts of the figure. Once you get it to work, add a class constant so that the size of the figure can be changed simply by changing the constant's value.

20. Write a Java program called `StarFigure` that produces the following output. Use nested for loops to capture the structure of the figure.

```
//////////////////\\\\\\\\\\\\\\\\\\
///////////********\\\\\\\\\\\\\\
////////****************\\\\\\\\
////********************\\\\
********************************
```

21. Modify your `StarFigure` program from the previous exercise to become a new program named `StarFigure2` that uses a global constant for the figure's height. (You may want to make loop tables first.) The previous output used a constant height of 5. The following are the outputs for constant heights of 3 and 6:

Height 3	Height 6
`////////\\\\\\\\`	`//////////////////////\\\\\\\\\\\\\\\\\\\\\\`
`////********\\\\`	`////////////////********\\\\\\\\\\\\\\\\\\\\`
`****************`	`//////////////****************\\\\\\\\\\\\\\\\`
	`////////****************************\\\\\\\\`
	`////********************************\\\\`
	`********************************************`

22. Write a Java program called `DollarFigure` that produces the following output. Use nested `for` loops to capture the structure of the figure.

```
$$$$$$$**************$$$$$$$
**$$$$$$************$$$$$$**
****$$$$$**********$$$$$****
******$$$$********$$$$******
********$$$******$$$********
**********$$****$$**********
************$**$************
```

23. Modify your `DollarFigure` program from the previous exercise to become a new program called `DollarFigure2` that uses a global constant for the figure's height. (You may want to make loop tables first.) The previous output used a constant height of 7.

Programming Projects

1. Write a program that produces the following output using nested `for` loops:

```
****** ///////////// ******
*****  ///////////\\  *****
****   ////////\\\\   ****
***    //////\\\\\\    ***
**     ////\\\\\\\\     **
*      //\\\\\\\\\\      *
       \\\\\\\\\\\\
```

2. Write a program that produces the following output using nested `for` loops:

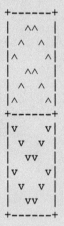

```
+-------+
|   ^^  |
|  ^  ^ |
| ^    ^|
|   ^^  |
|  ^  ^ |
| ^    ^|
+-------+
|v     v|
| v   v |
|  vv   |
|v     v|
| v   v |
|  vv   |
+-------+
```

3. Write a program that produces the following output using nested `for` loops:

```
+---------+
|    *    |
|   /*\   |
|  //*\\  |
| ///*\\\ |
| \\\*/// |
|  \\*//  |
|   \*/   |
|    *    |
+---------+
| \\\*/// |
|  \\*//  |
|   \*/   |
|    *    |
|    *    |
|   /*\   |
|  //*\\  |
| ///*\\\ |
+---------+
```

4. Write a program that produces the following hourglass figure as its output using nested `for` loops:

```
|"""""""""|
 \:::::::::/
  \:::::::/
   \:::::/
    \:::/
     ||
    /:::\
   /:::::\
  /:::::::\
 /:::::::::\
|"""""""""|
```

5. Write a program that produces the following output using nested `for` loops. Use a class constant to make it possible to change the number of stairs in the figure.

```
                    o  *******
                   /|\ *      *
                   / \ *      *
                o  ******     *`
               /|\ *          *
               / \ *          *
            o  ******          *
           /|\ *               *
           / \ *               *
        o  ******               *
       /|\ *                    *
       / \ *                    *
    o  ******                    *
   /|\ *                         *
   / \ *                         *
  *******************************
```

6. Write a program that produces the following rocket ship figure as its output using nested `for` loops. Use a class constant to make it possible to change the size of the rocket (the following output uses a size of 3).

```
       /**\
      //**\\
     ///**\\\
    ////**\\\\
   /////**\\\\\
  +=*=*=*=*=*=*=+
  |../\..../\..|
  |./\/\../\/\.|
  |/\/\/\/\/\/\|
  |\/\/\/\/\/\/|
  |.\/\/..\/\/.|
  |..\/....\/..|
  +=*=*=*=*=*=*=+
  |\/\/\/\/\/\/|
  |.\/\/..\/\/.|
  |..\/....\/..|
  |../\..../\..|
  |./\/\../\/\.|
  |/\/\/\/\/\/\|
  +=*=*=*=*=*=*=+
       /**\
      //**\\
     ///**\\\
    ////**\\\\
   /////**\\\\\
```

7. Write a program that produces the following figure (which vaguely resembles the Seattle Space Needle) as its output using nested `for` loops. Use a class constant to make it possible to change the size of the figure (the following output uses a size of 4).

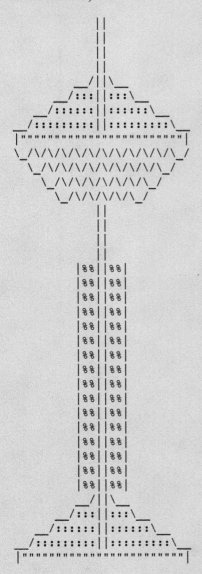

8. Write a program that produces the following figure (which vaguely resembles a textbook) as its output using nested `for` loops. Use a class constant to make it possible to change the size of the figure (the following output uses a size of 10).

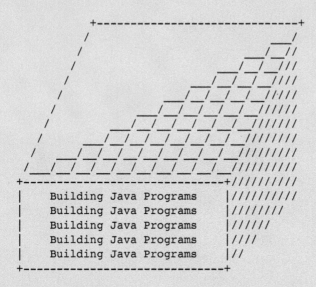

```
          +--------------------------------+
         /                                /
        /                             / __/
       /                          / __/ //
      /                       / __/ __/ ///
     /                    / __/ __/ __/ ////
    /                 / __/ __/ __/ __/ /////
   /              / __/ __/ __/ __/ __/ //////
  /           / __/ __/ __/ __/ __/ __/ ///////
 /        / __/ __/ __/ __/ __/ __/ __/ ////////
/     / __/ __/ __/ __/ __/ __/ __/ __/ /////////
+___/__/__/__/__/__/__/__/__/__/ //////////
+-----------------------------+//////////
|     Building Java Programs   |//////////
|     Building Java Programs   |////////
|     Building Java Programs   |//////
|     Building Java Programs   |////
|     Building Java Programs   |//
+-----------------------------+
```

Introduction to Parameters and Objects

Introduction

Chapter 2 introduced techniques for managing complexity, including the use of class constants, which make programs more flexible. This chapter explores a more powerful technique for obtaining such flexibility. Here, you will learn how to use parameters to create methods that solve not just single tasks, but whole families of tasks. Creating such methods requires you to generalize, or look beyond a specific task to find the more general category of task that it exemplifies. The ability to generalize is one of the most important qualities of a good software engineer, and the generalization technique you will study in this chapter is one of the most powerful techniques programmers use. After exploring parameters, we'll discuss some other issues associated with methods, such as the ability of a method to return a value.

This chapter then introduces the idea of objects and how to use them in Java programs. We aren't going to explore the details of defining objects for a while, but we want to begin using objects early. One of the most attractive features of Java is that it comes with a rich library of predefined objects that can be used to solve many common programming tasks.

The chapter concludes with an exploration of a very important kind of object known as a Scanner. Using a Scanner object, you can write programs that obtain values from the user. This feature will allow you to write interactive programs that prompt for input as well as producing output.

3.1 Parameters

Humans are very good at learning new tasks. When we learn, we often develop a single generalized solution for a family of related tasks. For example, someone might ask you to take 10 steps forward or 20 steps forward. These are different tasks, but they both involve taking a certain number of steps forward. We think of this action as a single task of taking steps forward, and we understand that the number of steps will vary from one task to another. In programming terms, we refer to the number of steps as a *parameter* that allows us to generalize the task.

> **Parameter (Parameterize)**
>
> Any of a set of characteristics that distinguish different members of a family of tasks. To parameterize a task is to identify a set of its parameters.

For a programming example, let's return to the `DrawFigure2` program of Chapter 2. It performs its task adequately, but there are several aspects of this program that we can improve. For example, there are many different places where a `for` loop writes out spaces. This approach is redundant and can be consolidated into a single method that performs all space-writing tasks.

Each space-writing task requires a different number of spaces, so you need some way to tell the method how many spaces to write. The methods you've written so far have a simple calling mechanism where you say:

```
writeSpaces();
```

One approach might be to set a variable to a particular value before the method is called:

```
int number = 10;
writeSpaces();
```

Then the method could look at the value of the variable `number` to see how many spaces to write. Unfortunately, this approach won't work. Recall from Chapter 2 that scope rules determine where variables can be accessed. Following those rules, the variable `number` would be a local variable in `main` that could not be seen inside `writeSpaces`.

Instead, you can specify one or more parameters to a method. The idea is that instead of writing a method that performs just one version of a task, you write a more flexible version that solves a family of related tasks that all differ by one or more parameters. In the case of the `writeSpaces` method, the parameter is the number of spaces to write.

The following is the definition of `writeSpaces` with a parameter for the number of spaces to write:

```
public static void writeSpaces(int number) {
    for (int i = 1; i <= number; i++) {
        System.out.print(" ");
    }
}
```

The parameter appears in the method header, after the name and inside the parentheses that you have, up to this point, been leaving empty. The writeSpaces method uses a parameter called number of type int. As we indicated earlier, you can no longer call the parameterized method by using just its name:

```
writeSpaces();
```

You must now say something like

```
writeSpaces(10);
```

When a call like this is made, the value 10 is used to initialize the number parameter. You can think of this as information flowing into the method from the call:

The parameter number is a local variable, but it gets its initial value from the call. Calling this method with the value 10 is equivalent to including the following declaration at the beginning of the writeSpaces method:

```
int number = 10;
```

Of course, this mechanism is more flexible than a specific variable declaration, because you can instead say

```
writeSpaces(20);
```

and it will be as if you had said

```
int number = 20;
```

at the beginning of the method. You can even use an integer expression for the call:

```
writeSpaces(3 * 4 − 5);
```

In this case, Java evaluates the expression to get the value 7 and then calls writeSpaces, initializing number to 7.

Computer scientists use the word "parameter" broadly to mean both what appears in the method header (the *formal parameter*) and what appears in the method call (the *actual parameter*).

> **Formal Parameter**
>
> A variable that appears inside parentheses in the header of a method that is used to generalize the method's behavior.

> **Actual Parameter**
>
> A specific value or expression that appears inside parentheses in a method call.

The term "formal parameter" does not describe its purpose. A better name would be "generalized parameter." In the `writeSpaces` method, `number` is the generalized parameter that appears in the method declaration. It is a placeholder for some unspecified value. The values appearing in the method calls are the actual parameters, because each call indicates a specific task to perform. In other words, each call provides an actual value to fill the placeholder.

The word "argument" is often used as a synonym for "parameter," as in "These are the arguments I'm passing to this method." Some people prefer to reserve the word "argument" for actual parameters and the word "parameter" for formal parameters.

Let's look at an example of how you might use this `writeSpaces` method. Remember that the `DrawFigure2` program had the following method, called `drawTop`:

```
// produces the top half of the hourglass figure
public static void drawTop() {
    for (int line = 1; line <= SUB_HEIGHT; line++) {
        System.out.print("|");
        for (int i = 1; i <= (line - 1); i++) {
            System.out.print(" ");
        }
        System.out.print("\\");
        int dots = 2 * SUB_HEIGHT - 2 * line;
        for (int i = 1; i <= dots; i++) {
            System.out.print(".");
        }
        System.out.print("/");
        for (int i = 1; i <= (line - 1); i++) {
            System.out.print(" ");
        }
        System.out.println("|");
    }
}
```

Using the `writeSpaces` method, you can rewrite this as follows:

```java
public static void drawTop() {
    for (int line = 1; line <= SUB_HEIGHT; line++) {
        System.out.print("|");
        writeSpaces(line - 1);
        System.out.print("\\");
        int dots = 2 * SUB_HEIGHT - 2 * line;
        for (int i = 1; i <= dots; i++) {
            System.out.print(".");
        }
        System.out.print("/");
        writeSpaces(line - 1);
        System.out.println("|");
    }
}
```

Notice that `writeSpaces` is called two different times, specifying how many spaces are required in each case. You could modify the `drawBottom` method from the `DrawFigure2` program similarly to simplify it.

The Mechanics of Parameters

VideoNote

When Java executes a call on a method, it initializes the method's parameters. For each parameter, it first evaluates the expression passed as the actual parameter and then uses the result to initialize the local variable whose name is given by the formal parameter. Let's use an example to clarify this process:

```java
 1  public class ParameterExample {
 2      public static void main(String[] args) {
 3          int spaces1 = 3;
 4          int spaces2 = 5;
 5
 6          System.out.print("*");
 7          writeSpaces(spaces1);
 8          System.out.println("*");
 9
10          System.out.print("!");
11          writeSpaces(spaces2);
12          System.out.println("!");
13
14          System.out.print("'");
15          writeSpaces(8);
16          System.out.println("'");
```

```
17
18              System.out.print("<");
19              writeSpaces(spaces1 * spaces2 - 5);
20              System.out.println(">");
21          }
22
23      // writes "number" spaces on the current output line
24      public static void writeSpaces(int number) {
25          for (int i = 1; i <= number; i++) {
26              System.out.print(" ");
27          }
28      }
29  }
```

In the first two lines of the main method, the computer finds instructions to allocate and initialize two variables:

The next three lines of code produce an output line with three spaces bounded by asterisks on either side:

```
System.out.print("*");
writeSpaces(spaces1);
System.out.println("*");
```

You can see where the asterisks come from, but look at the method call that produces the spaces. When Java executes the call on writeSpaces, it must set up its parameter. To set up the parameter, Java first evaluates the expression being passed as the actual parameter. The expression is simply the variable spaces1, which has the value 3. Therefore, the expression evaluates to 3. Java uses this result to initialize a local variable called number.

The following diagram indicates how the computer's memory would look as the writeSpaces method is entered the first time. Because there are two methods involved (main and writeSpaces), the diagram indicates which variables are local to main (spaces1 and spaces2) and which are local to writeSpaces (the parameter number):

The net effect of this process is that the writeSpaces method has a local copy of the value stored in the variable spaces1 from the main method. The println that comes after the call on writeSpaces puts an asterisk at the end of the line and then completes the line of output.

Let's now trace the next three lines of code:

```
System.out.print("!");
writeSpaces(spaces2);
System.out.println("!");
```

The first line prints an exclamation mark on the second line of output, then calls writeSpaces again, this time with the variable spaces2 as its actual parameter. The computer evaluates this expression, obtaining the result 5. This value is used to initialize number. Thus, this time it creates a copy of the value stored in the variable spaces2 from the main method:

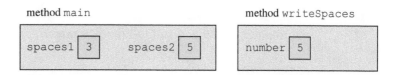

Because number has a different value this time (5 instead of 3), the method produces a different number of spaces. After the method executes, the println finishes the line of output with a second exclamation mark.

Here are the next three lines of code:

```
System.out.print("'");
writeSpaces(8);
System.out.println("'");
```

This code writes a single quotation mark at the beginning of the third line of output and then calls writeSpaces again. This time it uses the integer literal 8 as the expression, which means that it initializes the parameter number as a copy of the number 8:

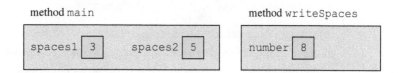

Again, the method will behave differently because of the different value of number. It prints eight spaces on the line and finishes executing. Then the println completes the line of output by printing another single quotation mark at the end of the line.

Finally, the last three lines of code in the `main` method are:

```
System.out.print("<");
writeSpaces(spaces1 * spaces2 - 5);
System.out.println(">");
```

This code prints a less-than character at the beginning of the fourth line of output and then makes a final call on the `writeSpaces` method. This time the actual parameter is an expression, not just a variable or literal value. Thus, before the call is made, the computer evaluates the expression to determine its value:

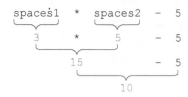

The computer uses this result to initialize `number`:

method `main`   method `writeSpaces`

spaces1	3		spaces2	5			number	10

Now `number` is a copy of the value described by this complex expression. Therefore, the total output of this program is

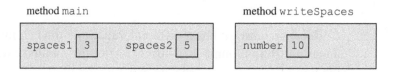

Common Programming Error

Confusing Actual and Formal Parameters

Many students get used to seeing declarations of formal parameters and mistakenly believe that their syntax is identical to that for passing actual parameters. It's a common mistake to write the type of a variable as it's being passed to a parameter:

```
writeSpaces(int spaces1); // this doesn't work
```

Continued on next page

Continued from previous page

This confusion is due to the fact that parameters' types are written in the declaration of the method, like this:

```
public static void writeSpaces(int number)
```

Types must be written when variables or parameters are declared, but when variables are used, such as when the code calls a method and passes the variables as actual parameters, their types are not written. Actual parameters are not declarations; therefore, types should not be written before them:

```
writeSpaces(spaces1); // much better!
```

Limitations of Parameters

We've seen that a parameter can be used to provide input to a method. But while you can use a parameter to send a value into a method, you can't use a parameter to get a value out of a method.

When a parameter is set up, a local variable is created and is initialized to the value being passed as the actual parameter. The net effect is that the local variable is a copy of the value coming from the outside. Since it is a local variable, it can't influence any variables outside the method. Consider the following sample program:

```
1  public class ParameterExample2 {
2      public static void main(String[] args) {
3          int x = 17;
4          doubleNumber(x);
5          System.out.println("x = " + x);
6          System.out.println();
7
8          int number = 42;
9          doubleNumber(number);
10         System.out.println("number = " + number);
11     }
12
13     public static void doubleNumber(int number) {
14         System.out.println("Initial value = " + number);
15         number = number * 2;
16         System.out.println("Final value = " + number);
17     }
18 }
```

This program begins by declaring and initializing an integer variable called x with the value 17:

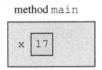

It then calls the method `doubleNumber`, passing x as a parameter. The value of x is used to initialize the parameter `number` as a local variable of the method called `doubleNumber`:

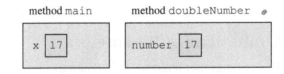

The program then executes the statements inside of `doubleNumber`. First, `doubleNumber` prints the initial value of `number` (17). Then it doubles `number`:

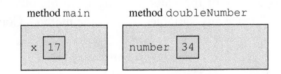

Notice that this has no effect on the variable x. The parameter called `number` is a copy of x, so even though they started out the same, changing the value of `number` does not affect x. Next, `doubleNumber` reports the new value of `number` (34).

At this point, `doubleNumber` finishes executing and we return to `main`:

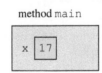

The next statement in the `main` method reports the value of x, which is 17. Then it declares and initializes a variable called `number` with the value 42:

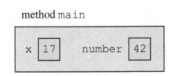

The following statement calls doubleNumber again, this time passing it the value of number. This is an odd situation because the parameter has the same name as the variable in main, but Java doesn't care. It always creates a new local variable for the doubleNumber method:

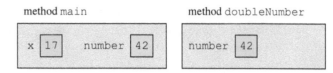

So, at this point there are two different variables called number, one in each method. Now it's time to execute the statements of doubleNumber again. It first reports the value of number (42), then doubles it:

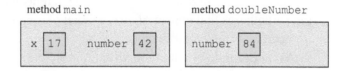

Again, notice that doubling number inside doubleNumber has no effect on the original variable number in main. These are separate variables. The method then reports the new value of number (84) and returns to main:

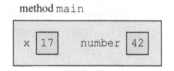

The program then reports the value of number and terminates. So, the overall output of the program is as follows:

```
Initial value = 17
Final value = 34
x = 17

Initial value = 42
Final value = 84
number = 42
```

The local manipulations of the parameter do not change these variables outside the method. The fact that variables are copied is an important aspect of parameters. On the positive side, we know that the variables are protected from change because the parameters are copies of the originals. On the negative side, it means that although parameters will allow us to send values into a method, they will not allow us to get values back out of a method.

Multiple Parameters

So far, our discussion of parameter syntax has been informal. It's about time that we wrote down more precisely the syntax we use to declare static methods with parameters. Here it is:

```
public static void <name>(<type> <name>, ..., <type> <name>) {
    <statement>;
    <statement>;
    ...
    <statement>;
}
```

This template indicates that we can declare as many parameters as we want inside the parentheses that appear after the name of a method in its header. We use commas to separate different parameters.

As an example of a method with multiple parameters, let's consider a variation of `writeSpaces`. It is convenient that we can use the method to write different numbers of spaces, but it always writes spaces. What if we want 18 asterisks or 23 periods or 17 question marks? We can generalize the task even further by having the method take two parameters—a character and a number of times to write that character:

```
public static void writeChars(char ch, int number) {
    for (int i = 1; i <= number; i++) {
        System.out.print(ch);
    }
}
```

The character to be printed is a parameter of type `char`, which we will discuss in more detail in the next chapter. Recall that character literals are enclosed in single quotation marks.

The syntax template for calling a method that accepts parameters is the following:

```
<method name>(<expression>, <expression>, ..., <expression>);
```

By calling the `writeChars` method you can write code like the following:

```
writeChars('=', 20);
System.out.println();
for (int i = 1; i <= 10; i++) {
    writeChars('>', i);
    writeChars(' ', 20 - 2 * i);
    writeChars('<', i);
    System.out.println();
}
```

This code produces the following output:

```
=====================
>                    <
>>                  <<
>>>                <<<
>>>>              <<<<
>>>>>            <<<<<
>>>>>>          <<<<<<
>>>>>>>        <<<<<<<
>>>>>>>>      <<<<<<<<
>>>>>>>>>    <<<<<<<<<
>>>>>>>>>><<<<<<<<<<
```

Using the `writeChars` method we can write an even better version of the `drawTop` method from the `DrawFigure2` program of Chapter 2. We saw earlier that using `writeChars` we could eliminate two of the inner loops, but this left us with the inner loop to print dots. Now we can eliminate all three of the inner loops and produce a much more readable version of the method:

```java
public static void drawTop() {
    for (int line = 1; line <= SUB_HEIGHT; line++) {
        System.out.print("|");
        writeChars(' ', line - 1);
        System.out.print("\\");
        writeChars('.', 2 * SUB_HEIGHT - 2 * line);
        System.out.print("/");
        writeChars(' ', line - 1);
        System.out.println("|");
    }
}
```

You can include as many parameters as you want when you define a method. Each method call must provide exactly that number of parameters, in the same order. For example, consider the first call on `writeChars` in the preceding code fragment and the header for `writeChars`. Java lines up the parameters in sequential order (with the first actual parameter going into the first formal parameter and the second actual parameter going into the second formal parameter):

```
writeChars('=', 20);
```

```
public static void writeChars(char ch, int number) {
    ...
}
```

We've seen that methods can call other methods; this is equally true of methods that take parameters. For example, here is a method for drawing a box of a given height and width that calls the writeChars method:

```java
public static void drawBox(int height, int width) {
    // draw top of box
    writeChars('*', width);
    System.out.println();

    // draw middle lines
    for (int i = 1; i <= height - 2; i++) {
        System.out.print('*');
        writeChars(' ', width - 2);
        System.out.println("*");
    }

    // draw bottom of box
    writeChars('*', width);
    System.out.println();
}
```

Notice that drawBox is passed values for its parameters called height and width and that these parameters are used to form expressions that are passed as values to writeChars. For example, inside the for loop we call writeChars asking it to produce width − 2 spaces. (We subtract 2 because we print a star at the beginning and the end of the line.) Here is a sample call on the method:

```java
drawBox(5, 10);
```

This code produces the following output:

```
**********
*        *
*        *
*        *
**********
```

When you're writing methods that accept many parameters, the method header can become very long. It is common to *wrap* long lines (ones that exceed roughly 80 characters in length) by inserting a line break after an operator or parameter and indenting the line that follows by twice the normal indentation width:

```java
// this method's header is too long, so we'll wrap it
public static void printTriangle(int xCoord1, int yCoord1,
        int xCoord2, int yCoord2, int xCoord3, int yCoord3) {
    ...
}
```

Parameters versus Constants

In Chapter 2, you saw that class constants are a useful mechanism to increase the flexibility of your programs. By using such constants, you can make it easy to modify a program to behave differently. Parameters provide much of the same flexibility, and more. Consider the `writeSpaces` method. Suppose you wrote it using a class constant:

```
public static final int NUMBER_OF_SPACES = 10;
```

This approach would give you the flexibility to produce a different number of spaces, but it has one major limitation: The constant can change only from execution to execution; it cannot change within a single execution. In other words, you can execute the program once with one value, edit the program, recompile, and then execute it again with a different value, but you can't use different values in a single execution of the program using a class constant.

Parameters are more flexible. Because you specify the value to be used each time you call the method, you can use several different values in a single program execution. As you have seen, you can call the method many different times within a single program execution and have it behave differently every time. However, using parameters involves more work for the programmer than using class constants. It makes your method headers and method calls more tedious, not to mention making the execution (and, thus, the debugging) more complex.

Therefore, you will probably find occasion to use each technique. The basic rule is to use a class constant when you only want to change the value from execution to execution. If you want to use different values within a single execution, use a parameter.

Overloading of Methods

You'll often want to create slight variations of the same method, passing different parameters. For example, you could have a `drawBox` method that allows you to specify a particular height and width, but you might also want to have a version that draws a box of default size. In other words, sometimes you want to specify these values, as in

```
drawBox(8, 10);
```

and other times you want to just draw a box with the standard height and width:

```
drawBox();
```

Some programming languages require you to come up with different names for these versions, such as `drawBox` and `drawDefaultBox`. As you can imagine, coming up with new names for each variation becomes tedious. Fortunately, Java allows you to have more than one method with the same name, as long as they have different parameters. This is called *overloading*. The primary requirement for overloading is that the different methods that you define must have different *method signatures*.

> **Method Overloading**
>
> The ability to define two or more different methods with the same name but different method signatures.

> **Method Signature**
>
> The name of a method, along with its number and type of parameters.

The two example `drawBox` versions clearly have different method signatures, because one has two parameters and the other has zero parameters. It would be obvious from any call on the method which version to use: If you see two parameters, you execute the version with two parameters; if you see zero parameters, you execute the version with zero parameters.

The situation gets more complicated when overloading involves the same number of parameters, but this turns out to be one of the most useful applications of overloading. For example, the `println` method is actually a series of overloaded methods. We can call `println` passing it a `String`, an `int`, a `double`, and so on. This flexibility is implemented as a series of different methods, all of which take one parameter: One version takes a `String`, another version takes an `int`, another version takes a `double`, and so on. Obviously, you do slightly different things to print one of these kinds of data versus another, which is why it's useful to have these different versions of the method.

3.2 Methods That Return Values

The last few methods we've looked at have been action-oriented methods that perform some specific task. You can think of them as being like commands that you could give someone, as in "Draw a box" or "Draw a triangle." Parameters allow these commands to be more flexible, as in "Draw a box that is 10 by 20."

You will also want to be able to write methods that compute values. These methods are more like questions, as in "What is the square root of 2.5?" or "What do you get when you carry 2.3 to the 4th power?" Consider, for example, a method called `sqrt` that would compute the square root of a number.

It might seem that the way to write such a method would be to have it accept a parameter of type `double` and `println` its square root to the console. But you may want to use the square root as part of a larger expression or computation, such as solving a quadratic equation or computing the distance between points on an *x*/*y* plane.

A better solution would be a square root command that passes the number of interest as a parameter and returns its square root back to the program as a result. You could then use the result as part of an expression, store it in a variable, or print it to the console. Such a command is a new type of method that is said to *return* a value.

> **Return**
>
> To send a value out as the result of a method that can be used in an expression in your program. Void methods do not return any value.

If you had such a method, you could ask for the square root of 2.5 by writing code like this:

```
// assuming you had a method named sqrt
double answer = sqrt(2.5);
```

The `sqrt` method has a parameter (the number whose square root you want to find), and it also returns a value (the square root). The actual parameter `2.5` goes "into" the method, and the square root comes out. In the preceding code, the returned result is stored in a variable called `answer`.

You can tell whether or not a method returns a value by looking at its header. All the methods you've written so far have begun with `public static void`. The word `void` is known as the *return type* of the method.

The `void` return type is a little odd because, as its name implies, the method returns nothing. A method can return any legal type: an `int`, a `double`, or any other type. In the case of the `sqrt` method, you want it to return a `double`, so you would write its header as follows:

```
public static double sqrt(double n)
```

As in the previous case, the word that comes after `public static` is the return type of the method:

$$
\text{public static } \underbrace{\text{double}}_{\text{return type}} \text{ sqrt(double n)}
$$

Fortunately, you don't actually need to write a method for computing the square root of a number, because Java has one that is built in. The method is included in a class known as `Math` that includes many useful computing methods. So, before we discuss the details of writing methods that return values, let's explore the `Math` class and what it has to offer.

The Math Class

In Chapter 1 we mentioned that a great deal of predefined code, collectively known as the Java class libraries, has been written for Java. One of the most useful classes is `Math`. It includes predefined mathematical constants and a large number of common mathematical functions. The `Math` class should be available on any machine on which Java is properly installed.

As we noted in the previous section, the `Math` class has a method called `sqrt` that computes the square root of a number. The method has the following header:

```
public static double sqrt(double n)
```

This header says that the method is called `sqrt`, that it takes a parameter of type `double`, and that it returns a value of type `double`.

Unfortunately, you can't just call this method directly by referring to it as `sqrt` because it is in another class. Whenever you want to refer to something declared in another class, you use *dot notation:*

```
<class name>.<element>
```

So you would refer to this method as `Math.sqrt`. Here's a sample program that uses the method:

```
1   public class WriteRoots {
2       public static void main(String[] args) {
3           for (int i = 1; i <= 20; i++) {
4               double root = Math.sqrt(i);
5               System.out.println("sqrt(" + i + ") = " + root);
6           }
7       }
8   }
```

This program produces the following output:

```
sqrt(1) = 1.0
sqrt(2) = 1.4142135623730951
sqrt(3) = 1.7320508075688772
sqrt(4) = 2.0
sqrt(5) = 2.23606797749979
sqrt(6) = 2.449489742783178
sqrt(7) = 2.6457513110645907
sqrt(8) = 2.8284271247461903
sqrt(9) = 3.0
sqrt(10) = 3.1622776601683795
sqrt(11) = 3.3166247903554
sqrt(12) = 3.4641016151377544
sqrt(13) = 3.605551275463989
sqrt(14) = 3.7416573867739413
sqrt(15) = 3.872983346207417
sqrt(16) = 4.0
sqrt(17) = 4.123105625617661
sqrt(18) = 4.242640687119285
sqrt(19) = 4.358898943540674
sqrt(20) = 4.47213595499958
```

Table 3.1   Math Constants

Constant	Description
E	base used in natural logarithms (2.71828 . . .)
PI	ratio of circumference of a circle to its diameter (3.14159 . . .)

Notice that we passed a value of type int to Math.sqrt, but the header says that it expects a value of type double. Remember that if Java is expecting a double and gets an int, it converts the int into a corresponding double.

The Math class also defines two frequently used constants: e and π (see Table 3.1). Following the Java convention, we use all uppercase letters for their names and refer to them as Math.E and Math.PI.

Table 3.2 lists some of the most useful static methods from the Math class. You can see a complete list of methods defined in the Math class by checking out the API

Table 3.2   Useful Static Methods in the Math Class

Method	Description	Example
abs	absolute value	Math.abs(−308) returns 308
ceil	ceiling (rounds upward)	Math.ceil(2.13) returns 3.0
cos	cosine (radians)	Math.cos(Math.PI) returns −1.0
exp	exponent base e	Math.exp(1) returns 2.7182818284590455
floor	floor (rounds downward)	Math.floor(2.93) returns 2.0
log	logarithm base e	Math.log(Math.E) returns 1.0
log10	logarithm base 10	Math.log10(1000) returns 3.0
max	maximum of two values	Math.max(45, 207) returns 207
min	minimum of two values	Math.min(3.8, 2.75) returns 2.75
pow	power (general exponentiation)	Math.pow(3, 4) returns 81.0
random	random value	Math.random() returns a random double value k such that $0.0 \leq k < 1.0$
round	round real number to nearest integer	Math.round(2.718) returns 3
sin	sine (radians)	Math.sin(0) returns 0.0
sqrt	square root	Math.sqrt(2) returns 1.4142135623730951
toDegrees	converts from radians to degrees	Math.toDegrees(Math.PI) returns 180.0
toRadians	converts from degrees to radians	Math.toRadians(270.0) returns 4.71238898038469

documentation for your version of Java. The API describes how to use the standard libraries that are available to Java programmers. It can be a bit overwhelming, because the Java libraries are vast. Wander around a bit if you are so inclined, but don't be dismayed that there are so many libraries to choose from in Java.

If you do look into the Math API, you'll notice that the Math class has several overloaded methods. For example, there is a version of the absolute value method (Math.abs) for integers and another for doubles. The rules that govern which method is called are complex, so we won't cover them here. The basic idea, though, is that Java tries to find the method that is the best fit. For the most part, you don't have to think much about this issue; you can just let Java choose for you, and it will generally make the right choice.

Defining Methods That Return Values

VideoNote

You can write your own methods that return values by using a special statement known as a return statement. For example, we often use a method that returns a value to express an equation. There is a famous story about the mathematician Carl Friedrich Gauss that illustrates the use of such a method. When Gauss was a boy, his teacher asked the class to add up the integers 1 through 100, thinking that it would take a while for them to complete the task. Gauss immediately found a formula and presented his answer to the teacher. He used a simple trick of adding two copies of the series together, one in forward order and one in backward order. This method allowed him to pair up values from the two copies so that their sum was the same:

First series	Second series	Sum
1	100	101
2	99	101
3	98	101
4	97	101
. . .	. . .	. . .
100	1	101

Every entry in the right-hand column is equal to 101 and there are 100 rows in this table, so the overall sum is $100 \times 101 = 10{,}100$. Of course, that's the sum of two copies of the sequence, so the actual answer is half that. Using this approach, Gauss determined that the sum of the first 100 integers is 5050. When the series goes from 1 to n, the sum is $(n + 1) \times n / 2$.

We can use Gauss' formula to write a method that computes the sum of the first n integers:

```java
public static int sum(int n) {
    return (n + 1) * n / 2;
}
```

The sum method could be used by the `main` method in code such as the following:

```
int answer = sum(100);
System.out.println("The sum of 1 through 100 is " + answer);
```

A diagram of what happens when this code is executed follows. The method is invoked with the parameter n being initialized to 100. Plugging this value into the formula, we get a value of 5050, which is sent back to be stored in the variable called `answer`:

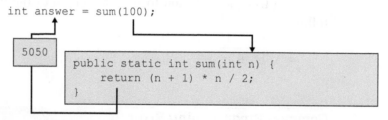

```
System.out.println("The sum of 1 through 100 is " + answer);
```

Notice once again that in the header for the method the familiar word `void` (indicating no return value) has been replaced with the word `int`. Remember that when you declare a method that returns a value, you have to tell Java what kind of value it will return. Thus, we can update our syntax template for static methods once more to clarify that the header includes a return type (`void` for none):

```
public static <type> <name>(<type> <name>, ..., <type> <name>) {
    <statement>;
    <statement>;
    ...
    <statement>;
}
```

The syntax of the `return` statement is:

```
return <expression>;
```

When Java encounters a `return` statement, it evaluates the given expression and immediately terminates the method, returning the value it obtained from the expression. As a result, it's not legal to have any other statements after a `return` statement; the `return` must be the last statement in your method. It is also an error for a Java method with a return type other than `void` to terminate without a `return`.

There are exceptions to the previous rules, as you'll see later. For example, it is possible for a method to have more than one `return` statement; this will come up in the next chapter, when we discuss conditional execution using `if` and `if`/`else` statements.

Let's look at another example method that returns a value. In *The Wizard of Oz*, the Scarecrow after being given a diploma demonstrates his intelligence by saying, "The sum of the square roots of any two sides of an isosceles triangle is equal to the square root of the remaining side. Oh, joy, oh, rapture. I've got a brain!" Probably he was trying to state the Pythagorean theorem, although it's not clear whether the writers were bad at math or whether they were making a comment about the value of a diploma. In an episode of *The Simpsons,* Homer repeats the Scarecrow's mistaken formula after putting on a pair of Henry Kissinger's glasses that he finds in a bathroom at the Springfield nuclear power plant.

The correct Pythagorean theorem refers only to right triangles and says that the length of the hypotenuse of a right triangle is equal to the square root of the sums of the squares of the two remaining sides. If you know the lengths of two sides *a* and *b* of a right triangle and want to find the length of the third side *c,* you compute it as follows:

$$c = \sqrt{a^2 + b^2}$$

Common Programming Error

Ignoring the Returned Value

When you call a method that returns a value, the expectation is that you'll do something with the value that's returned. You can print it, store it in a variable, or use it as part of a larger expression. It is legal (but unwise) to simply call the method and ignore the value being returned from it:

```
sum(1000);    // doesn't do anything
```

The preceding call doesn't print the sum or have any noticeable effect. If you want the value printed, you must include a println statement:

```
int answer = sum(1000);    // better
System.out.println("Sum up to 1000 is " + answer);
```

A shorter form of the fixed code would be the following:

```
System.out.println("Sum up to 1000 is " + sum(1000));
```

Say you want to print out the lengths of the hypotenuses of two right triangles, one with side lengths of 5 and 12, and the other with side lengths of 3 and 4. You could write code such as the following:

```
double c1 = Math.sqrt(Math.pow(5, 2) + Math.pow(12, 2));
System.out.println("hypotenuse 1 = " + c1);
double c2 = Math.sqrt(Math.pow(3, 2) + Math.pow(4, 2));
System.out.println("hypotenuse 2 = " + c2);
```

The preceding code is correct, but it's a bit hard to read, and you'd have to duplicate the same complex math a third time if you wanted to include a third triangle. A better solution would be to create a method that computes and returns the hypotenuse length when given the lengths of the two other sides as parameters. Such a method would look like this:

```
public static double hypotenuse(double a, double b) {
    double c = Math.sqrt(Math.pow(a, 2) + Math.pow(b, 2));
    return c;
}
```

This method can be used to craft a more concise and readable `main` method, as shown here.

```
1   public class Triangles {
2       public static void main(String[] args) {
3           System.out.println("hypotenuse 1 = " + hypotenuse(5, 12));
4           System.out.println("hypotenuse 2 = " + hypotenuse(3, 4));
5       }
6
7       public static double hypotenuse(double a, double b) {
8           double c = Math.sqrt(Math.pow(a, 2) + Math.pow(b, 2));
9           return c;
10      }
11  }
```

A few variations of this program are possible. For one, it isn't necessary to store the hypotenuse method's return value into the variable c. If you prefer, you can simply compute and return the value in one line. In this case, the body of the `hypotenuse` method would become the following:

```
return Math.sqrt(Math.pow(a, 2) + Math.pow(b, 2));
```

Also, some programmers avoid using `Math.pow` for low powers such as 2 and just manually do the multiplication. Using that approach, the body of the hypotenuse method would look like this:

```
return Math.sqrt(a * a + b * b);
```

Common Programming Error

Statement after Return

It's illegal to place other statements immediately after a `return` statement, because those statements can never be reached or executed. New programmers often accidentally do this when trying to print the value of a variable after returning. Say you've written the `hypotenuse` method but have accidentally written the parameters to `Math.pow` in the wrong order, so the method is not producing the right answer. You would try to debug this by printing the value of `c` that is being returned. Here's the faulty code:

```
// trying to find the bug in this buggy version of hypotenuse
public static double hypotenuse(double a, double b) {
    double c = Math.sqrt(Math.pow(2, a) + Math.pow(2, b));
    return c;
    System.out.println(c);  // this doesn't work
}
```

The compiler complains about the `println` statement being unreachable, since it follows a `return` statement. The compiler error output looks something like this:

```
Triangles.java:10: error: unreachable statement
        System.out.println(c);
        ^

Triangles.java:11: error: missing return statement
    }
    ^
2 errors
```

The fix is to move the `println` statement earlier in the method, before the `return` statement:

```
public static double hypotenuse(double a, double b) {
    double c = Math.sqrt(Math.pow(2, a) + Math.pow(2, b));
    System.out.println(c);  // better
    return c;
}
```

3.3 Using Objects

We've spent a considerable amount of time discussing the primitive types in Java and how they work, so it's about time that we started talking about objects and how they work.

The idea for objects came from the observation that as we start working with new kinds of data (integers, reals, characters, text, etc.), we find ourselves writing a lot of methods that operate on that data. Rather than completely separating the basic operations from the data, it seemed to make sense to include them together. This packaging of data and operations into one entity is the central idea behind objects. An *object* stores some data and has methods that act on its data.

> **Object**
>
> A programming entity that contains state (data) and behavior (methods).

As we said in Chapter 1, classes are the basic building blocks of Java programs. But classes also serve another purpose: to describe new types of objects.

> **Class**
>
> A category or type of object.

When it is used this way, a class is like a blueprint of what the object looks like. Once you've given Java the blueprint, you can ask it to create actual objects that match that blueprint. We sometimes refer to the individual objects as *instances* of the class. We tend to use the words "instance" and "object" interchangeably.

This concept is difficult to understand in the abstract. To help you come to grips with what it means and how it works, we'll look at several different classes. In keeping with our idea of focusing on fundamental concepts first, in this chapter we'll study how to use existing objects that are already part of Java, but we aren't going to study how to define our own new types of objects just yet. We'll get to that in Chapter 8, after we've had time to practice using objects.

Using objects differs from using primitive types, so we'll have to introduce some new syntax and concepts. It would be nice if Java had a consistent model for using all types of data, but it doesn't. Consequently, if you want to understand how your programs operate, you'll have to learn two sets of rules: one for primitives and one for objects.

String Objects

VideoNote

`String` objects are one of the most useful and most commonly used types of objects in Java, so they make a good starting point. They aren't the best example of objects, though, because there are a lot of special rules that apply only to `string`s. In the next section, we'll look at a more typical kind of object.

One special property of `string` objects is that there are literals that represent them (string literals). We've been using them in `println` statements since Chapter 1. What we haven't discussed is that these literal values represent objects of type `String` (instances of the `string` class). For example, in the same way that you can say

```
int x = 8;
```

you can say

```
String s = "hello there";
```

You can declare variables of type `String` and use the assignment statement to give values to these variables. You can also write code that involves `String` expressions:

```
String s1 = "hello";
String s2 = "there";
String combined = s1 + " " + s2;
```

This code defines two `String`s that each represent a single word and a third `String` that represents the concatenation of the two words with a space in between. You'll notice that the type `String` is capitalized (as are the names of all object types in Java), unlike the primitive types such as `double` and `int`.

These examples haven't shown what's special about `String` objects, but we're getting there. Remember that the idea behind objects was to include basic operations with the data itself, the way we make cars that have controls built in. The data stored in a `String` is a sequence of characters. There are all sorts of operations you might want to perform on this sequence of characters. For example, you might want to know how many characters there are in the `String`. `String` objects have a `length` method that returns this information.

If the `length` method were static, you would call it by saying something like

```
length(s)      // this isn't legal
```

But when you perform operations on objects, you use a different syntax. Objects store data and methods, so the method to report a `String`'s length actually exists inside that `String` object itself. To call an object's method, you write the name of the variable first, followed by a dot, and then the name of the method:

```
s.length()
```

Think of it as talking to the `String` object. When you ask for `s.length()`, you're saying, "Hey, s. I'm talking to you. What's your length?" Of course, different `String` objects have different lengths, so you will get different answers when you communicate with different `String` objects.

The general syntax for calling a method of an object is the following:

```
<variable>.<method name>(<expression>, <expression>, ..., <expression>)
```

For example, suppose that you have initialized two `String` variables as follows:

```
String s1 = "hello";
String s2 = "how are you?";
```

You can use a `println` to examine the length of each `String`:

```
System.out.println("Length of s1 = " + s1.length());
System.out.println("Length of s2 = " + s2.length());
```

This code produces the following output:

```
Length of s1 = 5
Length of s2 = 12
```

What else might you want to do with a `String` object? With the `length` method, you can figure out how many characters there are in a `String`, but what about getting the individual characters themselves? There are several ways to do this, but one of the most common is to use a method called `charAt` that returns the character at a specific location in the string.

This leads us to the problem of how to specify locations in a sequence. Obviously there is a first character, a second character, and so on, so it makes sense to use an integer to refer to a specific location. We call this the *index*.

> **Index**
>
> An integer used to specify a location in a sequence of values. Java generally uses zero-based indexing (with 0 as the first index value, followed by 1, 2, 3, and so on).

Each character of a `String` object is assigned an index value, starting with 0. For example, for the variable `s1` that refers to the string `"hello"`, the indexes are:

```
  0   1   2   3   4
+---+---+---+---+---+
| h | e | l | l | o |
+---+---+---+---+---+
```

It may seem intuitive to consider the letter "h" to be at position 1, but there are advantages to starting with an index of 0. It's a convention that was adopted by the designers of the C language and that has been followed by the designers of C++ and Java, so it's a convention you'll have to learn to live with.

For the longer `String s2`, the positions are:

```
  0   1   2   3   4   5   6   7   8   9  10  11
+---+---+---+---+---+---+---+---+---+---+---+---+
| h | o | w |   | a | r | e |   | y | o | u | ? |
+---+---+---+---+---+---+---+---+---+---+---+---+
```

Notice that the spaces in this `String` have positions as well (here, positions 3 and 7). Also notice that the indexes for a given string always range from 0 to one less than the length of the string.

Using the `charAt` method, you can request specific characters of a string. The return type is `char`. For example, if you ask for `s1.charAt(1)` you'll get `'e'` (the 'e' in "hello"). If you ask for `s2.charAt(5)`, you'll get `'r'` (the 'r' in "how are you?"). For any `String`, if you ask for `charAt(0)`, you'll get the first character of the string.

When you are working with `String` objects, you'll often find it useful to write a `for` loop to handle the different characters of the `String`. Because `Strings` are indexed starting at 0, this task is easier to write with `for` loops that start with 0 rather than 1. Consider, for example, the following code that prints out the individual characters of `s1`:

```
String s1 = "hello";
for (int i = 0; i < s1.length(); i++) {
    System.out.println(i + ": " + s1.charAt(i));
}
```

This code produces the following output:

```
0: h
1: e
2: l
3: l
4: o
```

Remember that when we start loops at 0, we usually test with less than (<) rather than less than or equal to (<=). The string `s1` has five characters in it, so the call on `s1.length()` will return 5. But because the first index is 0, the last index will be one less than 5, or 4. This convention takes a while to get used to, but zero-based indexing is used throughout Java, so you'll eventually get the hang of it.

Another useful `String` method is the `substring` method. It takes two integer arguments representing a starting and ending index. When you call the `substring` method, you provide two of these indexes: the index of the first character you want and the index just past the last index that you want.

Recall that the `String` `s2` has the following positions:

0	1	2	3	4	5	6	7	8	9	10	11
h	o	w		a	r	e		y	o	u	?

If you want to pull out the individual word "how" from this string, you'd ask for

```
s2.substring(0, 3)
```

Remember that the second value that you pass to the `substring` method is supposed to be one beyond the end of the substring you are forming. So, even though there is a space at position 3 in the original string, it will not be part of what you get from the call on `substring`. Instead, you'll get all the characters just before position 3.

Following this rule means that sometimes you will give a position to a substring at which there is no character. For instance, the last character in the string to which `s2` refers is at index 11 (the question mark). If you want to get the substring "you?" including the question mark, you'd ask for

```
s2.substring(8, 12)
```

There is no character at position 12 in s2, but this call asks for characters starting at position 8 that come before position 12, so this actually makes sense.

You have to be careful about what indexes you use, though. With the substring method you can ask for the position just beyond the end of the String, but you can't ask for anything beyond that. For example, if you ask for

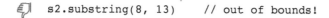

```
s2.substring(8, 13)     // out of bounds!
```

your program will generate an execution error. Similarly, if you ask for the charAt at a nonexistent position, your program will generate an execution error. These errors are known as *exceptions*.

Exceptions are runtime errors as mentioned in Chapter 1.

> **Exception**
>
> A runtime error that prevents a program from continuing its normal execution.

We say that an exception is *thrown* when an error is encountered. When an exception is thrown, Java looks to see if you have written code to handle it. If not, program execution is halted and you will see what is known as a *stack trace* or *back trace*. The stack trace shows you the series of methods that have been called, in reverse order. In the case of bad String indexes, the exception prints a message such as the following to the console:

```
Exception in thread "main"
        java.lang.StringIndexOutOfBoundsException:
        String index out of range: 13
        at java.lang.String.substring(Unknown Source)
        at ExampleProgram.main(ExampleProgram.java:3)
```

You can use Strings as parameters to methods. For example, the following program uses String parameters to eliminate some of the redundancy in a popular children's song:

```java
1 public class BusSong {
2       public static void main(String[] args) {
3           verse("wheels", "go", "round and round");
4           verse("wipers", "go", "swish, swish, swish");
5           verse("horn", "goes", "beep, beep, beep");
6       }
7
8       public static void verse(String item, String verb, String sound) {
9           System.out.println("The " + item + " on the bus " +
10                              verb + " " + sound + ",");
```

```
11          System.out.println(sound + ",");
12          System.out.println(sound + ".");
13          System.out.println("The " + item + " on the bus " +
14                             verb + " " + sound + ",");
15          System.out.println("All through the town.");
16          System.out.println();
17      }
18  }
```

It produces the following output:

```
The wheels on the bus go round and round,
round and round,
round and round.
The wheels on the bus go round and round,
All through the town.

The wipers on the bus go swish, swish, swish,
swish, swish, swish,
swish, swish, swish.
The wipers on the bus go swish, swish, swish,
All through the town.

The horn on the bus goes beep, beep, beep,
beep, beep, beep,
beep, beep, beep.
The horn on the bus goes beep, beep, beep,
All through the town.
```

Table 3.3 lists some of the most useful methods that you can call on `String` objects. `String`s in Java are *immutable*, which means that once they are constructed, their values can never be changed.

> **Immutable Object**
>
> An object whose value cannot be changed.

It may seem odd that `String`s are immutable and yet have methods like `toUpperCase` and `toLowerCase`. But if you read the descriptions in the table carefully, you'll see that these methods don't actually change a given `String` object; instead they return a new string. Consider the following code:

```
String s = "Hello, Maria";
s.toUpperCase();
System.out.println(s);
```

Table 3.3   Useful Methods of `String` Objects

Method	Description	Example (assuming s is `"hello"`)
`charAt(index)`	character at a specific index	`s.charAt(1)` returns `'e'`
`endsWith(text)`	whether or not the string ends with some text	`s.endsWith("llo")` returns `true`
`indexOf(text)`	index of a particular character or `String` (–1 if not present)	`s.indexOf("o")` returns 4
`length()`	number of characters in the string	`s.length()` returns 5
`replace(s1, s2)`	replace all occurrences of one substring with another	`s.replace("l", "y")` returns `"heyyyyo"`
`startsWith(text)`	whether or not the string starts with some text	`s.startsWith("hi")` returns `false`
`substring(start, stop)`	characters from start index to just before stop index	`s.substring(1, 3)` returns `"el"`
`toLowerCase()`	a new string with all lowercase letters	`s.toLowerCase()` returns `"hello"`
`toUpperCase()`	a new string with all uppercase letters	`s.toUpperCase()` returns `"HELLO"`

You might think that this will turn the string s into its uppercase equivalent, but it doesn't. The second line of code constructs a new string that has the uppercase equivalent of the value of s, but we don't do anything with this new value. In order to turn the string into uppercase, the key is to either store this new string in a different variable or reassign the variable s to point to the new string:

```
String s = "Hello, Maria";
s = s.toUpperCase();
System.out.println(s);
```

This version of the code produces the following output:

```
HELLO, MARIA
```

The `toUpperCase` and `toLowerCase` methods are particularly helpful when you want to perform string comparisons in which you ignore the case of the letters involved.

Another useful method found in String objects is the `replace` method. It accepts two parameters: a string to search for, and a new string to replace all occurrences of it with.

```
String s = "Tweedle Dee";
```

Interactive Programs and Scanner Objects

VideoNote

As you've seen, you can easily produce output in the console window by calling `System.out.println` and `System.out.print`. You can also write programs that pause and wait for the user to type a response. Such programs are known as *interactive* programs, and the responses typed by the user are known as *console input*.

> **Console Input**
>
> Responses typed by the user when an interactive program pauses for input.

When you refer to `System.out`, you are accessing an object in the `System` class known as the standard output stream, or "standard out" for short. There is a corresponding object for standard input known as `System.in`, but Java wasn't designed for console input, and `System.in` has never been particularly easy to use for this purpose. Fortunately for us, there is an easier way to read console input: `Scanner` objects.

Most objects have to be explicitly constructed by calling a special method known as a *constructor*.

> **Constructor (Construct)**
>
> A method that creates and initializes an object. Objects in Java programs must be constructed before they can be used.

Remember that a class is like a blueprint for a family of objects. Calling a constructor is like sending an order to the factory asking it to follow the blueprint to get you an actual object that you can manipulate. When you send in your order to the factory, you sometimes specify certain parameters (e.g., what color you want the object to be).

In Java, constructors are called using the special keyword `new`, followed by the object's type and any necessary parameters. For example, to construct a specific `Scanner` object, you have to pass information about the source of input. In particular, you have to provide an input stream. To read from the console window, pass it `System.in`:

```
Scanner console = new Scanner(System.in);
```

Once you've constructed the `Scanner`, you can ask it to return a value of a particular type. A number of methods, all beginning with the word "next," are available to obtain the various types of values. Table 3.4 lists them.

Typically, you will use variables to keep track of the values returned by these methods. For example, you might say:

```
int n = console.nextInt();
```

Table 3.4   Scanner Methods

Method	Description
`next()`	reads and returns the next token as a `String`
`nextDouble()`	reads and returns a `double` value
`nextInt()`	reads and returns an `int` value
`nextLine()`	reads and returns the next line of input as a `String`

The call on the `console` object's `nextInt` method pauses for user input. Whenever the computer pauses for input, it will pause for an entire line of input. In other words, it will wait until the user hits the Enter key before continuing to execute the program.

You can use the `Scanner` class to read input line by line using the `nextLine` method, although we won't be using `nextLine` very much for now. The other "next" methods are all *token*-based (that is, they read single elements of input rather than entire lines).

> **Token**
>
> A single element of input (e.g., one word, one number).

By default, the `Scanner` uses *whitespace* to separate tokens.

> **Whitespace**
>
> Spaces, tab characters, and new line characters.

A `Scanner` object looks at what the user types and uses the whitespace on the input line to break it up into individual tokens. For example, the line of input

```
hello     there. "how are"        "you?"  all-one-token
```

would be split into six tokens:

```
hello
there.
"how
are"
"you?"
all-one-token
```

Notice that the `Scanner` includes punctuation characters such as periods, question marks, and quotation marks in the tokens it generates. It also includes dashes, so because there is no whitespace in the middle to break it up into different tokens, we get just one token for "all-one-token." It's possible to control how a `Scanner` turns things into tokens (a process called *tokenizing* the input), but we won't be doing anything that fancy.

It is possible to read more than one value from a `Scanner`, as in:

```
double x = console.nextDouble();
double y = console.nextDouble();
```

Because there are two different calls on the `console` object's `nextDouble` method, this code will cause the computer to pause until the user has entered two numeric values. The values can be entered on the same line or on separate lines. In general, the computer continues to pause for user input until it has obtained whatever values you have asked the `Scanner` to obtain.

If a user types something that isn't an integer when you call `nextInt`, such as `xyzzy`, the `Scanner` object generates an exception. Recall from the section on `String` objects that exceptions are runtime errors that halt program execution. In this case, you'll see runtime error output such as the following:

```
Exception in thread "main" java.util.InputMismatchException
        at java.util.Scanner.throwFor(Unknown Source)
        at java.util.Scanner.next(Unknown Source)
        at java.util.Scanner.nextInt(Unknown Source)
        at Example.main(Example.java:13)
```

You will see in a later chapter how to test for user errors. In the meantime, we will assume that the user provides appropriate input.

Sample Interactive Program

Using the `Scanner` class, we can write a complete interactive program that performs a useful computation for the user. If you ever find yourself buying a house, you'll want to know what your monthly mortgage payment is going to be. The following is a complete program that asks for information about a loan and prints the monthly payment:

```
1    // This program prompts for information about a loan and
2    // computes the monthly mortgage payment.
3
4    import java.util.*;    // for Scanner
5
6    public class Mortgage {
7        public static void main(String[] args) {
8            Scanner console = new Scanner(System.in);
9
10           // obtain values
11           System.out.println("This program computes monthly " +
12                                  "mortgage payments.");
13           System.out.print("loan amount     : ");
14           double loan = console.nextDouble();
15           System.out.print("number of years : ");
16           int years = console.nextInt();
17           System.out.print("interest rate    : ");
18           double rate = console.nextDouble();
19           System.out.println();
20
21           // compute result and report
22           int n = 12 * years;
23           double c = rate / 12.0 / 100.0;
```

```
24              double payment = loan * c * Math.pow(1 + c, n) /
25                                  (Math.pow(1 + c, n) - 1);
26              System.out.println("payment = $" + (int) payment);
27          }
28      }
```

The following is a sample execution of the program (user input is in bold):

```
This program computes monthly mortgage payments.
loan amount      : 275000
number of years : 30
interest rate    : 4.25


payment = $1352
```

The first thing we do in the program is construct a `Scanner` object, which we will use for console input. Next, we explain what the program is going to do, printing a description to the console. This is essential for interactive programs. You don't want a program to pause for user input until you've explained to the user what is going to happen.

Below the `println`, you'll notice several pairs of statements like these:

```
System.out.print("loan amount      : ");
double loan = console.nextDouble();
```

The first statement is called a *prompt,* a request for information from the user. We use a `print` statement instead of a `println` so that the user will type the values on the same line as the prompt (i.e., to the right of the prompt). The second statement calls the `nextDouble` method of the `console` object to read a value of type `double` from the user. This value is stored in a variable called `loan`. This pattern of prompt/read statements is common in interactive programs.

After prompting for values, the program computes several values. The formula for computing monthly mortgage payments involves the loan amount, the total number of months involved (a value we call n), and the monthly interest rate (a value we call c). The payment formula is given by the following equation:

$$payment = loan \; \frac{c(1 + c)^n}{(1 + c)^n - 1}$$

You will notice in the program that we use the `Math.pow` method for exponentiation to translate this formula into a Java expression.

The final line of the program prints out the monthly payment. You might imagine that we would simply say:

```
System.out.println("payment = $" + payment);
```

However, because the payment is stored in a variable of type `double`, such a statement would print all the digits of the number. For example, for the log listed above, it would print the following:

```
payment = $1352.8347004685593
```

That is a rather strange-looking output for someone who is used to dollars and cents. For the purposes of this simple program, it's easy to cast the `double` to an `int` and report just the dollar amount of the payment:

```
System.out.println("payment = $" + (int) payment);
```

Most people trying to figure out their mortgage payments aren't that interested in the pennies, so the program is still useful. In the next section, we will see how to round a `double` to two decimal places.

There is something new at the beginning of this class file called an *import declaration*. Remember that Java has a large number of classes included in what are collectively known as the Java class libraries. To help manage these classes, Java provides an organizational unit known as a *package*. Related classes are combined together into a single package. For example, the `Scanner` class is stored in a package known as `java.util`. Java programs don't normally have access to a package unless they include an import declaration.

> **Package**
> A collection of related Java classes.

> **Import Declaration**
> A request to access a specific Java package.

We haven't needed an `import` declaration yet because Java automatically imports every class stored in a package called `java.lang`. The `java.lang` package includes basic classes that most Java programs are likely to use (e.g., `System`, `String`, `Math`). Because Java does not automatically import `java.util`, you have to do it yourself.

Java allows you to use an asterisk to import all classes from a package:

```
import java.util.*;
```

But some people prefer to specifically mention each class they import. The import declaration allows you to import just a single class from a package, as in

```
import java.util.Scanner;
```

The problem is that once you start importing one class from a package, you're likely to want to import others as well. We will use the asterisk version of `import` in this book to keep things simple.

3.4 Case Study: Projectile Trajectory

It's time to pull together the threads of this chapter with a more complex example that will involve parameters, methods that return values, mathematical computations, and the use of a `Scanner` object for console input.

Physics students are often asked to calculate the trajectory that a projectile will follow, given its initial velocity and its initial angle relative to the horizontal. For example, the projectile might be a football that someone has kicked. We want to compute the path it follows given Earth's gravity. To keep the computation reasonable, we will ignore air resistance.

There are several questions relating to this problem that we might want to answer:

- When does the projectile reach its highest point?
- How high does it reach?
- How long does it take to come back to the ground?
- How far does it land from where it was launched?

There are several ways to answer these questions. One simple approach is to provide a table that displays the trajectory step by step, indicating the *x* position, *y* position, and elapsed time.

To make such a table, we need to obtain three values from the user: the initial velocity, the angle relative to the horizontal, and the number of steps to include in the table we will produce. We could ask for the velocity in either meters/second or feet/second, but given that this is a physics problem, we'll stick to the metric system and ask for meters/second.

We also have to think about how to specify the angle. Unfortunately, most of the Java methods that operate on angles require angles in radians rather than degrees. We could request the angle in radians, but that would be highly inconvenient for the user, who would be required to make the conversion. Instead, we can allow the user to enter the angle in degrees and then convert it to radians using the built-in method `Math.toRadians`.

So, the interactive part of the program will look like this:

```java
Scanner console = new Scanner(System.in);
System.out.print("velocity (meters/second)? ");
double velocity = console.nextDouble();
System.out.print("angle (degrees)? ");
double angle = Math.toRadians(console.nextDouble());
System.out.print("number of steps to display? ");
int steps = console.nextInt();
```

Notice that for the velocity and angle we call the `nextDouble` method of the console object, because we want to let the user specify any number (including one with a decimal point), but for the number of steps we call `nextInt`, because the number of lines in our table needs to be an integer.

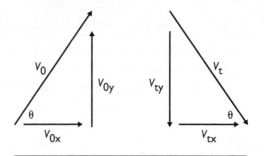

Figure 3.1   Initial and Final Velocity of Projectile

Look more closely at this line of code:

```
double angle = Math.toRadians(console.nextDouble());
```

Some beginners would write this as two separate steps:

```
double angleInDegrees = console.nextDouble();
double angle = Math.toRadians(angleInDegrees);
```

Both approaches work and are reasonable, but keep in mind that you don't need to divide this operation into two separate steps. You can write it in the more compact form as a single line of code.

Once we have obtained these values from the user, we are ready to begin the computations for the trajectory table. The x/y-position of the projectile at each time increment is determined by its velocity in each dimension and by the acceleration on the projectile due to gravity. Figure 3.1 shows the projectile's initial velocity v_0 and angle θ just as it is thrown and final velocity v_t just as it hits the ground.

We need to compute the x component of the velocity versus the y component of the velocity. From physics, we know that these can be computed as follows:

```
double xVelocity = velocity * Math.cos(angle);
double yVelocity = velocity * Math.sin(angle);
```

Because we are ignoring the possibility of air resistance, the x-velocity will not change. The y-velocity, however, is subject to the pull of gravity. Physics tells us that on the surface of the Earth, acceleration due to gravity is approximately 9.81 meters/second[2]. This is an appropriate value to define as a class constant:

```
public static final double ACCELERATION = -9.81;
```

Notice that we define gravity acceleration as a negative number because it decreases the y-velocity of an object (pulling it down as opposed to pushing it away).

Our goal is to display x, y, and elapsed time as the object goes up and comes back down again. The y-velocity decreases steadily until it becomes 0. From physics, we know that the graph of the projectile will be symmetrical. The projectile will go upward until its *y*-velocity reaches 0, and then it will follow a similar path back down that takes an equal amount of time. Thus, the total time involved in seconds can be computed as follows:

```
double totalTime = -2.0 * yVelocity / ACCELERATION;
```

Now, how do we compute the values of *x*, *y*, and elapsed time to include in our table? It is relatively simple to compute two of these. We want steady time increments for each entry in the table, so we can compute the time increment by dividing the total time by the number of steps we want to include in our table:

```
double timeIncrement = totalTime / steps;
```

As noted earlier, the *x*-velocity does not change, so for each of these time increments, we move the same distance in the *x*-direction:

```
double xIncrement = xVelocity * timeIncrement;
```

The tricky value to compute here is the *y*-position. Because of acceleration due to gravity, the *y*-velocity changes over time. But from physics, we have the following general formula for computing the displacement of an object given the velocity *v*, time *t*, and acceleration *a*:

$$\text{displacement} = vt + \frac{1}{2}at^2$$

In our case, the velocity we want is the *y*-velocity and the acceleration is from the Earth's gravity constant. Here, then, is a pseudocode description of how to create the table:

```
set all of x, y, and t to 0.
for (given number of steps) {
    add timeIncrement to t.
    add xIncrement to x.
    reset y to yVelocity * t + 0.5 * ACCELERATION * t * t.
    report step #, x, y, t.
}
```

We are fairly close to having real Java code here, but we have to think about how to report the values of x, y, and t in a table. They will all be of type `double`, which means they are likely to produce a large number of digits after the decimal point. But we aren't interested in seeing all those digits, because they aren't particularly relevant and because our computations aren't that accurate.

Before we try to complete the code for the table, let's think about the problem of displaying only some of the digits of a number. The idea is to truncate the digits so that we don't see all of them. One way to truncate is to cast a `double` to an `int`, which truncates all of the digits after the decimal point. We could do that, but we probably want at least some of those digits. Say, for example, that we want to report two digits after the decimal point. The trick is to bring the two digits we want to the other side of the decimal point. We can do that by multiplying by 100 and then casting to `int`:

```
(int) (n * 100.0)
```

This expression gets us the digits we want, but now the decimal point is in the wrong place. For example, if n is initially `3.488834`, the preceding expression will give us `348`. We have to divide this result by 100 to turn it back into the number 3.48:

```
(int) (n * 100.0) / 100.0
```

While we're at it, we can make one final improvement. Notice that the original number was `3.488834`. If we do simple truncation we get `3.48`, but really this number is closer to `3.49`. We can round to the nearest digit by calling the `Math.round` method on the number instead of casting it:

```
Math.round(n * 100.0) / 100.0
```

This is an operation that we are likely to want to perform on more than one number, so it deserves to be included in a method:

```
public static double round2(double n) {
    return Math.round(n * 100.0) / 100.0;
}
```

Getting back to our pseudocode for the table, we can incorporate calls on the `round2` method to get a bit closer to actual Java code:

```
set all of x, y, and t to 0.
for (given number of steps) {
    add timeIncrement to t.
    add xIncrement to x.
    reset y to yVelocity * t + 0.5 * ACCELERATION * t * t.
    report step #, round2(x), round2(y), round2(t).
}
```

It would be nice if the values in the table were aligned. To get numbers that line up nicely, we would have to use formatted output, which we will discuss in Chapter 4. For now, we can at least get the numbers to line up in columns by separating them with tab characters. Remember that the escape sequence \t represents a single tab.

If we're going to have a table with columns, it also makes sense to have a header for the table. And we probably want to include a line in the table showing the initial condition, where x, y, and time are all equal to 0. So we can expand our pseudocode into the following Java code:

```java
double x = 0.0;
double y = 0.0;
double t = 0.0;
System.out.println("step\tx\ty\ttime");
System.out.println("0\t0.0\t0.0\t0.0");
for (int i = 1; i <= steps; i++) {
    t += timeIncrement;
    x += xIncrement;
    y = yVelocity * t + 0.5 * ACCELERATION * t * t;
    System.out.println(i + "\t" + round2(x) + "\t" +
                          round2(y) + "\t" + round2(t));
}
```

Unstructured Solution

We can put all of these pieces together to form a complete program. Let's first look at an unstructured version that includes most of the code in main. This version also includes some new println statements at the beginning that give a brief introduction to the user:

```java
1   // This program computes the trajectory of a projectile.
2
3   import java.util.*; // for Scanner
4
5   public class Projectile {
6       // constant for Earth acceleration in meters/second^2
7       public static final double ACCELERATION = -9.81;
8
9       public static void main(String[] args) {
10          Scanner console = new Scanner(System.in);
11
12          System.out.println("This program computes the");
13          System.out.println("trajectory of a projectile given");
14          System.out.println("its initial velocity and its");
15          System.out.println("angle relative to the");
16          System.out.println("horizontal.");
17          System.out.println();
18
19          System.out.print("velocity (meters/second)? ");
20          double velocity = console.nextDouble();
21          System.out.print("angle (degrees)? ");
22          double angle = Math.toRadians(console.nextDouble());
```

```
23            System.out.print("number of steps to display? ");
24            int steps = console.nextInt();
25            System.out.println();
26
27            double xVelocity = velocity * Math.cos(angle);
28            double yVelocity = velocity * Math.sin(angle);
29            double totalTime = -2.0 * yVelocity / ACCELERATION;
30            double timeIncrement = totalTime / steps;
31            double xIncrement = xVelocity * timeIncrement;
32
33            double x = 0.0;
34            double y = 0.0;
35            double t = 0.0;
36            System.out.println("step\tx\ty\ttime");
37            System.out.println("0\t0.0\t0.0\t0.0");
38            for (int i = 1; i <= steps; i++) {
39                t += timeIncrement;
40                x += xIncrement;
41                y = yVelocity * t + 0.5 * ACCELERATION * t * t;
42                System.out.println(i + "\t" + round2(x) + "\t" +
43                                        round2(y) + "\t" + round2(t));
44            }
45        }
46
47        public static double round2(double n) {
48            return Math.round(n * 100.0) / 100.0;
49        }
50  }
```

The following is a sample execution of the program:

```
This program computes the
trajectory of a projectile given
its initial velocity and its
angle relative to the
horizontal.

velocity (meters/second)? 30
angle (degrees)? 50
number of steps to display? 10

step   x       y       time
0      0.0     0.0     0.0
1      9.03    9.69    0.47
```

2	18.07	17.23	0.94
3	27.1	22.61	1.41
4	36.14	25.84	1.87
5	45.17	26.92	2.34
6	54.21	25.84	2.81
7	63.24	22.61	3.28
8	72.28	17.23	3.75
9	81.31	9.69	4.22
10	90.35	0.0	4.69

From the log of execution, you can see that the projectile reaches a maximum height of 26.92 meters after 2.34 seconds (the fifth step) and that it lands 90.35 meters from where it began after 4.69 seconds (the tenth step).

This version of the program works, but we don't generally want to include so much code in the `main` method. The next section explores how to break up the program into smaller pieces.

Structured Solution

There are three major blocks of code in the `main` method of the `Projectile` program: a series of `println` statements that introduce the program to the user, a series of statements that prompt the user for the three values used to produce the table, and then the code that produces the table itself.

So, in pseudocode, the overall structure looks like this:

```
give introduction.
prompt for velocity, angle, and number of steps.
produce table.
```

The first and third steps are easily turned into methods, but not the middle step. This step prompts the user for values that we need to produce the table. If we turned it into a method, it would have to somehow return three values back to `main`. A method can return only a single value, so unfortunately we can't turn this step into a method. We could turn it into three different methods, one for each of the three values, but each of those methods would be just two lines long, so it's not clear that doing so would improve the overall structure.

The main improvement we can make, then, is to split off the introduction and the table into separate methods. Another improvement we can make is to turn the physics displacement formula into its own method. It is always a good idea to turn equations into methods. Introducing those methods, we get the following structured version of the program:

```
1  // This program computes the trajectory of a projectile.
2
3  import java.util.*;      // for Scanner
4
5  public class Projectile2 {
```

```
 6        // constant for Earth acceleration in meters/second^2
 7        public static final double ACCELERATION = -9.81;
 8
 9        public static void main(String[] args) {
10            Scanner console = new Scanner(System.in);
11            giveIntro();
12
13            System.out.print("velocity (meters/second)? ");
14            double velocity = console.nextDouble();
15            System.out.print("angle (degrees)? ");
16            double angle = Math.toRadians(console.nextDouble());
17            System.out.print("number of steps to display? ");
18            int steps = console.nextInt();
19            System.out.println();
20
21            printTable(velocity, angle, steps);
22        }
23
24        // prints a table showing the trajectory of an object given
25        // its initial velocity and angle and including the given
26        // number of steps in the table
27        public static void printTable(double velocity,
28                                      double angle, int steps) {
29            double xVelocity = velocity * Math.cos(angle);
30            double yVelocity = velocity * Math.sin(angle);
31            double totalTime = -2.0 * yVelocity / ACCELERATION;
32            double timeIncrement = totalTime / steps;
33            double xIncrement = xVelocity * timeIncrement;
34
35            double x = 0.0;
36            double y = 0.0;
37            double t = 0.0;
38            System.out.println("step\tx\ty\ttime");
39            System.out.println("0\t0.0\t0.0\t0.0");
40            for (int i = 1; i <= steps; i++) {
41                t += timeIncrement;
42                x += xIncrement;
43                y = displacement(yVelocity, t, ACCELERATION);
44                System.out.println(i + "\t" + round2(x) + "\t" +
45                                   round2(y) + "\t" + round2(t));
46            }
47        }
48
49        // gives a brief introduction to the user
```

```
50      public static void giveIntro() {
51          System.out.println("This program computes the");
52          System.out.println("trajectory of a projectile given");
53          System.out.println("its initial velocity and its");
54          System.out.println("angle relative to the");
55          System.out.println("horizontal.");
56          System.out.println();
57      }
58
59      // returns the vertical displacement for a body given
60      // initial velocity v, elapsed time t, and acceleration a
61      public static double displacement(double v, double t,
62                                        double a) {
63          return v * t + 0.5 * a * t * t;
64      }
65
66      // rounds n to 2 digits after the decimal point
67      public static double round2(double n) {
68          return Math.round(n * 100.0) / 100.0;
69      }
70  }
```

This version executes the same way as the earlier version.

Chapter Summary

Methods may be written to accept parameters, which are sets of characteristics that distinguish different members of a family of tasks. Parameters allow data values to flow into a method, which can change the way the method executes. A method declared with a set of parameters can perform an entire family of similar tasks instead of exactly one task.

When primitive values such as those of type int or double are passed as parameters, their values are copied into the method. Primitive parameters send values into a method but not out of it; the method can use the data values but cannot affect the value of any variables outside it.

Two methods can have the same name if they declare different parameters. This is called overloading.

Methods can be written to return values to the calling code. This feature allows a method to perform a complex computation and then provide its result back to the calling code. The type of the return value must be declared in the method's header and is called the method's return type.

Java has a class called Math that contains several useful static methods that you can use in your programs, such as powers, square roots, and logarithms.

An object is an entity that combines data and operations. Some objects in Java include Strings, which are sequences of text characters, and Scanners, which read user input.

Objects contain methods that implement their behavior. To call a method on an object, write its name, followed by a dot, followed by the method name.

_____

A `String` object holds a sequence of characters. The characters have indexes, starting with 0 for the first character.

_____

An exception is an error that occurs when a program has performed an illegal action and is unable to continue executing normally.

_____

Some programs are interactive and respond to input from the user. These programs should print a message to the user, also called a prompt, asking for the input.

_____

Java has a class called `Scanner` that reads input from the keyboard. A `Scanner` can read various pieces of input (also called tokens) from an input source. It can read either one token at a time or an entire line at a time.

_____

Self-Check Problems

Section 3.1: Parameters

1. Which of the following is the correct syntax for a method header with parameters?

   a. `public static void example(x, y) {`
   b. `public static (int x, int y) example() {`
   c. `public static void example(int x,y) {`
   d. `public static void example(x: int, y: int) {`
   e. `public static void example(int x, int y) {`

2. What output is produced by the following program?

```
1   public class MysteryNums {
2       public static void main(String[] args) {
3           int x = 15;
4           sentence(x, 42);
5
6           int y = x - 5;
7           sentence(y, x + y);
8       }
9
10      public static void sentence(int num1, int num2) {
11          System.out.println(num1 + " " + num2);
12      }
13  }
```

3. The following program has 9 mistakes. What are they?

```
1   public class Oops3 {
2       public static void main() {
3           double bubble = 867.5309;
4           double x = 10.01;
5           printer(double x, double y);
```

```
 6              printer(x);
 7              printer("barack", "obama");
 8              System.out.println("z = " + z);
 9          }
10
11      public static void printer(x, y double) {
12              int z = 5;
13              System.out.println("x = " + double x + " and y = " + y);
14              System.out.println("The value from main is: " + bubble);
15          }
16  }
```

4. What output is produced by the following program?

```
 1  public class Odds {
 2      public static void main(String[] args) {
 3              printOdds(3);
 4              printOdds(17 / 2);
 5
 6              int x = 25;
 7              printOdds(37 - x + 1);
 8          }
 9
10      public static void printOdds(int n) {
11              for (int i = 1; i <= n; i++) {
12                      int odd = 2 * i - 1;
13                      System.out.print(odd + " ");
14              }
15              System.out.println();
16          }
17  }
```

5. What is the output of the following program?

```
 1  public class Weird {
 2      public static void main(String[] args) {
 3              int number = 8;
 4              halfTheFun(11);
 5              halfTheFun(2 - 3 + 2 * 8);
 6              halfTheFun(number);
 7              System.out.println("number = " + number);
 8          }
 9
10      public static void halfTheFun(int number) {
11              number = number / 2;
12              for (int count = 1; count <= number; count++) {
13                      System.out.print(count + " ");
```

```
14              }
15              System.out.println();
16          }
17  }
```

6. What is the output of the following program?

```
 1  public class MysteryNumbers {
 2      public static void main(String[] args) {
 3          String one = "two";
 4          String two = "three";
 5          String three = "1";
 6          int number = 20;
 7
 8          sentence(one, two, 3);
 9          sentence(two, three, 14);
10          sentence(three, three, number + 1);
11          sentence(three, two, 1);
12          sentence("eight", three, number / 2);
13      }
14
15      public static void sentence(String three, String one, int number) {
16          System.out.println(one + " times " + three + " = " + (number * 2));
17      }
18  }
```

7. What output is produced by the following program?

```
 1  public class MysteryWho {
 2      public static void main(String[] args) {
 3          String whom = "her";
 4          String who = "him";
 5          String it = "who";
 6          String he = "it";
 7          String she = "whom";
 8
 9          sentence(he, she, it);
10          sentence(she, he, who);
11          sentence(who, she, who);
12          sentence(it, "stu", "boo");
13          sentence(it, whom, who);
14      }
15
16      public static void sentence(String she, String who, String whom) {
17          System.out.println(who + " and " + whom + " like " + she);
18      }
19  }
```

8. What output is produced by the following program?

```
1   public class MysteryTouch {
2       public static void main(String[] args) {
3           String head = "shoulders";
4           String knees = "toes";
5           String elbow = "head";
6           String eye = "eyes and ears";
7           String ear = "eye";
8
9           touch(ear, elbow);
10          touch(elbow, ear);
11          touch(head, "elbow");
12          touch(eye, eye);
13          touch(knees, "Toes");
14          touch(head, "knees " + knees);
15      }
16
17      public static void touch(String elbow, String ear) {
18          System.out.println("touch your " + elbow + " to your " + ear);
19      }
20  }
```

9. What output is produced by the following program?

```
1   public class MysterySoda {
2       public static void main(String[] args) {
3           String soda = "Coke";
4           String pop = "Pepsi";
5           String Coke = "pop";
6           String Pepsi = "soda";
7           String say = pop;
8
9           carbonated(Coke, soda, pop);
10          carbonated(pop, Pepsi, Pepsi);
11          carbonated("pop", pop, "Kool-Aid");
12          carbonated(say, "say", pop);
13      }
14      public static void carbonated(String Coke, String soda, String pop) {
15          System.out.println("say " + soda + " not " + pop + " or " + Coke);
16      }
17  }
```

10. Write a method called `printStrings` that accepts a `String` and a number of repetitions as parameters and prints that `String` the given number of times with a space after each time. For example, the call

```
printStrings("abc", 5);
```

will print the following output:

```
abc abc abc abc abc
```

11. The `System.out.println` command works on many different types of values, such as integers or doubles. What is the term for such a method?

Section 3.2: Methods That Return Values

12. What is wrong with the following program?

```
1   public class Temperature {
2       public static void main(String[] args) {
3           double tempf = 98.6;
4           double tempc = 0.0;
5           ftoc(tempf, tempc);
6           System.out.println("Body temp in C is: " + tempc);
7       }
8
9       // converts Fahrenheit temperatures to Celsius
10      public static void ftoc(double tempf, double tempc) {
11          tempc = (tempf - 32) * 5 / 9;
12      }
13  }
```

13. Evaluate the following expressions:

a. `Math.abs(-1.6)`

b. `Math.abs(2 + -4)`

c. `Math.pow(6, 2)`

d. `Math.pow(5 / 2, 6)`

e. `Math.ceil(9.1)`

f. `Math.ceil(115.8)`

g. `Math.max(7, 4)`

h. `Math.min(8, 3 + 2)`

i. `Math.min(-2, -5)`

j. `Math.sqrt(64)`

k. `Math.sqrt(76 + 45)`

l. `100 + Math.log10(100)`

m. `13 + Math.abs(-7) - Math.pow(2, 3) + 5`

n. `Math.sqrt(16) * Math.max(Math.abs(-5), Math.abs(-3))`

o. `7 - 2 + Math.log10(1000) + Math.log(Math.pow(Math.E, 5))`

p. `Math.max(18 - 5, Math.ceil(4.6 * 3))`

14. What output is produced by the following program?

```
1   public class MysteryReturn {
2       public static void main(String[] args) {
3           int x = 1, y = 2, z = 3;
4           z = mystery(x, z, y);
5           System.out.println(x + " " + y + " " + z);
```

```
 6              x = mystery(z, z, x);
 7              System.out.println(x + " " + y + " " + z);
 8              y = mystery(y, y, z);
 9              System.out.println(x + " " + y + " " + z);
10         }
11
12         public static int mystery(int z, int x, int y) {
13              z--;
14              x = 2 * y + z;
15              y = x - 1;
16              System.out.println(y + " " + z);
17              return x;
18         }
19    }
```

15. Write the result of each expression. Note that a variable's value changes only if you reassign it using the = operator.

```
double grade = 2.7;
Math.round(grade);                                      // grade =
grade = Math.round(grade);                              // grade =

double min = Math.min(grade, Math.floor(2.9));   //    min =

double x = Math.pow(2, 4);                        //      x =
x = Math.sqrt(64);                                //      x =

int count = 25;
Math.sqrt(count);                                       // count =
count = (int) Math.sqrt(count);                         // count =

int a = Math.abs(Math.min(-1, -3));               //      a =
```

16. Write a method called min that takes three integers as parameters and returns the smallest of the three values; for example, a call of min(3, -2, 7) would return -2, and a call of min(19, 27, 6) would return 6. Use Math.min to write your solution.

17. Write a method called countQuarters that takes an int representing a number of cents as a parameter and returns the number of quarter coins represented by that many cents. Don't count any whole dollars, because those would be dispensed as dollar bills. For example, countQuarters(64) would return 2, because 64 cents is equivalent to 2 quarters with 14 cents left over. A call of countQuarters(1278) would return 3, because after the 12 dollars are taken out, 3 quarters remain in the 78 cents that are left.

Section 3.3: Using Objects

18. What output is produced by the following code?

```
String first = "James";
String last = "Kirk";
String middle = "T.";
System.out.println(last);
System.out.println("My name is " + first);
System.out.println(first + " " + last);
```

```
System.out.println(last + ", " + first + " " + middle);
System.out.println(middle + " is for Tiberius");
```

19. Assuming that the following variables have been declared:

```
//         index 0123456789012345
String str1 = "Frodo Baggins";
String str2 = "Gandalf the GRAY";
```

evaluate the following expressions:

a. str1.length()

b. str1.charAt(7)

c. str2.charAt(0)

d. str1.indexOf("o")

e. str2.toUpperCase()

f. str1.toLowerCase().indexOf("B")

g. str1.substring(4)

h. str2.substring(3, 14)

i. str2.replace("a", "oo")

j. str2.replace("gray", "white")

k. "str1".replace("r", "range")

20. Assuming that the following variables have been declared:

```
String str1 = "Q.E.D.";
String str2 = "Arcturan Megadonkey";
String str3 = "Sirius Cybernetics Corporation";
```

evaluate the following expressions:

a. str1.length()

b. str2.length()

c. str1.toLowerCase()

d. str2.toUpperCase()

e. str1.substring(2, 4)

f. str2.substring(10, 14)

g. str1.indexOf("D")

h. str1.indexOf(".")

i. str2.indexOf("donkey")

j. str3.indexOf("X")

k. str2 + str3.charAt(17)

l. str3.substring(9, str3.indexOf("e"))

m. str3.substring(7, 12)

n. str2.toLowerCase().substring(9, 13) + str3.substring(18, str3.length() − 7)

21. Consider the following String:

```
String quote = "Four score and seven years ago";
```

What expression produces the new String "SCORE"? What expression produces "four years"?

22. Write a program that outputs "The Name Game," where the user inputs a first and last name and a song in the following format is printed about their first, then last, name. Use a method to avoid redundancy.

```
What is your name? Fifty Cent
Fifty Fifty, bo-Bifty
Banana-fana fo-Fifty
Fee-fi-mo-Mifty
FIFTY!
Cent, Cent, bo-Bent
Banana-fana fo-Fent
Fee-fi-mo-Ment
CENT!
```

23. Consider the following code fragment:

```
Scanner console = new Scanner(System.in);
System.out.print("How much money do you have? ");
double money = console.nextDouble();
```

Describe what will happen when the user types each of the following values. If the code will run successfully, describe the value that will be stored in the variable money.

a. 34.50
b. 6
c. $25.00
d. million
e. 100*5
f. 600x000
g. none
h. 645

24. Write Java code to read an integer from the user, then print that number multiplied by 2. You may assume that the user types a valid integer.

25. Consider the following program. Modify the code to use a Scanner to prompt the user for the values of low and high.

```
1  public class SumNumbers {
2      public static void main(String[] args) {
3          int low = 1;
4          int high = 1000;
5          int sum = 0;
6          for (int i = low; i <= high; i++) {
7              sum += i;
8          }
9          System.out.println("sum = " + sum);
10     }
11 }
```

Below is a sample execution in which the user asks for the sum of the values 1 through 10:

```
low? 1
high? 10
sum = 55
```

26. Write Java code that prompts the user for a phrase and a number of times to repeat it, then prints the phrase the requested number of times. Here is an example dialogue with the user:

```
What is your phrase? His name is Robert Paulson.
How many times should I repeat it? 3
His name is Robert Paulson.
His name is Robert Paulson.
His name is Robert Paulson.
```

Exercises

1. Write a method called `printNumbers` that accepts a maximum number as an argument and prints each number from 1 up to that maximum, inclusive, boxed by square brackets. For example, consider the following calls:

```
printNumbers(15);
printNumbers(5);
```

These calls should produce the following output:

```
[1] [2] [3] [4] [5] [6] [7] [8] [9] [10] [11] [12] [13] [14] [15]
[1] [2] [3] [4] [5]
```

You may assume that the value passed to `printNumbers` is 1 or greater.

2. Write a method called `printPowersOf2` that accepts a maximum number as an argument and prints each power of 2 from 2^0 (1) up to that maximum power, inclusive. For example, consider the following calls:

```
printPowersOf2(3);
printPowersOf2(10);
```

These calls should produce the following output:

```
1 2 4 8
1 2 4 8 16 32 64 128 256 512 1024
```

You may assume that the value passed to `printPowersOf2` is 0 or greater. (The `Math` class may help you with this problem. If you use it, you may need to cast its results from `double` to `int` so that you don't see a `.0` after each number in your output. Also try to write this program without using the `Math` class.)

3. Write a method called `printPowersOfN` that accepts a base and an exponent as arguments and prints each power of the base from base^0 (1) up to that maximum power, inclusive. For example, consider the following calls:

```
printPowersOfN(4, 3);
printPowersOfN(5, 6);
printPowersOfN(-2, 8);
```

These calls should produce the following output:

```
1 4 16 64
1 5 25 125 625 3125 15625
1 -2 4 -8 16 -32 64 -128 256
```

You may assume that the exponent passed to `printPowersOfN` has a value of 0 or greater. (The `Math` class may help you with this problem. If you use it, you may need to cast its results from `double` to `int` so that you don't see a `.0` after each number in your output. Also try to write this program without using the `Math` class.)

4. Write a method called `printSquare` that accepts a minimum and maximum integer and prints a square of lines of increasing numbers. The first line should start with the minimum, and each line that follows should start with the next-higher number. The sequence of numbers on a line wraps back to the minimum after it hits the maximum. For example, the call

```
printSquare(3, 7);
```

should produce the following output:

```
34567
45673
56734
67345
73456
```

If the maximum passed is less than the minimum, the method produces no output.

5. Write a method called `printGrid` that accepts two integers representing a number of rows and columns and prints a grid of integers from 1 to (rows * columns) in column major order. For example, the call

```
printGrid(4, 6);
```

should produce the following output:

```
1 5 9 13 17 21
2 6 10 14 18 22
3 7 11 15 19 23
4 8 12 16 20 24
```

6. Write a method called `largerAbsVal` that takes two integers as parameters and returns the larger of the two absolute values. A call of `largerAbsVal(11, 2)` would return 11, and a call of `largerAbsVal(4, -5)` would return 5.

7. Write a variation of the `largestAbsVal` method from the last exercise that takes three integers as parameters and returns the largest of their three absolute values. For example, a call of `largestAbsVal(7, -2, -11)` would return 11, and a call of `largestAbsVal(-4, 5, 2)` would return 5.

8. Write a method called `quadratic` that solves quadratic equations and prints their roots. Recall that a quadratic equation is a polynomial equation in terms of a variable x of the form $ax^2 + bx + c = 0$. The formula for solving a quadratic equation is

$$x = \frac{-b \pm \sqrt{b^2 - 4ac}}{2a}$$

Here are some example equations and their roots:

$$x^2 - 7x + 12: x = 4, x = 3$$
$$x^2 - 3x + 2: x = -2, x = -1$$

Your method should accept the coefficients a, b, and c as parameters and should print the roots of the equation. You may assume that the equation has two real roots, though mathematically this is not always the case.

9. Write a method called `lastDigit` that returns the last digit of an integer. For example, `lastDigit(3572)` should return 2. It should work for negative numbers as well. For example, `lastDigit(-947)` should return 7.

10. Write a method called `area` that accepts as a parameter the radius of a circle and that returns the area of the circle. For example, the call `area(2.0)` should return `12.566370614359172`. Recall that area can be computed as pi (π) times the radius squared and that Java has a constant called `Math.PI`.

11. Write a method called `distance` that accepts four integer coordinates x_1, y_1, x_2, and y_2 as parameters and computes the distance between points (x_1, y_1) and (x_2, y_2) on the Cartesian plane. The equation for the distance is

$$d = \sqrt{(x_2 - x_1)^2 + (y_2 - y_1)^2}$$

For example, the call of distance(1, 0, 4, 4) would return 5.0 and the call of distance(10, 2, 3, 15) would return 14.7648230602334.

12. Write a method called scientific that accepts a real number base and an exponent as parameters and computes the base times 10 to the exponent, as seen in scientific notation. For example, the call of scientific(6.23, 5) would return 623000.0 and the call of scientific(1.9, −2) would return 0.019.

13. Write a method called pay that accepts two parameters: a real number for a TA's salary, and an integer for the number of hours the TA worked this week. The method should return how much money to pay the TA. For example, the call pay(5.50, 6) should return 33.0. The TA should receive "overtime" pay of $1\frac{1}{2}$ times the normal salary for any hours above 8. For example, the call pay(4.00, 11) should return (4.00 * 8) + (6.00 * 3) or 50.0.

14. Write a method called cylinderSurfaceArea that accepts a radius and height as parameters and returns the surface area of a cylinder with those dimensions. For example, the call cylinderSurfaceArea(3.0, 4.5) should return 141.3716694115407. The formula for the surface area of a cylinder with radius r and height h is the following:
surface area $= 2\pi r^2 + 2\pi rh$

15. Write a method called sphereVolume that accepts a radius as a parameter and returns the volume of a sphere with that radius. For example, the call sphereVolume(2.0) should return 33.510321638291124. The formula for the volume of a sphere with radius r is the following:
volume $= \frac{4}{3}\pi r^3$

16. Write a method called triangleArea that accepts the three side lengths of a triangle as parameters and returns the area of a triangle with those side lengths. For example, the call triangleArea(8, 5.2, 7.1) should return 18.151176098258745. To compute the area, use Heron's formula, which states that the area of a triangle whose three sides have lengths a, b, and c, is the following. The formula is based on the computed value s, a length equal to half the perimeter of the triangle:
$$area = \sqrt{s(s-a)(s-b)(s-c)}$$
$$s = \frac{a+b+c}{2}$$

17. Write a method called padString that accepts two parameters: a string and an integer representing a length. The method should pad the parameter string with spaces until its length is the given length. For example, padString("hello", 8) should return "hello   ". (This sort of method is useful when trying to print output that lines up horizontally.) If the string's length is already at least as long as the length parameter, your method should return the original string. For example, padString("congratulations", 10) should return "congratulations".

18. Write a method called vertical that accepts a string as its parameter and prints each letter of the string on separate lines. For example, a call of vertical("hey now") should produce the following output:

h

e

y

n

o

w

19. Write a method called printReverse that accepts a string as its parameter and prints the characters in opposite order. For example, a call of printReverse("hello there!") should print "!ereht olleh". If the empty string is passed, the method should produce no output.

20. Write a method called `inputBirthday` that accepts a `Scanner` for the console as a parameter and prompts the user to enter a month, day, and year of birth, then prints the birthdate in a suitable format. Here is an example dialogue with the user:

```
On what day of the month were you born? 8
What is the name of the month in which you were born? May
During what year were you born? 1981
You were born on May 8, 1981. You're mighty old!
```

21. Write a method called `processName` that accepts a `Scanner` for the console as a parameter and prompts the user to enter a full name, then prints the name in reverse order (i.e., last name, first name). Here is an example dialogue with the user:

```
Please enter your full name: Sammy Jankis
Your name in reverse order is Jankis, Sammy
```

22. Write a program that outputs "The Name Game," where the user inputs a first and last name and a song in the following format is printed about their first, then last, name. Use a method to avoid redundancy.

```
What is your name? Fifty Cent


Fifty Fifty, bo-Bifty
Banana-fana fo-Fifty
Fee-fi-mo-Mifty
FIFTY!


Cent, Cent, bo-Bent
Banana-fana fo-Fent
Fee-fi-mo-Ment
CENT!
```

Programming Projects

1. Write a program that produces images of Christmas trees as output. It should have a method with two parameters: one for the number of segments in the tree and one for the height of each segment. For example, the tree shown here on the left has three segments of height 4 and the one on the right has two segments of height 5:

```
     *                   *
    ***                 ***
   *****               *****
  *******             *******
    ***             *********
   *****               ***
  *******             *****
 *********           *******
   *****           *********
  *******         ***********
 *********             *
***********            *
     *             *******
     *
  *******
```

2. A certain bank offers 6.5% interest on savings accounts, compounded annually. Create a table that shows how much money a person will accumulate over a period of 25 years, assuming that the person makes an initial investment of $1000 and deposits $100 each year after the first. Your table should indicate for each year the current balance, the interest, the new deposit, and the new balance.

3. Write a program that shows the total number of presents that the person in the song "The Twelve Days of Christmas" received on each day, as indicated in Table 3.5.

Table 3.5   Twelve Days of Christmas

Day	Presents Received	Total Presents
1	1	1
2	2	3
3	3	6
4	4	10
5	5	15
. . .	. . .	. . .

4. Write a program that prompts for the lengths of the sides of a triangle and reports the three angles.

5. Write a program that computes the spherical distance between two points on the surface of the Earth, given their latitudes and longitudes. This is a useful operation because it tells you how far apart two cities are if you multiply the distance by the radius of the Earth, which is roughly 6372.795 km.

   Let φ_1, λ_1, and φ_2, λ_2 be the latitude and longitude of two points, respectively. $\Delta\lambda$, the longitudinal difference, and $\Delta\sigma$, the angular difference/distance in radians, can be determined as follows from the spherical law of cosines:

   $$\Delta\sigma = \arccos(\sin \varphi_1 \sin \varphi_2 + \cos \varphi_1 \cos \varphi_2 \cos \Delta\lambda)$$

   For example, consider the latitude and longitude of two major cities:

   - Nashville, TN: N 36°7.2′, W 86°40.2′
   - Los Angeles, CA: N 33°56.4′, W 118°24.0′

   You must convert these coordinates to radians before you can use them effectively in the formula. After conversion, the coordinates become

   - Nashville: $\varphi_1 = 36.12° = 0.6304$ rad, $\Delta_1 = -86.67° = -1.5127$ rad
   - Los Angeles: $\varphi_2 = 33.94° = 0.5924$ rad, $\Delta_2 = -118.40° = -2.0665$ rad

   Using these values in the angular distance equation, you get

   $$r\Delta\sigma = 6372.795 \times 0.45306 = 2887.259 \text{ km}$$

   Thus, the distance between these cities is about 2887 km, or 1794 miles. (Note: To solve this problem, you will need to use the `Math.acos` method, which returns an arccosine angle in radians.)

6. Write a program that produces calendars as output. Your program should have a method that outputs a single month's calendar like the one below, given parameters to specify how many days are in the month and what the date of the first Sunday is in that month. In the month shown below, these values are 31 and 6, respectively.

```
    Sun     Mon     Tue     Wed     Thu     Fri     Sat
  +------+------+------+------+------+------+------+
  |      |      |   1  |   2  |   3  |   4  |   5  |
  |   6  |   7  |   8  |   9  |  10  |  11  |  12  |
  |  13  |  14  |  15  |  16  |  17  |  18  |  19  |
  |  20  |  21  |  22  |  23  |  24  |  25  |  26  |
  |  27  |  28  |  29  |  30  |  31  |      |      |
  +------+------+------+------+------+------+------+
```

One tricky part of this program is making the various columns line up properly with proper widths. We will learn better ways of formatting output in the next chapter. For now, you may copy the following `helper` method into your program and call it to turn a number into a left-padded string of a given exact width. For example, the call `System.out.print(padded(7, 5));` prints "   7" (the number 7 with four leading spaces).

```java
// Returns a string of the number n, left-padded
// with spaces until it is at least the given width.
public static String padded(int n, int width) {
    String s = "" + n;
    for (int i = s.length(); i < width; i++) {
        s = " " + s;
    }
    return s;
}
```

Supplement 3G
Graphics (Optional)

Introduction

One of the most compelling reasons to learn about using objects is that they allow us to draw graphics in Java. Graphics are used for games, computer animations, and modern graphical user interfaces (GUIs), and to render complex images. Graphics are also a good way to practice the use of parameters as discussed in the previous chapter.

In this optional supplement we will examine a few of the basic classes from Java's graphical framework and use them to draw patterned two-dimensional figures of shapes and text onto the screen.

3G.1 Introduction to Graphics

VideoNote

Java's original graphical tools were collectively known as the Abstract Window Toolkit (AWT). The classes associated with the AWT reside in the package `java.awt`. In order to create graphical programs like the ones you'll see in this section, you'll need to include the following `import` declaration at the top of your programs:

```
import java.awt.*;   // for graphics
```

To keep things simple, we'll use a custom class called `DrawingPanel` that was written by the authors of this textbook to simplify some of the more esoteric details of Java graphics. Its core code is less than a page long, so we aren't hiding much. You won't need to import `DrawingPanel`, but you will need to place the file `DrawingPanel.java` in the same folder as your program.

The drawing panel keeps track of the overall image, but the actual drawing will be done with an object of type `Graphics`. The `Graphics` class is also part of the `java.awt` library.

DrawingPanel

You can create a graphical window on your screen by constructing a `DrawingPanel` object. You must specify the width and height of the drawing area. When the following line executes, a window appears immediately on the screen:

```
DrawingPanel <name> = new DrawingPanel(<width>, <height>);
```

`DrawingPanel` objects have two public methods, listed in Table 3G.1.

The typical way that you'll use `DrawingPanel` will be to construct a panel of a particular height and width, set its background color (if you don't want the default white background), and then draw something on it using its `Graphics` object. The `DrawingPanel` appears on the screen at the time that you construct it.

All coordinates are specified as integers. Each (x, y) position corresponds to a different pixel on the computer screen. The word *pixel* is shorthand for "picture element" and represents a single dot on the computer screen.

> **Pixel**
> A single small dot on a computer screen.

Table 3G.1 Useful Methods for `DrawingPanel`

Method	Description
getGraphics()	returns a `Graphics` object that can be used to draw onto the panel
setBackground(color)	sets the background color of the panel to the given color (the default is white)

The coordinate system assigns the upper-left corner of a panel the position (0, 0). As you move to the right of this position, the *x* value increases. As you move down from this position, the *y* value increases. For example, suppose that you construct a `DrawingPanel` object with a width of 200 pixels and a height of 100 pixels. The upper-left corner will have the coordinates (0, 0), and the lower-right corner will have the coordinates (199, 99) as shown in Figure 3G.1.

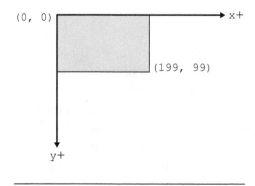

Figure 3G.1   The (*x*, *y*) Coordinate Space

This is likely to be confusing at first, because you're probably used to coordinate systems where *y* values decrease as you move down. However, you'll soon get the hang of it.

Drawing Lines and Shapes

So, how do you actually draw something? To draw shapes and lines, you don't talk directly to the `DrawingPanel`, but rather to a related object of type `Graphics`. Think of the `DrawingPanel` as a canvas and the `Graphics` object as the paintbrush. The `DrawingPanel` class has a method called `getGraphics` that returns its `Graphics` object:

```
Graphics g = <panel>.getGraphics();
```

One of the simplest drawing commands is `drawLine`, which takes four integer arguments.

For example, the method:

```
g.drawLine(<x1>, <y1>, <x2>, <y2>);
```

draws a line from the point (*x1*, *y1*) to the point (*x2*, *y2*). The `drawLine` method is just one of many commands a `Graphics` object understands; see Table 3G.2 for others. The `Graphics` object has many more methods in addition to the ones discussed here. You can read about them in the Java API documentation.

Here is a sample program that puts these pieces together:

```
1   // Draws a line onto a DrawingPanel.
2
3   import java.awt.*;   // for graphics
4
```

Table 3G.2 Some Useful Methods of `Graphics` Objects

Method	Description
`drawLine(x1, y1, x2, y2)`	draws a line between the points $(x1, y1)$ and $(x2, y2)$
`drawOval(x, y, width, height)`	draws the outline of the largest oval that fits within the specified rectangle
`drawRect(x, y, width, height)`	draws the outline of the specified rectangle
`drawString(message, x, y)`	draws the given text with its lower-left corner at (x, y)
`fillOval(x, y, width, height)`	fills the largest oval that fits within the specified rectangle using the current color
`fillRect(x, y, width, height)`	fills the specified rectangle using the current color
`setColor(color)`	sets this graphics context's current color to the specified color (all subsequent graphics operations using this graphics context use this specified color)
`setFont(font)`	sets this graphics context's current font to the specified font (all subsequent strings drawn using this graphics context use this specified font)

```
5   public class DrawLine1 {
6       public static void main(String[] args) {
7           // create the drawing panel
8           DrawingPanel panel = new DrawingPanel(200, 100);
9
10          // draw a line on the panel using
11          // the Graphics paintbrush
12          Graphics g = panel.getGraphics();
13          g.drawLine(25, 75, 175, 25);
14      }
15  }
```

When you run this program, the window shown in Figure 3G.2 appears. Though it isn't text on the console, as in previous chapters, we'll still refer to this as the "output" of the program.

(Java can be run on a variety of systems. Depending on your operating system, your output may differ slightly from the screenshots in this chapter.)

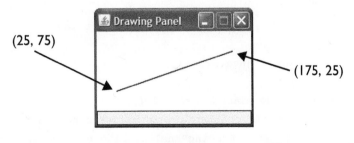

Figure 3G.2 Output of `DrawLine1`

The first statement in `main` constructs a `DrawingPanel` with a width of 200 and a height of 100. Once it has been constructed, the window will pop up on the screen. The second statement draws a line from (25, 75) to (175, 25). The first point is in the lower-left part of the window (25 over from the left, 75 down from the top). The second point is in the upper-right corner (175 over from the left, 25 down from the top).

Notice these particular lines of code:

```
Graphics g = panel.getGraphics();
g.drawLine(25, 75, 175, 25);
```

You might wonder why you can't just say:

```
panel.drawLine(25, 75, 175, 25);   // this is illegal
```

The problem is that there are two different objects involved in this program: the `DrawingPanel` itself (the canvas) and the `Graphics` object associated with the panel (the paintbrush). The panel doesn't know how to draw a line; only the `Graphics` object knows how to do this. You have to be careful to make sure that you are talking to the right object when you give a command.

This requirement can be confusing, but it is common in Java programs. In fact, in a typical Java program, there are hundreds (if not thousands) of objects interacting with each other. These interactions aren't so unlike interactions between people. If you want to schedule a meeting, a busy corporate executive might tell you, "Talk to my secretary about that." Or if you're asking difficult legal questions, a person might tell you, "Talk to my lawyer about that." In this case, the `DrawingPanel` doesn't know how to draw, so if it could talk it would say, "Talk to my `Graphics` object about that."

It's also legal to use the `Graphics` object without storing it in a variable, like this:

```
panel.getGraphics().drawLine(25, 75, 175, 25);   // also legal
```

But you'll often want to send several commands to the `Graphics` object, so it's more convenient to give it a name and store it in a variable.

Let's look at a more complicated example:

```
1  // Draws three lines to make a triangle.
2
3  import java.awt.*;
4
5  public class DrawLine2 {
6      public static void main(String[] args) {
7          DrawingPanel panel = new DrawingPanel(200, 100);
8
```

```
 9               // draw a triangle on the panel
10               Graphics g = panel.getGraphics();
11                 g.drawLine(25, 75, 100, 25);
12                 g.drawLine(100, 25, 175, 75);
13                 g.drawLine(25, 75, 175, 75);
14         }
15  }
```

This program draws three different lines to form a triangle, as shown in Figure 3G.3. The lines are drawn between three different points. In the lower-left corner we have the point (25, 75). In the middle at the top we have the point (100, 25). And in the lower-right corner we have the point (175, 75). The various calls on drawLine simply draw the lines that connect these three points.

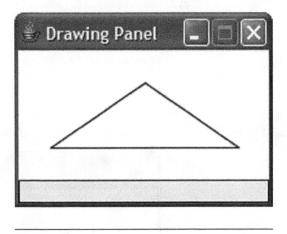

Figure 3G.3   Output of DrawLine2

The Graphics object also has methods for drawing particular shapes. For example, you can draw rectangles with the drawRect method:

```
g.drawRect(<x>, <y>, <width>, <height>);
```

This draws a rectangle with upper-left coordinates (*x*, *y*) and the given height and width.

Another figure you'll often want to draw is a circle or, more generally, an oval. But how do you specify where it appears and how big it is? What you actually specify is what is known as the "bounding rectangle" of the circle or oval. Java will draw the largest oval possible that fits inside that rectangle. So, the method:

```
g.drawOval(<x>, <y>, <width>, <height>);
```

draws the largest oval that fits within the rectangle with upper-left coordinates (*x*, *y*) and the given height and width.

Notice that the first two values passed to drawRect and drawOval are coordinates, while the next two values are a width and a height. For example, here is a short program that draws two rectangles and two ovals:

```
1   // Draws several shapes.
2
3   import java.awt.*;
4
5   public class DrawShapes1 {
6       public static void main(String[] args) {
7           DrawingPanel panel = new DrawingPanel(200, 100);
8
9           Graphics g = panel.getGraphics();
10          g.drawRect(25, 50, 20, 20);
11          g.drawRect(150, 10, 40, 20);
12          g.drawOval(50, 25, 20, 20);
13          g.drawOval(150, 50, 40, 20);
14      }
15  }
```

Figure 3G.4 shows the output of the program.

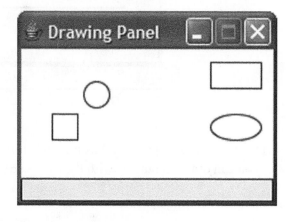

Figure 3G.4   Output of DrawShapes1

The first rectangle has its upper-left corner at the coordinates (25, 50). Its width and height are each 20, so this is a square. The coordinates of its lower-right corner would be (45, 70), or 20 more than the (x, y) coordinates of the upper-left corner. The program also draws a rectangle with its upper-left corner at (150, 10) that has a width of 40 and a height of 20 (wider than it is tall). The bounding rectangle of the first oval has upper-left coordinates (50, 25) and a width and height of 20. In other words, it's a circle. The bounding rectangle of the second oval has upper-left coordinates (150, 50), a width of 40, and a height of 20 (it's an oval that is wider than it is tall).

Sometimes you don't just want to draw the outline of a shape; you want to paint the entire area with a particular color. There are variations of the drawRect and drawOval methods known as fillRect and fillOval that do exactly that, drawing a rectangle or oval and filling it in with the current color of paint (the default is black). Let's change two of the calls in the previous program to be "fill" operations instead of "draw" operations:

```
1   // Draws and fills several shapes.
2
3   import java.awt.*;
4
5   public class DrawShapes2 {
6       public static void main(String[] args) {
7           DrawingPanel panel = new DrawingPanel(200, 100);
8
9           Graphics g = panel.getGraphics();
10          g.fillRect(25, 50, 20, 20);
11          g.drawRect(150, 10, 40, 20);
12          g.drawOval(50, 25, 20, 20);
13          g.fillOval(150, 50, 40, 20);
14      }
15  }
```

Now we get the output shown in Figure 3G.5 instead.

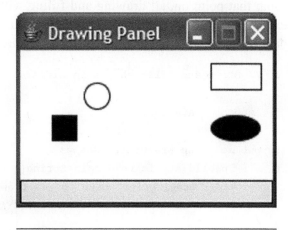

Figure 3G.5   Output of DrawShapes2

Colors

All of the shapes and lines drawn by the preceding programs were black, and all of the panels had a white background. These are the default colors, but you can change the background color of the panel, and you can change the color being used by the Graphics object as many times as you like. To change these colors, you use the standard Color class, which is part of the java.awt package.

Table 3G.3   Color Constants

Color.BLACK	Color.GREEN	Color.RED
Color.BLUE	Color.LIGHT_GRAY	Color.WHITE
Color.CYAN	Color.MAGENTA	Color.YELLOW
Color.DARK_GRAY	Color.ORANGE	
Color.GRAY	Color.PINK	

There are a number of predefined colors that you can refer to directly. They are defined as class constants in the Color class (a lot like the constants we used in Chapter 2). The names of these constants are all in uppercase and are self-explanatory. To refer to one of these colors, you have to precede it with the class name and a dot, as in Color.GREEN or Color.BLUE. The predefined Color constants are listed in Table 3G.3.

As mentioned earlier, the DrawingPanel object has a method that can be used to change the background color that covers the entire panel:

```
<panel>.setBackground(<color>);
```

Likewise, the Graphics object has a method that can be used to change the current color that draws or fills shapes and lines:

```
g.setColor(<color>);
```

Calling setColor is like dipping your paintbrush in a different color of paint. From that point on, all drawing and filling will be done in the specified color. For example, here is another version of the previous program that uses a cyan (light blue) background color and fills in the oval and square with white instead of black:

```
1   // Draws and fills shapes in different colors.
2
3   import java.awt.*;
4
5   public class DrawColoredShapes {
6       public static void main(String[] args) {
7           DrawingPanel panel = new DrawingPanel(200, 100);
8           panel.setBackground(Color.CYAN);
9
10          Graphics g = panel.getGraphics();
11          g.drawRect(150, 10, 40, 20);
12          g.drawOval(50, 25, 20, 20);
13          g.setColor(Color.WHITE);
14          g.fillOval(150, 50, 40, 20);
15          g.fillRect(25, 50, 20, 20);
16      }
17  }
```

This program produces the output shown in Figure 3G.6. (The figures shown in this textbook may not match the colors you would see on your screen.)

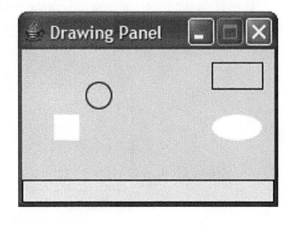

Figure 3G.6   Output of `DrawColoredShapes`

Notice that you tell the panel to set the background color, while you tell the `Graphics` object to set the foreground color. The reasoning is that the background color is a property of the entire window, while the foreground color affects only the particular shapes that you draw.

Notice also that the order of the calls has been rearranged. The two drawing commands appear first, then the call on `setColor` that changes the color to white, then the two filling commands. This ensures that the drawing is done in black and the filling is done in white. The order of operations is very important in these drawing programs, so you'll have to keep track of what your current color is each time you give a new command to draw or fill something.

Common Programming Error

Misunderstanding Draw vs. Fill

Some new programmers think that a shape must be drawn (such as with `drawRect`) before it can be filled in (such as with `fillRect`). This is not the case. In fact, when you are trying to draw an outlined shape, this is exactly the wrong thing to do. Suppose you want to draw a 60 × 30 green rectangle with a black border at (20, 50). You might write the following code:

```
g.setColor(Color.BLACK);   // incorrect code
g.drawRect(20, 50, 60, 30);
g.setColor(Color.GREEN);
g.fillRect(20, 50, 60, 30);
```

Continued on next page

Continued from previous page

However, the fill command covers the same pixels as the draw command, and the green interior will be drawn over the black outline, leading to the following appearance:

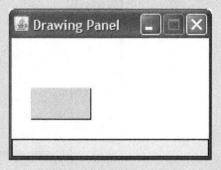

Instead, the code should fill the interior of the rectangle first, then draw the black outline, to make sure that the outline shows on top of the filling. The following is the correct code and its output:

```
g.setColor(Color.GREEN);    // corrected code
g.fillRect(20, 50, 60, 30);
g.setColor(Color.BLACK);
g.drawRect(20, 50, 60, 30);
```

Drawing with Loops

In each of the preceding examples we used simple constants for the drawing and filling commands, but it is possible to use expressions. For example, suppose that we stick with our DrawingPanel size of 200 pixels wide and 100 pixels tall and we want to produce a diagonal series of four rectangles that extend from the upper-left corner to the lower-right corner, each with a white oval inside. In other words, we want to produce the output shown in Figure 3G.7.

The overall width of 200 and overall height of 100 are divided evenly into four rectangles, which means that they must all be 50 pixels wide and 25 pixels high. So, width and height values for the four rectangles are the same, but the positions of their

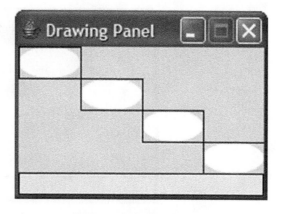

Figure 3G.7   Desired Output of `DrawLoop1`

upper-left corners are different. The first rectangle's upper-left corner is at (0, 0), the second is at (50, 25), the third is at (100, 50), and the fourth is at (150, 75). We need to write code to generate these different coordinates.

This is a great place to use a `for` loop. Using the techniques introduced in Chapter 2, we can make a table and develop a formula for the coordinates. In this case it is easier to have the loop start with 0 rather than 1, which will often be the case with drawing programs. Here is a program that makes a good first stab at generating the desired output:

```
1   // Draws boxed ovals using a for loop (flawed version).
2
3   import java.awt.*;
4
5   public class DrawLoop1 {
6       public static void main(String[] args) {
7           DrawingPanel panel = new DrawingPanel(200, 100);
8           panel.setBackground(Color.CYAN);
9
10          Graphics g = panel.getGraphics();
11          for (int i = 0; i < 4; i++) {
12              g.drawRect(i * 50, i * 25, 50, 25);
13              g.setColor(Color.WHITE);
14              g.fillOval(i * 50, i * 25, 50, 25);
15          }
16      }
17  }
```

This program produces the output shown in Figure 3G.8.

The coordinates and sizes are right, but not the colors. Instead of getting four black rectangles with white ovals inside, we're getting one black rectangle and three white rectangles. That's because we only have one call on `setColor` inside the loop. Initially the color will be set to black, which is why the first rectangle comes out

Figure 3G.8   Output of DrawLoop1

black. But once we make a call on setColor changing the color to white, every subsequent drawing and filling command is done in white, including the second, third,
and fourth rectangles.

So, we need to include calls to set the color to black, to draw the rectangles, and to
set the color to white to draw the filled ovals. While we're at it, it's a good idea to
switch the order of these tasks. The rectangles and ovals overlap slightly, and we would
rather have the rectangle drawn over the oval than the other way around. The following
program produces the correct output:

```
1   // Draws boxed ovals using a for loop.
2
3   import java.awt.*;
4
5   public class DrawLoop2 {
6       public static void main(String[] args) {
7           DrawingPanel panel = new DrawingPanel(200, 100);
8           panel.setBackground(Color.CYAN);
9
10          Graphics g = panel.getGraphics();
11          for (int i = 0; i < 4; i++) {
12              g.setColor(Color.WHITE);
13              g.fillOval(i * 50, i * 25, 50, 25);
14              g.setColor(Color.BLACK);
15              g.drawRect(i * 50, i * 25, 50, 25);
16          }
17      }
18  }
```

It's also possible to create custom Color objects of your own, rather than
using the constant colors provided in the Color class. Computer monitors use red,
green, and blue (RGB) as their primary colors, so when you construct a Color

object you pass your own parameter values for the redness, greenness, and blueness of the color:

```
new Color(<red>, <green>, <blue>)
```

The red/green/blue components should be integer values between 0 and 255. The higher the value, the more of that color is mixed in. All 0 values produce black, and all 255 values produce white. Values of (0, 255, 0) produce a pure green, while values of (128, 0, 128) make a dark purple color (because red and blue are mixed). Search for "RGB table" in your favorite search engine to find tables of many common colors.

The following program demonstrates the use of custom colors. It uses a class constant for the number of rectangles to draw and produces a blend of colors from black to white:

```
 1   // Draws a smooth color gradient from black to white.
 2
 3   import java.awt.*;
 4
 5   public class DrawColorGradient {
 6       public static final int RECTS = 32;
 7
 8       public static void main(String[] args) {
 9           DrawingPanel panel = new DrawingPanel(256, 256);
10           panel.setBackground(new Color(255, 128, 0)); // orange
11
12           Graphics g = panel.getGraphics();
13
14           // from black to white, top left to bottom right
15           for (int i = 0; i < RECTS; i++) {
16               int shift = i * 256 / RECTS;
17               g.setColor(new Color(shift, shift, shift));
18               g.fillRect(shift, shift, 20, 20);
19           }
20       }
21   }
```

This program produces the output shown in Figure 3G.9.

It is also legal to store a Color object into a variable or pass it as a parameter. For example, we could have written the coloring code in the preceding program as follows:

```
Color c = new Color(shift, shift, shift);
g.setColor(c);
...
```

We will use this idea later when parameterizing colors in this chapter's Case Study.

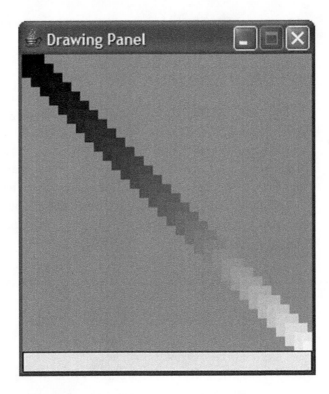

Figure 3G.9 Output of `DrawColorGradient`

Text and Fonts

Another drawing command worth mentioning can be used to include text in your drawings. The `drawString` method of the `Graphics` object draws the given `String` with its lower-left corner at coordinates (*x*, *y*):

```
g.drawString(<message>, <x>, <y>);
```

This is a slightly different convention than we used for `drawRect`. With `drawRect`, we specified the coordinates of the upper-left corner. Here we specify the coordinates of the lower-left corner. By default, text is drawn approximately 10 pixels high. Here is a sample program that uses a loop to draw a particular `string` 10 different times, each time indenting it 5 pixels to the right and moving it down 10 pixels from the top:

```
1   // Draws a message several times.
2
3   import java.awt.*;
4
5   public class DrawStringMessage1 {
6       public static void main(String[] args) {
7           DrawingPanel panel = new DrawingPanel(200, 100);
```

```
 8              panel.setBackground(Color.YELLOW);
 9
10              Graphics g = panel.getGraphics();
11              for (int i = 0; i < 10; i++) {
12                      g.drawString("There is no place like home",
13                              i * 5, 10 + i * 10);
14              }
15      }
16 }
```

This program produces the output shown in Figure 3G.10.

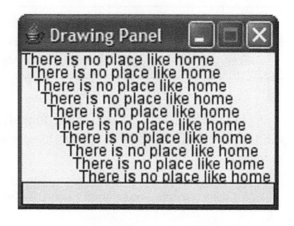

Figure 3G.10   Output of `DrawStringMessage`

Fonts are used to describe different styles for writing characters on the screen. If you'd like to change the style or size of the onscreen text, you can use the `setFont` method of the `Graphics` object.

> **Font**
>
> An overall design for a set of text characters, including the style, size, weight, and appearance of each character.

This method changes the text size and style in which strings are drawn.

The parameter to `setFont` is a `Font` object. A `Font` object is constructed by passing three parameters—the font's name as a `String`, its style (such as bold or italic), and its size as an integer:

```
new Font(<name>, <style>, <size>)
```

Common font styles such as bold are implemented as constants in the `Font` class. The available constants and some popular font names are listed in Tables 3G.4 and 3G.5.

Table 3G.4   Useful Constants of the Font Class

Constant	Displays
Font.BOLD	**Bold text**
Font.ITALIC	*Italic text*
Font.BOLD + Font.ITALIC	***Bold/Italic text***
Font.PLAIN	Plain text

Table 3G.5   Common Font Names

Name	Description
"Monospaced"	a typewriter font, such as Courier New
"SansSerif"	a font without curves (serifs) at letter edges, such as Arial
"Serif"	a font with curved edges, such as Times New Roman

As in the case of colors, setting the font affects only strings that are drawn after the font is set. The following program sets several fonts and uses them to draw strings:

```
1   // Draws several messages using different fonts.
2
3   import java.awt.*;
4
5   public class DrawFonts {
6       public static void main(String[] args) {
7           DrawingPanel panel = new DrawingPanel(200, 100);
8           panel.setBackground(Color.PINK);
9
10          Graphics g = panel.getGraphics();
11          g.setFont(new Font("Monospaced",
12                  Font.BOLD + Font.ITALIC, 36));
13          g.drawString("Too big", 20, 40);
14
15          g.setFont(new Font("SansSerif", Font.PLAIN, 10));
16          g.drawString("Too small", 30, 60);
17
18          g.setFont(new Font("Serif", Font.ITALIC, 18));
19          g.drawString("Just right", 40, 80);
20      }
21  }
```

This program produces the output shown in Figure 3G.11.

Figure 3G.11   Output of `DrawFonts`

Images

The `DrawingPanel` is also capable of displaying images loaded from files in formats such as JPEG, PNG, and GIF. To display an image, first you must find an image file (such as one on the internet or on your computer) and place it into the same directory as your code project. Images are displayed in two steps: first the image must be loaded from the hard drive into an `Image` object, and then your panel's `Graphics` object can display the image.

```
Image <name> = <panel>.loadImage("<filename>");
g.drawImage(<name>, <x>, <y>, <panel>);
```

The *x* and *y* coordinates passed when drawing the image represent its top/left corner pixel position.

There are a few quirks to the syntax. One is that we use the `DrawingPanel` to load the image, while you use the `Graphics` object to draw it. It's easy to accidentally get the two mixed up. Also, unlike the other drawing commands, `drawImage` requires you to pass the `DrawingPanel` as a last parameter to the method. This is required by Java's `Graphics` class in order for the code to compile.

For example, the following program loads an image that looks like a drawing of a rainbow and draws it onto the `DrawingPanel` with a text string underneath it.

```
// This program displays a rainbow from an image file.
import java.awt.*;

public class DrawRainbow {
    public static void main(String[] args) {
```

```
DrawingPanel panel = new DrawingPanel(280, 200);
Image rainbow = panel.loadImage("rainbow.png");
Graphics g = panel.getGraphics();
g.drawImage(rainbow, 0, 0, panel);
g.drawString("Somewhere over the rainbow...", 10, 180);
    }
}
```

The program produces the output shown in Figure 3G.12.

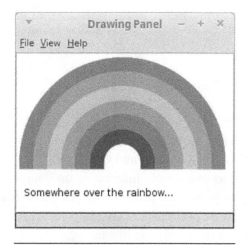

Figure 3G.12   Output of `DrawRainbow`

If you want to draw the same image multiple times on the panel, you don't need to repeat the `loadImage` part of the process. It is much more efficient to load the image a single time and then draw it as many times as you like. The following code would draw several copies of an image in a file named `smiley.png`, which is 100×100 pixels in size. The output of this code is shown in Figure 3G.13.

```
Image smileyFace = panel.loadImage("smiley.png");
Graphics g = panel.getGraphics();
for (int i = 0; i < 4; i++) {
    g.drawImage(smileyFace, i * 110 + 10, 10, panel);
}
```

Figure 3G.13 Smiley face output

3G.2 Procedural Decomposition with Graphics

VideoNote

If you write complex drawing programs, you will want to break them down into several static methods to structure the code and to remove redundancy. When you do this, you'll have to pass the Graphics object to each static method that you introduce. For a quick example, the DrawStringMessage1 program from the previous section could be split into a main method and a drawText method, as follows:

```
1   // Draws a message several times using a static method.
2
3   import java.awt.*;
4
5   public class DrawStringMessage2 {
6       public static void main(String[] args) {
7           DrawingPanel panel = new DrawingPanel(200, 100);
8           panel.setBackground(Color.YELLOW);
9
10          Graphics g = panel.getGraphics();
11          drawText(g);
12      }
13
14      public static void drawText(Graphics g) {
15          for (int i = 0; i < 10; i++) {
16              g.drawString("There is no place like home",
17                           i * 5, 10 + i * 10);
18          }
19      }
20  }
```

This program produces the same output as the original program (Figure 3G.10).

The program wouldn't compile without passing Graphics g to the drawText method, because g is needed to call drawing methods such as drawString and fillRect.

A Larger Example: `DrawDiamonds`

Now let's consider a slightly more complicated task: drawing the largest diamond figure that will fit into a box of a particular size. The largest diamond that can fit into a box of size 50 × 50 is shown in Figure 3G.14.

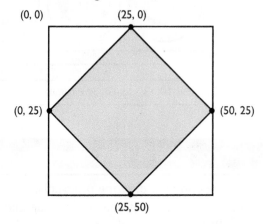

Figure 3G.14   Diamond

The code to draw such a diamond would be the following:

```
g.drawRect(0, 0, 50, 50);
g.drawLine(0, 25, 25, 0);
g.drawLine(25, 0, 50, 25);
g.drawLine(50, 25, 25, 50);
g.drawLine(25, 50, 0, 25);
```

Now imagine that we wish to draw three such 50 × 50 diamonds at different locations. We can turn our diamond-drawing code into a `drawDiamond` method that we'll call three times. Since each diamond will be in a different position, we can pass the *x*- and *y*-coordinates as parameters to our `drawDiamond` method.

A diamond enclosed by a box with top-left corner at the location (78, 22) is shown in Figure 3G.15.

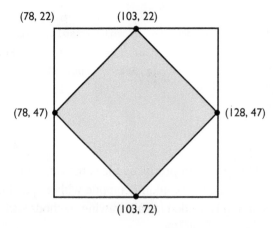

Figure 3G.15   Diamond at (78, 22)

The code to draw this diamond would be the following:

```
g.drawRect(78, 22, 50, 50);
g.drawLine(78, 47, 103, 22);
g.drawLine(103, 22, 128, 47);
g.drawLine(128, 47, 103, 72);
g.drawLine(103, 72, 78, 47);
```

As you can see, the parameter values passed to the drawRect and drawLine methods are very similar to those of the first diamond, except that they're shifted by 78 in the *x*-direction and 22 in the *y*-direction (except for the third and fourth parameters to drawRect, since these are the rectangle's width and height). This (78, 22) shift is called an *offset*.

We can generalize the coordinates to pass to Graphics g's drawing commands so that they'll work with any diamond if we pass that diamond's top-left *x*- and *y*-offset. For example, we'll generalize the line from (0, 25) to (25, 0) in the first diamond and from (78, 47) to (103, 22) in the second diamond by saying that it is a line from $(x, y + 25)$ to $(x + 25, y)$, where (x, y) is the offset of the given diamond.

The following program uses the drawDiamond method to draw three diamonds without redundancy:

```
1   // This program draws several diamond figures of size 50x50.
2
3   import java.awt.*;
4
5   public class DrawDiamonds {
6       public static void main(String[] args) {
7           DrawingPanel panel = new DrawingPanel(250, 150);
8           Graphics g = panel.getGraphics();
9
10          drawDiamond(g, 0, 0);
11          drawDiamond(g, 78, 22);
12          drawDiamond(g, 19, 81);
13      }
14
15      // draws a diamond in a 50x50 box
16      public static void drawDiamond(Graphics g, int x, int y) {
17          g.drawRect(x, y, 50, 50);
18          g.drawLine(x, y + 25, x + 25, y);
19          g.drawLine(x + 25, y, x + 50, y + 25);
20          g.drawLine(x + 50, y + 25, x + 25, y + 50);
21          g.drawLine(x + 25, y + 50, x, y + 25);
22      }
23  }
```

This program produces the output shown in Figure 3G.16.

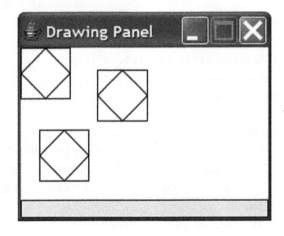

Figure 3G.16   Output of DrawDiamonds

It's possible to draw patterned figures in loops and to have one drawing method call another. For example, if we want to draw five diamonds, starting at (12, 15) and spaced 60 pixels apart, we just need a for loop that repeats five times and shifts the *x*-coordinate by 60 each time. Here's an example loop:

```
for (int i = 0; i < 5; i++) {
    drawDiamond(g, 12 + 60 * i, 15);
}
```

If we created another method to draw the line of five diamonds, we could call it from main to draw many lines of diamonds. Here's a modified version of the DrawDiamonds program with two graphical methods:

```
1   // This program draws several diamond figures of size 50x50.
2
3   import java.awt.*;
4
5   public class DrawDiamonds2 {
6       public static void main(String[] args) {
7           DrawingPanel panel = new DrawingPanel(360, 160);
8           Graphics g = panel.getGraphics();
9
10          drawManyDiamonds(g, 12, 15);
11          g.setColor(Color.RED);
12          drawManyDiamonds(g, 55, 100);
13      }
14
15      // draws five diamonds in a horizontal line
```

```
16      public static void drawManyDiamonds(Graphics g,
17                                          int x, int y) {
18          for (int i = 0; i < 5; i++) {
19              drawDiamond(g, x + 60 * i, y);
20          }
21      }
22
23      // draws a diamond in a 50x50 box
24      public static void drawDiamond(Graphics g, int x, int y) {
25          g.drawRect(x, y, 50, 50);
26          g.drawLine(x, y + 25, x + 25, y);
27          g.drawLine(x + 25, y, x + 50, y + 25);
28          g.drawLine(x + 50, y + 25, x + 25, y + 50);
29          g.drawLine(x + 25, y + 50, x, y + 25);
30      }
31  }
```

This program produces the output shown in Figure 3G.17.

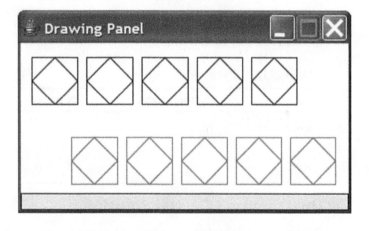

Figure 3G.17   Output of `DrawDiamonds2`

3G.3 Case Study: Pyramids

Imagine that you've been asked to write a program that will draw the images in Figure 3G.18 onto a `DrawingPanel`.

The overall drawing panel has a size of 350 × 250. Each pyramid is 100 pixels high and 100 pixels wide. The pyramids consist of centered flights of colored stairs

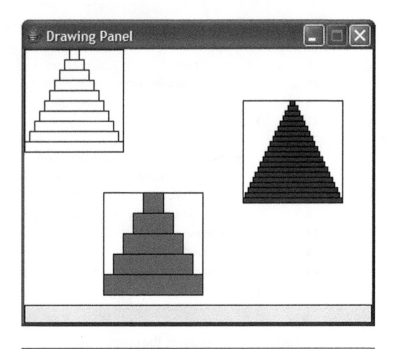

Figure 3G.18   Desired Pyramids Output

that widen toward the bottom, with black outlines around each stair. Table 3G.6 lists the attributes of each pyramid.

Table 3G.6   **Pyramid Attributes**

Fill color	Top-left corner	Number of stairs	Height of each stair
white	(0, 0)	10 stairs	10 pixels
red	(80, 140)	5 stairs	20 pixels
blue	(220, 50)	20 stairs	5 pixels

Unstructured Partial Solution

When trying to solve a larger and more complex problem like this, it's important to tackle it piece by piece and make iterative enhancements toward a final solution. Let's begin by trying to draw the top-left white pyramid correctly.

Each stair is centered horizontally within the pyramid. The top stair is 10 pixels wide. Therefore, it is surrounded by $\frac{90}{2}$ or 45 pixels of empty space on either side.

That means that the 10×10 rectangle's top-left corner is at (45, 0). The second stair is 20 pixels wide, meaning that it's surrounded by $\frac{80}{2}$ or 40 pixels on each side:

(0, 0)

← 45 ———→   10   ←——— 45 →

← 40 →   20   ← 40 →

The following program draws the white pyramid in the correct position:

```
1   import java.awt.*;
2
3   // Draws the first pyramid only, with a lot of redundancy.
4   public class Pyramids1 {
5       public static void main(String[] args) {
6           DrawingPanel panel = new DrawingPanel(350, 250);
7           Graphics g = panel.getGraphics();
8
9           // draws the border rectangle
10          g.drawRect(0, 0, 100, 100);
11
12          // draws the 10 "stairs" in the white pyramid
13          g.drawRect(45,  0,  10, 10);
14          g.drawRect(40, 10,  20, 10);
15          g.drawRect(35, 20,  30, 10);
16          g.drawRect(30, 30,  40, 10);
17          g.drawRect(25, 40,  50, 10);
18          g.drawRect(20, 50,  60, 10);
19          g.drawRect(15, 60,  70, 10);
20          g.drawRect(10, 70,  80, 10);
21          g.drawRect( 5, 80,  90, 10);
22          g.drawRect( 0, 90, 100, 10);
23      }
24  }
```

Looking at the code, it's clear that there's a lot of redundancy among the 10 lines to draw the stairs. Examining the patterns of numbers in each column reveals that the x value decreases by 5 each time, the y value increases by 10 each time, the width increases by 10 each time, and the height stays the same.

Another way of describing a stair's x value is to say that it is half of the overall 100 minus the stair's width. With that in mind, the following for loop draws the 10 stairs without the previous redundancy:

```
for (int i = 0; i < 10; i++) {
    int stairWidth = 10 * (i + 1);
    int stairHeight = 10;
    int stairX = (100 - stairWidth) / 2;
    int stairY = 10 * i;
    g.drawRect(stairX, stairY, stairWidth, stairHeight);
}
```

Generalizing the Drawing of Pyramids

Next let's add code to draw the bottom (red) pyramid. Its (x, y) position is (80, 140) and it has only five stairs. That means each stair is twice as tall and wide as those in the white pyramid.

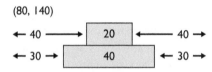

Given this information, we can determine that the top stair's upper-left corner is at (120, 140) and its size is 20×20, the second stair's upper-left corner is at (110, 160) and its size is 40×20, and so on.

For the moment, let's focus on getting the coordinates of the stairs right and not worry about the red fill color. Here is a redundant bit of code to draw the red pyramid's stairs, without the coloring:

```
// draws the border rectangle
g.drawRect(80, 140, 100, 100);
// draws the 5 "stairs" of the red pyramid
g.drawRect(120, 140, 20, 20);
g.drawRect(110, 160, 40, 20);
g.drawRect(100, 180, 60, 20);
g.drawRect( 90, 200, 80, 20);
g.drawRect( 80, 220, 100, 20);
```

Again we have redundancy among the five lines to draw the stairs, so let's look for a pattern. We'll use a loop to eliminate the redundancy like we did for the last pyramid, but with appropriate modifications. Each stair's height is now 20 pixels, and each stair's width is now 20 times the number for that stair. The x- and y-coordinates are a bit trickier. The x-coordinate formula is similar to the (100 − stairWidth) / 2 from before, but this time it must be shifted right by 80 to account for the position of its bounding box's top-left corner. The y-coordinate must similarly be shifted downward by 140 pixels. Here's the correct loop:

```
// draws the 5 "stairs" of the red pyramid
for (int i = 0; i < 5; i++) {
    int stairWidth = 20 * (i + 1);
    int stairHeight = 20;
    int stairX = 80 + (100 - stairWidth) / 2;
    int stairY = 140 + 20 * i;
    g.drawRect(stairX, stairY, stairWidth, stairHeight);
}
```

Can you spot the pattern between the two `for` loops used to draw the stairs of the pyramids? The *x*- and *y*-coordinates differ only in the addition of the offset from (0, 0) in the second loop. The stairs' widths and heights differ only in that one pyramid's stairs are 20 pixels tall and the other pyramid's stairs are 10 pixels tall (the result of dividing the overall size of 100 by the number of stairs).

Using the preceding information, let's turn the code for drawing a pyramid into a method that we can call three times to avoid redundancy. The parameters will be the (*x*, *y*) coordinates of the top-left corner of the pyramid's bounding box and the number of stairs in the pyramid. We'll also need to pass `Graphics g` as a parameter so that we can draw onto the `DrawingPanel`. We'll modify the `for` loop to compute the stair height first, then use the height to compute the stair width, and finally use the width and height to help compute the (*x*, *y*) coordinates of the stair. Here's the code:

```
public static void drawPyramid(Graphics g, int x,
                               int y, int stairs) {
    // draws the border rectangle
    g.drawRect(x, y, 100, 100);

    // draws the stairs of the pyramid
    for (int i = 0; i < stairs; i++) {
        int stairHeight = 100 / stairs;
        int stairWidth = stairHeight * (i + 1);
        int stairX = x + (100 - stairWidth) / 2;
        int stairY = y + stairHeight * i;
        g.drawRect(stairX, stairY, stairWidth, stairHeight);

    }
}
```

The preceding code is now generalized to draw a pyramid at any location with any number of stairs. But one final ingredient is missing: the ability to give a different color to each pyramid.

Complete Structured Solution

The preceding code is correct except that it doesn't allow us to draw the pyramids in the proper colors. Let's add an additional parameter, a `Color`, to our method and use it to fill the pyramid stairs as needed. We'll pass `Color.WHITE` as this parameter's value for the first white pyramid; it'll fill the stairs with white, even though this isn't necessary.

The way to draw a filled shape with an outline of a different color is to first fill the shape, then use the outline color to draw the same shape. For example, to get red rectangles with black outlines, first we'll use `fillRect` with red, then we'll use `drawRect` with black with the same parameters.

Here's the new version of the `drawPyramid` method that uses the fill color as a parameter:

```java
public static void drawPyramid(Graphics g, Color c,
                               int x, int y, int stairs) {
    g.drawRect(x, y, 100, 100);

    for (int i = 0; i < stairs; i++) {
        int stairHeight = 100 / stairs;
        int stairWidth = stairHeight * (i + 1);
        int stairX = x + (100 - stairWidth) / 2;
        int stairY = y + stairHeight * i;

        g.setColor(c);
        g.fillRect(stairX, stairY, stairWidth, stairHeight);
        g.setColor(Color.BLACK);
        g.drawRect(stairX, stairY, stairWidth, stairHeight);
    }
}
```

Using this method, we can now draw all three pyramids easily by calling `drawPyramid` three times with the appropriate parameters:

```java
drawPyramid(g, Color.WHITE, 0, 0, 10);
drawPyramid(g, Color.RED, 80, 140, 5);
drawPyramid(g, Color.BLUE, 220, 50, 20);
```

One last improvement we can make to our `Pyramids` program is to turn the overall pyramid size of 100 into a constant, so there aren't so many 100s lying around in the code. Here is the complete program:

```java
1   // This program draws three colored pyramid figures.
2
3   import java.awt.*;
4
5   public class Pyramids {
6       public static final int SIZE = 100;
7
8       public static void main(String[] args) {
9           DrawingPanel panel = new DrawingPanel(350, 250);
10          Graphics g = panel.getGraphics();
11
12          drawPyramid(g, Color.WHITE, 0, 0, 10);
13          drawPyramid(g, Color.RED, 80, 140, 5);
14          drawPyramid(g, Color.BLUE, 220, 50, 20);
15      }
16
17      // draws one pyramid figure with the given
```

```
18          // number of stairs at the given (x, y) position
19          // with the given color
20          public static void drawPyramid(Graphics g, Color c,
21                                          int x, int y, int stairs) {
22
23              // draws the border rectangle
24              g.drawRect(x, y, SIZE, SIZE);
25
26              // draws the stairs of the pyramid
27              for (int i = 0; i < stairs; i++) {
28                  int stairHeight = SIZE / stairs;
29                  int stairWidth = stairHeight * (i + 1);
30                  int stairX = x + (SIZE - stairWidth) / 2;
31                  int stairY = y + stairHeight * i;
32
33                  // fills the rectangles with the fill colors
34                  g.setColor(c);
35                  g.fillRect(stairX, stairY, stairWidth, stairHeight);
36
37                  // draws the black rectangle outlines
38                  g.setColor(Color.BLACK);
39                  g.drawRect(stairX, stairY, stairWidth, stairHeight);
40              }
41          }
42      }
```

Chapter Summary

DrawingPanel is a custom class provided by the authors to easily show a graphical window on the screen. A DrawingPanel contains a Graphics object that can be used to draw lines, text, and shapes on the screen using different colors.

———————

A Graphics object has many useful methods for drawing shapes and lines, such as drawLine, fillRect, and setColor. Shapes can be "drawn" (drawing only the outline) or "filled" (coloring the entire shape).

———————

The Graphics object can write text on the screen with its drawString method. You can specify different font styles and sizes with the setFont method.

———————

Graphical programs that are decomposed into methods must pass appropriate parameters to those methods (for example, the Graphics object, as well as any (x, y) coordinates, sizes, or other values that guide the figures to be drawn).

———————

Self-Check Problems

Section 3G.1: Introduction to Graphics

1. Which of the following is the correct syntax to draw a rectangle?

   a. `Graphics g.drawRect(10, 20, 50, 30);`

   b. `g.drawRect(10, 20, 50, 30);`

   c. `g.draw.rectangle(10, 20, 50, 30);`

   d. `Graphics.drawRect(10, 20, 50, 30);`

   e. `g.drawRect(x = 10, y = 20, width = 50, height = 30);`

2. There are two mistakes in the following code, which attempts to draw a line from coordinates (50, 86) to (20, 35). What are they?

   ```
   DrawingPanel panel = new DrawingPanel(200, 200);
   panel.drawLine(50, 20, 86, 35);
   ```

3. The following code attempts to draw a black-filled outer rectangle with a white-filled inner circle inside it:

   ```
   DrawingPanel panel = new DrawingPanel(200, 100);
   Graphics g = panel.getGraphics();
   g.setColor(Color.WHITE);
   g.fillOval(10, 10, 50, 50);
   g.setColor(Color.BLACK);
   g.fillRect(10, 10, 50, 50);
   ```

   However, the graphical output looks like Figure 3G.19 instead. What must be changed for it to look as intended?

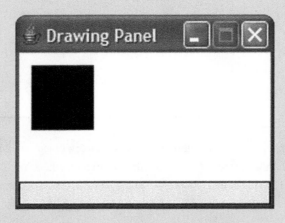

Figure 3G.19   Graphical output of Self-Check 3G.3

4. The following code attempts to draw a black rectangle from (10, 20) to (50, 40) with a line across its diagonal:

   ```
   DrawingPanel panel = new DrawingPanel(200, 100);
   Graphics g = panel.getGraphics();
   g.drawRect(10, 20, 50, 40);
   g.drawLine(10, 20, 50, 40);
   ```

   However, the graphical output looks like Figure 3G.20 instead. What must be changed for it to look as intended?

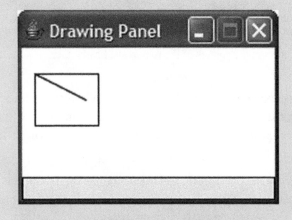

Figure 3G.20   Graphical output of Self-Check 3G.4

5. What sort of figure will be drawn by the following program? Can you draw a picture that will approximately match its appearance without running it first?

```
1   import java.awt.*;
2
3   public class Draw7 {
4       public static void main(String[] args) {
5           DrawingPanel panel = new DrawingPanel(200, 200);
6           Graphics g = panel.getGraphics();
7           for (int i = 0; i < 20; i++) {
8               g.drawOval(i * 10, i * 10, 200 - (i * 10), 200 - (i * 10));
9           }
10      }
11  }
```

Exercises

1. Write a program that uses the DrawingPanel to draw Figure 3G.21.

Figure 3G.21   Expected graphical output of Exercise 3G.1

The window is 220 pixels wide and 150 pixels tall. The background is yellow. There are two blue ovals of size 40×40 pixels. They are 80 pixels apart, and the left oval's top-left corner is located at position (50, 25). There is a red square whose top two corners exactly intersect the centers of the two ovals. Lastly, there is a black horizontal line through the center of the square.

2. Modify your program from the previous exercise to draw the figure by a method called `drawFigure`. The method should accept three parameters: the `Graphics g` of the `DrawingPanel` on which to draw, and a pair of (x, y) coordinates specifying the location of the top-left corner of the figure. Use the following heading for your method:

```
public static void drawFigure(Graphics g, int x, int y)
```

Set your `DrawingPanel`'s size to 450×150 pixels, and use your `drawFigure` method to place two figures on it, as shown in Figure 3G.22. One figure should be at position (50, 25) and the other should be at position (250, 45).

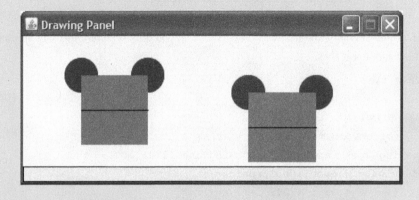

Figure 3G.22   Expected graphical output of Exercise 3G.2

3. Suppose you have the following existing program called `Face` that uses the `DrawingPanel` to draw the face figure shown in Figure 3G.23. Modify the program to draw the modified output shown in Figure 3G.24. Do so by writing a parameterized method that draws a face at different positions. The window size should be changed to 320×180 pixels, and the two faces' top-left corners are at (10, 30) and (150, 50).

Figure 3G.23   Initial graphical output of Exercise 3G.3

```
1   public class Face {
2       public static void main(String[] args) {
3           DrawingPanel panel = new DrawingPanel(220, 150);
```

```
4              Graphics g = panel.getGraphics();

5

6              g.setColor(Color.BLACK);
7              g.drawOval(10, 30, 100, 100);    // face outline

8

9              g.setColor(Color.BLUE);
10             g.fillOval(30, 60, 20, 20);      // eyes
11             g.fillOval(70, 60, 20, 20);

12

13             g.setColor(Color.RED);           // mouth
14             g.drawLine(40, 100, 80, 100);
15         }
16     }
```

Figure 3G.24   Expected graphical output of Exercise 3G.3

4. Modify your previous Face program to draw the new output shown in Figure 3G.25. The window size should be changed to 520 × 180 pixels, and the faces' top-left corners are at (10, 30), (110, 30), (210, 30), (310, 30), and (410, 30).

Figure 3G.25   Expected graphical output of Exercise 3G.4

5. Write a program called ShowDesign that uses the DrawingPanel to draw Figure 3G.26.

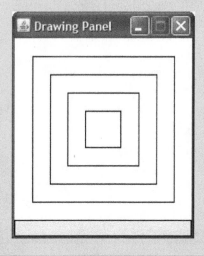

Figure 3G.26   Expected graphical output of Exercise 3G.5

The window is 200 pixels wide and 200 pixels tall. The background is white and the foreground is black. There are 20 pixels between each of the four rectangles, and the rectangles are concentric (their centers are at the same point). Use a loop to draw the repeated rectangles.

6. Modify your ShowDesign program from the previous exercise so that it has a method that accepts parameters for the window width and height and displays the rectangles at the appropriate sizes. For example, if your method was called with values of 300 and 100, the window would look like Figure 3G.27.

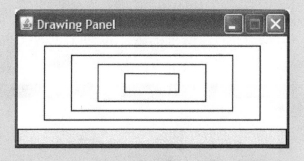

Figure 3G.27   Expected graphical output of Exercise 3G.6

7. Write a program called Squares that uses the DrawingPanel to draw the shape shown in Figure 3G.28.

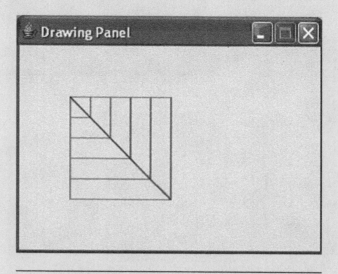

Figure 3G.28 Expected graphical output of Exercise 3G.7

The DrawingPanel is 300 pixels wide by 200 pixels high. Its background is cyan. The horizontal and vertical lines are drawn in red and the diagonal line is drawn in black. The upper-left corner of the diagonal line is at (50, 50). Successive horizontal and vertical lines are spaced 20 pixels apart.

8. Modify your code from the previous exercise to produce the pattern shown in Figure 3G.29.

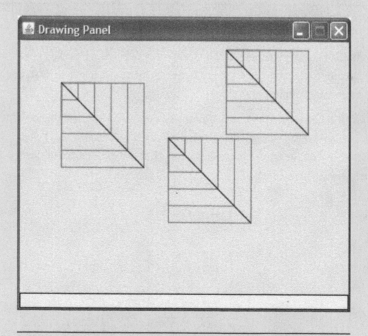

Figure 3G.29 Expected graphical output of Exercise 3G.8

The DrawingPanel is now 400 × 300 pixels in size. The first figure is at the same position, (50, 50). The other figures are at positions (250, 10) and (180, 115), respectively. Use one or more parameterized static methods to reduce the redundancy of your solution.

9. Modify your code from the previous exercise to produce the pattern shown in Figure 3G.30.

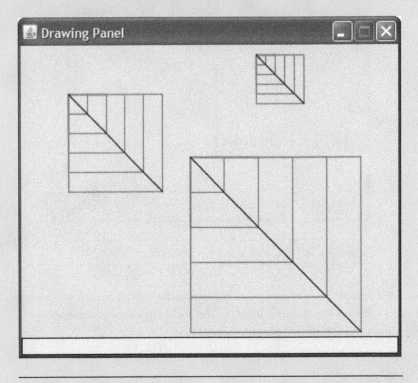

Figure 3G.30   Expected graphical output of Exercise 3G.9

The `DrawingPanel` is the same except that now each figure has a different size. The left figure has its original size of 100, the top-right figure has a size of 50, and the bottom-right figure has a size of 180. Use parameterized static methods to reduce the redundancy of your solution.

10. Write a program called `Stairs` that uses the `DrawingPanel` to draw the figure shown in Figure 3G.31. The first stair's top-left corner is at position (5, 5). The first stair is 10 × 10 pixels in size. Each stair is 10 pixels wider than the one above it. Make a table with the (*x, y*) coordinates and (*width × height*) sizes of the first five stairs. Note which values change and which ones stay the same.

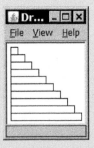

Figure 3G.31   Expected graphical output of Exercise 3G.10

11. Modify your previous `Stairs` program to draw each of the outputs shown in Figure 3G.32. Modify only the body of your loop. (You may want to make a new table to find the expressions for *x*, *y*, *width*, and *height* for each new output.)

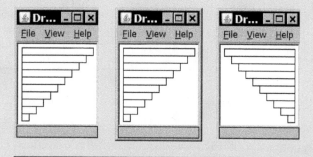

Figure 3G.32   Expected graphical outputs of Exercise 3G.11

12. Write a program called `Triangle` that uses the `DrawingPanel` to draw the figure shown in Figure 3G.33.

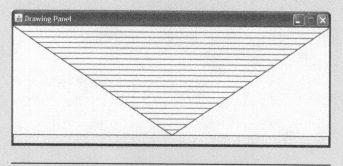

Figure 3G.33   Expected graphical output of Exercise 3G.12

The window is 600×200 pixels in size. The background is yellow and the lines are blue. The lines are 10 pixels apart vertically, and the diagonal lines intersect at the bottom of the figure in its horizontal center.

13. Write a program called `Football` that uses the `DrawingPanel` to draw the figure shown in Figure 3G.34. Though the figure looks to contain curves, it is entirely made of straight lines.

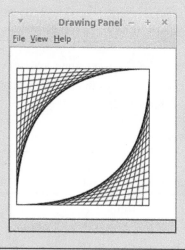

Figure 3G.34   Expected graphical output of Exercise 3G.13

The window is 250×250 pixels in size. There is an outer rectangle from (10, 30) to (210, 230), and a set of black lines drawn around the edges every 10 pixels. For example, along the top-left there is a line from (10, 200) to (20, 30), a line from (10, 190) to (30, 30), a line from (10, 180) to (40, 30), . . . and along the bottom-right there is a line from (20, 210) to (210, 200), a line from (30, 210) to (210, 190), and so on.

Programming Projects

1. Write a program that draws the patterns shown in Figure 3G.35 onto a `DrawingPanel`.

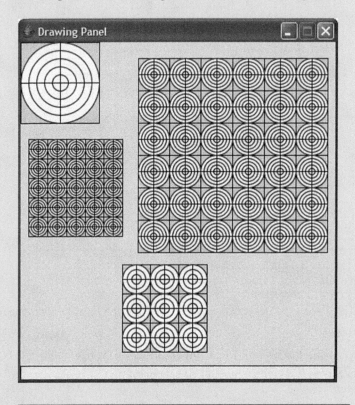

Figure 3G.35   Expected graphical output of Programming Project 3G.1

The `DrawingPanel`'s size is 400×400 pixels and its background color is cyan. It contains four figures of concentric yellow circles with black outlines, all surrounded by a green rectangle with a black outline. The four figures on your `DrawingPanel` should have the properties shown in Table 3G.7.

Table 3G.7   Circle Figure Properties

Description	(x, y) position	Size of subfigures	Number of circles	Number of rows/cols
top left	(0, 0)	100×100	5	1×1
bottom left	(10, 120)	24×24	4	5×5
top right	(150, 20)	40×40	5	6×6
bottom right	(130, 275)	36×36	3	3×3

Break down your program into methods for drawing one subfigure as well as larger grids of subfigures, such as the 5×5 grid at (10, 120).

2. Write a program that draws the image shown in Figure 3G.36 onto a `DrawingPanel` of size 200 × 200. Each stamp is 50 × 50 pixels in size.

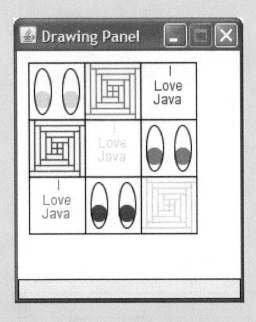

Figure 3G.36 Expected graphical output of Programming Project 3G.2

3. Write a program that draws checkerboards like these shown in Figure 3G.37 onto a `DrawingPanel` of size 420 × 300.

Figure 3G.37 Expected graphical output of Programming Project 3G.3

4. Write a modified version of the `Projectile` case study program from Chapter 3 that draws a graph of the projectile's flight onto a `DrawingPanel` of size 420 × 220. For example, the panel shown in Figure 3G.38 draws a projectile with an initial velocity of 30 meters per second, an angle of 50 degrees, and 10 steps.

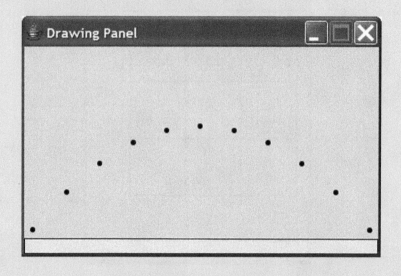

Figure 3G.38   Expected graphical output of Programming Project 3G.4

5. Write a program that draws the image shown in Figure 3G.39 onto a `DrawingPanel` of size 650 × 400. The image represents a famous optical illusion called the "Cafe Wall," in which a series of straight squares appears to be slanted.

Figure 3G.39   Expected graphical output of Programming Project 3G.5

The image has a gray background and many rows of black and white squares with a blue X drawn through each black square. The two free-standing rows in the diagram have the following properties:

Table 3G.8 Cafe Wall Row Properties

Description	(x, y) position	Number of pairs	Size of each box
upper-left	(0, 0)	4	20
mid-left	(50, 70)	5	30

The diagram has four grids of rows of squares, with 2 pixels of vertical space between adjacent rows. A key aspect of the optical illusion is that every other row is shifted horizontally by a particular offset. The four grids have the following properties:

Table 3G.9 Cafe Wall Grid Properties

Description	(x, y) position	Number of pairs	Size of each box	2nd row offset
lower-left	(10, 150)	4	25	0
lower-middle	(250, 200)	3	25	10
lower-right	(425, 180)	5	20	10
upper-right	(400, 20)	2	35	35

Chapter 4
Conditional Execution

Introduction

In the last few chapters, you've seen how to solve complex programming problems using for loops to repeat certain tasks many times. You've also seen how to introduce some flexibility into your programs by using class constants and how to read values input by the user with a Scanner object. Now we are going to explore a much more powerful technique for writing code that can adapt to different situations.

In this chapter, we'll look at *conditional execution* in the form of a control structure known as the if/else statement. With if/else statements, you can instruct the computer to execute different lines of code depending on whether certain conditions are true. The if/else statement, like the for loop, is so powerful that you will wonder how you managed to write programs without it.

This chapter will also expand your understanding of common programming situations. It includes an exploration of loop techniques that we haven't yet examined and includes a discussion of text-processing issues. Adding conditional execution to your repertoire will also require us to revisit methods, parameters, and return values so that you can better understand some of the fine points. The chapter concludes with several rules of thumb that help us to design better procedural programs.

4.1 `if/else` Statements

You will often find yourself writing code that you want to execute some of the time but not all of the time. For example, if you are writing a game-playing program, you might want to print a message each time the user achieves a new high score and store that score. You can accomplish this by putting the required two lines of code inside an `if` statement:

```
if (currentScore > maxScore) {
    System.out.println("A new high score!");
    maxScore = currentScore;
}
```

The idea is that you will sometimes want to execute the two lines of code inside the `if` statement, but not always. The test in parentheses determines whether or not the statements inside the `if` statement are executed. In other words, the test describes the conditions under which we want to execute the code.

The general form of the `if` statement is as follows:

```
if (<test>) {
    <statement>;
    <statement>;
    ...
    <statement>;
}
```

The `if` statement, like the `for` loop, is a control structure. Notice that we once again see a Java keyword (`if`) followed by parentheses and a set of curly braces enclosing a series of controlled statements.

The diagram in Figure 4.1 indicates the flow of control for the simple `if` statement. The computer performs the test, and if it evaluates to `true`, the computer executes the controlled statements. If the test evaluates to `false`, the computer skips the controlled statements.

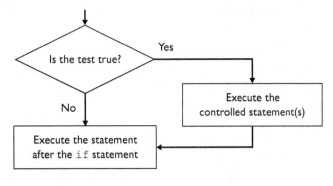

Figure 4.1   Flow of `if` statement

You'll use the simple `if` statement when you have code that you want to execute sometimes and skip other times. Java also has a variation known as the `if/else` statement that allows you to choose between two alternatives. Suppose, for example, that you want to set a variable called `answer` to the square root of a number:

```
answer = Math.sqrt(number);
```

You don't want to ask for the square root if the number is negative. To avoid this potential problem, you could use a simple `if` statement:

```
if (number >= 0) {
    answer = Math.sqrt(number);
}
```

This code will avoid asking for the square root of a negative number, but what value will it assign to `answer` if `number` is negative? In this case, you'll probably want to give a value to `answer` either way. Suppose you want `answer` to be −1 when `number` is negative. You can express this pair of alternatives with the following `if/else` statement:

```
if (number >= 0) {
    answer = Math.sqrt(number);
} else {
    answer = −1;
}
```

The `if/else` statement provides two alternatives and executes one or the other. So, in the code above, you know that `answer` will be assigned a value regardless of whether `number` is positive or negative.

The general form of the `if/else` statement is:

```
if (<test>) {
    <statement>;
    <statement>;
    ...
    <statement>;
} else {
    <statement>;
    <statement>;
    ...
    <statement>;
}
```

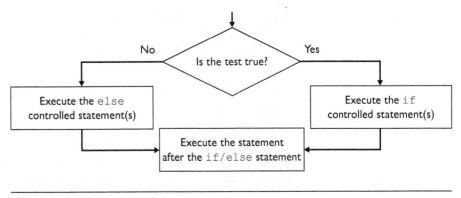

Figure 4.2   Flow of `if/else` statement

This control structure is unusual in that it has two sets of controlled statements and two different keywords (`if` and `else`). Figure 4.2 indicates the flow of control. The computer performs the test and, depending upon whether the code evaluates to `true` or `false`, executes one or the other group of statements.

As in the case of the `for` loop, if you have a single statement to execute, you don't need to include curly braces. However, the Java convention is to include the curly braces even if you don't need them, and we follow that convention in this book.

Relational Operators

An `if/else` statement is controlled by a test. Simple tests compare two expressions to see if they are related in some way. Such tests are themselves expressions of the following form and return either `true` or `false`:

```
<expression> <relational operator> <expression>
```

To evaluate a test of this form, first evaluate the two expressions and then see whether the given relation holds between the value on the left and the value on the right. If the relation holds, the test evaluates to `true`. If not, the test evaluates to `false`.

The relational operators are listed in Table 4.1. Notice that the equality operator consists of two equals signs (`==`), to distinguish it from the assignment operator (`=`).

Table 4.1   **Relational Operators**

Operator	Meaning	Example	Value
`==`	equal to	`2 + 2 == 4`	`true`
`!=`	not equal to	`3.2 != 4.1`	`true`
`<`	less than	`4 < 3`	`false`
`>`	greater than	`4 > 3`	`true`
`<=`	less than or equal to	`2 <= 0`	`false`
`>=`	greater than or equal to	`2.4 >= 1.6`	`true`

Table 4.2   Java Operator Precedence

Description	Operators
unary operators	++, −−, +, −
multiplicative operators	*, /, %
additive operators	+, −
relational operators	<, >, <=, >=
equality operators	==, !=
assignment operators	=, +=, −=, *=, /=, %=

Because we use the relational operators as a new way of forming expressions, we must reconsider precedence. Table 4.2 is an updated version of Table 2.5 that includes these new operators. You will see that, technically, the equality comparisons have a slightly different level of precedence than the other relational operators, but both sets of operators have lower precedence than the arithmetic operators.

Let's look at an example. The following expression is made up of the constants 3, 2, and 9 and contains addition, multiplication, and equality operations:

```
3 + 2 * 2 == 9
```

Which of the operations is performed first? Because the relational operators have a lower level of precedence than the arithmetic operators, the multiplication is performed first, then the addition, then the equality test. In other words, Java will perform all of the "math" operations first before it tests any relationships. This precedence scheme frees you from the need to place parentheses around the left and right sides of a test that uses a relational operator. When you follow Java's precedence rules, the sample expression is evaluated as follows:

```
3   +   2   *   2   ==   9
            ⌣
3   +       4       ==   9
    ⌣
        7           ==   9
        ⌣
            false
```

You can put arbitrary expressions on either side of the relational operator, as long as the types are compatible. Here is a test with complex expressions on either side:

```
(2 − 3 * 8) / (435 % (7 * 2)) <= 3.8 − 4.5 / (2.2 * 3.8)
```

One limitation of the relational operators is that they should be used only with primitive data. Later in this chapter we will talk about how to compare objects for equality, and in a later chapter we'll discuss how to perform less-than and greater-than comparisons on objects.

Nested `if/else` Statements

VideoNote

Many beginners write code that looks like this:

```
if (<test1>) {
    <statement1>;
}
if (<test2>) {
    <statement2>;
}
if (<test3>) {
    <statement3>;
}
```

This sequential structure is appropriate if you want to execute any combination of the three statements. For example, you might write this code in a program for a questionnaire with three optional parts, any combination of which might be applicable for a given person.

Figure 4.3 shows the flow of the sequential `if` code. Notice that it's possible for the computer to execute none of the controlled statements (if all tests are false), just one of them (if only one test happens to be true), or more than one of them (if multiple tests are true).

Often, however, you only want to execute one of a series of statements. In such cases, it is better to *nest* the `if` statements, stacking them one inside another:

```
if (<test1>) {
    <statement1>;
} else {
    if (<test2>) {
        <statement2>;
    } else {
        if (<test3>) {
            <statement3>;
        }
    }
}
```

When you use this construct, you can be sure that the computer will execute at most one statement: the statement corresponding to the first test that evaluates to `true`. If no tests evaluate to `true`, no statement is executed. If executing at most

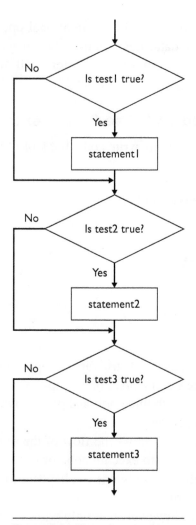

Figure 4.3   Flow of sequential `if`s

one statement is your objective, this construct is more appropriate than the sequential `if` statements. It reduces the likelihood of errors and simplifies the testing process.

As you can see, nesting `if` statements like this leads to a lot of indentation. The indentation isn't very helpful, because this construct is really intended to allow the choice of one of a number of alternatives. K&R style has a solution for this as well. If an `else` is followed by an `if`, we put them on the same line:

```
if (<test1>) {
    <statement1>;
} else if (<test2>) {
    <statement2>;
} else if (<test3>) {
    <statement3>;
}
```

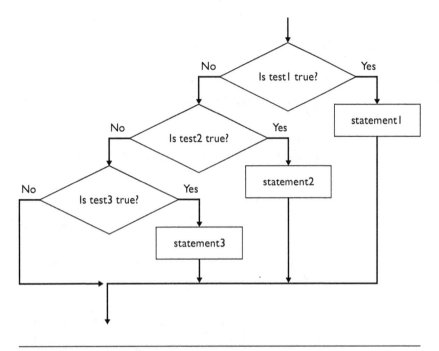

Figure 4.4   Flow of nested `if`s ending in test

When you follow this convention, the various statements all appear at the same level of indentation. We recommend that nested `if/else` statements be indented in this way.

Figure 4.4 shows the flow of the nested `if/else` code. Notice that it is possible to execute one of the controlled statements (the first one that evaluates to `true`) or none (if no tests evaluate to `true`).

In a variation of this structure, the final statement is controlled by an `else` instead of a test:

```
if (<test1>) {
    <statement1>;
} else if (<test2>) {
    <statement2>;
} else {
    <statement3>;
}
```

In this construct, the computer will always select the final branch when all the tests fail, and thus the construct will always execute exactly one of the three statements. Figure 4.5 shows the flow of this modified nested `if/else` code.

To explore these variations, consider the task of having the computer state whether a number is positive, negative, or zero. You could structure this task as three simple `if` statements as follows:

```
if (number > 0) {
    System.out.println("Number is positive.");
}
if (number == 0) {
    System.out.println("Number is zero.");
}
if (number < 0) {
    System.out.println("Number is negative.");
}
```

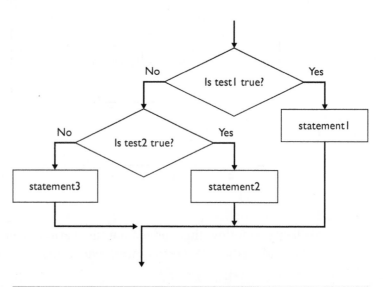

Figure 4.5   Flow of nested `if`s ending in `else`

To determine how many of the `println`s are potentially executed, you have to stop and think about the tests being performed. But you shouldn't have to put that much effort into understanding this code. The code is clearer if you nest the `if` statements:

```
if (number > 0) {
    System.out.println("Number is positive.");
} else if (number == 0) {
    System.out.println("Number is zero.");
} else if (number < 0) {
    System.out.println("Number is negative.");
}
```

This solution has a problem, however. You know that you want to execute one and only one `println` statement, but this nested structure does not preclude the possibility of no statement being executed (which would happen if all three tests failed). Of course, with these particular tests that will never happen: If a number is neither positive nor zero, it must be negative. Thus, the final test here is unnecessary and misleading. You must think about the tests to determine whether or not it is possible for all three tests to fail and all three branches to be skipped.

In this case, the best solution is the nested `if/else` approach with a final branch that is always taken if the first two tests fail:

```java
if (number > 0) {
    System.out.println("Number is positive.");
} else if (number == 0) {
    System.out.println("Number is zero.");
} else {
    System.out.println("Number is negative.");
}
```

You can glance at this construct and see immediately that exactly one `println` will be executed. You don't have to look at the tests being performed in order to realize this; it is a property of this kind of nested `if/else` structure. If you want, you can include a comment to make it clear what is going on:

```java
if (number > 0) {
    System.out.println("Number is positive.");
} else if (number == 0) {
    System.out.println("Number is zero.");
} else { // number must be negative
    System.out.println("Number is negative.");
}
```

One final benefit of this approach is efficiency. When the code includes three simple `if` statements, the computer will always perform all three tests. When the code uses the nested `if/else` approach, the computer carries out tests only until a match is found, which is a better use of resources. For example, in the preceding code we only need to perform one test for positive numbers and at most two tests overall.

When you find yourself writing code to choose among alternatives like these, you have to analyze the particular problem to figure out how many of the branches you potentially want to execute. If it doesn't matter what combination of branches is taken, use sequential `if` statements. If you want one or none of the branches to be taken, use nested `if/else` statements with a test for each statement. If you want exactly one branch to be taken, use nested `if/else` statements with a final branch controlled by an `else` rather than by a test. Table 4.3 summarizes these choices.

Table 4.3   `if/else` Options

Situation	Construct	Basic form
You want to execute any combination of controlled statements	Sequential `ifs`	```if (<test1>) { <statement1>; } if (<test2>) { <statement2>; } if (<test3>) { <statement3>; }```
You want to execute zero or one of the controlled statements	Nested `ifs` ending in test	```if (<test1>) { <statement1>; } else if (<test2>) { <statement2>; } else if (<test3>) { <statement3>; }```
You want to execute exactly one of the controlled statements	Nested `ifs` ending in `else`	```if (<test1>) { <statement1>; } else if (<test2>) { <statement2>; } else { <statement3>; }```

Common Programming Error

Choosing the Wrong `if/else` Construct

Suppose that your instructor has told you that grades will be determined as follows:

A for scores ≥ 90
B for scores ≥ 80
C for scores ≥ 70
D for scores ≥ 60
F for scores < 60

You can translate this scale into code as follows:

```
String grade;
if (score >= 90) {
    grade = "A";
```

Continued on next page

Continued from previous page

```
}
if (score >= 80) {
    grade = "B";
}
if (score >= 70) {
    grade = "C";
}
if (score >= 60) {
    grade = "D";
}
if (score < 60) {
    grade = "F";
}
```

However, if you then try to use the variable `grade` after this code, you'll get this error from the compiler:

```
variable grade might not have been initialized
```

This is a clue that there is a problem. The Java compiler is saying that it believes there are paths through this code that will leave the variable `grade` uninitialized. In fact, the variable will always be initialized, but the compiler cannot figure this out. We can fix this problem by giving an initial value to `grade`:

```
String grade = "no grade";
```

This change allows the code to compile. But if you compile and run the program, you will find that it gives out only two grades: D and F. Anyone who has a score of at least 60 ends up with a D and anyone with a grade below 60 ends up with an F. And even though the compiler complained that there was a path that would allow `grade` not to be initialized, no one ever gets a grade of "no grade."

The problem here is that you want to execute exactly one of the assignment statements, but when you use sequential `if` statements, it's possible for the program to execute several of them sequentially. For example, if a student has a score of 95, that student's `grade` is set to `"A"`, then reset to `"B"`, then reset to `"C"`, and finally reset to `"D"`. You can fix this problem by using a nested `if/else` construct:

```
String grade;
if (score >= 90) {
    grade = "A";
} else if (score >= 80) {
```

Continued on next page

Continued from previous page

```
    grade = "B";
} else if (score >= 70) {
    grade = "C";
} else if (score >= 60) {
    grade = "D";
} else { // score < 60
    grade = "F";
}
```

You don't need to set `grade` to `"no grade"` now because the compiler can see that no matter what path is followed, the variable `grade` will be assigned a value (exactly one of the branches will be executed).

Object Equality

You saw earlier in the chapter that you can use the `==` and `!=` operators to test for equality and nonequality of primitive data, respectively. Unfortunately, these operators do not work the way you might expect when you test for equality of objects like strings. You will have to learn a new way to test objects for equality.

For example, you might write code like the following to read a token from the console and to call one of two different methods depending on whether the user responded with "yes" or "no." If the user types neither word, this code is supposed to print an error message:

```
System.out.print("yes or no? ");
String s = console.next();
if (s == "yes") {
    processYes();
} else if (s == "no") {
    processNo();
} else {
    System.out.println("You didn't type yes or no");
}
```

Unfortunately, this code does not work. No matter what the user enters, this program always prints "You didn't type yes or no". We will explore in detail in Chapter 8 why this code doesn't work. For now the important thing to know is that Java provides a second way of testing for equality that is intended for use with objects. Every Java object has a method called `equals` that takes another object as an argument. You can use this method to ask an object whether it equals another object. For example, we can fix the previous code as follows:

```
System.out.print("yes or no? ");
String s = console.next();
```

```
if (s.equals("yes")) {
    processYes();
} else if (s.equals("no")) {
    processNo();
} else {
    System.out.println("You didn't type yes or no");
}
```

Remember when you're working with strings that you should always call the equals method rather than using ==.

The String class also has a special variation of the equals method called equalsIgnoreCase that ignores case differences (uppercase versus lowercase letters). For example, you could rewrite the preceding code as follows to recognize responses like "Yes," "YES," "No," "NO," yES", and so on:

```
System.out.print("yes or no? ");
String s = console.next();
if (s.equalsIgnoreCase("yes")) {
    processYes();
} else if (s.equalsIgnoreCase("no")) {
    processNo();
} else {
    System.out.println("You didn't type yes or no");
}
```

Factoring if/else Statements

VideoNote

Suppose you are writing a program that plays a betting game with a user and you want to give different warnings about how much cash the user has left. The nested if/else construct that follows distinguishes three different cases: funds less than $500, which is considered low; funds between $500 and $1000, which is considered okay; and funds over $1000, which is considered good. Notice that the user is given different advice in each case:

```
if (money < 500) {
    System.out.println("You have $" + money + " left.");
    System.out.print("Cash is dangerously low. Bet carefully.");
    System.out.print("How much do you want to bet? ");
    bet = console.nextInt();
} else if (money < 1000) {
    System.out.println("You have $" + money + " left.");
    System.out.print("Cash is somewhat low. Bet moderately.");
    System.out.print("How much do you want to bet? ");
    bet = console.nextInt();
} else {
```

```
    System.out.println("You have $" + money + " left.");
    System.out.print("Cash is in good shape. Bet liberally.");
    System.out.print("How much do you want to bet? ");
    bet = console.nextInt();
}
```

This construct is repetitious and can be made more efficient by using a technique called *factoring*. Using this simple technique, you factor out common pieces of code from the different branches of the if/else construct. In the preceding program, three different branches can execute, depending on the value of the variable money. Start by writing down the series of actions being performed in each branch and comparing them, as in Figure 4.6.

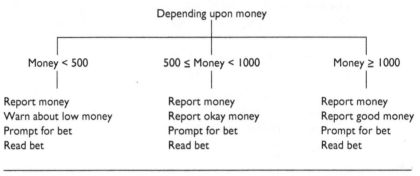

Figure 4.6   if/else branches before factoring

You can factor at both the top and the bottom of a construct like this. If you notice that the top statement in each branch is the same, you factor it out of the branching part and put it before the branch. Similarly, if the bottom statement in each branch is the same, you factor it out of the branching part and put it after the loop. You can factor the top statement in each of these branches and the bottom two statements, as in Figure 4.7.

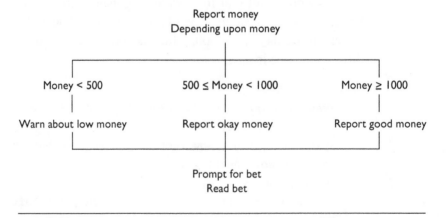

Figure 4.7   if/else branches after factoring

Thus, the preceding code can be reduced to the following more succinct version:

```
System.out.println("You have $" + money + " left.");
if (money < 500) {
```

```
    System.out.print("Cash is dangerously low. Bet carefully.");
} else if (money < 1000) {
    System.out.print("Cash is somewhat low. Bet moderately.");
} else {
    System.out.print("Cash is in good shape. Bet liberally.");
}
System.out.print("How much do you want to bet? ");
bet = console.nextInt();
```

Testing Multiple Conditions

When you are writing a program, you often find yourself wanting to test more than one condition. For example, suppose you want the program to take a particular course of action if a number is between 1 and 10. You might say:

```
if (number >= 1) {
    if (number <= 10) {
        doSomething();
    }
}
```

In these lines of code, you had to write two statements: one testing whether the number was greater than or equal to 1 and one testing whether the number was less than or equal to 10.

Java provides an efficient alternative: You can combine the two tests by using an operator known as the logical AND operator, which is written as two ampersands with no space in between (`&&`). Using the AND operator, we can write the preceding code more simply:

```
if (number >= 1 && number <= 10) {
    doSomething();
}
```

As its name implies, the AND operator forms a test that requires that both parts of the test evaluate to `true`. There is a similar operator known as logical OR that evaluates to `true` if either of two tests evaluates to `true`. The logical OR operator is written using two vertical bar characters (`||`). For example, if you want to test whether a variable `number` is equal to 1 or 2, you can say:

```
if (number == 1 || number == 2) {
    processNumber(number);
}
```

We will explore the logical AND and logical OR operators in more detail in the next chapter.

4.2 Cumulative Algorithms

The more you program, the more you will find that certain patterns emerge. Many common algorithms involve accumulating an answer step by step. In this section, we will explore some of the most common *cumulative algorithms*.

> **Cumulative Algorithm**
>
> An operation in which an overall value is computed incrementally, often using a loop.

For example, you might use a cumulative algorithm over a set of numbers to compute the average value or to find the largest number.

Cumulative Sum

You'll often want to find the sum of a series of numbers. One way to do this is to declare a different variable for each value you want to include, but that would not be a practical solution: If you have to add a hundred numbers together, you won't want to declare a hundred different variables. Fortunately, there is a simpler way.

The trick is to keep a running tally of the result and process one number at a time. For example, to add to a variable called sum, you would write the following line of code:

```
sum = sum + next;
```

Alternatively, you could use the shorthand assignment operator:

```
sum += next;
```

The preceding statement takes the existing value of sum, adds the value of a variable called next, and stores the result as the new value of sum. This operation is performed for each number to be summed. Notice that when you execute this statement for the first time sum does not have a value. To get around this, you initialize sum to a value that will not affect the answer: 0.

Here is a pseudocode description of the cumulative sum algorithm:

```
sum = 0.
for (all numbers to sum) {
    obtain "next".
    sum += next.
}
```

To implement this algorithm, you must decide how many times to go through the loop and how to obtain a next value. Here is an interactive program that prompts the user for the number of numbers to add together and for the numbers themselves:

```
1 // Finds the sum of a sequence of numbers.
2
3 import java.util.*;
4
5 public class ExamineNumbers1 {
6     public static void main(String[] args) {
7         System.out.println("This program adds a sequence of");
8         System.out.println("numbers.");
9         System.out.println();
10
11        Scanner console = new Scanner(System.in);
12
13        System.out.print("How many numbers do you have? ");
14        int totalNumber = console.nextInt();
15
16        double sum = 0.0;
17        for (int i = 1; i <= totalNumber; i++) {
18            System.out.print("    #" + i + "? ");
19            double next = console.nextDouble();
20            sum += next;
21        }
22        System.out.println();
23
24        System.out.println("sum = " + sum);
25    }
26 }
```

The program's execution will look something like this (as usual, user input is boldface):

```
This program adds a sequence of
numbers.

How many numbers do you have? 6
    #1? 3.2
    #2? 4.7
    #3? 5.1
    #4? 9.0
    #5? 2.4
    #6? 3.1

sum = 27.5
```

Let's trace the execution in detail. Before we enter the for loop, we initialize the variable sum to 0.0:

sum   0.0

On the first execution of the `for` loop, we read in a value of `3.2` from the user and add this value to `sum`:

sum `3.2`   next `3.2`

The second time through the loop, we read in a value of `4.7` and add this to the value of `sum`:

sum `7.9`   next `4.7`

Notice that the `sum` now includes both of the numbers entered by the user, because we have added the new value, `4.7`, to the old value, `3.2`. The third time through the loop, we add in the value `5.1`:

sum `13.0`   next `5.1`

Notice that the variable `sum` now contains the sum of the first three numbers (`3.2 + 4.7 + 5.1`). Now we read in `9.0` and add it to the sum:

sum `22.0`   next `9.0`

Then we add in the fifth value, `2.4`:

sum `24.4`   next `2.4`

Finally, we add in the sixth value, `3.1`:

sum `27.5`   next `3.1`

We then exit the `for` loop and print the value of `sum`.

There is an interesting scope issue in this particular program. Notice that the variable `sum` is declared outside the loop, while the variable `next` is declared inside the loop. We have no choice but to declare `sum` outside the loop because it needs to be initialized and it is used after the loop. But the variable `next` is used only inside the loop, so it can be declared in that inner scope. It is best to declare variables in the innermost scope possible.

The cumulative sum algorithm and variations on it will be useful in many of the programming tasks you solve. How would you do a cumulative product? Here is the pseudocode:

```
product = 1.
for (all numbers to multiply) {
    obtain "next".
    product = product * next.
}
```

Min/Max Loops

Another common programming task is to keep track of the maximum and/or minimum values in a sequence. For example, consider the task of deciding whether it will be viable to build a living area on the Moon inhabited by humans. One obstacle is that the average daily surface temperature on the Moon is a chilly −50 degrees Fahrenheit. But a much more daunting problem is the wide range of values; it ranges from a minimum of −240 degrees to a maximum of 250 degrees.

To compute the maximum of a sequence of values, you can keep track of the largest value you've seen so far and use an `if` statement to update the maximum if you come across a new value that is larger than the current maximum. This approach can be described in pseudocode as follows:

```
initialize max.
for (all numbers to examine) {
    obtain "next".
    if (next > max) {
        max = next.
    }
}
```

Initializing the maximum isn't quite as simple as it sounds. For example, novices often initialize `max` to `0`. But what if the sequence of numbers you are examining is composed entirely of negative numbers? For example, you might be asked to find the maximum of this sequence:

$$-84, -7, -14, -39, -410, -17, -41, -9$$

The maximum value in this sequence is –7, but if you've initialized `max` to `0`, the program will incorrectly report `0` as the maximum.

There are two classic solutions to this problem. First, if you know the range of the numbers you are examining, you can make an appropriate choice for `max`. In that case, you can set `max` to the lowest value in the range. That seems counterintuitive because normally we think of the maximum as being large, but the idea is to set `max` to the smallest possible value it could ever be so that anything larger will cause `max` to be reset to that value. For example, if you knew that the preceding sequence of numbers consisted of temperatures in degrees Fahrenheit, you would know that they temperatures could never be smaller than absolute zero (around −460 degrees Fahrenheit), so you could initialize `max` to that value.

The second possibility is to initialize `max` to the first value in the sequence. That won't always be convenient because it means obtaining one of the numbers outside the loop.

When you combine these two possibilities, the pseudocode becomes:

```
initialize max either to lowest possible value or to first value.
for (all numbers to examine) {
    obtain "next".
    if (next > max) {
        max = next;
    }
}
```

The pseudocode for computing the minimum is a slight variation of this code:

```
initialize min either to highest possible value or to first value.
for (all numbers to examine) {
    obtain "next".
    if (next < min) {
        min = next.
    }
}
```

To help you understand this better, let's put the pseudocode into action with a real problem. In mathematics, there is an open problem that involves what are known as *hailstone sequences*. These sequences of numbers often rise and fall in unpredictable patterns, which is somewhat analogous to the process that forms hailstones.

A hailstone sequence is a sequence of numbers in which each value x is followed by:

$(3x + 1)$, if x is odd

$\left(\dfrac{x}{2}\right)$ if x is even

For example, if you start with 7 and construct a sequence of length 10, you get the sequence:

7, 22, 11, 34, 17, 52, 26, 13, 40, 20

In this sequence, the maximum and minimum values are 52 and 7, respectively. If you extend this computation to a sequence of length 20, you get the sequence:

7, 22, 11, 34, 17, 52, 26, 13, 40, 20, 10, 5, 16, 8, 4, 2, 1, 4, 2, 1

In this case, the maximum and minimum values are 52 and 1, respectively.

You will notice that once 1, 2, or 4 appears in the sequence, the sequence repeats itself. It is conjectured that all integers eventually reach 1, like hailstones that fall to the ground. This is an unsolved problem in mathematics. Nobody has been able to disprove it, but nobody has proven it either.

Let's write a method that takes a starting value and a sequence length and prints the maximum and minimum values obtained in a hailstone sequence formed with that starting value and of that length. Our method will look like this:

```
public static void printHailstoneMaxMin(int value, int length) {
    ...
}
```

We can use the starting value to initialize max and min:

```
int min = value;
int max = value;
```

We then need a loop that will generate the other values. The user will input a parameter telling us how many times to go through the loop, but we don't want to execute the loop body `length` times: Remember that the starting value is part of the sequence, so if we want to use a sequence of the given length, we have to make sure that the number of iterations is one less than `length`. Combining this idea with the `max`/`min` pseudocode, we know the loop will look like this:

```
for (int i = 1; i <= length - 1; i++) {
    compute next number.
    if (value > max) {
        max = value.
    } else if (value < min) {
        min = value.
    }
}
print max and min.
```

To fill out the pseudocode for "compute next number," we need to translate the hailstone formula into code. The formula is different, depending on whether the current value is odd or even. We can use an `if`/`else` statement to solve this task. For the test, we can use a "mod 2" test to see what remainder we get when we divide by 2. Even numbers have a remainder of 0 and odd numbers have a remainder of 1. So the test should look like this:

```
if (value % 2 == 0) {
    do even computation.
} else {
    do odd computation.
}
```

Translating the hailstone mathematical formulas into Java, we get the following code:

```
if (value % 2 == 0) {
    value = value / 2;
} else {
    value = 3 * value + 1;
}
```

The only part of our pseudocode that we haven't filled in yet is the part that prints the result. This part comes after the loop and is fairly easy to complete. Here is the complete method:

```
public static void printHailstoneMaxMin(int value, int length) {
    int min = value;
    int max = value;
```

```
for (int i = 1; i <= length - 1; i++) {
    if (value % 2 == 0) {
        value = value / 2;
    } else {
        value = 3 * value + 1;
    }
    if (value > max) {
        max = value;
    } else if (value < min) {
        min = value;
    }
}
System.out.println("max = " + max);
System.out.println("min = " + min);
}
```

Cumulative Sum with `if`

Let's now explore how you can use `if`/`else` statements to create some interesting variations on the cumulative sum algorithm. Suppose you want to read a sequence of numbers and compute the average. This task seems like a straightforward variation of the cumulative sum code. You can compute the average as the sum divided by the number of numbers:

```
double average = sum / totalNumber;
System.out.println("average = " + average);
```

But there is one minor problem with this code. Suppose that when the program asks the user how many numbers to process, the user enters 0. Then the program will not enter the cumulative sum loop, and your code will try to compute the value of 0 divided by 0. Java will then print that the average is NaN, a cryptic message that is short for "Not a Number." It would be better for the program to print out some other kind of message which indicates that there aren't any numbers to average. You can use an `if`/`else` statement for this purpose:

```
if (totalNumber <= 0) {
    System.out.println("No numbers to average");
} else {
    double average = sum / totalNumber;
    System.out.println("average = " + average);
}
```

Another use of `if` statements would be to count how many negative numbers the user enters. You will often want to count how many times something occurs in a program.

This goal is easy to accomplish with an `if` statement and an integer variable called a *counter*. You start by initializing the counter to 0:

```
int negatives = 0;
```

You can use any name you want for the variable. Here we used `negatives` because that is what you're counting. The other essential step is to increment the counter inside the loop if it passes the test of interest:

```
if (next < 0) {
    negatives++;
}
```

When you put this all together and modify the comments and introduction, you end up with the following variation of the cumulative sum program:

```
1  // Finds the average of a sequence of numbers as well as
2  // reporting how many of the user-specified numbers were negative.
3
4  import java.util.*;
5
6  public class ExamineNumbers2 {
7      public static void main(String[] args) {
8          System.out.println("This program examines a sequence");
9          System.out.println("of numbers to find the average");
10         System.out.println("and count how many are negative.");
11         System.out.println();
12
13         Scanner console = new Scanner(System.in);
14
15         System.out.print("How many numbers do you have? ");
16         int totalNumber = console.nextInt();
17
18         int negatives = 0;
19         double sum = 0.0;
20         for (int i = 1; i <= totalNumber; i++) {
21             System.out.print("    #" + i + "? ");
22             double next = console.nextDouble();
23             sum += next;
24             if (next < 0) {
25                 negatives++;
26             }
27         }
28         System.out.println();
29
30         if (totalNumber <= 0) {
```

```
31                System.out.println("No numbers to average");
32            } else {
33                double average = sum / totalNumber;
34                System.out.println("average = " + average);
35            }
36            System.out.println("# of negatives = " + negatives);
37        }
38 }
```

The program's execution will look something like this:

```
This program examines a sequence
of numbers to find the average
and count how many are negative.

How many numbers do you have? 8
     #1? 2.5
     #2? 9.2
     #3? -19.4
     #4? 208.2
     #5? 42.3
     #6? 92.7
     #7? -17.4
     #8? 8

average = 40.7625
# of negatives = 2
```

Roundoff Errors

As you explore cumulative algorithms, you'll discover a particular problem that you should understand. For example, consider the following execution of the previous ExamineNumbers2 program with different user input:

```
This program examines a sequence
of numbers to find the average
and count how many are negative.

How many numbers do you have? 4
     #1? 2.1
     #2? -3.8
     #3? 5.4
     #4? 7.4

average = 2.7750000000000004
# of negatives = 1
```

If you use a calculator, you will find that the four numbers add up to 11.1. If you divide this number by 4, you get 2.775. Yet Java reports the result as 2.7750000000000004. Where do all of those zeros come from, and why does the number end in 4? The answer is that floating-point numbers can lead to *roundoff errors.*

> **Roundoff Error**
>
> A numerical error that occurs because floating-point numbers are stored as approximations rather than as exact values.

Roundoff errors are generally small and can occur in either direction (slightly high or slightly low). In the previous case, we got a roundoff error that was slightly high.

Floating-point numbers are stored in a format similar to scientific notation, with a set of digits and an exponent. Consider how you would store the value one-third in scientific notation using base-10. You would state that the number is 3.33333 (repeating) times 10 to the −1 power. We can't store an infinite number of digits on a computer, though, so we'll have to stop repeating the 3s at some point. Suppose we can store 10 digits. Then the value for one-third would be stored as 3.333333333 times 10 to the −1. If we multiply that number by 3, we don't get back 1. Instead, we get 9.999999999 times 10 to the −1 (which is equal to 0.9999999999).

You might wonder why the numbers we used in the previous example caused a problem when they didn't have any repeating digits. You have to remember that the computer stores numbers in base-2. Numbers like 2.1 and 5.4 might look like simple numbers in base-10, but they have repeating digits when they are stored in base-2.

Roundoff errors can lead to rather surprising outcomes. For example, consider the following short program:

```
1 public class Roundoff {
2     public static void main(String[] args) {
3         double n = 1.0;
4         for (int i = 1; i <= 10; i++) {
5             n += 0.1;
6             System.out.println(n);
7         }
8     }
9 }
```

This program presents a classic cumulative sum with a loop that adds 0.1 to the number n each time the loop executes. We start with n equal to 1.0 and the loop iterates 10 times, which we might expect to print the numbers 1.1, 1.2, 1.3, and so on through 2.0. Instead, it produces the following output:

```
1.1
1.2000000000000002
1.3000000000000003
```

```
1.4000000000000004
1.5000000000000004
1.6000000000000005
1.7000000000000006
1.8000000000000007
1.9000000000000008
2.000000000000001
```

The problem occurs because 0.1 cannot be stored exactly in base-2 (it produces a repeating set of digits, just as one-third does in base-10). Each time through the loop the error is compounded, which is why the roundoff error gets worse each time.

As another example, consider the task of adding together the values of a penny, a nickel, a dime, and a quarter. If we use variables of type `int`, we will get an exact answer regardless of the order in which we add the numbers:

```java
int cents1 = 1 + 5 + 10 + 25;
int cents2 = 25 + 10 + 5 + 1;
System.out.println(cents1);
System.out.println(cents2);
```

The output of this code is as follows:

```
41
41
```

Regardless of the order, these numbers always add up to 41 cents. But suppose that instead of thinking of these values as whole cents, we think of them as fractions of a dollar that we store as `doubles`:

```java
double dollars1 = 0.01 + 0.05 + 0.10 + 0.25;
double dollars2 = 0.25 + 0.10 + 0.05 + 0.01;
System.out.println(dollars1);
System.out.println(dollars2);
```

This code has surprising output:

```
0.41000000000000003
0.41
```

Even though we are adding up exactly the same numbers, the fact that we add them in a different order makes a difference. The reason is roundoff errors.

There are several lessons to draw from this:

- Be aware that when you store floating-point values (e.g., `doubles`), you are storing approximations and not exact values. If you need to store an exact value, store it using type `int`.

- Don't be surprised when you see numbers that are slightly off from the expected values.
- Don't expect to be able to compare variables of type `double` for equality.

To follow up on the third point, consider what the preceding code would lead to if we were to perform the following test:

```
if (dollars1 == dollars2) {
    ...
}
```

The test would evaluate to `false` because the values are very close, but not close enough for Java to consider them equal. We rarely use a test for exact equality when we work with `doubles`. Instead, we can use a test like this to see if numbers are close to one another:

```
if (Math.abs(dollars1 – dollars2) < 0.001) {
    ...
}
```

We use the absolute value (`abs`) method from the `Math` class to find the magnitude of the difference and then test whether it is less than some small amount (in this case, `0.001`).

Later in this chapter, we'll introduce a variation on `print/println` called `printf` that will make it easier to print numbers like these without all of the extra digits.

4.3 Text Processing

Programmers commonly face problems that require them to create, edit, examine, and format text. Collectively, we call these tasks *text processing*.

> **Text Processing**
> Editing and formatting strings of text.

In this section, we'll look in more detail at the `char` primitive type and introduce a new command called `System.out.printf`. Both of these tools are very useful for text-processing tasks.

The char Type

The primitive type `char` represents a single character of text. It's legal to have variables, parameters, and return values of type `char` if you so desire. Literal values of type `char` are expressed by placing the character within single quotes:

```
char ch = 'A';
```

Table 4.4   Differences between `char` and `String`

	char	String
Type of value	primitive	object
Memory usage	2 bytes	depends on length
Methods	none	`length, toUpperCase, . . .`
Number of letters	exactly 1	0 to many
Surrounded by	apostrophes: `'c'`	quotes: `"Str"`
Comparing	`<, >=, ==, . . .`	`equals`

It is also legal to create a char value that represents an escape sequence:

```
char newline = '\n';
```

In the previous chapter, we discussed `String` objects. The distinction between char and `String` is a subtle one that confuses many new Java programmers. The main difference is that a `String` is an object, but a char is a primitive value. A char occupies a very small amount of memory, but it has no methods. Table 4.4 summarizes several of the differences between the types.

Why does Java have two types for such similar data? The char type exists primarily for historical reasons; it dates back to older languages such as C that influenced the design of Java.

So why would a person ever use the char type when `String` is available? It's often necessary to use char because some methods in Java's API use it as a parameter or return type. But there are also a few cases in which using char can be more useful or simpler than using `String`.

The characters of a `String` are stored inside the object as values of type char. You can access the individual characters through the object's charAt method, which accepts an integer index as a parameter and returns the character at that index. We often loop over a string to examine or change its characters. For example, the following method prints each character of a string on its own line:

```
public static void printVertical(String message) {
    for (int i = 0; i < message.length(); i++) {
        char ch = message.charAt(i);
        System.out.println(ch);
    }
}
```

char versus int

Values of type char are stored internally as 16-bit integers. A standard encoding scheme called Unicode determines which integer value represents each character. (Unicode will be covered in more detail later in this chapter.) Since characters are really integers, Java automatically converts a value of type `char` into an `int` whenever it is expecting an `int`:

```java
char letter = 'a' + 2; // stores 'c'
```

It turns out that the integer value for `'a'` is 97, so the expression's result is 99, which is stored as the character `'c'`. An `int` can similarly be converted into a `char` using a type cast. (The cast is needed as a promise to the compiler, because not every possible `int` value corresponds to a valid character.) Below is an example of a code segment that uses a type cast to convert an `int` value to a value of type `char`:

```java
int code = 66;
char grade = (char) code; // stores 'B'
```

Because values of type `char` are really integers, they can also be compared by using relational operators such as `<` or `==`. In addition, they can be used in loops to cover ranges of letters. For example, the following code prints every letter of the alphabet:

```java
for (char letter = 'a'; letter <= 'z'; letter++) {
    System.out.print(letter);
}
if (c == '8') {... // true
```

You can learn more about the character-to-integer equivalences by searching the web for Unicode tables.

Cumulative Text Algorithms

Strings of characters are often used in cumulative algorithms as discussed earlier in this chapter. For example, you might loop over the characters of a string searching for a particular letter. The following method accepts a string and a character and returns the number of times the character occurs in the string:

```java
public static int count(String text, char c) {
    int found = 0;
    for (int i = 0; i < text.length(); i++) {
        if (text.charAt(i) == c) {
            found++;
        }
    }
    return found;
}
```

A `char` can be concatenated with a `String` using the standard `+` operator. Using this idea, a `String` can be built using a loop, starting with an empty string and

Table 4.5   Useful Methods of the `Character` Class

Method	Description	Example
`getNumericValue(ch)`	Converts a character that looks like a number into that number	`Character.getNumericValue('6')` returns 6
`isDigit(ch)`	Whether or not the character is one of the digits `'0'` through `'9'`	`Character.isDigit('X')` returns `false`
`isLetter(ch)`	Whether or not the character is in the range `'a'` to `'z'` or `'A'` to `'Z'`	`Character.isLetter('f')` returns `true`
`isLowerCase(ch)`	Whether or not the character is a lowercase letter	`Character.isLowerCase('Q')` returns `false`
`isUpperCase(ch)`	Whether or not the character is an uppercase letter	`Character.isUpperCase('Q')` returns `true`
`toLowerCase(ch)`	The lowercase version of the given letter	`Character.toLowerCase('Q')` returns `'q'`
`toUpperCase(ch)`	The uppercase version of the given letter	`Character.toUpperCase('x')` returns `'X'`

concatenating individual characters in the loop. This is called a *cumulative concatenation*. The following method accepts a string and returns the same characters in the reverse order:

```java
public static String reverse(String phrase) {
    String result = "";
    for (int i = 0; i < phrase.length(); i++) {
        result = phrase.charAt(i) + result;
    }
    return result;
}
```

For example, the call of `reverse("Tin man")` returns `"nam niT"`.

Several useful methods can be called to check information about a character or convert one character into another. Remember that `char` is a primitive type, which means that you can't use the dot syntax used with `String`s. Instead, the methods are static methods in a class called `Character`; the methods accept `char` parameters and return appropriate values. Some of the most useful `Character` methods are listed in Table 4.5.

The following method counts the number of letters A–Z in a `String`, ignoring all nonletter characters such as punctuation, numbers, and spaces:

```java
public static int countLetters(String phrase) {
    int count = 0;
    for (int i = 0; i < phrase.length(); i++) {
        char ch = phrase.charAt(i);
```

```
        if (Character.isLetter(ch)) {
            count++;
        }
    }
    return count;
}
```

For example, the call of countLetters("gr8 JoB!") returns 5.

System.out.printf

So far we've used System.out.println and System.out.print for console output. There's a third method, System.out.printf, which is a bit more complicated than the others but gives us some useful new abilities. The "f" in printf stands for "formatted," implying that System.out.printf gives you more control over the format in which your output is printed.

Imagine that you'd like to print a multiplication table from 1 to 10. The following code prints the correct numbers, but it doesn't look very nice:

```
for (int i = 1; i <= 10; i++) {
    for (int j = 1; j <= 10; j++) {
        System.out.print(i * j + " ");
    }
    System.out.println();
}
```

The output is the following. Notice that the numbers don't line up vertically:

```
1 2 3 4 5 6 7 8 9 10
2 4 6 8 10 12 14 16 18 20
3 6 9 12 15 18 21 24 27 30
4 8 12 16 20 24 28 32 36 40
5 10 15 20 25 30 35 40 45 50
6 12 18 24 30 36 42 48 54 60
7 14 21 28 35 42 49 56 63 70
8 16 24 32 40 48 56 64 72 80
9 18 27 36 45 54 63 72 81 90
10 20 30 40 50 60 70 80 90 100
```

We could separate the numbers by tabs, which would be better. But this separation doesn't give us very much control over the appearance of the table. Every number would be exactly eight spaces apart on the screen, and the numbers would appear left-aligned. It would be a pain to try to right-align the numbers manually, because you'd have to use if/else statements to check whether a given number was in a certain range and, if necessary, pad it with a given number of spaces.

Did You Know?

ASCII and Unicode

We store data on a computer as binary numbers (sequences of 0s and 1s). To store textual data, we need an encoding scheme that will tell us what sequence of 0s and 1s to use for any given character. Think of it as a giant secret decoder ring that says things like, "If you want to store a lowercase 'a,' use the sequence 01100001."

In the early 1960s, IBM developed an encoding scheme called *EBCDIC* that worked well with the company's punched cards, which had been in use for decades before computers were even invented. But it soon became clear that EBCDIC wasn't a convenient encoding scheme for computer programmers. There were gaps in the sequence that made characters like 'i' and 'j' appear far apart even though they follow one directly after the other.

In 1967, the American Standards Association published a scheme known as *ASCII* (pronounced "AS-kee") that has been in common use ever since. The acronym is short for "American Standard Code for Information Interchange." In its original form, ASCII defined 128 characters that each could be stored with 7 bits of data.

The biggest problem with ASCII is that it is an *American* code. There are many characters in common use in other countries that were not included in ASCII. For example, the British pound (£) and the Spanish variant of the letter n (ñ) are not included in the standard 128 ASCII characters. Various attempts have been made to extend ASCII, doubling it to 256 characters so that it can include many of these special characters. However, it turns out that even 256 characters is simply not enough to capture the incredible diversity of human communication.

Around the time that Java was created, a consortium of software professionals introduced a new standard for encoding characters known as *Unicode*. They decided that the 7 bits of standard ASCII and the 8 bits of extended ASCII were simply not big enough and chose not to set a limit on how many bits they might use for encoding characters. At the time of this writing, the consortium has identified over 110,000 characters, which require a little over 16 bits to store. Unicode includes the characters used in most modern languages and even some ancient languages. Egyptian hieroglyphs were added in 2007, although it still does not include Mayan hieroglyphs, and the consortium has rejected a proposal to include Klingon characters.

The designers of Java used Unicode as the standard for the type char, which means that Java programs are capable of manipulating a full range of characters. Fortunately, the Unicode Consortium decided to incorporate the ASCII encodings, so ASCII can be seen as a subset of Unicode. If you are curious about the actual ordering of characters in ASCII, type "ASCII table" into your favorite search engine and you will find millions of hits to explore.

A much easier way to print values aligned in fixed-width fields is to use the `System.out.printf` command. The `printf` method accepts a specially written `String` called a *format string* that specifies the general appearance of the output, followed by any parameters to be included in the output:

```
System.out.printf(<format string>, <parameter>, ..., <parameter>);
```

A format string is like a normal `String`, except that it can contain placeholders called *format specifiers* that allow you to specify a location where a variable's value should be inserted, along with the format you'd like to give that value. Format specifiers begin with a `%` sign and end with a letter specifying the kind of value, such as `d` for decimal integers (`int`) or `f` for floating-point numbers (real numbers of type `double`). Consider the following `printf` statement:

```
int x = 38, y = -152;
System.out.printf("location: (%d, %d)\n", x, y);
```

This statement produces the following output:

```
location: (38, -152)
```

The `%d` is not actually printed but is instead replaced with the corresponding parameter written after the format string. The number of format specifiers in the format string must match the number of parameters that follow it. The first specifier will be replaced by the first parameter, the second specifier by the second parameter, and so on. `System.out.printf` is unusual because it can accept a varying number of parameters.

The `printf` command is like `System.out.print` in that it doesn't move to a new line unless you explicitly tell it to do so. Notice that in the previous code we ended our format string with `\n` to complete the line of output.

Since a format specifier uses `%` as a special character, if you want to print an actual `%` sign in a `printf` statement, instead write two `%` characters in a row. For example:

```
int score = 87;
System.out.printf("You got %d%% on the exam!\n", score);
```

The code produces the following output:

```
You got 87% on the exam!
```

A format specifier can contain information after its `%` sign to specify the width, precision, and alignment of the value being printed. For example, `%8d` specifies an integer right-aligned in an 8-space-wide area, and `%12.4f` specifies a `double` value right-aligned in a 12-space-wide area, rounded to four digits past the decimal point. Table 4.6 lists some common format specifiers that you may wish to use in your programs.

Table 4.6   **Common Format Specifiers**

Specifier	Result
%d	Integer
%8d	Integer, right-aligned, 8-space-wide field
%-6d	Integer, left-aligned, 6-space-wide field
%f	Floating-point number
%12f	Floating-point number, right-aligned, 12-space-wide field
%.2f	Floating-point number, rounded to nearest hundredth
%16.3f	Floating-point number, rounded to nearest thousandth, 16-space-wide field
%s	String
%8s	String, right-aligned, 8-space-wide field
%-9s	String, left-aligned, 9-space-wide field

As a comprehensive example, suppose that the following variables have been declared to represent information about a student:

```
int score = 87;
double gpa = 3.18652;
String name = "Jessica";
```

The following code sample prints the preceding variables with several format specifiers:

```
System.out.printf("student name: %10s\n", name);
System.out.printf("exam score  : %10d\n", score);
System.out.printf("GPA         : %10.2f\n", gpa);
```

The code produces the following output:

```
student name:     Jessica
exam score  :          87
GPA         :        3.19
```

The three values line up on their right edge, because we print all of them with a width of 10. The `printf` method makes it easy to line up values in columns in this way. Notice that the student's GPA rounds to 3.19, because of the 2 in that variable's format specifier. The specifier `10.2` makes the value fit into an area 10 characters wide with exactly 2 digits after the decimal point.

Let's return to our multiplication table example. Now that we know about `printf`, we can print the table with right-aligned numbers relatively easily. We'll right-align the numbers into fields of width 5:

```
for (int i = 1; i <= 10; i++) {
    for (int j = 1; j <= 10; j++) {
```

```
        System.out.printf("%5d", i * j);
    }
    System.out.println();
}
```

This code produces the following output:

```
    1    2    3    4    5    6    7    8    9   10
    2    4    6    8   10   12   14   16   18   20
    3    6    9   12   15   18   21   24   27   30
    4    8   12   16   20   24   28   32   36   40
    5   10   15   20   25   30   35   40   45   50
    6   12   18   24   30   36   42   48   54   60
    7   14   21   28   35   42   49   56   63   70
    8   16   24   32   40   48   56   64   72   80
    9   18   27   36   45   54   63   72   81   90
   10   20   30   40   50   60   70   80   90  100
```

The `printf` method can also solve the problem with the `Roundoff` program introduced earlier in this chapter. Fixing the precision of the `double` value ensures that it will be rounded to avoid the tiny roundoff mistakes that result from `double` arithmetic. Here is the corrected program:

```
1  // Uses System.out.printf to correct roundoff errors.
2  public class Roundoff2 {
3      public static void main(String[] args) {
4          double n = 1.0;
5          for (int i = 1; i <= 10; i++) {
6              n += 0.1;
7              System.out.printf("%3.1f\n", n);
8          }
9      }
10 }
```

The program produces the following output:

```
1.1
1.2
1.3
1.4
1.5
1.6
1.7
1.8
1.9
2.0
```

4.4 Methods with Conditional Execution

We introduced a great deal of information about methods in Chapter 3, including how to use parameters to pass values into a method and how to use a `return` statement to have a method return a value. Now that we've introduced conditional execution, we need to revisit these issues so that you can gain a deeper understanding of them.

Preconditions and Postconditions

Every time you write a method you should think about exactly what that method is supposed to accomplish. You can describe how a method works by describing the *preconditions* that must be true before it executes and the *postconditions* that will be true after it has executed.

> **Precondition**
>
> A condition that must be true before a method executes in order to guarantee that the method can perform its task.

> **Postcondition**
>
> A condition that the method guarantees will be true after it finishes executing, as long as the preconditions were true before the method was called.

For example, if you are describing the task of a person on an automobile assembly line, you might use a postcondition like, "The bolts that secure the left front tire are on the car and tight." But postconditions are not the whole story. Employees on an assembly line depend on one another. A line worker can't add bolts and tighten them if the left tire isn't there or if there are no bolts. So, the assembly line worker might have preconditions like, "The left tire is mounted properly on the car, there are at least eight bolts in the supply box, and a working wrench is available." You describe the task fully by saying that the worker can make the postcondition(s) true if the precondition(s) are true before starting.

Like workers on an assembly line, methods need to work together, each solving its own portion of the task in order for them all to solve the overall task. The preconditions and postconditions describe the dependencies between methods.

Throwing Exceptions

We have seen several cases in which Java might throw an exception. For example, if we have a console `Scanner` and we call `nextInt`, the program will throw an exception if the user types something that isn't an `int`. In Appendix C, we examine how you can handle exceptions. For now, we just want to explore some of the ways in which exceptions can occur and how you might want to generate them in your own code.

Ideally programs execute without generating any errors, but in practice various problems arise. If you ask the user for an integer, the user may accidentally or perhaps even maliciously type something that is not an integer. Or your code might have a bug in it.

The following program always throws an exception because it tries to compute the value of 1 divided by 0, which is mathematically undefined:

```
1 public class CauseException {
2     public static void main(String[] args) {
3         int x = 1 / 0;
4         System.out.println(x);
5     }
6 }
```

When you run the program, you get the following error message:

```
Exception in thread "main" java.lang.ArithmeticException: / by zero
        at CauseException.main(CauseException.java:3)
```

The problem occurs in line 3, when you ask Java to compute a value that can't be stored as an `int`. What is Java supposed to do with that value? It throws an exception that stops the program from executing and warns you that an arithmetic exception occurred while the program was executing that specific line of code.

It is worth noting that division by zero does not always produce an exception. You won't get an exception if you execute this line of code:

```
double x = 1.0 / 0.0;
```

In this case, the program executes normally and produces the output `Infinity`. This is because floating-point numbers follow a standard from the Institute of Electrical and Electronics Engineers (IEEE) that defines exactly what should happen in these cases, and there are special values representing infinity and `"NaN"` (not a number).

You may want to throw exceptions yourself in the code you write. In particular, it is a good idea to throw an exception if a precondition fails. For example, suppose that you want to write a method for computing the factorial of an integer. The factorial is defined as follows:

$n!$ (which is read as "n factorial") $= 1 * 2 * 3 * ... * n$

You can write a Java method that uses a cumulative product to compute this result:

```
public static int factorial(int n) {
    int product = 1;
    for (int i = 2; i <= n; i++) {
```

```
        product = product * i;
    }
    return product;
}
```

You can then test the method for various values with a loop:

```
for (int i = 0; i <= 10; i++) {
    System.out.println(i + "! = " + factorial(i));
}
```

The loop produces the following output:

```
0! = 1
1! = 1
2! = 2
3! = 6
4! = 24
5! = 120
6! = 720
7! = 5040
8! = 40320
9! = 362880
10! = 3628800
```

It seems odd that the `factorial` method should return 1 when it is asked for 0!, but that is actually part of the mathematical definition of the factorial function. It returns 1 because the local variable `product` in the `factorial` method is initialized to 1, and the loop is never entered when the parameter n has the value 0. So, this is actually desirable behavior for 0!.

But what if you're asked to compute the factorial of a negative number? The method returns the same value, 1. The mathematical definition of factorial says that the function is undefined for negative values of n, so it actually shouldn't even compute an answer when n is negative. Accepting only numbers that are zero or positive is a precondition of the method that can be described in the documentation:

```
// pre : n >= 0
// post: returns n factorial (n!)
```

Adding comments about this restriction is helpful, but what if someone calls the `factorial` method with a negative value anyway? The best solution is to throw an exception. The general syntax of the `throw` statement is:

```
throw <exception>;
```

In Java, exceptions are objects. Before you can throw an exception, you have to construct an exception object using new. You'll normally construct the object as you are throwing the exception, because the exception object includes information about what was going on when the error occurred. Java has a class called IllegalArgumentException that is meant to cover a case like this where someone has passed an inappropriate value as an argument. You can construct the exception object and include it in a throw statement as follows:

```
throw new IllegalArgumentException();
```

Of course, you'll want to do this only when the precondition fails, so you need to include the code inside an if statement:

```
if (n < 0) {
    throw new IllegalArgumentException();
}
```

You can also include some text when you construct the exception that will be displayed when the exception is thrown:

```
if (n < 0) {
    throw new IllegalArgumentException("negative n: " + n);
}
```

Incorporating the pre/post comments and the exception code into the method definition, you get the following code:

```
// pre : n >= 0
// post: returns n factorial (n!)
public static int factorial(int n) {
    if (n < 0) {
        throw new IllegalArgumentException("negative n: " + n);
    }
    int product = 1;
    for (int i = 2; i <= n; i++) {
        product = product * i;
    }
    return product;
}
```

You don't need an else after the if that throws the exception, because when an exception is thrown, it halts the execution of the method. So, if someone calls the factorial method with a negative value of n, Java will never execute the code that follows the throw statement.

You can test this code with the following `main` method:

```
public static void main(String[] args) {
    System.out.println(factorial(-1));
}
```

When you execute this program, it stops executing and prints the following message:

```
Exception in thread "main"
java.lang.IllegalArgumentException: negative n: -1
        at Factorial2.factorial(Factorial2.java:8)
        at Factorial2.main(Factorial2.java:3)
```

The message indicates that the program `Factorial2` stopped running because an `IllegalArgumentException` was thrown with a negative n of −1. The system then shows you a backward trace of how it got there. The illegal argument appeared in line 8 of the `factorial` method of the `Factorial2` class. It got there because of a call in line 3 of the `main` of the `Factorial2` class. This kind of information is very helpful when you want to find the bugs in your programs.

Throwing exceptions is an example of *defensive programming.* We don't intend to have bugs in the programs we write, but we're only human, so we want to build in mechanisms that will give us feedback when we make mistakes. Writing code that will test the values passed to methods and throw an `IllegalArgumentException` when a value is not appropriate is a great way to provide that feedback.

Revisiting Return Values

VideoNote

In Chapter 3 we looked at some examples of simple calculating methods that return a value, as in this method for finding the sum of the first *n* integers:

```
public static int sum(int n) {
    return (n + 1) * n / 2;
}
```

Now that you know how to write `if/else` statements, we can look at some more interesting examples involving return values. For example, earlier in this chapter you saw that the `Math` class has a method called `max` that returns the larger of two values. There are actually two different versions of the method, one that finds the larger of two integers and one that finds the larger of two `doubles`. Recall that when two methods have the same name (but different parameters), it is called overloading.

Let's write our own version of the `max` method that returns the larger of two integers. Its header will look like this:

```
public static int max(int x, int y) {
    ...
}
```

We want to return either `x` or `y`, depending on which is larger. This is a perfect place to use an `if/else` construct:

```
public static int max(int x, int y) {
    if (x > y) {
        return x;
    } else {
        return y;
    }
}
```

This code begins by testing whether `x` is greater than `y`. If it is, the computer executes the first branch by returning `x`. If it is not, the computer executes the `else` branch by returning `y`. But what if `x` and `y` are equal? The preceding code executes the `else` branch when the values are equal, but it doesn't actually matter which `return` statement is executed when `x` and `y` are equal.

Remember that when Java executes a `return` statement, the method stops executing. It's like a command to Java to "get out of this method right now." That means that this method could also be written as follows:

```
public static int max(int x, int y) {
    if (x > y) {
        return x;
    }
    return y;
}
```

This version of the code is equivalent in behavior because the statement `return x` inside the `if` statement will cause Java to exit the method immediately and Java will not execute the `return` statement that follows the `if`. On the other hand, if we don't enter the `if` statement, we proceed directly to the statement that follows it (`return y`).

Whether you choose to use the first form or the second in your own programs depends somewhat on personal taste. The `if/else` construct makes it more clear that the method is choosing between two alternatives, but some people prefer the second alternative because it is shorter.

As another example, consider the `indexOf` method of the `String` class. We'll define a variable `s` that stores the following `String`:

```
String s = "four score and seven years ago";
```

Now we can write expressions like the following to determine where a particular character appears in the String:

```
int r = s.indexOf('r');
int v = s.indexOf('v');
```

This code sets r to 3 because 3 is the index of the first occurrence of the letter 'r' in the String. It sets v to 17 because that is the index of the first occurrence of the letter 'v' in the String.

The indexOf method is part of the String class, but let's see how we could write a different method that performs the same task. Our method would be called differently because it is a static method outside the String object. We would have to pass it both the String and the letter:

```
int r = indexOf('r', s);
int v = indexOf('v', s);
```

So, the header for our method would be:

```
public static int indexOf(char ch, String s) {
    ...
}
```

Remember that when a method returns a value, we must include the return type after the words public static. In this case, we have indicated that the method returns an int because the index will be an integer.

This task can be solved rather nicely with a for loop that goes through each possible index from first to last. We can describe this in pseudocode as follows:

```
for (each index i in the string) {
    if the char is at position i, we've found it.
}
```

To flesh this out, we have to think about how to test whether the character at position i is the one we are looking for. Remember that String objects have a method called charAt that allows us to pull out an individual character from the String, so we can refine our pseudocode as follows:

```
for (int i = 0; i < s.length(); i++) {
    if (s.charAt(i) == ch) {
        we've found it.
    }
}
```

To complete this code, we have to refine what to do when "we've found it." If we find the character, we have our answer: the current value of the variable `i`. And if that is the answer we want to return, we can put a `return` statement there:

```
for (int i = 0; i < s.length(); i++) {
    if (s.charAt(i) == ch) {
        return i;
    }
}
```

To understand this code, you have to understand how the `return` statement works. For example, if the `String s` is the one from our example ("four score...") and we are searching for the character `'r'`, we know that when `i` is equal to 3 we will find that `s.charAt(3)` is equal to `'r'`. That case causes our code to execute the `return` statement, effectively saying:

```
return 3;
```

When a `return` statement is executed, Java immediately exits the method, which means that we break out of the loop and return 3 as our answer. Even though the loop would normally increment `i` to 4 and keep going, our code doesn't do that because we hit the `return` statement.

There is only one thing missing from our code. If we try to compile it as it is, we get this error message from the Java compiler:

```
missing return statement
```

This error message occurs because we haven't told Java what to do if we never find the character we are searching for. In that case, we will execute the `for` loop in its entirety and reach the end of the method without having returned a value. This is not acceptable. If we say that the method returns an `int`, we have to guarantee that every path through the method will return an `int`.

If we don't find the character, we want to return some kind of special value to indicate that the character was not found. We can't use the value 0, because 0 is a legal index for a `String` (the index of the first character). So, the convention in Java is to return –1 if the character is not found. It is easy to add the code for this `return` statement after the `for` loop:

```
public static int indexOf(char ch, String s) {
    for (int i = 0; i < s.length(); i++) {
        if (s.charAt(i) == ch) {
            return i;
        }
    }
    return -1;
}
```

Common Programming Error

String Index Out of Bounds

It's very easy to forget that the last index of a `String` of length n is actually $n - 1$. Forgetting this fact can cause you to write incorrect text-processing loops like this one:

```java
// This version of the code has a mistake!
// The test should be i < s.length()
public static int indexOf(char ch, String s) {
    for (int i = 0; i <= s.length(); i++) {
        if (s.charAt(i) == ch) {
            return i;
        }
    }
    return -1;
}
```

The program will throw an exception if the loop runs past the end of the `String`. On the last pass through the loop, the value of the variable `i` will be equal to `s.length()`. When it executes the `if` statement test, the program will throw the exception. The error message will resemble the following:

```
Exception in thread "main"
    java.lang.StringIndexOutOfBoundsException:
    String index out of range: 11
        at java.lang.String.charAt(Unknown Source)
        at OutOfBoundsExample.indexOf(OutOfBoundsExample.java:9)
        at OutOfBoundsExample.main(OutOfBoundsExample.java:4)
```

An interesting thing about the bug in this example is that it only occurs if the `String` does not contain the character `ch`. If `ch` is contained in the `String`, the `if` test will be `true` for one of the legal indexes in `s`, so the code will return that index. Only if all the characters from `s` have been examined without finding `ch` will the loop attempt its last fatal pass.

It may seem strange that we don't have a test for the final `return` statement that returns -1, but remember that the `for` loop tries every possible index of the `String` searching for the character. If the character appears anywhere in the `String`, the `return` statement inside the loop will be executed and we'll never get to the `return` statement after the loop. The only way to get to the `return` statement after the loop is to find that the character appears nowhere in the given `String`.

Reasoning about Paths

The combination of `if`/`else` and `return` is powerful. It allows you to solve many complex problems in the form of a method that accepts some input and computes a result. But you have to be careful to think about the different paths that exist in the code that you write. At first this process might seem annoying, but when you get the hang of it, you will find that it allows you to simplify your code.

For example, suppose that we want to convert scores on the SAT into a rating to be used for college admission. Each of the three components of the SAT ranges from 200 to 800, so the overall total ranges from 600 to 2400. Suppose that a hypothetical college breaks up this range into three subranges with totals below 1200 considered not competitive, scores of at least 1200 but less than 1800 considered competitive, and scores of 1800 to 2400 considered highly competitive.

Let's write a method called `rating` that will take the total SAT score as a parameter and will return a string with the appropriate text. We can use the AND operator described earlier to write an `if`/`else` construct that has tests for each of these ranges:

```java
public static String rating(int totalSAT) {
    if (totalSAT >= 600 && totalSAT < 1200) {
        return "not competitive";
    } else if (totalSAT >= 1200 && totalSAT < 1800) {
        return "competitive";
    } else if (totalSAT >= 1800 && totalSAT <= 2400) {
        return "highly competitive";
    }
}
```

This method has been written in a logical manner with specific tests for each of the three cases, but it doesn't compile. The compiler indicates at the end of the method that there was a "missing return statement." That seems odd because there are three different `return` statements in this method. We have included a `return` for each of the different cases, so why is there a compiler error?

When the compiler encounters a method that is supposed to return a value, it computes every possible path through the method and makes sure that each path ends with a call on `return`. The method we have written has four paths through it. If the first test succeeds, then the method returns `"not competitive"`. Otherwise, if the second test succeeds, then the method returns `"competitive"`. If both of those tests fail but the third test succeeds, then the method returns `"highly competitive"`. But what if all three tests fail? That case would constitute a fourth path that doesn't have a `return` statement associated with it. Instead, we would reach the end of the method without having returned a value. That is not acceptable, which is why the compiler produces an error message.

It seems annoying that we have to deal with a fourth case because we know that the total SAT score will always be in the range of 600 to 2400. Our code covers all of the cases that we expect for this method, but that isn't good enough. Java insists that we cover every possible case.

Understanding this idea can simplify the code you write. If you think in terms of paths and cases, you can often eliminate unnecessary code. For our method, if we really want to return just one of three different values, then we don't need a third test. We can make the final branch of the nested if/else be a simple else:

```java
public static String rating(int totalSAT) {
    if (totalSAT >= 600 && totalSAT < 1200) {
        return "not competitive";
    } else if (totalSAT >= 1200 && totalSAT < 1800) {
        return "competitive";
    } else {   // totalSAT >= 1800
        return "highly competitive";
    }
}
```

This version of the method compiles and returns the appropriate string for each different case. We were able to eliminate the final test because we know that we want only three paths through the method. Once we have specified two of the paths, then everything else must be part of the third path.

We can carry this idea one step further. We've written a method that compiles and computes the right answer, but we can make it even simpler. Consider the first test, for example. Why should we test for the total being greater than or equal to 600? If we expect that it will always be in the range of 600 to 2400, then we can simply test whether the total is less than 1200. Similarly, to test for the highly competitive range, we can simply test whether the score is at least 1800. Of the three ranges, these are the two simplest to test for. So we can simplify this method even further by including tests for the first and third subranges and assume that all other totals are in the middle range:

```java
public static String rating(int totalSAT) {
    if (totalSAT < 1200) {
        return "not competitive";
    } else if (totalSAT >= 1800) {
        return "highly competitive";
    } else {   // 1200 <= totalSAT < 1800
        return "competitive";
    }
}
```

Whenever you write a method like this, you should think about the different cases and figure out which ones are the simplest to test for. This will allow you to avoid writing an explicit test for the most complex case. As in these examples, it is a good idea to include a comment on the final else branch to describe that particular case in English.

Before we leave this example, it is worth thinking about what happens when the method is passed an illegal SAT total. If it is passed a total less than 600, then it classifies it as not competitive and if it passed a total greater than 2400, it will classify it as highly competitive. Those aren't bad answers for the program to give, but the right thing to do is to document the fact that there is a precondition on the total. In addition, we can add an extra test for this particular case and throw an exception if the precondition is violated. Testing for the illegal values is a case in which the logical OR is appropriate because illegal values will either be too low or too high (but not both):

```java
// pre: 600 <= totalSAT <= 2400 (throws IllegalArgumentException if not)
public static String rating(int totalSAT) {
    if (totalSAT < 600 || totalSAT > 2400) {
        throw new IllegalArgumentException("total: " + totalSAT);
    } else if (totalSAT < 1200) {
        return "not competitive";
    } else if (totalSAT >= 1800) {
        return "highly competitive";
    } else {   // 1200 <= totalSAT < 1800
        return "competitive";
    }
}
```

4.5 Case Study: Body Mass Index

Individual body mass index has become a popular measure of overall health. The Centers for Disease Control and Prevention (CDC) website about body mass index (http://www.cdc.gov/healthyweight/assessing/bmi/index.html) explains:

> Body Mass Index (BMI) is a number calculated from a person's weight and height. BMI provides a reliable indicator of body fatness for most people and is used to screen for weight categories that may lead to health problems.

It has also become popular to compare the statistics for two or more individuals who are pitted against one another in a "fitness challenge," or to compare two sets of numbers for the same person to get a sense of how that person's BMI will vary if a person loses weight. In this section, we will write a program that prompts the user for the height and weight of two individuals and reports the overall results for the two people. Here is a sample execution for the program we want to write:

```
This program reads data for two
people and computes their body
mass index and weight status.
```

```
Enter next person's information:
height (in inches)? 73.5
weight (in pounds)? 230

Enter next person's information:
height (in inches)? 71
weight (in pounds)? 220.5

Person #1 body mass index = 29.93
overweight
Person #2 body mass index = 30.75
obese
```

In Chapter 1 we introduced the idea of *iterative enhancement,* in which you develop a complex program in stages. Every professional programmer uses this technique, so it is important to learn to apply it yourself in the programs you write.

In this case, we eventually want our program to explain to the user what it does and compute BMI results for two different people. We also want the program to be well structured. But we don't have to do everything at once. In fact, if we try to do so, we are likely to be overwhelmed by the details. In writing this program, we will go through three different stages:

1. First, we'll write a program that computes results for just one person, without an introduction. We won't worry about program structure yet.

2. Next, we'll write a complete program that computes results for two people, including an introduction. Again, we won't worry about program structure at this point.

3. Finally, we will put together a well-structured and complete program.

One-Person Unstructured Solution

Even the first version of the program will prompt for user input, so we will need to construct a Scanner object to read from the console:

```
Scanner console = new Scanner(System.in);
```

To compute the BMI for an individual, we will need to know the height and weight of that person. This is a fairly straightforward "prompt and read" task. The only real decision here is with regard to the type of variable to use for storing the height and weight. People often talk about height and weight in whole numbers, but the question to ask is whether or not it makes sense for people to use fractions. Do people ever describe their heights using half-inches? The answer is yes. Do people ever describe their weights using half-pounds? Again the answer is yes. So it makes sense to store the values as doubles, to allow people to enter either integer values or fractions:

```
System.out.println("Enter next person's information:");
System.out.print("height (in inches)? ");
```

```
double height1 = console.nextDouble();
System.out.print("weight (in pounds)? ");
double weight1 = console.nextDouble();
```

Once we have the person's height and weight, we can compute the person's BMI. The CDC website gives the following BMI formula for adults:

$$\frac{\text{weight (lb)}}{[\text{height (in)}]^2} \times 703$$

This formula is fairly easy to translate into a Java expression:

```
double bmi1 = weight1 / (height1 * height1) * 703;
```

If you look closely at the sample execution, you will see that we want to print blank lines to separate different parts of the user interaction. The introduction ends with a blank line, then there is a blank line after the "prompt and read" portion of the interaction. So, after we add an empty `println` and put all of these pieces together, our `main` method looks like this:

```
public static void main(String[] args) {
    Scanner console = new Scanner(System.in);
    System.out.println("Enter next person's information:");
    System.out.print("height (in inches)? ");
    double height1 = console.nextDouble();
    System.out.print("weight (in pounds)? ");
    double weight1 = console.nextDouble();
    double bmi1 = weight1 / (height1 * height1) * 703;
    System.out.println();
    ...
}
```

This program prompts for values and computes the BMI. Now we need to include code to report the results. We could use a `println` for the BMI:

```
System.out.println("Person #1 body mass index = " + bmi1);
```

This would work, but it produces output like the following:

```
Person #1 body mass index = 29.930121708547368
```

The long sequence of digits after the decimal point is distracting and implies a level of precision that we simply don't have. It is more appropriate and more appealing to the user to list just a few digits after the decimal point. This is a good place to use a `printf`:

```
System.out.printf("Person #1 body mass index = %5.2f\n", bmi1);
```

Table 4.7   Weight Status by BMI

BMI	Weight status
below 18.5	underweight
18.5–24.9	normal
25.0–29.9	overweight
30.0 and above	obese

In the sample execution we also see a report of the person's weight status. The CDC website includes the information shown in Table 4.7. There are four entries in this table, so we need four different `println` statements for the four possibilities. We will want to use `if` or `if/else` statements to control the four `println` statements. In this case, we know that we want to print exactly one of the four possibilities. Therefore, it makes most sense to use a nested `if/else` construct that ends with an `else`.

But what tests do we use for the nested `if/else`? If you look closely at Table 4.7, you will see that there are some gaps. For example, what if your BMI is 24.95? That number isn't between 18.5 and 24.9 and it isn't between 25.0 and 29.9. It seems clear that the CDC intended its table to be interpreted slightly differently. The range is probably supposed to be 18.5–24.999999 (repeating), but that would look rather odd in a table. In fact, if you understand nested `if/else` statements, this is a case in which a nested `if/else` construct expresses the possibilities more clearly than a table like the CDC's. The nested `if/else` construct looks like this:

```
if (bmi1 < 18.5) {
    System.out.println("underweight");
} else if (bmi1 < 25) {
    System.out.println("normal");
} else if (bmi1 < 30) {
    System.out.println("overweight");
} else {   // bmi1 >= 30
    System.out.println("obese");
}
```

So, putting all this together, we get a complete version of the first program:

```
1   import java.util.*;
2
3   public class BMI1 {
4       public static void main(String[] args) {
5           Scanner console = new Scanner(System.in);
6
7           System.out.println("Enter next person's information:");
8           System.out.print("height (in inches)? ");
```

```
 9              double height1 = console.nextDouble();
10              System.out.print("weight (in pounds)? ");
11              double weight1 = console.nextDouble();
12              double bmi1 = weight1 / (height1 * height1) * 703;
13              System.out.println();
14
15              System.out.printf("Person #1 body mass index = %5.2f\n", bmi1);
16              if (bmi1 < 18.5) {
17                  System.out.println("underweight");
18              } else if (bmi1 < 25) {
19                  System.out.println("normal");
20              } else if (bmi1 < 30) {
21                  System.out.println("overweight");
22              } else {   // bmi1 >= 30
23                  System.out.println("obese");
24              }
25          }
26  }
```

Here is a sample execution of the program:

```
Enter next person's information:
height (in inches)? 73.5
weight (in pounds)? 230


Person #1 body mass index = 29.93
overweight
```

Two-Person Unstructured Solution

Now that we have a program that computes one person's BMI and weight status, let's expand it to handle two different people. Experienced programmers would probably begin by adding structure to the program before trying to make it handle two sets of data, but novice programmers will find it easier to consider the unstructured solution first.

To make this program handle two people, we can copy and paste a lot of the code and make slight modifications. For example, instead of using variables called height1, weight1, and bmi1, for the second person we will use variables height2, weight2, and bmi2.

We also have to be careful to do each step in the right order. Looking at the sample execution, you'll see that the program prompts for data for both individuals first and then reports results for both. Thus, we can't copy the entire program and simply paste a second copy; we have to rearrange the order of the statements so that all of the prompting happens first and all of the reporting happens later.

We've also decided that when we move to this second stage, we will add code for the introduction. This code should appear at the beginning of the program and should include an empty `println` to produce a blank line to separate the introduction from the rest of the user interaction.

We now combine these elements into a complete program:

```java
1   // This program finds the body mass index (BMI) for two
2   // individuals.
3
4   import java.util.*;
5
6   public class BMI2 {
7       public static void main(String[] args) {
8           System.out.println("This program reads data for two");
9           System.out.println("people and computes their body");
10          System.out.println("mass index and weight status.");
11          System.out.println();
12
13          Scanner console = new Scanner(System.in);
14
15          System.out.println("Enter next person's information:");
16          System.out.print("height (in inches)? ");
17          double height1 = console.nextDouble();
18          System.out.print("weight (in pounds)? ");
19          double weight1 = console.nextDouble();
20          double bmi1 = weight1 / (height1 * height1) * 703;
21          System.out.println();
22
23          System.out.println("Enter next person's information:");
24          System.out.print("height (in inches)? ");
25          double height2 = console.nextDouble();
26          System.out.print("weight (in pounds)? ");
27          double weight2 = console.nextDouble();
28          double bmi2 = weight2 / (height2 * height2) * 703;
29          System.out.println();
30
31          System.out.printf("Person #1 body mass index = %5.2f\n", bmi1);
32          if (bmi1 < 18.5) {
33              System.out.println("underweight");
34          } else if (bmi1 < 25) {
35              System.out.println("normal");
36          } else if (bmi1 < 30) {
37              System.out.println("overweight");
38          } else {   // bmi1 >= 30
```

```
39                      System.out.println("obese");
40              }
41
42          System.out.printf("Person #2 body mass index = %5.2f\n", bmi2);
43          if (bmi2 < 18.5) {
44              System.out.println("underweight");
45          } else if (bmi2 < 25) {
46              System.out.println("normal");
47          } else if (bmi2 < 30) {
48              System.out.println("overweight");
49          } else {   // bmi2 >= 30
50              System.out.println("obese");
51          }
52      }
53  }
```

This program compiles and works. When we execute it, we get exactly the interaction we wanted. However, the program lacks structure. All of the code appears in `main`, and there is significant redundancy. That shouldn't be a surprise, because we created this version by copying and pasting. Whenever you find yourself using copy and paste, you should wonder whether there isn't a better way to solve the problem. Usually there is.

Two-Person Structured Solution

Let's explore how static methods can improve the structure of the program. Looking at the code, you will notice a great deal of redundancy. For example, we have two code segments that look like this:

```
System.out.println("Enter next person's information:");
System.out.print("height (in inches)? ");
double height1 = console.nextDouble();
System.out.print("weight (in pounds)? ");
double weight1 = console.nextDouble();
double bmi1 = weight1 / (height1 * height1) * 703;
System.out.println();
```

The only difference between these two code segments is that the first uses variables `height1`, `weight1`, `bmi1`, and the second uses variables `height2`, `weight2`, and `bmi2`. We eliminate redundancy by moving code like this into a method that we can call twice. So, as a first approximation, we can turn this code into a more generic form as the following method:

```
public static void getBMI(Scanner console) {
    System.out.println("Enter next person's information:");
    System.out.print("height (in inches)? ");
```

```
    double height = console.nextDouble();
    System.out.print("weight (in pounds)? ");
    double weight = console.nextDouble();
    double bmi = weight / (height * height) * 703;
    System.out.println();
}
```

We have to pass in the `Scanner` from `main`. Otherwise we have made all the variables local to this method. From `main` we can call this method twice:

```
getBMI(console);
getBMI(console);
```

Unfortunately, introducing this change breaks the rest of the code. If we try to compile and run the program, we find that we get error messages in `main` whenever we refer to the variables `bmi1` and `bmi2`.

The problem is that the method computes a `bmi` value that we need later in the program. We can fix this by having the method return the `bmi` value that it computes:

```
public static double getBMI(Scanner console) {
    System.out.println("Enter next person's information:");
    System.out.print("height (in inches)? ");
    double height = console.nextDouble();
    System.out.print("weight (in pounds)? ");
    double weight = console.nextDouble();
    double bmi = weight / (height * height) * 703;
    System.out.println();
    return bmi;
}
```

Notice that the method header now lists the return type as `double`. We also have to change `main`. We can't just call the method twice the way we would call a `void` method. Because each call returns a BMI result that the program will need later, for each call we have to store the result coming back from the method in a variable:

```
double bmi1 = getBMI(console);
double bmi2 = getBMI(console);
```

Study this change carefully, because this technique can be one of the most challenging for novices to master. When we write the method, we have to make sure that it returns the BMI result. When we write the call, we have to make sure that we store the result in a variable so that we can access it later.

After this modification, the program will compile and run properly. But there is another obvious redundancy in the `main` method: The same nested `if/else` construct appears twice. The only difference between them is that in one case we use the variable `bmi1`, and in the other case we use the variable `bmi2`. The construct is easily generalized with a parameter:

```java
public static void reportStatus(double bmi) {
    if (bmi < 18.5) {
        System.out.println("underweight");
    } else if (bmi < 25) {
        System.out.println("normal");
    } else if (bmi < 30) {
        System.out.println("overweight");
    } else {   // bmi >= 30
        System.out.println("obese");
    }
}
```

Using this method, we can replace the code in `main` with two calls:

```java
System.out.printf("Person #1 body mass index = %5.2f\n", bmi1);
reportStatus(bmi1);
System.out.printf("Person #2 body mass index = %5.2f\n", bmi2);
reportStatus(bmi2);
```

That change takes care of the redundancy in the program, but we can still use static methods to improve the program by better indicating structure. It is best to keep the `main` method short if possible, to reflect the overall structure of the program. The problem breaks down into three major phases: introduction, the computation of the BMI, and the reporting of the results. We already have a method for computing the BMI, but we haven't yet introduced methods for the introduction and reporting of results. It is fairly simple to add these methods.

There is one other method that we should add to the program. We are using a formula from the CDC website for calculating the BMI of an individual given the person's height and weight. Whenever you find yourself programming a formula, it is a good idea to introduce a method for that formula so that it is easy to spot and so that it has a name.

Applying all these ideas, we end up with the following version of the program:

```java
 1  // This program finds the body mass index (BMI) for two
 2  // individuals. This variation includes several methods
 3  // other than main.
 4
 5  import java.util.*;
 6
 7  public class BMI3 {
 8      public static void main(String[] args) {
 9          giveIntro();
```

```java
10              Scanner console = new Scanner(System.in);
11              double bmi1 = getBMI(console);
12              double bmi2 = getBMI(console);
13              reportResults(bmi1, bmi2);
14          }
15
16      // introduces the program to the user
17      public static void giveIntro() {
18              System.out.println("This program reads data for two");
19              System.out.println("people and computes their body");
20              System.out.println("mass index and weight status.");
21              System.out.println();
22          }
23
24      // prompts for one person's statistics, returning the BMI
25      public static double getBMI(Scanner console) {
26              System.out.println("Enter next person's information:");
27              System.out.print("height (in inches)? ");
28              double height = console.nextDouble();
29              System.out.print("weight (in pounds)? ");
30              double weight = console.nextDouble();
31              double bmi = BMIFor(height, weight);
32              System.out.println();
33              return bmi;
34          }
35
36      // this method contains the body mass index formula for
37      // converting the given height (in inches) and weight
38      // (in pounds) into a BMI
39      public static double BMIFor(double height, double weight) {
40              return weight / (height * height) * 703;
41          }
42
43      // reports the overall bmi values and weight status
44      public static void reportResults(double bmi1, double bmi2) {
45              System.out.printf("Person #1 body mass index = %5.2f\n", bmi1);
46              reportStatus(bmi1);
47              System.out.printf("Person #2 body mass index = %5.2f\n",bmi2);
48              reportStatus(bmi2);
49          }
50
51      // reports the weight status for the given BMI value
52      public static void reportStatus(double bmi) {
53              if (bmi < 18.5) {
```

```
54                    System.out.println("underweight");
55              } else if (bmi < 25) {
56                    System.out.println("normal");
57              } else if (bmi < 30) {
58                    System.out.println("overweight");
59              } else {   // bmi >= 30
60                    System.out.println("obese");
61              }
62         }
63    }
```

This solution interacts with the user the same way and produces the same results as the unstructured solution, but it has a much nicer structure. The unstructured program is in a sense simpler, but the structured solution is easier to maintain if we want to expand the program or make other modifications. These structural benefits aren't so important in short programs, but they become essential as programs become longer and more complex.

Procedural Design Heuristics

There are often many ways to divide (decompose) a problem into methods, but some sets of methods are better than others. Decomposition is often vague and challenging, especially for larger programs that have complex behavior. But the rewards are worth the effort, because a well-designed program is more understandable and more modular. These features are important when programmers work together or when revisiting a program written earlier to add new behavior or modify existing code. There is no single perfect design, but in this section we will discuss several *heuristics* (guiding principles) for effectively decomposing large programs into methods.

Consider the following alternative poorly structured implementation of the single-person BMI program. We'll use this program as a counterexample, highlighting places where it violates our heuristics and giving reasons that it is worse than the previous complete version of the BMI program.

```
1    // A poorly designed version of the BMI case study program.
2
3    import java.util.*;
4
5    public class BadBMI {
6        public static void main(String[] args) {
7            System.out.println("This program reads data for one");
8            System.out.println("person and computes his/her body");
9            System.out.println("mass index and weight status.");
10           System.out.println();
11
12           Scanner console = new Scanner(System.in);
13           person(console);
```

```
14          }
15
16      public static void person(Scanner console) {
17          System.out.println("Enter next person's information:");
18          System.out.print("height (in inches)? ");
19          double height = console.nextDouble();
20          getWeight(console, height);
21      }
22
23      public static void getWeight(Scanner console, double height) {
24          System.out.print("weight (in pounds)? ");
25          double weight = console.nextDouble();
26          reportStatus(console, height, weight);
27      }
28
29      public static void reportStatus(Scanner console, double height,
30                                      double weight) {
31          double bmi = weight / (height * height) * 703;
32          System.out.println("Person #1 body mass index = " + bmi);
33          if (bmi < 18.5) {
34              System.out.println("underweight");
35          } else if (bmi < 25) {
36              System.out.println("normal");
37          } else if (bmi < 30) {
38              System.out.println("overweight");
39          } else {
40              System.out.println("obese");
41          }
42      }
43  }
```

The methods of a program are like workers in a company. The author of a program acts like the director of a company, deciding what employee positions to create, how to group employees together into working units, which work to task to which group, and how groups will interact. Suppose a company director were to divide work into three major departments, two of which are overseen by middle managers:

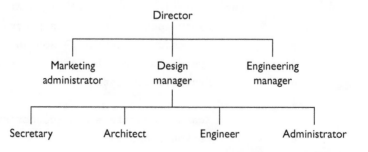

A good structure gives each group clear tasks to complete, avoids giving any particular person or group too much work, and provides a balance between workers and management. These guidelines lead to the first of our procedural design heuristics.

1. Each method should have a coherent set of responsibilities. In our analogy to a company, each group of employees must have a clear idea of what work it is to perform. If any of the groups does not have clear responsibilities, it's difficult for the company director to keep track of who is working on what task. When a new job comes in, two departments might both try to claim it, or a job might go unclaimed by any department.

The analogous concept in programming is that each method should have a clear purpose and set of responsibilities. This characteristic of computer programs is called *cohesion.*

> **Cohesion**
>
> A desirable quality in which the responsibilities of a method or process are closely related to each other.

A good rule of thumb is that you should be able to summarize each of your methods in a single sentence such as "The purpose of this method is to ... ." Writing a sentence like this is a good way to develop a comment for a method's header. It's a bad sign when you have trouble describing the method in a single sentence or when the sentence is long and uses the word "and" several times. Those indications can mean that the method is too large, too small, or does not perform a cohesive set of tasks.

The methods of the `BadBMI` example have poor cohesion. The `person` method's purpose is vague, and `getWeight` is probably too trivial to be its own method. The `reportStatus` method would be more readable if the computation of the BMI were its own method, since the formula is complex.

A subtler application of this first heuristic is that not every method must produce output. Sometimes a method is more reusable if it simply computes a complex result and returns it rather than printing the result that was computed. This format leaves the caller free to choose whether to print the result or to use it to perform further computations. In the `BadBMI` program, the `reportStatus` method both computes and prints the user's BMI. The program would be more flexible if it had a method to simply compute and return the BMI value, such as `BMIFor` in the `BMI3` version of the code. Such a method might seem trivial because its body is just one line in length, but it has a clear, cohesive purpose: capturing a complex expression that is used several times in the program.

2. No one method should do too large a share of the overall task. One subdivision of a company cannot be expected to design and build the entire product line for the year. This system would overwork that subdivision and would leave the other divisions without enough work to do. It would also make it difficult for the subdivisions to communicate effectively, since so much important information and responsibility would be concentrated among so few people.

Similarly, one method should not be expected to comprise the bulk of a program. This principle follows naturally from our first heuristic regarding cohesion, because a method that does too much cannot be cohesive. We sometimes refer to methods like these as "do-everything" methods because they do nearly everything involved in solving the problem. You may have written a "do-everything" method if one of your methods is much longer than the others, hoards most of the variables and data, or contains the majority of the logic and loops.

In the `BadBMI` program, the `person` method is an example of a do-everything method. This fact may seem surprising, since the method is not very many lines long. But a single call to `person` leads to several other calls that collectively end up doing all of the work for the program.

3. Coupling and dependencies between methods should be minimized. A company is more productive if each of its subdivisions can largely operate independently when completing small work tasks. Subdivisions of the company do need to communicate and depend on each other, but such communication comes at a cost. Interdepartmental interactions are often minimized and kept to meetings at specific times and places.

When we are programming, we try to avoid methods that have tight *coupling*.

> **Coupling**
>
> An undesirable state in which two methods or processes rigidly depend on each other.

Methods are coupled if one cannot easily be called without the other. One way to determine how tightly coupled two methods are is to look at the set of parameters one passes to the other. A method should accept a parameter only if that piece of data needs to be provided from outside and only if that data is necessary to complete the method's task. In other words, if a piece of data could be computed or gathered inside the method, or if the data isn't used by the method, it should not be declared as a parameter to the method.

An important way to reduce coupling between methods is to use `return` statements to send information back to the caller. A method should return a result value if it computes something that may be useful to later parts of the program. Because it is desirable for methods to be cohesive and self-contained, it is often better for the program to return a result than to call further methods and pass the result as a parameter to them.

None of the methods in the BadBMI program returns a value. Each method passes parameters to the next methods, but none of them returns the value. This is a lost opportunity because several values (such as the user's height, weight, or BMI) would be better handled as return values.

4. The main method should be a concise summary of the overall program. The top person in each major group or department of our hypothetical company reports to the group's director. If you look at the groups that are directly connected to the director at the top level of the company diagram, you can see a summary of the overall work: design, engineering, and marketing. This structure helps the director stay aware of what each group is doing. Looking at the top-level structure can also help the employees get a quick overview of the company's goals.

A program's main method is like the director in that it begins the overall task and executes the various subtasks. A main method should read as a summary of the overall program's behavior. Programmers can understand each other's code by looking at main to get a sense of what the program is doing as a whole.

A common mistake that prevents main from being a good program summary is the inclusion of a "do-everything" method. When the main method calls it, the do-everything method proceeds to do most or all of the real work.

Another mistake is setting up a program in such a way that it suffers from *chaining*.

Chaining

An undesirable design in which a "chain" of several methods call each other without returning the overall flow of control to main.

A program suffers from chaining if the end of each method simply calls the next method. Chaining often occurs when a new programmer does not fully understand returns and tries to avoid using them by passing more and more parameters down to the rest of the program. Figure 4.8 shows a hypothetical program with two designs. The flow of calls in a badly chained program might look like the diagram on the left.

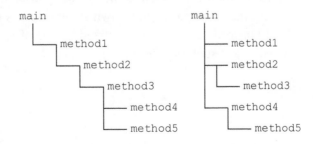

Figure 4.8   Sample code with chaining (left) and without chaining (right)

The `BadBMI` program suffers heavily from chaining. Each method does a small amount of work and then calls the next method, passing more and more parameters down the chain. The `main` method calls `person`, which calls `getWeight`, which calls `reportStatus`. Never does the flow of execution return to `main` in the middle of the computation. So when you read `main`, you don't get a very clear idea of what computations will be made.

One method should not call another simply as a way of moving on to the next task. A more desirable flow of control is to let `main` manage the overall execution of tasks in the program, as shown in the `BMI3` program and on the right side of Figure 4.8. This guideline doesn't mean that it is always bad for one method to call another method; it is okay for one method to call another when the second is a subtask within the overall task of the first, such as in `BMI3` when the `reportResults` method calls `reportStatus`.

5. Data should be "owned" at the lowest level possible. Decisions in a company should be made at the lowest possible level in the organizational hierarchy. For example, a low-level administrator can decide how to perform his or her own work without needing to constantly consult a manager for approval. But the administrator does not have enough information or expertise to design the entire product line; this design task goes to a higher authority such as the manager. The key principle is that each work task should be given to the lowest person in the hierarchy who can correctly handle it.

This principle has two applications in computer programs. The first is that the `main` method should avoid performing low-level tasks as much as possible. For example, in an interactive program `main` should not read the majority of the user input or contain lots of `println` statements.

The second application is that variables should be declared and initialized in the narrowest possible scope. A poor design is for `main` (or another high-level method) to read all of the input, perform heavy computations, and then pass the resulting data as parameters to the various low-level methods. A better design uses low-level methods to read and process the data, and return data to `main` only if they are needed by a later subtask in the program.

It is a sign of poor data ownership when the same parameter must be passed down several method calls, such as the `height` variable in the `BadBMI` program. If you are passing the same parameter down several levels of calls, perhaps that piece of data should instead be read and initialized by one of the lower-level methods (unless it is a shared object such as a `Scanner`).

Chapter Summary

An `if` statement lets you write code that will execute only if a certain condition is met. An `if/else` statement lets you execute one piece of code if a condition is met, and another if the condition is not met. Conditions are Boolean expressions and can be written using relational operators such as `<`, `>=` , and `!=` . You can test multiple conditions using the `&&` and `||` operators.

_____

You can nest `if/else` statements to test a series of conditions and execute the appropriate block of code on the basis of whichever condition is true.

_____

The `==` operator that tests primitive data for equality doesn't behave the way we would expect with objects, so we test objects for equality by calling their `equals` method instead.

_____

Common code that appears in every branch of an `if/else` statement should be factored out so that it is not replicated multiple times in the code.

_____

Cumulative algorithms compute values incrementally. A cumulative sum loop declares a sum variable and incrementally adds to that variable's value inside the loop.

_____

Since the `double` type does not store all values exactly, small roundoff errors can occur when the computer performs calculations on real numbers. Avoid these errors by providing a small amount of tolerance in your code for values near the values that you expect.

_____

The `char` type represents individual characters of text. Each letter of a `String` is stored internally as a `char` value, and you can use the `String`'s `charAt` method to access these characters with an index.

_____

The `System.out.printf` method prints formatted text. You can specify complex format strings to control the width, alignment, and precision by which values are printed.

_____

You can "throw" (generate) exceptions in your own code. This technique can be useful if your code ever reaches an unrecoverable error condition, such as the passing of an invalid argument value to a method.

_____

Self-Check Problems

Section 4.1: `if/else` Statements

1. Translate each of the following English statements into logical tests that could be used in an `if/else` statement. Write the appropriate `if` statement with your logical test. Assume that three `int` variables, x, y, and z, have been declared.

   a. `z` is odd.
   b. `z` is not greater than `y`'s square root.
   c. `y` is positive.
   d. Either `x` or `y` is even, and the other is odd.
   e. `y` is a multiple of `z`.
   f. `z` is not zero.
   g. `y` is greater in magnitude than `z`.
   h. `x` and `z` are of opposite signs.
   i. `y` is a nonnegative one-digit number.

j. z is nonnegative.

k. x is even.

l. x is closer in value to y than z is.

2. Given the variable declarations

```
int x = 4;
int y = -3;
int z = 4;
```

what are the results of the following relational expressions?

a. x == 4

b. x == y

c. x == z

d. y == z

e. x + y > 0

f. x - z != 0

g. y * y <= z

h. y / y == 1

i. x * (y + 2) > y - (y + z) * 2

3. Which of the following if statement headers uses the correct syntax?

a. if x = 10 then {

b. if [x == 10] {

c. if (x => y) {

d. if (x equals 42) {

e. if (x == y) {

4. The following program contains 7 mistakes! What are they?

```
1   public class Oops4 {
2       public static void main(String[] args) {
3           int a = 7, b = 42;
4           minimum(a, b);
5           if {smaller = a} {
6               System.out.println("a is the smallest!");
7           }
8       }
9
10      public static void minimum(int a, int b) {
11          if (a < b) {
12              int smaller = a;
13          } else (a => b) {
14              int smaller = b;
15          }
16          return int smaller;
17      }
18  }
```

5. Consider the following method:

```java
public static void ifElseMystery1(int x, int y) {
    int z = 4;
    if (z <= x) {
        z = x + 1;
    } else {
        z = z + 9;
    }
    if (z <= y) {
        y++;
    }
    System.out.println(z + " " + y);
}
```

What output is produced for each of the following calls?

a. `ifElseMystery1(3, 20);`

b. `ifElseMystery1(4, 5);`

c. `ifElseMystery1(5, 5);`

d. `ifElseMystery1(6, 10);`

6. Consider the following method:

```java
public static void ifElseMystery2(int a, int b) {
    if (a * 2 < b) {
        a = a * 3;
    } else if (a > b) {
        b = b + 3;
    }
    if (b < a) {
        b++;
    } else {
        a--;
    }
    System.out.println(a + " " + b);
}
```

What output is produced for each of the following calls?

a. `ifElseMystery2(10, 2);`

b. `ifElseMystery2(3, 8);`

c. `ifElseMystery2(4, 4);`

d. `ifElseMystery2(10, 30);`

7. Write Java code to read an integer from the user, then print even if that number is an even number or odd otherwise. You may assume that the user types a valid integer.

8. The following code contains a logic error:

```
Scanner console = new Scanner(System.in);
System.out.print("Type a number: ");
int number = console.nextInt();
if (number % 2 == 0) {
    if (number % 3 == 0) {
        System.out.println("Divisible by 6.");
    } else {
        System.out.println("Odd.");
    }
}
```

Examine the code and describe a case in which the code would print something that is untrue about the number that was entered. Explain why. Then correct the logic error in the code.

9. Describe a problem with the following code:

```
Scanner console = new Scanner(System.in);
System.out.print("What is your favorite color?");
String name = console.next();
if (name == "blue") {
    System.out.println("Mine, too!");
}
```

10. Factor out redundant code from the following example by moving it out of the if/else statement, preserving the same output.

```
if (x < 30) {
    a = 2;
    x++;
    System.out.println("Java is awesome! " + x);
} else {
    a = 2;
    System.out.println("Java is awesome! " + x);
}
```

11. The following code is poorly structured:

```
int sum = 1000;
Scanner console = new Scanner(System.in);
System.out.print("Is your money multiplied 1 or 2 times? ");
int times = console.nextInt();
if (times == 1) {
    System.out.print("And how much are you contributing? ");
    int donation = console.nextInt();
    sum = sum + donation;
    count1++;
    total = total + donation;
}
```

```
if (times == 2) {
    System.out.print("And how much are you contributing? ");
    int donation = console.nextInt();
    sum = sum + 2 * donation;
    count2++;
    total = total + donation;
}
```

Rewrite it so that it has a better structure and avoids redundancy. To simplify things, you may assume that the user always types 1 or 2. (How would the code need to be modified to handle any number that the user might type?)

12. The following code is poorly structured:

```
Scanner console = new Scanner(System.in);
System.out.print("How much will John be spending? ");
double amount = console.nextDouble();
System.out.println();
int numBills1 = (int) (amount / 20.0);
if (numBills1 * 20.0 < amount) {
    numBills1++;
}
System.out.print("How much will Jane be spending? ");
amount = console.nextDouble();
System.out.println();
int numBills2 = (int) (amount / 20.0);
if (numBills2 * 20.0 < amount) {
    numBills2++;
}
System.out.println("John needs " + numBills1 + " bills");
System.out.println("Jane needs " + numBills2 + " bills");
```

Rewrite it so that it has a better structure and avoids redundancy. You may wish to introduce a method to help capture redundant code.

13. Write a piece of code that reads a shorthand text description of a color and prints the longer equivalent. Acceptable color names are B for Blue, G for Green, and R for Red. If the user types something other than B, G, or R, the program should print an error message. Make your program case-insensitive so that the user can type an uppercase or lowercase letter. Here are some example executions:

```
What color do you want? B
You have chosen Blue.
```

```
What color do you want? g
You have chosen Green.
```

```
What color do you want? Bork
Unknown color: Bork
```

14. Write a piece of code that reads a shorthand text description of a playing card and prints the longhand equivalent. The shorthand description is the card's rank (2 through 10, J, Q, K, or A) followed by its suit (C, D, H, or S). You should expand the shorthand into the form "<Rank> of <Suit>". You may assume that the user types valid input. Here are two sample executions:

```
Enter a card: 9 S
Nine of Spades


Enter a card: K C
King of Clubs
```

Section 4.2: Cumulative Algorithms

15. What is wrong with the following code, which attempts to add all numbers from 1 to a given maximum? Describe how to fix the code.

```java
public static int sumTo(int n) {
    for (int i = 1; i <= n; i++) {
        int sum = 0;
        sum += i;
    }
    return sum;
}
```

16. What is wrong with the following code, which attempts to return the number of factors of a given integer n? Describe how to fix the code.

```java
public static int countFactors(int n) {
    for (int i = 1; i <= n; i++) {
        if (n % i == 0) {  // factor
            return i;
        }
    }
}
```

17. Write code to produce a cumulative product by multiplying together many numbers that are read from the console.

18. The following expression should equal 6.8, but in Java it does not. Why not?

```java
0.2 + 1.2 + 2.2 + 3.2
```

19. The following code was intended to print a message, but it actually produces no output. Describe how to fix the code to print the expected message.

```java
double gpa = 3.2;
if (gpa * 3 == 9.6) {
    System.out.println("You earned enough credits.");
}
```

Section 4.3: Text Processing

20. What output is produced by the following program?

```
 1 public class CharMystery {
 2     public static void printRange(char startLetter, char endLetter) {
 3         for (char letter = startLetter; letter <= endLetter; letter++) {
 4             System.out.print(letter);
 5         }
 6         System.out.println();
 7     }
 8
 9     public static void main(String[] args) {
10         printRange('e', 'g');
11         printRange('n', 's');
12         printRange('z', 'a');
13         printRange('q', 'r');
14     }
15 }
```

21. Write an `if` statement that tests to see whether a `String` begins with a capital letter.

22. What is wrong with the following code, which attempts to count the number occurrences of the letter `'e'` in a `String`, case-insensitively?

```
int count = 0;
for (int i = 0; i < s.length(); i++) {
    if (s.charAt(i).toLowerCase() == 'e') {
        count++;
    }
}
```

23. Consider a `String` stored in a variable called `name` that stores a person's first and last name (e.g., "Marla Singer"). Write the expression that would produce the last name followed by the first initial (e.g., "Singer, M.").

24. Write code to examine a `String` and determine how many of its letters come from the second half of the alphabet (that is, have values of `'n'` or subsequent letters). Compare case-insensitively, such that values of `'N'` through `'Z'` also count. Assume that every character in the `String` is a letter.

Section 4.4: Methods with Conditional Execution

25. Consider a method `printTriangleType` that accepts three integer arguments representing the lengths of the sides of a triangle and prints the type of triangle that these sides form. The three types are equilateral, isosceles, and scalene. An equilateral triangle has three sides of the same length, an isosceles triangle has two sides that are the same length, and a scalene triangle has three sides of different lengths.

However, certain integer values (or combinations of values) would be illegal and could not represent the sides of an actual triangle. What are these values? How would you describe the precondition(s) of the `printTriangleType` method?

26. Consider a method `getGrade` that accepts an integer representing a student's grade percentage in a course and returns that student's numerical course grade. The grade can be between `0.0` (failing) and `4.0` (perfect). What are the preconditions of such a method?

27. The following method attempts to return the median (middle) of three integer values, but it contains logic errors. In what cases does the method return an incorrect result? How can the code be fixed?

```
public static int medianOf3(int n1, int n2, int n3) {
    if (n1 < n2) {
        if (n2 < n3) {
            return n2;
        } else {
            return n3;
        }
    } else {
        if (n1 < n3) {
            return n1;
        } else {
            return n3;
        }
    }
}
```

28. One of the exercises in Chapter 3 asked you to write a method that would find the roots of a quadratic equation of the form $ax^2 + bx + c = 0$. The quadratic method was passed a, b, and c and then applied the following quadratic formula:

$$x = \frac{-b \pm \sqrt{b^2 - 4ac}}{2a}$$

Under what conditions would this formula fail? Modify the quadratic method so that it will reject invalid values of a, b, or c by throwing an exception. (If you did not complete the exercise in the previous chapter, just write the method's header and the exception-throwing code.)

29. Consider the following Java method, which is written incorrectly:

```
// This method should return how many of its three
// arguments are odd numbers.
public static void printNumOdd(int n1, int n2, int n3) {
    int count = 0;
    if (n1 % 2 != 0) {
        count++;
    } else if (n2 % 2 != 0) {
        count++;
```

```
    } else if (n3 % 2 != 0) {
        count++;
    }
    System.out.println(count + " of the 3 numbers are odd.");
}
```

Under what cases will the method print the correct answer, and when will it print an incorrect answer? What should be changed to fix the code? Can you think of a way to write the code correctly without any `if/else` statements?

Exercises

1. Write a method called `fractionSum` that accepts an integer parameter n and returns as a `double` the sum of the first n terms of the sequence

   $$\sum_{i=1}^{n} \frac{1}{i}$$

   In other words, the method should generate the following sequence:

   $$1 + \frac{1}{2} + \frac{1}{3} + \frac{1}{4} + \frac{1}{5} + \ldots$$

   You may assume that the parameter n is nonnegative.

2. Write a method called `repl` that accepts a `String` and a number of repetitions as parameters and returns the `String` concatenated that many times. For example, the call `repl("hello", 3)` should return `"hellohellohello"`. If the number of repetitions is zero or less, the method should return an empty string.

3. Write a method called `season` that takes as parameters two integers representing a month and day and returns a `String` indicating the season for that month and day. Assume that the month is specified as an integer between 1 and 12 (1 for January, 2 for February, and so on) and that the day of the month is a number between 1 and 31. If the date falls between 12/16 and 3/15, the method should return `"winter"`. If the date falls between 3/16 and 6/15, the method should return `"spring"`. If the date falls between 6/16 and 9/15, the method should return `"summer"`. And if the date falls between 9/16 and 12/15, the method should return `"fall"`.

4. Write a method called `daysInMonth` that takes a month (an integer between 1 and 12) as a parameter and returns the number of days in that month in this year. For example, the call `daysInMonth(9)` would return 30 because September has 30 days. Assume that the code is not being run during a leap year (that February always has 28 days). The following table lists the number of days in each month:

Month	1 Jan	2 Feb	3 Mar	4 Apr	5 May	6 Jun	7 Jul	8 Aug	9 Sep	10 Oct	11 Nov	12 Dec
Days	31	28	31	30	31	30	31	31	30	31	30	31

5. Write a method called `pow` that accepts a base and an exponent as parameters and returns the base raised to the given power. For example, the call `pow(3, 4)` should return `3 * 3 * 3 * 3`, or 81. Assume that the base and exponent are nonnegative.

6. Write a method called `printRange` that accepts two integers as arguments and prints the sequence of numbers between the two arguments, separated by spaces. Print an increasing sequence if the first argument is smaller than the second; otherwise, print a decreasing sequence. If the two numbers are the same, that number should be printed by itself. Here are some sample calls to `printRange`:

```
printRange(2, 7);
printRange(19, 11);
printRange(5, 5);
```

The output produced from these calls should be the following sequences of numbers:

```
2 3 4 5 6 7
19 18 17 16 15 14 13 12 11
5
```

7. Write a static method called xo that accepts an integer *size* as a parameter and prints a square of *size* by *size* characters, where all characters are "o" except that an "x" pattern of "x" characters has been drawn from the corners of the square. On the first line, the first and last characters are "x"; on the second line, the second and second-from-last characters are "x"; and so on. Here are two example outputs:

xo(5);	xo(6);
xooox	xooox
oxoxo	oxooxo
ooxoo	ooxxoo
oxoxo	ooxxoo
xooox	oxooxo
	xooox

8. Write a method called `smallestLargest` that accepts a `Scanner` for the console as a parameter and asks the user to enter numbers, then prints the smallest and largest of all the numbers supplied by the user. You may assume that the user enters a valid number greater than 0 for the number of numbers to read. Here is a sample execution:

```
How many numbers do you want to enter? 4
Number 1: 5
Number 2: 11
Number 3: -2
Number 4: 3
Smallest = -2
Largest = 11
```

9. Write a method called `evenSumMax` that accepts a `Scanner` for the console as a parameter. The method should prompt the user for a number of integers, then prompt the integer that many times. Once the user has entered all the integers, the method should print the sum of all the even numbers the user typed, along with the largest even number typed. You may assume that the user will type at least one nonnegative even integer. Here is an example dialogue:

```
How many integers? 4
Next integer? 2
```

```
Next integer? 9
Next integer? 18
Next integer? 4
Even sum = 24, Even max = 18
```

10. Write a method called `printGPA` that accepts a `Scanner` for the console as a parameter and calculates a student's grade point average. The user will type a line of input containing the student's name, then a number that represents the number of scores, followed by that many integer scores. Here are two example dialogues:

```
Enter a student record: Maria 5 72 91 84 89 78
Maria's grade is 82.8
```

```
Enter a student record: Jordan 4 86 71 62 90
Jordan's grade is 77.25
```

Maria's grade is 82.8 because her average of (72 + 91 + 84 + 89 + 78) / 5 equals 82.8.

11. Write a method called `longestName` that accepts a `Scanner` for the console and an integer n as parameters and prompts for n names, then prints the longest name (the name that contains the most characters) in the format shown below, which might result from a call of `longestName(console, 4)`:

```
name #1? Roy
name #2? DANE
name #3? sTeFaNiE
name #4? Mariana
Stefanie's name is longest
```

12. Write the method called `printTriangleType` referred to in Self-Check Problem 25. This method accepts three integer arguments representing the lengths of the sides of a triangle and prints the type of triangle that these sides form. Here are some sample calls to `printTriangleType`:

```
printTriangleType(5, 7, 7);
printTriangleType(6, 6, 6);
printTriangleType(5, 7, 8);
printTriangleType(2, 18, 2);
```

The output produced by these calls should be

```
isosceles
equilateral
scalene
isosceles
```

Your method should throw an `IllegalArgumentException` if passed invalid values, such as ones where one side's length is longer than the sum of the other two, which is impossible in a triangle. For example, the call of `printTriangleType(2, 18, 2);` should throw an exception.

13. Write a method called `average` that takes two integers as parameters and returns the average of the two integers.

14. Modify your `pow` method from Exercise 5 to make a new method called `pow2` that uses the type `double` for the first parameter and that works correctly for negative numbers. For example, the call `pow2(-4.0, 3)` should return −4.0 * −4.0 * −4.0, or −64.0, and the call `pow2(4.0, -2)` should return 1 / 16, or 0.0625.

15. Write a method called `getGrade` that accepts an integer representing a student's grade in a course and returns that student's numerical course grade. The grade can be between 0.0 (failing) and 4.0 (perfect). Assume that scores are in the range of 0 to 100 and that grades are based on the following scale:

Score	Grade
< 60	0.0
60–62	0.7
63	0.8
64	0.9
65	1.0
. . .	
92	3.7
93	3.8
94	3.9
>= 95	4.0

For an added challenge, make your method throw an `IllegalArgumentException` if the user passes a grade lower than 0 or higher than 100.

16. Write a method called `printPalindrome` that accepts a `Scanner` for the console as a parameter, prompts the user to enter one or more words, and prints whether the entered `String` is a palindrome (i.e., reads the same forward as it does backward, like `"abba"` or `"racecar"`).

For an added challenge, make the code case-insensitive, so that words like "Abba" and "Madam" will be considered palindromes.

17. Write a method called `stutter` that accepts a string parameter and returns that string with its characters repeated twice. For example, `stutter("Hello!")` returns `"HHeelllloo!!"`

18. Write a method called `wordCount` that accepts a `String` as its parameter and returns the number of words in the `String`. A word is a sequence of one or more nonspace characters (any character other than ' '). For example, the call `wordCount("hello")` should return 1, the call `wordCount("how are you?")` should return 3, the call `wordCount(" this  string  has  wide  spaces ")` should return 5, and the call `wordCount(" ")` should return 0.

19. Write a method called `quadrant` that accepts as parameters a pair of `double` values representing an (x, y) point and returns the quadrant number for that point. Recall that quadrants are numbered as integers from 1 to 4 with the upper-right quadrant numbered 1 and the subsequent quadrants numbered in a counterclockwise fashion:

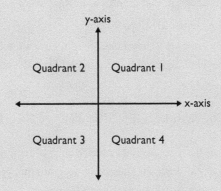

Notice that the quadrant is determined by whether the x and y coordinates are positive or negative numbers. Return 0 if the point lies on the x- or y-axis. For example, the call of `quadrant(-2.3, 3.5)` should return 2 and the call of `quadrant(4.5, -4.5)` should return 4.

20. Write a method called `numUnique` that takes three integers as parameters and returns the number of unique integers among the three. For example, the call `numUnique(18, 3, 4)` should return 3 because the parameters have three different values. By contrast, the call `numUnique(6, 7, 6)` should return 2 because there are only two unique numbers among the three parameters: 6 and 7.

21. Write a method called `perfectNumbers` that accepts an integer maximum as its parameter and prints all "perfect numbers" up to and including that maximum. A perfect number is an integer that is equal to the sum of its proper factors, that is, all numbers that evenly divide it other than 1 and itself. For example, 28 is a perfect number because 1 + 2 + 4 + 7 + 14 = 28. The call `perfectNumbers(500);` should produce the following output:

```
Perfect numbers up to 500: 6 28 496
```

Programming Projects

1. Write a program that prompts for a number and displays it in Roman numerals.

2. Write a program that prompts for a date (month, day, year) and reports the day of the week for that date. It might be helpful to know that January 1, 1601, was a Monday.

3. Write a program that compares two college applicants. The program should prompt for each student's GPA, SAT, and ACT exam scores and report which candidate is more qualified on the basis of these scores.

4. Write a program that prompts for two people's birthdays (month and day), along with today's month and day. The program should figure out how many days remain until each user's birthday and which birthday is sooner. Hint: It is much easier to solve this problem if you convert each date into an "absolute day" of year, from 1 through 365.

5. Write a program that computes a student's grade in a course. The course grade has three components: homework assignments, a midterm exam, and a final exam. The program should prompt the user for all information necessary to compute the grade, such as the number of homework assignments, the points earned and points possible for each assignment, the midterm and final exam scores, and whether each exam was curved (and, if so, by how much).

   Consider writing a variation of this program that reports what final exam score the student needs to get a certain course grade.

6. A useful technique for catching typing errors is to use a check digit. For example, suppose that a school assigns a six-digit number to each student. A seventh digit can be determined from the other digits with the use of the following formula:

   7th digit = (1 * (1st digit) + 2 * (2nd digit) + . . . + 6 * (6th digit)) % 10

   When a user types in a student number, the user types all seven digits. If the number is typed incorrectly, the check digit will fail to match in 90% of the cases. Write an interactive program that prompts for a six-digit student number and reports the check digit for that number, using the preceding formula.

7. Write a program that displays Pascal's triangle:

```
                    1
                  1   1
                1   2   1
              1   3   3   1
            1   4   6   4   1
          1   5  10  10   5   1
        1   6  15  20  15   6   1
      1   7  21  35  35  21   7   1
    1   8  28  56  70  56  28   8   1
  1   9  36  84 126 126  84  36   9  1
1  10  45 120 210 252 210 120  45  10   1
```

   Use `System.out.printf` to format the output into fields of width 4.

8. Write a program that produces a Caesar cipher of a given message string. A Caesar cipher, or rotation cipher, is formed by rotating each letter of a message by a given amount. For example, if you rotate by 3, every A becomes D; every B becomes E; and so on. Toward the end of the alphabet, you wrap around: X becomes A; Y becomes B; and Z becomes C. Your program should prompt for a message and an amount by which to rotate each letter and should output the encoded message.

```
Your message? Attack zerg at dawn
Encoding key? 3
Your message: DWWDFN CHUJ DW GDZQ
```

Program Logic and Indefinite Loops

Introduction

The chapter begins by examining a new construct called a while loop that allows you to loop an indefinite number of times. The while loop will allow you to solve a new class of programming problems in which you don't know in advance how many times you want a loop to execute. For example, game-playing programs often involve while loops because it is not possible to know beforehand how the user will play the game. Because we will be exploring game programs, we will also explore how to generate random numbers inside a Java program. We will also explore another class of algorithms known as fencepost algorithms that occur often in loop-programming tasks.

The chapter then discusses the fourth primitive type that we are going to examine in detail, boolean. The boolean type is used to store logical (true/false) information. Once you understand the details of the boolean type, you will be able to write complex loops involving multiple tests.

Next, we'll briefly examine the important topic of handling user errors.

The chapter concludes with a discussion of assertions. Using assertions, you can reason about the formal properties of programs (what is true at different points in program execution).

5.1 The `while` Loop

The `for` loops we have been writing since Chapter 2 are fairly simple loops that execute a predictable number of times. Recall that we call them *definite* loops because we know before the loops begin executing exactly how many times they will execute. Now we want to turn our attention to *indefinite* loops, which execute an unknown number of times. Indefinite loops come up often in interactive programs and file processing. For example, you don't know in advance how many times a user might want to play a game, and you won't know before you look at a file exactly how much data it stores.

The `while` loop is the first indefinite loop we will study. It has the following syntax:

```
while (<test>) {
    <statement>;
    <statement>;
    ...
    <statement>;
}
```

The diagram in Figure 5.1 indicates the flow of control for the `while` loop. The loop performs its test and, if the test evaluates to `true`, executes the controlled statements. It repeatedly tests and executes if the test evaluates to `true`. Only when the test evaluates to `false` does the loop terminate.

As Figure 5.1 indicates, the `while` loop performs its test at the top of the loop, before the body of the loop is executed. A `while` loop will not execute its controlled statements if its test evaluates to `false` the first time it is evaluated.

Here is an example of a `while` loop:

```
int number = 1;
while (number <= 200) {
    number = number * 2;
}
```

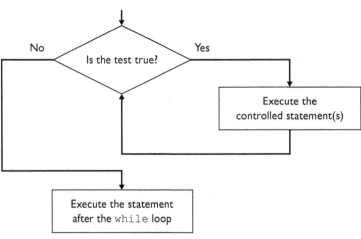

Figure 5.1   Flow of `while` loop

This loop initializes an integer variable called number to 1 and then doubles it while it is less than or equal to 200. On the surface, this operation is similar to using an if statement:

```
int number = 1;
if (number <= 200) {
    number = number * 2;
}
```

The difference between the two forms is that the while loop executes multiple times, looping until the test evaluates to false. The if statement executes the doubling statement only once, leaving number equal to 2. The while loop executes the doubling statement repeatedly, with number taking on the values 1, 2, 4, 8, 16, 32, 64, 128, and 256. The loop doesn't stop executing until the test evaluates to false. It executes the assignment statement eight times and terminates when number is set to the value 256 (the first power of 2 that is greater than 200).

Here is a while loop containing two statements:

```
int number = 1;
while (number <= max) {
    System.out.println("Hi there");
    number++;
}
```

This while loop is almost the same as the following for loop:

```
for (int number = 1; number <= max; number++) {
    System.out.println("Hi there");
}
```

The only difference between these two loops is the scope of the variable number. In the while loop, number is declared in the scope outside the loop. In the for loop, number is declared inside the loop.

A Loop to Find the Smallest Divisor

Suppose you want to find the smallest divisor of a number other than 1. Table 5.1 gives examples of what you are looking for.

Here is a pseudocode description of how you might find this value:

```
start divisor at 2.
while (the current value of divisor does not work) {
    increase divisor.
}
```

Table 5.1   Examples of Factors

Number	Factors	Smallest divisor
10	2 * 5	2
15	3 * 5	3
25	5 * 5	5
31	31	31
77	7 * 11	7

You don't start `divisor` at 1 because you are looking for the first divisor greater than 1. To refine this pseudocode, you must be more explicit about what makes a divisor work. A divisor of a number has no remainder when the number is divided by that divisor. You can rewrite this rule as the following pseudocode:

```
start divisor at 2.
while (the remainder of number/divisor is not 0) {
    increase divisor.
}
```

This exercise is a use for the mod operator, which gives the remainder for integer division. The following `while` loop performs the task:

```
int divisor = 2;
while (number % divisor != 0) {
    divisor++;
}
```

One problem you will undoubtedly encounter when you write `while` loops is the infamous infinite loop. Consider the following code:

```
int number = 1;
while (number > 0) {
    number++;
}
```

Because `number` begins as a positive value and the loop makes it larger, this loop will continue indefinitely. You must be careful when you formulate your `while` loops to avoid situations in which a piece of code will never finish executing. Every time you write a `while` loop, you should consider when and how it will finish executing.

Common Programming Error

Infinite Loop

It is relatively easy to write a while loop that never terminates. One reason it's so easy to make this mistake is that a while loop doesn't have an update step in its header like a for loop does. It's crucial for the programmer to include a correct update step because this step is needed to eventually cause the loop's test to fail.

Consider the following code, which is intended to prompt the user for a number and repeatedly print that number divided in half until 0 is reached. This first attempt doesn't compile:

```
Scanner console = new Scanner(System.in);
System.out.print("Type a number: ");

// this code does not compile
while (number > 0) {
    int number = console.nextInt();
    System.out.println(number / 2);
}
```

The problem with the preceding code is that the variable number needs to be in scope during the loop's test, so it cannot be declared inside the loop. An incorrect attempt to fix this compiler error would be to cut and paste the line initializing number outside the loop:

```
// this code has an infinite loop
int number = console.nextInt(); // moved out of loop

while (number > 0) {
    System.out.println(number / 2);
}
```

This version of the code has an infinite loop; if the loop is entered, it will never be exited. This problem arises because there is no update inside the while loop's body to change the value of number. If number is greater than 0, the loop will keep printing its value and checking the loop test, and the test will evaluate to true every time.

Continued on next page

Continued from previous page

The following version of the code solves the infinite loop problem. The loop contains an update step on each pass that divides the integer in half and stores its new value. If the integer hasn't reached 0, the loop repeats:

```
// this code behaves correctly
int number = console.nextInt(); // moved out of loop
while (number > 0) {
    number = number / 2; // update step: divide in half
    System.out.println(number);
}
```

The key idea is that every `while` loop's body should contain code to update the terms that are tested in the loop test. If the `while` loop test examines a variable's value, the loop body should potentially reassign a meaningful new value to that variable.

Random Numbers

We often want our programs to exhibit apparently random behavior. For example, we want game-playing programs to make up a number for the user to guess, shuffle a deck of cards, pick a word from a list for the user to guess, and so on. Programs are, by their very nature, predictable and nonrandom. But we can produce values that seem to be random. Such values are called *pseudorandom* because they are produced algorithmically.

> **Pseudorandom Numbers**
>
> Numbers that, although they are derived from predictable and well-defined algorithms, mimic the properties of numbers chosen at random.

Java provides several mechanisms for obtaining pseudorandom numbers. One option is to call the `random` method from the `Math` class to obtain a random value of type `double` that has the following property:

$$0.0 \leq \text{Math.random}() < 1.0$$

This method provides a quick and easy way to get a random number, and you can use multiplication to change the range of the numbers the method produces. Java also provides a class called `Random` that can be easier to use. It is included in the `java.util` package, so you have to include an import declaration at the beginning of your program to use it.

`Random` objects have several useful methods that are related to generating pseudorandom numbers, listed in Table 5.2. Each time you call one of these methods, Java will generate and return a new random number of the requested type.

Table 5.2 Useful Methods of Random Objects

Method	Description
nextInt()	Random integer between -2^{31} and ($2^{31} - 1$)
nextInt(max)	Random integer between 0 and (max $- 1$)
nextDouble()	Random real number between 0.0 (inclusive) and 1.0 (exclusive)
nextBoolean()	Random logical value of true or false

To create random numbers, you first construct a Random object:

```
Random r = new Random();
```

You can then call its nextInt method, passing it a maximum integer. The number returned will be between 0 (inclusive) and the maximum (exclusive). For example, if you call nextInt(100), you will get a number between 0 and 99. You can add 1 to the number to have a range between 1 and 100.

Let's look at a simple program that picks numbers between 1 and 10 until a particular number comes up. We'll use the Random class to construct an object for generating our pseudorandom numbers.

Our loop should look something like this (where number is the value the user has asked us to generate):

```
int result;
while (result != number) {
    result = r.nextInt(10) + 1; // random number from 1–10
    System.out.println("next number = " + result);
}
```

Notice that we have to declare the variable result outside the while loop, because result appears in the while loop test. The preceding code has the right approach, but Java won't accept it. The code generates an error message that the variable result might not be initialized. This is an example of a loop that needs *priming*.

> **Priming a Loop**
> Initializing variables before a loop to "prime the pump" and guarantee that the loop is entered.

We want to set the variable result to something that will cause the loop to be entered, but the value isn't important as long as it gets us into the loop. We do want to be careful not to set it to a value the user wants us to generate, though. We are dealing with values between 1 and 10 in this program, so we could set result to a value such as −1 that is clearly outside this range of numbers. We sometimes refer to this as a "dummy" value because we don't actually process it. Later in this chapter we will see a variation of the while loop that doesn't require this kind of priming.

The following is the complete program solution:

```java
1 import java.util.*;
2
3 public class Pick {
4     public static void main(String[] args) {
5         System.out.println("This program picks numbers from");
6         System.out.println("1 to 10 until a particular");
7         System.out.println("number comes up.");
8         System.out.println();
9
10        Scanner console = new Scanner(System.in);
11        Random r = new Random();
12
13        System.out.print("Pick a number between 1 and 10--> ");
14        int number = console.nextInt();
15
16        int result = -1; // set to -1 to make sure we enter the loop
17        int count = 0;
18        while (result != number) {
19            result = r.nextInt(10) + 1; // random number from 1-10
20            System.out.println("next number = " + result);
21            count++;
22        }
23        System.out.println("Your number came up after " +
24                            count + " times");
25    }
26 }
```

Depending on the sequence of numbers returned by the Random object, the program might end up picking the given number quickly, as in the following sample execution:

```
This program picks numbers from
1 to 10 until a particular
number comes up.

Pick a number between 1 and 10--> 2
next number = 7
next number = 8
next number = 2
Your number came up after 3 times
```

It's also possible that the program will take a while to pick the number, as in the following sample execution:

```
This program picks numbers from
1 to 10 until a particular
number comes up.

Pick a number between 1 and 10--> 10
next number = 9
next number = 7
next number = 7
next number = 5
next number = 8
next number = 8
next number = 1
next number = 5
next number = 1
next number = 9
next number = 7
next number = 10
Your number came up after 12 times
```

Common Programming Error

Misusing the Random Object

A Random object chooses a new random integer every time the nextInt method is called. When students are trying to produce a constrained random value, such as one that is odd, sometimes they mistakenly write code such as the following:

```java
// this code contains a bug
Random r = new Random();

if (r.nextInt() % 2 == 0) {
    System.out.println("Even number: " + r.nextInt());
} else {
    System.out.println("Odd number: " + r.nextInt());
}
```

The preceding code fails in many cases because the Random object produces one random integer for use in the if/else test, then another for use in whichever println statement is chosen to execute. For example, the if test might retrieve a random value of 47 from the Random object. The test would find

Continued on next page

Continued from previous page

that `47 % 2` does not equal `0`, so the code would proceed to the `else` statement. The `println` statement would then execute another call on `nextInt`, which would return a completely different number (say, `128`). The output of the code would then be the following bizarre statement:

```
Odd number: 128
```

The solution to this problem is to store the randomly chosen integer in a variable and call `nextInt` again only if another random integer is truly needed. The following code accomplishes this task:

```java
// this code behaves correctly
Random r = new Random();
int n = r.nextInt(); // save random number into a variable
if (n % 2 == 0) {
    System.out.println("Even number: " + n);
} else {
    System.out.println("Odd number: " + n);
}
```

Simulations

VideoNote

Traditional science and engineering involve a lot of real-world interaction. Scientists run experiments to test their hypotheses and engineers build prototypes to test their designs. But increasingly scientists and engineers are turning to computers as a way to increase their productivity by running simulations first to explore possibilities before they go out and run an actual experiment or build an actual prototype. A famous computer scientist named Jeanette Wing has argued that this increased use of computation by scientists and engineers will lead to computational thinking being viewed as fundamental in the same way that reading, writing, and arithmetic are considered fundamental today.

From a programming perspective, the two key ingredients in a simulation are pseudorandom numbers and loops. Some simulations can be written using `for` loops, but more often than not we use a `while` loop because the simulation should be run indefinitely until some condition is met.

As a simple example, let's look at how we would simulate the rolling of two dice until the sum of the dice is 7. We can use a `Random` object to simulate the dice, calling it once for each of the two dice. We want to loop until the sum is equal to 7 and we can print the various rolls that come up as we run the simulation. Here is a good first attempt:

```
Random r = new Random();
while (sum != 7) {
    // roll the dice once
    int roll1 = r.nextInt(6) + 1;
    int roll2 = r.nextInt(6) + 1;
    int sum = roll1 + roll2;
    System.out.println(roll1 + " + " + roll2 + " = " + sum);
}
```

The preceding code produces the following compiler error:

```
Dice.java:7: error: cannot find symbol
symbol : variable sum
location: class Dice
    while (sum != 7) {
          ^
```

```
1 error
```

The problem is that the while loop test refers to the variable sum, but the variable is declared inside the body of the loop. We can't declare the variable in the inner scope because we need to refer to it in the loop test. So we have to move the variable declaration before the loop. We also have to give the variable an initial value to guarantee that it enters the loop. This code is another example of a time when we need to prime the loop:

```
Random r = new Random();
int sum = 0; // set to 0 to make sure we enter the loop
while (sum != 7) {
    // roll the dice once
    int roll1 = r.nextInt(6) + 1;
    int roll2 = r.nextInt(6) + 1;
    sum = roll1 + roll2;
    System.out.println(roll1 + " + " + roll2 + " = " + sum);
}
```

This version of the code compiles and works properly. A sample execution follows:

```
1 + 4 = 5
5 + 6 = 11
1 + 3 = 4
4 + 3 = 7
```

do/while Loop

The while loop is the standard indefinite loop, but Java provides several alternatives. This section presents the do/while loop. Other variations are included in Appendix C.

As we have seen, the `while` loop tests at the "top" of the loop, before it executes its controlled statement. Java has an alternative known as the `do/while` loop that tests at the "bottom" of the loop. The `do/while` loop has the following syntax:

```
do {
    <statement>;
    ...
    <statement>;
} while (<test>);
```

Here is some sample code using a `do/while` loop:

```
int number = 1;
do {
    number *= 2;
} while (number <= 200);
```

This loop produces the same result as the corresponding `while` loop, doubling the variable `number` until its value reaches `256`, which is the first power of `2` greater than `200`. But unlike the `while` loop, the `do/while` loop always executes its controlled statements at least once. The diagram in Figure 5.2 shows the flow of control in a `do/while` loop.

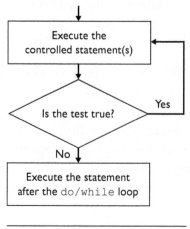

Figure 5.2   Flow of do/while loop

The `do/while` loop is most useful in situations in which you know you have to execute the loop at least once. For example, in the last section we wrote the following code that simulates the rolling of two dice until you get a sum of 7:

```
Random r = new Random();
int sum = 0; // set to 0 to make sure we enter the loop
while (sum != 7) {
    // roll the dice once
    int roll1 = r.nextInt(6) + 1;
```

```
    int roll2 = r.nextInt(6) + 1;
    sum = roll1 + roll2;
    System.out.println(roll1 + " + " + roll2 + " = " + sum);
}
```

We had to prime the loop by setting `sum` to 0 so that the computer would enter the loop. With a `do/while` loop, we can eliminate the priming:

```
Random r = new Random();
int sum;
do {
    // roll the dice once
    int roll1 = r.nextInt(6) + 1;
    int roll2 = r.nextInt(6) + 1;
    sum = roll1 + roll2;
    System.out.println(roll1 + " + " + roll2 + " = " + sum);
} while (sum != 7);
```

In this version, we always execute the body of the loop at least once, which ends up giving a value to the variable `sum` *before* it reaches the loop test that now appears at the bottom of the loop.

There are many programming problems in which using `do/while` loops is appropriate. These loops are often useful in interactive programs where you know you want to do something at least once. For example, you might have a loop that allows a user to play a game multiple times; you can be fairly sure that the user will want to play at least once. Likewise, if you are playing a guessing game with the user, you will always have to obtain at least one guess.

5.2 Fencepost Algorithms

VideoNote

A common programming problem involves a particular kind of loop known as a *fencepost loop*. Consider the following problem: You want to put up a fence that is 100 yards long, and you want to install a post every 10 yards. How many posts do you need? If you do a quick division in your head, you might think that you need 10 posts, but actually you need 11 posts. That's because fences begin and end with posts. In other words, a fence looks like Figure 5.3.

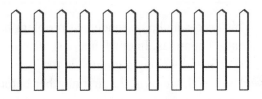

Figure 5.3 A typical fence

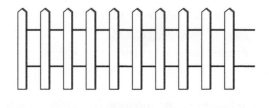

Figure 5.4   A flawed fence

Because you want posts on both the far left and the far right, you can't use the following simple loop (it doesn't plant the final post):

```
for (the length of the fence) {
    plant a post.
    attach some wire.
}
```

If you use the preceding loop, you'll get a fence that looks like Figure 5.4.

Switching the order of the two operations doesn't help, because then you miss the first post. The problem with this loop is that it produces the same number of posts as sections of wire, but we know we need an extra post. That's why this problem is also sometimes referred to as the "loop and a half" problem—we want to execute one half of this loop (planting a post) one additional time.

One solution is to plant one of the posts either before or after the loop. The usual solution is to do it before:

```
plant a post.
for (the length of the fence) {
    attach some wire.
    plant a post.
}
```

Notice that the order of the two operations in the body of the loop is now reversed because the initial post is planted before the loop is entered.

As a simple example, consider the problem of writing out the integers between 1 and 10, separated by commas. In other words, we want to get the following output:

```
1, 2, 3, 4, 5, 6, 7, 8, 9, 10
```

This task is a classic fencepost problem because we want to write out 10 numbers but only 9 commas. In our fencepost terminology, writing a number is the "post" part of the task and writing a comma is the "wire" part. So, implementing the pseudocode we developed, we print the first number before the loop:

```
System.out.print(1);
for (int i = 2; i <= 10; i++) {
```

```
    System.out.print(", " + i);
}
System.out.println();
```

Sentinel Loops

VideoNote

Suppose you want to read a series of numbers from the user and compute their sum. You could ask the user in advance how many numbers to read, as we did in the last chapter, but that isn't always convenient. What if the user has a long list of numbers to enter and hasn't counted them? One way around asking for the number is to pick some special input value that will signal the end of input. We call this a *sentinel value.*

> **Sentinel**
>
> A special value that signals the end of input.

For example, you could tell the user to enter the value –1 to stop entering numbers. But how do you structure your code to use this sentinel? In general, you'll want to use the following approach:

```
sum = 0.
while (we haven't seen the sentinel) {
    prompt and read.
    add it to the sum.
}
```

This approach doesn't quite work. Suppose, for example, that the user enters the numbers 10, 42, 5, and –1. As the pseudocode indicates, we'll prompt for and read each of these four values and add them to our sum until we encounter the sentinel value of –1. We initialize the sum to 0, so this computes (10 + 42 + 5 + –1), which is 56. But the right answer is 57. The sentinel value of –1 isn't supposed to be included in the sum.

This problem is a classic fencepost or "loop-and-a-half" problem: You want to prompt for and read a series of numbers, including the sentinel, and you want to add up most of the numbers, but you don't want to add the sentinel to the sum.

The usual fencepost solution works: We insert the first prompt-and-read instruction before the loop and reverse the order of the two steps in the body of the loop:

```
sum = 0.
prompt and read.
while (we haven't seen the sentinel) {
    add it to the sum.
    prompt and read.
}
```

You can then refine this pseudocode by introducing a variable for the number that is read from the user:

```
sum = 0.
prompt and read a value into n.
while (n is not the sentinel) {
    add n to the sum.
    prompt and read a value into n.
}
```

This pseudocode translates fairly easily into Java code:

```
Scanner console = new Scanner(System.in);
int sum = 0;
System.out.print("next integer (-1 to quit)? ");
int number = console.nextInt();
while (number != -1) {
    sum += number;
    System.out.print("next integer (-1 to quit)? ");
    number = console.nextInt();
}
System.out.println("sum = " + sum);
```

When the preceding code is executed, the interaction might look like this:

```
next integer (-1 to quit)? 34
next integer (-1 to quit)? 19
next integer (-1 to quit)? 8
next integer (-1 to quit)? 0
next integer (-1 to quit)? 17
next integer (-1 to quit)? 204
next integer (-1 to quit)? -1
sum = 282
```

Fencepost with `if`

Many of the fencepost loops that you write will require conditional execution. In fact, the fencepost problem itself can be solved with an `if` statement. Remember that the classic solution to the fencepost is to handle the first post before the loop begins:

```
plant a post.
for (the length of the fence) {
    attach some wire.
    plant a post.
}
```

This solution solves the problem, but it can be confusing because inside the loop the steps are apparently in reverse order. You can use an `if` statement and keep the original order of the steps:

```
for (the length of the fence) {
    plant a post.
    if (this isn't the last post) {
        attach some wire.
    }
}
```

This variation isn't used as often as the classic solution because it involves both a loop test and a test inside the loop. Often these tests are nearly identical, so it is inefficient to test the same thing twice each time the loop executes. But there will be situations in which you might use this approach. For example, in the classic approach, the lines of code that correspond to planting a post are repeated. If you were writing a program in which this step required a lot of code, you might decide that putting the `if` statement inside the loop was a better approach, even if it led to some extra testing.

As an example, consider writing a method called `multiprint` that will print a string a particular number of times. Suppose that you want the output on a line by itself, inside square brackets, and separated by commas. Here are two example calls:

```
multiprint("please", 4);
multiprint("beetlejuice", 3);
```

You would expect these calls to produce the following output:

```
[please, please, please, please]
[beetlejuice, beetlejuice, beetlejuice]
```

Your first attempt at writing this method might be a simple loop that prints square brackets outside the loop and prints the string and a comma inside the loop:

```
public static void multiprint(String s, int times) {
    System.out.print("[");
    for (int i = 1; i <= times; i++) {
        System.out.print(s + ", ");
    }
    System.out.println("]");
}
```

Unfortunately, this code produces an extraneous comma after the last value:

```
[please, please, please, please, ]
[beetlejuice, beetlejuice, beetlejuice, ]
```

Because the commas are separators, you want to print one more string than comma (e.g., two commas to separate the three occurrences of "beetlejuice"). You can use the classic solution to the fencepost problem to achieve this effect by printing one string outside the loop and reversing the order of the printing inside the loop:

```java
public static void multiprint(String s, int times) {
    System.out.print("[" + s);
    for (int i = 2; i <= times; i++) {
        System.out.print(", " + s);
    }
    System.out.println("]");
}
```

Notice that because you're printing one of the strings before the loop begins, you have to modify the loop so that it won't print as many strings as it did before. Adjusting the loop variable i to start at two accounts for the first value that is printed before the loop.

Unfortunately, this solution does not work properly either. Consider what happens when you ask the method to print a string zero times, as in:

```java
multiprint("please don't", 0);
```

This call produces the following incorrect output:

```
[please don't]
```

You want it to be possible for a user to request zero occurrences of a string, so the method shouldn't produce that incorrect output. The problem is that the classic solution to the fencepost problem involves printing one value before the loop begins. To get the method to behave correctly for the zero case, you can include an if/else statement:

```java
public static void multiprint(String s, int times) {
    if (times == 0) {
        System.out.println("[]");
    } else {
        System.out.print("[" + s);
        for (int i = 2; i <= times; i++) {
            System.out.print(", " + s);
        }
        System.out.println("]");
    }
}
```

Alternatively, you can include an `if` statement inside the loop (the double-test approach):

```java
public static void multiprint(String s, int times) {
    System.out.print("[");
    for (int i = 1; i <= times; i++) {
        System.out.print(s);
        if (i < times) {
            System.out.print(", ");
        }
    }
    System.out.println("]");
}
```

Although the preceding version of the code performs a similar test twice on each iteration, it is simpler than using the classic fencepost solution and its special case. Neither solution is better than the other, as there is a tradeoff involved. If you think that the code will be executed often and that the loop will iterate many times, you might be more inclined to use the efficient solution. Otherwise, you might choose the simpler code.

5.3 The boolean Type

VideoNote

George Boole was such a good logician that Java has a data type named after him. The Java type `boolean` is used to describe logical true/false relationships. Recall that `boolean` is one of the primitive types, like `int`, `double`, and `char`.

Novices often wonder why computer scientists are so interested in logic. The answer is that logic is fundamental to computing in the same way that physics is fundamental to engineering. Engineers study physics because they want to build real-world artifacts that are governed by the laws of physics. If you don't understand physics, you're likely to build a bridge that will collapse. Computer scientists build artifacts as well, but in a virtual world that is governed by the laws of logic. If you don't understand logic, you're likely to build computer programs that collapse.

Without realizing it, you have already used `boolean`s. All of the control structures we have looked at—`if`/`else` statements, `for` loops, and `while` loops—are controlled by expressions that specify tests. For example, the expression

```java
number % 2 == 0
```

is a test for divisibility by 2. It is also a Boolean expression. Boolean expressions are meant to capture the concepts of truth and falsity, so it is not surprising that the domain of type `boolean` has only two values: `true` and `false`. The words `true` and `false` are reserved words in Java. They are the literal values of type `boolean`. All Boolean expressions, when evaluated, will return one or the other of these literals. Don't confuse these special values with the string literals `"true"` and `"false"`. You don't need quotes to refer to the Boolean literals.

When you write a program that manipulates numerical values, you'll often want to compute a value and store it in a variable or write a method that captures some complex formula. We end up doing the same thing with type `boolean`. We might want to record a Boolean value in a variable and we often write methods that return Boolean results. For example, we have seen that the `String` class has methods that return a Boolean result, including `startsWith`, `endsWith`, `equals`, and `equalsIgnoreCase`.

To understand this better, remember what these terms mean for the type `int`. The literals of type `int` include 0, 1, 2, and so on. Because these are literals of type `int`, you can write expressions like the following ones with them:

```
int number1 = 1;
int number2 = 0;
```

Consider what you can do with variables of type `boolean`. Suppose you define two `boolean` variables, `test1` and `test2`. These variables can take on only two possible values: `true` and `false`. You can say:

```
boolean test1 = true;
boolean test2 = false;
```

You can also write a statement that copies the value of one `boolean` variable to another, as with variables of any other type:

```
test1 = test2;
```

Furthermore, you know that the assignment statement can use expressions like:

```
number1 = 2 + 2;
```

and that the simple tests you have been using are Boolean expressions. That means you can write statements like the following ones:

```
test1 = (2 + 2 == 4);
test2 = (3 * 100 < 250);
```

These assignment statements say, in effect, "Set this `boolean` variable according to the truth value returned by the following test." The first statement sets the variable `test1` to `true`, because the test evaluates to `true`. The second sets the variable `test2` to `false`, because the second test evaluates to `false`. You don't need to include parentheses, but they make the statements more readable.

Obviously, then, assignment is one of the operations you can perform on variables of type `boolean`.

Logical Operators

In Java, you can form complicated Boolean expressions using what are known as the *logical operators,* shown in Table 5.3.

Table 5.3 Logical Operators

Operator	Meaning	Example	Value
`&&`	AND (conjunction)	`(2 == 2) && (3 < 4)`	`true`
`||`	OR (disjunction)	`(1 < 2) || (2 == 3)`	`true`
`!`	NOT (negation)	`!(2 == 2)`	`false`

The NOT operator (`!`) reverses the truth value of its operand. If an expression evaluates to `true`, its negation evaluates to `false`, and vice versa. You can express this relationship in a truth table. The truth table that follows has two columns, one for a variable and one for its negation. For each value of the variable, the table shows the corresponding value of the negation.

Truth Table for NOT (`!`)

p	!p
`true`	`false`
`false`	`true`

In addition to the negation operator, there are two logical connectives you will use, AND (`&&`) and OR (`||`). You use these connectives to tie together two Boolean expressions, creating a new Boolean expression. The following truth table shows that the AND operator evaluates to `true` only when both of its individual operands are `true`.

Truth Table for AND (`&&`)

p	q	p && q
`true`	`true`	`true`
`true`	`false`	`false`
`false`	`true`	`false`
`false`	`false`	`false`

The following truth table shows that the OR operator evaluates to `true` except when both operands are `false`.

Truth Table for OR (| |)

p	q	p || q
true	true	true
true	false	true
false	true	true
false	false	false

The Java OR operator has a slightly different meaning from the English word "or." In English you say, "I'll study tonight or I'll go to a movie." One or the other will be true, but not both. The OR operator is more like the English expression "and/or": If one or both operands are `true`, the overall proposition is `true`.

You generally use logical operators when what you have to say cannot be reduced to a single test. For example, as we saw in the previous chapter, if you want to do a particular operation when a number is between 1 and 10, you might say,

```java
if (number >= 1) {
    if (number <= 10) {
        doSomething();
    }
}
```

But you can say this more easily using logical AND:

```java
if (number >= 1 && number <= 10) {
    doSomething();
}
```

People use the words "and" and "or" all the time, but Java only allows you to use them in the strict logical sense. Be careful not to write code like the following:

```java
// this does not compile
if (x == 1 || 2 || 3) {
    doSomething();
}
```

In English, we would read this as "x equals 1 or 2 or 3," which makes sense to us, but it doesn't make sense to Java. You might also be tempted to write code like the following:

```java
// this does not compile
if (1 <= x <= 10) {
    doSomethingElse();
}
```

In mathematics, this expression would make sense and would test whether x is between 1 and 10 inclusive. However, the expression doesn't make sense in Java.

You can only use the logical AND and OR operators to combine a series of Boolean expressions. Otherwise, the computer will not understand what you mean. To express the "1 or 2 or 3" idea, combine three different Boolean expressions with logical ORs:

```
if (x == 1 || x == 2 || x == 3) {
    doSomething();
}
```

To express the "between 1 and 10 inclusive" idea, combine two Boolean expressions with a logical AND:

```
if (1 <= x && x <= 10) {
    doSomethingElse();
}
```

Now that we've introduced the AND, OR, and NOT logical operators, it's time to revisit our precedence table. The NOT operator appears at the top, with the highest level of precedence. The other two logical operators have fairly low precedence, lower than the arithmetic and relational operators but higher than the assignment operators. The AND operator has a slightly higher level of precedence than the OR operator. Table 5.4 includes these new operators.

According to these rules of precedence, when Java evaluates an expression like the following one, the computer will evaluate the NOT first, the AND second, and then the OR.

```
if (test1 || !test2 && test3) {
    doSomething();
}
```

Table 5.4 Java Operator Precedence

Description	Operators
unary operators	!, ++, --, +, -
multiplicative operators	*, /, %
additive operators	+, -
relational operators	<, >, <=, >=
equality operators	==, !=
logical AND	&&
logical OR	||
assignment operators	=, +=, -=, *=, /=, %=, &&=, ||=

Short-Circuited Evaluation

In this section we will explore the use of the logical operators to solve a complex programming task, and we'll introduce an important property of these operators. We will write a method called `firstWord` that takes a `String` as a parameter and returns the first word in the string. To keep things simple, we will adopt the convention that a `String` is broken up into individual words by spaces. If the `String` has no words at all, the method should return an empty string. Here are a few example calls:

Method Call	Value Returned
firstWord("four score and seven years")	"four"
firstWord("all-one-word-here")	"all-one-word-here"
firstWord(" lots of space here")	"lots"
firstWord(" ")	""

Remember that we can call the `substring` method to pull out part of a string. We pass two parameters to the `substring` method: the starting index of the substring and the index one beyond the end of the substring. If the string is stored in a variable called s, our task basically reduces to the following steps:

```
set start to the first index of the word.
set stop to the index just beyond the word.
return s.substring(start, stop).
```

As a first approximation, let's assume that the starting index is 0. This starting index won't work for strings that begin with spaces, but it will allow us to focus on the second step in the pseudocode. Consider a string that begins with `"four score"`. If we examine the individual characters of the string and their indexes, we find the following pattern:

We set `start` to 0. We want to set the variable `stop` to the index just beyond the end of the first word. In this example, the word we want is `"four"`, and it extends from indexes 0 through 3. So, if we want the variable `stop` to be one beyond the end of the desired substring, we want to set it to index 4, the location of the first space in the string.

So how do we find the first space in the string? We use a `while` loop. We simply start at the front of the string and loop until we get to a space:

```
set stop to 0.
while (the character at index stop is not a space) {
    increase stop by 1.
}
```

This is easily converted into Java code. Combining it with our assumption that `start` will be 0, we get:

```
public static String firstWord(String s) {
    int start = 0;
    int stop = 0;
    while (s.charAt(stop) != ' ') {
        stop++;
    }
    return s.substring(start, stop);
}
```

This version of the method works for many cases, including our sample string, but it doesn't work for all strings. It has two major limitations. We began by assuming that the string did not begin with spaces, so we know we have to fix that limitation.

The second problem is that this version of `firstWord` doesn't work on one-word strings. For example, if we execute it with a string like `"four"`, it generates a `StringIndexOutOfBoundsException` indicating that 4 is not a legal index. The exception occurs because our code assumes that we will eventually find a space, but there is no space in the string `"four"`. So `stop` is incremented until it becomes equal to 4, and an exception is thrown because there is no character at index 4. This is sometimes referred to as "running off the end of the string."

To address this problem, we need to incorporate a test that involves the length of the string. Many novices attempt to do this by using some combination of `while` and `if`, as in the following code:

```
int stop = 0;
while (stop < s.length()) {
    if (s.charAt(stop) != ' ') {
        stop++;
    }
}
```

This code works for one-word strings like `"four"` because as soon as `stop` becomes equal to the length of the string, we break out of the loop. However, it doesn't work for the original multiword cases like `"four score"`. We end up in an infinite loop because once `stop` becomes equal to 4, we stop incrementing it, but we get trapped inside the loop because the test says to continue as long as `stop` is less than the length of the string. This approach of putting an `if` inside a `while` led to a world-famous bug on December 31, 2008, when Zune music players all over the world stopped working (see Self-Check Problem 21 for more details).

The point to recognize is that in this case we need to use two different conditions in controlling the loop. We want to continue incrementing `stop` only if we know that we haven't seen a space *and* that we haven't reached the end of the string. We can express that idea using the logical AND operator:

```
int stop = 0;
while (s.charAt(stop) != ' ' && stop < s.length()) {
    stop++;
}
```

Unfortunately, even this test does not work. It expresses the two conditions properly, because we want to make sure that we haven't reached a space and we want to make sure that we haven't reached the end of the string. But think about what happens just as we reach the end of a string. Suppose that s is "four" and stop is equal to 3. We see that the character at index 3 is not a space and we see that stop is less than the length of the string, so we increment one more time and stop becomes 4. As we come around the loop, we test whether s.charAt(4) is a space. This test throws an exception. We also test whether stop is less than 4, which it isn't, but that test comes too late to avoid the exception.

Java offers a solution for this situation. The logical operators && and || use *short-circuited evaluation*.

> ### Short-Circuited Evaluation
>
> The property of the logical operators && and || that prevents the second operand from being evaluated if the overall result is obvious from the value of the first operand.

In our case, we are performing two different tests and asking for the logical AND of the two tests. If either test fails, the overall result is false, so if the first test fails, it's not necessary to perform the second test. Because of short-circuited evaluation—that is, because the overall result is obvious from the first test—we don't perform the second test at all. In other words, the performance and evaluation of the second test are prevented (short-circuited) by the fact that the first test fails.

This means we need to reverse the order of our two tests:

```
int stop = 0;
while (stop < s.length() && s.charAt(stop) != ' ') {
    stop++;
}
```

If we run through the same scenario again with stop equal to 3, we pass both of these tests and increment stop to 4. Then, as we come around the loop again, we first test to see if stop is less than s.length(). It is not, which means the test evaluates to false. As a result, Java knows that the overall expression will evaluate to false and never evaluates the second test. This order of events prevents the exception from occurring, because we never test whether s.charAt(4) is a space.

This solution gives us a second version of the method:

```java
public static String firstWord(String s) {
    int start = 0;
    int stop = 0;
    while (stop < s.length() && s.charAt(stop) != ' ') {
        stop++;
    }
    return s.substring(start, stop);
}
```

But remember that we assumed that the first word starts at position 0. That won't necessarily be the case. For example, if we pass a string that begins with several spaces, this method will return an empty string. We need to modify the code so that it skips any leading spaces. Accomplishing that goal requires another loop. As a first approximation, we can write the following code:

```java
int start = 0;
while (s.charAt(start) == ' ') {
    start++;
}
```

This code works for most strings, but it fails in two important cases. The loop test assumes we will find a nonspace character. What if the string is composed entirely of spaces? In that case, we'll simply run off the end of the string, generating a `StringIndexOutOfBoundsException`. And what if the string is empty to begin with? We'll get an error immediately when we ask about `s.charAt(0)`, because there is no character at index 0.

We could decide that these cases constitute errors. After all, how can you return the first word if there is no word? So, we could document a precondition that the string contains at least one nonspace character, and throw an exception if we find that it doesn't. Another approach is to return an empty string in these cases.

To deal with the possibility of the string being empty, we need to modify our loop to incorporate a test on the length of the string. If we add it at the end of our `while` loop test, we get the following code:

```java
int start = 0;
while (s.charAt(start) == ' ' && start < s.length()) {
    start++;
}
```

But this code has the same flaw we saw before. It is supposed to prevent problems when `start` becomes equal to the length of the string, but when this situation occurs, a `StringIndexOutOfBoundsException` will be thrown before the computer reaches the test on the length of the string. So these tests also have to be reversed to take advantage of short-circuited evaluation:

```
int start = 0;
while (start < s.length() && s.charAt(start) == ' ') {
    start++;
}
```

To combine these lines of code with our previous code, we have to change the initialization of stop. We no longer want to search from the front of the string. Instead, we need to initialize stop to be equal to start. Putting these pieces together, we get the following version of the method:

```
public static String firstWord(String s) {
    int start = 0;
    while (start < s.length() && s.charAt(start) == ' ') {
        start++;
    }
    int stop = start;
    while (stop < s.length() && s.charAt(stop) != ' ') {
        stop++;
    }
    return s.substring(start, stop);
}
```

This version works in all cases, skipping any leading spaces and returning an empty string if there is no word to return.

boolean Variables and Flags

All if/else statements are controlled by Boolean tests. The tests can be boolean variables or Boolean expressions. Consider, for example, the following code:

```
if (number > 0) {
    System.out.println("positive");
} else {
    System.out.println("not positive");
}
```

This code could be rewritten as follows:

```
boolean positive = (number > 0);
if (positive) {
    System.out.println("positive");
} else {
    System.out.println("not positive");
}
```

Using boolean variables adds to the readability of your programs because it allows you to give names to tests. Consider the kind of code you would generate for a dating program. You might have some integer variables that describe certain attributes of a person: looks, to store a rough estimate of physical beauty (on a scale of 1–10); IQ, to store intelligence quotient; income, to store gross annual income; and snothers, to track intimate friends ("snother" is short for "significant other"). Given these variables to specify a person's attributes, you can develop various tests of suitability. As you are writing the program, you can use boolean variables to give names to those tests, adding greatly to the readability of the code:

```java
boolean cute = (looks >= 9);
boolean smart = (IQ > 125);
boolean rich = (income > 100000);
boolean available = (snothers == 0);
boolean awesome = cute && smart && rich && available;
```

You might find occasion to use a special kind of boolean variable called *a flag*. Typically we use flags within loops to record error conditions or to signal completion. Different flags test different conditions. As an analogy, consider a referee at a sports game who watches for a particular illegal action and throws a flag if it happens. You sometimes hear an announcer saying, "There is a flag down on the play."

Let's introduce a flag into the cumulative sum code we saw in the previous chapter:

```java
double sum = 0.0;
for (int i = 1; i <= totalNumber; i++) {
    System.out.print("    #" + i + "? ");
    double next = console.nextDouble();
    sum += next;
}
System.out.println("sum = " + sum);
```

Suppose we want to know whether the sum ever goes negative at any point. Notice that this situation isn't the same as the situation in which the sum ends up being negative. Like a bank account balance, the sum might switch back and forth between positive and negative. As you make a series of deposits and withdrawals, the bank will keep track of whether you overdraw your account along the way. Using a boolean flag, we can modify the preceding loop to keep track of whether the sum ever goes negative and report the result after the loop:

```java
double sum = 0.0;
boolean negative = false;
for (int i = 1; i <= totalNumber; i++) {
    System.out.print("    #" + i + "? ");
    double next = console.nextDouble();
```

```
        sum += next;
        if (sum < 0.0) {
            negative = true;
        }
    }
}
System.out.println("sum = " + sum);
if (negative) {
    System.out.println("Sum went negative");
} else {
    System.out.println("Sum never went negative");
}
```

Boolean Zen

In 1974, Robert Pirsig started a cultural trend with his book *Zen and the Art of Motorcycle Maintenance: An Inquiry into Values.* A slew of later books copied the title with *Zen and the Art of X,* where *X* was Poker, Knitting, Writing, Foosball, Guitar, Public School Teaching, Making a Living, Falling in Love, Quilting, Stand-up Comedy, the SAT, Flower Arrangement, Fly Tying, Systems Analysis, Fatherhood, Screenwriting, Diabetes Maintenance, Intimacy, Helping, Street Fighting, Murder, and on and on. There was even a book called *Zen and the Art of Anything.*

We now join this cultural trend by discussing Zen and the art of type `boolean`. It seems to take a while for many novices to get used to Boolean expressions. Novices often write overly complex expressions involving `boolean` values because they don't grasp the simplicity that is possible when you "get" how the `boolean` type works.

For example, suppose that you are writing a game-playing program that involves two-digit numbers, each of which is composed of two different digits. In other words, the program will use numbers like 42 that are composed of two distinct digits, but not numbers like 6 (only one digit), 394 (more than two digits), or 22 (both digits are the same). You might find yourself wanting to test whether a given number is legal for use in the game. You can restrict yourself to two-digit numbers with a test like the following one:

```
n >= 10 && n <= 99
```

You also have to test to make sure that the two digits aren't the same. You can get the digits of a two-digit number with the expressions `n / 10` and `n % 10`. So you can expand the test to ensure that the digits aren't the same:

```
n >= 10 && n <= 99 && (n / 10 != n % 10)
```

This test is a good example of a situation in which you could use a method to capture a complex Boolean expression. Returning a `boolean` will allow you to call the method as many times as you want without having to copy this complex expression each time, and you can give a name to this computation to make the program more readable.

Suppose you want to call the method `isTwoUniqueDigits`. You want the method to take a value of type `int` and return `true` if the `int` is composed of two unique digits and `false` if it is not. So, the method would look like the following:

```
public static boolean isTwoUniqueDigits(int n) {
    ...
}
```

How would you write the body of this method? We've already written the test, so we just have to figure out how to incorporate it into the method. The method has a `boolean` return type, so you want it to return the value `true` when the test succeeds and the value `false` when it fails. You can write the method as follows:

```
public static boolean isTwoUniqueDigits(int n) {
    if (n >= 10 && n <= 99 && (n % 10 != n / 10)) {
        return true;
    } else {
        return false;
    }
}
```

This method works, but it is more verbose than it needs to be. The preceding code evaluates the test that we developed. That expression is of type `boolean`, which means that it evaluates to either `true` or `false`. The `if/else` statement tells the computer to return `true` if the expression evaluates to `true` and to return `false` if it evaluates to `false`. But why use this construct? If the method is going to return `true` when the expression evaluates to `true` and return `false` when it evaluates to `false`, you can just return the value of the expression directly:

```
public static boolean isTwoUniqueDigits(int n) {
    return (n >= 10 && n <= 99 && (n % 10 != n / 10));
}
```

Even the preceding version can be simplified, because the parentheses are not necessary (although they make it clearer exactly what the method will return). This code evaluates the test that we developed to determine whether a number is composed of two unique digits and returns the result (`true` when it does, `false` when it does not).

Consider an analogy to integer expressions. To someone who understands Boolean Zen, the `if/else` version of this method looks as odd as the following code:

```
if (x == 1) {
    return 1;
} else if (x == 2) {
    return 2;
} else if (x == 3) {
    return 3;
```

```
} else if (x == 4) {
    return 4;
} else if (x == 5) {
    return 5;
}
```

If you always want to return the value of x, you should just say:

```
return x;
```

A similar confusion can occur when students use `boolean` variables. In the last section we looked at a variation of the cumulative sum algorithm that used a `boolean` variable called `negative` to keep track of whether or not the sum ever goes negative. We then used an `if/else` statement to print a message reporting the result:

```
if (negative) {
    System.out.println("Sum went negative");
} else {
    System.out.println("Sum never went negative");
}
```

Some novices would write this code as follows:

```
if (negative == true) {
    System.out.println("Sum went negative");
} else {
    System.out.println("Sum never went negative");
}
```

The comparison is unnecessary because the `if/else` statement expects an expression of type `boolean` to appear inside the parentheses. A `boolean` variable is already of the appropriate type, so we don't need to test whether it equals `true`; it either *is* `true` or it isn't (in which case it is `false`). To someone who understands Boolean Zen, the preceding test seems as redundant as saying:

```
if ((negative == true) == true) {
    ...
}
```

Novices also often write tests like the following:

```
if (negative == false) {
    ...
}
```

This makes some sense because the test is doing something useful, in that it switches the meaning of the `boolean` variable (evaluating to `true` if the variable is `false` and evaluating to `false` if the variable is `true`). But the negation operator is designed to do this kind of switching of `boolean` values, so this test is better written as follows:

```
if (!negative) {
    ...
}
```

You should get used to reading the exclamation mark as "not", so this test would be read as "if not negative." To those who understand Boolean Zen, that is a more concise way to express the test than to test whether `negative` is equal to `false`.

Negating Boolean Expressions

Programmers often find themselves needing to form the negation of a complex Boolean expression. For example, it is often easiest to reason about a loop in terms of an exit condition that would make us want to stop the loop, but the `while` loop requires us to express the code in terms of a continuation condition. Suppose that you want to write a loop that keeps prompting the user for an integer until that integer is a two-digit number. Because two-digit numbers range from 10 to 99, you can use the following lines of code to test whether a number has exactly two digits:

```
number >= 10 && number <= 99
```

To put this in a `while` loop, we have to turn the test around because the `while` loop test is a continuation test. In other words, we want to stay in the loop while this is *not* true (while the user has not yet given us a two-digit number). One approach is to use the logical NOT operator to negate this expression:

```
while (!(number >= 10 && number <= 99))
```

Notice that we need to parenthesize the entire Boolean expression and then put the NOT operator in front of it. While this approach works, it is generally considered bad style. It is best to simplify this expression.

A general approach to simplifying such expressions was formalized by the British logician Augustus De Morgan. We can apply one of two rules that are known as *De Morgan's laws*.

Table 5.5 shows De Morgan's laws. Notice that when you negate a Boolean expression, each operand is negated (p becomes `!p` and q becomes `!q`) and the logical operator flips. Logical OR becomes logical AND and vice versa when you compute the negation.

Table 5.5   De Morgan's Laws

Original expression	Negated expression	Simplified negation
p || q	!(p || q)	!p && !q
p && q	!(p && q)	!p || !q

We can use the first De Morgan's law for our two-digit number program because we are trying to find the negation of an expression that involves the logical OR operator. Instead of writing:

```
while (!(number >= 10 && number <= 99))
```

we can say:

```
while (number < 10 || number > 99)
```

Each individual test has been negated and the AND operator has been replaced with an OR operator.

Let's look at a second example that involves the other De Morgan's law. Suppose that you want to ask the user a question and you want to force the user to answer either "yes" or "no". If you have a `string` variable called `response`, you can use the following test to describe what you want to be true:

```
response.equals("yes") || response.equals("no")
```

If we're writing a loop to keep reading a response until this expression evaluates to `true`, then we want to write the loop so that it uses the negation of this test. So, once again, we could use the NOT operator for the entire expression:

```
while (!(response.equals("yes") || response.equals("no")))
```

Once again it is best to simplify the expression using De Morgan's law:

```
while (!response.equals("yes") && !response.equals("no"))
```

5.4 User Errors

In the previous chapter, you learned that it is good programming practice to think about the preconditions of a method and to mention them in the comments for the method. You also learned that in some cases your code can throw exceptions if preconditions are violated.

When you are writing interactive programs, the simplest approach is to assume that the user will provide good input. You can then document your preconditions and throw exceptions when the user input isn't what was expected. In general, though, it's better to write programs that don't make assumptions about user input. You've seen, for example, that the Scanner object can throw an exception if the user enters the wrong kind of data. It's preferable to write programs that can deal with user errors. Such programs are referred to as being *robust*.

> **Robust**
>
> Ability of a program to execute even when presented with illegal data.

In this section we will explore how to write robust interactive programs. Before you can write robust code, though, you have to understand some special functionality of the Scanner class.

Scanner Lookahead

The Scanner class has methods that allow you to perform a test before you read a value. In other words, it allows you to look before you leap. For each of the "next" methods of the Scanner class, there is a corresponding "has" method that tells you whether or not you can perform the given operation.

For example, you will often want to read an int using a Scanner object. But what if the user types something other than an int? Scanner has a method called hasNextInt that tells you whether or not reading an int is currently possible. To determine whether it is possible, the Scanner object looks at the next token and checks whether it can be interpreted as an integer.

We tend to interpret certain sequences of characters as particular types of data, but when we read tokens, they can be interpreted in different ways. The following program will allow us to explore this concept:

```java
1  import java.util.*;
2
3  public class ExamineInput1 {
4      public static void main(String[] args) {
5          System.out.println("This program examines the ways");
6          System.out.println("a token can be read.");
7          System.out.println();
8
9          Scanner console = new Scanner(System.in);
10
11         System.out.print("token? ");
12         System.out.println("  hasNextInt = " +
13                             console.hasNextInt());
14         System.out.println("  hasNextDouble = " +
15                             console.hasNextDouble());
```

```
16            System.out.println("  hasNext = " + console.hasNext());
17     }
18 }
```

Let's look at a few sample executions. Here is the output of the program when we enter the token 348:

```
This program examines the ways
a token can be read.

token? 348
  hasNextInt = true
  hasNextDouble = true
  hasNext = true
```

As you'd expect, the call on `hasNextInt` returns `true`, which means that we could interpret this token as an integer. The `Scanner` would also allow us to interpret this token as a double, so `hasNextDouble` also returns `true`. But notice that `hasNext()` returns `true` as well. That result means that we could call the `next` method to read in this token as a `String`.

Here's another execution, this time for the token 348.2:

```
This program examines the ways
a token can be read.

token? 348.2
  hasNextInt = false
  hasNextDouble = true
  hasNext = true
```

This token cannot be interpreted as an `int`, but it can be interpreted as a `double` or a `String`. Finally, consider this execution for the token `hello`:

```
This program examines the ways
a token can be read.

token? hello
  hasNextInt = false
  hasNextDouble = false
  hasNext = true
```

The token `hello` can't be interpreted as an `int` or `double`; it can only be interpreted as a `String`.

Handling User Errors

Consider the following code fragment:

```
Scanner console = new Scanner(System.in);
System.out.print("How old are you? ");
int age = console.nextInt();
```

What if the user types something that is not an integer? If that happens, the `Scanner` will throw an exception on the call to `nextInt`. We saw in the previous section that we can test whether or not the next token can be interpreted as an integer by using the `hasNextInt` method. So, we can test before reading an `int` whether the user has typed an appropriate value.

If the user types something other than an integer, we want to discard the input, print out some kind of error message, and prompt for a second input. We want this code to execute in a loop so that we keep discarding input and generating error messages as necessary until the user enters legal input.

Here is a first attempt at a solution in pseudocode:

```
while (user hasn't given us an integer) {
    prompt.
    discard input.
    generate an error message.
}
read the integer.
```

This reflects what we want to do, in general. We want to keep prompting, discarding, and generating error messages as long as the input is illegal, and when a legal value is entered, we want to read the integer. Of course, in that final case we don't want to discard the input or generate an error message. In other words, the last time through the loop we want to do just the first of these three steps (prompting, but not discarding and not generating an error message). This is another classic fencepost problem, and we can solve it in the usual way by putting the initial prompt before the loop and changing the order of the operations within the loop:

```
prompt.
while (user hasn't given us an integer) {
    discard input.
    generate an error message.
    prompt.
}
read the integer.
```

This pseudocode is fairly easy to turn into actual Java code:

```
Scanner console = new Scanner(System.in);
System.out.print("How old are you? ");
while (!console.hasNextInt()) {
    console.next(); // to discard the input
    System.out.println("Not an integer; try again.");
    System.out.print("How old are you? ");
}
int age = console.nextInt();
```

In fact, this is such a common operation that it is worth turning into a static method:

```
// prompts until a valid number is entered
public static int getInt(Scanner console, String prompt) {
    System.out.print(prompt);
    while (!console.hasNextInt()) {
        console.next(); // to discard the input
        System.out.println("Not an integer; try again.");
        System.out.print(prompt);
    }
    return console.nextInt();
}
```

Using this method, we can rewrite our original code as follows:

```
Scanner console = new Scanner(System.in);
int age = getInt(console, "How old are you? ");
```

When you execute this code, the interaction looks like this:

```
How old are you? what?
Not an integer; try again.
How old are you? 18.4
Not an integer; try again.
How old are you? ten
Not an integer; try again.
How old are you? darn!
Not an integer; try again.
How old are you? help
Not an integer; try again.
How old are you? 19
```

5.5 Assertions and Program Logic

Logicians concern themselves with declarative statements called *assertions*.

> **Assertion**
>
> A declarative sentence that is either true or false.

The following statements are all assertions:

- 2 + 2 equals 4.
- The sun is larger than the Earth.
- $x > 45$.
- It was raining.
- The rain in Spain falls mainly on the plain.

The following statements are not assertions (the first is a question and the second is a command):

- How much do you weigh?
- Take me home.

Some assertions are true or false depending upon their context:

- $x > 45$. (The validity of this statement depends on the value of x.)
- It was raining. (The validity of this statement depends on the time and location.)

You can pin down whether they are true or false by providing a context:

- When $x = 13$, $x > 45$.
- On July 4, 1776, in Philadelphia, it was raining.

To write programs correctly and efficiently, you must learn to make assertions about your programs and to understand the contexts in which those assertions will be true. For example, if you are trying to obtain a nonnegative number from the user, you want the assertion "Number is nonnegative" to be true. You can use a simple prompt and read:

```
System.out.print("Please give me a nonnegative number--> ");
double number = console.nextDouble();
// is number nonnegative?
```

But the user can ignore your request and input a negative number anyway. In fact, users often input values that you don't expect, usually because they are confused. Given the uncertainty of user input, this particular assertion may sometimes be true and sometimes false. But something later in the program may depend on the assertion being true. For example, if you are going to take the square root of that number, you must be sure the number is nonnegative. Otherwise, you might end up with a bad result.

Using a loop, you can guarantee that the number you get is nonnegative:

```
System.out.print("Please give me a nonnegative number--> ");
double number = console.nextDouble();
while (number < 0.0) {
    System.out.print("That is a negative number. Try again--> ");
    number = console.nextDouble();
}
// is number nonnegative?
```

You know that `number` will be nonnegative after the loop; otherwise, the program would not exit the `while` loop. As long as a user gives negative values, your program stays in the `while` loop and continues to prompt for input.

This doesn't mean that `number` *should* be nonnegative after the loop. It means that `number` *will* be nonnegative. By working through the logic of the program, you can see that this is a certainty, an assertion of which you are sure. You could even prove it if need be. Such an assertion is called a *provable assertion.*

> **Provable Assertion**
>
> An assertion that can be proven to be true at a particular point in program execution.

Provable assertions help to identify unnecessary bits of code. Consider the following statements:

```
int x = 0;
if (x == 0) {
    System.out.println("This is what I expect.");
} else {
    System.out.println("How can that be?");
}
```

The `if/else` construct is not necessary. You know what the assignment statement does, so you know that it sets x to 0. Testing whether x is 0 is as unnecessary as saying, "Before I proceed, I'm going to check that 2 + 2 equals 4." Because the `if` part of this `if/else` statement is always executed, you can prove that the following lines of code always do the same thing as the preceding lines:

```
int x = 0;
System.out.println("This is what I expect.");
```

This code is simpler and, therefore, better. Programs are complex enough without adding unnecessary code.

The concept of assertions has become so popular among software practitioners that many programming languages provide support for testing assertions. Java added support for testing assertions starting with version 1.4 of the language. You can read more about Java's `assert` statement in Appendix C.

Reasoning about Assertions

The focus on assertions comes out of a field of computer science known as *formal verification*.

> **Formal Verification**
>
> A field of computer science that involves reasoning about the formal properties of programs to prove the correctness of a program.

For example, consider the properties of the simple `if` statement:

```
if (<test>) {
    // test is always true here
    ...
}
```

You enter the body of the `if` statement only if the test is true, which is why you know that the test must be true if that particular line is reached in program execution. You can draw a similar conclusion about what is true in an `if`/`else` statement:

```
if (<test>) {
    // test is always true here
    ...
} else {
    // test is never true here
    ...
}
```

You can draw a similar conclusion about what is true inside the body of a `while` loop:

```
while (<test>) {
    // test is always true here
    ...
}
```

But in the case of the `while` loop, you can draw an even stronger conclusion. You know that as long as the test evaluates to `true`, you'll keep going back into the loop.

Thus, you can conclude that after the loop is done executing, the test can no longer be true:

```
while (<test>) {
    // test is always true here
    ...
}
// test is never true here
```

The test can't be true after the loop because if it had been true, the program would have executed the body of the loop again.

These observations about the properties of if statements, if/else statements, and while loops provide a good start for proving certain assertions about programs. But often, proving assertions requires a deeper analysis of what the code actually does. For example, suppose you have a variable x of type int and you execute the following if statement:

```
if (x < 0) {
    // x < 0 is always true here
    x = -x;
}
// but what about x < 0 here?
```

You wouldn't normally be able to conclude anything about x being less than 0 after the if statement, but you can draw a conclusion if you think about the different cases. If x was greater than or equal to 0 before the if statement, it will still be greater than or equal to 0 after the if statement. And if x was less than 0 before the if statement, it will be equal to −x after. When x is less than 0, −x is greater than 0. Thus, in either case, you know that after the if statement executes, x will be greater than or equal to 0.

Programmers naturally apply this kind of reasoning when writing programs. Computer scientists are trying to figure out how to do this kind of reasoning in a formal, verifiable way.

A Detailed Assertions Example

VideoNote

To explore assertions further, let's take a detailed look at a code fragment and a set of assertions we might make about the fragment. Consider the following method:

```
public static void printCommonPrefix(int x, int y) {
    int z = 0;
    // Point A
    while (x != y) {
        // Point B
        z++;
```

```
        // Point C
        if (x > y) {
            // Point D
            x = x / 10;
        } else {
            // Point E
            y = y / 10;
        }
        // Point F
    }
    // Point G
    System.out.println("common prefix = " + x);
    System.out.println("digits discarded = " + z);
}
```

This method finds the longest sequence of leading digits that two numbers have in common. For example, the numbers 32845 and 328929343 each begin with the prefix 328. This method will report that prefix and will also report the total number of digits that follow the common prefix and that are discarded.

We will examine the program to check whether various assertions are always true, never true, or sometimes true and sometimes false at various points in program execution. The comments in the method indicate the points of interest. The assertions we will consider are:

```
x > y
x == y
z == 0
```

Normally computer scientists write assertions in mathematical notation, as in z = 0, but we will use a Java expression to distinguish this assertion of equality from the practice of assigning a value to the variable.

We can record our answers in a table with the words "always," "never," or "sometimes." Our table will look like the following one:

	x > y	x == y	z == 0
Point A			
Point B			
...	...	...	...

Let's start at point A, which appears near the beginning of the method's execution:

```
public static void printCommonPrefix(int x, int y) {
    int z = 0;
    // Point A
```

The variables x and y are parameters and get their values from the call to the method. Many calls are possible, so we don't really know anything about the values of x and y. Thus, the assertion x > y could be true but doesn't have to be. The assertion is sometimes true, sometimes false at point A. Likewise, the assertion x == y could be true depending on what values are passed to the method, but it doesn't have to be true. However, we initialize the local variable z to 0 just before point A, so the assertion z == 0 will always be true at that point in execution. So, we can fill in the first line of the table as follows:

	x > y	x == y	z == 0
Point A	sometimes	sometimes	always

Point B appears just inside the `while` loop:

```
while (x != y) {
    // Point B
    z++;

    ...
}
```

We get to point B only by entering the loop, which means that the loop test must have evaluated to `true`. In other words, at point B it will always be true that x is not equal to y, so the assertion x == y will never be true at that point. But we don't know which of the two is larger. Therefore, the assertion x > y is sometimes true and sometimes false.

You might think that the assertion z == 0 would always be true at point B because we were at point A just before we were at point B, but that is not the right answer. Remember that point B is inside a `while` loop. On the first iteration of the loop we will have been at point A just before reaching point B, but on later iterations of the loop we will have been inside the loop just before reaching point B. And if you look at the line of code just after point B, you will see that it increments z. There are no other modifications to the variable z inside the loop. Therefore, each time the body of the loop executes, z will increase by 1. So, z will be 0 at point B the first time through the loop, but it will be 1 on the second iteration, 2 on the third iteration, and so forth. Therefore, the right answer for the assertion z == 0 at point B is that it is sometimes true, sometimes false. So, the second line of the table should look like this:

	x > y	x == y	z == 0
Point B	sometimes	never	sometimes

Point C is right after the increment of the variable z. There are no changes to the values of x and y between point B and point C, so the same answers apply at point C for the assertions x > y and x == y. The assertion z == 0 will never be true after the increment, even though z starts at 0 before the loop begins and there are no other manipulations of the variable inside the loop; once it is incremented, it will never be 0 again. Therefore, we can fill in the table for point C as follows:

	x > y	**x == y**	**z == 0**
Point C	sometimes	never	never

Points D and E are part of the if/else statement inside the while loop, so we can evaluate them as a pair. The if/else statement appears right after point C:

```
// Point C
if (x > y) {
    // Point D
    x = x / 10;
} else {
    // Point E
    y = y / 10;
}
```

No variables are changed between point C and points D and E. Java performs a test and branches in one of two directions. The if/else test determines whether x is greater than y. If the test is true, we go to point D. If not, we go to point E. So, for the assertion x > y, we know it is always true at point D and never true at point E. The assertion x == y is a little more difficult to work out. We know it can never be true at point D, but could it be true at point E? Solely on the basis of the if/else test, the answer is yes. But remember that at point C the assertion could never be true. The values of x and y have not changed between point C and point E, so it still can never be true.

As for the assertion z == 0, the variable z hasn't changed between point C and points D and E, and z is not included in the test. So whatever we knew about z before still holds. Therefore, the right answers to fill in for points D and E are as follows:

	x > y	**x == y**	**z == 0**
Point D	always	never	never
Point E	never	never	never

Point F appears after the if/else statement. To determine the relationship between x and y at point F, we have to look at how the variables have changed. The if/else statement either divides x by 10 (if it is the larger value) or divides y by 10 (if it is the larger value). So, we have to ask whether it is possible for the assertion x > y to be true at point F. The answer is yes. For example, x might have been 218 and y might have been 6 before the if/else statement. In that case, x would now be 21, which is still larger than y. But does it have to be larger than y? Not necessarily. The values might have been reversed, in which case y will be larger than x. So, that assertion is sometimes true and sometimes false at point F.

What about the assertion x == y? We know it doesn't have to be true because we have seen cases in which x is greater than y or y is greater than x. Is it possible for it to be true? Are there any values of x and y that would lead to this outcome? Consider the case in which x is 218 and y is 21. Then we would divide x by 10 to get 21, which would equal y. So, this assertion also is sometimes true and sometimes false.

There was no change to z between points D and E and point F, so we simply carry our answer down from the previous columns. So we would fill in the table as follows for point F:

	x > y	x == y	z == 0
Point F	sometimes	sometimes	never

Point G appears after the while loop:

```
while (x != y) {
    . . .
}
// Point G
```

We can escape the while loop only if x becomes equal to y. So, at point G we know that the assertion x == y is always true. That means that the assertion x > y can never be true. The assertion z == 0 is a little tricky. At point F it was never true, so you might imagine that at point G it can never be true. But we weren't necessarily at point F just before we reached point G. We might never have entered the while loop at all, in which case we would have been at point A just before point G. At point A the variable z was equal to 0. Therefore, the right answer for this assertion is that it is sometimes true, sometimes false at point G. The final row of our table thus looks like this:

	x > y	x == y	z == 0
Point G!	never	always	sometimes

When we combine this information, we can fill in our table as follows:

	x > y	x == y	z == 0
Point A	sometimes	sometimes	always
Point B	sometimes	never	sometimes
Point C	sometimes	never	never
Point D	always	never	never
Point E	never	never	never
Point F	sometimes	sometimes	never
Point G	never	always	sometimes

5.6 Case Study: `NumberGuess`

If we combine indefinite loops, the ability to check for user errors, and random number generation, it's possible for us to create guessing games in which the computer thinks of random numbers and the user tries to guess them. Let's consider an example game with the following rules. The computer thinks of a random two-digit number but keeps it secret from the player. We'll allow the program to accept positive numbers only, so the acceptable range of numbers is 00 through 99 inclusive. The player will try to guess the number the computer picked. If the player guesses correctly, the program will report the number of guesses that the player made.

To make the game more interesting, the computer will give the player a hint each time the user enters an incorrect guess. Specifically, the computer will tell the player how many digits from the guess are contained in the correct answer. The order of the digits doesn't affect the number of digits that match. For example, if the correct number is 57 and the player guesses 73, the computer will report one matching digit, because the correct answer contains a 7. If the player next guesses 75, the computer will report two matching digits. At this point the player knows that the computer's number must be 57, because 57 is the only two-digit number whose digits match those of 75.

Since the players will be doing a lot of console input, it's likely that they will type incorrect numbers or nonnumeric tokens by mistake. We'd like our guessing-game program to be robust against user input errors.

Initial Version without Hinting

In previous chapters, we've talked about the idea of iterative enhancement. Since this is a challenging program, we'll tackle it in stages. One of the hardest parts of the program is giving correct hints to the player. For now, we'll simply write a game that tells players whether they are correct or incorrect on each guess and, once the game is done, reports the number of guesses the players made. The program won't be robust against user input errors yet; that can be added later. To further simplify the game, rather than having the computer choose a random number, we'll choose a known value for the number so that the code can be tested more easily.

Since we don't know how many tries a player will need before correctly guessing the number, it seems that the main loop for this game will have to be a `while` loop. It might be tempting to write the code to match the following pseudocode:

```
// flawed number guess pseudocode
think of a number.
while (user has not guessed the number) {
    prompt and read a guess.
    report whether the guess was correct or incorrect.
}
```

But the problem with this pseudocode is that you can't start the `while` loop if you don't have a `guess` value from the player yet. The following code doesn't compile, because the variable `guess` isn't initialized when the loop begins:

```
// this code doesn't compile
int numGuesses = 0;
int number = 42; // computer always picks same number
int guess;

while (guess ! = number) {
    System.out.print("Your guess? ");
    guess = console.nextInt();
    numGuesses++;
    System.out.println("Incorrect.");
}

System.out.println("You got it right in " + numGuesses + " tries.");
```

It turns out that the game's main guess loop is a fencepost loop, because after each incorrect guess the program must print an "Incorrect" message (and later a hint). For n guesses, there are $n - 1$ hints. Recall the following general pseudocode for fencepost loops:

```
plant a post.
for (the length of the fence) {
    attach some wire.
    plant a post.
}
```

This particular problem is an indefinite fencepost using a `while` loop. Let's look at some more specific pseudocode. The "posts" are the prompts for guesses, and the "wires" are the "Incorrect" messages:

```
// specific number guess pseudocode
think of a number.
ask for the player's initial guess.
while (the guess is not the correct number) {
    inform the player that the guess was incorrect.
    ask for another guess.
}

report the number of guesses needed.
```

This pseudocode leads us to write the following Java program. Note that the computer always picks the value 42 in this version of the program:

```
1  import java.util.*;
2
3  public class NumberGuess1 {
4      public static void main(String[] args) {
5          Scanner console = new Scanner(System.in);
6          int number = 42; // always picks the same number
7
8          System.out.print("Your guess? ");
9          int guess = console.nextInt();
10         int numGuesses = 1;
11
12         while (guess != number) {
13             System.out.println("Incorrect.");
14             System.out.print("Your guess? ");
15             guess = console.nextInt();
16             numGuesses++;
17         }
18
19         System.out.println("You got it right in " +
20                             numGuesses + " tries.");
21     }
22 }
```

We can test our initial program to verify the code we've written so far. A sample dialogue looks like this:

```
Your guess? 65
Incorrect.
Your guess? 12
Incorrect.
Your guess? 34
Incorrect.
Your guess? 42
You got it right in 4 tries.
```

Randomized Version with Hinting

Now that we've tested the code to make sure our main game loops, let's make the game random by choosing a random value between 00 and 99 inclusive. To do so, we'll create a Random object and call its nextInt method, specifying the maximum value. Remember that the value passed to `nextInt` should be one more than the desired maximum, so we'll pass `100`:

```
// pick a random number between 00 and 99 inclusive
Random rand = new Random();
int number = rand.nextInt(100);
```

The next important feature our game should have is to give a hint when the player makes an incorrect guess. The tricky part is figuring out how many digits of the player's guess match the correct number. Since this code is nontrivial to write, let's make a method called `matches` that does the work for us. To figure out how many digits match, the `matches` method needs to use the guess and the correct number as parameters. It will return the number of matching digits. Therefore, its header should look like this:

```
public static int matches(int number, int guess) {
    ...
}
```

Our algorithm must count the number of matching digits. Either digit from the guess can match either digit from the correct number. Since the digits are somewhat independent—that is, whether the ones digit of the guess matches is independent of whether the tens digit matches—we should use sequential `if` statements rather than an `if/else` statement to represent these conditions.

The digit-matching algorithm has one special case. If the player guesses a number such as `33` that contains two of the same digit, and if that digit is contained in the correct answer (say the correct answer is `37`), it would be misleading to report that two digits match. It makes more sense for the program to report one matching digit. To handle this case, our algorithm must check whether the guess contains two of the same digit and consider the second digit of the guess to be a match only if it is different from the first.

Here is the pseudocode for the algorithm:

```
matches = 0.
if (the first digit of the guess matches
        either digit of the correct number) {
    we have found one match.
}

if (the second digit of the guess is different from the first digit,
        AND it matches either digit of the correct number) {
    we have found another match.
}
```

We need to be able to split the correct number and the guess into the two digits that compose each so that we can compare them. Recall from the Boolean Zen section that we can use the division and remainder operators to express the digits of any two-digit number n as n / 10 for the tens digit and n % 10 for the ones digit.

Let's write the statement that compares the tens digit of the guess against the correct answer. Since the tens digit of the guess can match either of the correct number's digits, we'll use an OR test with the || operator:

```
int matches = 0;

// check the first digit for a match
if (guess / 10 == number / 10 || guess / 10 == number % 10) {
    matches++;
}
```

Writing the statement that compares the ones digit of the guess against the correct answer is slightly trickier, because we have to take into consideration the special case described previously (in which both digits of the guess are the same). We'll account for this by counting the second digit as a match only if it is unique *and* matches a digit from the correct number:

```
// check the second digit for a match
if (guess / 10 ! = guess % 10 &&
        (guess % 10 == number / 10 || guess % 10 == number % 10)) {
    matches++;
}
```

The following version of the program uses the hinting code we've just written. It also adds the randomly chosen number and a brief introduction to the program:

```
1  // Two-digit number-guessing game with hinting.
2  import java.util.*;
3
4  public class NumberGuess2 {
5      public static void main(String[] args) {
6          System.out.println("Try to guess my two-digit");
7          System.out.println("number, and I'll tell you how");
8          System.out.println("many digits from your guess");
9          System.out.println("appear in my number.");
10         System.out.println();
11
12         Scanner console = new Scanner(System.in);
13
14         // pick a random number from 0 to 99 inclusive
```

```
15              Random rand = new Random();
16              int number = rand.nextInt(100);
17
18              // get first guess
19              System.out.print("Your guess? ");
20              int guess = console.nextInt();
21              int numGuesses = 1;
22
23              // give hints until correct guess is reached
24              while (guess != number) {
25                  int numMatches = matches(number, guess);
26                  System.out.println("Incorrect (hint: " +
27                                      numMatches + " digits match)");
28                  System.out.print("Your guess? ");
29                  guess = console.nextInt();
30                  numGuesses++;
31              }
32
33              System.out.println("You got it right in " +
34                                  numGuesses + " tries.");
35          }
36
37      // returns how many digits from the given
38      // guess match digits from the given correct number
39      public static int matches(int number, int guess) {
40          int numMatches = 0;
41
42          if (guess / 10 == number / 10 ||
43              guess / 10 == number % 10) {
44              numMatches++;
45          }
46
47          if (guess / 10 ! = guess % 10 &&
48                  (guess % 10 == number / 10 ||
49                  guess % 10 == number % 10)) {
50              numMatches++;
51          }
52
53          return numMatches;
54      }
55 }
```

The following is a sample log of the program execution:

```
Try to guess my two-digit
number, and I'll tell you how
many digits from your guess
appear in my number.

Your guess? 13
Incorrect (hint: 0 digits match)
Your guess? 26
Incorrect (hint: 0 digits match)
Your guess? 78
Incorrect (hint: 1 digits match)
Your guess? 79
Incorrect (hint: 1 digits match)
Your guess? 70
Incorrect (hint: 2 digits match)
Your guess? 7
You got it right in 6 tries.
```

Final Robust Version

The last major change we'll make to our program is to make it robust against invalid user input. There are two types of bad input that we may see:

1. Nonnumeric tokens.
2. Numbers outside the range of 0–99.

Let's deal with these cases one at a time. Recall the `getInt` method that was discussed earlier in this chapter. It repeatedly prompts the user for input until an integer is typed. Here is its header:

```
public static int getInt(Scanner console, String prompt)
```

We can make use of `getInt` to get an integer between 0 and 99. We'll repeatedly call `getInt` until the integer that is returned is within the acceptable range. The postcondition we require before we can stop prompting for guesses is:

```
guess >= 0 && guess <= 99
```

To ensure that this postcondition is met, we can use a `while` loop that tests for the opposite condition. Using De Morgan's law, we know that the opposite of the previous test would be the following:

```
guess < 0 || guess > 99
```

The reversed test is used in our new `getGuess` method to get a valid guess between 0 and 99. Now whenever we want to read user input in the main program, we'll call `getGuess`. It's useful to separate the input prompting in this way, to make sure that we don't accidentally count invalid inputs as guesses.

The final version of our code is the following:

```java
1  // Robust two-digit number-guessing game with hinting.
2  import java.util.*;
3
4  public class NumberGuess3 {
5      public static void main(String[] args) {
6          giveIntro();
7          Scanner console = new Scanner(System.in);
8
9          // pick a random number from 0 to 99 inclusive
10         Random rand = new Random();
11         int number = rand.nextInt(100);
12
13         // get first guess
14         int guess = getGuess(console);
15         int numGuesses = 1;
16
17         // give hints until correct guess is reached
18         while (guess != number) {
19             int numMatches = matches(number, guess);
20             System.out.println("Incorrect (hint: " +
21                                    numMatches + " digits match)");
22             guess = getGuess(console);
23             numGuesses++;
24         }
25
26         System.out.println("You got it right in " +
27                                numGuesses + " tries.");
28     }
29
30     public static void giveIntro() {
31         System.out.println("Try to guess my two-digit");
32         System.out.println("number, and I'll tell you how");
33         System.out.println("many digits from your guess");
34         System.out.println("appear in my number.");
35         System.out.println();
36     }
37
38     // returns # of matching digits between the two numbers
```

```
39          // pre: number and guess are unique two-digit numbers
40          public static int matches(int number, int guess) {
41              int numMatches = 0;
42
43              if (guess / 10 == number / 10 ||
44                      guess / 10 == number % 10) {
45                  numMatches++;
46              }
47
48              if (guess / 10 != guess % 10 &&
49                      (guess % 10 == number / 10 ||
50                      guess % 10 == number % 10)) {
51                  numMatches++;
52              }
53
54              return numMatches;
55          }
56
57          // prompts until a number in proper range is entered
58          // post: guess is between 0 and 99
59          public static int getGuess(Scanner console) {
60              int guess = getInt(console, "Your guess? ");
61              while (guess < 0 || guess >= 100) {
62                  System.out.println("Out of range; try again.");
63                  guess = getInt(console, "Your guess? ");
64              }
65
66              return guess;
67          }
68
69          // prompts until a valid number is entered
70          public static int getInt(Scanner console, String prompt) {
71              System.out.print(prompt);
72              while (!console.hasNextInt()) {
73                  console.next(); // to discard the input
74                  System.out.println("Not an integer; try again.");
75                  System.out.print(prompt);
76              }
77              return console.nextInt();
78          }
79  }
```

The following sample log of execution demonstrates the new input robustness of this program:

```
Try to guess my two-digit
number, and I'll tell you how
many digits from your guess
appear in my number.

Your guess? 12
Incorrect (hint: 0 digits match)
Your guess? okay
Not an integer; try again.
Your guess? 34
Incorrect (hint: 1 digits match)
Your guess? 35
Incorrect (hint: 1 digits match)
Your guess? 67
Incorrect (hint: 0 digits match)
Your guess? 89
Incorrect (hint: 0 digits match)
Your guess? 3
Incorrect (hint: 2 digits match)
Your guess? 300
Out of range; try again.
Your guess? 30
You got it right in 7 tries.
```

Notice that we're careful to comment our code to document relevant preconditions and postconditions of our methods. The precondition of the `matches` method is that the two parameters are unique two-digit numbers. The postcondition of our new `getGuesses` method is that it returns a guess between 0 and 99 inclusive. Also, note that the program does not count invalid input (`okay` and `300` in the previous sample log of execution) as guesses.

Chapter Summary

Java has a `while` loop in addition to its `for` loop. The `while` loop can be used to write indefinite loops that keep executing until some condition fails.

Java can generate pseudorandom numbers using objects of the `Random` class.

Priming a loop means setting the values of variables that will be used in the loop test, so that the test will be sure to succeed the first time and the loop will execute.

The do/while loop is a variation on the `while` loop that performs its loop test at the end of the loop body. A do/while loop is guaranteed to execute its body at least once.

A fencepost loop executes a "loop-and-a-half" by executing part of a loop's body once before the loop begins.

_____

A sentinel loop is a kind of fencepost loop that repeatedly processes input until it is passed a particular value, but does not process the special value.

_____

The `boolean` primitive type represents logical values of either `true` or `false`. Boolean expressions are used as tests in `if` statements and loops. Boolean expressions can use relational operators such as `<` or `!=` as well as logical operators such as `&&` or `!`.

_____

Complex Boolean tests with logical operators such as `&&` or `||` are evaluated lazily: If the overall result is clear from evaluating the first part of the expression, later parts are not evaluated. This is called short-circuited evaluation.

_____

`Boolean` variables (sometimes called "flags") can store Boolean values and can be used as loop tests.

_____

A complex Boolean expression can be negated using a set of rules known as De Morgan's laws, in which each sub-expression is negated and all AND and OR operations are swapped.

_____

A robust program checks for errors in user input. Better robustness can be achieved by looping and reprompting the user to enter input when he or she types bad input. The `Scanner` class has methods like `hasNextInt` that you can use to "look ahead" for valid input.

_____

Assertions are logical statements about a particular point in a program. Assertions are useful for proving properties about how a program will execute. Two useful types of assertions are preconditions and postconditions, which are claims about what will be true before and after a method executes.

_____

Self-Check Problems

Section 5.1: The while Loop

1. For each of the following `while` loops, state how many times the loop will execute its body. Remember that "zero," "infinity," and "unknown" are legal answers. Also, what is the output of the code in each case?

   a.
   ```java
   int x = 1;
   while (x < 100) {
       System.out.print(x + " ");
       x += 10;
   }
   ```
   b.
   ```java
   int max = 10;
   while (max < 10) {
       System.out.println("count down: " + max);
       max--;
   }
   ```
   c.
   ```java
   int x = 250;
   while (x % 3 != 0) {
       System.out.println(x);
   }
   ```

```
   d. int x = 2;
      while (x < 200) {
          System.out.print(x + " ");
          x *= x;
      }
   e. String word = "a";
      while (word.length() < 10) {
          word = "b" + word + "b";
      }
      System.out.println(word);
   f. int x = 100;
      while (x > 0) {
          System.out.println(x / 10);
          x = x / 2;
      }
```

2. Convert each of the following for loops into an equivalent while loop:

```
   a. for (int n = 1; n <= max; n++) {
          System.out.println(n);
       }
   b. int total = 25;
      for (int number = 1; number <= (total / 2); number++) {
          total = total - number;
          System.out.println(total + " " + number);
      }
   c. for (int i = 1; i <= 2; i++) {
          for (int j = 1; j <= 3; j++) {
              for (int k = 1; k <= 4; k++) {
                  System.out.print("*");
              }
              System.out.print("!");
          }
          System.out.println();
      }
   d. int number = 4;
      for (int count = 1; count <= number; count++) {
          System.out.println(number);
          number = number / 2;
      }
```

3. Consider the following method:

```
   public static void mystery(int x) {
       int y = 1;
       int z = 0;
       while (2 * y <= x) {
           y = y * 2;
```

```
            z++;
        }
        System.out.println(y + " " + z);
    }
```

For each of the following calls, indicate the output that the preceding method produces:

```
mystery(1);
mystery(6);
mystery(19);
mystery(39);
mystery(74);
```

4. Consider the following method:

```
public static void mystery(int x) {
    int y = 0;
    while (x % 2 == 0) {
        y++;
        x = x / 2;
    }
    System.out.println(x + " " + y);
}
```

For each of the following calls, indicate the output that the preceding method produces:

```
mystery(19);
mystery(42);
mystery(48);
mystery(40);
mystery(64);
```

5. Consider the following code:

```
Random rand = new Random();
int a = rand.nextInt(100);
int b = rand.nextInt(20) + 50;
int c = rand.nextInt(20 + 50);
int d = rand.nextInt(100) - 20;
int e = rand.nextInt(10) * 4;
```

What range of values can each variable (a, b, c, d, and e) have?

6. Write code that generates a random integer between 0 and 10 inclusive.

7. Write code that generates a random odd integer (not divisible by 2) between 50 and 99 inclusive.

8. For each of the do/while loops that follow, state the number of times that the loop will execute its body. Remember that "zero," "infinity," and "unknown" are legal answers. Also, what is the output of the code in each case?

```
a. int x = 1;
   do {
```

```
        System.out.print(x + " ");
        x = x + 10;
    } while (x < 100);
b. int max = 10;
   do {
        System.out.println("count down: " + max);
        max--;
   } while (max < 10);
c. int x = 250;
   do {
        System.out.println(x);
   } while (x % 3 != 0);
d. int x = 100;
   do {
        System.out.println(x);
        x = x / 2;
   } while (x % 2 == 0);
e. int x = 2;
   do {
        System.out.print(x + " ");
        x *= x;
   } while (x < 200);
f. String word = "a";
   do {
        word = "b" + word + "b";
   } while (word.length() < 10);
   System.out.println(word);
g. int x = 100;
   do {
        System.out.println(x / 10);
        x = x / 2;
   } while (x > 0);
h. String str = "/\\";
   do {
        str += str;
   } while (str.length() < 10);
   System.out.println(str);
```

9. Write a do/while loop that repeatedly prints a certain message until the user tells the program to stop. The do/while is appropriate because the message should always be printed at least one time, even if the user types n after the first message appears. The message to be printed is as follows:

```
She sells seashells by the seashore.
Do you want to hear it again? y
She sells seashells by the seashore.
Do you want to hear it again? y
```

```
She sells seashells by the seashore.
Do you want to hear it again? n
```

10. Write a method called `zeroDigits` that accepts an integer parameter and returns the number of digits in the number that have the value 0. For example, the call `zeroDigits(5024036)` should return 2, and `zeroDigits(743)` should return 0. The call `zeroDigits(0)` should return 1. (We suggest you use a `do/while` loop in your solution.)

11. Write a `do/while` loop that repeatedly prints random numbers between 0 and 1000 until a number above 900 is printed. At least one line of output should always be printed, even if the first random number is above 900. Here is a sample execution:

```
Random number: 235
Random number: 15
Random number: 810
Random number: 147
Random number: 915
```

Section 5.2: Fencepost Algorithms

12. Consider the flawed method `printLetters` that follows, which accepts a `String` as its parameter and attempts to print the letters of the `String`, separated by dashes. For example, the call of `printLetters("Rabbit")` should print R-a-b-b-i-t. The following code is incorrect:

```java
public static void printLetters(String text) {
    for (int i = 0; i < text.length(); i++) {
        System.out.print(text.charAt(i) + "-");
    }
    System.out.println(); // to end the line of output
}
```

What is wrong with the code? How can it be corrected to produce the desired behavior?

13. Write a sentinel loop that repeatedly prompts the user to enter a number and, once the number −1 is typed, displays the maximum and minimum numbers that the user entered. Here is a sample dialogue:

```
Type a number (or −1 to stop): 5
Type a number (or −1 to stop): 2
Type a number (or −1 to stop): 17
Type a number (or −1 to stop): 8
Type a number (or −1 to stop): −1
Maximum was 17
Minimum was 2
```

If −1 is the first number typed, no maximum or minimum should be printed. In this case, the dialogue would look like this:

```
Type a number (or −1 to stop): −1
```

Section 5.3: The boolean Type

14. Consider the following variable declarations:

```
int x = 27;
int y = −1;
```

```
int z = 32;
boolean b = false;
```

What is the value of each of the following Boolean expressions?

a. `!b`

b. `b || true`

c. `(x > y) && (y > z)`

d. `(x == y) || (x <= z)`

e. `!(x % 2 == 0)`

f. `(x % 2 != 0) && b`

g. `b && !b`

h. `b || !b`

i. `(x < y) == b`

j. `!(x / 2 == 13) || b || (z * 3 == 96)`

k. `(z < x) == false`

l. `!((x > 0) && (y < 0))`

15. Write a method called `isVowel` that accepts a character as input and returns `true` if that character is a vowel (a, e, i, o, or u). For an extra challenge, make your method case-insensitive.

16. The following code attempts to examine a number and return whether that number is prime (i.e., has no factors other than 1 and itself). A flag named `prime` is used. However, the Boolean logic is not implemented correctly, so the method does not always return the correct answer. In what cases does the method report an incorrect answer? How can the code be changed so that it will always return a correct result?

```java
public static boolean isPrime(int n) {
    boolean prime = true;
    for (int i = 2; i < n; i++) {
        if (n % i == 0) {
            prime = false;
        } else {
            prime = true;
        }
    }

    return prime;
}
```

17. The following code attempts to examine a `String` and return whether it contains a given letter. A flag named `found` is used. However, the Boolean logic is not implemented correctly, so the method does not always return the correct answer. In what cases does the method report an incorrect answer? How can the code be changed so that it will always return a correct result?

```java
public static boolean contains(String str, char ch) {
    boolean found = false;
    for (int i = 0; i < str.length(); i++) {
        if (str.charAt(i) == ch) {
            found = true;
```

```
        } else {
            found = false;
        }
    }
    return found;
}
```

18. Using "Boolean Zen," write an improved version of the following method, which returns whether the given `String` starts and ends with the same character:

```
public static boolean startEndSame(String str) {
    if (str.charAt(0) == str.charAt(str.length() - 1)) {
        return true;
    } else {
        return false;
    }
}
```

19. Using "Boolean Zen," write an improved version of the following method, which returns whether the given number of cents would require any pennies (as opposed to being an amount that could be made exactly using coins other than pennies):

```
public static boolean hasPennies(int cents) {
    boolean nickelsOnly = (cents % 5 == 0);
    if (nickelsOnly == true) {
        return false;
    } else {
        return true;
    }
}
```

20. Consider the following method:

```
public static int mystery(int x, int y) {
    while (x != 0 && y != 0) {
        if (x < y) {
            y -= x;
        } else {
            x -= y;
        }
    }
    return x + y;
}
```

For each of the following calls, indicate the value that is returned:

```
mystery(3, 3)
mystery(5, 3)
mystery(2, 6)
```

```
mystery(12, 18)
mystery(30, 75)
```

21. The following code is a slightly modified version of actual code that was in the Microsoft Zune music player in 2008. The code attempts to calculate today's date by determining how many years and days have passed since 1980. Assume the existence of methods for getting the total number of days since 1980 and for determining whether a given year is a leap year:

```
int days = getTotalDaysSince1980();
year = 1980;
while (days > 365) { // subtract out years
    if (isLeapYear(year)) {
        if (days > 366) {
            days -= 366;
            year += 1;
        }
    } else {
        days -= 365;
        year += 1;
    }
}
```

Thousands of Zune players locked up on January 1, 2009, the first day after the end of a leap year since the Zune was released. (Microsoft quickly released a patch to fix the problem.) What is the problem with the preceding code, and in what cases will it exhibit incorrect behavior? How can it be fixed?

22. Which of the following is a properly reversed version of the following Boolean expression, according to De Morgan's Laws?

```
(2 == 3) && (-1 < 5) && isPrime(n)
```

a. `(2 != 3) && (-1 > 5) && isPrime(n)`

b. `(2 == 3) || (-1 < 5) || isPrime(n)`

c. `!(2 == 3) && !(-1 < 5) && !isPrime(n)`

d. `(2 != 3) || (-1 >= 5) || !isPrime(n)`

e. `!(2 != 3) || !(-1 < 5) || isNotPrime(n)`

Section 5.4: User Errors

23. The following code is not robust against invalid user input. Describe how to change the code so that it will not proceed until the user has entered a valid age and grade point average (GPA). Assume that any `int` is a legal age and that any `double` is a legal GPA.

```
Scanner console = new Scanner(System.in);
System.out.print("Type your age: ");
int age = console.nextInt();
System.out.print("Type your GPA: ");
double gpa = console.nextDouble();
```

For an added challenge, modify the code so that it rejects invalid ages (for example, numbers less than 0) and GPAs (say, numbers less than 0.0 or greater than 4.0).

24. Consider the following code:

```
Scanner console = new Scanner(System.in);
System.out.print("Type something for me! ");
if (console.hasNextInt()) {
   int number = console.nextInt();
   System.out.println("Your IQ is " + number);
} else if (console.hasNext()) {
   String token = console.next();
   System.out.println("Your name is " + token);
}
```

What is the output when the user types the following values?

a. Jane   b. 56   c. 56.2

25. Write a piece of code that prompts the user for a number and then prints a different message depending on whether the number was an integer or a real number. Here are two sample dialogues:

```
Type a number: 42.5
You typed the real number 42.5


Type a number: 3
You typed the integer 3
```

26. Write code that prompts for three integers, averages them, and prints the average. Make your code robust against invalid input. (You may want to use the getInt method discussed in this chapter.)

Section 5.5: Assertions and Program Logic

27. Identify the various assertions in the following code as being always true, never true, or sometimes true and sometimes false at various points in program execution. The comments indicate the points of interest:

```
public static int mystery(Scanner console, int x) {
    int y = console.nextInt();
    int count = 0;

    // Point A
    while (y < x) {
        // Point B
        if (y == 0) {
            count++;
            // Point C
        }
        y = console.nextInt();
        // Point D
    }

    // Point E
    return count;
}
```

Categorize each assertion at each point with ALWAYS, NEVER, or SOMETIMES:

	y < x	y == 0	count > 0
Point A			
Point B			
Point C			
Point D			
Point E			

28. Identify the various assertions in the following code as being always true, never true, or sometimes true and sometimes false at various points in program execution. The comments indicate the points of interest:

```java
public static int mystery(int n) {
    Random r = new Random();
    int a = r.nextInt(3) + 1;
    int b = 2;
    // Point A
    while (n > b) {
        // Point B
        b = b + a;
        if (a > 1) {
            n--;
            // Point C
            a = r.nextInt(b) + 1;
        } else {
            a = b + 1;

            // Point D
        }
    }
    // Point E
    return n;
}
```

Categorize each assertion at each point with ALWAYS, NEVER, or SOMETIMES:

	n > b	a > 1	b > a
Point A			
Point B			
Point C			
Point D			
Point E			

29. Identify the various assertions in the following code as being always true, never true, or sometimes true and sometimes false at various points in program execution. The comments indicate the points of interest:

```java
public static int mystery(Scanner console) {
    int prev = 0;
    int count = 0;
    int next = console.nextInt();
    // Point A
    while (next != 0) {
        // Point B
        if (next == prev) {
            // Point C
            count++;
        }
        prev = next;
        next = console.nextInt();
        // Point D
    }
    // Point E
    return count;
}
```

Categorize each assertion at each point with ALWAYS, NEVER, or SOMETIMES:

	next == 0	prev == 0	next == prev
Point A			
Point B			
Point C			
Point D			
Point E			

Exercises

1. Write a method called showTwos that shows the factors of 2 in a given integer. For example, consider the following calls:

```java
showTwos(7);
showTwos(18);
showTwos(68);
showTwos(120);
```

These calls should produce the following output:

```
7 = 7
18 = 2 * 9
68 = 2 * 2 * 17
120 = 2 * 2 * 2 * 15
```

2. Write a method called gcd that accepts two integers as parameters and returns the greatest common divisor (GCD) of the two numbers. The GCD of two integers a and b is the largest integer that is a factor of both a and b.

One efficient way to compute the GCD of two numbers is to use Euclid's algorithm, which states the following:

GCD (a, b) = GCD $(b, a \% b)$

GCD $(a, 0)$ = Absolute value of a

3. Write a method called toBinary that accepts an integer as a parameter and returns a String containing that integer's binary representation. For example, the call of printBinary(44) should return "101100".

4. Write a method called randomX that prints a lines that contain a random number of "x" characters (between 5 and 20 inclusive) until it prints a line that contains 16 or more characters. For example, the output might look like the following:

```
xxxxxxx
xxxxxxxxxxxxxxx
xxxxxxxxxxxx
xxxxxxxxxxxxxx
xxxxxx
xxxxxxxxxxx
xxxxxxxxxxxxxxxxxx
```

5. Write a method called randomLines that prints between 5 and 10 random strings of letters (between "a" and "z"), one per line. Each string should have random length of up to 80 characters.

6. Write a method called makeGuesses that guesses numbers between 1 and 50 inclusive until it makes a guess of at least 48. It should report each guess and at the end should report the total number of guesses made. Here is a sample execution:

```
guess = 43
guess = 47
guess = 45
guess = 27
guess = 49
total guesses = 5
```

7. Write a method called diceSum that accepts a Scanner for the console as a parameter and prompts for a desired sum, then repeatedly simulates the rolling of 2 six-sided dice until their sum is the desired sum. Here is a sample dialogue with the user:

```
Desired dice sum: 9
4 and 3 = 7
3 and 5 = 8
5 and 6 = 11
5 and 6 = 11
1 and 5 = 6
6 and 3 = 9
```

8. Write a method called `randomWalk` that performs steps of a random one-dimensional walk. The random walk should begin at position 0. On each step, you should either increase or decrease the position by 1 (each with equal probability). Your code should continue making steps until a position of 3 or −3 is reached, and then report the maximum position that was reached during the walk. The output should look like the following:

```
position = 1
position = 0
position = -1
position = -2
position = -1
position = -2
position = -3
max position = 1
```

9. Write a method called `printFactors` that accepts an integer as its parameter and uses a fencepost loop to print the factors of that number, separated by the word `"and"`. For example, the factors of the number 24 should print as the following:

```
1 and 2 and 3 and 4 and 6 and 8 and 12 and 24
```

You may assume that the parameter's value is greater than 0, or you may throw an exception if it is 0 or negative. Your method should print nothing if the empty string (`""`) is passed.

10. Write a method called `hopscotch` that accepts an integer number of "hops" as its parameter and prints a pattern of numbers that resembles a hopscotch board. A "hop" is a three-number sequence where the output shows two numbers on a line, followed by one number on its own line. 0 hops is a board up to 1; one hop is a board up to 4; two hops is a board up to 7; and so on. For example, the call of `hopscotch(3);` should print the following output:

```
    1
2       3
    4
5       6
    7
8       9
   10
```

A call of `hopscotch(0);` should print only the number 1. If it is passed a negative value, the method should produce no output.

11. Write a method called `threeHeads` that repeatedly flips a coin until the results of the coin toss are three heads in a row. You should use a `Random` object to make it equally likely that a head or a tail will appear. Each time the coin is flipped, display H for heads or T for tails. When three heads in a row are flipped, the method should print a congratulatory message. Here is a possible output of a call to the method:

```
T T H T T T H T H T H H H
Three heads in a row!
```

12. Write a method called `printAverage` that uses a sentinel loop to repeatedly prompt the user for numbers. Once the user types any number less than zero, the method should display the average of all nonnegative numbers typed. Display the average as a `double`. Here is a sample dialogue with the user:

```
Type a number: 7
Type a number: 4
Type a number: 16
Type a number: -4
Average was 9.0
```

If the first number that the user types is negative, do not print an average:

```
Type a number: -2
```

13. Write a method called `consecutive` that accepts three integers as parameters and returns `true` if they are three consecutive numbers—that is, if the numbers can be arranged into an order such that, assuming some integer k, the parameters' values are k, $k + 1$, and $k + 2$. Your method should return `false` if the integers are not consecutive. Note that order is not significant; your method should return the same result for the same three integers passed in any order.

For example, the calls `consecutive(1, 2, 3)`, `consecutive(3, 2, 4)`, and `consecutive(-10, -8, -9)` would return `true`. The calls `consecutive(3, 5, 7)`, `consecutive(1, 2, 2)`, and `consecutive(7, 7, 9)` would return `false`.

14. Write a method called `hasMidpoint` that accepts three integers as parameters and returns `true` if one of the integers is the midpoint between the other two integers; that is, if one integer is exactly halfway between them. Your method should return `false` if no such midpoint relationship exists. For example, the call `hasMidpoint(7, 4, 10)` should return `true` because 7 is halfway between 4 and 10. By contrast, the call `hasMidpoint(9, 15, 8)` should return `false` because no integer is halfway between the other two. The integers could be passed in any order; the midpoint could be the 1st, 2nd, or 3rd. You must check all cases. If your method is passed three of the same value, return `true`.

15. Write a method called `dominant` that accepts three integers as parameters and returns `true` if any one of the three integers is larger than the sum of the other two integers. The integers might be passed in any order, so the largest value could be any of the three. For example, the call `dominant(4, 9, 2)` returns `true` because 9 is larger than 4 + 2. Assume that none of the numbers is negative.

16. Write a method called `anglePairs` that accepts three angles (integers), measured in degrees, as parameters and returns whether or not there exist both complementary and supplementary angles among the three angles passed. Two angles are complementary if their sum is exactly 90 degrees; two angles are supplementary if their sum is exactly 180 degrees. Therefore, the method should return `true` if any two of the three angles add up to 90 degrees and also any two of the three angles add up to 180 degrees. For example, the call `anglePairs(120, 60, 30)` returns `true`. Assume that each angle passed is nonnegative.

17. Write a method called `monthApart` that accepts four integer parameters, *m1*, *d1*, *m2*, and *d2*, representing two calendar dates. Each date consists of a month (1 through 12) and a day (1 through the number of days in that month [28–31]). Assume that all parameter values passed are valid. The method should return `true` if the dates are at least a month apart and `false` otherwise. For example, the call of `monthApart(4, 15, 5, 22)` would return `true` while the call of `monthApart(9, 19, 10, 17)` would return `false`. Assume that all the dates in this problem occur during the same year. Note that the first date could come before or after the second date.

18. Write a method called `digitSum` that accepts an integer as a parameter and returns the sum of the digits of that number. For example, the call `digitSum(29107)` returns $2 + 9 + 1 + 0 + 7$ or 19. For negative numbers, return the same value that would result if the number were positive. For example, `digitSum(-456)` returns $4 + 5 + 6$ or 15. The call `digitSum(0)` returns 0.

19. Write a method called `firstDigit` that returns the first (most significant) digit of an integer. For example, `firstDigit(3572)` should return 3. It should work for negative numbers as well; `firstDigit(-947)` should return 9.

20. Write a method called `digitRange` that accepts an integer as a parameter and returns the range of values of its digits. The range is defined as 1 more than the difference between the largest and smallest digit value. For example, the call of `digitRange(68437)` would return 6 because the largest digit value is 8 and the smallest is 3, so $8 - 3 + 1 = 6$. If the number contains only one digit, return 1. You should solve this problem without using a `String`.

21. Write a method called `swapDigitPairs` that accepts an integer n as a parameter and returns a new integer whose value is similar to n's but with each pair of digits swapped in order. For example, the call of `swapDigitPairs(482596)` would return 845269. Notice that the 9 and 6 are swapped, as are the 2 and 5, and the 4 and 8. If the number contains an odd number of digits, leave the leftmost digit in its original place. For example, the call of `swapDigitPairs(1234567)` would return 1325476. You should solve this problem without using a `String`.

22. Write a method called `allDigitsOdd` that returns whether every digit of a positive integer is odd. Return `true` if the number consists entirely of odd digits (1, 3, 5, 7, 9) and `false` if any of its digits are even (0, 2, 4, 6, 8). For example, the call `allDigitsOdd(135319)` returns `true` but `allDigitsOdd(9145293)` returns `false`.

23. Write a method called `hasAnOddDigit` that returns whether a given positive integer has at least one digit whose value is odd. Return `true` if the number has at least one odd digit and `false` if none of its digits are odd. For example, the call `hasAnOddDigit(4822116)` should return `true` and `hasAnOddDigit(2448)` should return `false`.

24. Write a method called `isAllVowels` that returns whether a string consists entirely of vowels (a, e, i, o, or u, case-insensitively). If and only if every character of the string is a vowel, your method should return `true`. For example, the call `isAllVowels("eIEiO")` returns `true` and `isAllVowels("oink")` returns `false`. You should return `true` if passed the empty string, since it does not contain any non-vowel characters.

Programming Projects

1. Write an interactive program that reads lines of input from the user and converts each line into "Pig Latin." Pig Latin is English with the initial consonant sound moved to the end of each word, followed by "ay." Words that begin with vowels simply have an "ay" appended. For example, the phrase

    `The deepest shade of mushroom blue`

    would have the following appearance in Pig Latin:

    `e-Thay eepest-day ade-shay of-ay ushroom-may ue-blay`

    Terminate the program when the user types a blank line.

2. Write a reverse Hangman game in which the user thinks of a word and the computer tries to guess the letters in that word. The user tells the computer how many letters the word contains.

3. Write a program that plays a guessing game with the user. The program should generate a random number between 1 and some maximum (such as 100), then prompt the user repeatedly to guess the number. When the user guesses incorrectly, the game should give the user a hint about whether the correct answer is higher or lower than the guess. Once the user guesses correctly, the program should print a message showing the number of guesses that the user made.

Consider extending this program by making it play multiple games until the user chooses to stop and then printing statistics about the player's total and average number of guesses.

4. Write a program that plays a reverse guessing game with the user. The user thinks of a number between 1 and 10, and the computer repeatedly tries to guess it by guessing random numbers. It's fine for the computer to guess the same random number more than once. At the end of the game, the program reports how many guesses it made. Here is a sample execution:

```
This program has you, the user, choose a number
between 1 and 10. Then I, the computer, will try
my best to guess it.
Is it 8? (y/n) n
Is it 7? (y/n) n
Is it 5? (y/n) n
Is it 1? (y/n) n
Is it 8? (y/n) n
Is it 1? (y/n) n
Is it 9? (y/n) y
I got your number of 9 correct in 7 guesses.
```

For an added challenge, consider having the user hint to the computer whether the correct number is higher or lower than the computer's guess. The computer should adjust its range of random guesses on the basis of the hint.

5. Write a game that plays many rounds of Rock Paper Scissors. The user and computer will each choose between three items: rock (defeats scissors, but loses to paper), paper (defeats rock, but loses to scissors), and scissors (defeats paper, but loses to rock). If the player and computer choose the same item, the game is a tie.

You could extend this program to include different algorithmic strategies for choosing the best item. Should the computer pick randomly? Should it always pick a particular item or a repeating pattern of items? Should it count the number of times the opponent chooses various items and base its strategy on this history?

6. Write a program that draws a graphical display of a 2D random walk using a DrawingPanel. Start a pixel walker in the middle of the panel. On each step, choose to move 1 pixel up, down, left, or right, then redraw the pixel. (You can draw a single pixel by drawing a rectangle of size 1×1.)

7. Write a program that plays the dice game "Pig." Pig is a two-player game where the players take turns repeatedly rolling a single 6-sided die; a player repeatedly rolls the die until one of two events occurs. Either the player chooses to stop rolling, in which case the sum of that player's roll are added to his/her total points; or if the player rolls a 1 at any time, all points for that turn are lost and the turn ends immediately. The first player to reach a score of at least 100 points wins.

File Processing

Introduction

In Chapter 3 we discussed how to construct a `Scanner` object to read input from the console. Now we will look at how to construct `Scanner` objects to read input from files. The idea is fairly straightforward, but Java does not make it easy to read from input files. This is unfortunate because many interesting problems can be formulated as file-processing tasks. Many introductory computer science classes have abandoned file processing altogether and left the topic for the second course because it is considered too advanced for novices.

There is nothing intrinsically complex about file processing, but Java was not designed for it and the designers of Java have not been particularly eager to provide a simple solution. They did, however, introduce the `Scanner` class as a way to simplify some of the details associated with reading files. The result is that file reading is still awkward in Java, but at least the level of detail is manageable.

Before we start writing file-processing programs, we have to explore some issues related to Java exceptions. Remember that exceptions are errors that halt the execution of a program. In the case of file processing, trying to open a file that doesn't exist or trying to read beyond the end of a file generates an exception.

6.1 File-Reading Basics

In this section, we'll look at the most basic issues related to file processing. What are files and why do we care about them? What are the most basic techniques for reading files in a Java program? Once you've mastered these basics, we'll move on to a more detailed discussion of the different techniques you can use to process files.

Data, Data Everywhere

People are fascinated by data. When the field of statistics emerged in the nineteenth century, there was an explosion of interest in gathering and interpreting large amounts of data. Mark Twain reported that the British statesman Benjamin Disraeli complained to him, "There are three kinds of lies: lies, damn lies, and statistics."

The advent of the Internet has only added fuel to the fire. Today, every person with an Internet connection has access to a vast array of databases containing information about every facet of our existence. Here are just a few examples:

- If you visit http://www.landmark-project.com and click on the link for "Raw Data," you will find data files about earthquakes, air pollution, baseball, labor, crime, financial markets, U.S. history, geography, weather, national parks, a "world values survey," and more.

- At http://www.gutenberg.org you'll find thousands of online books, including the complete works of Shakespeare and works by Sir Arthur Conan Doyle, Jane Austen, H.G. Wells, James Joyce, Albert Einstein, Mark Twain, Lewis Carroll, T.S. Eliot, Edgar Allan Poe, and many others.

- A wealth of genomic data is available from sites like http://www.ncbi.nlm.nih.gov/guide/. Biologists have decided that the vast quantities of data describing the human genome and the genomes of other organisms should be publicly available to everyone to study.

- Many popular web sites, such as the Internet Movie Database, make their data available for download as simple data files (see http://www.imdb.com/interfaces).

- The U.S. government produces reams of statistical data. The web site http://www.fedstats.gov provides a lengthy list of available downloads, including maps and statistics on employment, climate, manufacturing, demographics, health, crime, and more.

Files and File Objects

When you store data on your own computer, you store it in a *file*.

> **File**
>
> A collection of information that is stored on a computer and assigned a particular name.

As we have just noted, every file has a name. For example, if you were to download the text of *Hamlet* from the Gutenberg site, you might store it on your computer

Origin of Data Processing

The field of data processing predates computers by over half a century. It is often said that necessity is the mother of invention, and the emergence of data processing is a good example of this principle. The crisis that spawned the industry came from a requirement in Article 1, Section 2, of the U.S. Constitution, which indicates that each state's population will determine how many representatives that state gets in the House of Representatives. To calculate the correct number, you need to know the population, so the Constitution says, "The actual Enumeration shall be made within three Years after the first Meeting of the Congress of the United States, and within every subsequent Term of ten Years, in such Manner as they shall by Law direct."

The first census was completed relatively quickly in 1790. Since then, every 10 years the U.S. government has had to perform another complete census of the population. This process became more and more difficult as the population of the country grew larger. By 1880 the government discovered that using old-fashioned hand-counting techniques, it barely completed the census within the 10 years allotted to it. So the government announced a competition for inventors to propose machines that could be used to speed up the process.

Herman Hollerith won the competition with a system involving punched cards. Clerks punched over 62 million cards that were then counted by 100 counting machines. This system allowed the 1890 tabulation to be completed in less than half the time it had taken to hand-count the 1880 results, even though the population had increased by 25 percent.

Hollerith struggled for years to turn his invention into a commercial success. His biggest problem initially was that he had just one customer: the U.S. government. Eventually he found other customers, and the company that he founded merged with competitors and grew into the company we now know as International Business Machines Corporation, or IBM.

We think of IBM as a computer company, but it sold a wide variety of data-processing equipment involving Hollerith cards long before computers became popular. Later, when it entered the computer field, IBM used Hollerith cards for storing programs and data. These cards were still being used when one of this book's authors took his freshman computer programming class in 1978.

in a file called `hamlet.txt`. A file name often ends with a special suffix that indicates the kind of data it contains or the format in which it has been stored. This suffix is known as a *file extension*. Table 6.1 lists some common file extensions.

Table 6.1   Common File Extensions

Extension	Description
.txt	text file
.java	Java source code file
.class	compiled Java bytecode file
.doc	Microsoft Word file
.xls	Microsoft Excel file
.pdf	Adobe Portable Document File
.mp3	audio file
.jpg	image file
.zip	compressed archive
.html	hypertext markup language files (most often web pages)
.exe	executable file

Files can be classified into text files and binary files depending on the format that is used. Text files can be edited using simple text editors. Binary files are stored using an internal format that requires special software to process. Text files are often stored using the .txt extension, but other file formats are also text formats, including .java and .html files.

To access a file from inside a Java program, you need to construct an internal object that will represent the file. The Java class libraries include a class called File that performs this duty.

You construct a File object by passing in the name of a file, as in the following line of code:

```
File f = new File("hamlet.txt");
```

Once you've constructed the object, you can call a number of methods to manipulate the file. For example, the following program calls a method that determines whether a file exists, whether it can be read, what its length is (i.e., how many characters are in the file), and what its absolute path is (i.e., where it is stored on the computer):

```
1 // Report some basic information about a file.
2
3 import java.io.*; // for File
4
5 public class FileInfo {
6     public static void main(String[] args) {
7         File f = new File("hamlet.txt");
```

```
8              System.out.println("exists returns " + f.exists());
9              System.out.println("canRead returns " + f.canRead());
10             System.out.println("length returns " + f.length());
11             System.out.println("getAbsolutePath returns "
12                               + f.getAbsolutePath());
13      }
14 }
```

Notice that the program includes an import from the package `java.io`, because the `File` class is part of that package. The term "io" (or I/O) is jargon used by computer science professionals to mean "input/output." Assuming you have stored the file `hamlet.txt` in the same directory as the program, you'll get output like the following when you run the program:

```
exists returns true
canRead returns true
length returns 191734
getAbsolutePath returns C:\data\hamlet.txt
```

The fact that we use a call on `new` to construct a `File` object can be misleading. We aren't constructing an actual file by constructing this object. The `File` object is an internal object that allows us to access files that already exist on the computer. Later in the chapter we will see how to write a program that creates a file as output.

Table 6.2 lists some useful methods for `File` objects.

Reading a File with a Scanner

The `Scanner` class that we have been using since Chapter 3 is flexible in that `Scanner` objects can be attached to many different kinds of input (see Figure 6.1).

Table 6.2 Useful Methods of `File` Objects

Method	Description
`canRead()`	Whether or not this file exists and can be read
`delete()`	Deletes the given file
`exists()`	Whether or not this file exists on the system
`getAbsolutePath()`	The full path where this file is located
`getName()`	The name of this file as a `String`, without any path attached
`isDirectory()`	Whether this file represents a directory/folder on the system
`isFile()`	Whether this file represents a file (nonfolder) on the system
`length()`	The number of characters in this file
`renameTo(file)`	Changes this file's name to the given file's name

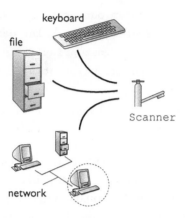

Figure 6.1   Scanners can be connected to many input sources.

You can think of a `Scanner` object as being like a faucet that you can attach to a pipe that has water flowing through it. The water can come from various sources. For example, in a house you'd attach a faucet to a pipe carrying water from the city water supply or from a well, but faucets in places like mobile homes and airplanes have different sources of water.

Thus far, we have been constructing `Scanner` objects by passing `System.in` to the `Scanner` constructor:

```
Scanner console = new Scanner(System.in);
```

This line of code instructs the computer to construct a `Scanner` that reads from the console (i.e., pauses for input from the user).

Instead of passing `System.in` to the constructor, you can pass a `File` object:

```
File f = new File("hamlet.txt");
Scanner input = new Scanner(f);
```

In this case the variable `f` is not necessary, so we can shorten this code to the following:

```
Scanner input = new Scanner(new File("hamlet.txt"));
```

This line of code, or something like it, will appear in all of your file-processing programs. When we were reading from the console window, we called our `Scanner` variable `console`. When you read from an input file, you may want to call the variable `input`. Of course, you can name the variable anything you want, as long as you refer to it in a consistent way.

Unfortunately, when you try to compile a program that constructs a `Scanner` in this manner, you'll run into a snag. Say you write a `main` method that begins by opening a `Scanner` as follows:

```java
// flawed method--does not compile
public static void main(String[] args) {
    Scanner input = new Scanner(new File("hamlet.txt"));

    ...

}
```

This program does not compile. It produces a message like the following:

```
CountWords.java:8:
unreported exception java.io.FileNotFoundException;
must be caught or declared to be thrown
        Scanner input = new Scanner(new File(hamlet.txt));
                    ^

1 error
```

The issue involves exceptions, which were described in Chapter 3. Remember that exceptions are errors that prevent a program from continuing normal execution. In this case the compiler is worried that it might not be able to find a file called `hamlet.txt`. What is it supposed to do if that happens? It won't have a file to read from, so it won't have any way to continue executing the rest of the code.

If the program is unable to locate the specified input file, it will generate an error by throwing what is known as a `FileNotFoundException`. This particular exception is known as a *checked exception*.

> **Checked Exception**
>
> An exception that *must* be caught or specifically declared in the header of the method that might generate it.

Because `FileNotFoundException` is a checked exception, you can't just ignore it. Java provides a construct known as the `try/catch` statement for handling such errors (described in Appendix C), but it allows you to avoid handling this error as long as you clearly indicate the fact that you aren't handling it. All you have to do is include a *throws clause* in the header for the `main` method to clearly state the fact that your `main` method might generate this exception.

> **`throws` Clause**
>
> A declaration that a method will not attempt to handle a particular type of exception.

Here's how to modify the header for the `main` method to include a `throws` clause indicating that it may throw a `FileNotFoundException`:

```
public static void main(String[] args)
        throws FileNotFoundException {
    Scanner input = new Scanner(new File("hamlet.txt"));
    ...
}
```

With the `throws` clause, the line becomes so long that we have to break it into two lines to allow it to fit in the margins of the textbook. On your own computer, you will probably include all of it on a single line.

After this modification, the program compiles. Once you've constructed the `Scanner` so that it reads from the file, you can manipulate it like any other `Scanner`. Of course, you should always prompt before reading from the console to give the user an indication of what kind of data you want, but when reading from a file, you don't need to prompt because the data is already there, stored in the file. For example, you could write a program like the following to count the number of words in *Hamlet*:

```
 1 // Counts the number of words in Hamlet.
 2
 3 import java.io.*;
 4 import java.util.*;
 5
 6 public class CountWords {
 7     public static void main(String[] args)
 8             throws FileNotFoundException {
 9         Scanner input = new Scanner(new File("hamlet.txt"));
10         int count = 0;
11         while (input.hasNext()) {
12             String word = input.next();
13             count++;
14         }
15         System.out.println("total words = " + count);
16     }
17 }
```

Note that you have to include an import from `java.util` for the `Scanner` class and an import from `java.io` for the `File` class. The program generates the following output:

```
total words = 31956
```

Common Programming Error

Reading Beyond the End of a File

As you learn how to process input files, you are likely to write programs that accidentally attempt to read data when there is no data left to read. For example, the `CountWords` program we just saw uses a `while` loop to keep reading words from the file as long as there are still words left to read. After the `while` loop, you might include an extra statement to read a word:

```
while (input.hasNext()) {
    String word = input.next();
    count++;
}
String extra = input.next(); // illegal, no more input
```

This new line of code causes the computer to try to read a word when there is no word to read. Java throws an exception when this occurs:

```
Exception in thread "main" java.util.NoSuchElementException
        at java.util.Scanner.throwFor(Scanner.java:817)
        at java.util.Scanner.next(Scanner.java:1317)
        at CountWords.main(CountWords.java:15)
```

As usual, the most important information appears at the end of this list of line numbers. The exception indicates that the error occurred in line 15 of `CountWords`. The other line numbers come from the `Scanner` class and aren't helpful.

If you find yourself getting a `NoSuchElementException`, it is probably because you have somehow attempted to read beyond the end of the input. The `Scanner` is saying, "You've asked me for some data, but I don't have any such value to give you."

Common Programming Error

Forgetting `"new File"`

Suppose that you intend to construct a `Scanner` the way we've learned:

```
Scanner input = new Scanner(new File("hamlet.txt"));
```

But you accidentally forget to include the `File` object and instead write this line of code:

```
Scanner input = new Scanner("hamlet.txt"); // not right
```

Continued on next page

Continued from previous page

The line of code may seem correct because it mentions the name of the file, but it won't work because it doesn't include the `File` object.

Normally, when you make a mistake like this Java warns you that you have done something illegal. In this case, however, you'll get no warning from Java. This is because, as you'll see later in this chapter, it is possible to construct a `Scanner` from a `String`, in which case Java reads from the `String` itself.

If you were to make this mistake in the `CountWords` program, you would get the following output:

```
total words = 1
```

The program would report just one word because the `String` `"hamlet.txt"` looks like a single word to the `Scanner`. So, whenever you construct a `Scanner` that is supposed to read from an input file, make sure that you include the call on `new File` to construct an appropriate `File` object.

6.2 Details of Token-Based Processing

VideoNote

Now that we've introduced some of the basic issues involved in reading an input file, let's explore reading from a file in more detail. One way to process a file is token by token.

> **Token-Based Processing**
>
> Processing input token by token (i.e., one word at a time or one number at a time).

Recall from Chapter 3 the primary token-reading methods for the `Scanner` class:

- `nextInt` for reading an `int` value
- `nextDouble` for reading a `double` value
- `next` for reading the next token as a `String`

For example, you might want to create a file called `numbers.dat` with the following content:

```
308.2 14.9 7.4
2.8


3.9 4.7 -15.4
2.8
```

You can create such a file with an editor like Notepad on a Windows machine or TextEdit on a Macintosh. Then you might write a program that processes this input file and produces some kind of report. For example, the following program reads the first five numbers from the file and reports their sum:

```java
 1  // Program that reads five numbers and reports their sum.
 2
 3  import java.io.*;
 4  import java.util.*;
 5
 6  public class ShowSum1 {
 7      public static void main(String[] args)
 8              throws FileNotFoundException {
 9          Scanner input = new Scanner(new File("numbers.dat"));
10
11          double sum = 0.0;
12          for (int i = 1; i <= 5; i++) {
13              double next = input.nextDouble();
14              System.out.println("number " + i + " = " + next);
15              sum += next;
16          }
17          System.out.println("Sum = " + sum);
18      }
19  }
```

This program uses a variation of the cumulative sum code from Chapter 4. Remember that you need a `throws` clause in the header for `main` because there is a potential `FileNotFoundException`. The program produces the following output:

```
number 1 = 308.2
number 2 = 14.9
number 3 = 7.4
number 4 = 2.8
number 5 = 3.9
Sum = 337.19999999999993
```

Notice that the reported sum is not 337.2. This result is another example of a roundoff error (also described in Chapter 4).

The preceding program reads exactly five numbers from the file. More typically, you'll continue to read numbers as long as there are more numbers to read while a `while` loop is executing. Remember that the `Scanner` class includes a series of `hasNext` methods that parallel the various `next` methods. In this case, `nextDouble` is being used to read a value of type `double`, so you can use `hasNextDouble` to test whether there is such a value to read:

```
1  // Reads an input file of numbers and prints the numbers and
2  // their sum.
3
4  import java.io.*;
5  import java.util.*;
6
7  public class ShowSum2 {
8      public static void main(String[] args)
9              throws FileNotFoundException {
10         Scanner input = new Scanner(new File("numbers.dat"));
11
12         double sum = 0.0;
13         int count = 0;
14         while (input.hasNextDouble()) {
15             double next = input.nextDouble();
16             count++;
17             System.out.println("number " + count + " = " + next);
18             sum += next;
19         }
20         System.out.println("Sum = " + sum);
21     }
22 }
```

This program would work on an input file with any number of numbers; `numbers.dat` happens to contain eight. This version of the program produces the following output:

```
number 1 = 308.2
number 2 = 14.9
number 3 = 7.4
number 4 = 2.8
number 5 = 3.9
number 6 = 4.7
number 7 = -15.4
number 8 = 2.8
Sum = 329.29999999999995
```

Structure of Files and Consuming Input

We think of text as being two-dimensional, like a sheet of paper, but from the computer's point of view, each file is just a one-dimensional sequence of characters. For example, consider the file `numbers.dat` that we used in the previous section:

```
308.2 14.9 7.4
2.8


3.9 4.7 -15.4
2.8
```

We think of this as a six-line file with text going across and down and two blank lines in the middle. However, the computer views the file differently. When you typed the text in this file, you hit the Enter key to go to a new line. This key inserts special "new line" characters in the file. You can annotate the file with \n characters to indicate the end of each line:

```
308.2 14.9 7.4\n
2.8\n
\n
\n
3.9 4.7 -15.4\n
2.8\n
```

Common Programming Error

Reading the Wrong Kind of Token

It's easy to write code that accidentally reads the wrong kind of data. For example, the ShowSum1 program always reads exactly five doubles from the input file numbers.dat. But suppose that the input file has some extraneous text in it:

```
308.2 14.9 7.4
hello
2.8

3.9 4.7 -15.4
2.8
```

The first line of the file contains three numbers that the program will read properly. But when it attempts to read a fourth number, the computer finds that the next token in the file is the text "hello". This token cannot be interpreted as a double, so the program generates an exception:

```
number 1 = 308.2
number 2 = 14.9
number 3 = 7.4
Exception in thread "main" java.util.InputMismatchException
```

Continued on next page

Continued from previous page

```
        at java.util.Scanner.throwFor(Scanner.java:819)
        at java.util.Scanner.next(Scanner.java:1431)
        at java.util.Scanner.nextDouble(Scanner.java:2335)
        at ShowSum1.main(ShowSum1.java:13)
```

Once again, the useful line number appears at the bottom of this list. The last line indicates that the exception occurred in line 13 of the `ShowSum1` class. The other line numbers are from the `Scanner` class and aren't helpful.

You saw earlier that when you attempt to read beyond the end of a file, the `Scanner` throws a `NoSuchElementException`. In the case of this program that attempts to read the wrong kind of token, the `Scanner` throws an `InputMismatchException`. By paying attention to the kind of exception the `Scanner` throws, you can get better feedback about what the problem is.

When you mark the end of each line in your program, you no longer need to use a two-dimensional representation. You can collapse this text to a one-dimensional sequence of characters:

```
308.2 14.9 7.4\n2.8\n\n\n3.9 4.7 -15.4\n2.8\n
```

This sequence is how the computer views the file: as a one-dimensional sequence of characters including special characters that represent "new line". On some systems, including Windows machines, there are two different "new line" characters, but we'll use just \n here—objects like `Scanner` handle these differences for you, so you can generally ignore them. (For those who are interested, the brief explanation is that Windows machines end each line with a \r followed by a \n.)

When it is processing a file, the `Scanner` object keeps track of the current position in the file. You can think of this as an *input cursor* or pointer into the file.

Input Cursor

A pointer to the current position in an input file.

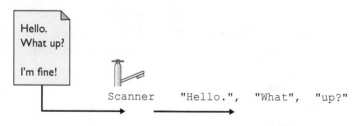

Figure 6.2   Scanners treat files as one-dimensional strings of characters and convert their contents into a series of whitespace-separated tokens.

When a `Scanner` object is first constructed, the cursor points to the beginning of the file. But as you perform various next operations, the cursor moves forward. The `ShowSum2` program from the last section processes the file through a series of calls on `nextDouble`. Let's take a moment to examine in detail how that works. Again, when the `Scanner` is first constructed, the input cursor will be positioned at the beginning of the file (indicated with an up-arrow pointing at the first character):

```
308.2 14.9 7.4\n2.8\n\n\n3.9 4.7 -15.4\n2.8\n
↑
input
cursor
```

After the first call on `nextDouble` the cursor will be positioned in the middle of the first line, after the token "308.2":

```
308.2 14.9 7.4\n2.8\n\n\n3.9 4.7 -15.4\n2.8\n
      ↑
      input
      cursor
```

We refer to this process as *consuming input.*

> **Consuming Input**
> Moving the input cursor forward past some input.

The process of consuming input doesn't actually change the file, it just changes the corresponding `Scanner` object so that it is positioned at a different point in the file.

The first call on `nextDouble` consumes the text "308.2" from the input file and leaves the input cursor positioned at the first character after this token. Notice that this leaves the input cursor positioned at a space. When the second call is made on `nextDouble`, the `Scanner` first skips past this space to get to the next token, then consumes the text "14.9" and leaves the cursor positioned at the space that follows it:

```
308.2 14.9 7.4\n2.8\n\n\n3.9 4.7 -15.4\n2.8\n
           ↑
           input
           cursor
```

The third call on `nextDouble` skips that space and consumes the text "7.4":

```
308.2 14.9 7.4\n2.8\n\n\n3.9 4.7 -15.4\n2.8\n
              ↑
              input
              cursor
```

At this point, the input cursor is positioned at the new line character at the end of the first line of input. The fourth call on `nextDouble` skips past this new line character and consumes the text "2.8":

```
308.2 14.9 7.4\n2.8\n\n\n3.9 4.7 -15.4\n2.8\n
                   ↑
                 input
                 cursor
```

Notice that when it skipped past the first new line character, the input cursor moved into data stored on the second line of input. At this point, the input cursor is positioned at the end of the second line of input, because it has consumed the "2.8" token. When a fifth call is made on `nextDouble`, the `Scanner` finds three new line characters in a row. This isn't a problem for the `Scanner`, because it simply skips past any leading white-space characters (spaces, tabs, new line characters) until it finds an actual token. So, it skips all three of these new line characters and consumes the text "3.9":

```
308.2 14.9 7.4\n2.8\n\n\n3.9 4.7 -15.4\n2.8\n
                          ↑
                        input
                        cursor
```

At this point the input cursor is positioned in the middle of the fifth line of input. (The third and fourth lines were blank). The program continues reading in this manner, consuming the remaining three numbers in the input file. After it reads the final token, "2.8", the input cursor is positioned at the new line character at the end of the file:

```
308.2 14.9 7.4\n2.8\n\n\n3.9 4.7 -15.4\n2.8\n
                                          ↑
                                        input
                                        cursor
```

If you attempted to call `nextDouble` again, it would throw a `NoSuchElementException` because there are no more tokens left to process. But remember that the `ShowSum2` program has a `while` loop that calls `hasNextDouble` before it calls `nextDouble`. When you call methods like `hasNextDouble`, the `Scanner` looks ahead in the file to see whether there is a next token and whether it is of the specified type (in this case, a `double`). So, the `ShowSum2` program will continue executing until it reaches the end of the file or until it encounters a token that cannot be interpreted as a `double`.

When the input cursor reaches the new line character at the end of the file, the `Scanner` notices that there are no more `double` values to read and returns `false` when `hasNextDouble` is called. That return stops the `while` loop from executing and causes the program to exit.

Scanner objects are designed for file processing in a forward manner. They provide a great deal of flexibility for looking ahead in an input file, but no support for reading the input backward. There are no "previous" methods, and there's no mechanism for resetting a Scanner back to the beginning of the input. Instead, you would have to construct a new Scanner object that would be positioned at the beginning of the file. We will see an example of this technique in the case study at the end of the chapter.

Scanner Parameters

Novices are sometimes surprised that the input cursor for a Scanner does not reset to the beginning of the file when it is passed as a parameter to a method. For example, consider the following variation of the ShowSum1 program. It has a method that takes a Scanner as input and an integer specifying how many numbers to process:

```java
 1 // Demonstrates a Scanner as a parameter to a method that
 2 // can consume an arbitrary number of tokens.
 3
 4 import java.io.*;
 5 import java.util.*;
 6
 7 public class ShowSum3 {
 8     public static void main(String[] args)
 9             throws FileNotFoundException {
10         Scanner input = new Scanner(new File("numbers.dat"));
11         processTokens(input, 2);
12         processTokens(input, 3);
13         processTokens(input, 2);
14     }
15
16     public static void processTokens(Scanner input, int n) {
17         double sum = 0.0;
18         for (int i = 1; i <= n; i++) {
19             double next = input.nextDouble();
20             System.out.println("number " + i + " = " + next);
21             sum += next;
22         }
23         System.out.println("Sum = " + sum);
24         System.out.println();
25     }
26 }
```

The main method creates a Scanner object that is tied to the numbers.dat file. It then calls the processTokens method several times, indicating the number of tokens to process. The first call instructs the method to process two tokens. It operates on the first two tokens of the file, generating the following output:

```
number 1 = 308.2
number 2 = 14.9
Sum = 323.09999999999997
```

The second call on the method indicates that three tokens are to be processed. Some people expect the method to process the first three tokens of the file, but that's not what happens. Remember that the Scanner keeps track of where the input cursor is positioned. After the first call on the method, the input cursor is positioned beyond the first two tokens. So the second call on the method processes the next three tokens from the file, producing the following output:

```
number 1 = 7.4
number 2 = 2.8
number 3 = 3.9
Sum = 14.1
```

The final call on the method asks the Scanner to process the next two tokens from the file, so it ends up processing the sixth and seventh numbers from the file:

```
number 1 = 4.7
number 2 = −15.4
Sum = −10.7
```

The program then terminates, never having processed the eighth number in the file.

The key point to remember is that a Scanner keeps track of the position of the input cursor, so you can process an input file piece by piece in a very flexible manner. Even when the Scanner is passed as a parameter to a method, it remembers how much of the input file has been processed so far.

Paths and Directories

Files are grouped into *folders*, also called *directories*. Directories are organized in a hierarchy, starting from a root directory at the top. For example, most Windows machines have a disk drive known as c:. At the top level of this drive is the *root* directory, which we can describe as c:\. This root directory will contain various top-level directories. Each top-level directory can have subdirectories, each of which also has subdirectories, and so on. All files are stored in one of these directories. The description of how to get from the top-level directory to the particular directory that stores a file is known as the *path* of the file.

> **File Path**
>
> A description of a file's location on a computer, starting with a drive and including the path from the root directory to the directory where the file is stored.

We read the path information from left to right. For example, if the path to a file is `C:\school\data\hamlet.txt`, we know that the file is on the `C:` drive in a folder called `school` and in a subfolder called `data`.

In the previous section, the program used the file name `numbers.dat`. When Java encounters a simple name like that (also called a *relative* file path), it looks in the *current directory* to find the file.

> **Current Directory (a.k.a. Working Directory)**
>
> The directory that Java uses as the default when a program uses a simple file name.

The default directory varies with the Java environment you are using. In most environments, the current directory is the one in which your program appears. We'll assume that this is the case for the examples in this textbook.

You can also use a *fully qualified*, or complete, file name (sometimes called an *absolute file path*). However, this approach works well only when you know exactly where your file is going to be stored on your system. For example, if you are on a Windows machine and you have stored the file in the `C:\data` directory, you could use a file name like the following:

```java
Scanner input = new Scanner(new File("C:/data/numbers.dat"));
```

Notice that the path is written with forward-slash characters rather than backslash characters. On Windows you would normally use a backslash, but Java allows you to use a forward slash instead. If you wanted to use a backslash, you would have to use a `\\` escape sequence. Most programmers choose the simpler approach of using forward-slash characters because Java does the appropriate translation on Windows machines.

You can also specify a file using a *relative path*. To write a relative path you omit the drive specification at the beginning of the string. You can still specify subdirectory relationships that will be relative to the current directory. For example, the relative path `"data/numbers.dat"` indicates a file called `numbers.dat` in a subdirectory of the working directory called `data`.

Sometimes, rather than writing a file's path name in the code yourself, you'll ask the user for a file name. For example, here is a variation of `ShowSum2` that prompts the user for the file name:

```java
1  // Variation of ShowSum2 that prompts for a file name.
2
3  import java.io.*;
4  import java.util.*;
5
6  public class ShowSum4 {
7      public static void main(String[] args)
8              throws FileNotFoundException {
```

```
 9              System.out.println("This program will add a series");
10              System.out.println("of numbers from a file.");
11              System.out.println();
12
13              Scanner console = new Scanner(System.in);
14              System.out.print("What is the file name? ");
15              String name = console.nextLine();
16              Scanner input = new Scanner(new File(name));
17              System.out.println();
18
19              double sum = 0.0;
20              int count = 0;
21              while (input.hasNextDouble()) {
22                  double next = input.nextDouble();
23                  count++;
24                  System.out.println("number " + count + " = " + next);
25                  sum += next;
26              }
27              System.out.println("Sum = " + sum);
28          }
29  }
```

Notice that the program has two different Scanner objects: one for reading from the console and one for reading from the file. We read the file name using a call on nextLine to read an entire line of input from the user, which allows the user to type in file names that have spaces in them. Notice that we still need the throws FileNotFoundException in the header for main because even though we are prompting the user to enter a file name, there won't necessarily be a file of that name.

If we have this program read from the file numbers.dat used earlier, it will produce the following output:

```
This program will add a series
of numbers from a file.

What is the file name? numbers.dat

number 1 = 308.2
number 2 = 14.9
number 3 = 7.4
number 4 = 2.8
number 5 = 3.9
number 6 = 4.7
number 7 = -15.4
number 8 = 2.8
Sum = 329.29999999999995
```

The user also has the option of specifying a full file path:

```
This program will add a series
of numbers from a file.

What is the file name? C:\data\numbers.dat

number 1 = 308.2
number 2 = 14.9
number 3 = 7.4
number 4 = 2.8
number 5 = 3.9
number 6 = 4.7
number 7 = -15.4
number 8 = 2.8
Sum = 329.29999999999995
```

Notice that the user doesn't have to type two backslashes to get a single backslash. The `Scanner` object that reads the user's input is able to read it without escape sequences.

A More Complex Input File

Suppose an input file contains information about how many hours each employee of a company has worked. It might look like the following:

```
Erica 7.5 8.5 10.25 8 8.5
Erin 10.5 11.5 12 11 10.75
Simone 8 8 8
Ryan 6.5 8 9.25 8
Kendall 2.5 3
```

Suppose you want to find out the total number of hours worked by each individual. You can construct a `Scanner` object linked to this file to solve this task. As you start writing more complex file-processing programs, you will want to divide the program into methods to break up the code into logical subtasks. In this case, you can open the file in `main` and write a separate method to process the file.

Most file processing will involve `while` loops, because you won't know in advance how much data the file contains. You'll need to write different tests, depending on the particular file being processed, but they will almost all be calls on the various `hasNext` methods of the `Scanner` class. You basically want to say, "While you have more data for me to process, let's keep reading."

In this case, the data is a series of input lines that each begins with a name. For this program you can assume that names are simple, with no spaces in the middle.

That means you can read them with a call on the next method. As a result, the while loop test involves seeing whether there is another name in the input file:

```
while (input.hasNext()) {
    process next person.
}
```

So, how do you process each person? You have to read that person's name and then read that person's list of hours. If you look at the sample input file, you will see that the list of hours is not always the same length. For example, some employees worked on five days, while others worked only two or three days. This unevenness is a common occurrence in input files. You can deal with it by using a nested loop. The outer loop will handle one person at a time and the inner loop will handle one number at a time. The task is a fairly straightforward cumulative sum:

```
double sum = 0.0;
while (input.hasNextDouble()) {
    sum += input.nextDouble();
}
```

When you put the parts of the program together, you end up with the following complete program:

```
 1 // This program reads an input file of hours worked by various
 2 // employees and reports the total hours worked by each.
 3
 4 import java.io.*;
 5 import java.util.*;
 6
 7 public class HoursWorked {
 8     public static void main(String[] args)
 9             throws FileNotFoundException {
10         Scanner input = new Scanner(new File("hours.dat"));
11         process(input);
12     }
13
14     public static void process(Scanner input) {
15         while (input.hasNext()) {
16             String name = input.next();
17             double sum = 0.0;
18             while (input.hasNextDouble()) {
19                 sum += input.nextDouble();
20             }
21             System.out.println("Total hours worked by " + name
22                     + " = " + sum);
```

```
23            }
24      }
25 }
```

Notice that you need to put the `throws FileNotFoundException` in the header for `main`. You don't need to include it in the `process` method because the code to open the file appears in method `main`.

If you put the input data into a file called `hours.dat` and execute the program, you get the following result:

```
Total hours worked by Erica = 42.75
Total hours worked by Erin = 55.75
Total hours worked by Simone = 24.0
Total hours worked by Ryan = 31.75
Total hours worked by Kendall = 5.5
```

6.3 Line-Based Processing

VideoNote

So far we have been looking at programs that process input token by token. However, you'll often find yourself working with input files that are line-based: Each line of input represents a different case, to be handled separately from the rest. These types of files lend themselves to a second style of file processing called *line-based processing.*

> **Line-Based Processing**
> The practice of processing input line by line (i.e., reading in entire lines of input at a time).

Most file processing involves a combination of line- and token-based styles, and the `Scanner` class is flexible enough to allow you to write programs that include both styles of processing. For line-based processing, you'll use the `nextLine` and `hasNextLine` methods of the `Scanner` object. For example, here is a program that echoes an input file in uppercase:

```
1 // Reads a file and echoes it in uppercase.
2
3 import java.io.*;
4 import java.util.*;
5
6 public class EchoUppercase {
7     public static void main(String[] args)
8             throws FileNotFoundException {
9         Scanner input = new Scanner(new File("poem.txt"));
10        while (input.hasNextLine()) {
```

```
11                    String text = input.nextLine();
12                    System.out.println(text.toUpperCase());
13            }
14        }
15 }
```

This loop reads the input line by line and prints each line in uppercase until it runs out of lines to process. It reads from a file called `poem.txt`. Suppose that the file has the following contents:

```
My candle burns at both ends
It will not last the night;
But ah, my foes, and oh, my friends -
It gives a lovely light.


   --Edna St. Vincent Millay
```

If you run the preceding program on this input, it will produce the following output:

```
MY CANDLE BURNS AT BOTH ENDS
IT WILL NOT LAST THE NIGHT;
BUT AH, MY FOES, AND OH, MY FRIENDS -
IT GIVES A LOVELY LIGHT.


   --EDNA ST. VINCENT MILLAY
```

Notice that you could not have accomplished the same task with token-based processing. In this example, the line breaks are significant because they are part of the poem. Also, when you read a file token by token, you lose the spacing within the line because the `Scanner` skips any leading whitespace when it reads a token. The final line of this input file is indented because it is the name of the author and not part of the poem. That spacing would be lost if the file was read as a series of tokens.

String Scanners and Line/Token Combinations

In the last section we looked at a program called `HoursWorked` that processed the following data file:

```
Erica 7.5 8.5 10.25 8 8.5
Erin 10.5 11.5 12 11 10.75
Simone 8 8 8
Ryan 6.5 8 9.25 8
Kendall 2.5 3
```

The data are line-oriented, each employee's information appearing on a different line of input, but this aspect of the data wasn't incorporated into the program. The program processed the file in a token-based manner. However, that approach won't always work. For example, consider a slight variation in the data in which each line of input begins with an employee ID rather than just a name:

```
101 Erica 7.5 8.5 10.25 8 8.5
783 Erin 10.5 11.5 12 11 10.75
114 Simone 8 8 8
238 Ryan 6.5 8 9.25 8
156 Kendall 2.5 3
```

This addition seems like a fairly simple change that shouldn't require major changes to the code. Recall that the program uses a method to process the file:

```java
public static void process(Scanner input) {
    while (input.hasNext()) {
        String name = input.next();
        double sum = 0.0;
        while (input.hasNextDouble()) {
            sum += input.nextDouble();
        }
        System.out.println("Total hours worked by " + name +
                            " = " + sum);
    }
}
```

Suppose you add a line of code to read the employee ID and modify the `println` to report it:

```java
public static void process(Scanner input) {
    while (input.hasNext()) {
        int id = input.nextInt();
        String name = input.next();
        double sum = 0.0;
        while (input.hasNextDouble()) {
            sum += input.nextDouble();
        }
        System.out.println("Total hours worked by " + name +
                        " (id#" + id + ") = " + sum);
    }
}
```

When you run this new version of the program on the new input file, you'll get one line of output and then Java will throw an exception:

```
Total hours worked by Erica (id#101) = 825.75
Exception in thread "main" java.util.InputMismatchException
        at java.util.Scanner.throwFor(Scanner.java:819)
        at java.util.Scanner.next(Scanner.java:1431)
        at java.util.Scanner.nextInt(Scanner.java:2040)
        ...
```

The program correctly reads Erica's employee ID and reports it in the `println` statement, but then it crashes. Also, notice that the program reports Erica's total hours worked as 825.75, when the number should be 42.75. Where did it go wrong?

If you compute the difference between the reported sum of 825.75 hours and the correct sum of 42.75 hours, you'll find it is equal to 783. That number appears in the data file: It's the employee ID of the second employee, Erin. When the program was adding up the hours for Erica, it accidentally read Erin's employee ID as more hours worked by Erica and added this number to the sum. That's also why the exception occurs—on the second iteration of the loop, the program tries to read an employee ID for Erin when the next token in the file is her name, not an integer.

The solution is to somehow get the program to stop reading when it gets to the end of an input line. Unfortunately, there is no easy way to do this with a token-based approach. The loop asks whether the `Scanner` has a next `double` value to read, and the employee ID looks like a `double` that can be read. You might try to write a complex test that looks for a `double` that is not also an integer, but even that won't work because some of the hours are integers.

To make this program work, you need to write a more sophisticated version that pays attention to the line breaks. The program must read an entire line of input at a time and process that line by itself. Recall the `main` method for the program:

```
public static void main(String[] args)
        throws FileNotFoundException {
    Scanner input = new Scanner(new File("hours2.dat"));
    process(input);
}
```

If you incorporate a line-based loop, you'll end up with the following method:

```
public static void main(String[] args)
        throws FileNotFoundException {
    Scanner input = new Scanner(new File("hours2.dat"));
    while (input.hasNextLine()) {
```

```
        String text = input.nextLine();
        processLine(text);
    }
}
```

Reading the file line by line guarantees that you don't accidentally combine data for two employees. The downside to this approach is that you have to write a method called `processLine` that takes a `String` as a parameter, and you have to pull apart that `String`. It contains the employee ID, followed by the employee name, followed by the numbers indicating how many hours the employee worked on different days. In other words, the input line is composed of several pieces (tokens) that you want to process piece by piece. It's much easier to process this data in a token-based manner than to have it in a `String`.

Fortunately, there is a convenient way to do this. You can construct a `Scanner` object from an individual `String`. Remember that just as you can attach a faucet to different sources of water (a faucet in a house attached to city or well water versus a faucet on an airplane attached to a tank of water), you can attach a `Scanner` to different sources of input. You've seen how to attach it to the console (`System.in`) and to a file (passing a `File` object). You can also attach it to an individual `String`. For example, consider the following line of code:

```
Scanner input = new Scanner("18.4 17.9 8.3 2.9");
```

This code constructs a `Scanner` that gets its input from the `String` used to construct it. This `Scanner` has an input cursor just like a `Scanner` linked to a file. Initially the input cursor is positioned at the first character in the `String`, and it moves forward as you read tokens from the `Scanner`.

The following short program demonstrates this solution:

```
 1  // Simple example of a Scanner reading from a String.
 2
 3  import java.util.*;
 4
 5  public class StringScannerExample {
 6      public static void main(String[] args) {
 7          Scanner input = new Scanner("18.4 17.9 8.3 2.9");
 8          while (input.hasNextDouble()) {
 9              double next = input.nextDouble();
10              System.out.println(next);
11          }
12      }
13  }
```

This program produces the following output:

```
18.4
17.9
8.3
2.9
```

Notice that the program produces four lines of output because there are four numbers in the `String` used to construct the `Scanner`.

When a file requires a combination of line-based and token-based processing, you can construct a `String`-based `Scanner` for each line of the input file. Using this approach, you end up with a lot of `Scanner` objects. You have a `Scanner` object that is keeping track of the input file, and you use that `Scanner` to read entire lines of input. In addition, each time you read a line of text from the file, you construct a mini-`Scanner` for just that line of input. You can then use token-based processing for these mini-`Scanner` objects, because each contains just a single line of data.

This combination of line-based and token-based processing is powerful. You will find that you can use this approach (and slight variations on it) to process a large variety of input files. To summarize, this approach involves a two-step process:

1. Break the file into lines with a `Scanner` using calls on `hasNextLine` and `nextLine`.

2. Break apart each line by constructing a `Scanner` just for that line of input and making calls on token-based methods like `hasNext` and `next`.

Following this approach, if you have a file composed of n lines of input, you end up constructing $n + 1$ different `Scanner` objects–one for each of the n individual lines (step 2) and one extra `Scanner` that is used to process the overall file line by line (step 1).

In the `HoursWorked` program, each input line contains information for a single employee. Processing the input line involves making a `Scanner` for the line and then reading its various parts (employee ID, name, hours) in a token-based manner. You can put this all together into a new version of the program:

```java
1 // Variation of HoursWorked that includes employee IDs.
2
3 import java.io.*;
4 import java.util.*;
5
6 public class HoursWorked2 {
7     public static void main(String[] args)
8                 throws FileNotFoundException {
9         Scanner input = new Scanner(new File("hours2.dat"));
```

```
10              while (input.hasNextLine()) {
11                  String text = input.nextLine();
12                  processLine(text);
13              }
14          }
15
16      // processes the given String (ID, name, and hours worked)
17      public static void processLine(String text) {
18          Scanner data = new Scanner(text);
19          int id = data.nextInt();
20          String name = data.next();
21          double sum = 0.0;
22          while (data.hasNextDouble()) {
23              sum += data.nextDouble();
24          }
25          System.out.println("Total hours worked by " + name +
26                              " (id#" + id + ") = " + sum);
27      }
28  }
```

Notice that the main method includes line-based processing to read entire lines of input from the file. Each such line is passed to the processLine method. Each time the program calls processLine, it makes a mini-Scanner for just that line of input and uses token-based processing (calling the methods nextInt, next, and nextDouble).

This new version of the program produces the following output:

```
Total hours worked by Erica (id#101) = 42.75
Total hours worked by Erin (id#783) = 55.75
Total hours worked by Simone (id#114) = 24.0
Total hours worked by Ryan (id#238) = 31.75
Total hours worked by Kendall (id#156) = 5.5
```

While this version of the program is a little more complex than the original, it is much more flexible because it pays attention to line breaks.

6.4 Advanced File Processing

In this section, we'll explore two advanced topics related to file processing: producing output files and guaranteeing that files can be read.

Output Files with PrintStream

All of the programs we've studied so far have sent their output to the console window by calling System.out.print or System.out.println. But just as you can read input from a file instead of reading from the console, you can write output to a file instead of writing it to the console. There are many ways to accomplish this task. The simplest approach is to take advantage of what you already know. You've already learned all about how `print` and `println` statements work, and you can leverage that knowledge to easily create output files.

If you look at the Java documentation, you will find that `System.out` is a variable that stores a reference to an object of type `PrintStream`. The `print` and `println` statements you've been writing are calls on methods that are part of the `PrintStream` class. The variable `System.out` stores a reference to a special `PrintStream` object that is tied to the console window. However, you can construct other `PrintStream` objects that send their output to other places. Suppose, for example, that you want to send output to a file called `results.txt`. You can construct a `PrintStream` object as follows:

```java
PrintStream output = new PrintStream(new File("results.txt"));
```

This line of code looks a lot like the one we used to construct a `Scanner` tied to an input file. In this case, the computer is creating an output file. If no such file already exists, the program creates it. If such a file does exist, the computer overwrites the current version. Initially, the file will be empty. It will end up containing whatever output you tell it to produce through calls on `print` and `println`.

The line of code that constructs a `PrintStream` object can generate an exception if Java is unable to create the file you've described. There are many reasons that this might happen: You might not have permission to write to the directory, or the file might be locked because another program is using it. Like the line of code that creates a file-based `Scanner`, this line of code potentially throws a `FileNotFoundException`. Therefore, Java requires you to include the `throws` clause in whatever method contains this line of code. The simplest approach is to put this line in `main`. In fact, it is common practice to have the `main` method begin with the lines of code that deal with the input and output files.

Once you have constructed a `PrintStream` object, how do you use it? You should already have a good idea of what to do. We have been making calls on `System.out.print` and `System.out.println` since Chapter 1. If you recall everything you know about `System.out` you'll have a good idea of what to do, but for this program, you will call `output.print` instead of `System.out.print` and `output.println` instead of `System.out.println`.

As a simple example, remember that in Chapter 1 we looked at the following variation of the simple "hello world" program that produces several lines of output:

```java
1  public class Hello2 {
2      public static void main(String[] args) {
3          System.out.println("Hello, world!");
4          System.out.println();
```

```
5            System.out.println("This program produces four");
6            System.out.println("lines of output.");
7        }
8    }
```

Here is a variation that sends its output to a file called `hello.txt`:

```
1   // Variation of Hello2 that prints to a file.
2
3   import java.io.*;
4
5   public class Hello4 {
6       public static void main(String[] args)
7               throws FileNotFoundException {
8           PrintStream output =
9               new PrintStream(new File("hello.txt"));
10          output.println("Hello, world.");
11          output.println();
12          output.println("This program produces four");
13          output.println("lines of output.");
14      }
15  }
```

When you run this new version of the program, a curious thing happens. The program doesn't seem to do anything; no output appears on the console at all. You're so used to writing programs that send their output to the console that this might seem confusing at first. We don't see any output in the console window when we run this program because the output was directed to a file instead. After the program finishes executing, you can open up the file called `hello.txt` and you'll find that it contains the following:

```
Hello, world.

This program produces four
lines of output.
```

The main point is that everything you've learned to do with `System.out`, you can also do with `PrintStream` objects that are tied to files.

You can also write methods that take `PrintStream` objects as parameters. For example, consider the task of fixing the spacing for a series of words. Say that you have a line of text with erratic spacing, like the following line:

```
a        new   nation,      conceived   in      liberty
```

Suppose that you want to print this text with exactly one space between each pair of words:

```
a new nation, conceived in liberty
```

How do you do that? Assume that you are writing a method that is passed a `String` to echo and a `PrintStream` object to which the output should be sent:

```java
public static void echoFixed(String text, PrintStream output) {
    ...
}
```

You can construct a `Scanner` from the `String` and then use the `next` method to read one word at a time. Recall that the `Scanner` class ignores whitespace, so you'll get just the individual words without all of the spaces between them. As you read words, you'll need to echo them to the `PrintStream` object. Here's a first attempt:

```java
Scanner data = new Scanner(text);
while (data.hasNext()) {
    output.print(data.next());
}
```

This code does a great job of deleting the long sequences of spaces from the `String`, but it goes too far: It eliminates all of the spaces. To get one space between each pair of words, you'll have to include some spaces:

```java
Scanner data = new Scanner(text);
while (data.hasNext()) {
    output.print(data.next() + " ");
}
```

This method produces results that look pretty good, but it prints an extra space at the end of the line. To get rid of that space so that you truly have spaces appearing only between pairs of words, you'll have to change the method slightly. This is a classic fencepost problem; you want to print one more word than you have spaces. You can use the typical solution of processing the first word before the loop begins and swapping the order of the other two operations inside the loop (printing a space and then the word):

```java
Scanner data = new Scanner(text);
output.print(data.next());
while (data.hasNext()) {
    output.print(" " + data.next());
}
```

This version of the program works well for almost all cases, but by including the fencepost solution, which echoes the first word before the loop begins, you've introduced an assumption that there is a first word. If the `string` has no words at all, this call on `next` will throw an exception. So, you need a test for the case in which the `String` doesn't contain any words. If you also want this program to produce a complete line of output, you'll have to include a call on `println` to complete the line of output after printing the individual words. Incorporating these changes, you get the following code:

```java
public static void echoFixed(String text, PrintStream output) {
    Scanner data = new Scanner(text);
    if (data.hasNext()) {
        output.print(data.next());
        while (data.hasNext()) {
            output.print(" " + data.next());
        }
    }
    output.println();
}
```

Notice that you're now calling `output.print` and `output.println` instead of calling `System.out.print` and `System.out.println`. An interesting aspect of this method is that it can be used not only to send output to an output file, but also to send it to `System.out`. The method header indicates that it works on any `PrintStream`, so you can call it to send output either to a `PrintStream` object tied to a file or to `System.out`.

The following complete program uses this method to fix the spacing in an entire input file of text. To underscore the flexibility of the method, the program sends its output both to a file (`words2.txt`) and to the console:

```java
 1  // This program removes excess spaces in an input file.
 2
 3  import java.io.*;
 4  import java.util.*;
 5
 6  public class FixSpacing {
 7      public static void main(String[] args)
 8              throws FileNotFoundException {
 9          Scanner input = new Scanner(new File("words.txt"));
10          PrintStream output =
11              new PrintStream(new File("words2.txt"));
12          while (input.hasNextLine()) {
13              String text = input.nextLine();
14              echoFixed(text, output);
```

```
15                        echoFixed(text, System.out);
16            }
17       }
18
19       public static void echoFixed(String text,
20                                      PrintStream output) {
21            Scanner data = new Scanner(text);
22            if (data.hasNext()) {
23                 output.print(data.next());
24                 while (data.hasNext()) {
25                      output.print(" " + data.next());
26                 }
27            }
28            output.println();
29       }
30  }
```

Consider the following input file:

```
    four          score      and
seven     years ago      our
   fathers brought   forth on this      continent
a        new nation,      conceived in      liberty
   and  dedicated    to  the  proposition      that
   all    men     are     created     equal
```

Using this input, the program produces the following output file, called `words2.txt`:

```
four score and
seven years ago our
fathers brought forth on this continent
a new nation, conceived in liberty
and dedicated to the proposition that
all men are created equal
```

The output also appears in the console window.

Guaranteeing That Files Can Be Read

The programs we have studied so far assume that the user will provide a legal file name. But what if the user accidentally types in the name of a file that doesn't exist or that can't be read for some reason? In this section we explore how to guarantee that a file can be read.

Let's explore how you might handle the task of prompting the user for a file name in the console window. If the user does not input a legal file name, you can keep prompting until the user does enter a legal name. The `File` class has a method called `canRead` that you can use to test whether a file exists and can be read. You can print an error message each time the file can't be read, until you get a good file name. This situation turns out to be a fencepost problem. If you end up prompting the user *n* times, you'll want to produce *n − 1* error messages. You can use the classic fencepost solution of prompting for the file name once before the loop:

```java
System.out.print("input file name? ");
File f = new File(console.nextLine());
while (!f.canRead()) {
    System.out.println("File not found. Try again.");
    System.out.print("input file name? ");
    f = new File(console.nextLine());
}
```

This code could be included in your `main` method, but there is enough code here that it makes sense to put it in its own method. Because it is prompting the user for input, the code requires a `Scanner` for reading from the console. It can return a `Scanner` that is tied to the input file to process.

When you try to create a method that includes this code, you again run into the problem of checked exceptions. Even though we are being very careful to make sure that the file exists and can be read, the Java compiler doesn't know that. From its point of view, this code might throw an exception. You still need to include a `throws` clause in the method header, just as you've been doing with `main`:

```java
public static Scanner getInput(Scanner console)
        throws FileNotFoundException {
    System.out.print("input file name? ");
    File f = new File(console.nextLine());
    while (!f.canRead()) {
        System.out.println("File not found. Try again.");
        System.out.print("input file name? ");
        f = new File(console.nextLine());
    }
    // now we know that f is a file that can be read
    return new Scanner(f);
}
```

Here is a variation of the `CountWords` program that prompts for a file name:

```java
1   // Variation of CountWords that prompts for a file name.
2
3   import java.io.*;
4   import java.util.*;
```

```
 5
 6  public class CountWords2 {
 7      public static void main(String[] args)
 8              throws FileNotFoundException {
 9          Scanner console = new Scanner(System.in);
10          Scanner input = getInput(console);
11
12          // and count words
13          int count = 0;
14          while (input.hasNext()) {
15              String word = input.next();
16              count++;
17          }
18          System.out.println("total words = " + count);
19      }
20
21      // Prompts the user for a legal file name; creates and
22      // returns a Scanner tied to the file
23      public static Scanner getInput(Scanner console)
24              throws FileNotFoundException {
25          System.out.print("input file name? ");
26          File f = new File(console.nextLine());
27          while (!f.canRead()) {
28              System.out.println("File not found. Try again.");
29              System.out.print("input file name? ");
30              f = new File(console.nextLine());
31          }
32          // now we know that f is a file that can be read
33          return new Scanner(f);
34      }
35  }
```

The following log of execution shows what happens when the user types in some illegal file names, ending with a legal file name:

```
input file name? amlet.txt
File not found. Try again.
input file name? hamlet.dat
File not found. Try again.
input file name? humlet.txt
File not found. Try again.
input file name? hamlet.txt
Total words = 31956
```

The code for opening a file is fairly standard and could be used without modification in many programs. We refer to this as *boilerplate code*.

Boilerplate Code

Code that tends to be the same from one program to another.

The getInput method is a good example of the kind of boilerplate code that you might use in many different file-processing programs.

6.5 Case Study: Zip Code Lookup

VideoNote

Knowing the distance between two locations turns out to be extremely helpful and valuable. For example, many popular Internet dating sites allow you to search for people on the basis of a target location. On Match.com, you can search for potential matches within a particular radius of a given city or zip code (5 miles, 10 miles, 15 miles, 25 miles, and so on). Obviously this is an important feature for a dating site because people are most interested in dating other people who live near them.

There are many other applications of this kind of proximity search. In the 1970s and 1980s there was an explosion of interest in what is known as direct mail marketing that has produced what we now call junk mail. Proximity searches are very important in direct mail campaigns. A local store, for example, might decide to mail out a brochure to all residents who live within 5 miles of the store. A political candidate might pay a membership organization like The Sierra Club or the National Rifle Association a fee to get the mailing addresses of all its members who live within a certain distance of a town or a city district.

Massive databases keep track of potential customers and voters. Direct-mail marketing organizations often want to find the distance between one of these individuals and some fixed location. The distance calculations are done almost exclusively with zip codes. There are over 40,000 five-digit zip codes in the United States. Some zip codes cover rural areas that are fairly large, but more often a zip code determines your location in a city or town to within a fraction of a mile. If you use the more specific Zip + 4 database, you can often pinpoint a location to within a few city blocks.

If you do a web search for "zip code database" or "zip code software" you will find that there are many people selling the data and the software to interpret the data. There are also some free databases, although the data aren't quite as accurate. The U.S. Census Bureau is the source of much of the free data.

To explore this application, let's write a program that finds all the zip codes within a certain proximity of another zip code. A web site like Match.com could use the logic of this program to find potential dates within a certain radius. You'd simply start with the zip code of interest, find all the other zip codes within a particular distance, and then find all the customers who have those zip codes. We don't have access to a massive dating database like Match.com, so we'll be working on just the first part of this task, finding the zip codes that are within a specified distance.

As we noted earlier, some free zip code databases are available online. Our sample program uses data compiled by software developer Schuyler Erle, whose data are distributed free through a Creative Commons license (obtained from http://www.boutell.com/zipcodes/).

We have reformatted the data to make it more convenient for us to work with it (a process known as *data munging*). We will be working with a file called `zipcode.txt` that has a series of 3-line entries, one for each zip code. The first line contains the zip code, the second line contains the city and state, and the third line contains two numbers that represent the latitude and longitude of the zip code. For example, the following is an entry for one of the authors' home zip codes:

```
98104
Seattle, WA
47.60252 -122.32855
```

The overall task is to prompt the user for a target zip code and a proximity and to show all zip codes within the given proximity of the target. Here is a first attempt at pseudocode for the overall task:

```
introduce program to user.
prompt for target zip code and proximity.
display matching zip codes from file.
```

This approach doesn't quite work. To display a match, you have to compare the target location to each of the different zip codes in the data file. You'll need the latitude and longitude information to make this comparison. But when you prompt the user, you're just asking for a zip code and proximity. You could alter the program to prompt for a latitude and longitude, but that wouldn't be a very friendly program for the user. Imagine if Match.com required you to know your latitude and longitude in order for you to search for people who live near you.

Instead, you can use the zip code data to find the latitude and longitude of the target zip code. As a result, you'll have to search the data twice. The first time through you will be looking for the target zip code, so that you can find its coordinates. The second time through you will display all the zip codes that are within the distance specified by the user. Here is a new version of the pseudocode:

```
introduce program to user.
prompt for target zip code and proximity.
find coordinates for target zip code.
display matching zip codes from file.
```

Introducing the program and prompting for the target zip code and proximity are fairly straightforward tasks that don't require detailed explanation. The real work of the program involves solving the third and fourth steps in this pseudocode. Each of these steps is sufficiently complex that it deserves to be included in a static method.

First consider the problem of finding the coordinates for the target zip code. You need to set up a Scanner to read from the file, and then you need to call the method that will do the search. But what information should the searching method return? You want the coordinates of the target zip code (the latitude and longitude). Your method can't return two different values, but these coordinates appear on a single line of input, so you can return that line of input as a String. That means that your main method will include the following code:

```java
Scanner input = new Scanner(new File("zipcode.txt"));
String targetCoordinates = find(target, input);
```

The method should read the input file line by line, searching for the target zip code. Remember that each entry in the file is composed of three different lines. As a result, you need a slight variation of the standard line-processing loop that reads three lines each time through the loop:

```java
public static String find(String target, Scanner input) {
    while (input.hasNextLine()) {
        String zip = input.nextLine();
        String city = input.nextLine();
        String coordinates = input.nextLine();
        ...
    }
    ...
}
```

As you read various zip code entries, you want to test each to see whether it matches the target. Remember that you need to use the equals method to compare strings for equality. If you find a match, you can print it and return the coordinates:

```java
public static String find(String target, Scanner input) {
    while (input.hasNextLine()) {
        String zip = input.nextLine();
        String city = input.nextLine();
        String coordinates = input.nextLine();
        if (zip.equals(target)) {
            System.out.println(zip + ": " + city);
            return coordinates;
        }
    }
    ...
}
```

This method isn't complete because you have to consider the case in which the target zip code doesn't appear in the file. In that case, you exit the loop without having returned a value. There are many things the program could do at this point, such as printing an error message or throwing an exception. To keep things simple, let's instead return a set of fake coordinates. If the program returns a latitude and longitude of (0, 0), there won't be any matches unless the user asks for an outrageously high proximity (over 4,000 miles):

```java
public static String find(String target, Scanner input) {
    while (input.hasNextLine()) {
        String zip = input.nextLine();
        String city = input.nextLine();
        String coordinates = input.nextLine();
        if (zip.equals(target)) {
            System.out.println(zip + ": " + city);
            return coordinates;
        }
    }
    // at this point we know the zip code isn't in the file
    // we return fictitious (no match) coordinates
    return "0 0";
}
```

This method completes the first of the two file-processing tasks. In the second task, you have to read the file and search for zip codes within the given proximity. The Scanner doesn't have a reset option for going back to the beginning of the file. Instead, you have to construct a second Scanner object that will be used for the second pass. Thus, your code in main will look like the following:

```java
input = new Scanner(new File("zipcode.txt"));
showMatches(targetCoordinates, input, miles);
```

The code for finding matches involves a similar file-processing loop that reads three lines of input at a time, printing matches as it finds them:

```java
public static void showMatches(String targetCoordinates,
                               Scanner input, double miles) {
    // compute lat1 and long1
    System.out.println("zip codes within " + miles + " miles:");
    while (input.hasNextLine()) {
        String zip = input.nextLine();
        String city = input.nextLine();
        String coordinates = input.nextLine();
        // compute lat2 and long2
        double distance = distance(lat1, long1, lat2, long2);
```

```
        if (distance <= miles) {
            // print zip code
        }
    }
}
```

Again, this is an incomplete version of the method. It indicates that before the loop begins you will compute two values known as `lat1` and `long1` that represent the latitude and longitude of the target coordinates. Inside the loop you compute values for `lat2` and `long2` that represent the latitude and longitude of the next entry from the data file. The latitude and longitude are stored in a `String`. You can construct a `Scanner` for each `String` that can be used to pull out the individual tokens. You also need to fill in the details of printing. This is a good place to use a `printf` to format the output:

```
public static void showMatches(String targetCoordinates,
                               Scanner input, double miles) {
    Scanner data = new Scanner(targetCoordinates);
    double lat1 = data.nextDouble();
    double long1 = data.nextDouble();
    System.out.println("zip codes within " + miles + " miles:");
    while (input.hasNextLine()) {
        String zip = input.nextLine();
        String city = input.nextLine();
        String coordinates = input.nextLine();
        data = new Scanner(coordinates);
        double lat2 = data.nextDouble();
        double long2 = data.nextDouble();
        double distance = distance(lat1, long1, lat2, long2);
        if (distance <= miles) {
            System.out.printf("    %s %s, %3.2f miles\n",
                              zip, city, distance);
        }
    }
}
```

This addition almost completes the program. The preceding code calls a method called `distance` that is intended to compute the distance between two points, given their latitude and longitude. This problem was included as Programming Project 5 in Chapter 3. You can use the following standard formula:

Let φ_1, λ_1, and φ_2, λ_2 be the latitude and longitude of two points, respectively. $\Delta\lambda$, the longitudinal difference, and $\Delta\sigma$, the angular difference/distance in radians, can be determined from the spherical law of cosines as:

$$\Delta\sigma = \arccos(\sin \varphi_1 \sin \varphi_2 + \cos \varphi_1 \cos \varphi_2 \cos \Delta\lambda)$$

We won't dwell on the math involved here, but a short explanation might be helpful. Imagine forming a triangle by connecting two points with the North Pole. From the two latitudes, you can compute the distance from each point to the North Pole. The difference between the two longitudes tells you the angle formed by these two sides of the triangle. You may recall from geometry class that if you know two sides and the angle between them, then you can compute the third side. We are using a special version of the law of cosines that works for spheres to compute the length of the third side of the triangle (which is the line connecting the two points on our sphere). We have to convert from degrees into radians and we have to include the radius of our sphere (in this case the Earth). The resulting calculation is included in the final version of the program.

Here is the complete version of the program:

```java
 1   // This program uses a file of zip code information to allow a user
 2   // to find zip codes within a certain distance of another zip code.
 3
 4   import java.util.*;
 5   import java.io.*;
 6
 7   public class ZipLookup {
 8       // radius of sphere. Here it's the Earth, in miles
 9       public static final double RADIUS = 3956.6;
10
11       public static void main(String[] args)
12               throws FileNotFoundException {
13           giveIntro();
14           Scanner console = new Scanner(System.in);
15
16           System.out.print("What zip code are you interested in? ");
17           String target = console.next();
18           System.out.print("And what proximity (in miles)? ");
19           double miles = console.nextDouble();
20           System.out.println();
21
22           Scanner input = new Scanner(new File("zipcode.txt"));
23           String targetCoordinates = find(target, input);
24           input = new Scanner(new File("zipcode.txt"));
25           showMatches(targetCoordinates, input, miles);
26       }
27
28       // introduces the program to the user
29       public static void giveIntro() {
30           System.out.println("Welcome to the zip code database.");
31           System.out.println("Give me a 5-digit zip code and a");
```

```
32          System.out.println("proximity, and I'll tell you where");
33          System.out.println("that zip code is located, along");
34          System.out.println("with a list of other zip codes");
35          System.out.println("within the given proximity.");
36          System.out.println();
37      }
38
39      // Searches for the given string in the input file; if found,
40      // returns the coordinates; otherwise returns (0, 0)
41      public static String find(String target, Scanner input) {
42          while (input.hasNextLine()) {
43              String zip = input.nextLine();
44              String city = input.nextLine();
45              String coordinates = input.nextLine();
46              if (zip.equals(target)) {
47                  System.out.println(zip + ": " + city);
48                  return coordinates;
49              }
50          }
51          // at this point we know the zip code isn't in the file
52          // we return fictitious (no match) coordinates
53          return "0 0";
54      }
55
56      // Shows all matches for the given coordinates within the
57      // given number of miles
58      public static void showMatches(String targetCoordinates,
59                                     Scanner input, double miles) {
60          Scanner data = new Scanner(targetCoordinates);
61          double lat1 = data.nextDouble();
62          double long1 = data.nextDouble();
63          System.out.println("zip codes within " + miles + " miles:");
64          while (input.hasNextLine()) {
65              String zip = input.nextLine();
66              String city = input.nextLine();
67              String coordinates = input.nextLine();
68              data = new Scanner(coordinates);
69              double lat2 = data.nextDouble();
70              double long2 = data.nextDouble();
71              double distance = distance(lat1, long1, lat2, long2);
72              if (distance <= miles) {
73                  System.out.printf("   %s %s, %3.2f miles\n",
74                                    zip, city, distance);
75              }
```

```
76              }
77          }
78
79          // Returns spherical distance in miles given the latitude
80          // and longitude of two points (depends on constant RADIUS)
81          public static double distance(double lat1, double long1,
82                                        double lat2, double long2) {
83              lat1 = Math.toRadians(lat1);
84              long1 = Math.toRadians(long1);
85              lat2 = Math.toRadians(lat2);
86              long2 = Math.toRadians(long2);
87              double theCos = Math.sin(lat1) * Math.sin(lat2) +
88                  Math.cos(lat1) * Math.cos(lat2) * Math.cos(long1 - long2);
89              double arcLength = Math.acos(theCos);
90              return arcLength * RADIUS;
91          }
92  }
```

Here is a sample execution:

```
Welcome to the zip code database.
Give me a 5-digit zip code and a
proximity, and I'll tell you where
that zip code is located, along
with a list of other zip codes
within the given proximity.

What zip code are you interested in? 98104
And what proximity (in miles)? 1

98104: Seattle, WA
zip codes within 1.0 miles:
    98101 Seattle, WA, 0.62 miles
    98104 Seattle, WA, 0.00 miles
    98154 Seattle, WA, 0.35 miles
    98164 Seattle, WA, 0.29 miles
    98174 Seattle, WA, 0.35 miles
```

There is an old saying that you get what you pay for, and these zip code data are no exception. There are several web sites that list zip codes within a mile of 98104, and they include many zip codes not included here. That's because the free zip code information is incomplete. Each of those web sites gives you the option of obtaining a better database for a small fee.

Chapter Summary

Files are represented in Java as `File` objects. The `File` class is found in the `java.io` package.

A `Scanner` object can read input from a file rather than from the keyboard. This task is achieved by passing new `File(`*filename*`)` to the `Scanner`'s constructor, rather than passing `System.in`.

A checked exception is a program error condition that must be caught or declared in order for the program to compile. For example, when constructing a `Scanner` that reads a file, you must write the phrase `throws FileNotFoundException` in the `main` method's header.

The `Scanner` treats an input file as a one-dimensional stream of data that is read in order from start to end. The input cursor consumes (moves past) input tokens as they are read and returns them to your program.

A `Scanner` that reads a file makes use of the various `hasNext` methods to discover when the file's input has been exhausted.

`Scanner`s can be passed as parameters to methods to read part or all of a file, since they are objects and therefore use reference semantics.

A file name can be specified as a relative path such as `data/text/numbers.dat`, which refers to a file called `numbers.dat` that exists in the `data/text/` subfolder of the current directory. Alternatively, you can specify a full file path such as `C:/Documents and Settings/user/My Documents/data/text/numbers.dat`.

In many files, input is structured by lines, and it makes sense to process those files line by line. In such cases, it is common to use nested loops: an outer loop that iterates over each line of the file and an inner loop that processes the tokens in each line.

Output to a file can be achieved with a `PrintStream` object, which is constructed with a `File` and has the same methods as `System.out`, such as `println` and `print`.

Self-Check Problems

Section 6.1: File-Reading Basics

1. What is a file? How can we read data from a file in Java?

2. What is wrong with the following line of code?

   ```java
   Scanner input = new Scanner("test.dat");
   ```

3. Which of the following is the correct syntax to declare a `Scanner` to read the file `example.txt` in the current directory?

   a. `Scanner input = new Scanner("C:\example.txt");`
   b. `Scanner input = new Scanner(new File("example.txt"));`
   c. `Scanner input = new File("\\example.txt");`
   d. `File input = new Scanner("/example.txt");`
   e. `Scanner input = new Scanner("C:/example.txt");`

4. Write code to construct a `Scanner` object to read the file `input.txt`, which exists in the same folder as your program.

Section 6.2: Details of Token-Based Processing

5. Given the following line of input, what tokens does a `Scanner` break the line apart into?

```
welcome...to the matrix.
```

   a. `"welcome"`, `"to"`, `"the"`, `"matrix"`
   b. `"welcome...to the matrix."`
   c. `"welcome...to"`, `"the"`, `"matrix."`
   d. `"welcome..."`, `"to"`, `"the matrix."`
   e. `"welcome"`, `"to the matrix"`

6. Given the following lines of input, what tokens does a `Scanner` break the line apart into?

```
in fourteen-hundred 92
columbus sailed the ocean blue :)
```

   a. `"in"`, `"fourteen-hundred"`, `"92"`
   b. `"in"`, `"fourteen-hundred"`, `"92"`, `"columbus"`, `"sailed"`, `"the"`, `"ocean"`, `"blue"`, `":)"`
   c. `"in"`, `"fourteen"`, `"hundred"`, `"92"`, `"columbus"`, `"sailed"`, `"the"`, `"ocean"`, `"blue"`
   d. `"in"`, `"fourteen-hundred"`, `"92\ncolumbus"`, `"sailed"`, `"the"`, `"ocean"`, `"blue :)"`
   e. `"in fourteen-hundred 92"`, `"columbus sailed the ocean blue :)"`

7. How many tokens are there in the following input, and what `Scanner` method(s) can be used to read each of the tokens?

```
Hello there,how are you?
I am "very well", thank you.
12 34 5.67 (8 + 9) "10"
```

8. What is wrong with the following line of code?

```
Scanner input = new Scanner(new File("C:\temp\new files\test.dat"));
```

   (Hint: Try printing the `String` in this line of code.)

9. Answer the following questions about a Java program located on a Windows machine in the folder `C:\Documents and Settings\amanda\My Documents\programs`:

   a. What are two legal ways you can refer to the file `C:\Documents and Settings\amanda\My Documents\programs\numbers.dat`?
   b. How can you refer to the file `C:\Documents and Settings\amanda\My Documents\programs\data\homework6\input.dat`?
   c. How many, and in what legal, ways can you refer to the file `C:\Documents and Settings\amanda\My Documents\homework\data.txt`?

10. Answer the following questions about a Java program located on a Linux machine in the folder `/home/amanda/Documents/hw6`:

   a. What are two legal ways you can refer to the file `/home/amanda/Documents/hw6/names.txt`?
   b. How can you refer to the file `/home/amanda/Documents/hw6/data/numbers.txt`?
   c. How many legal ways can you refer to the file `/home/amanda/download/saved.html`?

11. The following program contains 6 mistakes! What are they?

```
1   public class Oops6 {
2       public static void main(String[] args) {
3           Scanner in = new Scanner("example.txt");
4           countWords(in);
5       }
6
7       // Counts total lines and words in the input scanner.
8       public static void countWords(Scanner input) {
9           Scanner input = new Scanner("example.txt");
10          int lineCount = 0;
11          int wordCount = 0;
12
13          while (input.nextLine()) {
14              String line = input.line();     // read one line
15              lineCount++;
16              while (line.next()) {           // tokens in line
17                  String word = line.hasNext;
18                  wordCount++;
19              }
20          }
21      }
22  }
```

Section 6.3: Line-Based Processing

12. For the next several questions, consider a file called readme.txt that has the following contents:

```
6.7         This file has
        several input lines.

  10 20        30    40


test
```

What would be the output from the following code when it is run on the readme.txt file?

```
Scanner input = new Scanner(new File("readme.txt"));
int count = 0;
while (input.hasNextLine()) {
    System.out.println("input: " + input.nextLine());
    count++;
}
System.out.println(count + " total");
```

13. What would be the output from the code in the previous exercise if the calls to hasNextLine and nextLine were replaced by calls to hasNext and next, respectively?

14. What would be the output from the code in the previous exercise if the calls to `hasNextLine` and `nextLine` were replaced by calls to `hasNextInt` and `nextInt`, respectively? How about `hasNextDouble` and `nextDouble`?

15. Given the following file contents, what will be the output from each of the following code fragments?

```
the quick brown
    fox    jumps


        over
the lazy    dog
```

a.

```
Scanner input = new Scanner(new File("brownfox.txt"));
while (input.hasNextLine()) {
    String line = input.nextLine();
    System.out.println(line);
}
```

b.

```
Scanner input = new Scanner(new File("brownfox.txt"));
while (input.hasNext()) {
    String token = input.next();
    System.out.println(token);
}
```

16. Write a program that prints itself to the console as output. For example, if the program is stored in `Example.java`, it will open the file `Example.java` and print its contents to the console.

17. Write code that prompts the user for a file name and prints the contents of that file to the console as output. Assume that the file exists. You may wish to place this code into a method called `printEntireFile`.

18. Write a program that takes as input lines of text like the following:

```
This is some
text here.
```

The program should produce as output the same text inside a box, as in the following:

```
+--------------+
| This is some |
| text here.   |
+--------------+
```

Your program will have to assume some maximum line length (e.g., 12 in this case).

Section 6.4: Advanced File Processing

19. What object is used to write output to a file? What methods does this object have available for you to use?

20. Write code to print the following four lines of text into a file named `message.txt`:

```
Testing,
1, 2, 3.


This is my output file.
```

21. Write code that repeatedly prompts the user for a file name until the user types the name of a file that exists on the system. You may wish to place this code into a method called `getFileName`, which will return that file name as a `String`.

22. In Problem 16, you wrote a piece of code that prompted the user for a file name and printed that file's contents to the console. Modify your code so that it will repeatedly prompt the user for the file name until the user types the name of a file that exists on the system.

Exercises

1. Write a method called `boyGirl` that accepts a `Scanner` that is reading its input from a file containing a series of names followed by integers. The names alternate between boys' names and girls' names. Your method should compute the absolute difference between the sum of the boys' integers and the sum of the girls' integers. The input could end with either a boy or girl; you may not assume that it contains an even number of names. For example, if the input file contains the following text:

```
Erik 3 Rita 7 Tanner 14 Jillyn 13 Curtis 4 Stefanie 12 Ben 6
```

Then the method should produce the following console output, since the boys' sum is 27 and the girls' sum is 32:

```
4 boys, 3 girls
Difference between boys' and girls' sums: 5
```

2. Write a method called `evenNumbers` that accepts a `Scanner` reading input from a file with a series of integers, and report various statistics about the integers to the console. Report the total number of numbers, the sum of the numbers, the count of even numbers and the percent of even numbers. For example, if the input file contains the following text:

```
5 7 2 8 9 10 12 98 7 14 20 22
```

Then the method should produce the following console output:

```
12 numbers, sum = 214
8 evens (66.67%)
```

3. Write a method called `negativeSum` that accepts a `Scanner` reading input from a file containing a series of integers, and print a message to the console indicating whether the sum starting from the first number is ever negative. You should also return `true` if a negative sum can be reached and `false` if not. For example, suppose the file contains the following text:

```
38 4 19 -27 -15 -3 4 19 38
```

Your method would consider the sum of just one number (38), the first two numbers (38 + 4), the first three numbers (38 + 4 + 19), and so on to the end. None of these sums is negative, so the method would produce the following output and return `false`:

```
no negative sum
```

If the file instead contains the following numbers:

```
14 7 -10 9 -18 -10 17 42 98
```

The method finds that a negative sum of −8 is reached after adding the first six numbers. It should output the following to the console and return `true`:

```
sum of -8 after 6 steps
```

4. Write a method called countCoins that accepts a Scanner representing an input file whose data is a series of pairs of tokens, where each pair begins with an integer and is followed by the type of coin, which will be "pennies" (1 cent each), "nickels" (5 cents each), "dimes" (10 cents each), or "quarters" (25 cents each), case-insensitively. Add up the cash values of all the coins and print the total money. For example, if the input file contains the following text:

   ```
   3 pennies 2 quarters 1 Pennies 23 NiCkeLs 4 DIMES
   ```

   For the input above, your method should produce the following output:

   ```
   Total money: $2.09
   ```

5. Write a method called collapseSpaces that accepts a Scanner representing an input file as its parameter, then reads that file and outputs it with all its tokens separated by single spaces, collapsing any sequences of multiple spaces into single spaces. For example, consider the following text:

   ```
   many    spaces    on    this    line!
   ```

   If this text were a line in the file, the same line should be output as follows:

   ```
   many spaces on this line!
   ```

6. Write a method called readEntireFile that accepts a Scanner representing an input file as its parameter, then reads that file and returns its entire text contents as a String.

7. Write a method called flipLines that accepts a Scanner for an input file and writes to the console the same file's contents with each pair of lines reversed in order. If the file contains an odd number of lines, leave the last line unmodified. For example, if the file contains:

   ```
   Twas brillig and the slithy toves
   did gyre and gimble in the wabe.
   All mimsey were the borogroves,
   and the mome raths outgrabe.
   ```

   your method should produce the following output:

   ```
   did gyre and gimble in the wabe.
   Twas brillig and the slithy toves
   and the mome raths outgrabe.
   All mimsey were the borogroves,
   ```

8. Write a method called doubleSpace that accepts a Scanner for an input file and a PrintStream for an output file as its parameters, writing into the output file a double-spaced version of the text in the input file. You can achieve this task by inserting a blank line between each line of output.

9. Write a method called wordWrap that accepts a Scanner representing an input file as its parameter and outputs each line of the file to the console, word-wrapping all lines that are longer than 60 characters. For example, if a line contains 112 characters, the method should replace it with two lines: one containing the first 60 characters and another containing the final 52 characters. A line containing 217 characters should be wrapped into four lines: three of length 60 and a final line of length 37.

10. Modify the preceding wordWrap method so that it outputs the newly wrapped text back into the original file. (Be careful—don't output into a file while you are reading it!) Also, modify it to use a class constant for the maximum line length rather than hard-coding 60.

11. Modify the preceding wordWrap method so that it only wraps whole words, never chopping a word in half. Assume that a word is any whitespace-separated token and that all words are under 60 characters in length.

12. Write a method called stripHtmlTags that accepts a Scanner representing an input file containing an HTML web page as its parameter, then reads that file and prints the file's text with all HTML tags removed. A tag is any text between the characters < and >. For example, consider the following text:

```
<html>
<head>
<title>My web page</title>
</head>
<body>
<p>There are many pictures of my cat here,
as well as my <b>very cool</b> blog page,
which contains <font color="red">awesome
stuff about my trip to Vegas.</p>

Here's my cat now:<img src="cat.jpg">
</body>
</html>
```

If the file contained these lines, your program should output the following text:

```
My web page

There are many pictures of my cat here,
as well as my very cool blog page,
which contains awesome
stuff about my trip to Vegas.


Here's my cat now:
```

You may assume that the file is a well-formed HTML document and that there are no < or > characters inside tags.

13. Write a method called stripComments that accepts a Scanner representing an input file containing a Java program as its parameter, reads that file, and then prints the file's text with all comments removed. A comment is any text on a line from // to the end of the line, and any text between /* and */ characters. For example, consider the following text:

```
import java.util.*;

/* My program
by Suzy Student */
public class Program {
    public static void main(String[] args) {
        System.out.println("Hello, world!"); // a println
    }
```

```
    public static /* Hello there */ void foo() {
        System.out.println("Goodbye!"); // comment here
    } /* */
}
```

If the file contained this text, your program should output the following text:

```
import java.util.*;

public class Program {
    public static void main(String[] args) {
        System.out.println("Hello, world!");
    }

    public static  void foo() {
        System.out.println("Goodbye!");
    }
}
```

14. Write a method called `printDuplicates` that takes as a parameter a `Scanner` containing a series of lines. Your method should examine each line looking for consecutive occurrences of the same token on the same line and print each duplicated token, along with the number of times that it appears consecutively. Nonrepeated tokens are not printed. You may ignore the case of repetition across multiple lines (such as if a line ends with a given token and the next line starts with the same token). You may assume that each line of the file contains at least 1 token of input. For example, consider the following input:

```
hello how how are you you you you
I I I am Jack's Jack's smirking smirking smirking smirking revenge
bow wow wow yippee yippee  yo yippee  yippee yay yay yay
one fish two fish red fish blue fish
It's the Muppet Show, wakka wakka wakka
```

Your method should produce the following output:

```
how*2 you*4
I*3 Jack's*2 smirking*4
wow*2 yippee*2 yippee*2 yay*3

wakka*3
```

15. Write a method called `coinFlip` that accepts a `Scanner` representing an input file of coin flips that are heads (H) or tails (T). Consider each line to be a separate set of coin flips and output the number and percentage of heads in that line. If it is more than 50%, print "You win!". Consider the following file:

```
H T H H T
T t   t T h H
```

For the input above, your method should produce the following output:

```
3 heads (60.0%)
You win!

2 heads (33.3%)
```

16. Write a method called `mostCommonNames` that accepts a `Scanner` representing an input file with names on each line separated by spaces. Some names appear multiple times in a row on the same line. For each line, print the most commonly occurring name. If there's a tie, use the first name that had that many occurrences; if all names are unique, print the first name on the line. For example, if the file has this input:

```
Benson Eric    Eric  Kim   Kim Kim    Jenny  Nancy Nancy  Paul  Paul
Ethan   Jamie Jamie Alyssa Alyssa Helene   Helene Jessica Jessica
```

For the input above, your method should produce the following output:

```
Most common: Kim
Most common: Jamie
```

17. Write a method called `inputStats` that accepts a `Scanner` representing an input file and reports the number of lines, the longest line, the number of tokens on each line, and the length of the longest token on each line. If the file contains the following text:

```
Beware the Jabberwock, my son,
the jaws that bite, the claws that catch,
Beware the JubJub bird and shun
the frumious bandersnatch.
```

For the input above, your method should produce the following output:

```
Line 1 has 5 tokens (longest = 11)
Line 2 has 8 tokens (longest = 6)
Line 3 has 6 tokens (longest = 6)
Line 4 has 3 tokens (longest = 13)
Longest line: the jaws that bite, the claws that catch,
```

18. Write a method called `plusScores` that accepts a `Scanner` representing an input file containing a series of lines that represent student records. Each student record takes up two lines of input. The first line has the student's name and the second line has a series of plus and minus characters. Below is a sample input:

```
Kane, Erica
--+-+
Chandler, Adam
++-+
Martin, Jake
++++++
```

For each student you should produce a line of output with the student's name followed by a colon followed by the percent of plus characters. For the input above, your method should produce the following output:

```
Kane, Erica: 40.0% plus
Chandler, Adam: 75.0% plus
Martin, Jake: 100.0% plus
```

19. Write a method called `leetSpeak` that accepts two parameters: a `Scanner` representing an input file, and a `PrintStream` representing an output file. Convert the input file's text to "leet speak," where various letters are replaced by other letters/numbers, and output the new text to the given output file. Replace `"o"` with `"0"`, `"l"` (lowercase "L") with `"1"` (the number one), `"e"` with `"3"`, `"a"` with `"4"`, `"t"` with `"7"`, and an `"s"` at the end of a word with `"z"`. Preserve the original line breaks from the input. Also wrap each word of input in parentheses. For example, if the input file contains the following text:

```
four score and
seven years ago our
fathers brought forth on this continent
a new nation
```

For the input above, your method should produce the following in the output file:

```
(f0ur) (sc0r3) (4nd)
(s3v3n) (y34rZ) (4g0) (0ur)
(f47h3rZ) (br0ugh7) (f0r7h) (0n) (7hiZ) (c0n7in3n7)
(4) (n3w) (n47i0n)
```

Programming Projects

1. Students are often asked to write term papers containing a certain number of words. Counting words in a long paper is a tedious task, but the computer can help. Write a program that counts the number of words, lines, and total characters (not including whitespace) in a paper, assuming that consecutive words are separated either by spaces or end-of-line characters.

2. Write a program that compares two files and prints information about the differences between them. For example, consider a file `data1.txt` with the following contents:

```
This file has a great deal of
text in it which needs to

be processed.
```

Consider another file `data2.txt` that exists with the following contents:

```
This file has a grate deal of
text in it which needs to

bee procesed.
```

A dialogue with the user running your program might look like the following:

```
Enter a first file name: data1.txt
Enter a second file name: data2.txt
Differences found:
Line 1:
< This file has a great deal of
> This file has a grate deal of

Line 4:
< be processed.
> bee procesed.
```

3. Write a program that prompts the user for a file name, assuming that the file contains a Java program. Your program should read the file and print its contents properly indented. When you see a left-brace character ({) in the file, increase your indentation level by four spaces. When you see a right-brace character (}), decrease your indentation level by four spaces. You may assume that the file has only one opening or closing brace per line, that every block statement (such as if or for) uses braces rather than omitting them, and that every relevant occurrence of a { or } character in the file occurs at the end of a line. Consider using a class constant for the number of spaces to indent (4), so that it can easily be changed later.

4. Write a program that reads a file containing data about the changing popularity of various baby names over time and displays the data about a particular name. Each line of the file stores a name followed by integers representing the name's popularity in each decade: 1900, 1910, 1920, and so on. The rankings range from 1 (most popular) to 1000 (least popular), or 0 for a name that was less popular than the 1000th name. The following lines are a sample of the file format:

```
Sally 0 0 0 0 0 0 0 0 0 0 886
Sam 58 69 99 131 168 236 278 380 467 408 466
Samantha 0 0 0 0 0 0 272 107 26 5 7
Samir 0 0 0 0 0 0 0 0 920 0 798
```

Your program should prompt the user for a name and search the file for that name:

```
This program allows you to search through the
data from the Social Security Administration
to see how popular a particular name has been
since 1900.

Name? Sam
```

If the name is found, the program should display data about the name on the screen:

```
Statistics on name "Sam"
    1900: 58
    1910: 69
```

```
1920: 99
1930: 131
. . .
```

This program is more fun and challenging if you also draw the name's popularity on a `DrawingPanel` as a line graph. Plot the decades on the *x*-axis and the popularity on the *y*-axis.

5. Write a program that plays a game where a player is asked to fill in various words of a mostly complete story without being able to see the rest. Then the user is shown his/her story, which is often funny. The input for your program is a set of story files, each of which contains "placeholder" tokens surrounded by < and >, such as:

```
One of the most <adjective> characters in fiction is named
"Tarzan of the <plural-noun> ." Tarzan was raised by a/an
<noun> and lives in the <adjective> jungle in the
heart of darkest <place> .
```

The user is prompted to fill in each of the placeholders in the story, and then a resulting output file is created with the placeholders filled in. For example:

```
Input file name? story1.txt
Please enter an adjective: silly
Please enter a plural noun: socks
Please enter a noun: tree
Please enter an adjective: tiny
Please enter a place: Canada
```

The resulting output story would be:

```
One of the most silly characters in fiction is named
"Tarzan of the socks ." Tarzan was raised by a/an
tree and lives in the tiny jungle in the
heart of darkest Canada .
```

Introduction

The sequential nature of files severely limits the number of interesting things that you can do easily with them. The algorithms we have examined so far have all been sequential algorithms: algorithms that can be performed by examining each data item once, in sequence. An entirely different class of algorithms can be performed when you can access the data items multiple times and in an arbitrary order.

This chapter examines a new object called an array that provides this more flexible kind of access. The concept of arrays is not complex, but it can take a while for a novice to learn all of the different ways that an array can be used. The chapter begins with a general discussion of arrays and then moves into a discussion of common array manipulations as well as advanced array techniques. The chapter also includes a discussion of special rules known as reference semantics that apply only to objects like arrays and strings.

7.1 Array Basics

An *array* is a flexible structure for storing a sequence of values that are all of the same type.

> **Array**
>
> An indexed structure that holds multiple values of the same type.

The values stored in an array are called *elements*. The individual elements are accessed using an integer *index*.

> **Index**
>
> An integer indicating the position of a particular value in a data structure.

As an analogy, consider post office boxes. The boxes are indexed with numbers, so you can refer to an individual box by using a description like "P.O. Box 884." You already have experience using an index to indicate positions within a `String`; recall the methods `charAt` and `substring`. Like `String` indexes, array indexes start with 0. This is a convention known as *zero-based indexing*.

> **Zero-Based Indexing**
>
> A numbering scheme used throughout Java in which a sequence of values is indexed starting with 0 (element 0, element 1, element 2, and so on).

It might seem more natural to start indexes with 1 instead of 0, but Java uses the same indexing scheme that is used in C and C++.

Constructing and Traversing an Array

Suppose you want to store some different temperature readings. You could keep them in a series of variables:

```
double temperature1;
double temperature2;
double temperature3;
```

This isn't a bad solution if you have just 3 temperatures, but suppose you need to store 3000 temperatures. Then you would want a more flexible way to store the values. You can instead store the temperatures in an array.

When you use an array, you first need to declare a variable for it, so you have to know what type to use. The type will depend on the type of elements you want to have in your array. To indicate that you are creating an array, follow the type name with a set of square brackets: [ ]. If you are storing temperature values, you want a sequence of values of type `double`, so you use the type `double[ ]`. Thus, you can declare a variable for storing your array as follows:

```
double[] temperature;
```

Arrays are objects, which means that they must be constructed. Simply declaring a variable isn't enough to bring the object into existence. In this case you want an array of three `double` values, which you can construct as follows:

```
double[] temperature = new double[3];
```

This is a slightly different syntax than you've used previously to create a new object. It is a special syntax for arrays only. Notice that on the left-hand side you don't put anything inside the square brackets, because you're describing a type. The variable `temperature` can refer to any array of `double` values, no matter how many elements it has. On the right-hand side, however, you have to mention a specific number of elements because you are asking Java to construct an actual array object and it needs to know how many elements to include.

The general syntax for declaring and constructing an array is as follows:

```
<element type>[] <name> = new <element type>[<length>];
```

You can use any type as the element type, although the left and right sides of this statement have to match. For example, any of the following lines of code would be legal ways to construct an array:

```
int[] numbers = new int[10];        // an array of 10 ints
char[] letters = new char[20];      // an array of 20 chars
boolean[] flags = new boolean[5];   // an array of 5 booleans
String[] names = new String[100];   // an array of 100 Strings
Color[] colors = new Color[50];     // an array of 50 Colors
```

Some special rules apply when you construct an array of objects such as an array of `Strings` or an array of `Colors`, but we'll discuss those later in the chapter.

When it executes the line of code to construct the array of temperatures, Java will construct an array of three `double` values, and the variable `temperature` will refer to the array:

As you can see, the variable `temperature` is not itself the array. Instead, it stores a reference to the array. The array indexes are indicated in square brackets. To refer to an individual element of the array, you combine the name of the variable that

Table 7.1   Zero-Equivalent Auto-Initialization Values

Type	Value
int	0
double	0.0
char	'\0'
boolean	false
objects	null

refers to the array (`temperature`) with a specific index (`[0]`, `[1]`, or `[2]`). So, there is an element known as `temperature[0]`, an element known as `temperature[1]`, and an element known as `temperature[2]`.

In the `temperature` array diagram, each of the array elements has the value `0.0`. This is a guaranteed outcome when an array is constructed. Each element is initialized to a default value, a process known as *auto-initialization*.

> **Auto-Initialization**
>
> The initialization of variables to a default value, such as on an array's elements when it is constructed.

When Java performs auto-initialization, it always initializes to the zero-equivalent for the type. Table 7.1 indicates the zero-equivalent values for various types. The special value `null` will be explained later in this chapter.

Notice that the zero-equivalent for type `double` is `0.0`, which is why the array elements were initialized to that value. Using the indexes, you can store the specific temperature values that are relevant to this problem:

```
temperature[0] = 74.3;
temperature[1] = 68.4;
temperature[2] = 70.3;
```

This code modifies the array to have the following values:

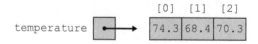

Obviously an array isn't particularly helpful when you have just three values to store, but you can request a much larger array. For example, you could request an array of 100 temperatures by writing the following line of code:

```
double[] temperature = new double[100];
```

This is almost the same line of code you executed before. The variable is still declared to be of type double[ ], but in constructing the array, you requested 100 elements instead of 3, which constructs a much larger array:

Notice that the highest index is 99 rather than 100 because of zero-based indexing.

You are not restricted to using simple literal values inside the brackets. You can use any integer expression. This flexibility allows you to combine arrays with loops, which greatly simplifies the code you write. For example, suppose you want to read a series of temperatures from a Scanner. You could read each value individually:

```
temperature[0] = input.nextDouble();
temperature[1] = input.nextDouble();
temperature[2] = input.nextDouble();
...
temperature[99] = input.nextDouble();
```

But since the only thing that changes from one statement to the next is the index, you can capture this pattern in a for loop with a control variable that takes on the values 0 to 99:

```
for (int i = 0; i < 100; i++) {
    temperature[i] = input.nextDouble();
}
```

This is a very concise way to initialize all the elements of the array. The preceding code works when the array has a length of 100, but you can change this to accommodate an array of a different length. Java provides a useful mechanism for making this code more general. Each array keeps track of its own length. You're using the variable temperature to refer to your array, which means you can ask for temperature.length to find out the length of the array. By using temperature.length in the for loop test instead of the specific value 100, you make your code more general:

```
for (int i = 0; i < temperature.length; i++) {
    temperature[i] = input.nextDouble();
}
```

Notice that the array convention is different from the string convention. When you are working with a string variable s, you ask for the length of the string by referring to s.length(). When you are working with an array variable, you don't include the parentheses after the word "length." This is another one of those unfortunate inconsistencies that Java programmers just have to memorize.

The previous code provides a pattern that you will see often with array-processing code: a `for` loop that starts at 0 and that continues while the loop variable is less than the length of the array, doing something with element `[i]` in the body of the loop. The program goes through each array element sequentially, which we refer to as *traversing* the array.

> **Array Traversal**
>
> Processing each array element sequentially from the first to the last.

This pattern is so useful that it is worth including it in a more general form:

```
for (int i = 0; i < <array>.length; i++) {
    <do something with array[i]>;
}
```

We will see this traversal pattern repeatedly as we explore common array algorithms.

Accessing an Array

As we discussed in the last section, we refer to array elements by combining the name of the variable that refers to the array with an integer index inside square brackets:

```
<array variable>[<integer expression>]
```

Notice in this syntax description that the index can be an arbitrary integer expression. To explore this feature, let's examine how we would access particular values in an array of integers. Suppose that we construct an array of length 5 and fill it up with the first five odd integers:

```
int[] list = new int[5];
for (int i = 0; i < list.length; i++) {
    list[i] = 2 * i + 1;
}
```

The first line of code declares a variable `list` of type `int[]` that refers to an array of length 5. The array elements are auto-initialized to `0`:

Then the code uses the standard traversing loop to fill in the array with successive odd numbers:

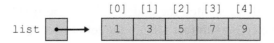

Suppose that we want to report the first, middle, and last values in the list. From an examination of the preceding diagram, we can see that these values occur at indexes 0, 2, and 4, which means we could write the following code:

```
// works only for an array of length 5
System.out.println("first = " + list[0]);
System.out.println("middle = " + list[2]);
System.out.println("last = " + list[4]);
```

This technique works when the array is of length 5, but suppose that we use an array of a different length? If the array has a length of 10, for example, this code will report the wrong values. We need to modify it to incorporate `list.length`, just as we modified the standard traversing loop.

The first element of the array will always be at index 0, so the first line of code doesn't need to change. You might at first think that we could fix the third line of code by replacing the 4 with `list.length`:

```
// doesn't work
System.out.println("last = " + list[list.length]);
```

However, this code doesn't work. The culprit is zero-based indexing. In our example, the last value is stored at index 4, not index 5, when `list.length` is 5. More generally, the last value will be at index `list.length` − 1. We can use this expression directly in our `println` statement:

```
// this one works
System.out.println("last = " + list[list.length − 1]);
```

Notice that what appears inside the square brackets is an integer expression (the result of subtracting 1 from `list.length`).

A simple approach to finding the middle value is to divide the length of the list in half:

```
// is this right?
System.out.println("middle = " + list[list.length / 2]);
```

When `list.length` is 5, this expression evaluates to 2, which prints the correct value. But what about when `list.length` is 10? In that case the expression evaluates to 5, and we would print `list[5]`. But when the list has an even length, there are actually two values in the middle. For a list of length 10, the two values are at `list[4]` and `list[5]`. In general, the preceding expression always returns the second of the two values in the middle when the list is of even length.

If we wanted the code to return the first of the two values in the middle instead, we could subtract 1 from the length before dividing it in half. Here is a complete set of println statements that follows this approach:

```
System.out.println("first = " + list[0]);
System.out.println("middle = " + list[(list.length - 1) / 2]);
System.out.println("last = " + list[list.length - 1]);
```

As you learn how to use arrays, you will find yourself wondering what types of operations you can perform on an array element that you are accessing. For example, for the array of integers called list, what exactly can you do with list[i]? The answer is that you can do anything with list[i] that you would normally do with any variable of type int. For example, if you have a variable called x of type int, any of the following expressions are valid:

```
x = 3;
x++;
x *= 2;
x--;
```

That means that the same expressions are valid for list[i] if list is an array of integers:

```
list[i] = 3;
list[i]++;
list[i] *= 2;
list[i]--;
```

From Java's point of view, because list is declared to be of type int[ ], an array element like list[i] is of type int and can be manipulated as such. For example, to increment every value in the array, you could use the standard traversing loop:

```
for (int i = 0; i < list.length; i++) {
    list[i]++;
}
```

This code would increment each value in the array, turning the array of odd numbers into an array of even numbers.

It is possible to refer to an illegal index of an array, in which case Java throws an exception. For example, for an array of length 5, the legal indexes are from 0 to 4. Any number less than 0 or greater than 4 is outside the bounds of the array:

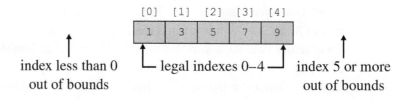

When you are working with this sample array, if you attempt to refer to `list[-1]` or `list[5]`, you are attempting to access an array element that does not exist. If your code makes such an illegal reference, Java will halt your program with an `ArrayIndexOutOfBoundsException`.

A Complete Array Program

Let's look at a program in which an array allows you to solve a problem that you couldn't solve before. If you tune in to any local news broadcast at night, you'll hear them report the high temperature for that day. It is usually reported as an integer, as in, "It got up to 78 today."

Suppose you want to examine a series of daily high temperatures, compute the average high temperature, and count how many days were above that average temperature. You've been using `Scanner`s to solve problems like this, and you can almost solve the problem that way. If you just wanted to know the average, you could use a `Scanner` and write a cumulative sum loop to find it:

```java
 1  // Reads a series of high temperatures and reports the average.
 2
 3  import java.util.*;
 4
 5  public class Temperature1 {
 6      public static void main(String[] args) {
 7          Scanner console = new Scanner(System.in);
 8          System.out.print("How many days' temperatures? ");
 9          int numDays = console.nextInt();
10          int sum = 0;
11          for (int i = 1; i <= numDays; i++) {
12              System.out.print("Day " + i + "'s high temp: ");
13              int next = console.nextInt();
14              sum += next;
15          }
16          double average = (double) sum / numDays;
17          System.out.println();
18          System.out.println("Average = " + average);
19      }
20  }
```

Did You Know?

Buffer Overruns

One of the earliest and still most common sources of computer security problems is a *buffer overrun* (also known as a *buffer overflow*). A buffer overrun is similar

Continued on next page

Continued from previous page

to an array index out of bounds exception. It occurs when a program writes data beyond the bounds of the buffer that is set aside for that data.

For example, you might have space allocated for the `string` "James T Kirk", which is 12 characters long, counting the spaces:

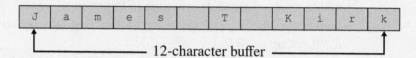

Suppose that you tell the computer to overwrite this buffer with the `string` "Jean Luc Picard". There are 15 letters in Picard's name, so if you write all of those characters into the buffer, you "overrun" it by writing three extra characters:

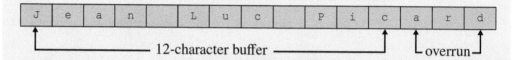

The last three letters of Picard's name ("ard") are being written to a part of memory that is beyond the end of the buffer. This is a very dangerous situation, because it will overwrite any data that is already there. An analogy would be a fellow student grabbing three sheets of paper from you and erasing anything you had written on them. You are likely to have had useful information written on those sheets of paper, so the overrun is likely to cause a problem.

When a buffer overrun happens accidentally, the program usually halts with some kind of error condition. However, buffer overruns are particularly dangerous when they are done on purpose by a malicious program. If the attacker can figure out just the right memory location to overwrite, the attacking software can take over your computer and instruct it to do things you haven't asked it to do.

Three of the most famous Internet worms were built on buffer overruns: the 1988 Morris worm, the 2001 Code Red worm, and the 2003 SQLSlammer worm.

Buffer overruns are often written as array code. You might wonder how such a malicious program could be written if the computer checks the bounds when you access an array. The answer is that older programming languages like C and C++ do not check bounds when you access an array. By the time Java was designed in the early 1990s, the danger of buffer overruns was clear and the designers of the language decided to include array-bounds checking so that Java would be more secure. Microsoft included similar bounds checking when it designed the language C# in the late 1990s.

The preceding program does a pretty good job. Here is a sample execution:

```
How many days' temperatures? 5
Day 1's high temp: 78
Day 2's high temp: 81
Day 3's high temp: 75
Day 4's high temp: 79
Day 5's high temp: 71
Average = 76.8
```

But how do you count how many days were above average? You could try to incorporate a comparison to the average temperature into the loop, but that won't work. The problem is that you can't figure out the average until you've gone through all of the data. That means you'll need to make a second pass through the data to figure out how many days were above average. You can't do that with a Scanner, because a Scanner has no "reset" option that allows you to see the data a second time. You'd have to prompt the user to enter the temperature data a second time, which would be silly.

Fortunately, you can solve the problem with an array. As you read numbers in and compute the cumulative sum, you can fill up an array that stores the temperatures. Then you can use the array to make the second pass through the data.

In the previous temperature example you used an array of double values, but here you want an array of int values. So, instead of declaring a variable of type double[], declare a variable of type int[]. You're asking the user how many days of temperature data to include, so you can construct the array right after you've read that information:

```
int numDays = console.nextInt();
int[] temps = new int[numDays];
```

Here is the old loop:

```
for (int i = 1; i <= numDays; i++) {
    System.out.print("Day " + i + "'s high temp: ");
    int next = console.nextInt();
    sum += next;
}
```

Because you're using an array, you'll want to change this to a loop that starts at 0 to match the array indexing. But just because you're using zero-based indexing inside the program doesn't mean that you have to confuse the user by asking for "Day 0's high temp." You can modify the println to prompt for day (i + 1). Furthermore, you no longer need the variable next because you'll be storing the values in the array instead. So, the loop code becomes

```
for (int i = 0; i < numDays; i++) {
    System.out.print("Day " + (i + 1) + "'s high temp: ");
```

```
    temps[i] = console.nextInt();
    sum += temps[i];
}
```

Notice that you're now testing whether the index is strictly less than `numDays`. After this loop executes, you compute the average as we did before. Then you write a new loop that counts how many days were above average using our standard traversing loop:

```
int above = 0;
for (int i = 0; i < temps.length; i++) {
    if (temps[i] > average) {
        above++;
    }
}
```

In this loop the test involves `temps.length`. You could instead have tested whether the variable is less than `numDays`; either choice works in this program because they should be equal to each other.

If you put these various code fragments together and include code to report the number of days that had an above-average temperature, you get the following complete program:

```
1   // Reads a series of high temperatures and reports the
2   // average and the number of days above average.
3
4   import java.util.*;
5
6   public class Temperature2 {
7       public static void main(String[] args) {
8           Scanner console = new Scanner(System.in);
9           System.out.print("How many days' temperatures? ");
10          int numDays = console.nextInt();
11          int[] temps = new int[numDays];
12
13          // record temperatures and find average
14          int sum = 0;
15          for (int i = 0; i < numDays; i++) {
16              System.out.print("Day " + (i + 1) + "'s high temp: ");
17              temps[i] = console.nextInt();
18              sum += temps[i];
19          }
20          double average = (double) sum / numDays;
21
22          // count days above average
23          int above = 0;
```

```
24            for (int i = 0; i < temps.length; i++) {
25                if (temps[i] > average) {
26                    above++;
27                }
28            }
29
30            // report results
31            System.out.println();
32            System.out.println("Average = " + average);
33            System.out.println(above + " days above average");
34        }
35    }
```

Here is a sample execution of the program:

```
How many days' temperatures? 9
Day 1's high temp: 75
Day 2's high temp: 78
Day 3's high temp: 85
Day 4's high temp: 71
Day 5's high temp: 69
Day 6's high temp: 82
Day 7's high temp: 74
Day 8's high temp: 80
Day 9's high temp: 87

Average = 77.88888888888889
5 days above average
```

Random Access

Most of the algorithms we have seen so far have involved *sequential access.*

Sequential Access

Manipulating values in a sequential manner from first to last.

A scanner object is often all you need for a sequential algorithm, because it allows you to access data by moving forward from the first element to the last. But as we have seen, there is no way to reset a scanner back to the beginning. The sample program we just studied uses an array to allow a second pass through the data, but even this is fundamentally a sequential approach because it involves two forward passes through the data.

An array is a powerful data structure that allows a more flexible kind of access known as *random access:*

> **Random Access**
>
> Manipulating values in any order whatsoever to allow quick access to each value.

An array can provide random access because it is allocated as a contiguous block of memory. The computer can quickly compute exactly where a particular value will be stored, because it knows how much space each element takes up in memory and it knows that all the elements are allocated right next to one another in the array.

When you work with arrays, you can jump around in the array without worrying about how much time it will take. For example, suppose that you have constructed an array of temperature readings that has 10,000 elements and you find yourself wanting to print a particular subset of the readings with code like the following:

```
System.out.println("#1394 = " + temps[1394]);
System.out.println("#6793 = " + temps[6793]);
System.out.println("#72 = " + temps[72]);
```

This code will execute quickly even though you are asking for array elements that are far apart from one another. Notice also that you don't have to ask for them in order. You can jump to element 1394, then jump ahead to element 6793, and then jump back to element 72. You can access elements in an array in any order that you like, and you will get fast access.

Later in the chapter we will explore several algorithms that would be difficult to implement without fast random access.

Common Programming Error

Off-by-One Bug

When you converted the `Temperature1` program to one that uses an array, you modified the `for` loop to start with an index of 0 instead of 1. The original `for` loop was written the following way:

```
for (int i = 1; i <= numDays; i++) {
    System.out.print("Day " + i + "'s high temp: ");
    int next = console.nextInt();
    sum += next;
}
```

Because you were storing the values into an array rather than reading them into a variable called `next`, you replaced `next` with `temps[i]`:

```
// wrong loop bounds
for (int i = 1; i <= numDays; i++) {
```

Continued on next page

Continued from previous page

```
    System.out.print("Day " + i + "'s high temp: ");
    temps[i] = console.nextInt();
    sum += temps[i];
}
```

Because the array is indexed starting at 0, you changed the bounds of the `for` loop to start at 0 and adjusted the `print` statement. Suppose those were the only changes you made:

```
// still wrong loop bounds
for (int i = 0; i <= numDays; i++) {
    System.out.print("Day " + (i + 1) + "'s high temp: ");
    temps[i] = console.nextInt();
    sum += temps[i];
}
```

This loop generates an error when you run the program. The loop asks for an extra day's worth of data and then throws an exception. Here's a sample execution:

```
How many days' temperatures? 5
Day 1's high temp: 82
Day 2's high temp: 80
Day 3's high temp: 79
Day 4's high temp: 71
Day 5's high temp: 75
Day 6's high temp: 83
Exception in thread "main"
    java.lang.ArrayIndexOutOfBoundsException: 5
        at Temperature2.main(Temperature2.java:18)
```

The problem is that if you're going to start the `for` loop variable at 0, you need to do a test to ensure that it is strictly less than the number of iterations you want. You changed the 1 to a 0 but left the `<=` test. As a result, the loop is performing an extra iteration and trying to make a reference to an array element `temps[5]` that doesn't exist.

This is a classic off-by-one error. The fix is to change the loop bounds to use a strictly less-than test:

```
// correct bounds
for (int i = 0; i < numDays; i++) {
    System.out.print("Day " + (i + 1) + "'s high temp: ");
    temps[i] = console.nextInt();
    sum += temps[i];
}
```

Arrays and Methods

You will find that when you pass an array as a parameter to a method, the method has the ability to change the contents of the array. We'll examine in detail later in the chapter why this occurs, but for now, the important point is simply to understand that methods can alter the contents of arrays that are passed to them as parameters.

Let's explore a specific example to better understand how to use arrays as parameters and return values for a method. Earlier in the chapter, we saw the following code for constructing an array of odd numbers and incrementing each array element:

```
int[] list = new int[5];
for (int i = 0; i < list.length; i++) {
    list[i] = 2 * i + 1;
}
for (int i = 0; i < list.length; i++) {
    list[i]++;
}
```

Let's see what happens when we move the incrementing loop into a method. It will need to take the array as a parameter. We'll rename it `data` instead of `list` to make it easier to distinguish it from the original array variable. Remember that the array is of type `int[ ]`, so we would write the method as follows:

```
public static void incrementAll(int[] data) {
    for (int i = 0; i < data.length; i++) {
        data[i]++;
    }
}
```

You might think this method will have no effect whatsoever, or that we have to return the array to cause the change to be remembered. But when we use an array as a parameter, this approach actually works. We can replace the incrementing loop in the original code with a call on our method:

```
int[] list = new int[5];
for (int i = 0; i < list.length; i++) {
    list[i] = 2 * i + 1;
}
incrementAll(list);
```

This code produces the same result as the original.

The key lesson to draw from this is that when we pass an array as a parameter to a method, that method has the ability to change the contents of the array. We don't need to return the array to allow this to happen.

To continue with this example, let's define a method for the initializing code that fills the array with odd numbers. We can accomplish this by moving the initializing loop into a method that takes the array as a parameter:

```
public static void fillWithOdds(int[] data) {
    for (int i = 0; i < data.length; i++) {
        data[i] = 2 * i + 1;
    }
}
```

We would then change our `main` method to call this `fillWithOdds` method:

```
int[] list = new int[5];
fillWithOdds(list);
incrementAll(list);
```

Like the `incrementAll` method, this method would change the array even though it does not return it. But this isn't the best approach to use in this situation. It seems odd that the `fillWithOdds` method requires you to construct an array and pass it as a parameter. Why doesn't `fillWithOdds` construct the array itself? That would simplify the call to the method, particularly if we ended up calling it multiple times.

If `fillWithOdds` is going to construct the array, it will have to return a reference to it. Otherwise, only the method will have a reference to the newly constructed array. In its current form, the `fillWithOdds` method assumes that the array has already been constructed, which is why we wrote the following two lines of code in `main`:

```
int[] list = new int[5];
fillWithOdds(list);
```

If the method is going to construct the array, it doesn't have to be passed as a parameter, but it will have to be returned by the method. Thus, we can rewrite these two lines of code from `main` as a single line:

```
int[] list = fillWithOdds();
```

Now, however, we have a misleading method name. The method isn't just filling an existing array, it is constructing one. Also notice that we can make the method more flexible by telling it how large to make the array. So if we rename it and pass the size as a parameter, then we'd call it this way:

```
int[] list = buildOddArray(5);
```

We can then rewrite the `fillWithOdds` method so that it constructs and returns the array:

```java
public static int[] buildOddArray(int size) {
    int[] data = new int[size];
    for (int i = 0; i < data.length; i++) {
        data[i] = 2 * i + 1;
    }
    return data;
}
```

Pay close attention to the header of the preceding method. It no longer has the array as a parameter, and its return type is `int[]` rather than `void`. It also ends with a `return` statement that returns a reference to the array that it constructs.

Putting this all together along with some code to print the contents of the array, we end up with the following complete program:

```java
 1  // Sample program with arrays passed as parameters
 2
 3  public class IncrementOdds {
 4      public static void main(String[] args) {
 5          int[] list = buildOddArray(5);
 6          incrementAll(list);
 7          for (int i = 0; i < list.length; i++) {
 8              System.out.print(list[i] + " ");
 9          }
10          System.out.println();
11      }
12
13      // returns array of given size composed of consecutive odds
14      public static int[] buildOddArray(int size) {
15          int[] data = new int[size];
16          for (int i = 0; i < data.length; i++) {
17              data[i] = 2 * i + 1;
18          }
19          return data;
20      }
21
22      // adds one to each array element
23      public static void incrementAll(int[] data) {
24          for (int i = 0; i < data.length; i++) {
25              data[i]++;
26          }
27      }
28  }
```

The program produces the following output:

```
2 4 6 8 10
```

The For-Each Loop

Java has a loop construct that simplifies certain array loops. It is known as the enhanced `for` loop, or the for-each loop. You can use it whenever you want to examine each value in an array. For example, the program `Temperature2` had an array variable called `temps` and the following loop:

```java
for (int i = 0; i < temps.length; i++) {
    if (temps[i] > average) {
        above++;
    }
}
```

We can rewrite this as a for-each loop:

```java
for (int n : temps) {
    if (n > average) {
        above++;
    }
}
```

This loop is normally read as, "For each `int n` in `temps`. . . ." The basic syntax of the for-each loop is

```java
for (<type> <name> : <array>) {
    <statement>;
    <statement>;
    ...
    <statement>;
}
```

There is nothing special about the variable name, as long as you keep it consistent within the body of the loop. For example, the previous loop could be written with the variable x instead of the variable n:

```java
for (int x : temps) {
    if (x > average) {
        above++;
    }
}
```

The for-each loop is most useful when you simply want to examine each value in sequence. There are many situations in which a for-each loop is not appropriate. For example, the following loop would double every value in an array called `list`:

```
for (int i = 0; i < list.length; i++) {
    list[i] *= 2;
}
```

Because the loop is changing the array, you can't replace it with a for-each loop:

```
for (int n : list) {
    n *= 2; // changes only n, not the array
}
```

As the comment indicates, the preceding loop doubles the variable n without changing the array elements.

In some cases, the for-each loop isn't the most convenient choice even when the code involves examining each array element in sequence. Consider, for example, the following loop that prints each array index along with the array value separated by a tab character:

```
for (int i = 0; i < data.length; i++) {
    System.out.println(i + "\t" + data[i]);
}
```

A for-each loop could be used to replace the array access:

```
for (int n : data) {
    System.out.println(i + "\t" + n); // not quite legal
}
```

However, this loop would cause a problem. We want to print the value of i, but we eliminated i when we converted the array access to a for-each loop. We would have to add extra code to keep track of the value of i:

```
// legal but clumsy
int i = 0;
for (int n : data) {
    System.out.println(i + "\t" + n);
    i++;
}
```

In this case, the for-each loop doesn't really simplify things, and the original version is probably clearer.

Initializing Arrays

Java has a special syntax for initializing an array when you know exactly what you want to put into it. For example, you could write the following code to initialize an array of integers to keep track of the number of days that are in each month ("Thirty days hath September . . .") and an array of strings to keep track of the abbreviations for the days of the week:

```
int[] daysIn = new int[12];
daysIn[0] = 31;
daysIn[1] = 28;
daysIn[2] = 31;
daysIn[3] = 30;
daysIn[4] = 31;
daysIn[5] = 30;
daysIn[6] = 31;
daysIn[7] = 31;
daysIn[8] = 30;
daysIn[9] = 31;
daysIn[10] = 30;
daysIn[11] = 31;
String[] dayNames = new String[7];
dayNames[0] = "Mon";
dayNames[1] = "Tue";
dayNames[2] = "Wed";
dayNames[3] = "Thu";
dayNames[4] = "Fri";
dayNames[5] = "Sat";
dayNames[6] = "Sun";
```

This code works, but it's a rather tedious way to declare these arrays. Java provides a shorthand:

```
int[] daysIn = {31, 28, 31, 30, 31, 30, 31, 31, 30, 31, 30, 31};
String[] dayNames = {"Mon", "Tue", "Wed", "Thu", "Fri", "Sat", "Sun"};
```

The general syntax for array initialization is as follows:

```
<element type>[] <name> = {<value>, <value>, ..., <value>};
```

You use the curly braces to enclose a series of values that will be stored in the array. The order of the values is important. The first value will go into index 0, the second value will go into index 1, and so on. Java counts how many values you include and constructs an array that is just the right size. It then stores the various values into the appropriate spots in the array.

This is one of only two examples we have seen in which Java will construct an object without the new keyword. The other place we saw this was with String literals, in which Java constructs String objects without your having to call new. Both of these techniques are conveniences for programmers. These tasks are so common that the designers of the language wanted to make it easy to do them.

The Arrays Class

Arrays have some important limitations that you should understand. Over the years Java has attempted to remedy these limitations by providing various utility methods in a class called Arrays. This class provides many methods that make it easier to work with arrays. The Arrays class is part of the java.util package, so you would have to include an import declaration in any program that uses it.

The first limitation you should be aware of is that you can't change the size of an array in the middle of program execution. Remember that arrays are allocated as a contiguous block of memory, so it is not easy for the computer to expand the array. If you find that you need a larger array, you should construct a new array and copy the values from the old array to the new array. The method Arrays.copyOf provides exactly this functionality. For example, if you have an array called data, you can create a copy that is twice as large with the following line of code:

```
int[] newData = Arrays.copyOf(data, 2 * data.length);
```

If you want to copy only a portion of an array, there is a similar method called Arrays.copyOfRange that accepts an array, a starting index, and an ending index as parameters.

The second limitation is that you can't print an array using a simple print or println statement. You will get odd output when you do so. The Arrays class once again offers a solution: The method Arrays.toString returns a conveniently formatted version of an array. Consider, for example, the following three lines of code:

```
int[] primes = {2, 3, 5, 7, 11, 13, 17, 19, 23};
System.out.println(primes);
System.out.println(Arrays.toString(primes));
```

It produces the following output:

```
[I@fee4648
[2, 3, 5, 7, 11, 13, 17, 19, 23]
```

Notice that the first line of output is not at all helpful. The second line, however, allows us to see the list of prime numbers in the array because we called Arrays.toString to format the array before printing it.

Table 7.2 Useful Methods of the **Arrays** Class

Method	Description
copyOf(array, newSize)	returns a copy of the array with the given size
copyOfRange(array, startIndex, endIndex)	returns a copy of the given subportion of the given array from startIndex (inclusive) to endIndex (exclusive)
equals(array1, array2)	returns true if the arrays contain the same elements
fill(array, value)	sets every element of the array to be the given value
sort(array)	rearranges the elements so that they appear in sorted (nondecreasing) order
toString(array)	returns a String representation of the array, as in [3, 5, 7]

The third limitation is that you can't compare arrays for equality using a simple == test. We saw that this was true of Strings as well. If you want to know whether two arrays contain the same set of values, you should call the Arrays.equals method:

```
int[] data1 = {1, 1, 2, 3, 5, 8, 13, 21};
int[] data2 = {1, 1, 2, 3, 5, 8, 13, 21};
if (Arrays.equals(data1, data2)) {
    System.out.println("They store the same data");
}
```

This code prints the message that the arrays store the same data. It would not do so if we used a direct comparison with ==.

The Arrays class provides other useful methods as well, including methods for sorting the array and for filling it up with a specific value. Table 7.2 contains a list of some of the most useful methods in the Arrays class.

7.2 Array-Traversal Algorithms

VideoNote

The previous section presented two standard patterns for manipulating an array. The first is the traversing loop, which uses a variable of type int to index each array value:

```
for (int i = 0; i < <array>.length; i++) {
    <do something with array[i]>;
}
```

The second is the for-each loop:

```
for (<type> <name> : <array>) {
    <statement>;
    <statement>;
```

```
    ...
    <statement>;
}
```

In this section we will explore some common array algorithms that can be implemented with these patterns. Of course, not all array operations can be implemented this way—the section ends with an example that requires a modified version of the standard code.

We will implement each operation as a method. Java does not allow you to write generic array code, so we have to pick a specific type. We'll assume that you are operating on an array of int values. If you are writing a program to manipulate a different kind of array, you'll have to modify the code for the type you are using (e.g., changing int[ ] to double[ ] if you are manipulating an array of double values).

Printing an Array

Suppose you have an array of int values like the following:

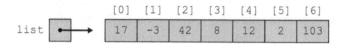

How would you go about printing the values in the array? For other types of data, you can use a println statement:

```
System.out.println(list);
```

Unfortunately, as mentioned in the Arrays class section of this chapter, with an array the println statement produces strange output like the following:

```
[I@6caf43
```

This is not helpful output, and it tells us nothing about the contents of the array. We saw that Java provides a solution to this problem in the form of a method called Arrays.toString that converts the array into a convenient text form. You can rewrite the println as follows to include a call on Arrays.toString:

```
System.out.println(Arrays.toString(list));
```

This line of code produces the following output:

```
[17, -3, 42, 8, 12, 2, 103]
```

This is a reasonable way to show the contents of the array, and in many situations it will be sufficient. However, for situations in which you want something different, you can write your own method.

Suppose that you want to write each number on a line by itself. In that case, you can use a for-each loop that does a println for each value:

```java
public static void print(int[] list) {
    for (int n : list) {
        System.out.println(n);
    }
}
```

You can then call this method with the variable list:

```java
print(list);
```

This call produces the following output:

```
17
-3
42
8
12
2
103
```

In some cases, the for-each loop doesn't get you quite what you want, though. For example, consider how the Arrays.toString method must be written. It produces a list of values that are separated by commas, which is a classic fencepost problem (e.g., seven values separated by six commas). To solve the fencepost problem, you'd want to use an indexing loop instead of a for-each loop so that you can print the first value before the loop:

```java
System.out.print(list[0]);
for (int i = 1; i < list.length; i++) {
    System.out.print(", " + list[i]);
}
System.out.println();
```

Notice that i is initialized to 1 instead of 0 because list[0] is printed before the loop. This code produces the following output for the preceding sample array:

```
17, -3, 42, 8, 12, 2, 103
```

Even this code is not correct, though, because it assumes that there is a list[0] to print. It is possible for arrays to be empty, with a length of 0, in which case this code will generate an ArrayIndexOutOfBoundsException. The version of the method that follows produces output that matches the String produced by

`Arrays.toString` . The printing statements just before and just after the loop have been modified to include square brackets, and a special case has been included for empty arrays:

```java
public static void print(int[] list) {
    if (list.length == 0) {
        System.out.println("[]");
    } else {
        System.out.print("[" + list[0]);
        for (int i = 1; i < list.length; i++) {
            System.out.print(", " + list[i]);
        }
        System.out.println("]");
    }
}
```

Searching and Replacing

Often you'll want to search for a specific value in an array. For example, you might want to count how many times a particular value appears in an array. Suppose you have an array of `int` values like the following:

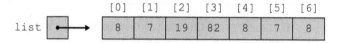

Counting occurrences is the simplest search task, because you always examine each value in the array and you don't need to change the contents of the array. You can accomplish this task with a for-each loop that keeps a count of the number of occurrences of the value for which you're searching:

```java
public static int count(int[] list, int target) {
    int count = 0;
    for (int n : list) {
        if (n == target) {
            count++;
        }
    }
    return count;
}
```

You can use this method in the following call to figure out how many 8s are in the list:

```java
int number = count(list, 8);
```

This call would set `number` to 3 for the sample array, because there are three occurrences of 8 in the list. If you instead made the call

```
int number = count(list, 2);
```

`number` would be set to 0, because there are no occurrences of 2 in the list.

Sometimes you want to find out where a value is in a list. You can accomplish this task by writing a method that will return the index of the first occurrence of the value in the list. Because you don't know exactly where you'll find the value, you might try including this method in a `while` loop, as in the following pseudocode:

```
int i = 0;
while (we haven't found it yet) {
    i++;
}
```

However, there is a simpler approach. Because you're writing a method that returns a value, you can return the appropriate index as soon as you find a match. That means you can use the standard traversal loop to solve this problem:

```
for (int i = 0; i < list.length; i++) {
    if (list[i] == target) {
        return i;
    }
}
```

Remember that a `return` statement terminates a method, so you'll break out of this loop as soon as the target value is found. But what if the value isn't found? What if you traverse the entire array and find no matches? In that case, the `for` loop will finish executing without ever returning a value.

There are many things you can do if the value is not found. The convention used throughout the Java class libraries is to return the value `-1` to indicate that the value is not anywhere in the list. So you can add an extra `return` statement after the loop that will be executed only when the target value is not found. Putting all this together, you get the following method:

```
public static int indexOf(int[] list, int target) {
    for (int i = 0; i < list.length; i++) {
        if (list[i] == target) {
            return i;
        }
    }
    return -1;
}
```

You can use this method in the following call to find the first occurrence of the value 7 in the list:

```
int position = indexOf(list, 7);
```

This call would set `position` to 1 for the sample array, because the first occurrence of 7 is at index 1. There is another occurrence of 7 later in the array, at index 5, but this code terminates as soon as it finds the first match.

If you instead made the call

```
int position = indexOf(list, 42);
```

`position` would be set to −1 because there are no occurrences of 42 in the list.

As a final variation, consider the problem of replacing all the occurrences of a value with some new value. This is similar to the counting task. You'll want to traverse the array looking for a particular value and replace the value with something new when you find it. You can't accomplish that task with a for-each loop, because changing the loop variable has no effect on the array. Instead, use a standard traversing loop:

```
public static void replaceAll(int[] list, int target, int replacement) {
    for (int i = 0; i < list.length; i++) {
        if (list[i] == target) {
            list[i] = replacement;
        }
    }
}
```

Notice that even though the method is changing the contents of the array, you don't need to return it in order to have that change take place.

As we noted at the beginning of this section, these examples involve an array of integers, and you would have to change the type if you were to manipulate an array of a different type (for example, changing `int[]` to `double[]` if you had an array of `double` values). But the change isn't quite so simple if you have an array of objects, such as `Strings`. In order to compare `String` values, you must make a call on the `equals` method rather than using a simple `==` comparison. Here is a modified version of the `replaceAll` method that would be appropriate for an array of `Strings`:

```
public static void replaceAll(String[] list, String target,
                              String replacement) {
    for (int i = 0; i < list.length; i++) {
        if (list[i].equals(target)) {
            list[i] = replacement;
        }
    }
}
```

Testing for Equality

Because arrays are objects, testing them for equality is more complex than testing primitive values like integers and `doubles` for equality. Two arrays are equivalent in value if they have the same length and store the same sequence of values. The method `Arrays.equals` performs this test:

```
if (Arrays.equals(list1, list2)) {
    System.out.println("The arrays are equal");
}
```

Like the `Arrays.toString` method, often the `Arrays.equals` method will be all you need. But sometimes you'll want slight variations, so it's worth exploring how to write the method yourself.

The method will take two arrays as parameters and will return a `boolean` result indicating whether or not the two arrays are equal. So, the method will look like this:

```
public static boolean equals(int[] list1, int[] list2) {
    ...
}
```

When you sit down to write a method like this, you probably think in terms of defining equality: "The two arrays are equal if their lengths are equal and they store the same sequence of values." But this isn't the easiest approach. For example, you could begin by testing that the lengths are equal, but what would you do next?

```
public static boolean equals(int[] list1, int[] list2) {
    if (list1.length == list2.length) {
        // what do we do?
        ...
    }
    ...
}
```

Methods like this one are generally easier to write if you think in terms of the opposite condition: What would make the two arrays *unequal?* Instead of testing for the lengths being equal, start by testing whether the lengths are unequal. In that case, you know exactly what to do. If the lengths are not equal, the method should return a value of `false`, and you'll know that the arrays are not equal to each other:

```
public static boolean equals(int[] list1, int[] list2) {
    if (list1.length != list2.length) {
        return false;
    }
    ...
}
```

If you get past the `if` statement, you know that the arrays are of equal length. Then you'll want to check whether they store the same sequence of values. Again, test for inequality rather than equality, returning `false` if there's a difference:

```java
public static boolean equals(int[] list1, int[] list2) {
    if (list1.length != list2.length) {
        return false;
    }
    for (int i = 0; i < list1.length; i++) {
        if (list1[i] != list2[i]) {
            return false;
        }
    }
    ...
}
```

If you get past the `for` loop, you'll know that the two arrays are of equal length and that they store exactly the same sequence of values. In that case, you'll want to return the value `true` to indicate that the arrays are equal. This addition completes the method:

```java
public static boolean equals(int[] list1, int[] list2) {
    if (list1.length != list2.length) {
        return false;
    }
    for (int i = 0; i < list1.length; i++) {
        if (list1[i] != list2[i]) {
            return false;
        }
    }
    return true;
}
```

This is a common pattern for a method like `equals`: You test all of the ways that the two objects might not be equal, returning `false` if you find any differences, and returning `true` at the very end so that if all the tests are passed the two objects are declared to be equal.

Reversing an Array

As a final example of common operations, let's consider the task of reversing the order of the elements stored in an array. For example, suppose you have an array that stores the following values:

One approach would be to create a new array and to store the values from the first array into the second array in reverse order. Although that approach would be reasonable, you should be able to solve the problem without constructing a second array. Another approach is to conduct a series of exchanges or swaps. For example, the value 3 at the front of the list and the value 78 at the end of the list need to be swapped:

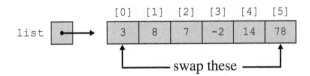

After swapping that pair, you can swap the next pair in (the values at indexes 1 and 4):

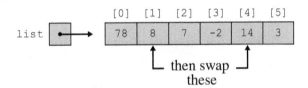

You can continue swapping until the entire list has been reversed. Before we look at the code that will perform this reversal, let's consider the general problem of swapping two values.

Suppose you have two integer variables x and y that have the values 3 and 78:

```
int x = 3;
int y = 78;
```

How would you swap these values? A naive approach is to simply assign the values to one another:

```
// will not swap properly
x = y;
y = x;
```

Unfortunately, this doesn't work. You start out with the following:

$$x\ \boxed{3}\quad y\ \boxed{78}$$

When the first assignment statement is executed, you copy the value of y into x:

$$x\ \boxed{78}\quad y\ \boxed{78}$$

You want x to eventually become equal to 78, but if you attempt to solve the problem this way, you lose the old value of x as soon as you assign the value of y to it. The second assignment statement then copies the new value of x, 78, back into y, which leaves you with two variables equal to 78.

The standard solution is to introduce a temporary variable that you can use to store the old value of x while you're giving x its new value. You can then copy the old value of x from the temporary variable into y to complete the swap:

```
int temp = x;
x = y;
y = temp;
```

You start by copying the old value of x into temp:

x   3   y   78   temp   3

Then you put the value of y into x:

x   78   y   78   temp   3

Next, you copy the old value of x from temp to y:

x   78   y   3   temp   3

At this point you have successfully swapped the values of x and y, so you don't need temp anymore.

In some programming languages, you can define this as a swap method that can be used to exchange two int values:

```
// this method won't work
public static void swap(int x, int y) {
    int temp = x;
    x = y;
    y = temp;
}
```

As you've seen, this kind of method won't work in Java because the x and y that are swapped will be copies of any integer values passed to them. But because arrays are stored as objects, you can write a variation of this method that takes an array and two indexes as parameters and swaps the values at those indexes:

```
public static void swap(int[] list, int i, int j) {
    int temp = list[i];
```

```
    list[i] = list[j];
    list[j] = temp;
}
```

The code in this method matches the code in the previous method, but instead of using x and y it uses list[i] and list[j]. This method will work because, instead of changing simple int variables, the method is changing the contents of the array.

Given this swap method, you can fairly easily write a reversing method. You just have to think about what combinations of values to swap. Start by swapping the first and last values. The sample array has a length of 6, which means that you will be swapping the values at indexes 0 and 5. But you want to write the code so that it works for an array of any length. In general, the first swap you'll want to perform is to swap element 0 with element (list.length − 1):

```
swap(list, 0, list.length − 1);
```

Then you'll want to swap the second value with the second-to-last value:

```
swap(list, 1, list.length − 2);
```

Then you'll swap the third value with the third-to-last value:

```
swap(list, 2, list.length − 3);
```

There is a pattern to these swaps that you can capture with a loop. If you use a variable i for the first parameter of the call on swap and introduce a local variable j to store an expression for the second parameter to swap, each of these calls will take the following form:

```
int j = list.length − i − 1;
swap(list, i, j);
```

To implement the reversal, you could put the method inside the standard traversal loop:

```
// doesn't quite work
for (int i = 0; i < list.length; i++) {
    int j = list.length − i − 1;
    swap(list, i, j);
}
```

If you were to test this code, though, you'd find that it seems to have no effect whatsoever. The list stores the same values after executing this code as it stores initially. The problem is that this loop does too much swapping. Here is a trace of the six swaps that are performed on the list [3, 8, 7, −2, 14, 78], with an indication of the values of i and j for each step:

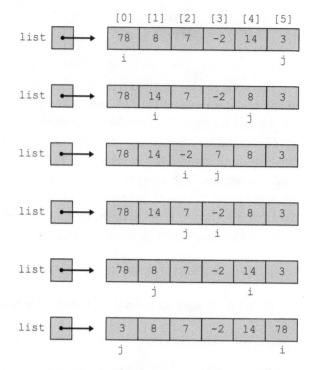

The values of i and j cross halfway through this process. As a result, the first three swaps successfully reverse the array, and then the three swaps that follow undo the work of the first three. To fix this problem, you need to stop it halfway through the process. This task is easily accomplished by changing the test:

```
for (int i = 0; i < list.length / 2; i++) {
    int j = list.length - i - 1;
    swap(list, i, j);
}
```

In the sample array, list.length is 6. Half of that is 3, which means that this loop will execute exactly three times. That is just what you want in this case (the first three swaps), but you should be careful to consider other possibilities. For example, what if list.length were 7? Half of that is also 3, because of truncating division. Is three the correct number of swaps for an odd-length list? The answer is yes. If there are an odd number of elements, the value in the middle of the list does not need to be swapped. So, in this case, a simple division by 2 turns out to be the right approach.

Including this code in a method, you end up with the following overall solution:

```
public static void reverse(int[] list) {
    for (int i = 0; i < list.length / 2; i++) {
        int j = list.length - i - 1;
        swap(list, i, j);
    }
}
```

String Traversal Algorithms

In Java we often think of a string as chunk of text, but you can also think of it as a sequence of individual characters. Viewed in this light, a string is a lot like an array. Recall that the individual elements of a string are of type char and that you can access the individual character values by calling the charAt method.

The same techniques we have used to write array traversal algorithms can be used to write string traversal algorithms. The syntax is slightly different, but the logic is the same. Our array traversal template looks like this:

```
for (int i = 0; i < <array>.length; i++) {
    <do something with array[i]>;
}
```

The corresponding string algorithm template looks like this:

```
for (int i = 0; i < <string>.length(); i++) {
    <do something with string.charAt(i)>;
}
```

Notice that with arrays you refer to length without using parentheses, but with a string you do use parentheses. Notice also that the array square bracket notation is replaced with a call on the charAt method.

For example, you can count the number of occurrences of the letter "i" in "Mississippi" with this code:

```
String s = "Mississippi";
int count = 0;
for (int i = 0; i < s.length(); i++) {
    if (s.charAt(i) == 'i') {
        count++;
    }
}
```

This code would correctly compute that there are four occurrences of "i" in the string. For another example, consider the task of computing the reverse of a string. You can traverse the string building up a new version that has the letters in reverse order by putting each new character at the front of string you are building up. Here is a complete method that uses this approach:

```
public static String reverse(String text) {
    String result = "";
    for (int i = 0; i < text.length(); i++) {
        result = text.charAt(i) + result;
    }
}
```

```
        return result;
    }
```

If you make the call `reverse("Mississippi")`, the method returns `"ippissis-`
`siM"`.

Functional Approach

Chapter 19 describes a different approach to manipulating arrays that leads to code
that looks quite different than the examples in this section. It relies on features added
to the Java programming language starting with version 8 that allow you to manipulate arrays and other data structures in a more declarative manner. Instead of specifying exactly how to traverse an array, you can instead tell Java what you want to
do with the array elements and allow Java to figure out how to do the traversal. The
addition of the for-each loop starting with version 5 of Java was an initial move in
this direction, but the new features go much further.

Suppose, for example, that you have an array of values defined as follows:

```
int[] numbers = {8, 3, 2, 17};
```

Let's look at the code you would write for two simple tasks: finding the sum and
printing the values. Using the standard traversal loops, you would write the following
code.

```
// sum an array of numbers and print them (for loop)
int sum = 0;
for (int i = 0; i < numbers.length; i++) {
    sum += numbers[i];
}
System.out.println("sum = " + sum);
for (int i = 0; i < numbers.length; i++) {
    System.out.println(numbers[i]);
}
```

This code produces the following output.

```
sum = 30
8
3
2
17
```

The for-each loop simplifies this code by specifying that you want to manipulate
each of the different values in the array in sequence, but it doesn't require you to
include an indexing variable to say exactly how that is done.

```
// sum an array of numbers and print them (for-each loop)
int sum = 0;
for (int n : numbers) {
    sum += n;
}
System.out.println("sum = " + sum);
for (int n : numbers) {
    System.out.println(n);
}
```

With the new Java 8 features, this becomes even simpler. The task of finding the sum of a sequence of values is so common that there is a built-in method that does it for you. And the task of printing each value with a call on the `println` method of `System.out` can also be expressed in a very concise manner.

```
// sum an array of numbers and print them (functional)
int sum = Arrays.stream(numbers).sum();
System.out.println("sum = " + sum);
Arrays.stream(numbers).forEach(System.out::println);
```

This code doesn't at all describe how the traversal is to be performed. Instead, you tell Java the operations you want to have performed on the values in the array and leave it up to Java to perform the traversal. See Chapter 19 for a more complete explanation of this approach.

7.3 Reference Semantics

In Java, arrays are objects. We have been using objects since Chapter 3 but we haven't yet discussed in detail how they are stored. It's about time that we explored the details. Objects are stored in the computer's memory in a different way than primitive data are stored. For example, when we declare the integer variable

```
int x = 8;
```

the variable stores the actual data. So, we've drawn pictures like the following:

The situation is different for arrays and other objects. With regard to objects, the variable doesn't store the actual data. Instead, the data are stored in an object and the variable stores a reference to the location at which the object is stored. So, we have two different elements in the computer's memory: the variable and the object. Thus, when we construct an array object such as

```
int[] list = new int[5];
```

we end up with the following:

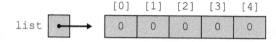

As the diagram indicates, two different values are stored in memory: the array itself, which appears on the right side of the diagram, and a variable called `list`, which stores a reference to the array (represented in this picture as an arrow). We say that `list` *refers* to the array.

It may take some time for you to get used to the two different approaches to storing data, but these approaches are so common that computer scientists have technical terms to describe them. The system for the primitive types like `int` is known as *value semantics,* and those types are often referred to as *value types.* The system for arrays and other objects is known as *reference semantics,* and those types are often referred to as *reference types.*

> **Value Semantics (Value Types)**
>
> A system in which values are stored directly and copying is achieved by creating independent copies of values. Types that use value semantics are called value types.

> **Reference Semantics (Reference Types)**
>
> A system in which references to values are stored and copying is achieved by copying these references. Types that use reference semantics are called reference types.

It will take us a while to explore all of the implications of this difference. The key thing to remember is that when you are working with objects, you are always working with references to data rather than the data itself.

At this point you are probably wondering why Java has two different systems. Java was designed for object-oriented programming, so the first question to consider is why Sun decided that objects should have reference semantics. There are two primary reasons:

- **Efficiency.** Objects can be complex, which means that they can take up a lot of space in memory. If we made copies of such objects, we would quickly run out of memory. A `string` object that stores a large number of characters might take up a lot of space in memory. But even if the `string` object is very large, a reference to it can be fairly small, in the same way that even a mansion has a simple street address. As another analogy, think how we use cell phones to communicate with people. The phones can be very tiny and easy to transport because cell phone numbers don't take up much space. Imagine that, instead of carrying around a set of cell phone numbers, you tried to carry around the actual people!

- **Sharing.** Often, having a copy of something is not good enough. Suppose that your instructor tells all of the students in the class to put their tests into a certain box. Imagine how pointless and confusing it would be if each student made a copy of the box. The obvious intent is that all of the students use the same box. Reference semantics allows you to have many references to a single object, which allows different parts of your program to share a certain object.

Without reference semantics, Java programs would be more difficult to write. Then why did Sun also decide to include primitive types that have value semantics? The reasons are primarily historical. Sun wanted to leverage the popularity of C and C++, which had similar types, and to guarantee that Java programs would run quickly, which was easier to accomplish with the more traditional primitive types. If Java's designers had a chance to redesign Java today, the company might well get rid of the primitive types and use a consistent object model with just reference semantics.

Multiple Objects

In the previous section, you saw how to manipulate a single array object. In this section, we will delve deeper into the implications of reference semantics by considering what happens when there are multiple objects and multiple references to the same object.

Consider the following code:

```
int[] list1 = new int[5];
int[] list2 = new int[5];
for (int i = 0; i < list1.length; i++) {
    list1[i] = 2 * i + 1;
    list2[i] = 2 * i + 1;
}
int[] list3 = list2;
```

Each call on new constructs a new object and this code has two calls on new, so that means we have two different objects. The code is written in such a way that list2 will always have the exact same length and sequence of values as list1. After the two arrays are initialized, we define a third array variable that is assigned to list2. This step creates a new reference but not a new object. After the computer executes the code, memory would look like this:

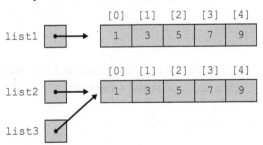

We have three variables but only two objects. The variables `list2` and `list3` both refer to the same array object. Using the cell phone analogy, you can think of this as two people who both have the cell phone number for the same person. That means that either one of them can call the person. Or, as another analogy, suppose that both you and a friend of yours know how to access your bank information online. That means that you both have access to the same account and that either one of you can make changes to the account.

The implication of this method is that `list2` and `list3` are in some sense both equally able to modify the array to which they refer. The line of code

```
list2[2]++;
```

will have exactly the same effect as the line

```
list3[2]++;
```

Since both variables refer to the same array object, you can access the array through either one.

Reference semantics help us to understand why a simple == test does not give us what we might expect. When this test is applied to objects, it determines whether two *references* are the same (not whether the objects to which they refer are somehow equivalent). In other words, when we test whether two references are equal, we are testing whether they refer to exactly the same object.

The variables `list2` and `list3` both refer to the same array object. As a result, if we ask whether `list2 == list3`, the answer will be yes (the expression evaluates to `true`). But if we ask whether `list1 == list2`, the answer will be no (the expression evaluates to `false`) even though we think of the two arrays as somehow being equivalent.

Sometimes you want to know whether two variables refer to exactly the same object, and for those situations, the simple == comparison will be appropriate. But you'll also want to know whether two objects are somehow equivalent in value, in which case you should call methods like `Arrays.equals` or the string `equals` method.

Understanding reference semantics also allows you to understand why a method is able to change the contents of an array that is passed to it as a parameter. Remember that earlier in the chapter we considered the following method:

```
public static void incrementAll(int[] data) {
    for (int i = 0; i < data.length; i++) {
        data[i]++;
    }
}
```

We saw that when our variable `list` was initialized to an array of odd numbers, we could increment all of the values in the array by means of the following line:

```
incrementAll(list);
```

When the method is called, we make a copy of the variable `list`. But the variable `list` is not itself the array; rather, it stores a reference to the array. So, when we make a copy of that reference, we end up with two references to the same object:

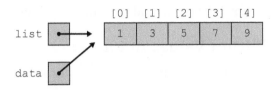

Because `data` and `list` both refer to the same object, when we change `data` by saying `data[i]++`, we end up changing the object to which `list` refers. That's why, after the loop increments each element of data, we end up with the following:

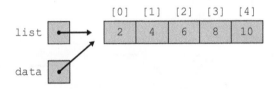

The key lesson to draw from this discussion is that when we pass an array as a parameter to a method, that method has the ability to change the contents of the array.

Before we leave the subject of reference semantics, we should describe in more detail the concept of the special value `null`. It is a special keyword in Java that is used to represent "no object".

> **null**
>
> A Java keyword signifying no object.

The concept of null doesn't have any meaning for value types like `int` and `double` that store actual values. But it can make sense to set a variable that stores a reference to `null`. This is a way of telling the computer that you want to have the variable, but you haven't yet come up with an object to which it should refer. So you can use `null` for variables of any object type, such as a `String` or array:

```
String s = null;
int[] list = null;
```

There is a difference between setting a variable to an empty string and setting it to `null`. When you set a variable to an empty string, there is an actual object to which your variable refers (although not a very interesting object). When you set a variable to `null`, the variable doesn't yet refer to an actual object. If you try to use the variable to access the object when it has been set to `null`, Java will throw a `NullPointerException`.

7.4 Advanced Array Techniques

VideoNote

In this section we'll discuss some advanced uses of arrays, such as algorithms that cannot be solved with straightforward traversals. We'll also see how to create arrays that store objects instead of primitive values.

Shifting Values in an Array

You'll often want to move a series of values in an array. For example, suppose you have an array of integers that stores the sequence of values [3, 8, 9, 7, 5] and you want to send the value at the front of the list to the back and keep the order of the other values the same. In other words, you want to move the 3 to the back, yielding the list [8, 9, 7, 5, 3]. Let's explore how to write code to perform that action.

Suppose you have a variable of type int[] called list of length 5 that stores the values [3, 8, 9, 7, 5]:

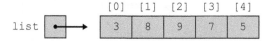

The shifting operation is similar to the swap operation discussed in the previous section, and you'll find that it is useful to use a temporary variable here as well. The 3 at the front of the list is supposed to go to the back of the list, and the other values are supposed to rotate forward. You can make the task easier by storing the value at the front of the list (3, in this example) into a local variable:

```
int first = list[0];
```

With that value safely tucked away, you now have to shift the other four values to the left by one position:

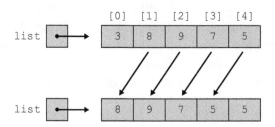

The overall task breaks down into four different shifting operations, each of which is a simple assignment statement:

```
list[0] = list[1];
list[1] = list[2];
list[2] = list[3];
list[3] = list[4];
```

Obviously you'd want to write this as a loop rather than writing a series of individual assignment statements. Each of the preceding statements is of the form

```
list[i] = list[i + 1];
```

You'll replace list element `[i]` with the value currently stored in list element `[i + 1]`, which shifts that value to the left. You can put this line of code inside a standard traversing loop:

```
for (int i = 0; i < list.length; i++) {
    list[i] = list[i + 1];
}
```

This loop is almost the right answer, but it has an off-by-one bug. This loop will execute five times for the sample array, but you only want to shift four values (you want to do the assignment for i equal to 0, 1, 2, and 3, but not for i equal to 4). So, this loop goes one too many times. On the last iteration of the loop, when i is equal to 4, the loop executes the following line of code:

```
list[i] = list[i + 1];
```

This line becomes:

```
list[4] = list[5];
```

There is no value `list[5]` because the array has only five elements, with indexes 0 through 4. So, this code generates an `ArrayIndexOutOfBoundsException`. To fix the problem, alter the loop so that it stops one iteration early:

```
for (int i = 0; i < list.length - 1; i++) {
    list[i] = list[i + 1];
}
```

In place of the usual `list.length`, use `(list.length - 1)`. You can think of the minus one in this expression as offsetting the plus one in the assignment statement.

Of course, there is one more detail you must address. After shifting the values to the left, you've made room at the end of the list for the value that used to be at the front of the list (which is currently stored in a local variable called `first`). When the loop has finished executing, you have to place this value at index 4:

```
list[list.length - 1] = first;
```

Here is the final method:

```
public static void rotateLeft(int[] list) {
    int first = list[0];
    for (int i = 0; i < list.length - 1; i++) {
        list[i] = list[i + 1];
    }
}
```

```
        list[list.length — 1] = first;
}
```

An interesting variation on this method is to rotate the values to the right instead of rotating them to the left. To perform this inverse operation, you want to take the value that is currently at the end of the list and bring it to the front, shifting the remaining values to the right. So, if a variable called `list` initially stores the values [3, 8, 9, 7, 5], it should bring the 5 to the front and store the values [5, 3, 8, 9, 7].

Begin by tucking away the value that is being rotated into a temporary variable:

```
int last = list[list.length — 1];
```

Then shift the other values to the right:

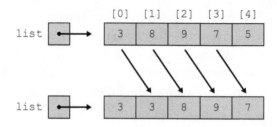

In this case, the four individual assignment statements would be the following:

```
list[1] = list[0];
list[2] = list[1];
list[3] = list[2];
list[4] = list[3];
```

A more general way to write this is the following line of code:

```
list[i] = list[i — 1];
```

If you put this code inside the standard `for` loop, you get the following:

```
// doesn't work
for (int i = 0; i < list.length; i++) {
    list[i] = list[i — 1];
}
```

There are two problems with this code. First, there is another off-by-one bug. The first assignment statement you want to perform would set `list[1]` to contain the value that is currently in `list[0]`, but this loop sets `list[0]` to `list[-1]`. Java generates an `ArrayIndexOutOfBoundsException` because there is no value `list[-1]`. You want to start i at 1, not 0:

```
// still doesn't work
for (int i = 1; i < list.length; i++) {
    list[i] = list[i — 1];
}
```

However, this version of the code doesn't work either. It avoids the exception, but think about what it does. The first time through the loop it assigns `list[1]` to what is in `list[0]`:

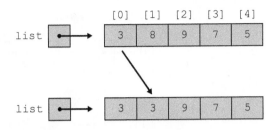

What happened to the value 8? It's overwritten with the value 3. The next time through the loop `list[2]` is set to be `list[1]`:

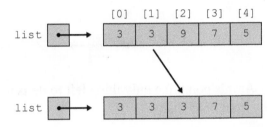

You might say, "Wait a minute . . . `list[1]` isn't a 3, it's an 8." It was an 8 when you started, but the first iteration of the loop replaced the 8 with a 3, and now the 3 has been copied into the spot where 9 used to be.

The loop continues in this way, putting 3 into every cell of the array. Obviously, that's not what you want. To make this code work, you have to run the loop in reverse order (from right to left instead of left to right). So let's back up to where we started:

[0] [1] [2] [3] [4]
list → | 3 | 8 | 9 | 7 | 5 |

We tucked away the final value of the list into a local variable. That frees up the final array position. Now, assign `list[4]` to be what is in `list[3]`:

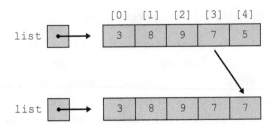

This wipes out the 5 that was at the end of the list, but that value is safely stored away in a local variable. And once you've performed this assignment statement, you free up list[3], which means you can now set list[3] to be what is currently in list[2]:

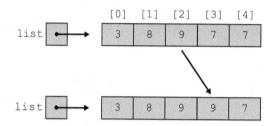

The process continues in this manner, copying the 8 from index 1 to index 2 and copying the 3 from index 0 to index 1, leaving you with the following:

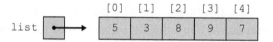

At this point, the only thing left to do is to put the 5 stored in the local variable at the front of the list:

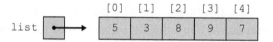

You can reverse the for loop by changing the i++ to i-- and adjusting the initialization and test. The final method is as follows:

```
public static void rotateRight(int[] list) {
    int last = list[list.length − 1];
    for (int i = list.length − 1; i >= 1; i−−) {
        list[i] = list[i − 1];
    }
    list[0] = last;
}
```

Arrays of Objects

All of the arrays we have looked at so far have stored primitive values like simple int values, but you can have arrays of any Java type. Arrays of objects behave slightly differently, though, because objects are stored as references rather than as data values. Constructing an array of objects is usually a two-step process, because you normally have to construct both the array and the individual objects.

As an example, Java has a `Point` class as part of its `java.awt` package. Each `Point` object is used for storing the (x, y) coordinates of a point in two-dimensional space. (We will discuss this class in more detail in the next chapter, but for now we will just construct a few objects from it.) Suppose that you want to construct an array of `Point` objects. Consider the following statement:

```
Point[] points = new Point[3];
```

This statement declares a variable called `points` that refers to an array of length 3 that stores references to `Point` objects. Using the new keyword to construct the array doesn't construct any actual `Point` objects. Instead it constructs an array of length 3, each element of which can store a reference to a `Point`. When Java constructs the array, it auto-initializes these array elements to the zero-equivalent for the type. The zero-equivalent for all reference types is the special value `null`, which indicates "no object":

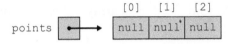

The actual `Point` objects must be constructed separately with the new keyword, as in the following code:

```
Point[] points = new Point[3];
points[0] = new Point(3, 7);
points[1] = new Point(4, 5);
points[2] = new Point(6, 2);
```

After these lines of code execute, your program will have created individual `Point` objects referred to by the various array elements:

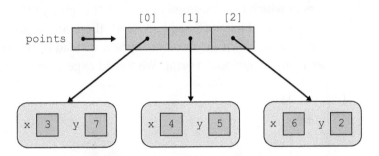

Notice that the new keyword is required in four different places, because there are four objects to be constructed: the array itself and the three individual `Point` objects. You could also use the curly brace notation for initializing the array, in which case you don't need the new keyword to construct the array itself:

```
Point[] points = {new Point(3, 7), new Point(4, 5), new Point(6, 2)};
```

Command-Line Arguments

As you've seen since Chapter 1, whenever you define a `main` method, you're required to include as its parameter `String[] args`, which is an array of `String` objects. Java itself initializes this array if the user provides what are known as *command-line arguments* when invoking Java. For example, the user could execute a Java class called `DoSomething` from a command prompt or terminal by using a command like:

```
java DoSomething
```

The user has the option to type extra arguments, as in the following:

```
java DoSomething temperature.dat temperature.out
```

In this case the user has specified two extra arguments that are file names that the program should use (e.g., the names of an input and output file). If the user types these extra arguments when starting up Java, the `String[] args` parameter to `main` will be initialized to an array of length 2 that stores these two `strings`:

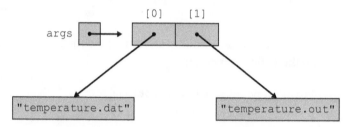

Nested Loop Algorithms

All of the algorithms we have seen have been written with a single loop. But many computations require nested loops. For example, suppose that you were asked to print all inversions in an array of integers. An inversion is defined as a pair of numbers in which the first number in the list is greater than the second number.

In a sorted list such as [1, 2, 3, 4], there are no inversions at all and there is nothing to print. But if the numbers appear instead in reverse order, [4, 3, 2, 1], then there are many inversions to print. We would expect output like the following:

```
(4, 3)
(4, 2)
(4, 1)
(3, 2)
(3, 1)
(2, 1)
```

Notice that any given number (e.g., 4 in the list above) can produce several different inversions, because it might be followed by several smaller numbers (1, 2, and

3 in the example). For a list that is partially sorted, as in [3, 1, 4, 2], there are only a few inversions, so you would produce output like this:

```
(3, 1)
(3, 2)
(4, 2)
```

This problem can't be solved with a single traversal because we are looking for pairs of numbers. There are many possible first values in the pair and many possible second values in the pair. Let's develop a solution using pseudocode.

We can't produce all pairs with a single loop, but we can use a single loop to consider all possible first values:

```
for (every possible first value) {
    print all inversions that involve this first value.
}
```

Now we just need to write the code to find all the inversions for a given first value. That requires us to write a second, nested loop:

```
for (every possible first value) {
    for (every possible second value) {
        if (first value > second value) {
            print(first, second).
        }
    }
}
```

This problem is fairly easy to turn into Java code, although the loop bounds turn out to be a bit tricky. For now, let's use our standard traversal loop for each:

```
for (int i = 0; i < data.length; i++) {
    for (int j = 0; j < data.length; j++) {
        if (data[i] > data[j]) {
            System.out.println("(" + data[i] + ", " + data[j] + ")");
        }
    }
}
```

The preceding code isn't quite right. Remember that for an inversion, the second value has to appear *after* the first value in the list. In this case, we are computing all possible combinations of a first and second value. To consider only values that come after the given first value, we have to start the second loop at i + 1 instead of starting at 0. We can also make a slight improvement by recognizing that because an inversion requires a pair of values, there is no reason to include the last number of the list as a possible first value. So the outer loop involving i can end one iteration earlier:

```java
for (int i = 0; i < data.length - 1; i++) {
    for (int j = i + 1; j < data.length; j++) {
        if (data[i] > data[j]) {
            System.out.println("(" + data[i] + ", " + data[j] + ")");
        }
    }
}
```

When you write nested loops like these, it is a common convention to use i for the outer loop, j for the loop inside the outer loop, and k if there is a loop inside the j loop.

7.5 Multidimensional Arrays

The array examples in the previous sections all involved what are known as one-dimensional arrays (a single row or a single column of data). Often, you'll want to store data in a multidimensional way. For example, you might want to store a two-dimensional grid of data that has both rows and columns. Fortunately, you can form arrays of arbitrarily many dimensions:

- double: one double
- double[]: a one-dimensional array of doubles
- double[][]: a two-dimensional grid of doubles
- double[][][]: a three-dimensional collection of doubles
- ...

Arrays of more than one dimension are called *multidimensional arrays*.

> **Multidimensional Array**
>
> An array of arrays, the elements of which are accessed with multiple integer indexes.

Rectangular Two-Dimensional Arrays

The most common use of a multidimensional array is a two-dimensional array of a certain width and height. For example, suppose that on three separate days you took a series of five temperature readings. You can define a two-dimensional array that has three rows and five columns as follows:

```java
double[][] temps = new double[3][5];
```

Notice that on both the left and right sides of this assignment statement, you have to use a double set of square brackets. When you are describing the type on the left, you have to make it clear that this is not just a one-dimensional sequence of values, which would be of type `double[]`, but instead a two-dimensional grid of values, which is of type `double[][]`. On the right, when you construct the array, you must specify the dimensions of the grid. The normal convention is to list the row first followed by the column. The resulting array would look like this:

As with one-dimensional arrays, the values are initialized to `0.0` and the indexes start with 0 for both rows and columns. Once you've created such an array, you can refer to individual elements by providing specific row and column numbers (in that order). For example, to set the fourth value of the first row to `98.3` and to set the first value of the third row to `99.4`, you would write the following code:

```
temps[0][3] = 98.3;   // fourth value of first row
temps[2][0] = 99.4;   // first value of third row
```

After the program executes these lines of code, the array would look like this:

It is helpful to think of referring to individual elements in a stepwise fashion, starting with the name of the array. For example, if you want to refer to the first value of the third row, you obtain it through the following steps:

`temps`	the entire grid
`temps[2]`	the entire third row
`temps[2][0]`	the first element of the third row

You can pass multidimensional arrays as parameters just as you pass one-dimensional arrays. You need to be careful about the type, though. To pass the temperature grid, you would have to use a parameter of type `double[][]` (with both sets of brackets). For example, here is a method that prints the grid:

```
public static void print(double[][] grid) {
    for (int i = 0; i < grid.length; i++) {
        for (int j = 0; j < grid[i].length; j++) {
            System.out.print(grid[i][j] + " ");
        }
```

```
            System.out.println();
    }
}
```

Notice that to ask for the number of rows you ask for `grid.length` and to ask for the number of columns you ask for `grid[i].length`.

The `Arrays.toString` method mentioned earlier in this chapter does work on multidimensional arrays, but it produces a poor result. When used with the preceding array `temps`, it produces output such as the following:

```
[[D@14b081b, [D@1015a9e, [D@1e45a5c]
```

This poor output is because `Arrays.toString` works by concatenating the `String` representations of the array's elements. In this case the elements are arrays themselves, so they do not convert into `String`s properly. To correct the problem you can use a different method called `Arrays.deepToString` that will return better results for multidimensional arrays:

```
System.out.println(Arrays.deepToString(temps));
```

The call produces the following output:

```
[[0.0, 0.0, 0.0, 98.3, 0.0], [0.0, 0.0, 0.0, 0.0, 0.0],
[99.4, 0.0, 0.0, 0.0, 0.0]]
```

Arrays can have as many dimensions as you want. For example, if you want a three-dimensional 4 by 4 by 4 cube of integers, you would write the following line of code:

```
int[][][] numbers = new int[4][4][4];
```

The normal convention for the order of values is the plane number, followed by the row number, followed by the column number, although you can use any convention you want as long as your code is written consistently.

Jagged Arrays

The previous examples have involved rectangular grids that have a fixed number of rows and columns. It is also possible to create a jagged array in which the number of columns varies from row to row.

To construct a jagged array, divide the construction into two steps: Construct the array for holding rows first, and then construct each individual row. For example, to construct an array that has two elements in the first row, four elements in the second row, and three elements in the third row, you can write the following lines of code:

```
int[][] jagged = new int[3][];
jagged[0] = new int[2];
jagged[1] = new int[4];
jagged[2] = new int[3];
```

This code would construct an array that looks like this:

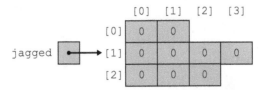

We can explore this technique by writing a program that produces the rows of what is known as *Pascal's triangle*. The numbers in the triangle have many useful mathematical properties. For example, row *n* of Pascal's triangle contains the coefficients obtained when you expand the equation:

$(x + y)^n$

Here are the results for *n* between 0 and 4:

$(x + y)^0 = 1$
$(x + y)^1 = x + y$
$(x + y)^2 = x^2 + 2xy + y^2$
$(x + y)^3 = x^3 + 3x^2y + 3xy^2 + y^3$
$(x + y)^4 = x^4 + 4x^3y + 6x^2y^2 + 4xy^3 + y^4$

If you pull out just the coefficients, you get the following values:

```
      1
    1   1
   1  2  1
 1   3  3 1
1  4  6  4  1
```

These rows of numbers form a five-row Pascal's triangle. One of the properties of the triangle is that if you are given any row, you can use it to compute the next row. For example, let's start with the last row from the preceding triangle:

```
1 4 6 4 1
```

We can compute the next row by adding adjacent pairs of values together. So, we add together the first pair of numbers (1 + 4), then the second pair of numbers (4 + 6), and so on:

```
5 10 10 5
```

$$\underbrace{(1 + 4)}_{5} \quad \underbrace{(4 + 6)}_{10} \quad \underbrace{(6 + 4)}_{10} \quad \underbrace{(4 + 1)}_{5}$$

Then we put a 1 at the front and back of this list of numbers, and we end up with the next row of the triangle:

```
        1
      1   1
    1   2   1
  1   3   3   1
1   4   6   4   1
1  5  10  10  5  1
```

This property of the triangle provides a technique for computing it. We can construct it row by row, computing each new row from the values in the previous row. In other words, we write the following loop (assuming that we have a two-dimensional array called `triangle` in which to store the answer):

```
for (int i = 0; i < triangle.length; i++) {
    construct triangle[i] using triangle[i - 1].
}
```

We just need to flesh out the details of how a new row is constructed. This is a jagged array because each row has a different number of elements. Looking at the triangle, you'll see that the first row (row 0) has one value in it, the second row (row 1) has two values in it, and so on. In general, row i has (i + 1) values, so we can refine our pseudocode as follows:

```
for (int i = 0; i < triangle.length; i++) {
    triangle[i] = new int[i + 1];
    fill in triangle[i] using triangle[i - 1].
}
```

We know that the first and last values in each row should be 1:

```
for (int i = 0; i < triangle.length; i++) {
    triangle[i] = new int[i + 1];
    triangle[i][0] = 1;
    triangle[i][i] = 1;
    fill in the middle of triangle[i] using triangle[i - 1].
}
```

And we know that the middle values come from the previous row. To figure out how to compute them, let's draw a picture of the array we are attempting to build:

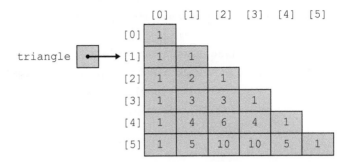

We have already written code to fill in the 1 that appears at the beginning and end of each row. We now need to write code to fill in the middle values. Look at row 5 for an example. The value 5 in column 1 comes from the sum of the values 1 in column 0 and 4 in column 1 in the previous row. The value 10 in column 2 comes from the sum of the values in columns 1 and 2 in the previous row.

More generally, each of these middle values is the sum of the two values from the previous row that appear just above and to the left of it. In other words, for column j the values are computed as follows:

```
triangle[i][j] = (value above and left) + (value above).
```

We can turn this into actual code by using the appropriate array indexes:

```
triangle[i][j] = triangle[i - 1][j - 1] + triangle[i - 1][j];
```

We need to include this statement in a for loop so that it assigns all of the middle values. The for loop is the final step in converting our pseudocode into actual code:

```
for (int i = 0; i < triangle.length; i++) {
    triangle[i] = new int[i + 1];
    triangle[i][0] = 1;
    triangle[i][i] = 1;
    for (int j = 1; j < i; j++) {
        triangle[i][j] = triangle[i - 1][j - 1] + triangle[i - 1][j];
    }
}
```

If we include this code in a method along with a printing method similar to the grid-printing method described earlier, we end up with the following complete program:

```
1   // This program constructs a jagged two-dimensional array
2   // that stores Pascal's Triangle. It takes advantage of the
3   // fact that each value other than the 1s that appear at the
4   // beginning and end of each row is the sum of two values
```

```
 5  // from the previous row.
 6
 7  public class PascalsTriangle {
 8      public static void main(String[] args) {
 9          int[][] triangle = new int[11][];
10          fillIn(triangle);
11          print(triangle);
12      }
13
14      public static void fillIn(int[][] triangle) {
15          for (int i = 0; i < triangle.length; i++) {
16              triangle[i] = new int[i + 1];
17              triangle[i][0] = 1;
18              triangle[i][i] = 1;
19              for (int j = 1; j < i; j++) {
20                  triangle[i][j] = triangle[i - 1][j - 1]
21                                 + triangle[i - 1][j];
22              }
23          }
24      }
25
26      public static void print(int[][] triangle) {
27          for (int i = 0; i < triangle.length; i++) {
28              for (int j = 0; j < triangle[i].length; j++) {
29                  System.out.print(triangle[i][j] + " ");
30              }
31              System.out.println();
32          }
33      }
34  }
```

This program produces the following output:

```
1
1 1
1 2 1
1 3 3 1
1 4 6 4 1
1 5 10 10 5 1
1 6 15 20 15 6 1
1 7 21 35 35 21 7 1
1 8 28 56 70 56 28 8 1
1 9 36 84 126 126 84 36 9 1
1 10 45 120 210 252 210 120 45 10 1
```

7.6 Arrays of Pixels

Recall from Supplement 3G that images are stored on computers as a two-dimensional grid of colored dots known as *pixels*. One of the most common applications of two-dimensional (2D) arrays is for manipulating the pixels of an image. Popular apps like Instagram provide filters and options for modifying images by applying algorithms to their pixels; for example, you can make an image black-and-white, sharpen it, enhance the colors and contrast, or make it look like an old faded photograph. The two-dimensional rectangular nature of an image makes a 2D array a natural way to represent for its pixel data.

Supplement 3G introduced the `DrawingPanel` class that we use to represent a window for drawing 2D shapes and colors. Recall that an image is composed of pixels whose locations are specified with integer coordinates starting from the top-left corner of the image at (0, 0). The various drawing commands of the panel's `Graphics` object, such as `drawRect` and `fillOval`, change the color of regions of pixels. Colors are usually specified by `Color` objects, but the full range of colors comes from mixtures of red, green, and blue elements specified by integers that range from 0 to 255 inclusive. Each combination of three integers specifies a particular color and is known as an *RGB value*.

The `DrawingPanel` includes several methods for getting and setting the color of pixels, listed in Table 7.3. You can interact with a single pixel, or you can grab all of the pixels of the image as a 2D array and manipulate the entire array. The array is in row-major order; that is, the first index of the array is the *y*-coordinate and the second is the *x*-coordinate. For example, $a[r][c]$ represents the pixel at position ($x=c$, $y=r$). For efficiency it is generally recommended to use the array-based versions of the methods; the individual-pixel methods run slowly when applied repeatedly over all pixels of a large image.

The following `DrawPurpleTriangle` example program uses `getPixels` and `setPixels` to fill a triangular region of the panel with a purple color. Figure 7.1 shows the graphical output of the program. Notice that you must call `setPixels` at the end to see the updated image; changing the array will not produce any effect on the screen until you tell the panel to update itself using the new contents of the array.

Table 7.3 `DrawingPanel` methods related to pixels

Method	Description
`getPixel(x, y)`	returns a pixel's color as a `Color` object
`getPixels()`	returns all pixels' colors as a 2D array of `Color` objects, in row-major order (*first index is row or y, second index is column or x*)
`setPixel(x, y, color)`	sets a pixel's color to the given `Color` object's color
`setPixels(pixels)`	sets all pixels' colors from given 2D array of `Color` objects, resizing the panel if necessary to match the array's dimensions

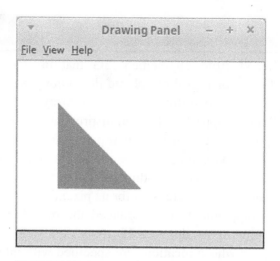

Figure 7.1 Output of `DrawPurpleTriangle`

```
1 // This program demonstrates the DrawingPanel's
2 // getPixels and setPixels methods for
3 // manipulating pixels of an image.
4
5 import java.awt.*;
6
7 public class DrawPurpleTriangle {
8     public static void main(String[] args) {
9         DrawingPanel panel = new DrawingPanel(300, 200);
10        Color[][] pixels = panel.getPixels();
11        for (int row = 50; row <= 150; row++) {
12            for (int col = 50; col <= row; col++) {
13                pixels[row][col] = Color.MAGENTA;
14            }
15        }
16        panel.setPixels(pixels);
17    }
18 }
```

You can use `getPixels` and `setPixels` to draw a shape like our purple triangle, but a more typical usage of these methods would be to grab the panel's existing state and alter it in some interesting way. The following `Mirror` program demonstrates the use of a 2D array of `Color` objects. The program's `mirror` method accepts a `DrawingPanel` parameter and flips the pixel contents horizontally, swapping each pixel's color with the one at the opposite horizontal location. The code uses the dimensions of the array to represent the size of the image; `pixels.length` is its height and `pixels[0].length` (the length of the first row of the 2D array) is its width. Figure 7.2 shows the program's graphical output before and after `mirror` is called.

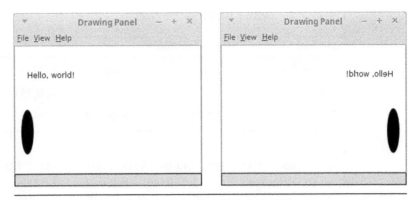

Figure 7.2 Output of `Mirror` before and after mirroring

```
1  // This program contains a mirror method that flips the appearance
2  // of a DrawingPanel horizontally pixel-by-pixel.
3
4  import java.awt.*;
5
6  public class Mirror {
7      public static void main(String[] args) {
8          DrawingPanel panel = new DrawingPanel(300, 200);
9          Graphics g = panel.getGraphics();
10         g.drawString("Hello, world!", 20, 50);
11         g.fillOval(10, 100, 20, 70);
12         mirror(panel);
13     }
14
15     // Flips the pixels of the given drawing panel horizontally.
16     public static void mirror(DrawingPanel panel) {
17         Color[][] pixels = panel.getPixels();
18         for (int row = 0; row < pixels.length; row++) {
19             for (int col = 0; col < pixels[0].length / 2; col++) {
20                 // swap with pixel at "mirrored" location
21                 int opposite = pixels[0].length - 1 - col;
22                 Color px = pixels[row][col];
23                 pixels[row][col] = pixels[row][opposite];
24                 pixels[row][opposite] = px;
25             }
26         }
27         panel.setPixels(pixels);
28     }
29 }
```

Often you'll want to extract the individual red, green, and blue components of a color to manipulate them. Each pixel's `Color` object has methods to help you do this.

Table 7.4 `Color` methods related to pixel RGB components

Method	Description
getRed()	returns the red component from 0-255
getGreen()	returns the green component from 0-255
getBlue()	returns the blue component from 0-255

The `getRed`, `getGreen`, and `getBlue` methods extract the relevant components out of an RGB integer. Table 7.4 lists the relevant methods.

The following code shows a method that computes the negative of an image, which is found by taking the opposite of each color's RGB values. For example, the opposite of (red = 255, green = 100, blue = 35) is (red = 0, green = 155, blue = 220). The simplest way to compute the negative is to subtract the pixel's RGB values from the maximum color value of 255. Figure 7.3 shows an example output.

```java
// Produces the negative of the given image by inverting all color
// values in the panel.
public static void negative(DrawingPanel panel) {
    Color[][] pixels = panel.getPixels();
    for (int row = 0; row < pixels.length; row++) {
        for (int col = 0; col < pixels[0].length; col++) {
            // extract red/green/blue components from 0-255
            int r = 255 - pixels[row][col].getRed();
            int g = 255 - pixels[row][col].getGreen();
            int b = 255 - pixels[row][col].getBlue();

            // update the pixel array with the new color value
            pixels[row][col] = new Color(r, g, b);
        }
    }
    panel.setPixels(pixels);
}
```

All of the previous examples have involved making changes to a 2D pixel array in place. But sometimes you want to create an image with different dimensions, or want to set each pixel based on the values of pixels around it, and therefore you need to create a new pixel array. The following example shows a `stretch` method that widens the contents of a `DrawingPanel` to twice their current width. To do so, it creates an array `newPixels` that is twice as wide as the existing one. (Remember that the first index of the 2D array is y and the second is x, so to widen the array, the code must double the array's second dimension.) The `setPixels` method will resize the panel if necessary to accommodate our new larger array of pixels.

Figure 7.3 Negative of an image (before and after)

The loop to fill the new array sets the value at each index to the value at half as large an x-index in the original array. So, for example, the original array's pixel value at (52, 34) is used to fill the new array's pixels at (104, 68) and (105, 68). Figure 7.4 shows the graphical output of the stretched image.

```java
// Stretches the given panel to be twice as wide.
// Any shapes and colors drawn on the panel are stretched to fit.
public static void stretch(DrawingPanel panel) {
    Color[][] pixels = panel.getPixels();
    Color[][] newPixels = new Color[pixels.length][2 * pixels[0].length];
    for (int row = 0; row < pixels.length; row++) {
        for (int col = 0; col < 2 * pixels[0].length; col++) {
            newPixels[row][col] = pixels[row][col / 2];
        }
    }
    panel.setPixels(newPixels);
}
```

Figure 7.4 Horizontally stretched image (before and after)

The pixel-based methods shown in this section are somewhat inefficient because they create large arrays of `Color` objects, which takes a lot of time and memory. These methods aren't efficient enough for an animation or a game. The `DrawingPanel` provides some additional methods like `getPixelsRGB` that use specially packed integers to represent red, green, and blue color information instead of `Color` objects to improve the speed and memory usage at the cost of a bit of code complexity. If you are interested, you can read about these additional methods in the online `DrawingPanel` documentation at buildingjavaprograms.com.

7.7 Case Study: Benford's Law

Let's look at a more complex program example that involves using arrays. When you study real-world data you will often come across a curious result that is known as *Benford's Law*, named after a physicist named Frank Benford who stated it in 1938.

Benford's Law involves looking at the first digit of a series of numbers. For example, suppose that you were to use a random number generator to generate integers in the range of 100 to 999 and you looked at how often the number begins with 1, how often it begins with 2, and so on. Any decent random number generator would spread the answers out evenly among the nine different regions, so we'd expect to see each digit about one-ninth of the time (11.1%). But with a lot of real-world data, we see a very different distribution.

When we examine data that matches the Benford distribution, we see a first digit of 1 over 30% of the time (almost one third) and, at the other extreme, a first digit of 9 only about 4.6% of the time (less than one in twenty cases). Table 7.5 shows the expected distribution for data that follows Benford's Law.

Why would the distribution turn out this way? Why so many 1s? Why so few 9s? The answer is that exponential sequences have different properties than simple linear sequences. In particular, exponential sequences have a lot more numbers that begin with 1.

Table 7.5 Expected Distribution Under Benford's Law

First Digit	Frequency
1	30.1%
2	17.6%
3	12.5%
4	9.7%
5	7.9%
6	6.7%
7	5.8%
8	5.1%
9	4.6%

To explore this phenomenon, let's look at two different sequences of numbers: one that grows linearly and one that grows exponentially. If you start with the number 1 and add 0.2 to it over and over, you get the following linear sequence:

1, 1.2, 1.4, 1.6, 1.8, 2, 2.2, 2.4, 2.6, 2.8, 3, 3.2, 3.4, 3.6, 3.8, 4, 4.2, 4.4, 4.6, 4.8, 5, 5.2, 5.4, 5.6, 5.8, 6, 6.2, 6.4, 6.6, 6.8, 7, 7.2, 7.4, 7.6, 7.8, 8, 8.2, 8.4, 8.6, 8.8, 9, 9.2, 9.4, 9.6, 9.8, 10

In this sequence there are five numbers that begin with 1, five numbers that begin with 2, five numbers that begin with 3, and so on. For each digit, there are five numbers that begin with that digit. That's what we expect to see with data that goes up by a constant amount each time.

But consider what happens when we make it an exponential sequence instead. Let's again start with 1 and continue until we get to 10, but this time let's multiply each successive number by 1.05 (we'll limit ourselves to displaying just two digits after the decimal, but the actual sequence takes into account all of the digits):

1.00, 1.05, 1.10, 1.16, 1.22, 1.28, 1.34, 1.41, 1.48, 1.55, 1.63, 1.71, 1.80, 1.89, 1.98, 2.08, 2.18, 2.29, 2.41, 2.53, 2.65, 2.79, 2.93, 3.07, 3.23, 3.39, 3.56, 3.73, 3.92, 4.12, 4.32, 4.54, 4.76, 5.00, 5.25, 5.52, 5.79, 6.08, 6.39, 6.70, 7.04, 7.39, 7.76, 8.15, 8.56, 8.99, 9.43, 9.91, 10.40

In this sequence there are 15 numbers that begin with 1 (31.25%), 8 numbers that begin with 2 (16.7%), and so on. There are only 2 numbers that begin with 9 (4.2%). In fact, the distribution of digits is almost exactly what you see in the table for Benford's Law.

There are many real-world phenomena that exhibit an exponential character. For example, population tends to grow exponentially in most regions. There are many other data sets that also seem to exhibit the Benford pattern, including sunspots, salaries, investments, heights of buildings, and so on. Benford's Law has been used to try to detect accounting fraud under the theory that when someone is making up data, he or she is likely to use a more random process that won't yield a Benford style distribution.

For our purposes, let's write a program that reads a file of integers and that shows the distribution of the leading digit. We'll read the data from a file and will run it on several sample inputs. First, though, let's consider the general problem of tallying.

Tallying Values

VideoNote

In programming we often find ourselves wanting to count the number of occurrences of some set of values. For example, we might want to know how many people got a 100 on an exam, how many got a 99, how many got a 98, and so on. Or we might want to know how many days the temperature in a city was above 100 degrees, how many days it was in the 90s, how many days it was in the 80s, and so on. The approach is very nearly the same for each of these tallying tasks. Let's look at a small tallying task in which there are only five values to tally.

Suppose that a teacher scores quizzes on a scale of 0 to 4 and wants to know the distribution of quiz scores. In other words, the teacher wants to know how many scores of 0 there are, how many scores of 1, how many scores of 2, how many scores of 3, and how many scores of 4. Suppose that the teacher has included all of the scores in a data file like the following:

```
1 4 1 0 3 2 1 4 2 0
3 0 2 3 0 4 3 3 4 1
2 4 1 3 1 4 3 3 2 4
2 3 0 4 1 4 4 1 4 1
```

The teacher could hand-count the scores, but it would be much easier to use a computer to do the counting. How can you solve the problem? First you have to recognize that you are doing five separate counting tasks: You are counting the occurrences of the number 0, the number 1, the number 2, the number 3, and the number 4. You will need five counters to solve this problem, which means that an array is a great way to store the data. In general, whenever you find yourself thinking that you need *n* of some kind of data, you should think about using an array of length *n*.

Each counter will be an `int`, so you want an array of five `int` values:

```
int[] count = new int[5];
```

This line of code will allocate the array of five integers and will auto-initialize each to `0`:

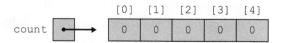

You're reading from a file, so you'll need a `Scanner` and a loop that reads scores until there are no more scores to read:

```
Scanner input = new Scanner(new File("tally.dat"));
while (input.hasNextInt()) {
    int next = input.nextInt();
    // process next
}
```

To complete this code, you need to figure out how to process each value. You know that `next` will be one of five different values: 0, 1, 2, 3, or 4. If it is 0, you want to increment the counter for 0, which is `count[0]`; if it is 1, you want to increment the counter for 1, which is `count[1]`, and so on. We have been solving problems like this one with nested `if`/`else` statements:

```
if (next == 0) {
    count[0]++;
} else if (next == 1) {
    count[1]++;
} else if (next == 2) {
    count[2]++;
} else if (next == 3) {
    count[3]++;
} else { // next == 4
    count[4]++;
}
```

But with an array, you can solve this problem much more directly:

```
count[next]++;
```

This line of code is so short compared to the nested `if/else` construct that you might not realize at first that it does the same thing. Let's simulate exactly what happens as various values are read from the file.

When the array is constructed, all of the counters are initialized to 0:

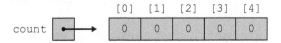

The first value in the input file is a 1, so the program reads that into `next`. Then it executes this line of code:

```
count[next]++;
```

Because `next` is 1, this line of code becomes

```
count[1]++;
```

So the counter at index `[1]` is incremented:

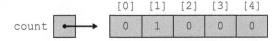

Then a 4 is read from the input file, which means `count[4]` is incremented:

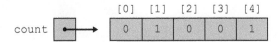

Next, another 1 is read from the input file, which increments `count[1]`:

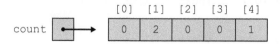

Then a 0 is read from the input file, which increments `count[0]`:

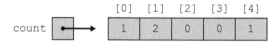

Notice that in just this short set of data you've jumped from index 1 to index 4, then back down to index 1, then to index 0. The program continues executing in this manner, jumping from counter to counter as it reads values from the file. This ability to jump around in the data structure is what's meant by random access.

After processing all of the data, the array ends up looking like this:

After this loop finishes executing, you can report the total for each score by using the standard traversing loop with a `println`:

```java
for (int i = 0; i < count.length; i++) {
    System.out.println(i + "\t" + count[i]);
}
```

With the addition of a header for the output, the complete program is as follows:

```java
1  // Reads a series of values and reports the frequency of
2  // occurrence of each value.
3
4  import java.io.*;
5  import java.util.*;
6
7  public class Tally {
8      public static void main(String[] args)
9              throws FileNotFoundException {
10         Scanner input = new Scanner(new File("tally.dat"));
11         int[] count = new int[5];
12         while (input.hasNextInt()) {
```

```
13              int next = input.nextInt();
14              count[next]++;
15          }
16          System.out.println("Value\tOccurrences");
17          for (int i = 0; i < count.length; i++) {
18              System.out.println(i + "\t" + count[i]);
19          }
20      }
21  }
```

Given the sample input file shown earlier, this program produces the following output:

```
Value   Occurrences
0       5
1       9
2       6
3       9
4       11
```

It is important to realize that a program written with an array is much more flexible than programs written with simple variables and if/else statements. For example, suppose you wanted to adapt this program to process an input file with exam scores that range from 0 to 100. The only change you would have to make would be to allocate a larger array:

```
int[] count = new int[101];
```

If you had written the program with an if/else approach, you would have to add 96 new branches to account for the new range of values. When you use an array solution, you just have to modify the overall size of the array. Notice that the array size is one more than the highest score (101 rather than 100) because the array is zero-based and because you can actually get 101 different scores on the test, including 0 as a possibility.

Completing the Program

Now that we've explored the basic approach to tallying, we can fairly easily adapt it to the problem of analyzing a data file to find the distribution of leading digits. As we stated earlier, we're assuming that we have a file of integers. To count the leading digits, we will need to be able to get the leading digit of each. This task is specialized enough that it deserves to be in its own method.

So let's first write a method called firstDigit that returns the first digit of an integer. If the number is a one-digit number, then the number itself will be the answer. If the number is not a one-digit number, then we can chop off its last digit because we don't need it. If we do the chopping in a loop, then eventually we'll get down to a one-digit number (the first digit). This leads us to write the following loop:

```
while (result >= 10) {
    result = result / 10;
}
```

We don't expect to get any negative numbers, but it's not a bad idea to make sure we don't have any negatives. So putting this into a method that also handles negatives, we get the following code:

```
public static int firstDigit(int n) {
    int result = Math.abs(n);
    while (result >= 10) {
        result = result / 10;
    }
    return result;
}
```

In the previous section we explored the general approach to tallying. In this case we want to tally the digits 0 through 9, so we want an array of length 10. Otherwise the solution is nearly identical to what we did in the last section. We can put the tallying code into a method that constructs an array and returns the tally:

```
public static int[] countDigits(Scanner input) {
    int[] count = new int[10];
    while (input.hasNextInt()) {
        int n = input.nextInt();
        count[firstDigit(n)]++;
    }
    return count;
}
```

Notice that instead of tallying n in the body of the loop, we are instead tallying firstDigit(n) (just the first digit, not the entire number).

The value 0 presents a potential problem for us. Benford's Law is meant to apply to data that comes from an exponential sequence. But even if you are increasing exponentially, if you start with 0, you never get beyond 0. As a result, it is best to eliminate the 0 values from the calculation. Often they won't occur at all.

When reporting results, then, let's begin by reporting the excluded zeros if they exist:

```
if (count[0] > 0) {
    System.out.println("excluding " + count[0] + " zeros");
}
```

For the other digits, we want to report the number of occurrences of each and also the percentage of each. To figure the percentage, we'll need to know the sum of the values. This is a good place to introduce a method that finds the sum of an array of integers. It's a fairly straightforward array traversal problem that can be solved with a for-each loop:

```java
public static int sum(int[] data) {
    int sum = 0;
    for (int n : data) {
        sum += n;
    }
    return sum;
}
```

Now we can compute the total number of digits by calling the method and subtracting the number of 0s:

```java
int total = sum(count) - count[0];
```

And once we have the total number of digits, we can write a loop to report each of the percentages. To compute the percentages, we multiply each count by 100 and divide by the total number of digits. We have to be careful to multiply by 100.0 rather than 100 to make sure that we are computing the result using `double` values. Otherwise we'll get truncated integer division and won't get any digits after the decimal point:

```java
for (int i = 1; i < count.length; i++) {
    double pct = count[i] * 100.0 / total;
    System.out.println(i + " " + count[i] + " " + pct);
}
```

Notice that the loop starts at 1 instead of 0 because we have excluded the zeros from our reporting.

Here is a complete program that puts these pieces together. It also uses `printf` statements to format the output and includes a header for the table and a total afterward:

```java
1   // This program finds the distribution of leading digits in a set
2   // of positive integers.  The program is useful for exploring the
3   // phenomenon known as Benford's Law.
4
5   import java.io.*;
6   import java.util.*;
7
8   public class Benford {
9       public static void main(String[] args)
```

```
10              throws FileNotFoundException {
11          Scanner console = new Scanner(System.in);
12          System.out.println("Let's count those leading digits...");
13          System.out.print("input file name? ");
14          String name = console.nextLine();
15          Scanner input = new Scanner(new File(name));
16          int[] count = countDigits(input);
17          reportResults(count);
18      }
19
20      // Reads integers from input, computing an array of counts
21      // for the occurrences of each leading digit (0-9).
22      public static int[] countDigits(Scanner input) {
23          int[] count = new int[10];
24          while (input.hasNextInt()) {
25              int n = input.nextInt();
26              count[firstDigit(n)]++;
27          }
28          return count;
29      }
30
31      // Reports percentages for each leading digit, excluding zeros
32      public static void reportResults(int[] count) {
33          System.out.println();
34          if (count[0] > 0) {
35              System.out.println("excluding " + count[0] + " zeros");
36          }
37          int total = sum(count) - count[0];
38          System.out.println("Digit Count Percent");
39          for (int i = 1; i < count.length; i++) {
40              double pct = count[i] * 100.0 / total;
41              System.out.printf("%5d %5d %6.2f\n", i, count[i], pct);
42          }
43          System.out.printf("Total %5d %6.2f\n", total, 100.0);
44      }
45
46      // returns the sum of the integers in the given array
47      public static int sum(int[] data) {
48          int sum = 0;
49          for (int n : data) {
50              sum += n;
51          }
```

```
52          return sum;
53      }
54
55      // returns the first digit of the given number
56      public static int firstDigit(int n) {
57          int result = Math.abs(n);
58          while (result >= 10) {
59              result = result / 10;
60          }
61          return result;
62      }
63  }
```

Now that we have a complete program, let's see what we get when we analyze various data sets. The Benford distribution shows up with population data because population tends to grow exponentially. Let's use data from the web page http://www.census.gov/popest/ which contains population estimates for various U.S. counties. The data set has information on 3000 different counties with populations varying from 100 individuals to over 9 million for the census year 2000. Here is a sample output of our program using these data:

```
Let's count those leading digits...
input file name? county.txt

Digit   Count   Percent
    1     970    30.90
    2     564    17.97
    3     399    12.71
    4     306     9.75
    5     206     6.56
    6     208     6.63
    7     170     5.24
    8     172     5.48
    9     144     4.59
Total    3139   100.00
```

These percentages are almost exactly the numbers predicted by Benford's Law.

Data that obey Benford's Law have an interesting property. It doesn't matter what scale you use for the data. So if you are measuring heights, for example, it doesn't matter whether you measure in feet, inches, meters, or furlongs. In our case, we counted the number of people in each U.S. county. If we instead count the number of human hands in each county, then we have to double each number. Look at the preceding output and see if you can predict the result when you double each number. Here is the actual result:

```
Let's count those leading digits...
input file name? county2.txt

Digit   Count   Percent
    1     900    28.67
    2     555    17.68
    3     415    13.22
    4     322    10.26
    5     242     7.71
    6     209     6.66
    7     190     6.05
    8     173     5.51
    9     133     4.24
Total    3139   100.00
```

Notice that there is very little change. Doubling the numbers has little effect because if the original data is exponential in nature, then the same will be true of the doubled numbers. Here is another sample run that triples the county population numbers:

```
Let's count those leading digits...
input file name? county3.txt

Digit   Count   Percent
    1     926    29.50
    2     549    17.49
    3     385    12.27
    4     327    10.42
    5     258     8.22
    6     228     7.26
    7     193     6.15
    8     143     4.56
    9     130     4.14
Total    3139   100.00
```

Another data set that shows Benford characteristics is the count of sunspots that occur on any given day. Robin McQuinn maintains a web page at http://sidc.oma.be/html/sunspot.html that has daily counts of sunspots going back to 1818. Here is a sample execution using these data:

```
Let's count those leading digits...
input file name? sunspot.txt

excluding 4144 zeros
Digit   Count   Percent
    1    5405    31.24
    2    1809    10.46
    3    2127    12.29
    4    1690     9.77
    5    1702     9.84
    6    1357     7.84
    7    1364     7.88
    8     966     5.58
    9     882     5.10
Total  17302   100.00
```

Notice that on this execution the program reports the exclusion of some 0 values.

Chapter Summary

An array is an object that groups multiple primitive values or objects of the same type under one name. Each individual value, called an element, is accessed with an integer index that ranges from 0 to one less than the array's length.

Attempting to access an array element with an index of less than 0 or one that is greater than or equal to the array's length will cause the program to crash with an `ArrayIndexOutOfBoundsException`.

Arrays are often traversed using `for` loops. The length of an array is found by accessing its length field, so the loop over an array can process indexes from 0 to `length − 1`. Array elements can also be accessed in order using a type of loop called a for-each loop.

Arrays have several limitations, such as fixed size and lack of support for common operations like `==` and `println`. To perform these operations, you must either use the `Arrays` class or write `for` loops that process each element of the array.

Several common array algorithms, such as printing an array or comparing two arrays to each other for equality, are implemented by traversing the elements and examining or modifying each one.

Java arrays are objects and use reference semantics, in which variables store references to values rather than to the actual values themselves. This means that two variables can refer to the same array or object. If the array is modified through one of its references, the modification will also be seen in the other.

Arrays of objects are actually arrays of references to objects. A newly declared and initialized array of objects actually stores `null` in all of its element indexes, so each element must be initialized individually or in a loop to store an actual object.

A multidimensional array is an array of arrays. These are often used to store two-dimensional data, such as data in rows and columns or xy data in a two-dimensional space.

Self-Check Problems

Section 7.1: Array Basics

1. Which of the following is the correct syntax to declare an array of ten integers?

    a. `int a[10] = new int[10];`

    b. `int[10] a = new int[10];`

    c. `[]int a = [10]int;`

    d. `int a[10];`

    e. `int[] a = new int[10];`

2. What expression should be used to access the first element of an array of integers called `numbers`? What expression should be used to access the last element of `numbers`, assuming it contains 10 elements? What expression can be used to access its last element, regardless of its length?

3. Write code that creates an array of integers named `data` of size 5 with the following contents:

	[0]	[1]	[2]	[3]	[4]
data →	27	51	33	-1	101

4. Write code that stores all odd numbers between −6 and 38 into an array using a loop. Make the array's size exactly large enough to store the numbers.

    Then, try generalizing your code so that it will work for any minimum and maximum values, not just –6 and 38.

5. What elements does the array `numbers` contain after the following code is executed?

    ```
    int[] numbers = new int[8];
    numbers[1] = 4;
    numbers[4] = 99;
    numbers[7] = 2;

    int x = numbers[1];
    numbers[x] = 44;
    numbers[numbers[7]] = 11; // uses numbers[7] as index
    ```

6. What elements does the array `data` contain after the following code is executed?

    ```
    int[] data = new int[8];
    data[0] = 3;
    data[7] = -18;
    data[4] = 5;
    data[1] = data[0];

    int x = data[4];
    data[4] = 6;
    data[x] = data[0] * data[1];
    ```

7. What is wrong with the following code?

```
int[] first = new int[2];
first[0] = 3;
first[1] = 7;
int[] second = new int[2];
second[0] = 3;
second[1] = 7;


// print the array elements
System.out.println(first);
System.out.println(second);


// see if the elements are the same
if (first == second) {
    System.out.println("They contain the same elements.");
} else {
    System.out.println("The elements are different.");
}
```

8. Which of the following is the correct syntax to declare an array of the given six integer values?

  a. `int[] a = {17, -3, 42, 5, 9, 28};`

  b. `int a {17, -3, 42, 5, 9, 28};`

  c. `int[] a = new int[6] {17, -3, 42, 5, 9, 28};`

  d. `int[6] a = {17, -3, 42, 5, 9, 28};`

  e. `int[] a = int [17, -3, 42, 5, 9, 28] {6};`

9. Write a piece of code that declares an array called `data` with the elements 7, -1, 13, 24, and 6. Use only one statement to initialize the array.

10. Write a piece of code that examines an array of integers and reports the maximum value in the array. Consider putting your code into a method called `max` that accepts the array as a parameter and returns the maximum value. Assume that the array contains at least one element.

11. Write a method called `average` that computes the average (arithmetic mean) of all elements in an array of integers and returns the answer as a `double`. For example, if the array passed contains the values `[1, -2, 4, -4, 9, -6, 16, -8, 25, -10]`, the calculated average should be `2.5`. Your method accepts an array of integers as its parameter and returns the average.

Section 7.2: Array-Traversal Algorithms

12. What is an array traversal? Give an example of a problem that can be solved by traversing an array.

13. Write code that uses a `for` loop to print each element of an array named `data` that contains five integers:

```
element [0] is 14
element [1] is 5
element [2] is 27
element [3] is -3
element [4] is 2598
```

Consider generalizing your code so that it will work on an array of any size.

14. What elements does the array `list` contain after the following code is executed?

```
int[] list = {2, 18, 6, -4, 5, 1};
for (int i = 0; i < list.length; i++) {
    list[i] = list[i] + (list[i] / list[0]);
}
```

15. Write a piece of code that prints an array of integers in reverse order, in the same format as the `print` method from Section 7.2. Consider putting your code into a method called `printBackwards` that accepts the array as a parameter.

16. Describe the modifications that would be necessary to change the `count` and `equals` methods developed in Section 7.2 to process arrays of `Strings` instead of arrays of integers.

17. Write a method called `allLess` that accepts two arrays of integers and returns `true` if each element in the first array is less than the element at the same index in the second array. Your method should return `false` if the arrays are not the same length.

Section 7.3: Reference Semantics

18. Why does a method to swap two array elements work correctly when a method to swap two integer values does not?

19. What is the output of the following program?

```
public class ReferenceMystery1 {
    public static void main(String[] args) {
        int x = 0;
        int[] a = new int[4];
        x = x + 1;
        mystery(x, a);
        System.out.println(x + " " + Arrays.toString(a));
        x = x + 1;
        mystery(x, a);
        System.out.println(x + " " + Arrays.toString(a));
    }
    public static void mystery(int x, int[] a) {
        x = x + 1;
        a[x] = a[x] + 1;
        System.out.println(x + " " + Arrays.toString(a));
    }
}
```

20. What is the output of the following program?

```
public class ReferenceMystery2 {
    public static void main(String[] args) {
        int x = 1;
        int[] a = new int[2];
        mystery(x, a);
        System.out.println(x + " " + Arrays.toString(a));
        x--;
        a[1] = a.length;
        mystery(x, a);
```

```
            System.out.println(x + " " + Arrays.toString(a));
        }

        public static void mystery(int x, int[] list) {
            list[x]++;
            x++;
            System.out.println(x + " " + Arrays.toString(list));
        }
    }
```

21. Write a method called `swapPairs` that accepts an array of integers and swaps the elements at adjacent indexes. That is, elements 0 and 1 are swapped, elements 2 and 3 are swapped, and so on. If the array has an odd length, the final element should be left unmodified. For example, the list `[10, 20, 30, 40, 50]` should become `[20, 10, 40, 30, 50]` after a call to your method.

Section 7.4: Advanced Array Techniques

22. What are the values of the elements in the array `numbers` after the following code is executed?

```
int[] numbers = {10, 20, 30, 40, 50, 60, 70, 80, 90, 100};
for (int i = 0; i < 9; i++) {
    numbers[i] = numbers[i + 1];
}
```

23. What are the values of the elements in the array `numbers` after the following code is executed?

```
int[] numbers = {10, 20, 30, 40, 50, 60, 70, 80, 90, 100};
for (int i = 1; i < 10; i++) {
    numbers[i] = numbers[i - 1];
}
```

24. Consider the following method, `mystery`:

```
public static void mystery(int[] a, int[] b) {
    for (int i = 0; i < a.length; i++) {
        a[i] += b[b.length - 1 - i];
    }
}
```

What are the values of the elements in array `a1` after the following code executes?

```
int[] a1 = {1, 3, 5, 7, 9};
int[] a2 = {1, 4, 9, 16, 25};
mystery(a1, a2);
```

25. Consider the following method, `mystery2`:

```
public static void mystery2(int[] a, int[] b) {
    for (int i = 0; i < a.length; i++) {
        a[i] = a[2 * i % a.length] - b[3 * i % b.length];
    }
}
```

What are the values of the elements in array a1 after the following code executes?

```
int[] a1 = {2, 4, 6, 8, 10, 12, 14, 16};
int[] a2 = {1, 1, 2, 3, 5, 8, 13, 21};
mystery2(a1, a2);
```

26. Consider the following method, mystery3:

```
public static void mystery3(int[] data, int x, int y) {
    data[data[x]] = data[y];
    data[y] = x;
}
```

What are the values of the elements in the array numbers after the following code executes?

```
int[] numbers = {3, 7, 1, 0, 25, 4, 18, -1, 5};
mystery3(numbers, 3, 1);
mystery3(numbers, 5, 6);
mystery3(numbers, 8, 4);
```

27. Consider the following method:

```
public static int mystery4(int[] list) {
    int x = 0;
    for (int i = 1; i < list.length; i++) {
        int y = list[i] - list[0];
        if (y > x) {
            x = y;
        }
    }
    return x;
}
```

What value does the method return when passed each of the following arrays?

a. {5}
b. {3, 12}
c. {4, 2, 10, 8}
d. {1, 9, 3, 5, 7}
e. {8, 2, 10, 4, 10, 9}

28. Consider the following method:

```
public static void mystery5(int[] nums) {
    for (int i = 0; i < nums.length - 1; i++) {
        if (nums[i] > nums[i + 1]) {
            nums[i + 1]++;
        }
    }
}
```

What are the final contents of each of the following arrays if each is passed to the above method?

a. {8}

b. {14, 7}

c. {7, 1, 3, 2, 0, 4}

d. {10, 8, 9, 5, 5}

e. {12, 11, 10, 10, 8, 7}

29. Write a piece of code that computes the average `String` length of the elements of an array of `Strings`. For example, if the array contains `{"belt", "hat", "jelly", "bubble gum"}`, the average length is `5.5`.

30. Write code that accepts an array of `Strings` as its parameter and indicates whether that array is a palindrome— that is, whether it reads the same forward as backward. For example, the array `{"alpha", "beta", "gamma", "delta", "gamma", "beta", "alpha"}` is a palindrome.

Section 7.5: Multidimensional Arrays

31. What elements does the array `numbers` contain after the following code is executed?

```java
int[][] numbers = new int[3][4];
for (int r = 0; r < numbers.length; r++) {
    for (int c = 0; c < numbers[0].length; c++) {
        numbers[r][c] = r + c;
    }
}
```

32. Assume that a two-dimensional rectangular array of integers called `data` has been declared with four rows and seven columns. Write a loop to initialize the third row of data to store the numbers 1 through 7.

33. Write a piece of code that constructs a two-dimensional array of integers with 5 rows and 10 columns. Fill the array with a multiplication table, so that array element `[i][j]` contains the value `i * j`. Use nested `for` loops to build the array.

34. Assume that a two-dimensional rectangular array of integers called `matrix` has been declared with six rows and eight columns. Write a loop to copy the contents of the second column into the fifth column.

35. Consider the following method:

```java
public static void mystery2d(int[][] a) {
    for (int r = 0; r < a.length; r++) {
        for (int c = 0; c < a[0].length - 1; c++) {
            if (a[r][c + 1] > a[r][c]) {
                a[r][c] = a[r][c + 1];
            }
        }
    }
}
```

If a two-dimensional array `numbers` is initialized to store the following integers, what are its contents after the call shown?

```java
int[][] numbers = {{3, 4, 5, 6},
                   {4, 5, 6, 7},
                   {5, 6, 7, 8}};
mystery2d(numbers);
```

36. Write a piece of code that constructs a jagged two-dimensional array of integers with five rows and an increasing number of columns in each row, such that the first row has one column, the second row has two, the third has three, and so on. The array elements should have increasing values in top-to-bottom, left-to-right order (also called row-major order). In other words, the array's contents should be the following:

```
1
2, 3
4, 5, 6
7, 8, 9, 10
11, 12, 13, 14, 15
```

Use nested `for` loops to build the array.

37. When examining a 2D array of pixels, how could you figure out the width and height of the image even if you don't have access to the `DrawingPanel` object?

38. Finish the following code for a method that converts an image into its red channel; that is, removing any green or blue from each pixel and keeping only the red component.

```java
public static void toRedChannel(DrawingPanel panel) {
    Color[][] pixels = panel.getPixels();
    for (int row = 0; row < pixels.length; row++) {
        for (int col = 0; col < pixels[0].length; col++) {
            // your code goes here
        }
    }
    panel.setPixels(pixels);
}
```

39. What is the result of the following code? What will the image look like?

```java
public static void pixelMystery(DrawingPanel panel) {
    Color[][] pixels = panel.getPixels();
    for (int row = 0; row < pixels.length; row++) {
        for (int col = 0; col < pixels[0].length; col++) {
            int n = Math.min(row + col, 255);
            pixels[row][col] = new Color(n, n, n);
        }
    }
    panel.setPixels(pixels);
}
```

Exercises

1. Write a method called `lastIndexOf` that accepts an array of integers and an integer value as its parameters and returns the last index at which the value occurs in the array. The method should return −1 if the value is not found. For example, in the array [74, 85, 102, 99, 101, 85, 56], the last index of the value 85 is 5.

2. Write a method called `range` that returns the range of values in an array of integers. The range is defined as 1 more than the difference between the maximum and minimum values in the array. For example, if an array called `list` contains the values [36, 12, 25, 19, 46, 31, 22], the call of range(list) should return 35 (46 − 12 + 1). You may assume that the array has at least one element.

3. Write a method called countInRange that accepts an array of integers, a minimum value, and a maximum value as parameters and returns the count of how many elements from the array fall between the minimum and maximum (inclusive). For example, in the array [14, 1, 22, 17, 36, 7, −43, 5], for minimum value 4 and maximum value 17, there are four elements whose values fall between 4 and 17.

4. Write a method called isSorted that accepts an array of real numbers as a parameter and returns true if the list is in sorted (nondecreasing) order and false otherwise. For example, if arrays named list1 and list2 store [16.1, 12.3, 22.2, 14.4] and [1.5, 4.3, 7.0, 19.5, 25.1, 46.2] respectively, the calls isSorted(list1) and isSorted(list2) should return false and true respectively. Assume the array has at least one element. A one-element array is considered to be sorted.

5. Write a method called mode that returns the most frequently occurring element of an array of integers. Assume that the array has at least one element and that every element in the array has a value between 0 and 100 inclusive. Break ties by choosing the lower value. For example, if the array passed contains the values [27, 15, 15, 11, 27], your method should return 15. (*Hint:* You may wish to look at the Tally program from this chapter to get an idea how to solve this problem.) Can you write a version of this method that does not rely on the values being between 0 and 100?

6. Write a method called stdev that returns the standard deviation of an array of integers. Standard deviation is computed by taking the square root of the sum of the squares of the differences between each element and the mean, divided by one less than the number of elements. (It's just that simple!) More concisely and mathematically, the standard deviation of an array a is written as follows:

$$stdev(a) = \sqrt{\frac{\sum_{i=0}^{a.length-1} (a[i] - average(a)^2)}{a.length - 1}}$$

For example, if the array passed contains the values [1, −2, 4, −4, 9, −6, 16, −8, 25, −10], your method should return approximately 11.237.

7. Write a method called kthLargest that accepts an integer k and an array a as its parameters and returns the element such that k elements have greater or equal value. If k = 0, return the largest element; if k = 1, return the second-largest element, and so on. For example, if the array passed contains the values [74, 85, 102, 99, 101, 56, 84] and the integer k passed is 2, your method should return 99 because there are two values at least as large as 99 (101 and 102). Assume that $0 \le k < a.length$. (*Hint:* Consider sorting the array or a copy of the array first.)

8. Write a method called median that accepts an array of integers as its parameter and returns the median of the numbers in the array. The median is the number that appears in the middle of the list if you arrange the elements in order. Assume that the array is of odd size (so that one sole element constitutes the median) and that the numbers in the array are between 0 and 99 inclusive. For example, the median of [5, 2, 4, 17, 55, 4, 3, 26, 18, 2, 17] is 5 and the median of [42, 37, 1, 97, 1, 2, 7, 42, 3, 25, 89, 15, 10, 29, 27] is 25. (*Hint:* You may wish to look at the Tally program from earlier in this chapter for ideas.)

9. Write a method called minGap that accepts an integer array as a parameter and returns the minimum difference or gap between adjacent values in the array, where the gap is defined as the later value minus the earlier value. For example, in the array [1, 3, 6, 7, 12], the first gap is 2 (3 − 1), the second gap is 3 (6 − 3), the third gap is 1 (7 − 6), and the fourth gap is 5 (12 − 7). So your method should return 1 if passed this array. The minimum gap could be a negative number if the list is not in sorted order. If you are passed an array with fewer than two elements, return 0.

10. Write a method called `percentEven` that accepts an array of integers as a parameter and returns the percentage of even numbers in the array as a real number. For example, if the array stores the elements [6, 2, 9, 11, 3], then your method should return 40.0. If the array contains no even elements or no elements at all, return 0.0.

11. Write a method called `isUnique` that accepts an array of integers as a parameter and returns a `boolean` value indicating whether or not the values in the array are unique (`true` for yes, `false` for no). The values in the list are considered unique if there is no pair of values that are equal. For example, if passed an array containing [3, 8, 12, 2, 9, 17, 43, −8, 46], your method should return `true`, but if passed [4, 7, 3, 9, 12, −47, 3, 74], your method should return `false` because the value 3 appears twice.

12. Write a method called `priceIsRight` that mimics the guessing rules from the game show *The Price Is Right*. The method accepts as parameters an array of integers representing the contestants' bids and an integer representing a correct price. The method returns the element in the bids array that is closest in value to the correct price without being larger than that price. For example, if an array called `bids` stores the values [200, 300, 250, 1, 950, 40], the call of `priceIsRight(bids, 280)` should return 250, since 250 is the bid closest to 280 without going over 280. If all bids are larger than the correct price, your method should return −1.

13. Write a method called `longestSortedSequence` that accepts an array of integers as a parameter and returns the length of the longest sorted (nondecreasing) sequence of integers in the array. For example, in the array [3, 8, 10, 1, 9, 14, −3, 0, 14, 207, 56, 98, 12], the longest sorted sequence in the array has four values in it (the sequence −3, 0, 14, 207), so your method would return 4 if passed this array. Sorted means nondecreasing, so a sequence could contain duplicates. Your method should return 0 if passed an empty array.

14. Write a method called `contains` that accepts two arrays of integers *a1* and *a2* as parameters and that returns a `boolean` value indicating whether or not the sequence of elements in *a2* appears in *a1* (`true` for yes, `false` for no). The sequence must appear consecutively and in the same order. For example, consider the following arrays:

```
int[] list1 = {1, 6, 2, 1, 4, 1, 2, 1, 8};
int[] list2 = {1, 2, 1};
```

The call of `contains(list1, list2)` should return `true` because the sequence of values in `list2` [1, 2, 1] is contained in `list1` starting at index 5. If `list2` had stored the values [2, 1, 2], the call of `contains(list1, list2)` would return `false`. Any two lists with identical elements are considered to contain each other. Every array contains the empty array, and the empty array does not contain any arrays other than the empty array itself.

15. Write a method called `collapse` that accepts an array of integers as a parameter and returns a new array containing the result of replacing each pair of integers with the sum of that pair. For example, if an array called `list` stores the values [7, 2, 8, 9, 4, 13, 7, 1, 9, 10], then the call of `collapse(list)` should return a new array containing [9, 17, 17, 8, 19]. The first pair from the original list is collapsed into 9 (7 + 2), the second pair is collapsed into 17 (8 + 9), and so on. If the list stores an odd number of elements, the final element is not collapsed. For example, if the list had been [1, 2, 3, 4, 5], then the call would return [3, 7, 5]. Your method should not change the array that is passed as a parameter.

16. Write a method called `append` that accepts two integer arrays as parameters and returns a new array that contains the result of appending the second array's values at the end of the first array. For example, if arrays `list1` and `list2` store [2, 4, 6] and [1, 2, 3, 4, 5] respectively, the call of `append(list1, list2)` should return a new array containing [2, 4, 6, 1, 2, 3, 4, 5]. If the call instead had been `append(list2, list1)`, the method would return an array containing [1, 2, 3, 4, 5, 2, 4, 6].

17. Write a method called `vowelCount` that accepts a `String` as a parameter and produces and returns an array of integers representing the counts of each vowel in the string. The array returned by your method should hold five

elements: the first is the count of As, the second is the count of Es, the third Is, the fourth Os, and the fifth Us. Assume that the string contains no uppercase letters. For example, the call `vowelCount("i think, therefore i am")` should return the array `[1, 3, 3, 1, 0]`.

18. Write a method called `wordLengths` that accepts a `Scanner` for an input file as its parameter. Your method should open the given file, count the number of letters in each token in the file, and output a result diagram of how many words contain each number of letters. For example, consider a file containing the following text:

```
Before sorting:
13 23 480 -18 75
hello how are you feeling today

After sorting:
-18 13 23 75 480
are feeling hello how today you
```

Your method should produce the following output to the console. Use tabs so that the stars line up:

```
1: 0
2: 6 ******
3: 10 **********
4: 0
5: 5 *****
6: 1 *
7: 2 **
8: 2 **
```

Assume that no token in the file is more than 80 characters in length.

19. Write a method called `matrixAdd` that accepts a pair of two-dimensional arrays of integers as parameters, treats the arrays as two-dimensional matrixes, and returns their sum. The sum of two matrixes A and B is a matrix C, where for every row `i` and column `j`, $C_{ij} = A_{ij} + B_{ij}$. You may assume that the arrays passed as parameters have the same dimensions.

20. Write a method called `isMagicSquare` that accepts a two-dimensional array of integers as a parameter and returns `true` if it is a magic square. A square matrix is a *magic square* if all of its row, column, and diagonal sums are equal. For example, `[[2, 7, 6], [9, 5, 1], [4, 3, 8]]` is a square matrix because all eight of the sums are exactly 15.

21. Write a method `grayscale` that converts a color image into a black-and-white image. This is done by averaging the red, green, and blue components of each pixel. For example, if a pixel has RGB values of (red = 100, green = 30, blue = 80), the average of the three components is $(100 + 30 + 80)/3 = 70$, so that pixel becomes (red = 70, green = 70, blue = 70).

22. Write a method `transpose` that accepts a `DrawingPanel` as a parameter and inverts the image about both the *x* and *y* axes. You may assume that the image is square, that is, that its width and height are equal.

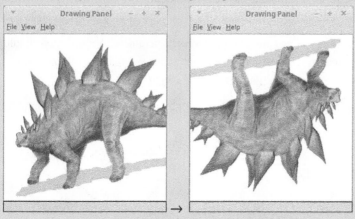

23. Write a method `zoomIn` that accepts a `DrawingPanel` as a parameter and converts it into an image twice as large in both dimensions. Each pixel from the original image becomes a cluster of 4 pixels (2 rows and 2 columns) in the new zoomed image.

24. Write methods `rotateLeft` and `rotateRight` that rotate the pixels of an image counter-clockwise or clockwise by 90 degrees respectively. You should not assume that the image is square in shape; its width and height might be different.

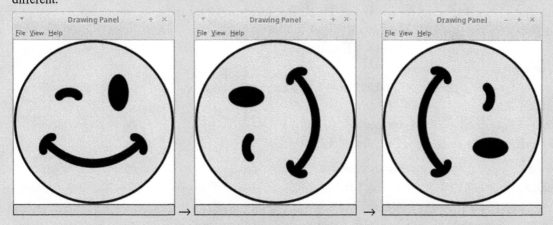

25. Write a method `blur` that makes an image look "blurry" using the following specific algorithm. Set each pixel to be the average of itself and the 8 pixels around it. That is, for the pixel at position (x, y), set its RGB value to be the average of the RGB values at positions $(x - 1, y - 1)$ through $(x + 1, y + 1)$. Be careful not to go out of bounds near the edge of the image; if a pixel lies along the edge of the image, average whatever neighbors it does have.

Programming Projects

1. Java's type `int` has a limit on how large an integer it can store. This limit can be circumvented by representing an integer as an array of digits. Write an interactive program that adds two integers of up to 50 digits each.

2. Write a game of Hangman using arrays. Allow the user to guess letters and represent which letters have been guessed in an array.

3. Write a program that plays a variation of the game of Mastermind with a user. For example, the program can use pseudorandom numbers to generate a four-digit number. The user should be allowed to make guesses until she gets the number correct. Clues should be given to the user indicating how many digits of the guess are correct and in the correct place and how many digits are correct but in the wrong place.

4. Write a program to score users' responses to the classic Myers–Briggs personality test. Assume that the test has 70 questions that determine a person's personality in four dimensions. Each question has two answer choices that we'll call the "A" and "B" answers. Questions are organized into 10 groups of seven questions, with the following repeating pattern in each group:

- The first question in each group (questions 1, 8, 15, 22, etc.) tells whether the person is introverted or extroverted.
- The next two questions (questions 2 and 3, 9 and 10, 16 and 17, 23 and 24, etc.) test whether the person is guided by his or her senses or intuition.
- The next two questions (questions 4 and 5, 11 and 12, 18 and 19, 25 and 26, etc.) test whether the person focuses on thinking or feeling.
- The final two questions in each group (questions 6 and 7, 13 and 14, 20 and 21, 27 and 28, etc.) test whether the person prefers to judge or be guided by perception.

In other words, if we consider introversion/extraversion (I/E) to be dimension 1, sensing/intuition (S/N) to be dimension 2, thinking/feeling (T/F) to be dimension 3, and judging/perception (J/P) to be dimension 4, the map of questions to their respective dimensions would look like this:

```
1223344122334412233441223344122334412233441223344122334412233441223344
BABAAAABAAAAAAABAAAABBAAAAAABAAAABABAABAAABABABABAABAAAAAABAAAAAABAAAAAA
```

The following is a partial sample input file of names and responses:

```
Betty Boop
BABAAAABAAAAAAABAAAABBAAAAAABAAAABABAABAAABABABABAABAAAAAABAAAAAABAAAAAA
Snoopy
AABBAABBBBBABABAAAAABABBAABBAAAABBBAAABAABAABABAAAABAABBBBAAABBAABABBB
```

If less than 50% of a person's responses are B for a given personality dimension, the person's type for that dimension should be the first of its two choices. If the person has 50% or more B responses, the person's type for that dimension is the second choice. Your program should output each person's name, the number of A and B responses for each dimension, the percentage of Bs in each dimension, and the overall personality type. The following should be your program's output for the preceding input data:

```
Betty Boop:
    1A—9B 17A—3B 18A—2B 18A—2B
    [90%, 15%, 10%, 10%] = ISTJ
Snoopy:
    7A—3B 11A—9B 14A—6B 6A—14B
    [30%, 45%, 30%, 70%] = ESTP
```

5. Use a two-dimensional array to write a game of Tic-Tac-Toe that represents the board.

6. Write a program that reads a file of DNA data and searches for protein sequences. DNA data consists of long `strings` of the letters A, C, G, and T, corresponding to chemical nucleotides called adenine, cytosine, guanine, and thymine. Proteins can be identified by looking for special triplet sequences of nucleotides that indicate the start and stop of a protein range. Store relevant data in arrays as you make your computation. See our textbook's web site for example DNA input files and more details about heuristics for identifying proteins.

7. Write a basic Photoshop or Instagram-inspired program with a menu of available image manipulation algorithms similar to those described in the exercises in this chapter. The user can load an image from a file and then select which manipulation to perform, such as grayscale, zoom, rotate, or blur.

index

Index